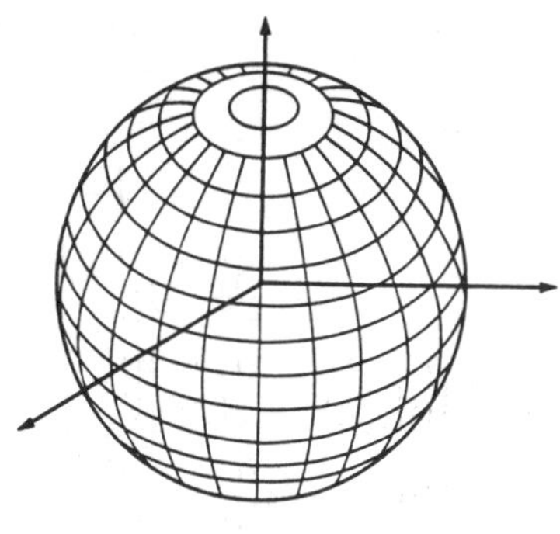

SPATIAL REASONING AND MULTI-SENSOR FUSION:
Proceedings of the 1987 Workshop

October 5-7, 1987
Pheasant Run Resort, St. Charles, Illinois
Sponsored by AAAI

Program Committee:
Su-shing Chen (Co-Chair)
Avi Kak (Co-Chair)
Jake Aggarwal
Ruzenna Bajscy
Tom Garvey
Tom Henderson
Tod Levitt
Linda Shapiro

Morgan Kaufmann Publishers, Inc.
95 First Street, Los Altos, California 94022

Editor and President   *Michael B. Morgan*
Coordinating Editor   *Todd R. Armstrong*
Production Manager   *Jennifer Ballentine*
Cover Designer   *Irene Imfeld*

Library of Congress Cataloging-in-Publication Data

Spatial reasoning and multi-sensor fusion.
    Proceedings of the Workshop on Spatial Reasoning and
Multi-Sensor Fusion, held at Pheasant Run (a resort hotel)
in St. Charles, Ill.; sponsored by the American
Association for Artificial Intelligence.
    Bibliography: p.
    Includes index.
    1. Artificial intelligence — Congresses. 2. Robotics —
Congresses. 3. Machine vision — Congresses. I. Kak,
Avinash C. II. Chen, Su-shing. III. Workshop on
Spatial Reasoning and Multi-Sensor Fusion (1987 :
Saint Charles, Ill.) IV. American Association
for Artificial Intelligence.
Q334.S635 1987   006.3   87-22646
ISBN 0-934613-59-1

MORGAN KAUFMANN PUBLISHERS, INC.
95 First Street, Suite 120
Los Altos, California 94022
© 1987 by Morgan Kaufmann Publishers, Inc.
All rights reserved.

No part of the publication may be reproduced, stored in a retrieval
system, or transmitted in any form or by any means — electronic, mechanical,
recording, or otherwise — without the prior written permission of the
publisher.

91 90 89 88 87   5 4 3 2 1

FOREWORD

This volume contains proceedings of the AAAI sponsored Workshop on Spatial Reasoning and Multi-Sensor Fusion. Spatial reasoning goes beyond computer vision in the sense that it also involves spatial task planning, navigation planning for mobile robots, representing and indexing large spatial databases, symbolic reasoning and the integration of such reasoning with geometrical constraints, accumulation of uncertain evidence, etc. To the extent spatial inferences must be made from information gathered from multiple sources, which may sometimes compete and sometimes cooperate, the techniques of Multi-Sensor Fusion are an important adjunct to Spatial Reasoning. Our hope is that this workshop will bring into focus these different aspects of Spatial Reasoning.

This workshop would not have come about without the great effort on the part of the members of the Program Committee. Each submission was reviewed by all the members of the committee. We are truly appreciative of their help. We also thank all those who agreed to be the main presenters at the workshop; consider the fact that their jobs are fraught with danger since they will be critically reviewing the papers of some of their peers, who will be right there to challenge them.

Avi Kak
Su-shing Chen

CONTENTS

WORKSHOP ON
SPATIAL REASONING AND MULTI-SENSOR FUSION

PROGRAM

SUNDAY, October 4

6:00 pm -- 7:30 pm   **Reception**

8:00 pm -- 9:30 pm   **Dinner**

MONDAY, October 5

7:30 am -- 9:00 am   **Breakfast**

9:00 am -- 9:15 am   **Introduction to the workshop**

9:15 am -- 10:30 am   **FRAMEWORKS FOR REASONING**

Presenter: TAKEO KANADE

Respondents: AVI KAK, JAMES RODGER, TERRY WEYMOUTH

TAKEO KANADE will present his perspectives on the subject and a critique of the papers:

Andress and Kak: *A Production System Environment for Integrating Knowledge with Vision Data*

Rodger and Browse: *An Object-Oriented Representation for Multisensory Robotic Perception*

Walker, Herman and Kanade: *A Framework for Representing and Reasoning about 3D Objects for Vision*

Weymouth: *Knowledge-Based Spatial Reasoning, Using a Blackboard Architecture*

10:45 am -- 12:00 pm   **SPATIAL DATABASES**

Presenter: TOD LEVITT

ix

x

Respondents: RICHARD ANTONY, CHRISTER BACKSTROM,
PRASANTA BOSE, RAMESH JAIN, SUKHAMAY KUNDU

TOD LEVITT will present his perspectives on the subject and a critique of the papers:

Antony: *Spatial Reasoning using an Object-Oriented Spatial DBMS*

Backstrom: *Static and Dynamic Logical Modeling of Mechanical Assembly Processes
in a Simplified Geometrical Environment*

Bose, Meng and Rajinikanth: *Planning Flight Paths in Dynamic Situations with
Incomplete Knowledge*

Jain and Grosky: *Hyper-Pyramidal Representation for Integration of Spatial Information*

Kundu and Singh: *Spatial Reasoning in Rectangular Dissection*

Levitt, Lawton, Chelberg and Nelson: *Visual Memory Structure for a Mobile Robot*

12:00 pm -- 1:00 pm   Lunch

1:00 pm -- 2:00 pm   Short nature walk down the **Prairie Path**

2:30 pm -- 3:45 pm   **COMPUTER VISION -- I**

Presenter: JAKE AGGARWAL

Respondents: BIJAN ARBAB, VINCENT HAYWARD, TERRANCE BOULT,
GEORGE STOCKMAN

JAKE AGGARWAL will present his perspectives on the subject and a critique of the papers:

Arbab: *Mask: An Object Identification Algorithm*

Aubry and Hayward: *Recursive Decomposition of Free-Space from Boundary Points*

Boult and Gross: *Recovery of Super-Quadrics from 3D Information*

Hu and Stockman: *3D Scene Analysis via Fusion of Light Striped Image and Intensity Image*

4:00 pm -- 5:15 pm   **SHAPE ANALYSIS**

Presenter: RAM NEVATIA

Respondents: JAKE AGGARWAL, MICHAEL LEYTON, TOYOAKI NISHIDA

RAM NEVATIA will present his perspectives on the subject and a critique of the papers:

Leyton: *A Process-Grammar for Representing Shape*

Nishida, Yamada and Doshita: *Figuring Out Most Plausible Interpretation from Constraints*

Rao, Nevatia and Medioni: *Obtaining Shape Descriptions from Sparse 3-D Data*

Vemuri and Aggarwal: *Resolving the Orientation and Identity of an Object from Range Data*

5:30 pm -- 6:30 pm   **NATURAL SYSTEMS AND GEOMETRICAL APPROACHES**

Presenter: DANA BALLARD

Respondents: STEVEN BRODD, SU-SHING CHEN

DANA BALLARD will present his perspectives on the subject and a critique of the papers:

Ballard: *Eye Movement and Visual Cognition*

Brodd: *A Strategy Planner for NASA Robotics Applications*

Chen: *A Geometric Approach to Multi-Sensor Fusion*

6:30 pm -- 8:00 pm   **Dinner**

8:00 pm -- 9:00 pm   **Round Table Discussions**

9:00 pm -- 11:00 pm   **Outdoor camp fire, etc. at Whispering Winds**

TUESDAY, October 6

7:30 am -- 8:30 am   **Breakfast**

9:00 am -- 10:15 am   **MOBILE AUTONOMOUS SYSTEMS**

Presenter: TOM STRAT

Respondents: DOUGLAS CHUBB, LARRY DAVIS, DAVID MILLER

TOM STRAT will present his perspectives on the subject and a critique of the papers:

Bixler and Miller: *A Sensory Input System for Autonomous Mobile Robots*

Chubb: *An Introduction and Analysis of a Straight Line Path Planning Algorithm for Use in Binary Domains*

Dickinson, LeMoigne, Waltzman and Davis: *An Expert Vision System for Autonomous Land Vehicle (ALV) Road Following*

Miller and Slack: *Efficient Navigation Through Dynamic Domains*

Strat: *The Management of Spatial Information in a Mobile Robot*

10:30 am -- 11:45 pm   COMPUTER VISION -- II

Presenter: LINDA SHAPIRO

Respondents: HAIM WOLFSON, MICHAEL MAGEE, JOHN KENDER, GARY SILVERMAN

LINDA SHAPIRO will present her perspectives on the subject and a critique of the papers:

Kishon and Wolfson: *3-D Curve Matching*

Magee and Nathan: *Spatial Reasoning, Sensor Repositioning and Disambiguation in 3D Model Based Recognition*

Moerdler and Kender: *An Approach to the Fusion of Multiple Shape from Texture Algorithms*

Silverman, Tsai and Levin: *Locating Polyhedral Objects from Edge Point Data*

12:00 pm -- 1:00 pm   Lunch

1:15 pm -- 2:45 pm   Nature walk down a primitive country road

3:00 pm -- 4:15 pm   MULTI-SENSOR FUSION -- I

Presenter: RUZENA BAJCSY

Respondents: JAMES CROWLEY, HUGH DURRANT-WHYTE, JACQUELINE LE MOIGNE

RUZENA BAJCSY will present her perspectives on the subject and a critique of the papers:

Crowley: *Mathematical Tools for Representing Uncertainty in Images*

Durrant-Whyte: *Sensor Models and Multi-Sensor Integration*

Hager and Mintz: *Searching for Information*

Le Moigne: *Control Strategies for Sensors*

4:30 pm -- 5:45 pm   MULTI-SENSOR FUSION -- II

Presenter: TOM HENDERSON

Respondents: JAMES DUNCAN, TERRANCE HUNTSBERGER, REN LUO, RANDY SMITH

TOM HENDERSON will present his perspectives on the subject and a critique of the papers:

Duncan, Gindi and Narendra: *Low Level Information Fusion, Multisensor Scene Segmentation Using Learning Automata*

Duncan and Staib: *Shape Determination from Incomplete and Noisy Multisensor Imagery*

Huntsberger and Jayaramamurthy: *A Framework for Multi-Sensor Fusion in the Presence of Uncertainty*

Luo, Lin and Scherp: *Multi-Sensor Integrated Intelligent Robot for Automated Assembly*

Smith, Self and Cheeseman: *A Stochastic Map for Uncertain Spatial Relationships*

6:00 pm -- 6:45 pm   NATURAL LANGUAGE PROCESSING AND SPATIAL REASONING

Presenter: VICTOR RASKIN

Respondents: GUDULA RETZ-SCHMIDT, SERGEI NIRENBURG

VICTOR RASKIN will present his perspectives on the subject and a critique of the papers:

Nirenburg and Raskin: *Dealing with Space in Natural Language Processing*

Retz-Schmidt: *Deictic and Intrinsic Use of Spatial Prepositions, A Multidisciplinary Comparison*

7:00 pm -- 8:00 pm   Dinner

8:30 pm -- 10:00 pm   Round Table Discussions Continued

WEDNESDAY, October 7

7:00 am -- 8:00 am   **Breakfast**

8:15 am -- 9:30 am   **PLANNING AND PERCEPTION**

Presenter: BEN KUIPERS

Respondents: TAPIO HEIKKILA, DERYL LAWTON, DREW McDERMOTT, A. MENG

BEN KUIPERS will present his perspectives on the subject and a critique of the papers:

Karkkainen, Heikkila and Nissila: *Monitoring an Assembly Task by Perception Requests*

Kuipers and Byun: *A Qualitative Approach to Robot Exploration and Map-Learning in an Unknown World*

Lawton and McConnell: *Perceptual Organization Using Interestingness*

McDermott and Gelsey: *Terrain Analysis for Tactical Situation Assessment*

Meng: *Free Space Modeling and Path Planning Under Uncertainty for Autonomous Air Robots*

9:30 am -- 10:30 am   **PANEL DISCUSSION**

Organizer: TOM GARVEY

Title: *Open Issues -- Needs, Expectations and Realities in Spatial Reasoning and Multisensor Fusion*

Panelists: to be announced

10:30 noon -- 12:30 pm   **Reports from Round-Table Discussion Leaders**

12:30 pm -- 1:30 pm   **Lunch**

A PRODUCTION SYSTEM ENVIRONMENT FOR INTEGRATING KNOWLEDGE WITH VISION DATA

K. M. Andress and A. C. Kak

Robot Vision Lab
School of Electrical Engineering
Purdue University
W. Lafayette, IN 47907

ABSTRACT

A description of work-in-progress on PSEIKI is presented. PSEIKI is a computer vision system designed to use multiple sources of knowledge to aid in the image understanding task. In this paper we describe how the incorporation of world knowledge can be used to make PSEIKI expectation driven. The world knowledge in the system is represented as a line drawing of the expected scene. The system is implemented as a 2 panel / 6 level blackboard and uses the Dempster-Shafer formalism to accomplish inexact reasoning in a hierarchical space.

1. INTRODUCTION

A large number of factors affect the intensity values of a photometric image: scene geometry, illumination sources, object reflectances and viewpoint. Because of this, a robust computer vision system must be able to use knowledge from a variety of sources when interpreting photometric scenes. Various knowledge sources have been used to improve computer vision system performance in the past; a few of these are: images taken from multiple viewpoints, multiple images taken over time, effects of perspective geometry and occlusion, and knowledge of the object's texture, or the position of the illuminating source. One source of additional knowledge that can aid in image interpretation is contained in the expected scene; this information can be expressed as a line drawing of the world that the system expects to see. This paper describes work in progress on PSEIKI [1], a Production System Environment for Integrating Knowledge with Images.

SYSTEM USES

PSEIKI originally was built as a prototypical system to investigate the integration of global map information with vision data to aid navigation for an autonomous mobile robot. The robot's task is to traverse a known network of sidewalks using sensor data to provide position information [2]. For various reasons, the robot's position and orientation never can be known with certainty. Therefore, for the purpose of self-location, the robot must attempt to integrate its map knowledge with the sensed image while the two are out of registration. Although PSEIKI originally was developed to aid in navigation, the system can be used in any application where a good estimate of the expected scene is available to the vision system. For example, other typical uses of PSEIKI would be as a task monitor in a robotic assembly cell or as a visual verification system.

Some of the aims of PSEIKI are

1)   One of the central aims of PSEIKI is to investigate how different sources of knowledge can be integrated into the image interpretation task. Although knowledge of the expected scene is the main source of information being investigated, the system is general enough to affect integration over multiple images in structural stereo or optic flow.

2)   PSEIKI also was developed to investigate the implementation of a domain independent vision system. PSEIKI contains two features that keep it domain independent. First, the knowledge used by PSEIKI consists of a line drawing of the expected scene (which in most applications would not be in registration with the observed image). The fact that the expected scene is represented as a line drawing lends the system a degree of domain independence. For example, the line drawings used for robot navigation can easily be generated from road maps. In more industrial 2D vision applications, computer graphics or CAD systems can be used directly to generate the line drawings of the expected scenes. The other feature that provides the system domain independence concerns how the system presents its results. The output of PSEIKI consists of a mapping from elements detected in the input image to elements in the expect scene.* This mapping is expressed by labeling the detected edges with the names of the corresponding lines in the expected scene. It is left to a higher level system to make global interpretations based on the mapping found.

3)   Another aim of PSEIKI is the investigation of how inexact reasoning can be achieved on hierarchical representation of scenes in symbolic form. Gordon and Shortliffe [3] discuss a technique that allows the Dempster-Shafer formalism [4] to be used in a system that hierarchically groups hypotheses. The article deals with diagnostic reasoning (in medicine) where the hypotheses can be grouped into strict hierarchies. It is not possible to use the methods of Gordon and Shortliffe directly because PSEIKI does not employ strict hierarchies (an edge can be a member of two faces if it is a part of the border between them). In the current implementation of PSEIKI, the blackboard architecture is exploited to permit exact and inexact reasoning in a tangled hierarchy. The Dempster-Shafer formalism is used for pooling uncertain evidence in the hierarchy.

---

* We will be referring to this mapping throughout the paper.

4)   PSEIKI is able to handle significant perspective effects. Many previous systems, again most notably aerial interpretation systems, were able to assume that the images were obtained by an orthographic imaging system. Although perspective distortions make image interpretation difficult because metric properties, such as length and orientation, depend on the object's position in the image, they also provide clues to the structure of objects in the image.

5)   PSEIKI also was developed to investigate how system control flow affects the image understanding task.

RELATED IMAGE UNDERSTANDING SYSTEMS

- ACRONYM (Brooks, et. al. [5]) is a model-based image understanding system. The system's task consists of finding instances of known objects in the image. To perform object identification, the system first builds a *Picture Graph* of the image and an *Observability Graph* that specifies information about objects that could be in the image. The system identifies instances of objects in the image by matching nodes of the Observability Graph with sets of nodes in the Picture Graph. The objects in the Observability Graph are represented in *slot - filler* structures where any slot that can accept numeric values can also accept algebraic constraints expresses as inequalities. The system can then manipulate these constraints and determine if properties of objects detected in the image meet these constraints. The objects used to generate the Observability Graph are represented as generalized cones. Inexact reasoning is not used and the system uses only backward chaining to arrive at an interpretation.

- Davis and Hwang describe the SIGMA image understanding system [6] for aerial image interpretation. The system uses both forward and backward chaining to arrive at an interpretation, and it represents its object classes hierarchically using frames. Furthermore, the system is able to integrate hypotheses about specific objects in the scene. The system does not use uncertain reasoning but instead is able to control its focus of attention based on the strength of a situation.

- SPAM [7], a system designed by McKeown, Harvey and McDermott is also an aerial image interpretation system. The system originally was constructed to interpret airport scenes but has been expanded with a rule generator so it can now interpret scenes from other domains. SPAM uses confidence values to aid labeling and can manipulate these values based on the consistency of the various labelings.

- VISIONS (Hanson and Riseman [8]) is a blackboard expert system designed to analyze color images. The system uses a flexible control scheme, hierarchical scene representation, and a number of knowledge sources to accomplish the scene interpretation task. VISIONS is domain independent but uses schemas to tune the system for a particular application.

- The image segmentation expert system developed by Nazif and Levine [9] contains two global memories. The global long term memory contains rules that are applied to the data stored in its short term memory. The system is rule based and uses modules to update lines, regions and areas in the image. The expert system also contains a set of metarules and can control its focus of attention.

- Barnard describes a system that deals with perspective images [10]. The system is able to use the Gaussian sphere to determine the vanishing points of the scene being analyzed. The backprojection of angles and curvatures also is used to aid the interpretation task.

- Barrow and Tenenbaum discuss the problem of interpreting line drawings in [11]. They are able to use junction libraries and knowledge of differential geometry to discriminate between extremal and discontinuity boundaries. This knowledge then is used to determine how the surfaces should be constrained.

PSEIKI differs from the above system in the following three main areas:

Firstly, PSEIKI's task differs from those of previous systems. Most of the other systems were designed to find object instances in the image and, through such discoveries, to arrive at a global interpretation of the image. PSEIKI's task is limited to integrating expected scene information with the observed image -- the result is a set of consistent labels, with associated belief values, for the edge elements in the image.

PSEIKI differs from SPAM and SIGMA, and to a certain extent VISIONS, in not relying on domain-dependent information. For example, SPAM uses airport design knowledge when interpreting airport scenes. Context-cues have also been used extensively in past computer vision systems. For example, if SIGMA has detected a driveway in an image, it would then search for a house and for roads connected to the driveway. Because PSEIKI is provided with a good estimate of the expected scene, it does not have to perform inferences of this type. Although it might be said that context-cues are indispensable for scene interpretation because they make deductions more powerful, their use necessarily introduces some domain dependence. Therefore, it is our philosophy to separate the generation of the mapping from the formation of an overall interpretation of the scene. If the use of context-cues is desired by a system using PSEIKI, then it is up to the higher level system to provide PSEIKI with a line drawing incorporating the information contained in the cues.

PSEIKI also differs from previous systems in its method of performing inexact reasoning. Many systems, including ACRONYM, SIGMA and the system by Nazif and Levine use no uncertain reasoning in the image interpretation process. Because of the overwhelming amount of data in an image, most of the inexact reasoning schemes used in the past have been fairly simple to avoid becoming bogged down in certainty value computations. On the other hand, inexact reasoning in PSEIKI is based on the Dempster-Shafer formalism in a tangled hierarchical space. The use of a hierarchy curtails the number of uncertainty calculations and is made possible by the use of the blackboard architecture.

OVERVIEW OF PSEIKI

There are two main sections to PSEIKI, a low-level preprocessor which performs pixel-to-symbol conversion and a rule-based edge labeler. PSEIKI's architecture is shown in figure 1. Because PSEIKI trys to establish a mapping from the input image to a line drawing of the expected scene, the preprocessor produces an edge-based segmentation. The final output of the preprocessor is a collection of edges detected in the image which are represented as piecewise-linear segments.

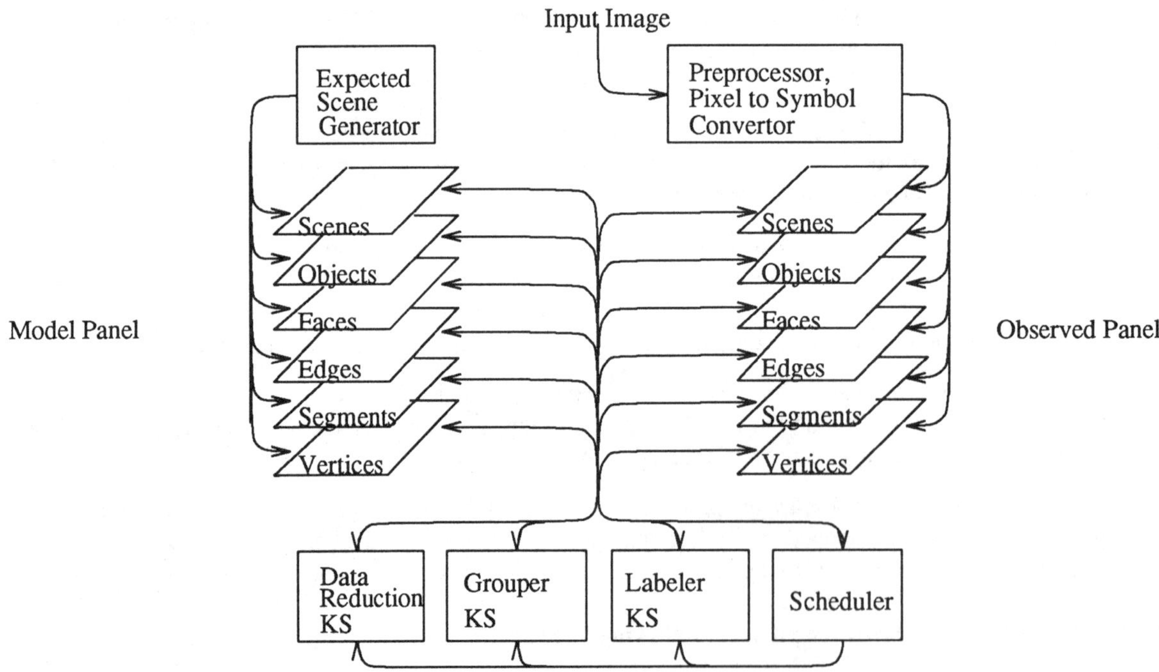

FIGURE 1. PSEIKI's Architecture

The rule based portion of PSEIKI is written in OPS83 and is implemented as a blackboard system. The expected and detected scenes are hierarchically represented on a 2 panel / 6 level blackboard. One panel of the blackboard is reserved for data defining the expected scene and is called the model panel. The other panel, called the observed panel, contains data derived from the input image.* Currently, data on the model panel is static once the expected scene data is deposited on it. However, it is thought that the data in this panel will be dynamic in future versions of the system. The ability to change the model panel could be exploited in future versions of PSEIKI.

For example, if the expected and observed scenes are misregistered by a large amount, then PSEIKI will not be able to establish a complete mapping. However, if it is able to provide the higher level system with a partial mapping, then the system may be able to generate an improved estimate of the expected scene. The improved estimate could then be deposited onto PSEIKI's model panel producing a greater correspondence between the expected and observed scenes. This new information would hopefully aid in the generation of the mapping. Currently, it is not necessary to perform this change because a high degree of correspondence is required between the observed and the expected scenes.

The ability to change the data in the model panel also could be used if multiple images were being fused to provide stereo vision capabilities. In this case, data from a second camera could replace the model information; PSEIKI should be able to use many of the same techniques to perform structural stereo fusion on the data in the two panels.

Each blackboard panel contains the following levels to represent the images: scenes, objects, faces, edges, segments and vertices. Each element in a level is defined by a finite collection of elements on lower levels. For example, a scene is made of a union of objects and a face is defined by the group of edges which form its borders. The following is a short description of the data stored at each level.

6)   Scenes -- The entire scene (expected or observed) is represented on this level. The scene is defined as the union of all objects in level 5 of the hierarchy. It provides a way of labeling multiple objects that otherwise would not be possible.

5)   Objects -- Each element on this level corresponds to a distinct physical object. The objects are defined as the union of all boundary faces from level 4.

4)   Faces -- The elements on this level represent the polygonal faces that form a boundary representation of the observable portion of the objects. A face is defined by the edges from level 3 which form its border.

3)   Edges -- These elements form the boundaries of the faces in level 4 of the hierarchy. This level is included to provide a way to compensate for segmentation deficiences. Highly collinear segments from level 2 are grouped to produce an edge in this level.

2)   Segments -- The piecewise linear segments produced by the low level vision system are represented on this level. It should be noted that this level and the Edge level are identical in the model panel because the line drawing depicting the expected scene should not need to be improved.

1)   Vertices -- The vertices are the endpoints of the segments and edges from the next two higher levels. Most of the vertices are also provided by the low level vision system.

Levels 1 - 4 are currently implemented; the rest will be implemented in the near future. It is thought these levels should be sufficient to accomplish the task of generating the mapping; however, some intermediate levels may be introduced in the future if it is thought that they will aid in solving the task.

---

* Note that these two panels correspond with the Observability and Picture graphs in ACRONYM.

Reasoning Scheme

PSEIKI has two main sub-processes that it uses to accomplish its goal of establishing a mapping from the observed to the expected scene; these processes are performed by the labeler and grouper knowledge sources (KSs). These processes can be understood by considering the data on the different levels of the hierarchy. The grouper KS determines which data elements in the lower levels of the hierarchy should be grouped to form a data element on a higher level. Since this process is primarily data driven, it is accomplished via a forward chaining scheme. The second activity that must be accomplished is the labeling of data elements; the labeler KS is used to perform this function. Because this process can be expressed most readily as a goal to be achieved, backward chaining is used.

These two subprocesses are heavily interdependent. For example, when some data elements are grouped into a higher level construct, a goal requesting that this new element be labeled is generated. Conversely, the labeler can also request that the data elements from lower levels be regrouped if it hypothesizes that the regrouping will aid in labeling. Control flow is opportunistic and is currently under investigation.

2. PSEIKI DETAILS

This section of the paper will describe the parts of PSEIKI that are currently implemented.

PREPROCESSING AND CONVERSION TO SYMBOLIC FORM.

The preprocessor accepts digitized images from the robot and outputs binary edges represented as piecewise linear segments. A block diagram representation of the preprocessor is shown in figure 2.

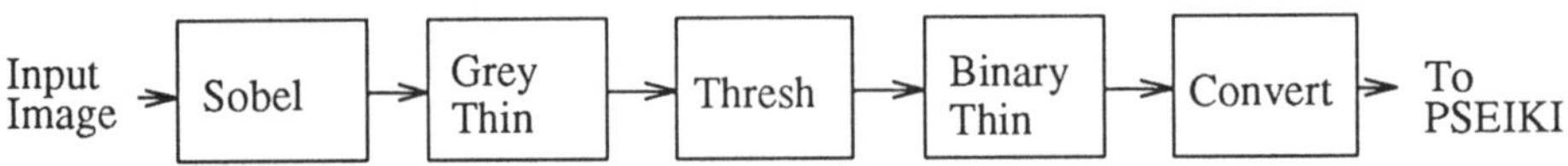

FIGURE 2. Block Diagram of PSEIKI's Preprocessor

To convert the image to a form usable by PSEIKI, the edges in the image are detected by applying a Sobel operator to the digitized gray scale image. These edges are then thinned via Eberlein's algorithm [12] and thresholded. The resulting binary images are thinned again to produce edges that are at most one pixel wide. Small edges are also deleted by the preprocessor. At this point, the image is ready to be converted into symbolic form.

The conversion to symbolic form is accomplished via an algorithm based on the Duda-Hart iterative end-point fit algorithm [13]. In this process, the following steps are performed. First, some pixels are labeled as vertices. The pixels so labeled are edge endpoints and the points at which two or more edges intersect. The edges in the segmented image are then traced from the starting to ending vertices and are represented as broken line segments. The symbolic form of each edge contains the following information: edge number, start vertex, end vertex, length and strength (average gradient magnitude). Likewise, each vertex contains the following information: row coordinate, column coordinate, vertex number and degree. Currently, low level processing is one of the most time consuming activities performed by PSEIKI; it is hoped that the speed of low level system will be increased by replacing much of it with a ridge-following algorithm.

EXPECTED SCENE GENERATION

It previously has been mentioned that one way that PSEIKI achieves domain independence is by accepting expected scene information as a line drawing. An obvious method of generating line drawings of an expected scene is via a CAD or computer graphics system; because any type of graphics system could be used to provide this information, it is considered to be separate from PSEIKI proper. However, PSEIKI does require that the graphics system be capable of performing hidden line removal. The fact that PSEIKI can be interfaced with a CAD system can be useful for 2D vision sensing in an integrated manufacturing environment where the same information used to specify a part could also be used by the vision system during the manufacturing process.

When the graphics system presents its data to PSEIKI, PSEIKI requires that the locations of the model vertices be defined first. Higher level constructs (segments, edges, etc.) are then defined by listing the subelements of which they are composed. The vertices of the edges in the expected scene can be specified in two ways: First of all, the locations of the model vertices can be specified in terms of their world coordinates. PSEIKI also can accept input in which the vertices of the model are specified by their pixel locations. If the input is of this form, PSEIKI uses its camera calibration information and immediately projects the vertices onto a plane (usually the ground plane for mobile robot applications). This projection is done so that PSEIKI can work in the world coordinate frame.

For example, a simple 2D graphics system is used to generate PSEIKI's line drawings when PSEIKI is being used to aid in the navigation of a mobile robot. This can be done because of the 2D nature of scenes typical of those gathered by the robot. To generate the expected scene, the graphics system first accounts for the robot's hypothesized current position and orientation by performing a coordinate transform on the global sidewalk map. Next, a clipping algorithm is applied to determine which edges of the sidewalk should be visible to the robot. Each section of sidewalk is then considered to be a face of a single-object scene. When the graphics system presents the data to PSEIKI, it passes the vertex coordinates in the world coordinate frame.

HIGH LEVEL VISION SYSTEM.

Currently, there are three knowledge sources in the PSEIKI system. Besides the grouper and labeler which have been discussed briefly, there is also a data reduction knowledge source. Each of these knowledge sources will be discussed in more detail in this section of the paper.

Data Reduction Knowledge Source

The goal of this knowledge source is to overcome segmentation deficiencies and reduce the amount of data seen by the sections that use inexact reasoning. This KS does not employ an uncertain reasoning scheme. The process performed by this KS is fairly conservative, but it does to reduce the amount of data by a significant amount. There are two main ways that the current segmentation is deficient.

First the segmentation procedure produces artifacts that break lines into smaller line segments. The system tries to compensate for this fact by rejoining these broken line segments. Also, if possible, the KS combines segments that are joined at a degree-two vertex into a single segment. The segmentation used also leaves small edges caused by noise. Although many of these edges are eliminated during the segmentation process, others remain because they are connected to longer segments. These "dangling" edges (all segments which are shorter than a specified length and have a degree one vertex) are eliminated by the data-reduction KS. The actions performed by this KS are shown in figure 3.

The overall result of these subprocesses is a cleaner image containing a substantially reduced number of line segments. Experimental results demonstrate that the amount of pruning is greater than 50%; this is obviously a large reduction in the amount of data.

Labeler Knowledge Source

The second subsystem performs element labeling and confidence estimation. This KS uses the Dempster-Shafer formalism to combine the certainty values used for uncertain reasoning. The combinatorial

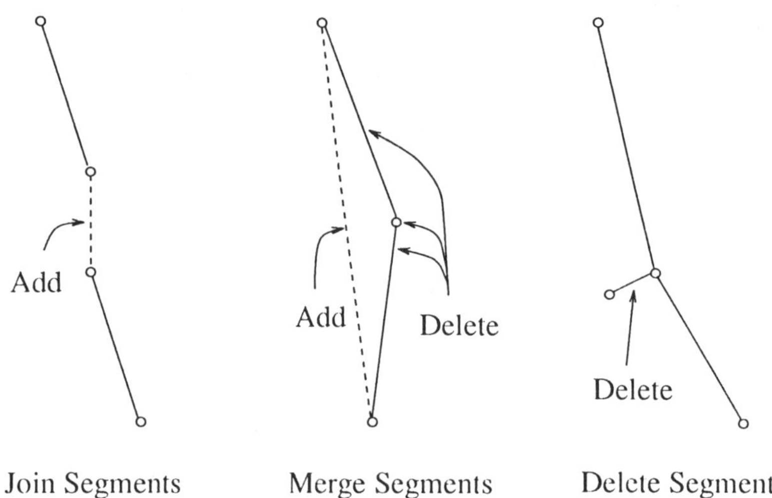

FIGURE 3. Actions performed by the Data Reduction KS

explosion of uncertainty calculations usually associated with the Dempster-Shafer scheme is avoided by the use of a hierarchical reasoning space.

The hierarchical structure of the blackboard data provides a natural basis for a hierarchical reasoning space. The levels of this space correspond naturally with the levels of the data elements on the blackboard. For example, assume on the model panel that face F_A is composed of edges $\{E_A, E_B, E_C, E_D\}$. Also assume that on the observed panel, edge E_1 is part of the group that composes face F_1. If F_1 is labeled as F_A, then E_1 can be labeled as one of $\{E_A, ..., E_D\}$ only. If the data were not arranged hierarchically, it would be necessary to consider every element on the model panel when assigning labels and when performing consistency checks. Because of the structure of PSEIKI's data, consistency checks cannot be made directly between two elements at the same level of the hierarchy if they do not have the same parent. However, consistency checks can be made indirectly by propagating an element's confidence value up through the hierarchy until a common ancestor is reached and then back down to the second element.

The frame of discernment for any element is defined by the labels which could be given to the element. In the example above, the frame of discerment for edge E_1 would be

$$\Theta = \{E_A, E_B, E_C, E_D\}$$

An element's label is defined to be the label of the element from its frame of discernment which has the greatest belief value attached to it. If the belief value of an element on an upper level of the hierarchy is changed, then all of its descendents must change their frame of discernment. However, the basic probability assignment (bpa) over the new frame of discernment incorporates the basic probability numbers from the old frame of discernment if possible. Thus, it is advantageous to perform compatibility checks between elements on upper levels of the hierarchy first to avoid performing unnecessary calculations on lower levels when frames of discernment are changed. The necessity for checking global consistency before checking local consistency seems reasonable.

Two metrics are required when updating the label belief functions for elements on any level of the hierarchy. The two metrics must provide measures of the <u>compatibility</u> and the <u>incompatibility</u> between two elements. To facilitate the correspondence between them and certainty values, both metrics should range between 0.0 and 1.0. Obviously, the metrics need not be the same for all levels of the hierarchy.

The two metrics need only provide a measure of the (in)compatibility of two elements if they are believed to correspond to the same model element. For example, if E_1 and E_2 are thought to correspond to the same model edge, then <u>collinearity(E_1, E_2)</u> is the measure of compatibility between them.

We have defined collinearity as:

$$\text{collinearity}(E_1, E_2) = \frac{D_{max} - D_{seg}}{D_{max}} \times \cos(\Theta)$$

Where Θ is the angle between the two segments; D_{seg} is the distance from the middle of E_2 to E_1 and D_{max} is the maximum possible distance between the two segments (see figure 4).

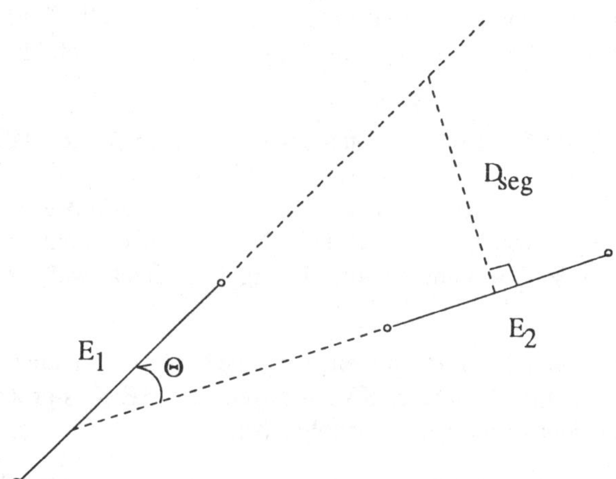

FIGURE 4. Geometry used in definition of collinearity

Likewise, the measure of incompatibility, noncollinearity(E_1, E_2), can be defined as:

$$\text{noncollinearity}(E_1, E_2) = \frac{D_{seg}}{D_{max}} \times \text{scale}(E_1) \times \sin(\Theta)$$

where $\text{scale}(E_1)$ depends on the length of E_1.

If two elements correspond to different model elements, a rigid motion transform is applied to one of them before the metric is applied. For example, if edges E_1 and E_2 are thought to correspond to model edges E_A and E_B respectively, then the measure of compatibility between E_1 and E_2 would be defined as

$$\text{compatibility}(E_1, E_2) = \text{collinearity}(E_1, T_{A,B}(E_2))$$

where $T_{A,B}$ is the rigid motion transformation that makes model edge E_B collinear with model edge E_A. In other words,

$$\text{collinearity}(E_A, T_{A,B}(E_B)) = 1.0$$

The initial bpa for segments in the observed panel is generated by finding their compatibility with edges in the model panel. When using data element B to update the belief function for data element A, the new evidence is defined to be

$$m(A) = SF * \text{compatibility}(B, A)$$

$$m(A^c) = SF * \text{incompatibility}(B, A)$$

Where SF is a scale factor $(0.0 \leq SF \leq 1.0)$ that determines the maximum amount of evidence that can be obtained by checking data element compatibility.

The labeler knowledge source used in PSEIKI uses backward chaining to establish initial labels and belief values of data elements. Although this procedure works satisfactorily during initial labeling, a simple forward-chaining procedure also is provided for updating labels. This provides a way to propagate confidence values to higher levels in the hierarchy when elements are regrouped or their labels are updated.

Grouper Knowledge Source

The grouper knowledge source builds the data elements on the upper levels of the hierarchy from the segments and vertices deposited by the low level vision system. It does this in a data-driven manner by first grouping segments into edges and then grouping the edges into faces, etc. The KS is triggered by a request to find the parent of a seed element. After the KS is triggered, it must find elements that could be members of the same group and then form the parent element on the next higher level of the hierarchy. To create the parent element, the grouper must first find all of its children. After the children are identified, they are grouped into the parent element.

In general, two elements on the same level must satisfy two requirements if they are to be grouped together. First, the elements must satisfy a level-specific adjacency constraint. These constraints usually force the KS to consider only elements that are physically close when it forms groups. The other requirement is obtained from the consistency metric used by the labeler KS; i.e., the elements must be highly consistent in order to be grouped. For example, two segments must be highly collinear and two edges must lie on a common plane to be grouped.

Although the KS should be able to group elements based solely on their geometry, it should also be able to use any label information that the labeler KS has provided. PSEIKI's grouper KS currently does this by refusing to group a data element with an incompatible label.

The grouper KS also can split elements into subelements if this is required. This can happen during the labeling process if the labeler determines that the elements were grouped incorrectly.

3. EXPERIMENTAL RESULTS

PSEIKI was run on data from a number of digitized images typical of those gathered by a mobile robot; the images in figure 5 show partial results for a typical scene. The example depicts a scene typical of what the robot would see when approaching an intersection. Figure 5a shows the edges representing the expected scene; each edge's label is indicated also. The observed scene is shown in figure 5b; note that it differs from the expected by a significant amount. Because the robot was slightly to the right of its expected position and its orientation also was slightly off, two edges that are in the expected scene are missing entirely. Shadows on the sidewalk are also a problem that the robot encounters frequently; the example also contains this type of degradation.

The other images in figure 5 show partial results produced by PSEIKI. The output of the preprocessor is shown in figure 5c. Figure 5d shows the output of the data reduction module; it was able to reduce the number of segments to 59 from 183 in the original image. The final result, figure 5e, shows the edges and labels provided by PSEIKI. Even though the expected and observed scenes differed by a significant amount, PSEIKI was able to label all but one edge. As figure 5 demonstrates, the results that PSEIKI produces are sufficient to provide a higher level navigation system the feedback need to successfully navigate a known sidewalk map.

4. CONCLUSIONS

This paper describes work in progress on PSEIKI, a domain independent vision system. It demonstrates how a line drawing of the expected scene can be used to aid in the image understanding task. It describes the architecture and reasoning schemes used by PSEIKI to accomplish its task. It details how the Dempster-Shafer theory of evidence can be applied to labeling and grouping processes in a hierarchical scene representation.

References

[1]   K. M. Andress and A. C. Kak, ''PSEIKI: A Production System Environment for Integrating Knowledge with images,'' Technical Report, School of Electrical Engineering, Purdue University.

[2]   A. C. Kak, B. A. Roberts, K. M. Andress and R. L. Cromwell, ''Experiments in the Integration of World Knowledge with Sensory Information for Mobile Robots,'' *Proc. IEEE Int. Conf. Robotics Automat.,* Vol 2., 1987, pp. 734-741.

[3]   J. Gordon and E. H. Shortliffe, ''A Method for Managing Evidential Reasoning in a Hierarchical Hypothesis Space,'' *Artificial Intelligence,* Vol. 26, 1985, pp. 323-357.

[4]   G. Shafer, *A Mathematical Theory of Evidence,* Princeton University Press, 1976.

[5]   R. A. Brooks, ''Symbolic Reasoning Among 3-D Models and 2-D Images,'' *Artificial Intelligence,* Vol. 17, 1981, pp. 285-348.

[6]   L. S. Davis and S. S. V. Hwang, ''The SIGMA Image Understanding System,'' *IEEE Proc. Comp. Vision: Rep. and Cont.,* 1985, pp. 19 - 26.

[7]   D. M. McKeown, Jr., W. A. Harvey, Jr. and J. McDermott, ''Rule-Based Interpretation of Aerial Imagery,'' *IEEE trans. on Pat. Anal. and Mach. Intel.,* Vol. PAMI-7, No. 5, 1985, pp. 570-585.

[8]   A. R. Hanson and E. M. Riseman ''VISIONS: A Computer System for Interpreting Scenes,'' *Computer Vision Systems* Academic Press, 1978, pp. 303-333.

[9]   A. M. Nazif and M. D. Levine ''Low Level Segmentation: An Expert System,'' *IEEE Trans. on Pattern Analysis and Machine Intelligence,* Vol. PAMI-6, No. 5, 1984 pp. 555-577

[10] S. T. Barnard, ''Interpreting Perspective Images,'' *Artificial Intelligence,* Vol. 21, 1983, pp. 435-462.

[11] H. G. Barrow and J. M. Tenenbaum, ''Interpreting Line Drawings as Three-Dimensional Surfaces,'' *Artificial Intelligence,* Vol. 17, 1981, pp. 75-116.

[12] R. B. Eberlein, ''An iterative gradient edge detection Algorithm,'' *Computer Graphics and Image Processing,* Vol. 5, 1976, pp. 245-253.

[13] R. O. Duda and P. E. Hart *Pattern Classification and Scene Analysis,* Wiley, New York, 1973.

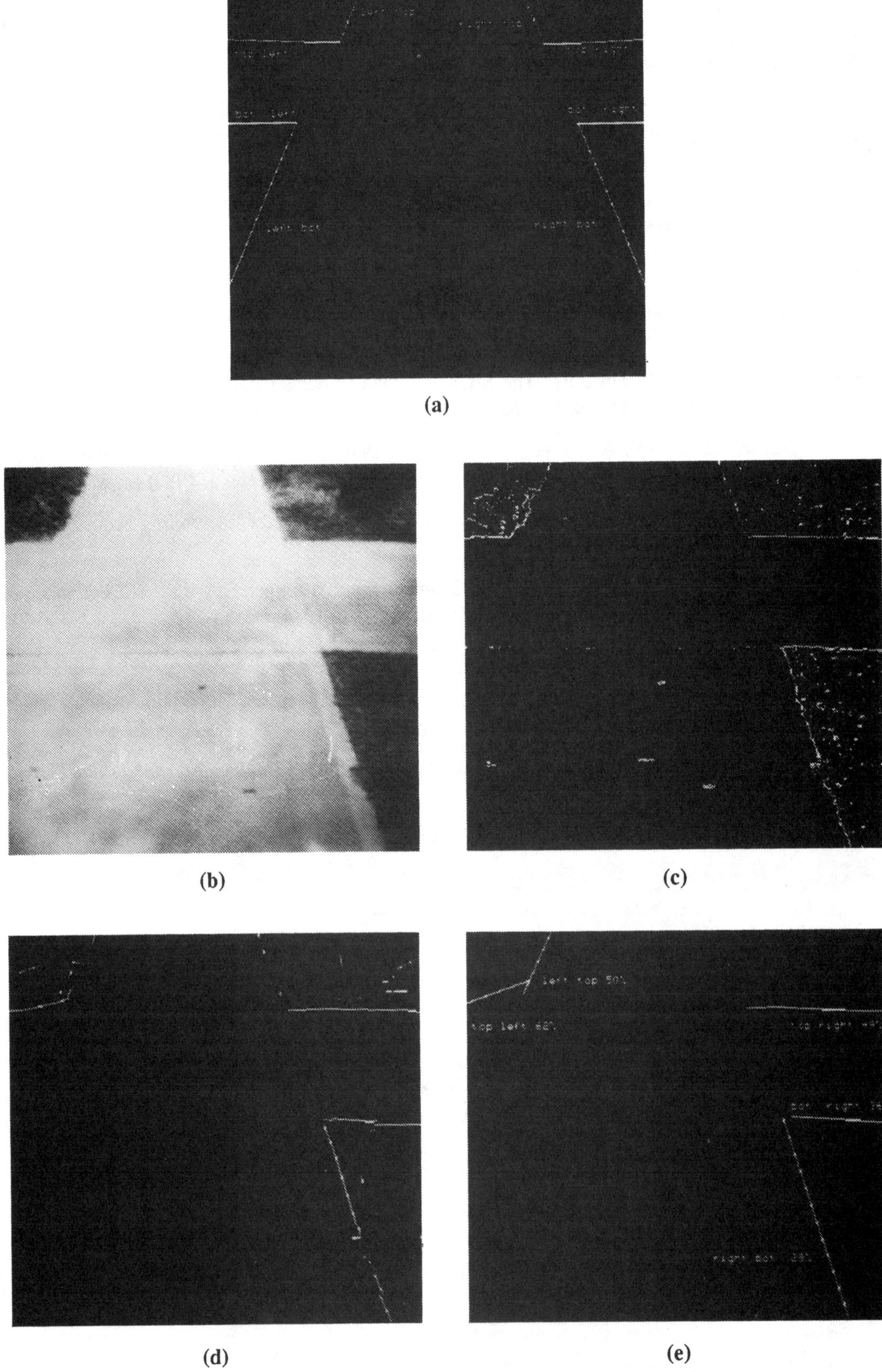

FIGURE 5. example images from PSEIKI.

AN OBJECT-BASED REPRESENTATION FOR MULTISENSORY ROBOTIC PERCEPTION

J.C. Rodger † and R.A. Browse † ‡
†Department of Computing and Information Science
‡Department of Psychology
Queen's University
Kingston, Ontario, Canada
K7L 3N6

ABSTRACT

The inclusion of multiple sensors in robot systems emphasizes the need for general techniques to combine data across sensor systems. This paper describes a simple, uniform, object-based representation and consistency scheme that facilitates the combining of input from an arbitrary number of sensors in order to recognize and locate objects. The approach assumes that raw sensor data yields features that invoke objects, together with associated orientation and location constraints. This makes it appropriate for model-based recognition systems using spatial sensors (eg. photometric, tactile, ranging). The uniform representation permits application of simple consistency operations to extract interpretations that are supported by all sensor inputs. This approach has been tested in a demonstration system that simulates the combination of photometric and force array sensing in order to recognize and locate modeled objects.

MULTISENSOR INTEGRATION

Recent reports (Allen & Bajcsy, 1985; Browse & Lederman, 1985a; Henderson & Fai, 1983; Giralt, 1985; Ellis, 1985; Durrant-Whyte, 1986) have recognized the potential of multisensory integration to improve robotic performance in tasks requiring flexible interaction with the environment. Complementary properties of distinct physical sensor systems may facilitate difficult tasks by enhancing robotic perception. The potential of distributed systems for acquisition and processing sensor data (Belzile et al, 1986) provides further support for multi-sensor systems.

The complex of related tasks involved in identifying, locating, grasping and manipulating objects constitutes a difficult robotic perception problem. In humans, vision and touch sensing cooperate elegantly in such tasks, suggesting that robotic perception may benefit from similar use of complementary sensors (Browse & Lederman, 1985a). The combination of photometric with force array sensing thus serves as a specific example of multisensory integration. In general, these sensor systems produce grey level images from visible light cameras and force/displacement arrays respectively. Continuing the analogy with human perceptual systems, we use the terms "vision" and "touch" for these categories. Of course multi-sensor integration need not be restricted to this specific combination. For example, Magee and Aggarwal (1985) described the complementary nature of intensity and range imaging systems.

Most existing multisensory systems include restricted sensor integration. For example, Luo, Tsai, and Lin (1984) described a system using moment-based features of binary images from an overhead camera and array force sensors mounted on parallel jaw grippers. Touch features were used only if necessary to disambiguate among residual possibilities following visual classification. Similarly, Allen and Bajcsy (1985) described a system using stereo vision and a finger-shaped tactile sensor to identify and locate objects. The sensor modules operated sequentially, with vision providing initial guidance for detailed tactile exploration. Though the sensors shared 3D feature representations the system accessed object models only through structural primitives derived by touch.

Several authors have proposed system properties and representation techniques for general models of multi-sensor systems. One approach (Henderson & Fai, 1983; Henderson & Shilcrat, 1984) provided a uniform interface to shared, high-level processing routines by encapsulating sensor-specific information in "logical" sensors. In addition, a common representation, the "spatial proximity graph" (Henderson, 1983), combined features from separate sensors in a single structure, prior to grouping operations. Another approach (Durrant-Whyte, 1986) combined input across sensors to maintain a network model of the environment. The technique modeled sensors as distributions of geometric observations, employing Bayesian methods to integrate sensor data. Updating one object's state to reflect new input required propagation over the network to maintain consistency. The approach assumed existence of an initial world model. An alternative general technique involved elaboration of object models to include functional properties (Ellis, 1985). Expanded models accommodated varying sensor characteristics by incorporating corresponding object properties.

A summary of general goals for multisensory systems includes: (1) accommodating an arbitrary number of sensors, while allowing full sensor interaction; (2) isolating sensor heterogeneity in low level modules; (3) allowing for sensor variations in reliability, noise and error; (4) maintaining one shared representation incorporating spatial relations; (5) increasing flexibility of object models to include sensor-specific properties.

A SIMPLE, UNIFORM REPRESENTATION

Our approach to multisensory integration extends a general principle for the use of sensory data in perceptual tasks. This principle (Browse, 1982; Witkin & Tenenbaum, 1983) holds that early extraction of structurally significant features facilitates performance by allowing knowledge of objects and their relations to contribute to early stages of the process. Early reference to object structure also provides the basis for a common representation across sensor systems.

The multisensory representation and consistency techniques described here were introduced as tools for implementing a tactile object recognition system (Browse & Lederman, 1985a; Browse, 1987). Browse (1987) noted that the source, order of acquisition, and number of tactile features were unimportant for the operation of the high-level recognition component, suggesting the generality of the techniques. The system assumed extraction of structurally significant features from raw sensor data. It included low-level, sensor-specific, processes using knowledge of object models and feature acquisition conditions to invoke sets of object possibilities and to associate orientation and location constraints with each possibility.

While the potential generality of the approach has not as yet been fully explored, an initial test of its extensibility combined the existing tactile system with a simple vision component (Rodger & Browse, 1986). The following description illustrates the application of the techniques in the implemented tactile/visual system.

The system defines objects as gravitationally stable polyhedra, resting on a support plane. Thus an object's placement is described by a single rotational and two translational parameters, referenced to a standard pose. Tests of the system supply an object, a transform to position it, and input features to simulate. The system uses the features to develop interpretations in terms of modeled objects, their orientation and location.

Visual features are straight line segments corresponding to perspective projections of object edges. There are three categories of tactile features - corner, edge, and flush contacts between the sensor and an object surface. Camera parameters and the location and orientation of the sensor at contact are assumed known.

Each sensor system uses the shared object models independently, constructing alternative representations to facilitate sensor-specific operations. Feature attributes are used to index into pre-computed structures that contain all possible candidate interpretations for each feature category. These initial interpretation possibilities are sets of object and edge/surface pairs. This uniform representation permits early consistency requirements across features, regardless of source. Input features are denoted by F_n, the set of candidate interpretations for the ith feature by C_i, and elements of the set by c_{jk}, indicating a candidate for edge/surface k of object model j. The system can then impose a single object consistency requirement, expressed as follows:

$$C_i = \left\{ c_{jk} \ \middle| \ \forall F_n \ \exists c_{jl} \left[c_{jl} \in C_n \right] \right\} \tag{1}$$

This ensures that any surviving candidate has support across all features.

The association of a spatial feature with part of an object imposes constraints on the object's orientation and location. The principal consistency operation depends on expansion of simple possibilities by adding the associated constraints on placement parameters. Computing these is again specific to each sensor system. The process requires an additional step for vision features, using the feature's image coordinates, the camera parameters and the model coordinates to invert the perspective projection. Both sensor systems then compute the transform parameters to take the model from the standard pose to that associated with the obtained feature.

Some feature/object pairings only yield parameter ranges. These are expanded by subdividing into equally spaced increments (to whatever resolution is desired), evaluating dependent parameters at each increment. Then the full consistency operation is applied, retaining only interpretations and associated placement parameter values with support across all features. Parameter consistency is operationalized as the matching of corresponding values within specified tolerances.

An expanded candidate may be denoted by $c\tau_{jk}$, where τ_{jk} represents the constraints on the placement parameters. The consistency requirement is expressed as:

$$C_i = \left\{ c\tau_{jk} \;\middle|\; \forall F_n \,\exists\, c\tau_{jl} \left[c\tau_{jl} \in C_n \,\wedge\, \left(\tau_{jk} \leftarrow \tau_{jk} \cap \tau_{jl} \right) \neq \phi \right] \right\} \tag{2}$$

The intersection operator is used in this expression to indicate the placement parameter values consistent over the two constraints. Only the consistent values are retained, and if there are none, the entire candidate interpretation is eliminated.

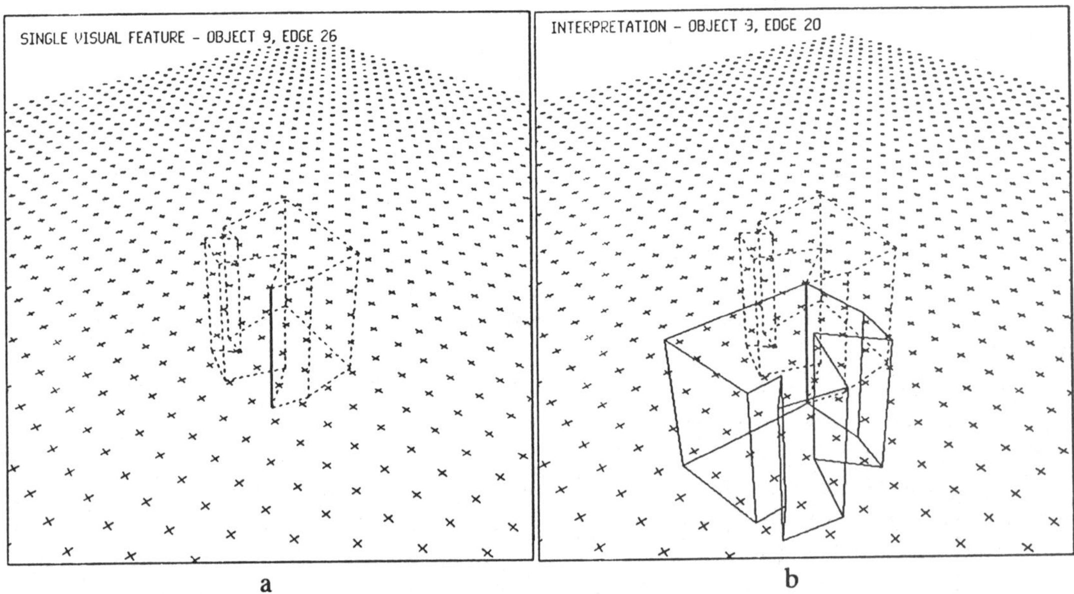

Figure 1. Single Visual Feature and Sample Interpretation.

To illustrate the operation of the system we develop an example, varying the input features. For the example, the system included nine object models. The camera parameters, input object, and placement were constant. In the figures the input object is shown by dashed lines, visual features by bold lines, tactile features by a stylized sensor, and interpretations by solid lines.

The first step used a single visual feature. Figure 1a shows the input. A visual feature due to a vertical edge fixes its location but could arise from many different combinations of parameter values. Figure 1b shows one interpretation. This single feature eliminated candidates from all but two objects, which are the same height. Figure 2a shows input for a single tactile feature, a corner contact on the same object edge. This least constraining tactile feature type admits all convex corners as possibilities. Part b of the figure shows one interpretation.

The next step integrated the previous two features (see Figure 3a). Together they allowed considerably more pruning of candidates. Part b of the figure shows one interpretation. The correct interpretation was among those generated by the system in this and the next two steps.

Figure 4a shows the integration of features from both sensors but different parts of the object. This provided more discriminatory power, yielding just three interpretations, each for a different edge of

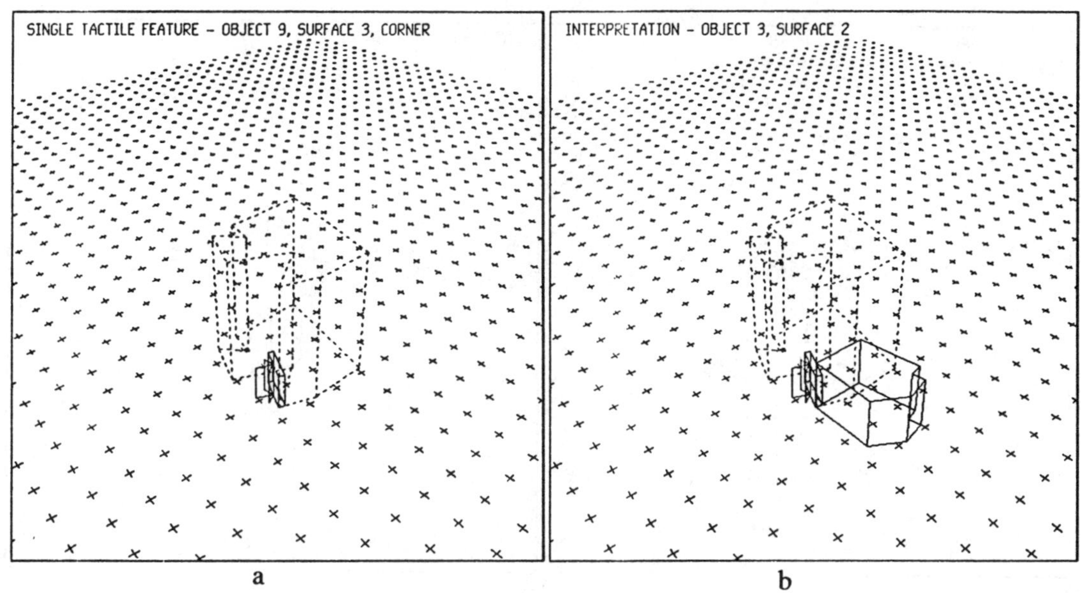

Figure 2. Single Tactile Feature and Sample Interpretation.

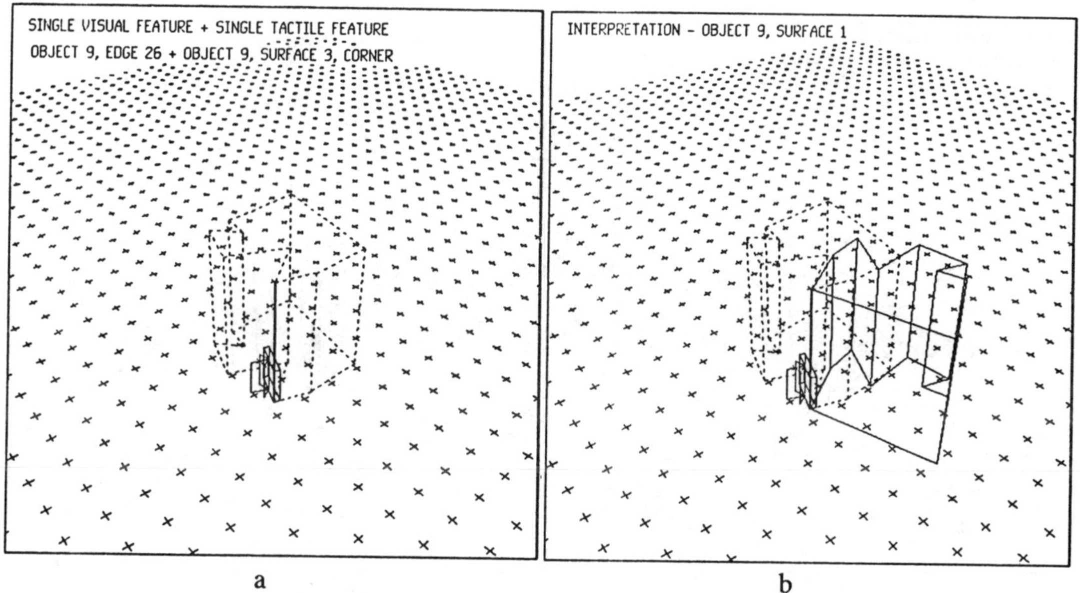

Figure 3. Visual + Tactile Feature and Sample Interpretation.

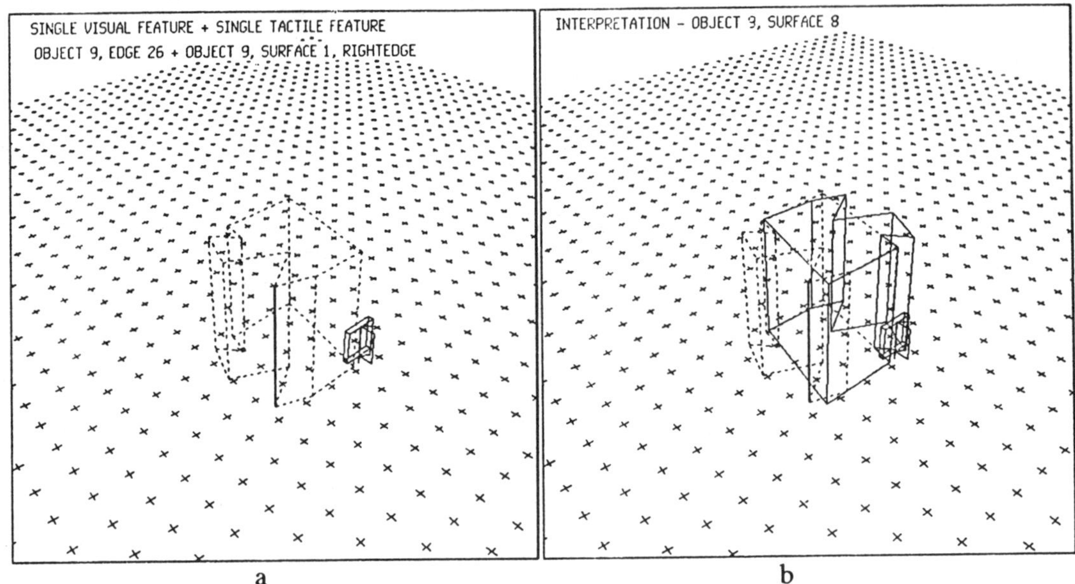

Figure 4. Separate Visual and Tactile Feature and Sample Interpretation.

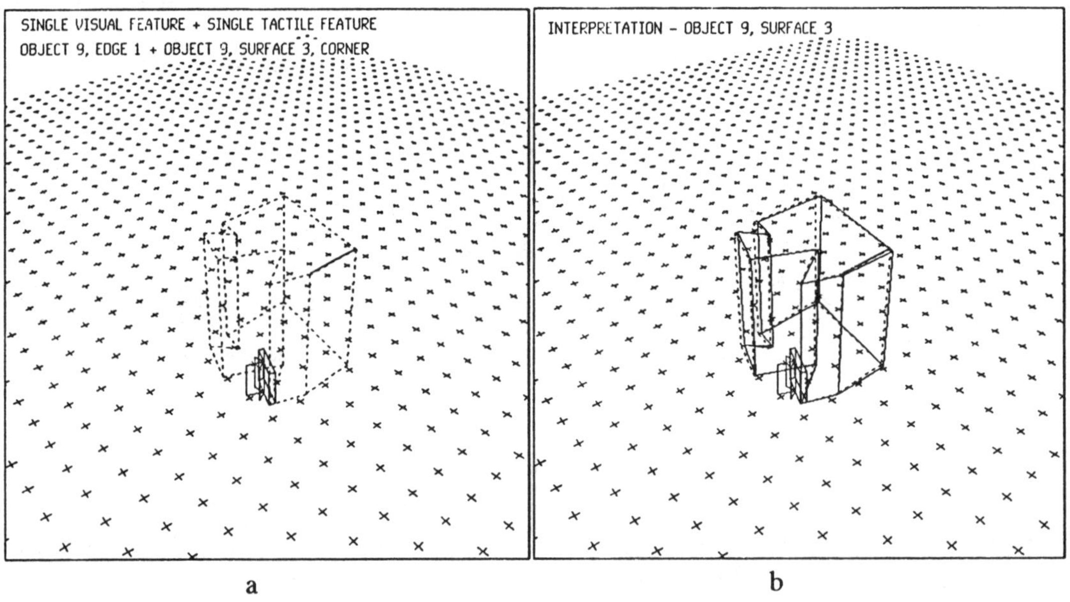

Figure 5. Separate Visual and Tactile Feature and Correct Interpretation.

the correct object. Figure 4b illustrates an incorrect interpretation. It shows a correctly located tactile contact, with an edge close to the input visual feature, the discrepancy reflecting placement parameter tolerances. The final step also used features from each sensor. This combination left only a single interpretation. Figure 5 shows the input and single surviving interpretation, which is correct to within the parameter tolerances.

Table 1 summarizes these results. The numbers in the "Consistent Candidates" column of the table demonstrate the advantage of integrating features over sensor systems. While there were 13 candidates for the single visual feature and 52 for the single tactile feature, the combination limited candidates to only 11. The feature pairs in the final two steps provided additional discriminatory power.

SUMMARY AND EXTENSIONS

The representation technique employed in the system described above appears to be a good candidate for a general approach to multisensory integration. It makes no assumptions about the number or nature of sensors, except that they provide spatial data that can be related to modeled objects. It allows data from all sensors to participate equally in forming system interpretations. Sensor-specific properties and processes are restricted to low-level modules that could run largely independently in a distributed system.

Though the techniques exhibit considerable generality, they clearly will require some elaboration in order to be completely general. For example, we recognize that the restricted classes of objects considered to date, and the limited freedom of object pose in demonstration systems both require generalization. It is a relatively simple matter to model more general classes of objects, but may result in much greater complexity at the level of associating constraints on placement parameters. We propose to investigate hierarchical consistency operations as a possible approach to handling the complexity resulting from six degree of freedom placement possibilities and elaborated object sets.

One potential problem with the proposed representation is that it does not explicitly accommodate probabilistic or confidence measures that may be associated with sensor input. While on one hand the uniformity of the representation means that failure of a particular sensor need not disable the entire system, on the other hand, one bad sensor input, if it resulted in the failure to activate the correct interpretation, could cause the system to fail to derive a consistent interpretation across sensors. The latter problem might be addressed several ways, within the same general framework.

A simple but computationally unattractive solution would be for the system to backtrack in the event of failure to find a consistent interpretation, considering subsets of the initial feature set. The present technique does not preclude attaching confidence estimates to input features. These could be used to order the inclusion of features in the consistency process. Another general technique that we would like to incorporate is the incremental use of the developing interpretation to guide active feature acquisition.

Table 1. Summary of Example.

Example Results with Varying Input Features						
Step	Visual Feature	Candidates	Tactile Feature	Candidates	Consistent Candidates	Total Interpretations
1	Edge 26	53	None	–	13	416
2	None	–	Corner S3	52	52	396
3	Edge 26	53	Corner S3	52	11	81
4	Edge 26	53	RtEdge S1	52	3	3
5	Edge 1	118	Corner S3	52	1	1

The maintenance of a complex model of space is outside the scope of the present version of the approach, although extension to multiple objects should be relatively straightforward, using subsets of features, perhaps grouped spatially. Addition of another layer could incorporate individual objects as nodes in a more general representation of the environment.

Acknowledgements

The research reported here was supported in part by the Natural Sciences and Engineering Research Council of Canada under Operating Grant number A2427.

References

Allen, P. & Bajcsy, R. (1985). Object recognition using vision and touch. *Proceedings of the Ninth International Joint Conference on Artificial Intelligence (Vol. 2),* Los Angeles CA., August 18-23, 1131-1137.

Belzile, C., Coulas, M., MacEwen, G.H., & Marquis, G. (1986). RNET: a hard real-time distributed programming system. *Proceedings of the Real-Time Systems Symposium,* New Orleans LA., December 2-4, 2-13.

Browse, R.A. (1982). Knowledge-based visual interpretation using declarative schemata. *Technical Report 82-12,* University of British Columbia, Vancouver, British Columbia, Canada.

Browse, R.A. (1987) Feature-Based Tactile Object Recognition. *IEEE Transactions on Pattern Analysis and Machine Intelligence.* in press.

Browse, R.A. & Lederman, S.J. (1985a). A framework for robotic perception. *TR-85-165,* Department of Computing and Information Science, Queen's University, Kingston, Ontario, Canada.

Browse, R.A. & Lederman, S.J. (1985b). Feature-based robotic tactile perception. *Proceedings of the IEEE Conference on Computer Aided Technologies, COMPINT-85,* Montréal Québec, September, 455-458.

Durrant-Whyte, H.F. (1986). Consistent integration and propagation of disparate sensor observations. *MS-CIS-86-08,* Department of Computer and Information Science, Moore School, University of Pennsylvania, Philadelphia PA 19104-6389.

Ellis, R.E. (1985). An approach to the integration of vision and touch for robot control. *COINS Technical Report 85-20,* Laboratory for Perceptual Robotics, Department of Computer and Information Science, University of Massachusetts, Amherst MA 01003.

Giralt, G. (1985). Research trends in decisional and multisensory aspects of third generation robots. In H. Hanafuso & H. Inoue (Eds.), *Robotics Research: The Second International Symposium* (pp. 512-520). Cambridge MA: MIT Press.

Henderson, T.C. & Fai, W.S. (1983). A multi-sensor integration and data acquisition system. *Proceedings of the Conference on Computer Vision and Pattern Recognition,* Washington D.C., June 1983, 274-279.

Henderson, T. & Shilcrat, E. (1984). Logical sensor systems. *Journal of Robotic Systems,* 1, 169-193.

Luo, R., Tsai, W. & Lin, J.C. (1984). Object recognition with combined tactile and visual information. In A. Pugh (Ed.), *Proceedings of the 4th International Conference on Robot Vision and Sensory Controls,* London UK, October 9-11, 183-196.

Magee, M.J. & Aggarwal, J.K. (1985). Using multisensory images to derive the structure of three-dimensional objects - a review. *Computer Vision, Graphics, and Image Processing,* 32, 145-157.

Rodger, J.C. & Browse, R.A. (1986). Combining visual and tactile perception for robotics. *Proceedings of the Sixth Canadian Conference on Artificial Intelligence,* Montréal Québec, May 21-23, 166-171.

Witkin, A.P. & Tenenbaum, J.M. (1983). On the role of structure in vision. In J. Beck, B. Hope, & A. Rosenfeld (Eds.), *Human and Machine Vision* (pp.481-543). New York NY: Academic Press.

A FRAMEWORK FOR REPRESENTING AND REASONING ABOUT THREE-DIMENSIONAL OBJECTS FOR VISION[*]

Ellen Lowenfeld Walker
Computer Science Department
Carnegie-Mellon University
Pittsburgh, PA 15213

Martin Herman
Robot Systems Division
National Bureau of Standards
Gaithersburg, MD 20899

Takeo Kanade
Computer Science Department
Carnegie-Mellon University
Pittsburgh, PA 15213

Abstract

The capabilities for representing and reasoning about three-dimensional objects are essential for knowledge-based, 3D photo-interpretation systems that combine domain knowledge with image processing, as demonstrated by such systems as 3D Mosaic and Acronym. Three-dimensional representation of objects is necessary for many additional applications such as robot navigation and 3D change detection. Geometric reasoning is especially important, since geometric relationships between object parts are a rich source of domain knowledge. A practical framework for geometric representation and reasoning must incorporate projections between a 2D image and a 3D scene, shape and surface properties of objects, and geometric and topological relationships between objects. In addition, it should allow easy modification and extension of the system's domain knowledge and be flexible enough to organize its reasoning efficiently to take advantage of the current available knowledge. We are developing such a framework, called the 3D FORM (Frame-based Object Recognition and Modelling) System. This system uses frames to represent objects such as buildings and walls, geometric features such as lines and planes, and geometric relationships such as parallel lines.

[*] This research was sponsored by the Defense Advanced Research Projects Agency (DOD), ARPA Order No. 4976, monitored by the Air Force Avionics Laboratory Under Contract F33615-84-K-1520. The views and conclusions contained in this document are those of the authors and should not be interpreted as representing the official policies, either expressed or implied, of the Defense Advanced Research Projects Agency or of the U. S. Government.

1. Introduction

We are developing the 3D FORM (Frame-based Object Recognition and Modelling) System, a framework for representing and reasoning about three-dimensional objects. This framework incorporates projections between a 2D image and a 3D scene, representations of shape and surface properties of objects and geometric and topological relationships between objects, and a geometric reasoning capability. Such a representation and reasoning capability is essential for knowledge-based, 3D photo-interpretation systems which combine domain knowledge with image processing, as demonstrated by such systems as 3D Mosaic [4, 5] and ACRONYM [2], and for many applications such as robot navigation, 3D change detection, and simulating the appearance of a scene from arbitrary viewpoints. The 3D FORM system uses frames to represent objects such as buildings and walls, geometric features such as lines and planes, and geometric relationships such as parallel lines. Active procedures attached to the frames dynamically compute values as needed. The order of processing is controlled largely by accessing objects' slots, so the system performs both top-down and bottom-up reasoning, depending on the current available knowledge.

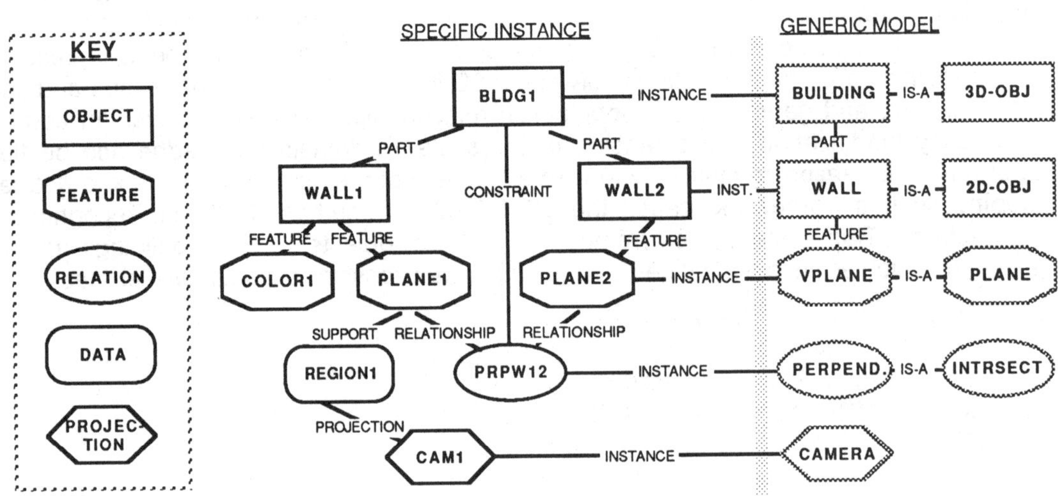

Figure 1: Portion of knowledge base for buildings

The 3D FORM system can include knowledge about model and data objects organized into IS-A and PART hierarchies, along with relationships between object features, and projections used to convert between model objects and data objects. The knowledge includes both generic object models and specific instances of objects. Figure 1 shows a portion of the knowledge that might be represented about a building. A BUILDING is a 3D-OBJECT, with a WALL, which is a 2D-OBJECT as one of its parts. The specific building BLDG1 has parts WALL1 and WALL2 whose geometric features are the primitive geometric objects PLANE1 and PLANE2, respectively. In addition to its geometric feature, WALL1 has the photometric feature COLOR1. The knowledge that a building's walls are mutually perpendicular is represented for BLDG1 by the instance PRPW12 of the PERPENDICULAR-PLANES relationship. The arguments to PRPW12 are PLANE1 and PLANE2, the geometric features of BLDG1's walls. The geometric feature PLANE1 is supported by the data object REGION1, which came from an image whose projection between 2D and 3D is CAM1.

In the current implementation, only 3D objects, geometric features, and geometric relationships are represented. The next section will discuss some of the issues in geometric reasoning for knowledge-based vision systems and how some existing systems have addressed them. The following sections will discuss the representations of primitive geometric objects, geometric relationships, and composite objects in the 3D FORM system. The final section will discuss the application of the representation to 3D data and present examples.

2. Geometric reasoning in knowledge-based vision systems

Domain knowledge has been used by previous vision systems to compensate for the inadequacies of low level image processing, as well as to generate reasonable assumptions to make it possible to recover 3D shape from 2D data. Shape, one of the most important cues for object recognition, must be included in any domain knowledge representation for a vision system. Therefore, a knowledge based vision system must be able to represent and reason about geometric objects. Geometric reasoning assists in both data acquisition (bottom-up reasoning) and model matching (top-down reasoning). The overall control of the system should be flexible enough to allow these two processes to be combined to achieve the best results based on the current state of the knowledge base. In addition, the system itself should be domain-independent, with the domain dependent portions collected into a separate replaceable module so the domain knowledge can be easily modified or extended. Each of the systems described in this section has met some of these goals, but no system has adequately addressed all of them.

The 3D Mosaic system [4, 5] used 3D geometric reasoning in the domain of aerial images of polyhedral buildings to acquire a scene description from images from multiple points of view. Using a polyhedral boundary geometric representation, it hypothesized missing parts of objects in the first view according to a weak model of the urban domain encoded into the program itself. With the domain models implicit in the system's code and no explicit representation of generic objects, it would be difficult to modify or extend 3D Mosaic's domain knowledge. For example, it would be a major programming effort to extend the 3D Mosaic system to make use of the colors of buildings or the textures of their surfaces. Since it was designed as a model acquisition system, the 3D Mosaic system was limited to bottom-up reasoning. When new information invalidated one of the hypotheses generated for missing parts, a complicated network of backpointers was followed to eliminate the effect of the failed hypothesis.

Unlike the 3D Mosaic system, ACRONYM [2] used explicit representation of generic objects, representing its geometric objects in a hierarchy of frames. Geometric relationships between objects were represented as quantified algebraic inequalities, and interpretation was done by an external graph matching procedure. To perform the matching, ACRONYM needed strong domain models. The graph matching procedure was primarily top-down, with special low-level objects (ribbons and ellipses) for its generalized cylinder representation of objects. Since the matching procedure was independent of the data, ACRONYM could not organize its search to match the most certain or most complete data first and restrict the search for the remainder of the data. The use of quantifiers removed the constraints one level from the data, making them more difficult to read, modify, and extend.

Mundy and others [1, 8, 10] are developing a system which combines algebraic methods for geometric reasoning with a hierarchical organization of knowledge (both object knowledge and knowledge about geometric reasoning). Algebraic constraints from the perspective projection are combined with additional constraints from the model to derive equations describing a family of interpretations for each object. Inequalities from line labeling [6] are then used to constrain the solutions to these equations. Since the relationships as well as the objects are represented in a concept hierarchy, the geometric reasoning component should be both flexible and extensible. The disadvantage of using algebraic methods is their inefficiency for handling inequalities, an important component of real-world geometric relationships.

Although Hwang's thesis [7] used only two-dimensional geometric reasoning, its method for representing relationships was unique. Each relationship was represented as two procedures attached to its arguments: one for top-down hypothesizing and the other for bottom-up verification. Representing the relationships as active components of the object representation allowed both top-down and bottom-up reasoning, although not at the same time. Only a restricted class of binary relationships was implemented.

Like ACRONYM and Hwang's system, the 3D FORM system uses frames to represent its objects. Frames are also used by the system to represent relationships between objects, and have active procedures (demons) attached to their arguments so that they are hypothesized or computed as needed. Primitive objects also have demons to compute missing parts of their descriptions from other parts. For example, a line has a demon to compute its vector from the known points on the line. Since both object and relationship knowledge are explicitly represented, extending the system to additional domains involves adding new frames but not modifying the code that manipulates the frames. The reasoning process is controlled largely by accessing objects, which are computed as needed, so the representation is equally amenable to top-down and bottom-up processing. In addition, there is no need for an external ordering mechanism such as a focus of attention. Instead, the dynamically computed COMPLETENESS value for each object is used to select the most complete object to match or relationship to evaluate next.

3. Representing primitive geometric objects

Geometric representation in the 3D FORM system has three parts: (1) representing primitive geometric objects such as points, lines, and planes; (2) representing primitive geometric relationships between these objects such as parallel lines and perpendicular planes; and (3) combining this information with a part hierarchy to represent composite objects such as faces and buildings. All objects and relationships are represented using frames. The *slots* of the frames are used to store parameters of the object or relationship. Each slot may have *demons* associated with it to compute or recompute the slot when necessary. In addition, some slots have *facets*, which contain constraints on the values that can fill those slots. Frames representing generic objects are arranged in an IS-A hierarchy, and each specific object has an INSTANCE slot pointing back to its generic object. Slots left empty in a particular instance of an object are inherited from the generic object across the INSTANCE link and by means of the IS-A hierarchy.

The primitive geometric objects represented in the current system are *points*, *lines*, and *planes*. For example, the generic line frame shown in Figure 2 has slots for points on the line, the line's vector, vectors of lines perpendicular to the line, and the error in fitting a line to the points. The slots PT1, VEC, ERR, and COMPLETENESS have if-needed demons (designated with N in the figure) to determine the value from other slots as needed. In addition, the slots PT1 and PTS have if-added demons to propagate the new information to other slots in the frame. For example, when additional points are added to a line, the line's old vector and error values are invalidated, so they are deleted. When one of these values is needed later, it is recomputed by fitting a line to the set of points. Often, the value of an object's slot may be computed in more than one way from other slots of that object. For example, the vector of a line may be computed either by fitting a line to its points, or by taking the cross product of its normal vectors. The if-needed demons take into account the available information in choosing a method to compute their results.

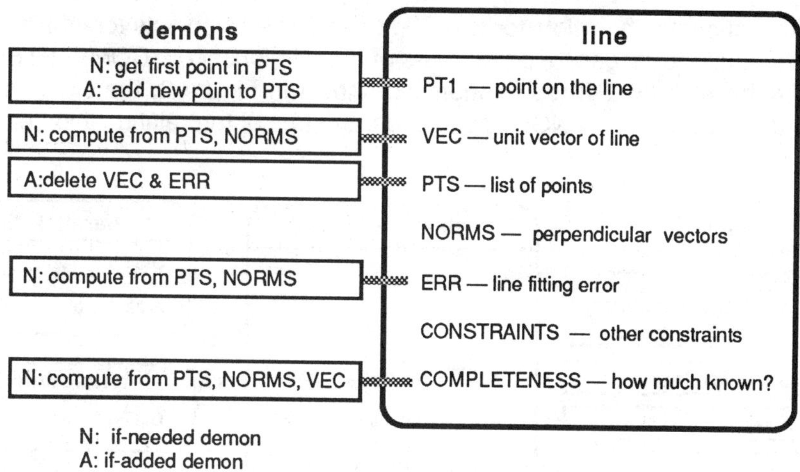

Figure 2:   Representation of a line

In addition to the slots for the parameters of the object, every geometric object has slots to represent knowledge used in computing its relationships and matching its instances. Currently, we have defined the following slots for this purpose:

- ERR contains the error in applying the geometric primitive to the given constraints (e.g. the error in fitting a line to a set of points). This value is used to constrain matches.

- CONSTRAINTS contains geometric constraints that cannot be represented by filling in any other slot. These constraints allow relationships to affect later matching. Each value consists of a function to compute the constraint and a pointer to the relationship that caused it, and is evaluated when sufficient information is added to the constrained object. For example, if two lines are supposed to intersect, but neither has any points specified yet, a constraint is placed on each line consisting of a function to compute the distance between the lines and a pointer back to the intersection relationship. When one line is further specified, the distance function is executed. If the distance is small enough, the constraint of intersection has been satisfied and is removed, and if the distance is too large, an error is returned to the process that changed the line. If the other line is not yet specified, the original relationship is re-evaluated to put a new constraint on the other line.

- COMPLETENESS contains a user-defined measure of the information stored in the object. This value is used for sorting relationship computation and matching operations so the most complete items are tried first. For example, the completeness of a line is greatest if two or more points are known, but greater if one point and the vector are known than if only one point or the vector is known.

4. Representing primitive geometric relationships

Like geometric objects, primitive geometric relationships are also represented by frames. The system currently considers relationships between pairs of lines, between pairs of planes, between lines and the planes they lie in, and between points and the lines they lie on. Each frame representing a primitive geometric relationship has slots for two or more geometric objects for which the relationship is defined, one or more numeric ranges for parameters of the relationship, a COMPLETENESS slot, and a COMPUTE slot. In the **related-2-lines** relationship shown in Figure 3, the slots L1, L2, and INTPT contain objects, and slots DIST and ANGLE contain parameters of the relationship between the objects.

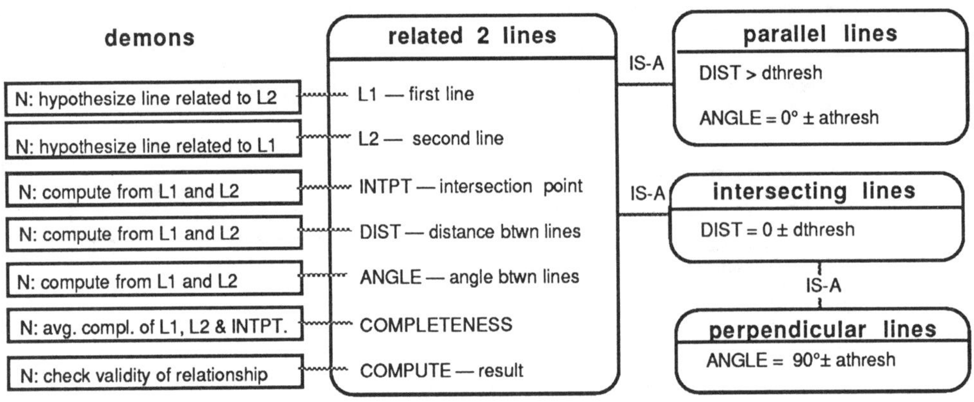

Figure 3:   Relationships between 2 lines

The COMPLETENESS slot and the COMPUTE slot are computed only when needed. A demon attached to the completeness slot of each relationship computes the average completeness value of the geometric object arguments of the relationship. A demon attached to the COMPUTE slot of each relationship evaluates the relationship. The evaluation function first attempts to fill in any missing slots by hypothesizing geometric objects or computing numeric ranges. When objects are hypothesized, only the slot values that are known are filled in. After attempting to hypothesize each missing argument, the evaluation function adds constraints derived from the relationship to each geometric object. For example, the **perpendicular-lines** relationship adds the vector of L1 to the norms of L2, the vector of L2 to the norms of L1, and the coordinates of INTPT to both lines. If the geometric arguments of the relationship are not fully specified, as much constraint as possible is applied to the remaining geometric objects. Finally, the evaluation function computes the true values for the numeric arguments of the relationship and determines whether they fall within the specified ranges.

The **related-2-lines** relationship has several specializations, also shown in Figure 3. The **parallel-lines** relationship is a **related-2-lines** relationship specialized to have the angle between the lines near zero and a positive distance between the lines. Similarly, an **perpendicular-lines** relationship is a specialization of **intersecting-lines,** which in turn is a specialization of **related-2-lines**.

5. Representing composite objects

Primitive geometric objects and their relationships are combined with a part hierarchy and other features to create composite objects. The slots of a composite object fall into three classes: features, which describe the object as a whole; parts, which are lower level objects; and constraints, which relate the features of an object and its parts. For example, Figure 4 shows the representation of a generic wall. Its parts are two vertical edges, two horizontal edges, and four vertices, and its geometric feature is a vertical plane. Among the constraints of the wall are a **perpendicular-planes** relationship between its geometric feature and the ground and **perpendicular-lines** relationships between the top edge and each of the two vertical edges.

Like primitive objects and relationships, all objects have COMPLETENESS and COMPUTE slots. The completeness of an object is computed by averaging the completeness values of its features and parts. Accessing an object's COMPUTE slot causes a conjunction of the object's constraints to be evaluated. As a side effect of computing an object, hypotheses for the object's parts and features may be derived.

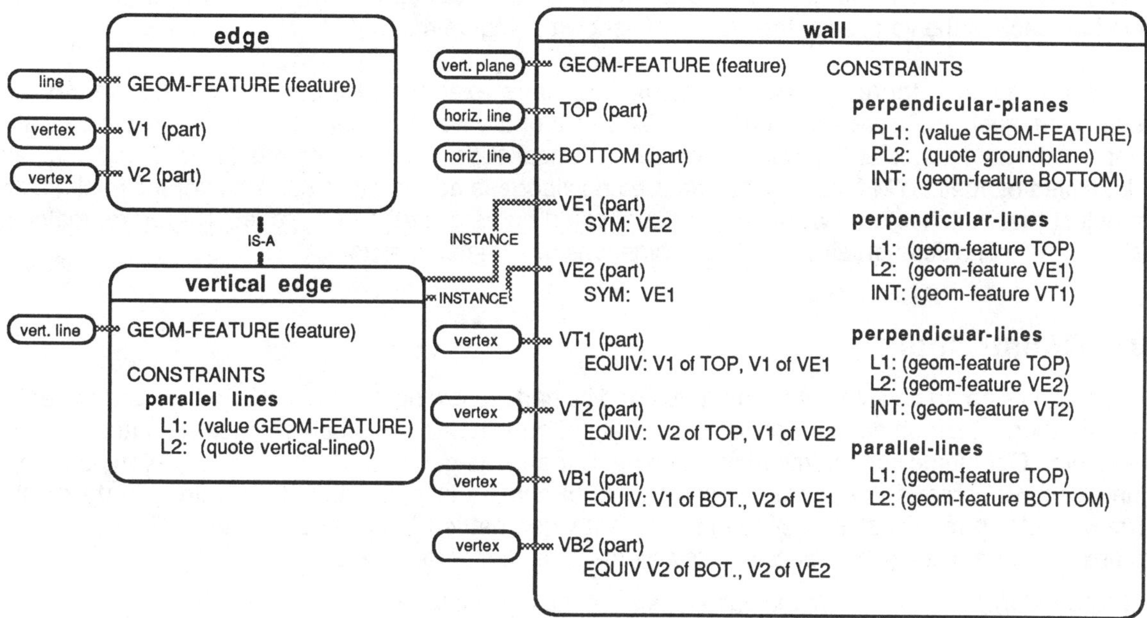

Figure 4: Representations of wall, vertical edge, and edge

5.1. Features

Object features include shape, color, texture, reflectance, and other object characteristics useful for matching world objects to their sensor representations. Currently, only shape is represented, with the GEOM-FEATURE slot of each object pointing to its underlying primitive geometric object. The INSTANCE facet of a feature points to the frame that must be instantiated to fill it in. Its value is used for type-checking in matching, and to instantiate new hypotheses for features. In Figure 4, for example, the geometric features of a wall, a vertical edge, and an edge respectively are a vertical plane, a vertical line, and a line. Each feature has its own primitive frame representation.

5.2. Parts

Objects are organized into a part hierarchy to allow the system to focus on an appropriate level of detail for the current evaluation (for example, to ignore windows until the walls are completed). Each object part is an instance of another object according to its INSTANCE facet. For example,the parts VE1 and VE2 of a wall are instances of vertical edges. The parts of an object participate in the object's constraint relationships, and objects are matched by recursively matching their parts.

Since an intersection relationship between two objects also refers to the object of intersection, the object of intersection is part of the parent object as well as both of the intersecting parts. For example, the vertex at the intersection of the top edge and one vertical edge of a wall is part of the wall, and also part of the top edge and the vertical edge. To enforce consistency between such equivalent parts, the EQUIV facet of each part of a parent object contains pointers to equivalent parts of the child objects, and demons check all equivalent parts whenever a part slot is accessed. If the values of the equivalent parts cannot be reconciled, an error is signalled to the process that accessed the slot. The EQUIV facet is defined for each of the vertices of the wall frame shown in Figure 4.

In some objects, there are pairs of parts that have exactly the same INSTANCE values and relationships, such as the vertical edges VE1 and VE2 of the wall in Figure 4. Each is perpendicular to the top and bottom edges and parallel to the other vertical edge. These slots are called *symmetric* , and are identified by their SYM facets. Until feature knowledge is added by filling in one of these slots, any data object that matches one will match both and could be assigned to either one. Therefore, matching must take into consideration all possible combinations of symmetric slots.

5.3. Constraints

Constraints on an object relate its features and its parts, allowing each to be hypothesized or verified from the other. Each object currently has two sets of constraints: geometric constraints and inclusion constraints. Geometric constraints relate an object's parts, its geometric feature, and prototype frames. Figure 4 shows some of the geometric constraints of a wall. Inclusion constraints are **points-on-line** or **lines-in-plane** relationships between the object's geometric feature and its parts. Each constraint is a template for a relationship specifying its arguments in one of four ways:

(**value** *slot*):	Use the value of *slot* in the current frame.
(**geom-feature** *slot*):	Use the GEOM-FEATURE of the value of *slot* in the current frame.
(**local** *var*):	Use the value of the local variable *var*, initializing to NIL if necessary. Local variables persist throughout the conjunction they are defined in.
expression:	Evaluate the expression, usually a prototype frame.

Thus, the first constraint of the wall in Figure 4 specifies that the wall's GEOM-FEATURE is perpendicular to the ground plane (a prototype frame) intersecting in the line that is the GEOM-FEATURE of the BOTTOM of the wall.

The evaluation function for an object computes a conjunction of the relationships specified by its constraints. A side effect of evaluating an object's relationships is to generate hypotheses for missing parts of the objects and fill in partially specified objects when possible.

6. Applying the representation to 3D wire frame data

A model of a particular domain is created by defining the generic objects found in that domain. In addition, features and relationships between the objects are defined using the facilities described in Sections 3-5. The 3D FORM system applies the domain model to real world data to recognize objects and hypothesize their missing parts. Top-down and bottom-up reasoning are combined to take best advantage of the available data, controlled by the procedural component of the knowledge representation. Given a simple domain model of rectangular prism buildings, the 3D FORM system interprets a set of 3D edges and vertices (such as the wire frames produced by the stereo and monocular components of the 3D Mosaic system) as buildings, hypothesizing missing edges, vertices, and faces as necessary. First, appropriate initial edge, line, vertex, and point frames are created from the input. The initial frames are then grouped into generic 2D and 3D objects, and the relationships between them are determined. Finally, the IS-A hierarchy is followed by means of a specialization procedure to find the most specific possible interpretation for each object and fill in its slots. Once all input features have been placed into object slots, the top-level objects are computed. The result is a completed building for each wire frame, including hypotheses for any previously missing parts. New 3D data may be used to verify these hypotheses.

6.1. Acquiring object frames from wire frames

The first step in data interpretation is to create initial object frames from the input points and lines. For each point, a point frame is instantiated, and the coordinates of the point are added to the new frame. If the point is a vertex between two lines, a vertex frame is also instantiated, and its GEOM-FEATURE is set to the point. For each line, a line frame is instantiated and its PTS slot is filled in. In addition, an edge frame is instantiated with its GEOM-FEATURE set to the line, and the edge's vertices, if any, are filled in.

Next, the initial object frames are grouped into more complex objects, and the relationships between them are determined. The dual space [9] is used to efficiently find parallel and coincident lines and planes. Each new line is added to a dual space database. For each pair of parallel or coincident lines found in the dual space, an appropriate relationship is instantiated. In addition, each pair of lines intersecting at a vertex is stored according to the dual of the plane spanned by the lines. The dual space database is then searched to group all sets of coplanar edges into faces, and to determine parallel relationships between faces. Finally, an intersection relationship is instantiated for each vertex and the pair of lines it intersects, and for each edge and the pair of planes it intersects. The angle of intersection for each of these relationships is automatically computed when it is needed or whenever the relationship itself is computed.

6.2. Specializing objects and relationships

After initial object creation and grouping, all objects are of the most general type, such as 3D-OBJECT. The next process in data interpretation is to search the IS-A hierarchy to find a more specialized interpretation for each object. An object can be specialized in one of three ways:

1. Fill in a slot of the object with a more specific value

2. Add a relationship constraining a feature of the object

3. Add new parts to the object and/or relationships between its parts (recursively specializing the object's parts and relationships)

The first method of specialization is the easiest to test for. The values in a frame's slot are matched with those of its possible specializations. For example, in Figure 3 the **intersecting-lines** relationship is specialized to a **perpendicular-lines** relationship by filling its angle slot with the value 90°. Specialization by slot value is used for relationships as well as objects.

To test whether objects can be specialized by the second method, a conjunction of the constraints for each feature of the new type is computed, using the current object's feature values. If this conjunction computes successfully for all features of the new type, the object may be specialized. Thus, in Figure 4, an edge is specialized to a vertical edge by adding a relationship constraining its GEOM-FEATURE to be parallel to the prototype vertical line.

To specialize an object by the third method, a correspondence between the parts of the candidate object and the parts of the specialized object is determined so that each part is an instance of the right object and all constraints are satisfied. For example to specialize a vertical face to a wall, the slots TOP, BOTTOM, VE1 and VE2 and the relationships between them are added. The correspondence of parts to slots is done in two phases. First, a list of matches using only local considerations is made, then this list is pruned by propagating relationship information. The considerations for local matching are:

- For each part, which slots have the right INSTANCE value?

- If a slot is filled in, can the part be successfully matched with the slot's current value?

For example, when specializing the face 2D-OBJECT161 in Figure 5b to a wall, the local matches for EDGE133 are VE1 and VE2 (see Figure 4), since EDGE133 is a vertical edge. Although EDGE134 (a horizontal edge) has the right INSTANCE value for both TOP and BOTTOM of the wall, the BOTTOM slot is already filled with the intersection of the wall plane and the ground plane. Since EDGE134 lies above the ground, its only possible local match is TOP.

If there is at least one possible match for each part, then relationship information is propagated by assigning one part to one of its possible slots, and pruning the possibilities for the other parts according to its relationships. This is done by matching the relationships of the current part with the relationship templates of its assigned slot. For example, when specializing 2D-OBJECT158 to a roof, after local matching, any of the edges of 2D-OBJECT158 can match any of the edge slots of the roof. However, once EDGE134 is assigned to the roof's edge 4, EDGE132, which is perpendicular to it, can no longer be assigned to the roof's edge 2, which is parallel to edge 4. From the remaining possibilities, a new assignment is chosen, and the propagation process is repeated until all parts are matched, all slots are filled, or a part cannot be matched. If there is an unmatched part and all slots were not filled, the specialization fails. Otherwise, hypotheses for missing parts of the object may be generated by accessing its COMPUTE slot. Two facets in the PARTS slot of the object are used to store information in case computing the object fails: the MATCHES-TRIED facet contains matches already tried, and the LOCAL-MATCH facet contains the original set of local matches for each part.

6.3. Controlling the matching process

Since matching is expensive, it is advantageous to limit the number of pairs of objects to be matched. One way this is done by the 3D FORM system is to specialize each data object as much as possible before any matching is attempted. Since only instances of the same generic objects can possibly match, specializing an object limits its possible matches. A second method of limiting the number of pairs of objects to match is to consider the relationships between the parts being matched, eliminating object pairs with conflicting relationships. These two methods of eliminating matches correspond to the two conditions for local matching used in specialization. However, even after local matching, multiple possibilities often remain.

Once it is determined that general matching must be done, processing is limited by making sure that the most likely matches are tried first, and if a match eventually fails, it fails as early as possible, cutting off the recursion tree near the top. Since empty objects match anything, the more complete an object is, the less likely it is to match a given object. Therefore, whenever there is a list of possible matches to be tried, they are sorted by the object's COMPLETENESS values, and the pair with the greatest average completeness is tried first. In the case of parts being matched to slots, these heuristics are applied by doing the local matches first, then choosing the object with the fewest possibilities, and finally choosing the possibility with the greatest average completeness.

6.4. Examples: from 3D wire frames to complete 3D objects

This section describes experiments in which 3D wire frames, generated from image edges by hand, were read into the frame database, specialized, and evaluated, generating hypotheses for missing edges. In the first example, a new edge was then entered manually, and the system matched it to one of the hypothesized edges of the object. The initial wire frame for the first experiment consisted of four edges, three horizontal and one vertical (see Figure 5a). During the initial processing, the three horizontal edges were combined into one face (2D-OBJECT158), and a second face (2D-OBJECT161) was created from the intersection of the vertical edge with one of the horizontal edges. Since the faces intersected at an edge, a 3D-OBJECT was created with both faces as its parts.

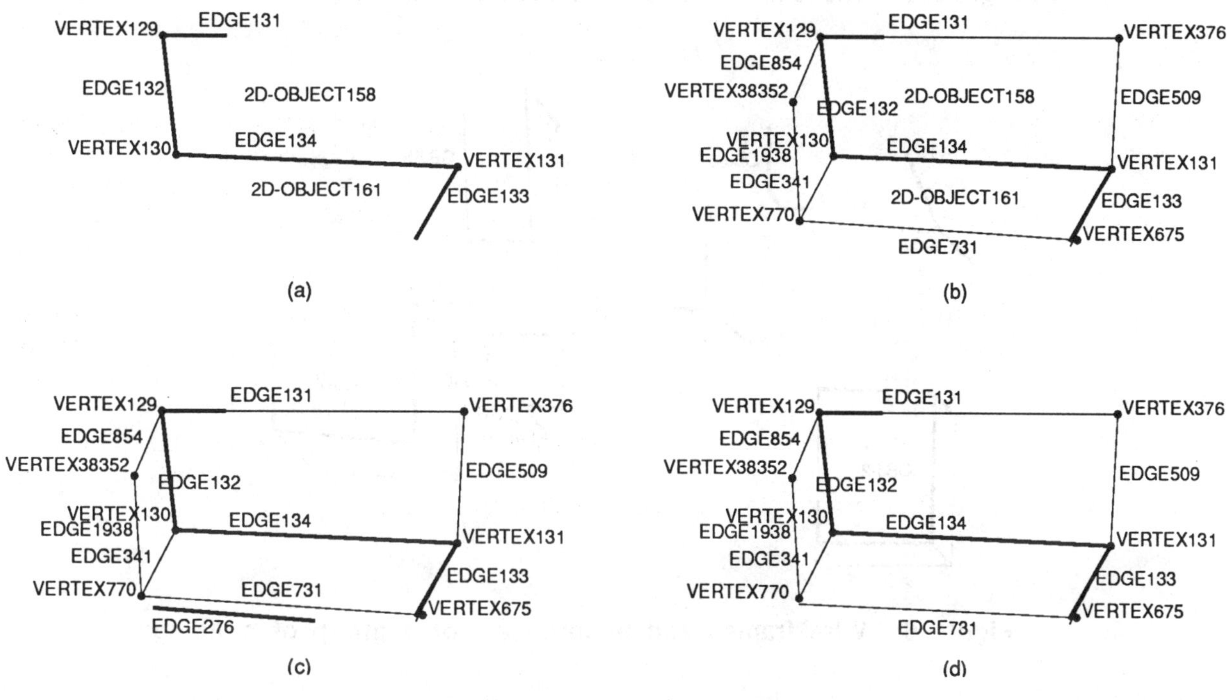

Figure 5: (a) initial wire frame; (b) visible faces of completed building; (c) completed building with new edge; (d) revised building after merging new edge

In the specialization process, the edges were divided into horizontal and vertical edges, and 2D-OBJECT161 was found to be a wall, since it was a vertical face. Since 2D-OBJECT158 is above the ground plane, it was found to be the roof, rather than the floor of the building. The parts of each of these objects were assigned to slots, as discussed in Section 6.2. The final result of specialization was a building with 2D-OBJECT158 as its roof and 2D-OBJECT161 as its 4th wall.

Next, the building was evaluated, providing hypotheses for the missing slots. Figure 5b shows the visible faces of the completed building. Notice that an extension to the input edge EDGE131 was hypothesized to complete the rectangular roof.

Finally, a new 3D edge was entered and matched to the existing building hypothesis. The algorithm used was to take the new data, specialize it as much as possible, and attempt to match the top-level object to all other instances of the same object until a match was found. The new edge, EDGE276, was found to match the hypothesized edge, EDGE731. Figure 5c shows the building and the new edge, and Figure 5d shows the result of merging the new edge with the old using this algorithm.

The second experiment evaluated a more realistic set of wire frames, finding three buildings in the image, and rejecting one object because it did not fit any models. Figure 6 shows the results of evaluating these wire frames. The bold lines are the initial wireframes, and the remaining lines were hypothesized when the buildings were evaluated. Objects 1 and 6 were rejected as buildings, since each had a non-perpendicular vertex. Objects 3 and 4 were considered to have too little information with only three edges each. The remaining objects were successfully completed.

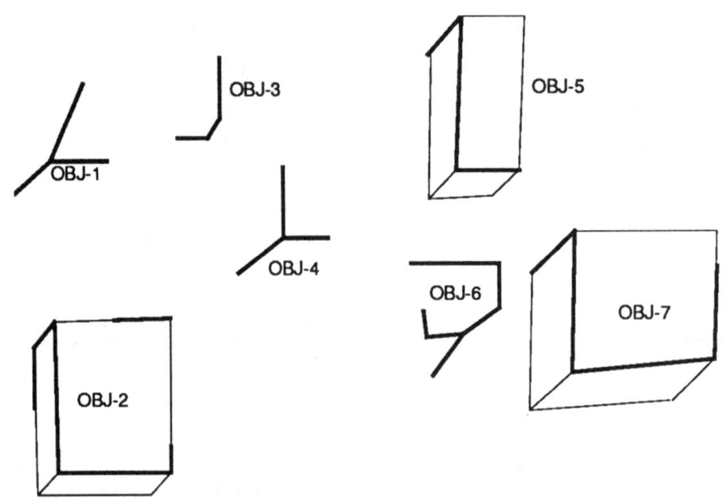

Figure 6: Wire frames and hypotheses for a group of buildings

References

[1]   Barry, M., Cyrluk, D. Kapur, D., and Mundy, J. A multi-level geometric reasoning system for vision. In Kapur, D. and Mundy, J. L. (ed.), *Proceedings of a Workshop on Geometric Reasoning*. Keble College - Oxford University, June, 1986. To appear as a special issue of Artificial Intelligence.

[2]   Brooks, R. A. Symbolic reasoning among 3-D models and 2-D images. *Artificial Intelligence* 17:285-348, 1981. Special volume on computer vision.

[3]   Carbonell, J. G. and Joseph, R. *The FrameKit+ reference manual.* 1986. CMU Computer Science Department internal paper.

[4]   Herman, M. Kanade, T. and Kuroe, S. Incremental acquisition of a three-dimensional scene model from images. *IEEE Transactions on Pattern Analysis and Machine Intelligence* 6(3):331-340, 1984.

[5]   Herman, M. and Kanade, T. Incremental reconstruction of 3-D scenes from multiple, complex images. *Artificial Intelligence* 30:289-341, 1986.

[6]   Huffman, D. A. Impossible objects as nonsense sentences. *Machine Intelligence.* Elsevier, New York, 1971.

[7]   Hwang, V. S. S. *Evidence accumulation for spatial reasoning in aerial image understanding.* PhD thesis, University of Maryland, November, 1984.

[8]   Kapur, D., Mundy, J., Musser, D, and Narendran, P. Reasoning about three dimensional space. In *1985 IEEE International Conference on Robotics and Automation.* IEEE, St. Louis, Missouri, March, 1985.

[9]   Mackworth, A. K. Interpreting pictures of polyhedral scenes. *Artificial Intelligence* 4:121-137, 1973.

[10]   Mundy, J. L. Image understanding research at General Electric. In *Proceedings of Image Understanding Workshop*, pages 83-88. 1985.

Incremental Inference:
Spatial Reasoning
Within a Blackboard Architecture

Terry E. Weymouth*

Computer Vision Research Laboratory
Department of Electrical Engineering and Computer Science
University of Michigan
Ann Arbor, MI 48109-2122

Abstract

Designing an automated scene interpretation system requires the integration of fine-grained, detailed knowledge into a control structure capable of dealing with uncertainty and error. One such control structure is knowledge-based inference using a best-first strategy. This control structure is typically used in blackboard architectures. The processing of information to construct an interpretation is performed by knowledge sources. Thus, each knowledge source represents a step in the inference process that ties together data from a sequence of images and the instances of object models which interpret that data.

The interpretation of dynamic scenes is itself a dynamic process that must take place at several levels of abstraction beginning with those partial interpretations that are best supported by the data but interacting with the tentative and partial instantiation of object model information. The blackboard architecture is especially suited for such opportunistic reasoning.

The design of a vision system is an exploratory task. Progress can best be made in restricted domains, demanding specialized knowledge sources. With each new domain, additional knowledge sources are designed and previous ones adapted. Over several such experiments, general knowledge sources emerge and become part of a more general system. The flexibility of the blackboard architecture makes this exploration and the resulting generalization possible.

---

*This research was supported in part by AFOSR Contract No. F33615-85-C-5105 and NASA Ames Grant No. 2-350

1   Introduction

Machine perception is based on the interactions between many related and uncertain sources of evidence. These must interact to select and group features from sensory information to match models corresponding to objects in the world. This process of grouping requires inference: each feature group constitutes a partial interpretation from which further interpretation can proceed or against which tentative model hypotheses can be confirmed. Partial, fragmentary interpretations, whether based on data, model appropriateness, or both, are stages in the inference of object existence from scene derived data. Aided by the redundancy of nature, the task of the system is to construct a consistent interpretation by such a process of inference.

We are investigating the design of a knowledge-based system founded on a blackboard architecture [Nii, 1986]. Within this architecture, frames are used to represent hypotheses and object model information, while knowledge sources represent the steps in inference under uncertainty. Each knowledge source uses object model information to construct hypotheses consistent with both the data and the object models in response to other hypotheses or data. The flow of control moves through the creation of hypotheses and is channeled by the selection of knowledge sources for activation. In addition, parallel activation of non-interacting knowledge sources provides the potential for a speedup of computation.

The study of scene interpretation using intensity images is a field that has seen a great division of effort. On one hand, many researchers have concentrated on developing sound theoretical underpinnings for methods of deriving information from image sequences (see [Brady, 1982] and [Horn, 1986]). Their efforts have led to mathematical models which, although powerful as tools of explanation, are only applicable under restricting assumptions. On the other hand, much research effort has gone into attempting automatic interpretation with the tools and techniques at hand. The systems for the interpretation of aerial photographs by Nagao and Matsuyama [Nagao, 1980], by Glicksman [Glicksman, 1982], and by Brooks [Brooks, 1981] were each designed to use general knowledge about image features and object characteristics along with specific knowledge about the objects expected in the images to guide interpretation and construct a description of the scene. The interpretation of natural outdoor scenes has also been an area that has yielded similar experimental systems, for example see [Ohta, 1980] and [Weymouth, 1986]. In each of these studies the argument has been made that the type of scene being interpreted and the system doing the interpretation should be as general as possible. However, the experiments and results are usually restricted to only a few examples of scenes from a very small class of scenes [Binford, 1982].

The development of powerful mathematical models of the process of image formation and its relation to surface shape and other object characteristics may eventually lead to useful tools. Meanwhile, many of the principles for reasoning and control in perception-based systems can be developed by taking a pragmatic approach to the problems of what can be inferred directly from the image. Using the best methods available, experimental systems can be developed which interpret scenes.

While we favor research that attempts to build working systems, and argue for the absolute necessity for experimental results on real images from scenes of some complexity, it is clear from the previous experimental results that a more moderate approach would be more fruitful. What is needed to better understand the science and engineering of scene

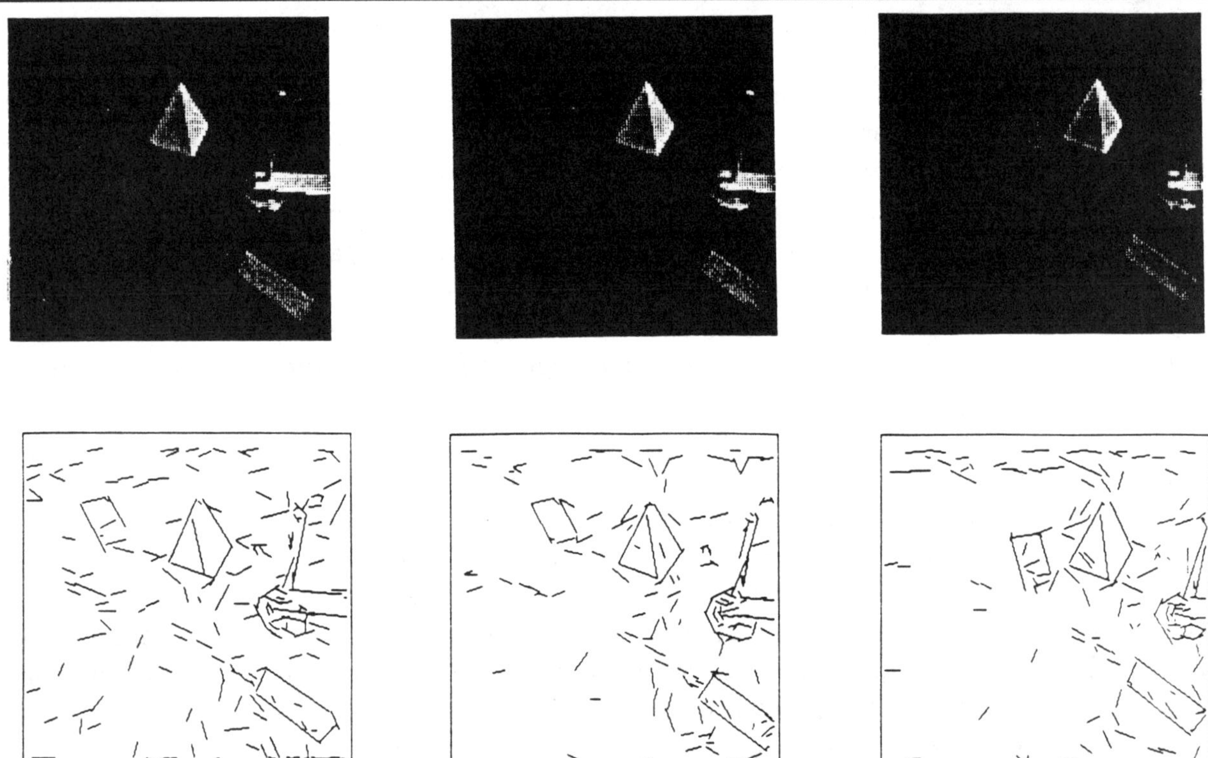

Figure 1: In the sequence of images shown across the top the camera and two objects are in motion. The faint block in the upper left is moving towards the camera and the block in the lower right is moving away. The pyramid and pencil-holder are stationary, while the camera is moving to the left. The images across the bottom were produced by a straight line extraction process [Burns, 1986] which looks for a strong light-to-dark transition which can be fit to a straight line.

interpretation is a series of detailed studies in restricted domains. This is not, however, to suggest that we should return to the type of "blocks world" study that relies on special control over the imaging environment. It would seem more reasonable to follow the lead of the limited success that has been gained from the interpretation of aerial photographs and seek other domains that have restrictions on the amount and complexity of the *knowledge* needed for interpretation.

We are developing an understanding of the diverse types of knowledge needed for interpretation through the construction of a series of scene interpretation systems for a variety of inspection tasks. Guided by the pragmatic requirements for each task, we are developing procedures for interpretation within a blackboard system architecture. Each of these procedures, called knowledge sources, embodies a small portion of the knowledge needed for interpretation within the specific inspection task. As we accumulate knowledge sources, some will emerge as being more general. In addition, the demands of the general framework of the blackboard architecture dictate that we identify the conditions under which each knowledge source applies. Thus, this collection of knowledge sources will constitute a toolbox of procedures, each of which will perform some small step in the process of interpretation.

2   Knowledge-Sources for Active Inference

Interpretation relies on knowledge of the world. We use information about objects, their interrelations, their functions, and their visual characteristics. The researcher in computer vision is faced with the problem of organizing that knowledge in an effective way so that it can be accessed, the appropriate facts brought to bear, and the correct description constructed from the application of that knowledge and those facts. When designing an interpretation system, it is difficult enough to understand the issues of appropriate representation and effective control. The task of attempting to understand general computer vision is confounded by the fact that large amounts of fine-grained knowledge must be represented. Consider the task set forth in Figure 1. Object recognition relies on the active organization of active primitive elements at several levels of abstraction.

In our experiments, we begin by examining the issues of controlling processing: this is the key to dealing with errorful partial results. When results of intermediate steps of the interpretation system can be classified as to the confidence in their fidelity, then the best of those results can be used to guide subsequent interpretation. This general strategy of searching for a solution by extending better results has been used successfully in the field of Speech Understanding. The HEARSAY system [Erman, 1980] was able to interpret speech signals under errorful and uncertain conditions by applying syntactic and semantic knowledge. We are applying a similar technique to image understanding.

The choices of the type of representation and of the method of control are intertwined. Each style and implementation of control affects the way in which information is represented. Choosing a control strategy for computer vision seems to be dictated by the need to combine declarative and procedural information. Much of the knowledge needed for image interpretation is symbolic in nature: relations between objects, color and texture labels, object part placement, and object labels; but many of the symbols are derived by processes that are essentially numeric (e.g., statistical measures, mechanisms for determining varying thresholds, and feature extraction). More importantly, given our current understanding, the strategies for when and how to extract symbolic information are more easily and naturally expressed as programs [Weymouth, 1986]. This requires that the processes employed to initiate and drive the use of the symbolic information be an integral part of the object representation.

Consider the sequence of images shown in Figure 2. By first matching elements from frame to frame (a restricted version of the correspondence problem) and hypothesizing groupings of objects under similar motion parameters, a hypothesis of object position and motion can be constructed. To avoid a combinitorial explosion, we must exploit the consistency of object motion over long sequences [Haynes, 1986], and rely inferences to generate hypotheses groupings through searches that start from only those correspondences that are very reliable. Interpretation works outward from initial hypotheses that are of high confidence, through the inferences of the knowledge sources, across the bridge of the redundancy of nature, to include the consistent but less reliable future, past and neighboring hypotheses.

Unfortunately, many of the groupings of image features are consistent only if they are first interpreted as three dimensional structures. The reliance on object geometry presents a classical problem: recognition rests on derived structure and that derived structure evolves from recognition. Thus, it is necessary to pursue the tracking of image events at several levels of abstraction simultaneously. For short sequences, image features can be tracked

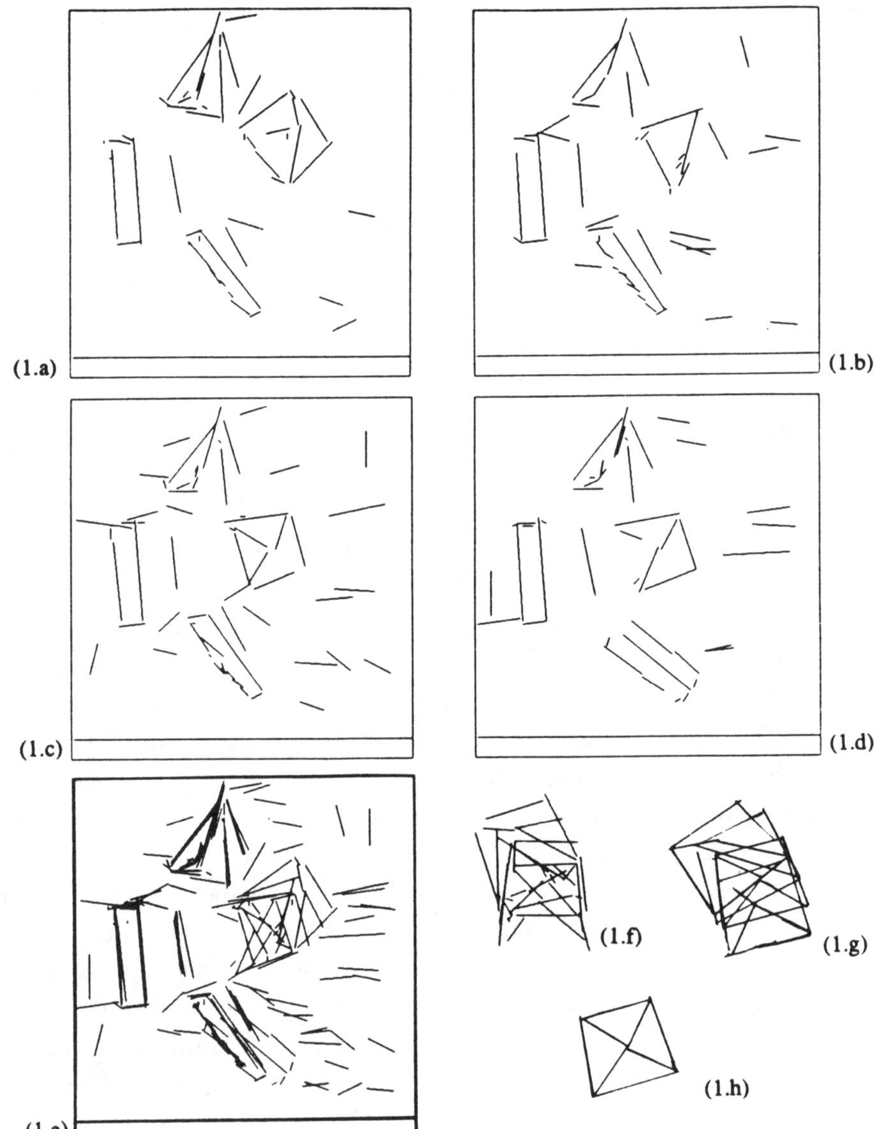

Figure 2: Shown in 2a-2d, four frames of a motion sequence processes to extract straight lines [Burns, 1986]. Shown in 2e, a superimposing of those four frames to illustrate relative motion of linear features. Moving lines can be grouped (2f), on common motion features, and extended to form closed figures (2g), shown here still superimposed. The hypothesis after four frames (2h) shows the projection of a pyramidal solid which can be used for tracking. Matching in further frames can be used to infer three-dimensional characteristics.

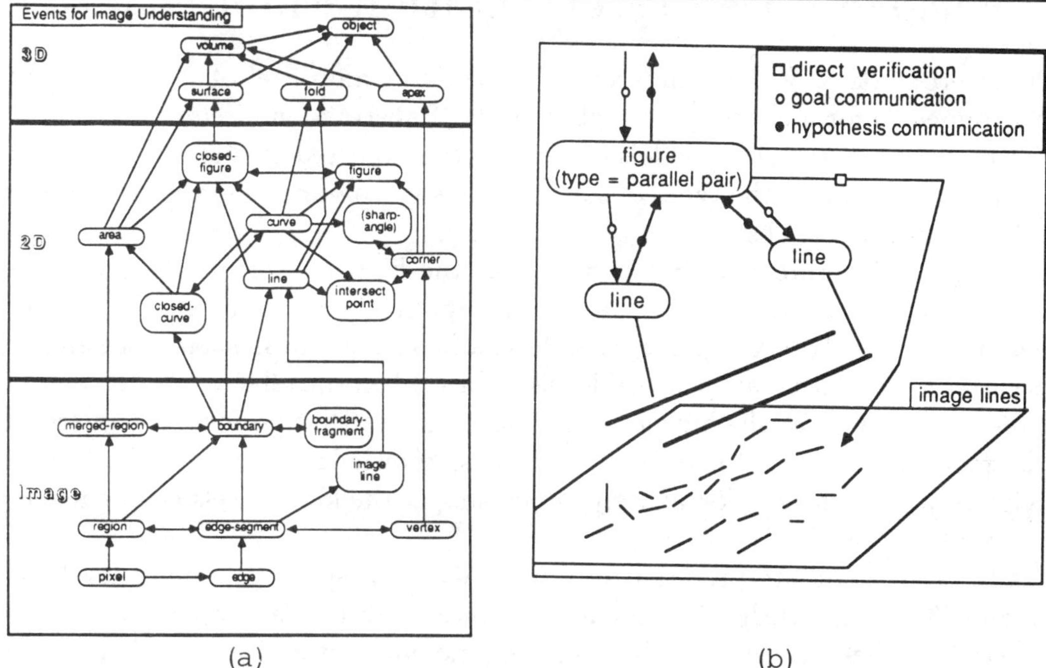

Figure 3: (a) The active elements for tracking visual events over time can be distributed over several levels of abstraction. During processing these levels interact. (b) The information propagates from the lowest level of abstraction to higher levels under the control of knowledge sources; verification of hypotheses, however, causes interactions which are directed by higher levels of abstraction towards lower levels. The frequency of updating necessary to maintain consistency with the data decreases at higher levels of abstraction where processing is more complex and global.

within the image, especially if there is some prediction as to what their expected motion is. For longer sequences, rather than track image features we must track object features – by tracking the expected position of the image features that are inferred from hypothesized three dimensional structure.

This suggests that interpretation itself is a dynamic process. Tentative hypotheses of feature groupings are advanced to explain unaccounted-for data. Hypotheses are grouped if they are consistent at some level of abstraction: moving feature, moving surface, moving object. Models are instantiated to account for hypothesized groupings and, in turn, they interact with the interpretation process by accounting for additional data (see Figure 3). Hypotheses that are inconsistent languish for lack of data; models without support fail to serve in the tracking of events in the image. Thus, over time, a consistent interpretation of the objects emerges from these processes. It is through the actions of the knowledge sources that interpretation is carried forward.

3   Knowledge-Based Interpretation Maintenance

During the interpretation of dynamic scenes, elements at any level of abstraction can be selectively grouped to form elements at higher levels of abstraction. Geometric information guides this grouping process. The models of objects, the expected configurations of surfaces, and general knowledge about the types of surface and edge conjunctions all are used to make inferences between levels of abstraction.

The character of interpretation maintenance at the higher levels of abstraction differs from that of the lower levels. The more abstract hypotheses are more global and need be updated less frequently. For example, a hypothesis of an object in motion, normally will be consistent with the hypothesis at the lower levels. Thus, when the relatively rare event occurs that requires maintenance at the higher levels, the processes that perform the inference can afford to be more elaborate and expensive. Whereas, knowledge-sources at the lower levels must be relatively inexpensive. Fortunately, processing at the lower levels can be made more local.

In overall character an interpretation system for dynamic scenes is a multi-level tracking system (Figure 3c). Knowledge sources at the lowest levels are simple procedures that maintain local hypothesis consistency by matching moving picture element. This process is aided by projected model information from the higher levels, when it is available. Knowledge sources at the highest levels are qualitative and geometric reasoning processes for maintaining global information about object placement and motion.

4   Conclusion

A computer vision system must deal with the uncertainty associated with noisy data and the misapplication of assumptions by feature extraction processes. The "best first" interpretation strategies typical of blackboard systems are a reasonable approach to this problem. Within a blackboard system, the knowledge sources represent the primitive steps of inference under uncertainty. In the application of knowledge sources to the problem of dynamic scene interpretation, the knowledge sources have the added feature of tracking changing elements over time.

References

[Binford, 1982] Binford, T. "Survey of Model Based Image Analysis Systems," *International Journal of Robotics Research*, Vol. 1, No. 1, Spring 1982, pp. 18-64.

[Brady, 1982] Brady, M., "Computational Approaches to Image Understanding," *ACM Computing Surveys*, Vol.14, 1982, pp. 3-71.

[Brooks, 1981] Brooks, R., "Symbolic Reasoning Among 3-D Models and 2-D Images," Technical Report STAN-CS-81-861, Department of Computer Science, Stanford University, Stanford, California, June 1981.

[Burns, 1986] Burns, J. B., Hanson, A. R., and Riseman, E. M., "Extracting Straight Lines," PAMI-8, 4, 425-255, 1986.

[Erman, 1980] Erman, L., Hayes-Roth, F., Lesser, V. and Reddy, D., "The Hearsay-II Speech-Understanding System: Integrating Knowledge to Resolve Uncertainty," *Computing Surveys*, 12(2), June 1980, pp. 213-253.

[Glicksman, 1982] Glicksman, J., "A Cooperative Scheme for Image Understanding Using Multiple Sources of Information," Ph. D. Dissertation, University of British Columbia, November 1982.

[Haynes, 1986] Haynes, S. M. and Jain, R., "Event Detection and Correspondance," *Optical Engineering*, Vol. 25, No. 3, March, 1986.

[Horn, 1986] Horn, B. K. P., *Robot Vision*, 1986, M.I.T. Press, Cambridge, MA.

[Nagao, 1980] Nagao, M. and Matsuyama, T., *A Structural Analysis of Complex Aerial Photographs*, Plenum Press, New York, 1980.

[Nii, 1986] Nii, H. P., "Blackboard Systems (parts I and II)," *The AI Magazine*, Vol. 7, Nos. 2 and 3, pp. 38-53 and pp. 82-106, 1986.

[Ohta, 1980] Ohta, Y., "A Region-Oriented Image-Analysis System by Computer," Ph. D. Dissertation, Kyoto University, Department of Information Science, Kyoto, Japan, 1980.

[Weymouth, 1986] Weymouth, T. E., "Using Object Descriptions in a Schema Network for Machine Vision," Ph. D. Dissertation, available as COINS Technical Report 86-35, University of Massachusetts, Amherst, May 1986.

SPATIAL REASONING USING AN OBJECT-ORIENTED SPATIAL DBMS

Richard Antony
Center for Signals Warfare
U. S. Army Communications Electronics Command
Warrenton, VA 22186-5100

ABSTRACT

A spatial database management system (SDBMS) based on an integrated hierarchical, object-oriented and hierarchical, true spatial representation is proposed that can significantly enhance the performance of correlation, fusion, target recognition, situation assessment, autonomous vehicle control and planning systems. By tailoring the database structure to the typical object (e.g., hierarchical, relational) and spatial-oriented (e.g., spatial distance, direction, intersection) queries that underlie spatial problem solving, significant reductions in search space size and required compute-and-test operations can be achieved. In contrast, spatial problem solving using conventional database management systems (DBMS) tend to require intensive search and computation (e.g., find the closest road to an arbitrary point in space).

A hybrid data structure consisting of vector, pyramid, quadtree, and frame-based components is discussed that offers efficient representation of both uniformly and non-uniformly sampled point, line and region object attributes. Search algorithms that exploit the proposed database structure are presented that accomplish complex object and spatial oriented 1) Boolean operations, such as region intersection and spatial templating, 2) hierarchical path development based on recursive, multiple resolution goal-seeking under spatial constraints and 3) generalized metric computations based on hierarchical region-growing techniques. A true spatial representation supports sophisticated, high performance image processing and image understanding algorithms for database abstraction and generalization. The proposed search and manipulation algorithms form the basis of a generic, low-level spatial reasoning and maintenance system that supports a high level database interface. For large-scale, real time applications, the spatial database management system can be implemented on a distributed multiple processor network to provide concurrent search and large on-line memory capacity.

INTRODUCTION

Spatial reasoning plays a key role in numerous domains, including battlefield sensor fusion, situation assessment, object classification, autonomous vehicle control and mission planning/replanning. The spatial relationships among entities and their relationship to cultural and terrain features represent important contextual knowledge for reasoning in these domains.

Because of the potentially enormous size of spatial databases and the complexity of the search requirements, conventional relational database management systems (DBMS) can represent a serious processing bottleneck in automated spatial reasoning systems. Object-oriented representations offer an alternative approach that provides a powerful conceptual framework for maintaining both dynamic, as well as relatively static domain knowledge. This paper explores the search space reduction potential of an integrated spatial representation that provides a "window" into an object-oriented database. If, in addition, both the object-oriented and spatial-oriented representations are hierarchical, additional reductions in search space size and subsequent improvements in problem solving efficiency can be achieved through the use of recursive, multiple resolution reasoning. Such a database structure appears to have wide applicability in the automation of many complex decisionmaking processes since it offers a representation that supports complex reasoning processes metaphorically similiar to human problem solving approaches.

In a DBMS which consists of host-resident software and disk-resident data, access time depends on both the search space size and the disk retrieval time. In the next section, the database bottleneck problem is attacked on two fronts. First, a fully integrated object and spatial oriented database organization, referred to as a spatial DBMS (SDBMS), is developed that supports efficient access and manipulation of the knowledge base. Second, a distributed processor implementation is suggested that allows the entire active knowledge base to be resident in random access memory (RAM) and at the same time support concurrent search. In the third section, low level spatial reasoning involving Boolean operations, path development and metric computation are outlined that exploit the rich structure of the proposed SDBMS. Elements of automated low level generic spatial reasoning are discussed that support a high level intelligent database interface. In the fourth section, higher level spatial reasoning relevant to terrain analysis, battlefield information fusion and autonomous vehicle control is presented. The final section summarizes the key requirements for and the advantages of the SDBMS for situation representation and complex spatial, temporal and hierarchical reasoning.

PROPOSED SPATIAL DATABASE MANAGEMENT SYSTEM

In this section, a spatial database representation is recommended that exploits the power of the human's spatial reasoning style. Targets, events, and geographic and cultural features can be treated as objects possessing inherent spatial properties (e.g., position, shape, orientation). The proposed database organization integrates the object-oriented and spatial representations as depicted conceptually in Fig. 1. Such an organization supports uniform reasoning both within a class of features (e.g., targets) and between classes of features (e.g., target and geographic databases). Although the recommended SDBMS provides robust and economical representations of spatially-organized objects and features, its primary benefits are reduction in search space size and computational requirements in support of complex spatial, temporal and hierarchical reasoning.

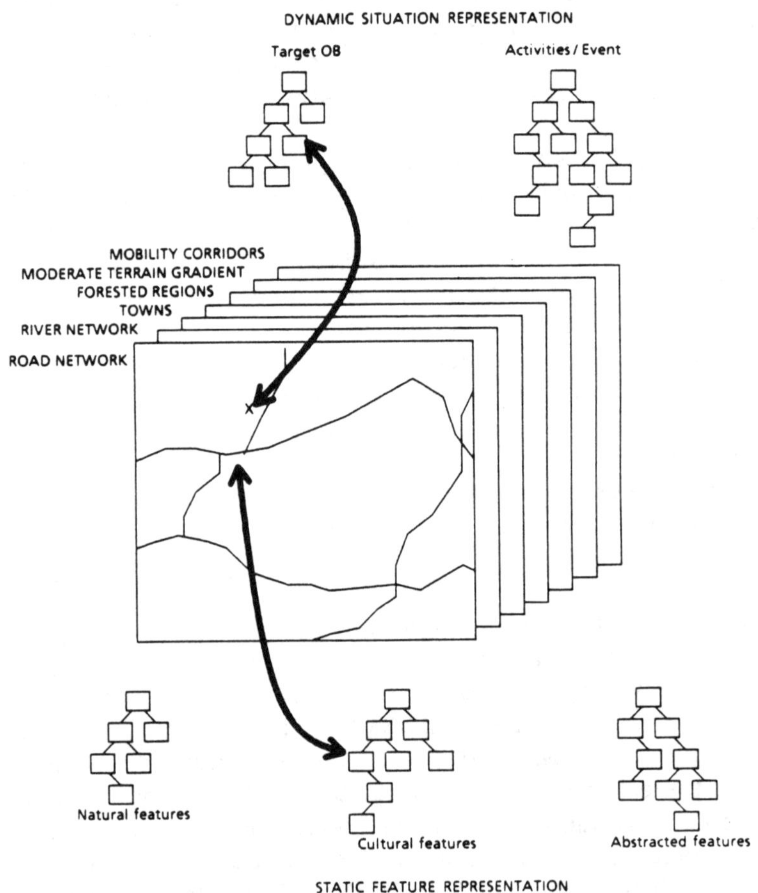

FIGURE 1. Conceptual organization of the SDBMS.

DATABASE REPRESENTATION

The proposed SDBMS is a hybrid representation consisting of 1) a pyramidal multiple resolution spatial representation, 2) the region quadtree (Samet, 1984), 3) generalized frame structures and 4) an object-oriented database system. In essence, the pyramid provides a hierarchical spatial indexing scheme for the detailed point, line (vector-represented) and region (quadtree represented) features.

Spatial reasoning is inherently a hierarchical process which can be performed at two levels of abstraction: low resolution and high resolution. Low resolution spatial reasoning supports global decisionmaking by restricting the search space required to perform more refined reasoning. At a low resolution, map and target data appear to be reasonably homogeneous; as the resolution is increased, such data tends to become non-homogeneous. Thus, an efficient database design should provide both uniform and non-uniform representations in support of both low resolution and higher resolution spatial reasoning, respectively. Figure 2 shows the essential components of the proposed spatial database representation.

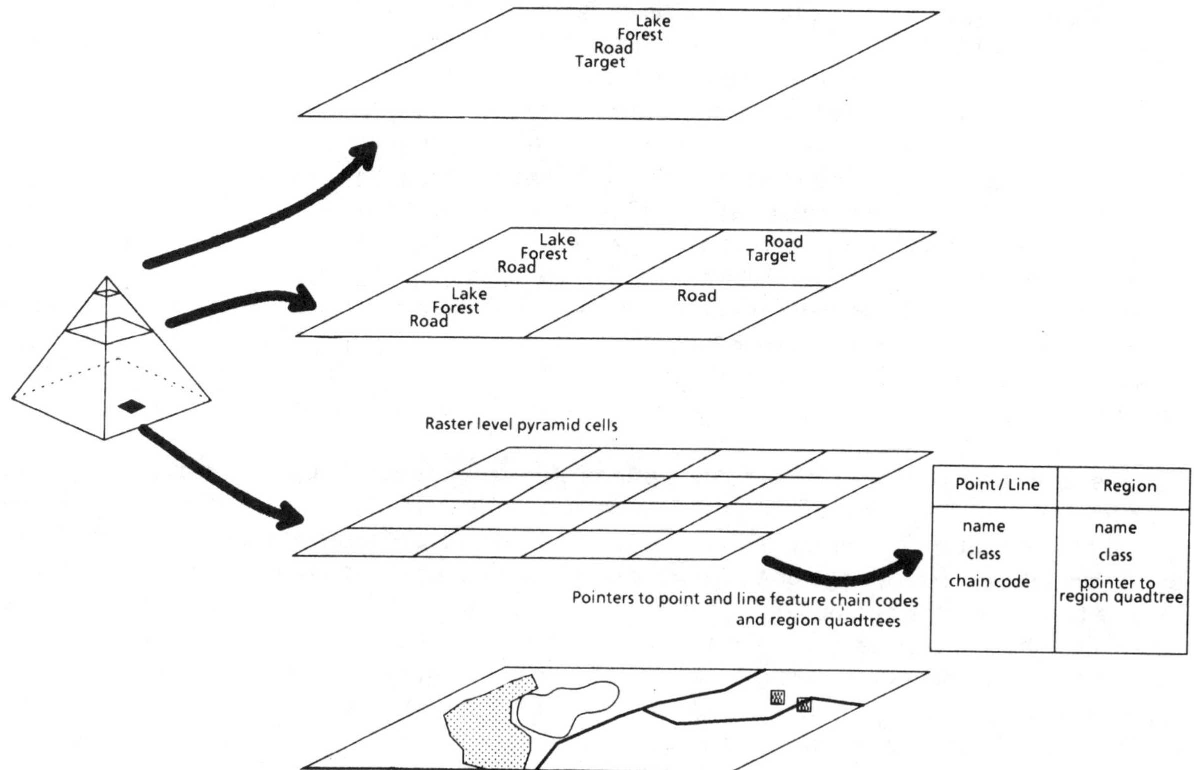

FIGURE 2. Pyramid representation structure

In the present application, the pyramid provides a uniform hierarchical spatial representation that supports low resolution spatial reasoning. The features present in each resolution cell are represented in a generalized frame structure that provides a concise semantic description of a particular geographic region. A default implementation of the non-raster level frame structure is a bit-coded feature vector representation that summarizes the generic features present in each cell. Assuming a pyramid base of (m x n) raster level cells, for spatial-oriented search, search space reductions over non-spatially-indexed representations of on the order of m*n can be achieved.

As mentioned above, only a non-uniform representation can efficiently represent non-homogeneous high resolution data. In the proposed representation, high resolution data utilizes vectors to represent points and lines and minimal region quadtrees to represent individual regions. An efficient quadtree nearest neighbor move algorithm is presented in (Antony, 1987a). Since a pyramid representation uses fundamentally the same hierarchical, regular decomposition of space as the region quadtree, the pyramid can be implemented as a complete quadtree. The pyramid requires only 1.33 times the total number of minimum resolution cell (raster) nodes and can be implemented using a simple, pointerless, direct access coding scheme. The complete quadtree-based pyramid with its frame-based cell representation will be referred to as the frame-based quadtree. By proper choice of the minimum frame-based quadtree resolution size, an important tradeoff between memory requirements, computational and search efficiency of the proposed SDBMS can be achieved.

The point, line and region features that occur within each minimum resolution frame-based quadtree node are represented as shown in Fig. 2. The raster level cells point to the appropriate point, line and region database representations. Point and line features are stored by a name, an object class, associated chain code representation, and other optional attributes (e.g., time stamp). Point features within the minimum resolution quadtree cell have a straightforward mapping to the object-oriented database. For the inverse mapping, the object frame points to a single minimum resolution frame-based quadtree node, which in turn maintains the precise location of the object. Since, for lines and regions, the links between the spatial and object representations are not 1:1, other conventions must be adopted. Within a minimum resolution frame-based quadtree node, line features are represented as vertices of piecewise linear functions stored in a quadtree node-offset form. The node-offset form expresses x and y position offsets relative to the center of the respective minimum resolution frame-based quadtree node. Explicit representation of entrance and exit points resolves ambiguity and avoids discontinuities between data in adjacent cells due to computational effects such as roundoff or truncation. For a 1 km minimum frame based quadtree size, 1 m accuracy can be achieved by the use of 10 bit position offsets.

General properties of line features are inherited from general object classes (e.g., generic road frame), as well as, a specific instance frame (e.g., Interstate 66). An explicit pointer links the spatial representation of the named line segment to the specific object frame. The inverse link points from the object frame to one or more frame-based quadtree nodes associated with that line feature (e.g., line centroid, beginning node). Any part of the line can then be accessed by simple nearest neighbor quadtree moves within the minimum resolution pyramid cells, followed by the use of the corresponding vector data. Since search regions can have arbitrary spatial configurations, and within a window, the intersection of multiple point, line and region data is often required, the hybrid pyramid/vector representation (with its uniform low resolution representation) offers advantages over strictly non-uniform lineal spatial data structures such as the k-d tree and its variants.

The spatial representation of a named region is represented as the minimal quadtree whose root node is the smallest single parent node of the region. The pyramid provides a hierarchical spatial indexing scheme to all generic region classes. If a region root node is larger than the size of the pyramid raster level cell, the region name, feature class and pointer to the minimal quadtree representation is stored in the pyramid cell corresponding to the region root node; if the region root node is equal to or smaller than the pyramid raster cell size, the information is stored within the respective pyramid raster cell. Each region occurring within the minimum resolution cells of the frame-based quadtree points to the named object frame for the respective region. In the inverse mapping, the region object frames point to the minimal quadtree representation (and hence the region root node in the pyramid) of each named region.

Thus, point objects are linked directly to the appropriate minimum resolution pyramid cell. For line features or objects, the object frame points to one or more minimum resolution frame-based quadtree nodes; the line feature is then constructively developed by nearest neighbor moves in the pyramid and use of the underlying vector database. For region features or objects, the object frame points to the corresponding quadtree root node. The spatial-to-object representation link for points, lines and regions is an explicit pointer from the spatial frame to the appropriate object oriented frame representation. Thus, the SDBMS provides two important capabilities: 1) a true two-dimensional representation of object and feature attributes and 2) a natural spatial "window" into the object-oriented database.

DATABASE IMPLEMENTATION

Because of the recursive symmetry of the quadtree representation, as well as the natural decomposition of object classes, the proposed SDBMS lends itself to highly parallel, tree-structured, multiple processor implementations. A system to handle large, high resolution areal databases could be implemented as a network of microprocessors where individual processors maintain either disjoint spatial or object class databases. Such a multiple processor implementation reduces the execution time required to perform database search and spatial reasoning, as well as reduces the execution speed and memory requirements of the individual processing elements. A 128 node system with 8 Mbytes of local processor memory provides 1 Gbyte of random access storage plus powerful local processing resources. For highly mobile forces or an autonomous vehicle, such distributed spatial databases allow dynamic migration of the overall digital database (residing on disk) to the multiprocessor network with little or no disruption in database operation. Because of the natural hierachical property inheritance structure of the pyramid, the region quadtree and the object-oriented representations, the required database maintenance operations following additions, deletions or modifications of the underlying database is straightforward . If the database resides on dedicated hardware, database maintenance overhead will not compete for resources with application software.

SPATIAL WINDOWS

Spatial windows offer important focus-of-attention capabilities in a spatially organized database. In data fusion, for instance, sensor messages must be correlated with the historically derived situation assessment in real time. With conventional database organizations, a significant portion of the entire target database may need to be queried and tested. Important search space reduction advantages can be achieved if only that portion of the target database that falls within some spatial window need be considered.

In general, a spatial window has an arbitrary two-dimensional shape that can be represented by a minimal quadtree. Window size can be scaled by a factor of 2^n (where n is an arbitrary positive or negative integer) by merely rescaling all quadtree node levels (depth); the window centroid (or any node, for that matter) can then be translated to an arbitrary quadtree node by calculating the directed distance between the current and desired centroid and applying the appropriate set of x and y offsets to all nodes within the original window or by constructing the new window based on nearest neighbor relationships within the original window (Antony, 1987a). Because of the recursive symmetry of the quadtree representation, the rotation of arbitrary regions by integer multiples of 90 degrees is a relatively straightforward operation.

LOW LEVEL SPATIAL REASONING

The primary categories of spatial reasoning to be discussed in this paper deal with: 1) Boolean operations, 2) path strategies and 3) Euclidean and non-Euclidean distance metric computation. Local spatial reasoning, such as nearest neighbor path development (e.g., road, treeline, minimum terrain gradient following strategies) is straightforward. In addition, because of both the hierarchical and spatial organization, search for the three nearest river crossing sites (out of perhaps thousands of possible sites) or the highest ground in a specific spatial window or spatial direction are easily accommodated. Without a hierarchical, spatially-organized database, real time global reasoning may be impractical for very large, high resolution databases.

The proposed database system will support real time manual or automated tasking where the detailed spatial/object-oriented database organization, manipulation and maintenance software can be completely transparent to the user. By providing generic low level spatial reasoning capability, the proposed SDBMS can be developed into a powerful, knowledge based system capable of high level database access and manipulation.

BOOLEAN OPERATIONS

A general Boolean database query can be expressed as concatenated queries of the form:

$$
\text{Find} \begin{pmatrix} n \\ all \end{pmatrix} \begin{pmatrix} \text{point feature} \\ \text{line feature} \\ \text{region "} \end{pmatrix} \begin{pmatrix} \text{intersect} \\ \text{union} \\ \text{difference} \end{pmatrix} \begin{pmatrix} \text{point feature} \\ \text{line feature} \\ \text{region "} \end{pmatrix} \text{cond} \begin{pmatrix} \text{spatial} \\ \text{window} \end{pmatrix}
$$

For the proposed SDBMS, the intersection of regions is a straightforward logical AND of corresponding region trees; intersection among the other feature classes is trivial. In a similiar way, the union of points, lines and regions yields the composite of all addends and the difference yields the nodes not contained within the intersection. Containment can be easily implemented by observing that $A \subset B$ if $A \cap B = A$.

The recognition of spatial patterns of terrain, cultural features, vehicles, or weapon systems is another aspect of intersection processing. Consider the apparently simple task of assigning N emitters to candidate K-member radio nets based on proximity. With a non-spatially-organized database, as many as $(N!/(K!*(N-K)!))$ locational comparisions may be required. The combinatorial explosion can be avoided if the target location database has a true two-dimensional spatial representation. First, a spatial window of dimensions comparable to a nominal net size is overlaid on all unassociated emitters. The window centroid is then moved to each of the emitters present within the window and the number of previously unassociated emitters is determined. When the window centroid reaches the net centroid, the maximum number of emitters appears within the window. The detailed spatial pattern, parametrics and semantics on this reduced candidate set can then be evaluated to complete the decision process.

PATH STRATEGIES

Path development, as considered in this paper, involves the creation and assessment of target routes based on local and global movement strategies that are terrain, weather and vehicle-class dependent. Local strategies involve some form of nearest-neighbor move which includes both directional and feature-following. With a hierarchical, spatially-organized database, global path-finding can be implemented using recursive search algorithms. A path is defined as a continuous set of connected-cells (quadtree nodes that share at least part of an edge or a corner) between two points that satisfy given spatial constraints. A simple multiple resolution, recursive algorithm considers all neighbor nodes of the head of the evolving path that satisfy a spatial constraint set and chooses the best next cell in the path based on various heuristics. Passage into a node is blocked if the node contains no features within the spatial constraint set. A simple look ahead algorithm allows the selected best next node to be decomposed an arbitrary number of levels to guarantee that passage through the cell is actually possible. The look-ahead algorithm adds a depth first search capability so as to minimize later backtracking that would be required in the case of premature path termination. In subsequent stages of the algorithm, the offspring nodes (next higher resolution pyramid level) of the path set from the last iteration are used to develop a new refined path based on these same spatial constraints and path selection heuristics. The recursion terminates when the connected-cell path is developed to some specified resolution. The path development algorithm supports the continuum between a strictly local (high resolution single pass) and a global (hierarchical multiple resolution) strategy which is particularly valuable for autonomous vehicle route planning and replanning. An example of the path-finding algorithm is given in (Antony, 1986) and an efficient region line-of-sight algorithm is developed as a special case of this algorithm in (Antony, 1987a).

DISTANCE METRIC

Using an image processing approach, efficient computation of both absolute and relative metrics between arbitrary combinations of point, line and region features can be developed. Since points and lines are merely degenerate regions, in general, distance can be developed by incrementally growing regions by either a fixed or variable quadtree node size, testing for intersection and continuing the region growth until an intersection occurs. Consider the simple example of finding the closest road to point (x,y). In a non-spatially-organized database, the distance between (x,y) and all vectorized line segments for all roads may need to be computed. With the proposed SDBMS, the quadtree node containing the point feature can be grown uniformly until an intersection with a node containing a road segment occurs. Even for such a simple query, a quadtree based representation is seen to offer significant computational advantages over conventional vector-oriented and certain non-uniform lineal representation algorithms. This advantage is particularly important for the autonomous vehicle application where the required high resolution road database is extremely large for real world applications. The search space can be restricted to certain spatial directions or regions by simply growing the region within these spatial constraints. By defining membership functions such as "near", "close", "high", and "rough", the system can easily support fuzzy reasoning processes.

HIGHER LEVEL SPATIAL REASONING

Military intelligence analysts and data fusion experts depend heavily on graphic, spatially-organized map products and the human's facility at spatial reasoning. Similiarly, an AI-based spatial reasoning system capable of approaching human-level performance must interpret and reason about spatially-organized data. Because of the true spatial representation aspect of the SDBMS, image processing and image understanding tools and techniques can be employed to automate certain aspects of spatial reasoning. Normally both image processing and image understanding tools are used to process and interpret unknown, raw data scenes. Since, in the present application, the "scene" is a fully understood (i.e., fully segmented and labelled) low level spatial knowledge base which is to be processed to yield higher level features or knowledge base abstractions, high level performance of such algorithms can be expected.

As an example of the use of image processing and understanding techniques, consider the automated development of mobility corridor maps. Mobility corridors require connected, trafficable regions of some minimum width. A first-cut mobility corridor map can be developed using the hierarchical path development algorithm. The path width can be controlled by defining a minimum quadtree resolution size for the top-down hierarchical search algorithm. Once potential corridors are determined, a true mobility corridor map can be generated by growing the path into the maximal region that satisfies the spatial constraint set. Finally, the "rolling ball" algorithm can be used to test the mobility corridor for natural or man-made bottlenecks (Antony, 1987a).

In battlefield sensor fusion, objects and events must be observed, understood and correlated over time and space to maintain a current picture of the dynamically evolving battlefield situation. Sensor reports are correlated with the current situation assessment using available domain knowledge of sensors, targets, doctrine, tactics and the environment. A key element of the data fusion process (Antony, 1987b) is the ability to implicitly and explicitly represent, manipulate and dynamically interpret the hierarchical semantic and spatial relationships among objects (targets, geographic, cultural features, and events).

Since asynchronous space/time correlation represents perhaps the first level of fusion processing, a spatially-organized and temporally coded target location database allows efficient access to candidate events that are "close" in time and space to a new detection. The cross correlation (i.e., intersection) of radar footprints, ELINT error ellipses and human intelligence locational estimates are examples of spatial reasoning that are fundamental to battlefield sensor fusion. Vehicle movement over time is constrained by vehicle class characteristics and geographic and cultural features. Since terrain affects the mobility of ground targets in relatively predictable ways, such knowledge can be used to interpolate or extrapolate vehicle movement, as well as, in the vehicle classification process. Since units have known doctrinal deployment and mobility requirements (e.g., patterns, trafficability requirements) and communication constraints (eg., line-of-sight requirements), traffic analysis, hierarchical target aggregation and tactics assessment are supported by efficient spatial templating and route-finding capability based on the proposed SDBMS.

The blackboard is an important artificial intelligence-based concept that supports distributed problem solving among a group of cooperating/competing processes. For a large scale data fusion system, the blackboard could represent the dynamic Order of Battle (OB) or situation assessment picture of the battlefield. The proposed SDBMS provides a natural blackboard representation structure that supports efficient, hierarchical object and spatial oriented database access and manipulation for a wide spectrum of data fusion tasks.

Autonomous vehicle control shares many of the same requirements and characteristics of terrain analysis and multi-sensor fusion. In the dynamic control of autonomous vehicles, the correlation of on-board sensors must be merged with vehicle constraints relative to terrain, cultural, weather and other spatial features. A true spatial representation of domain constraints allows vehicle-centered coordinate system access to the database which supports local control and registration, as well as global planning to fulfill both general and specific mission objectives under multiple and possibly time-varying spatial constraints. Rapid search of spatial features near the vehicle, efficient development of off-road paths in complex domains and generalized metric computation supports efficient local planning and control. The hierarchical structure of the database supports complex global planning/replanning.

SUMMARY

Since the accomplishment of many important military domain tasks depend on a human's facility for spatial problem solving, automation of such tasks demands a capability of performing real time, dynamic spatial reasoning. Efficient problem solving depends heavily on the efficiency of the knowledge base search process; search efficiency depends in large measure on the organization of the database. Automated spatial reasoning was shown to benefit from the use of an integrated spatially and semantically organized DBMS. A frame-based quadtree organization integrated with vector, region quadtree and object-oriented representations was recommended as a powerful and robust, spatial database management system (SDBMS) that provides an efficient capability for storage, search and manipulation of both spatial and object-organized knowledge.

The intrinsic advantages of a two stage spatial representation and reasoning process were emphasized. In the first stage, a hierarchically organized, uniformly sampled spatial representation provides efficient search space reduction by supporting both top-down and spatially-windowed search. In the second stage, non-uniformly sampled spatial representations provide memory efficient, refined representations of point, line and region features. High speed access to the knowledge base depends on both efficient search and effective implementation. In a conventional DBMS, with host-resident software and disk-resident data, data access time depends both on the search space size and the disk retrieval time. The proposed SDBMS supports reduction in the search space size; a multi processor implementation was recommended to eliminate host overhead and disk retrieval time. In the proposed implementation, the entire database is resident within active memory of the processor network. In addition to the speed advantage of RAM access relative to disk access, such an implementation offers the potential for sophisticated concurrent search and manipulation.

Spatial reasoning was discussed in terms of the proposed hybrid SDBMS. Efficient local and global extrapolation and route-planning strategies can be implemented using simple recursive search algorithms. Various distance metric and spatial templating algorithms were shown to be well supported by the true spatial representation. The potential role of image processing and image understanding techniques in the generation of higher level map-like and target abstraction products was discussed. The proposed SDBMS appears to provide a natural representation framework for an advanced distributed blackboard architecture for use in complex, distributed data fusion, situation assessment, autonomous vehicle control, and mission planning systems.

References

R. Antony. A Hybrid Spatial/Object-Oriented Database to Support Complex Spatial, Temporal and Hierarchical Reasoning. CECOM, Center for Signals Warfare, TR-CSW-87-2, (1987a)

R. Antony. A Framework for Automated Tactical Data Fusion. 1987 Data Fusion Symposium, Johns Hopkins Applied Physics Laboratory, Laurel MD, (1987b)

R. Antony. Spatial Reasoning and Knowledge Representation. Geographic Information Systems in the Government Workshop Proceedings, edited by Bruce Opitz, A. Deepak Publishing, (1986)

H. Samet. The Quadtree and Related Hierarchical Data Structures. Comp. Surv. 16, No. 2, pp187-260, (1984)

STATIC AND DYNAMIC LOGICAL MODELLING OF MECHANICAL ASSEMBLY PROCESSES IN A SIMPLIFIED GEOMETRICAL ENVIRONMENT

Christer Bäckström
Dept. of Computer and Information Science
Linköping University
S-581 83 Linköping, SWEDEN

Abstract:

This paper describes a logical model for geometric reasoning about assembly processes in a simplified world called the $2D^+$ world. The $2D^+$ world is a restricted 2^+-dimensional world, which is powerful enough to express most of the interesting assembly problems. A static description of this world in first order predicate calculus, and a dynamic description of assembly operations is provided. Assembly operations are expressed in a dynamic logic, extended with two new very restrictedly used operators to attack the frame problem.

The reason for using a logical geometry model instead of the usual procedural models, is that logical descriptions are better suited to symbolic reasoning than procedural ones. This is especially important since the combination of geometric and symbolic reasoning (geombolic reasoning) is known to be a very hard problem.

INTRODUCTION

Among the currently most challenging and important problems in robotics is how to automatically perform and plan automated assembly of mechanical details. The importance of research in this area is stressed in [Nev80],saying: *"Assembly is a process performed by people and is poorly understood.* To automate assembly requires an information-control approach which accurately describes the process, the workpieces and the assembly equipment so that reproducible systems can be designed." This quotation points at one of the key questions, namely how to model the robot and its environment, which is a question further stressed in [Alb84]: "The representation of knowledge about the world in an internal model is absolutely crucial to both the processing of sensory data and the decomposition of tasks and goals." A candidate model for this purpose must describe both the static and dynamic aspects of the robot world, and that in a way suitable to planning and other reasoning processes.

The static aspects of the model must describe the geometry of objects and the geometrical relationships between objects. A lot of geometric models have been suggested, but most of them focus on computer graphics applications. Developing commercial CAD systems have been the major driving force here, and a good survey of geometric models for such applications is given in [Req80]. The research about geometric reasoning in robotics has mainly focused on models for vision, while very little is done regarding models for reasoning about the geometry itself..

The problem of dynamic modelling is much less understood than static modelling, and not very much is done in this area. Most research about dynamic modelling in robotics have been more concerned about higher level planning (STRIPS [Fik71] and PFR [Sch86]) than lower level geometric reasoning. Other examples of dynamic modelling are mainly in the area of computer animation, e.g. MOSS-4 [Nic85].

The combination of geometric and symbolic reasoning is well known to be a hard problem, which [Rot83] has stated as: *"Many design problems require reasoning about spatial relations. Reasoning about distance, shapes and contours demand considerable computational resources. Good methods of reasoning approximately or qualitatively about shape and spatial relations do not yet exist."* Other good papers on this subject are [Bal84], [Ten84] describing the breakdown of a geometric reasoning project and [Ten86] where the term "geombolic reasoning" is coined for the combination of geometric and symbolic reasoning.

MODELLING THE ASSEMBLY PROCESS

This paper describes a purely logical model for both static and dynamic modelling of the assembly process, while previous work in this area has used procedural models, e.g. [Wes80]. Logic descriptions are better suited to reasoning processes than the more procedural approaches used in conventional geometric models [Req80], but hardly any research is done in this area. The logical geometry model also has the feature that dynamic descriptions in logic are more general than procedural ones.

The model must be able to express the important geometrical aspects of the assembly process, such as the composite structures of objects. Some of these aspects to describe are:
- Elementary bodies
- Holes in bodies

- Contact between bodies and attachment of bodies, thus forming larger structures
- Constraints in relative movability when bodies are in contact with or fixed to each other.

Since the real 3-dimensional world is very hard to model, a simpler experimental $2D^+$ world is choosen for study. The $2D^+$ world is a 2-dimensional world with the restriction that all bodies are axis parallel rectangles, but with holes allowed in them. Holes are also axis parallel rectangles, but an important feature of the 2D+ world is that through holes are allowed without splitting a body into two, thus preserving most of the topologically interesting problems of the real world. This validates the 2-dimensionality and is the reason for the name $2D^+$.
Fig. 1 shows a sample set of $2D^+$ structures, ranging from simple elementary bodies to more complex structures such as bolt junctions..

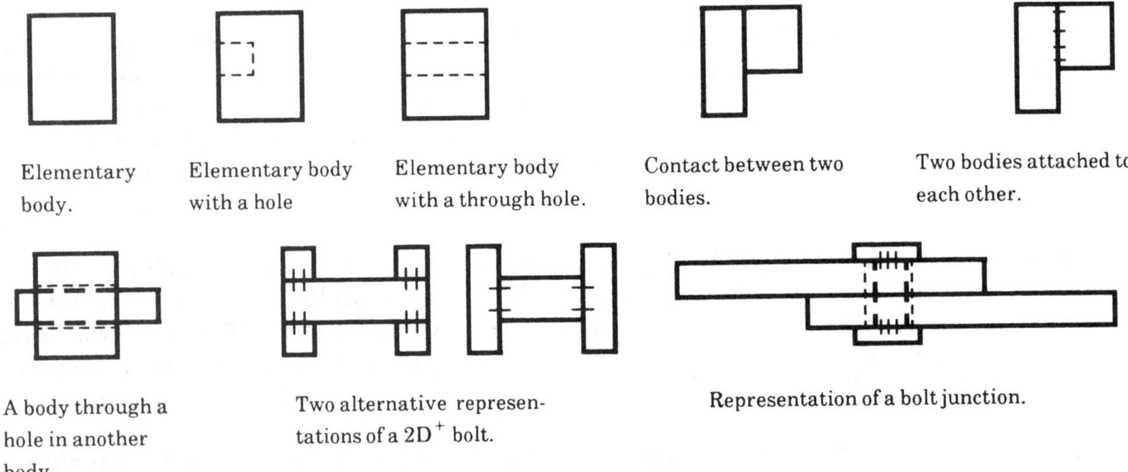

Elementary body.

Elementary body with a hole

Elementary body with a through hole.

Contact between two bodies.

Two bodies attached to each other.

A body through a hole in another body.

Two alternative representations of a $2D^+$ bolt.

Representation of a bolt junction.

Fig. 1. Some examples of $2D^+$ structures

STATIC DESCRIPTION OF THE $2D^+$ WORLD

OBJECT DOMAINS

B is the set of bodies (currently only axis parallel rectangles).
H is the set of holes in objects of **B**. (also axis parallel rectangles).
O is the total domain of objects, i.e. $O = B \cup H$.
S is a set of structures.
A structure is a tuple $<E,P>$, where $E \subseteq O$ and **P** is a consistent set of facts about the objects/structures in **E**. An interesting modification could be to let $E \subseteq O \cup S$.

The 2-dimensional coordinate space is discrete and bounded, where vectors and points in the space are denoted [x,y], with x and y being integers. The + sign is defined for vectors, denoting ordinary vector addition.

The following conventions for variables will be used in the rest of thepaper: $b_n \in B$, $h_n \in H$, $o_n \in O$, x_n, y_n are components of vectors and p_n denote points in the coordinate space.

FUNCTIONS

Only a sample of functions is given here. For a complete list see [Bäc87].

$\text{Xpart}([x,y]) = x$	*X component of vector.*
$\text{Xproj}([x,y]) = [x,0]$	*Projection of vector onto x axis.*
$\text{Dim}(o) = [x,y] \leftrightarrow \text{Dim}(o,x,y)$	*Returns the dimension of the object o as a vector.*
$\text{Llpos}(o) = [x,y] \leftrightarrow \text{Pos}(o,[x,y])$	*Lower left corner position of object o.*
$\text{Lrpos}(o) = \text{Llpos}(o) + \text{Xproj}(\text{Dim}(o))$	*Lower right corner position of object o.*

PRIMITIVE PREDICATES

Like STRIPS [Fik71], a distinction is made between primitive predicates and derivable predicates. Primitive predicates are predicates that can't be derived from other predicates, and thus must be explicitly asserted.

$\text{Dim}(o,x,y)$ — *Indicates that object o is x units wide and y units high (note that the dimension is with respect to global coordinates and not the object itself, and the dimesion of o might thus change if o is rotated).*

$\text{Pos}(o,[x,y])$ — *Indicates that the lower left corner of object o is at absolute coordinate [x,y] (which is thus equal to Llpos(o)).*

$\text{Hole}(b,h)$ — *Indicates that the hole h is a hole in the body b.*

$\text{Attached}(b_1,b_2)$ — *Indicates that the bodies b_1 and b_2 are somehow attached to each other.*

DERIVABLE PREDICATES

The derivable predicates are not asserted and must thus be derived from the primitive predicates. Only a few predicates are listed here. A complete list can be found in [Bäc87].

$\text{Xbetween}(p_1,p_2,p_3) \leftrightarrow \text{Xpart}(p_1) \leq \text{Xpart}(p_2) \leq \text{Xpart}(p_3) \wedge$
$\text{Ypart}(p_1) = \text{Ypart}(p_2) = \text{Ypart}(p_3)$
True if p_2 is on a horizontal line between p_1 and p_3.

$\text{Pinside}(o,p) \leftrightarrow p_1 = \text{Llpos}(o) \wedge p_2 = \text{Urpos}(o) \wedge \text{Xpart}(p_1) \leq p \leq \text{Xpart}(p_2) \wedge$
$\text{Ypart}(p_1) \leq p \leq \text{Ypart}(p_2)$
True if p is a point inside o.

$\text{Spinside}(o,p) \leftrightarrow p_1 = \text{Llpos}(o) \wedge p_2 = \text{Urpos}(o) \wedge \text{Xpart}(p_1) < p < \text{Xpart}(p_2) \wedge$
$\text{Ypart}(p_1) < p < \text{Ypart}(p_2)$
True if p is a point strictly inside o.

$\text{Onedge}(o,p) \leftrightarrow \text{Pinside}(o,p) \wedge \neg\text{Spinside}(o,p)$
True if p is on one of the edges of o.

$\text{Overlap}(o_1,o_2) \leftrightarrow \exists p((\text{Pinside}(o_1,p) \wedge \text{Spinside}(o_2,p)) \vee (\text{Spinside}(o_1,p) \wedge$
$\text{Pinside}(o_2,p)))$
True if o_1 and o_2 overlaps each other.

The following predicates are used to check whether bodies are in contact with each other. A complete list of the predicates used by Pcontact, how these predicates were arrived at, and a thorough analysis of the possible contact cases is given in [Bäc87].

$\text{Outerpcontact}(b_1,b_2,p) \leftrightarrow \neg\text{Overlap}(b_1,b_2) \wedge \text{Onedge}(b_1,p) \wedge \text{Onedge}(b_2,p) \wedge$
$\neg\text{Edgexcp}(b_1,p) \wedge \neg\text{Edgexcp}(b_2,p)$
True if b_1 and b_2 are in contact at p without overlapping at any point.

Pcontact(b_1,b_2,p) ↔   Outerpcontact(b_1,b_2,p)∨Innerpcontact(b_1,b_2,p)
True if b_1 and b_2 are in contact with each other at p.
Contact(b_1,b_2,p_1,p_2) ↔   Online(p_1,p_2)∧ ∀p_3((Xbetween(p_1,p_3,p_2)∨Ybetween(p_1,p_3,p_2))→
Pcontact(b_1,b_2,p_3))
True if b_1 and b_2 are in contact with each other along a line between p_1 and p_2.

CONSTRAINT AXIOMS

Axioms constraining the relations between objects:

{**A1**}   ∀h∃b(Hole(b,h)∧Inside(b,h))
All holes must be inside bodies.
{**A2**}   ∀$h_1$$h_2$b(Hole(b,$h_1$)∧Hole(b,$h_2$)→ ¬Overlap($h_1$,$h_2$))
Two holes in the same body must not overlap.
{**A3**}   ∀$b_1$$b_2$($b_1$ ≠ b_2→(¬Overlap(b_1,b_2)∨∀p(Pinside(b_1,p)∧Pinside(b_2,p)→
∃h((Hole(b_1,h)∨Hole(b_2,h))∧Pinside(h,p))
Bodies must not overlap, but a body can be located in a hole in another body.
{**A4**}   ∀$b_1$$b_2$(Attached($b_1$,$b_2$)→∃$p_1$$p_2$Contact($b_1$,$b_2$,$p_1$,$p_2$))
Bodies cannot be attached to each other without being in contact along a line.

DYNAMIC DESCRIPTION

Since the problem domain is mainly about assembly of details, three principal types of operations seems to be sufficient, namely:

- Translation
- Rotation
- Attachment/Detachment

The following basic set of operations is thus suggested:

Lmove(b)   *Move the body b the distance 1 unit to the left.*
Pturn(b)   *Rotate the body b 90° in positive direction.*
Attach(b_1,b_2)   *Attach bodies b_1 and b_2 to each other.*
Rmove(b), Umove(b),Dmove(b),Nturn(b), Detach(b_1,b_2) are defined analogously.

No other operations than the above mentioned seems to be indispensible. [Bäc87].gives the reasons for only allowing 1 unit moves, and also briefly addresses the problems of collision detection and some other peculiar anomalies of the $2D^+$ world.

USING DYNAMIC LOGIC TO DESCRIBE OPERATIONS

Dynamic logic is a variant of modal logic, where the possible worlds correspond to world states and where there are several accesibility relations. The accesibility relations correspond to different operations that can be performed upon the world, and they describe how the world state changes as an effect of certain operations being performed. The modal operators in dynamic logic are the box operator (denoted [a]) meaning necessity and the diamond operator (denoted <a>) meaning possibility. For a thorough description of dynamic logic, see [Har79].

An extended version of dynamic logic is here used to form rules describing the effects of operations. The current rules only use the box operator, and they have the form φ→[a]ψ, meaning that if φ holds then ψ must necesarily hold after performing the operation a. A simple description of the Lmove operator could be the rule Pos(o,[x,y])→[Lmove(o)]Pos(o,[x-1,y]), if we assume that no other object than o is affected. The possible world interpretation of this rule is shown in fig. 2.

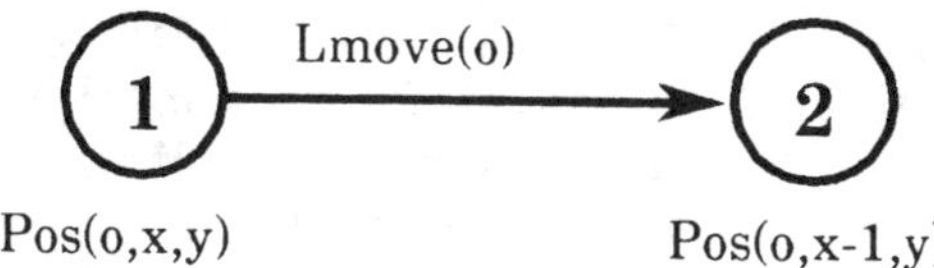

Fig. 2. Lmove operation.

Obviously the fact Pos(o,[x-1,y]) must be asserted in the world state succeding the Lmove(o) operation. What is obvious to a human but not expressed in the rule is that the old fact Pos(o,[x,y]) must be retracted in the new world state. Another problem is that any fact present in state 1 and not affected by the operation should still be true in state 2. Trying to write rules specifying everything that is not affected by a certain operation would result in an enormous amount of rules, and would be practically impossible. This is a classical problem in AI, which is referred to as the *frame problem*, and some good papers on the subject are [Hay71, San71]

One way to cope with the problem is to include default inheritance into the system, i.e. letting a state inherit all consistent facts from its previous state. In this case there must be some method to prevent a state from inheriting the no longer valid facts of the previous state. So far, two different methods for doing this have been investigated.

INTRODUCING THE M OPERATOR

One way to introduce default inheritance is to introduce an **M** operator, where **M**ϕ means "consistent to assume ϕ", here interpreted as: **M**ϕ is true if $\neg \phi$ is not asserted in the current world state. A general default inheritance rule of the type $\phi \rightarrow [\alpha](M\phi \rightarrow \phi)$ could then be introduced.The ϕ stands for P(-) or $\neg$P(-), where P is any primitive predicate. The idea here is that for any fact that should no longer be true, its negation should be asserted in the new state, and thereby preventing it from being inherited. This method will be called method A.

To see how method A works, lets suppose that we have a predicate P taking one argument (or argument vector), and also suppose that we have two operations α and β described by the rules:

P(a)→[α](P(b)∧¬P(a))

P(b)→[β](P(c)∧¬P(b))

Note that the $\neg$P(a) and $\neg$P(b) clauses are present to prevent P(a) and P(b) respectively to be inherited. We let δ denote any operation that does not affect the predicate P. Now consider the example in fig. 3.

From this example it can be seen that a retracted fact will have its negation asserted in all succeding states, and the effect of this is that the number of facts (true or negated) will increase over time. One way to solve this problem would be to avoid inheritance of negated facts. This would however mean that all predicates that are meaningful to assert negated (like e.g. Attached) would have to have a complementary predicate to express their negation. The reason for this is that a fact like Attached(b_1,b_2) would be inherited, but its negation $\neg$Attached(b_1,b_2) would not. Therefore an extra predicate Detached meaning $\neg$Attached would be needed. This problem does of course not exist if we assume a closed world where only positive facts are stored. It can be argued that the previously described $2D^+$ world is closed, but a more realistic world description would probably not be closed.It is naturally possible to use complementary predicates like the *Attached/Detached* pair, but it is awkward and extra axioms should be added for every

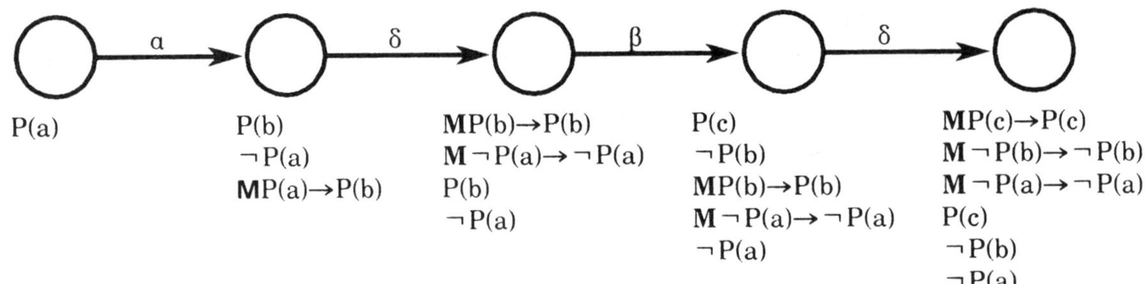

Fig. 3.

complementary pair in order to assure consistency.
Another problem arises with rules of the following kind:

$$P(x) \rightarrow [a(d)](P(x+d) \wedge \neg P(x))$$

Performing the operation $a(0)$ would now lead to an inconsistency. This could be avoided by adding an axiom saying:

$$\forall xy.(x \neq y \wedge P(x) \rightarrow \neg P(y)).$$

Such axioms must however be added for every predicate that is constrained in this way. Another solution is to rewrite the rule as:

$$d \neq 0 \wedge P(x) \rightarrow [a(d)](P(x+d) \wedge \neg P(x))$$

Method A seems to work, but requires a lot of extra qualifications and restrictions, so a more natural and simple method will be introduced below.

INTRODUCING THE D OPERATOR

In order not to depend on a closed world assumption, method A is refined to method B, where a **D** operator is introduced. $D\phi$ will mean "ϕ deleted", i.e. that the fact ϕ is no longer true, for any ϕ denoting $P(-)$ or $\neg P(-)$ as in method A. The **D** operator is intended to be used in the right hand side of operation rules to indicate what will no longer hold after performing a certain operation. In conjunction with the **D** operator there must also be a default inheritance rule of the form $\phi \rightarrow [a](M \neg D\phi \rightarrow \phi)$, i.e. everything that holds before performing an operation, and that is not explicitly invalidated by that operation, will also hold after performing the operation. Method B slightly resembles the STRIPS approach [Fik71], where add and delete lists are used to indicate what facts changes between succeding states.

Now consider method b. The rules corresponding to the previous example would be

$$P(a) \rightarrow [a](P(b) \wedge DP(a))$$
$$P(b) \rightarrow [\beta](P(c) \wedge DP(b))$$

Obviously these rules are almost equal to the previous rules, with the exception that the negation signs are changed to **D** operators in the rules. Fig. 4 describes the previous example, but with the new rules and method B used.
With this method a retracted fact will show up with a **D** operator in the succeding state and disappear totally in the thereafter succeding states. If an object has earlier been located at 4312 different positions, the current state will not contain 4312 facts stating 4312 certain positions that the object is currently not loacted at, as would have been the case with method A.

Method B does also allow assertion of negated predicates, as can be seen from the following example. Consider the rules:

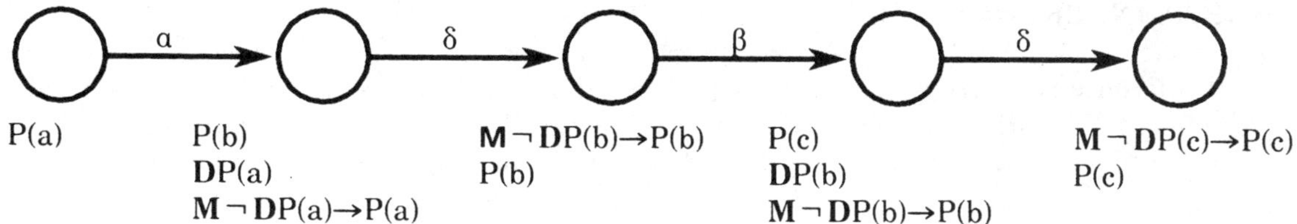

Fig. 4.

$$\neg p \rightarrow [\alpha](p \wedge \mathbf{D} \neg p)$$
$$p \rightarrow [\beta](\neg p \wedge \mathbf{D}p)$$

The operation δ denotes any operation that does not affect p, and fig. 5 shows an example using the rules above..

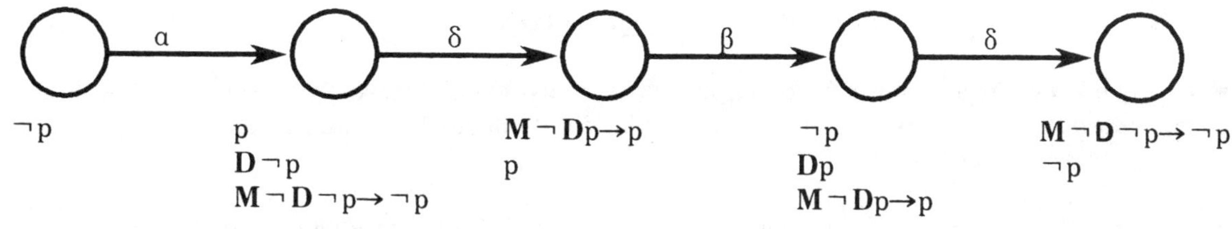

Fig. 5.

Since method B is more general than method A and does not assume a closed world, it is the method considered in the rest of thisp aper.

EXTRA PREDICATES

Predicates like the following must be added in the dynamic description:

Lfbase$(o_1,o_2) \leftrightarrow$ Attached$(o_1,o_2) \vee$ Hole$(o_1,o_2) \vee$
$\exists p_1 p_2$(Ybetween(Lrpos$(o_2),p_1,p_2) \wedge$ Ybetween$(p_1,p_2,$Urpos$(o_2)) \wedge$
Contact$(o_1,o_2,$Lrpos$(o_2),p_1) \wedge$ Contact$(o_1,o_2,p_2,$Urpos$(o_2)))$

True if o2 is in contact with o1 in such a way that it will follow (be dragged, pushed or otherwise forced by) o1 if o1 is translated to the left.

Lfollows$(o_1,o_2) \leftrightarrow$ Lfbase$(o_1,o_2) \vee \exists o_3(o_1 \neq o_2 \wedge o_1 \neq o_3 \wedge o_2 \neq o_3 \wedge$
Lfollows$(o_1,o_3) \wedge$ Lfbase$(o_3,o_2))$

Transitive closure of Lfbase.

INFERENCE RULES DESCRIBING OPERATIONS

Rules for Lmove and Attach are given below. Rules for some more operations can be found in [Bäc87].

$$Pos(o,[x,y]) \wedge (b = o \vee Lfollows(b,o)) \rightarrow [Lmove(b)]Pos(o,[x-1,y])$$
$$Pos(o,[x,y]) \wedge (b = o \vee Lfollows(b,o)) \rightarrow [Lmove(b)]\mathbf{D}Pos(o,[x,y])$$

$$\exists p_1 p_2 Contact(b_1,b_2,p_1,p_2) \rightarrow [Attach(b_1,b_2)]Attached(b_1,b_2)$$
$$\exists p_1 p_2 Contact(b_1,b_2,p_1,p_2) \rightarrow [Attach(b_1,b_2)]\mathbf{D} \neg Attached(b_1,b_2)$$

GENERAL INFERENCE RULES

All inference rules from first order logic are valid, but they can naturally only be used to derive facts from the primitive facts within a certain state. There is also the default rule:

$$\phi \to [\alpha](\mathbf{M} \neg \mathbf{D}\phi \to \phi)$$

where ϕ is of the form P(-) or $\neg$ P(-) for any primitive predicate P, and where α is any operation.

AXIOMS

The axioms {**A1**} to {**A4**} are still necessary, but {**A1**} to {**A2**} must only be checked for the initial state, while {**A3**} to {**A4**} must be checked for every new state.

CONCLUSION

- The $2D^+$ world is powerful enough to study most of the interesting problems in automated assembly, and it is expected to be a sufficient model for a large class of real assembly problems, [Bäc87].

- The $2D^+$ world can be statically described in first order predicate calculus, although the formulas become very complex and would require large amounts of computational resources. This problem is true for all other known model for geometric reasoning too, so it is hardly a step backwards, but rather stresses that geometric reasoning is a hard problem in itself independent of representation. Some methods to attack this problem are suggested in [Bäc87].

- The dynamic model uses an augmented dynamic logic, but in such a simple and restricted way that it should not cause any serious problems to implement. The formal semantics for this logic is still an open issue though.

- The method used to attack the frame problem does of course not solve it, but provides a fairly good and simple way to tackle it. Some further improvements are suggested in [Bäc87].

Acknowledgements

Many thanks goes to Erik Sandewall for initial ideas and support, and to Erik Tengvald, Roland Almgren, Arne Jönsson and Jalal Maleki for interesting ideas, comments and discussions.

References

[Alb84]   **Albus, J. S.**: *Robotics*, NATO ASI Series, vol. F11, Robotics and Artificial Intelligence, (eds. Brady, M. & Gerhardt, L. A. et. al.), Berlin: Springer Verlag 1984.

[Bal84]   **Ballard, D. H.**: *Task frames in robot manipulation*, Proc. AAAI-84 conference, pp. 16-22, Austin 1984.

[Bäc87]   **Bäckström, C.**: *Logical modelling of simplified geometrical objects and mechanical assembly processes*, Report: LITH-IDA-87-05, Dept. of Computer and Information Science, Linköping University 1987.

[Fik71]   **Fikes, R & Nilsson, N.**: *STRIPS - A new approach to the application of theorem proving to problem solving*, AI magazine 2 (3,4), pp. 189-208, 1971

[Har79]   **Harel, D.**: *First Order Dynamic Logic*, Lecture Notes in Computer Science, vol. 68. Berlin: Springer Verlag, 1979.

[Hay71]   **Hayes, P.**: *The frame problem and related problems in Artificial Intelligence*, Memo AIM-153, Stanford Artificial Intelligence Project , Stanford 1971.

[Nev80]   **Nevins, J. L. & Whitney, D. E.**: *Assembly Research*, Automatica, vol. 16, No. 6, Peragmon Press 1980.

[Nic85]   **Nicol, C. J.**: *Modelling solids in four dimensions*, Computer Graphics Forum, vol. 4, No. 3, pp. 239-244, North-Holland, September 1985.

[Req80]   **Requicha, A.**: *Representations for rigid solids: Theory, Methods and Systems*, Computing Surveys, vol 12, No 4, pp 437-464, (eds. Goldberg, A. & Mandelbaum, M. et. al.), ACM 1980.

[Rot83]   **Hayes-Roth, F. & Waterman, D. & Lenat, D.**: *Building Expert Systems*, p. 85 (end of first paragraph), Addison Wesley Publishing Company Inc 1983.

[San72]   **Sandewall, E.**: *An approach to the frame problem and its implementation*, Machine Intelligence 7, pp. 195-204, (eds. Meltzer, B. & Mitchie, D.), Edinburgh: Edinburgh University Press 1972.

[Sch86]   **Schmolze, J. G.**: *Physics for Robots*, Proc. AAAI-86 conference, pp.626-631, Philadelphia 1986.

[Ten84]   **Tengvald, E.**: *The design of Expert Planning Systems: An Experimental Operations Planning System for Turning*, Linköping Studies in Science and Technology PhD Dissertation No. 111, Dept. of Computer and Information Science, Linköping University 1984.

[Ten86]   **Tengvald, E.**: *Description of the AIM project: Artificial Intelligence for manufacturing*, Unpublished memo, ver. 6, Dept. of Computer and Information Science, Linköping University 1986.

[Wes80]   **Wesley, M.A. & Lozano-Perez, T.** et.al.: *A Geometric Modelling System for Automated Mechanical Assembly*, IBM Journal of Research and Development, vol. 24, Number 1, pp. 64-74, January 1980.

Planning Flight Paths In Dynamic Situations with Incomplete Knowledge

Prasanta K. Bose

A. C-C. Meng

M. Rajinikanth

Artificial Intelligence Laboratory

Computer Science Center

Texas Instruments Inc.

MS 238,Dallas, Texas 75266

Abstract

This paper describes the spatial representations and the planning process of a system designed to support the critical decision making required of an autonomous robot executing air navigation tasks in dynamic environments. The spatial planning and replanning problems that are encountered in the control and execution of such air tasks are very complex. One major source of the complexity is due to incomplete and uncertain knowledge about the world. Another source of complexity is controlling the search for a feasible course of actions that meets the goals of an air-navigation task.

Some of the functional components of an implemented system, KAMPR, are described here in terms of the knowledge of the environment, its representation and the spatial reasoning processes that endow the system with the capabilities to plan and act reactively. The design of the system is based on a computational methodology that makes explicit the causal connection of relevant situational parameters to a flight plan to aid in the execution monitoring and reactive replanning to adapt to changes in the real world.

Introduction

Designing intelligent robots that can execute air navigation tasks in dynamic situations is a complex problem. Several factors contribute to the complexity of the problem. Spatial reasoning in 3-D space to obtain collision-free paths is of exponential complexity. Since perceptual processes give partial evidence of the environment, the model of the environment is incomplete. Such incompleteness have to be modeled and taken into account in the plan generation process. Moreover, the world being dynamic, it is not feasible to predict all changes and take account of those changes in the plan generation process. Hence the plan chosen must be adaptable to the world changes that may affect its successful execution.

In this paper we are primarily concerned with the generation of reactive flight plans, their execution monitoring and replanning. Problems caused by uncertainty and incompleteness about the situation, plays the key role in defining the computational methodology used in the design of the system. The criticality factor is due to the dynamic elements that can cause a task to fail. The capabilities needed in the system to support handling of some of the above problems can be stated in more functional terms. In generating the flight plan the system has to represent and reason about the spatial properties of the terrain such as terrain obstacles and the free space that is flight-safe. Monitoring execution of plans and the causal effects of sensed information on the plan in execution requires the capability to maintain and update a model of the situation in relation to the flight-plan. To be able to replan or repair some plan would require the system to detect failing components of the plan, be able to compute in real time, the modifications to the plan and evaluate the impact of modifications to current plan.

Representation of Spatial Information

For a given large area in a 3-D space, the number of all the possible paths satisfying the high level air mission task are combinatorially explosive, and searching for a solution in this space is of exponential complexity. Traditionally there have been two main approaches to the path finding problem: one represents the obstacles explicitly as geometrical shapes, like polygons, and the free space is defined implicitly by being outside of those obstacles. For 2-D space, this representation is adequate to determine the shortest distance path by searching the spatial graph known as the Visibility Graph. [LOZANO-PEREZ-WESLEY79]. This graph represents all the visible paths between vertices of obstacles and start and goal locations.

But to extend this approach to the 3D shortest path problem incurs a very high computational cost [SHARIR-SCHORR84]. The other basic approach represents the free space explicitly and finds the path directly inside the free space. Brooks [BROOKS83] represents the free space as generalized cones where the central axes of these cones form a connected graph of passing channels. The path finding process searches for the path on the connectivity graph. By definition, the path found is therefore a safe path, i.e. collision-free, but not the shortest path. This paper follows a similar approach in a way which will allow modelling of the free space bounded by randomly shaped obstacles. Certain constraints can also be imposed on the path to be planned besides being collision-free. Currently, some systems have explored the approach of associating cost to each point in a 3-D digitized space and reduce the planning problem into a numeric optimization problem of finding the minimum cost path. Such approaches use techniques of dynamic programming. But cost functions are hard to generate and this scheme cannot represent qualitative information and plan tasks in situations where knowledge is incomplete.

In **KAMPR** the 3-D space is approximated with a sequence of layered 2-D maps. Within each 2-D map, the space is classified into adjacent regions, using the Voronoi Region Classification scheme ([MENG87]). Semantically a region in this scheme is the area which is dominated uniquely by an obstacle. A more formal definition of Voronoi regions is that each point inside a particular region is closer to the obstacle in that region than to any other regions. The edge curve between two obstacles consists of those points that are equidistant from them. Figure 1 shows the Voronoi regions extracted from a digital map data.

The vornoi region classification process finally leads to the creation of two representations that are used in spatial planning. They are the obstacle centered region-connectivity graph and the dual of that, the vornoi-edges connectivity graph. The obstacle centered region-connectivity graph representation is used to generate the direction of flight in terms of a sequence of adjacent regions. The vornoi-edges connectivity graph is a representation of the free space and is used for the path plan or moves plan generation. The abstract directional-plan in terms of the region-sequence is utilised to prune the search space for a plausible moves path plan.

The basic entities that represent the spatial information are the voronoi regions and voronoi path segments. The spatial information like natural landmarks, topographic features, tactical information and lethality are then associated with each region and path segment. When searching for a air-navigation plan, at the level of flight-moves, the decision to take an action of type *traverse-way-through* between region X and region Y, is dependent on certain types information related to these two regions. This information is related to traversibility of that vornoi path segment between region X and region Y. The traversibility of a path segment is causally dependent on such data as the existence of obstacles in the neighbouring regions, their types, weather traversibility, and landmarks. At a lower level, the traversibility depends on the motion constraints of the robot, such as turn radius and speed. Hence to make an intelligent local decision about a move, the planner needs to reason about terrain properties of regions such as visibility and trafficability, obstacle features such as the mobility and such spatial properties as connectivity and local geometry of the neighbouring obstacles. These spatial properties are represented as relations and are indexed with reference to obstacles and the associated free space between obstacles, i.e. the vornoi path segment. For example, we can express some spatial information related to the path segment between two regions C1 and C2 as follows:

$F2$:   *landmark(landmark-id(TOWER3),betw-obsts(C1,C2))*.

The following if-then inference rule exemplies how the above information may be utilized to infer the traversibility of a path segment:

$R6$:   **if***(weather-traversible(waythru(?X,?Y)),*
           vehicle-sensor-type(range-finder, status(operational)),
           landmark(landmark-id(?L),betw-obsts(?X,?Y)))
              ==>
        then*(traversible(waythru(?X,?Y)))*.

The Reasoning Mechanism in KAMPR

KAMPR uses a tool for assumption-based reasoning with truth-maintenance, ARMS ([BOSE86a]), to reason about actions and and changes in the world that affect actions and goals. The functionality of ARMS is similar to that of ATMS ([DEKL86]). ARMS works in the logic programming environment of Explorer Prolog ([TIPR87]). ARMS has two components. The inference component of ARMS reasons with each action and determines the dependency information which is relevant for its successful execution. These causal dependencies of actions on world conditions obtained by the inference component is communicated to the truth-maintenance component. The truth-maintenance component does management of the information that model the world and the intended actions whose executability depend on such information.

To illustrate briefly how KAMPR reasons with incomplete world models consider the KB (knowledge base) of *F2* and *R6* (from the previous section) with the additional knowledge:

F4:   *vehicle-sensor-type(range-finder,status(operational))*,

R8:   **if(assumable(***waythru(betw-obsts(C1,C2),weather(LOW-CLOUD))***)**
          ==>
        then(*weather-traversible(waythru(?X,?Y))***).*

The *assumable* predicated antecedent in rule *R8* allows the system to make default inferences, i.e. conclusions to be drawn in the absence of any contradictory information in the knowledge base. This is essential to making decisions with incomplete knowledge about the situation. When KAMPR attempts to decide the feasability of an action to traverse between region C1 and C2, it backward-chains on *F5*:

F5:   *traversible(waythru(C1,C2))*.

and with the default assumption *F6* (assuming that its negation is not present):

F6:   *waythru(betw-obsts(C1,C2),weather(LOW-CLOUD))*.

it concludes *F7* from rule *R8* and *F6*:

F7:   *weather-traversible(waythru(C1,C2))*.

and from *R6*, *F7*, *F4* and *F2* it concludes that F6 is valid and hence the action is feasible. The truth-maintenance component maintains the dependency information of *F5*, *F6* and *F7*. If the KB is then updated with the information that the weather has changed from *Low-Cloud* to *High-Cloud* in the region between C1 and C2, the assumed fact *F6* (which contradicts the new information update, assuming that the KB knows about facts which are contradictory) looses its validity status. Hence the previously believed facts *F7* and *F5* are no longer warranted. The KB after the update is:

F2:   *landmark(landmark-id(TOWER3),betw-obsts(C1,C2))*.

F4:   *vehicle-sensor-type(range-finder,status(operational))*,

F8:   *waythru(betw-obsts(C1,C2),weather(HIGH-CLOUD))*.

The system then needs to replan the action of flying between region C1 and C2, unless there is an alternative justification which makes that action feasible.

The Plan Generation Process

The higher level planning activity involves finding the sequence of adjacent regions from base to destination which satisfy the constraints generated from the high-level task goals. It produces a set of plausible directional plans. A directional plan is the sequence of regions to traverse in order to go from the base to the destination. Each directional plan is evaluated in terms of risks involved in following that direction.

The minimum risk directional plan is then expanded to give rise to a set of plausible moves plan with contingencies as shown in Figure 2. A moves plan is a sequence of actions, each action being of type:

$$traverse\text{-}waythru(between(?C1,?C2),from(?X),to(?Y)).$$

The set of plausible moves plan are then further evaluated in terms of resource cost like fuel and other risks. The minimum cost moves plan is then checked against the world knowledge base to see if it is feasible. A moves plan is feasible if the conditions necessary for executing each move is valid in the world situation model. These conditions are known as the protection conditions. The process of determining the feasibility of a plausible moves plan, results in the creation of a dependency network. The dependency network explicates all the the protection conditions that need to hold good for the plan to succeed. The protection conditions also in a sense model the rationale for choosing a particular plan of action.

Replanning in Dynamic Situations

The protection conditions of a moves plan step are conditions about the state of world that need to hold true, before, during or after the execution of the step. The assumption-based reasoning and truth-maintenance mechanism derives these conditions at the time of checking the feasability of a moves plan. This dependency information may involve both facts which are known to be true at plan generation time and defualt assumptions which can be believed to be true in the absence of any contradictory information. Once a moves plan is chosen for execution, the truth-maintenance subsystem, monitors the continuous validity of these protection conditions. The explication of the dependency information of a plan on the world conditions and truth-maintenance of those conditions makes it possible for the system to be reactive to changes that can be modelled in the knowledge base. Updates to the world situation may causally lead to changing the belief status of a protection condition and affect adversely a plan step or the whole plan. In such a situation the plan execution monitor can locate the failing steps of the plan and trigger the replanning process.

The replanning process tries to repair the current plan by making use of the contingent plans database. If that is not possible, it evokes the plan generation process. For this to happen, the replanning process will have to determine which assumptions made in the air-naviagtion plan are affected by the reported changes. If the assumptions affected by the new information lead to failure of some steps of the the initial plan, the replanner will seek to modify the plan by replacing failing actions with contingent plans which can be validated in the modified world scenario. If the effect of the changes is such that a major portion of the plan is affected, then the replanner will attempt to use an alternative existing plan (which might have been rejected earlier in comparison to the failing plan) which satisfies the new set of constraints or a major subset thereof and modify this alternative plan if need be, before redoing the planning from scratch. A KAMPR display of the choice of an alternative path plan caused by failure of the previous path plan due to a situation update is shown in Figure 3. For more details on KAMPR replanning process refer to [BOSE87b].

Summary

This paper describes KAMPR, a system for planning spatial actions in critical situations. The key problems addressed are to do with coping with the complexity of the search space and doing reactive planning and replanning with incomplete knowledge of the environment. The first problem is dealt through the use of an abstract obstacle-centered representation in searching for a directional plan and then using a dual of that representation to search for a between-obstacles moves plan. The characteristic properties of the spatial representation in terms of Vornoi regions and edges ensures generation of a collision-free path in real-time. The plan protection conditions generation process makes the plan reactive to changes in the world. These conditions may be defualt assumptions as a result of incomplete knowledge about the environment. The assumption-based truth maintenance process is utilised to handle the effects of changing information on the model of the world and the action plan chosen based on that model.

References

[BOSE86a] P. K. Bose, "ARMS : An Assumption-based Reasoning System in a Logic Programming Environment", TI Tech Report.

[BOSE87b] P. K. Bose, A. Meng and M. Rajinikanth, "Planning and Re-planning Air Navigation Tasks in Dynamic Situations", Technical Report, CSC, Texas Instruments, in preparation.

[BROOKS83] R. Brooks "Solving the Find-Path Problem by Good Representation of Free Space" IEEE Trans. on system, man, and cybernetics. Vol. SMC-13 No. 3, 1983. Also in AAAI 82.

[DEKL86] de Kleer,J., "ATMS: An Assumption-Based TMS " Artificial Intelligence, Vol. 28, 1986.

[DONALD83] "Hypothesizing Channels Through Free-Space In Solving the Find-Path Problem" MIT, AI Memo 736.

[LOZANO-PEREZ-WESLEY79] T. Lozano-perez and M. A. Wesley "A Algorithm for Planning Collision-Free Paths Among Polyhedra Obstacles" CACM, Vol. 22, Oct. 1979.

[MENG87] A. C-C. Meng, "Free Space Modeling and Geometric Motion Planning Under Location Uncertainty," Proceeding of the Workshop On Spatial Reasoning and Multi-Sensor Fusion, 1987

[SHARIR-SCHORR84] M. Sharir and A Schorr "On Shortest Paths in Polyhedra Spaces" Proceeding of 16th ACM Symp. on the theory of Computer, 1984

[TIPR87] Texas Instruments Prolog, Data Systems Group, Texas Instruments, Austin, Texas.

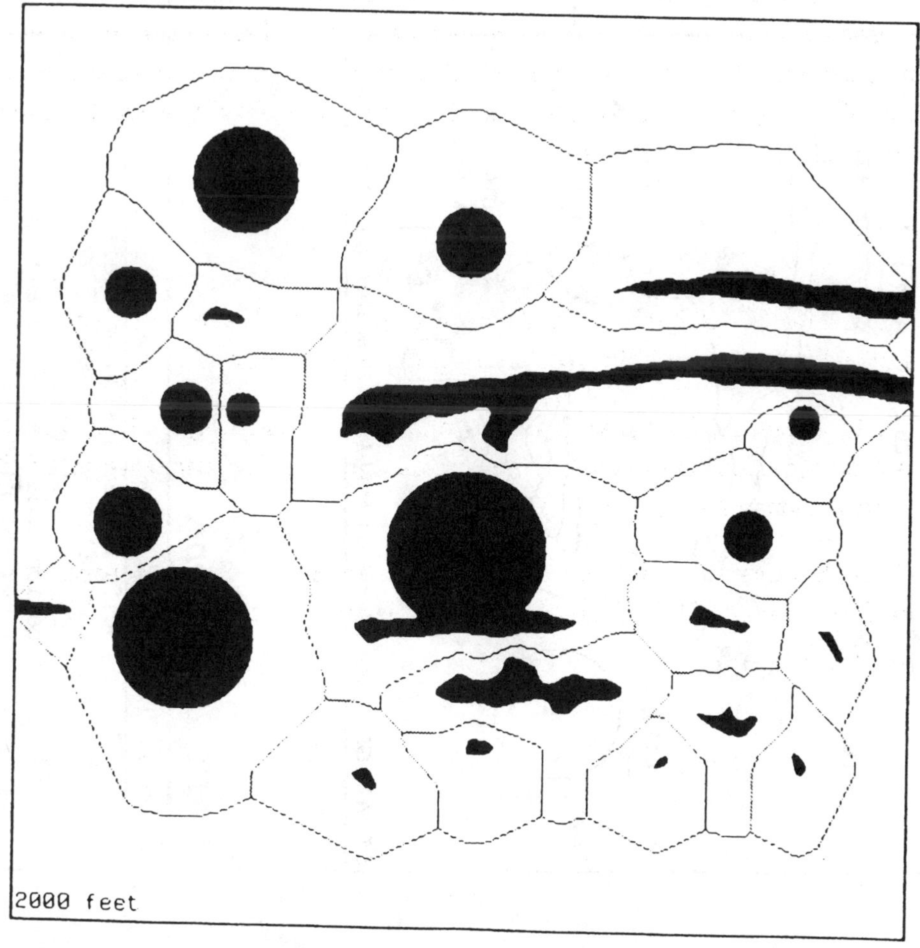

FIGURE -1

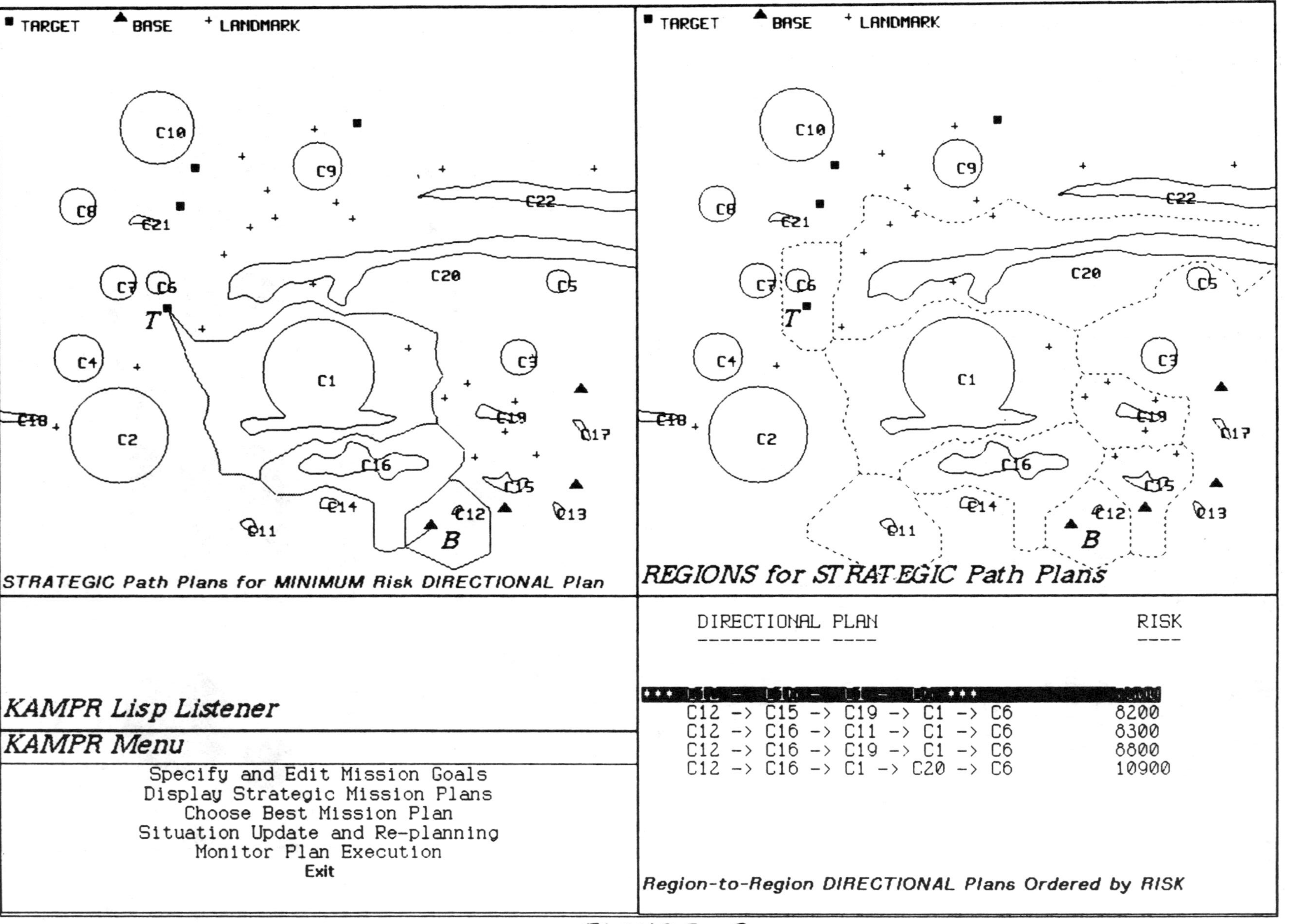

TARGET   BASE   + LANDMARK
C10
C9
C8
C21
C7 C6
T
C4
C2
C18
C1
C19
C17
C16
C15
C14
C12
C11
B
C13
C20
C22
C5
C3
STRATEGIC Path Plans for MINIMUM Risk DIRECTIONAL Plan
KAMPR Lisp Listener
KAMPR Menu
Specify and Edit Mission Goals
Display Strategic Mission Plans
Choose Best Mission Plan
Situation Update and Re-planning
Monitor Plan Execution
Exit
TARGET   BASE   + LANDMARK
C10
C9
C8
C21
C7 C6
T
C4
C2
C18
C1
C19
C17
C16
C15
C14
C12
C11
B
C13
C20
C22
C5
C3
REGIONS for STRATEGIC Path Plans
DIRECTIONAL PLAN   RISK
C12 -> C15 -> C19 -> C1 -> C6   8200
C12 -> C16 -> C11 -> C1 -> C6   8300
C12 -> C16 -> C19 -> C1 -> C6   8800
C12 -> C16 -> C1 -> C20 -> C6   10900
Region-to-Region DIRECTIONAL Plans Ordered by RISK

FIGURE - 2

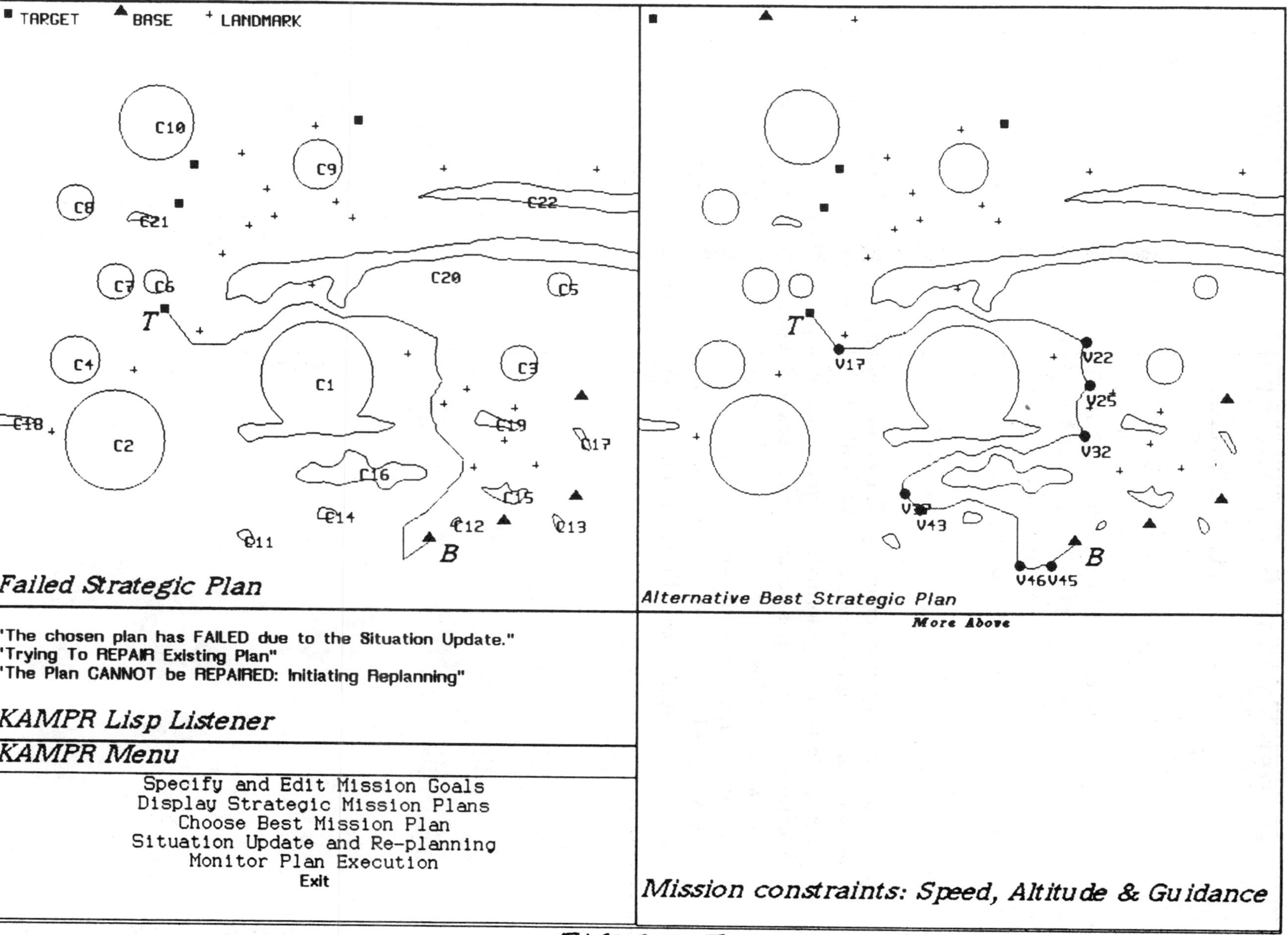

■ TARGET   ▲ BASE   + LANDMARK
C10
C9
C8
C21
C22
C7 C6
C20
C5
T
C4
C1
C3
C18
C2
C19
C17
C16
C14
C15
C11
C12
C13
B
Failed Strategic Plan
"The chosen plan has FAILED due to the Situation Update."
"Trying To REPAIR Existing Plan"
"The Plan CANNOT be REPAIRED: Initiating Replanning"
KAMPR Lisp Listener
KAMPR Menu
Specify and Edit Mission Goals
Display Strategic Mission Plans
Choose Best Mission Plan
Situation Update and Re-planning
Monitor Plan Execution
Exit
T
V17
V22
V25
V32
V38
V43
V46 V45
B
Alternative Best Strategic Plan
More Above
Mission constraints: Speed, Altitude & Guidance

FIGURE 3.

Hyper-Pyramids for Integration of Spatial Information

Ramesh Jain and William I Grosky
Computer Vision Research Laboratory
Electrical Engineering and Computer Science
The University of Michigan
Ann Arbor, Michigan 48109

Abstract

An intelligent autonomous system working in an unstructured, changing environment requires a world model to direct all its actions. This model is used in integration of information acquired using disparate sensors. The representations used for this model should work with both spatial and symbolic information. In this paper we present a hierachical representation using re-linkable hyperpyramids for world modeling. This structure will be combined with a graph-based representation of objects to integrate and assimilate information about objects in the environment for navigation of a mobile robot.

1   Introduction

A very important problem in a robotic or autonomous system is the integration and assimilation of spatial information. Most autonomous tasks require a close coordination between *sensors, manipulators, and planners.* The amount of contribution from each component depends on the nature and complexity of both the task and the environment. In general, the more unstructured an environment is, the more demanding the sensing and planning needs of the system are. A system may acquire information about the environment using many types of sensors, and then use this information to control the action of a machine.

An intelligent autonomous system working in an unstructured, changing environment must maintain a world model to direct all its actions. There are several questions about the world model, including:

- How to prepare this world model?

- What information to keep in it?

- How to combine information coming from disparate sources?

- How to combine uncertain and imprecise information?, and

- How to assimilate information in the world model?

In a complex mult-robot multi-sensor system, each robot and sensor will have an *ego-world* model. This model will contain an *ego-centered* description of the world. Knowledge about the goals, current states, and strategies of other robots and sensors will also be a part of the ego-world model. As more information is acquired, the model will be updated. Based on the ego-world model, each module will decide what it can do to improve its model and to help other module in accompalishing their task. Based on this reasoning, appropriate information will be communicated to other modules.

2   Representation

The representations used for combining information should be able to work with both both spatial and symbolic information. This information may be represented at different abstraction levels. The information must be represented at the following levels:

- Volumetric,

- Surface Descriptors, and

- Features.

At the most detailed level, one may require volumetric representation of a scene in the world model. This representation will be independent of individual sensor locations at a particular time instant. This exhaustive representation may be used to store characteristics, such as color, compliance, and temperature, of the entity at that location in the space. At the next level the surface descriptors may be used. Range sensors give explicit information for determining surface descriptors. For intensity and tactile images also many techniques are being developed for determining surface descriptors. Though the techniques for determining these surface descriptors from intensity and range data are still in the developmental phase, this appears to be the proper level for interaction among sensors and among ego-world models of sensors and the world model of the system. Individual sensors may use different features for recognizing objects and may use these features to participate in the object recognition process.

In this hierarchical model, each sensor has its own representations, but communicates with the world model using 3-D spatial information. The lowest level of representation should contain different properties at points in space. For this level, a volumetric representation is needed. The highest level should contain information about objects, their properties, and relations among the objects. This symbolic level should be related to the exhausive volumetric level. In between these two extremes there should be several resolutions. In the next section we discuss hyperpyramids for representing lower levels in the world representation.

3   Hyperpyramids

We would like to define a space-efficient data structure which can represent property values defined at various points in a 3-D workspace in such a way that connected regions of similar property values, called *3-D property segments*, can be efficiently accessed and processed with respect to a given semantics. This semantics should be one in which 3-D regions are represented in a hierarchical manner in terms of subregions, the leaves being these 3-D property segments. Such a representation of semantically meaningful regions will lend itself to the identification of these regions with real world objects in that properties of objects and relationships among objects can easily be computed from similar computations on their subobjects, these computations being realized on their corresponding regions in the data structure.

Such a data structure has been formulated. Particularized to a single property, it resembles pyramids [1,2,3] and octrees [5]. Like octrees, when a region of space is reached for which the given property has a uniform value, it is not further subdivided. Like relinkable pyramids, a given node has a set of possible fathers. We refer to this factored data structure as a *relinkable octree*.

Recall that in a standard octree of $N+1$ levels, a node at level j, $0 \le j \le N$, represents a cubic region of size $L/2^j \times L/2^j \times L/2^j$ for a workspace of size $L \times L \times L$. Put another way, if the workspace if divided into $R \times R \times R$ voxels, for R the *resolution* of the workspace, a node on level j represents a cube which contains $R^{N-j} \times R^{N-j} \times R^{N-j}$ voxels. A node of an octree is called a *border* node if the cubic region it represents has a face which is included in a border face of the workspace. Note that each non-border node has 8 children. We associate a coordinate tuple, (*level*, *plane*, *row*, *column*), with each node of an octree. The root will have coordinate $(0,0,0,0)$, while if a particular node has coordinate (n,p,r,c), then the jth child of that node, $1 \le j \le 8$, will have coordinate $(n+1, 2p+j_2, 2r+j_1, 2c+j_0)$, for $j_2 j_1 j_0$ the base 2 expansion of $j-1$. These children are called a node's *standard* children.

A *relinkable octree* can be looked at as an octree in which some of a node's standard children migrate to one of the given node's siblings. That is, a child of node (n,p,r,c) could be any of the standard children of node $(n, p+\Delta_p, r+\Delta_r, c+\Delta_c)$, for $\Delta_p, \Delta_r, \Delta_c \in \{-1,0,1\}$, whose corresponding voxel in a standard octree has a face which is included in a face of the voxel which is represented by (n,p,r,c) in a standard octree. Thus, node (n,p,r,c) can have as children any subset of $\{(n+1, 2p+\Delta_p, 2r+\Delta_r, 2c+\Delta_c)|\Delta_p, \Delta_r, \Delta_c \in \{-1,0,1,2\}\}$, or from 0 to 64 children. Note that each node except the root still has a single father. For the workspace shown in Figure 1, Figure 2 exhibits a corresponding relinkable octree.

Figure 3 shows the tree of Figure 2 with some flags added to each node. These flags are *root* and *hidden*. A node whose *root* flag is true is the root of a subtree some of whose leaves comprise a 3-D property segment, while a node whose *hidden* flag is true is the root of a subtree, one of whose other nodes has a true *root* flag. The 3-D property segment corresponding to this latter node is called a *hidden* 3-D property segment. These hidden segments provide a means of organizing the 3-D property segments together so that they all can be accessed from the root of the relinkable octree and so that the computation of segment properties and relationships do not conflict with each other. Hidden segments also provide a hierarchical decomposition of segments into subsegments in such a way that the organization of a particular segment in terms of its subsegments becomes transparent.

Our unfactored data structure, which is called a *hyper-pyramid*, can be considered to be a collection of relinkable octrees, one for each represented property. It consists of a *backbone*, which is a standard octree of processing element (p.e.) nodes. Each backbone node has a non-empty set of associated property nodes. The backbone nodes hold information that is common to each of its associated properties, such as its coordinates. For a given property, the set of property nodes forms a relinkable octree. See Figure 6 for our representation of a hyper-pyramid which combines the relinkable octrees of Figures 2 and 5, assuming they result from different properties.

Our approach allows the definition of multiple properties, each property having one of the 4 datatypes *integer*, *real*, *string*, or *greylevel*. Each property has values defined over the workspace, which is divided into $R \times R \times R$ voxels, for R the resolution of the workspace. This resolution may be changed at any time.

Property values may be input in 2 ways:

1. The entire workspace may have values specified. This consists of an input file containing R^3 values. Any previous values of the property are destroyed.

2. A particular value may be specified for a particular plane, row, and column. This approach may be used by various sensors to input their values. Note that by redefining the resolution, entire regions of constant values may be input in a single step. For example, suppose a $4 \times 4 \times 4$ workspace has been input via Method 1 above. Changing the resolution

to 2 and specifying a value for *plane* $= 1$, *row* $= 1$, and *column* $= 1$ will then input this value for a $2 \times 2 \times 2$ set of voxels.

A given property's values may also be segmented as previous described based on a user defined notion of closeness of values. This performs relinking so that each 3-D property segment corresponds to a subtree whose leaves are the actual voxels belongning to this segment and whose root is as close to the hyper-pyramid root as possible. The notion of hidden segments are also supported so that each segment may be accessed as efficiently as possible. Our present approach to segmentation is more powerful than our previous one [3] for the following reasons:

1. Our underlying data structure is octree-based rather than pyramid-based, resulting in savings in space utilization.

2. There are no disabled nodes. Nodes which cannot be relinked cause extra nodes in the data structure. These extra nodes are minimized by a more powerful relinking algorithm. This algorithm causes fewer nodes which would have become disabled in our previous approach.

3. Our algorithm goes through only as many passes as it needs to for the segmentation.

4. Any relinking done after a change in property values is restricted to a small neighborhood surrounding each of the changes. Thus, incremental changes in the workspace result in an incremental amount of effort spent in relinking.

4   Current Status and Future Research

We have implemented algorithms for input of different properties and relinking for segmentation based on properties. This segmentation results in the representation of objects at a higher level in the octree. We developed an approach for recovering depth using qualitative information. That approach represents object relationships in a graph structure that is updated as more information is acquired in a dynamic environment [4]. We will now integrate that representation with the above representation for integration and assimilation of information for a mobile robot.

References

[1] H. J. Antoniss, "Image segmentation in pyramids", *Computer Graphics and Image Processing*, vol. 19, pp. 367-383, 1982.

[2] J.M. Chibulskis and C.R. Dyer, " An analysis of node linking in over-lapped pyramids", *IEEE Trans. on Systems, Man, and Cybernetics*, vol SMC-14, pp. 424-436, 1984.

[3] W.I. Grosky and R. Jain, "Pyramid-based approach to segmentation applied to region matching", *IEEE Trans. on Pattern Analysis and Machine Intelligence*, vol. PAMI-8, pp.639-650, 1986.

[4] S.M. Haynes and R. Jain, "A Qualitive approach for recovering relative depths in dynamic scenes", Tech Report 11, Cognitive Science and Machine Intelligence Lab, The University of Michigan, June 1987.

[5] C.L. Jackins and S.L. Tanimoto, "Oct-trees and their use in representing three-dimensional objects", *Computer Graphics and Image Processing*, vol. 14, pp.249-270, 1980.

a	a	a	b
a	a	b	b
c	c	c	c
d	d	c	c

z	z	y	y
z	z	y	y
z	w	y	y
u	w	x	x

P_1 - No background values

P_2 - No background values

FIGURE   1

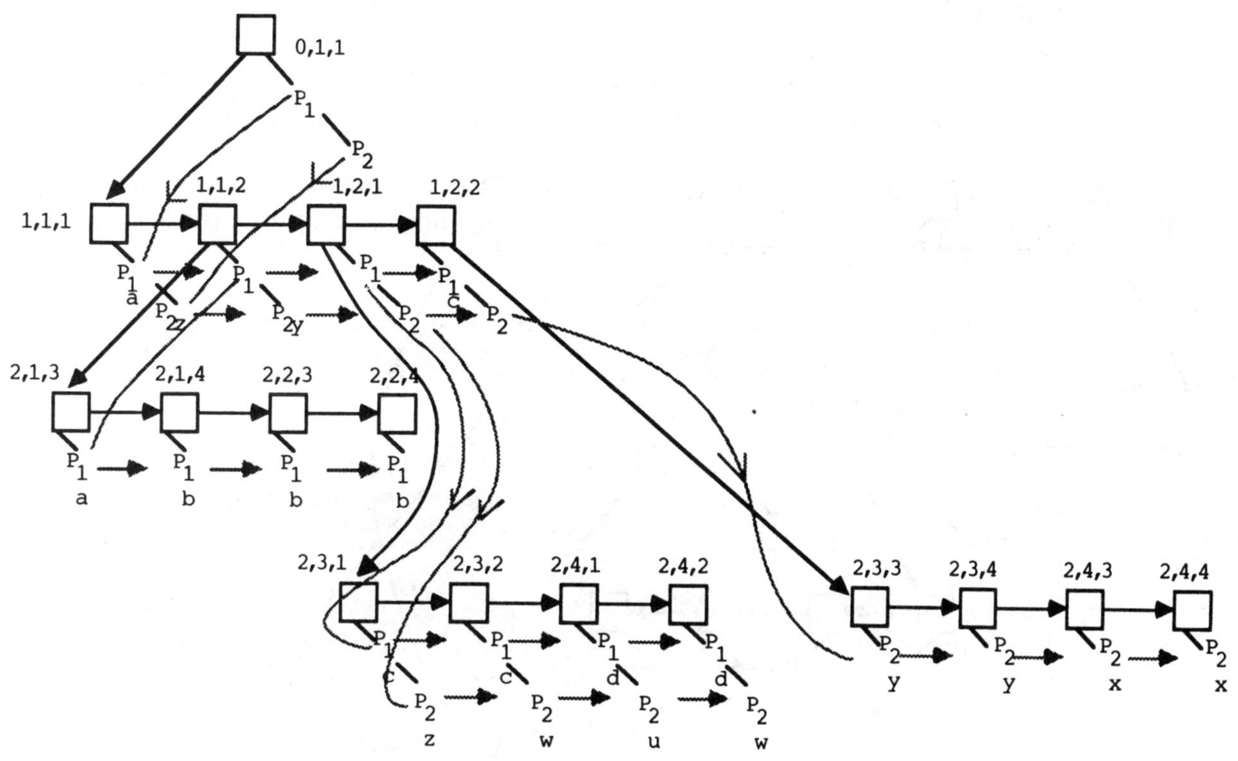

FIGURE 2

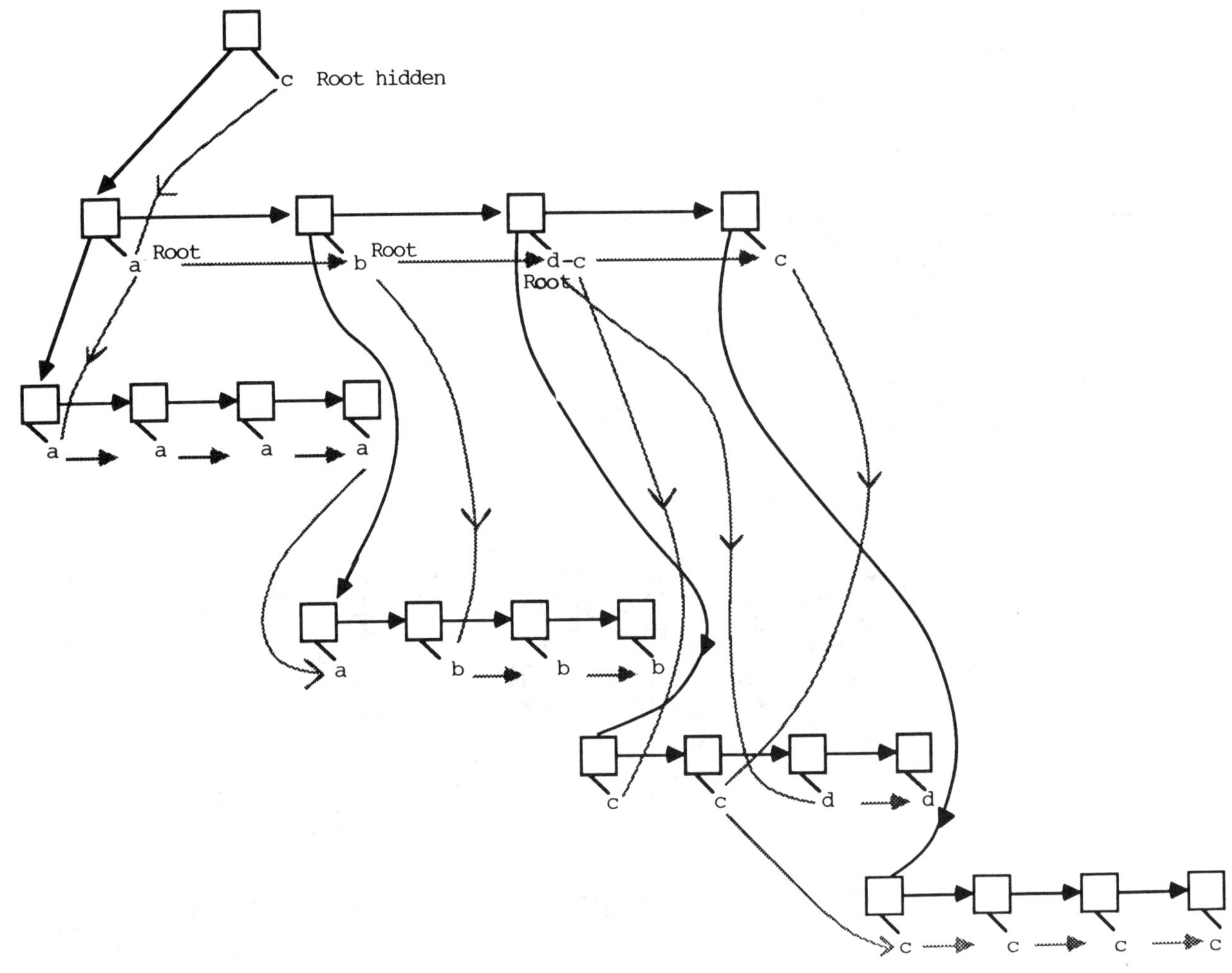

FIGURE 3 - P_1 relinked

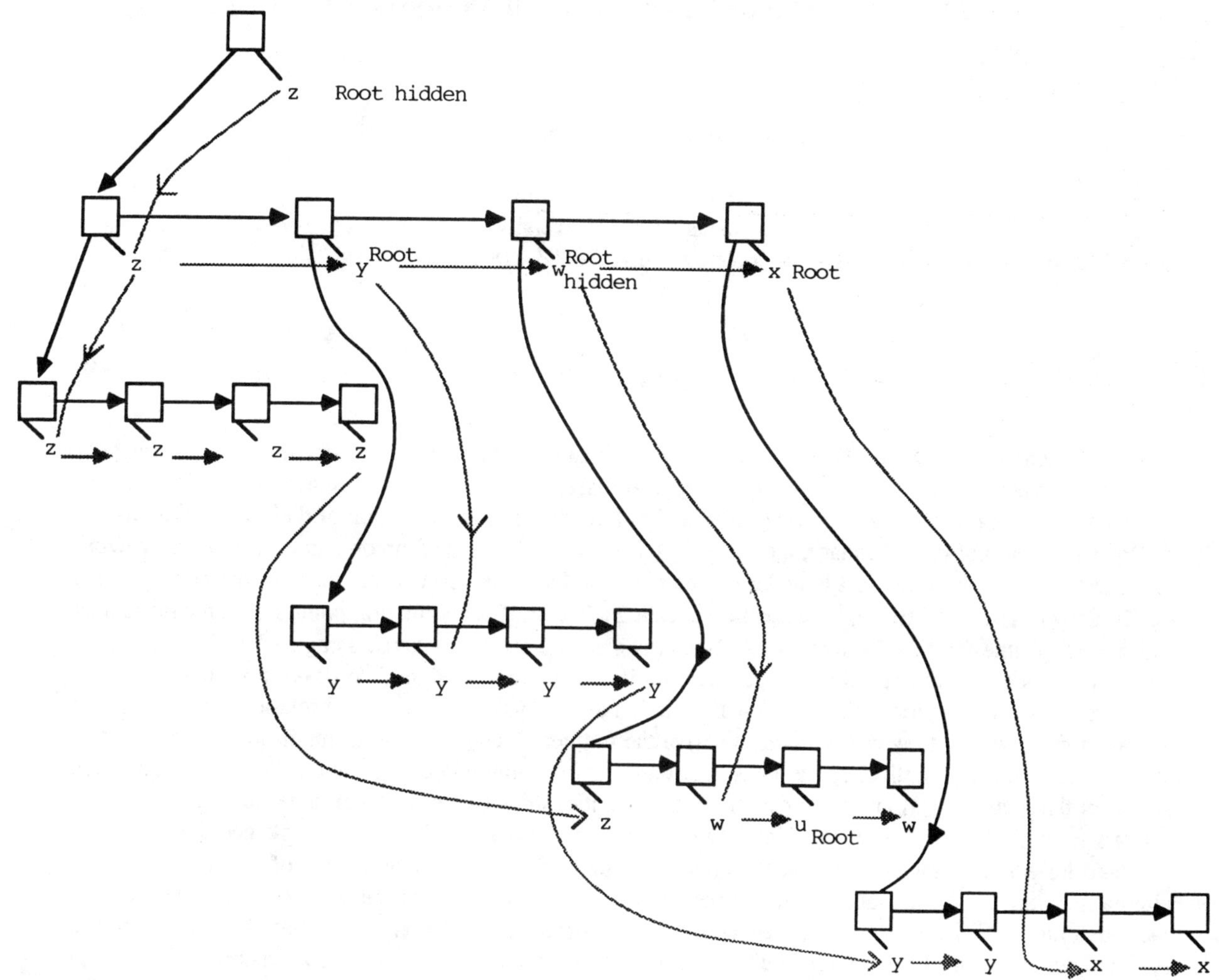

FIGURE 4 - P_2 relinked

SPATIAL REASONING IN RECTANGULAR DISSECTION

Sukhamay Kundu and Rajiv Singh

Computer Science Department
Louisiana State University
Baton Rouge, LA 70803, USA

ABSTRACT

A rectangular dissection D is a partition of a rectangular space R into $n \geq 1$ non-overlapping rectangular subspaces or basic regions $\{r_1, r_2, ..., r_n\}$. A dissection D defines two elementary spatial relationships among the basic regions: (1) h(i, j), if r_i and r_j have in common a portion of their *vertical* boundary and r_i is to the left of that boundary, and (2) v(i, j), if r_i and r_j have in common a portion of their *horizontal* boundary and r_i is above that boundary. The horizontal and the vertical relationships define the graphs $G_h(D)$ and $G_v(D)$, respectively. A dissection is called a T-plan if each junction point between a horizontal and a vertical line forms a T-junction. A T-plan is a model for space partitioning in VLSI design, path planning in robot motion, and floor-space planning in architectural design. We develop several inference rules for the vertical relationships v(i, j) and their "dual" forms for the horizontal relationships h(i, j) of a T-plan, and show how they can be used to derive the implied h- and v-relationships from a given set of h- and v-relationships. In particular, we focus here on the inferencing process for determining all missing v(i, j)'s from the graph $G_h(D)$ and one or more vertical relationships (the problem of determining the missing h(i, j)'s from $G_v(D)$ etc. is similar). The inference rules given here are based on simple geometric properties, and have the characteristics that the conclusion-part of some of them consist of a large number of alternatives (an "or"-combination). Such rules are known as indefinite inference-rules. One drawback of the indefinite inference-rules is that their application in deriving new facts from other given facts require separate continuation of the inference-chain from each of the alternatives in the conclusion of a rule, and this makes the inferencing process computationally inefficient. This calls for an alternative approach for deriving the missing hv-relationships. We develop here such an approach for a subclass of T-plans, called T_*-plans. A T_*-plan is a T-plan which is obtained by repeated application of the following partitioning operations: the horizontal partitioning, the vertical partitioning, the left-spiral partitioning, and the right-spiral partitioning. An important property of a T_*-plan D is that the successive partitioning operations which generate D can be represented as a tree T(D), called the structure tree of D. The inferencing of the v(i, j)'s is accomplished in two stages: first the tree T(D) is determined (upto certain ambiguities) from $G_h(D)$, and then the inference rules are applied using T(D) as a guide. The algorithm for determining the structure tree T(D) of T_*-plan from its h-graph $G_h(D)$ is given here. The details of how to use the tree T(D) in guiding the application of inference rules is described elsewhere. The tree T(D) essentially helps to capture certain global properties of the T_*-plan D and this in turn facilitates the inferencing process by localizing it to the substructures within D. The inferencing at a global level is also facilitated via certain abstractions of D defined by T(D). Once the v(i, j)'s have been determined, and hence the graph G(D) = $G_h(D) \cup G_v(D)$, one can completely determine the topological layout of D from G(D) [5].

Keywords: Rectangular dissection, Inference rules, Structure tree, Algorithm.

1. INTRODUCTION

A *subregion* of a T-plan is a subset of its basic regions which together form a rectangular subspace of the total space R. (See Abstract for other notations and terminologies.) The subregions of a T-plan D form a hierarchical tree structure, denoted by T(D). Each terminal node of T(D) represents a basic region and each intermediate node correspond to a non-trivial subregion; the root of T(D) represents the whole design space R. For a T_*-plan, the subregions of D are in 1-1 correspondence with the non-terminal nodes of T(D). A non-backtracking algorithm for determining the layout of a T_*-plan from its hv-adjacency graph G(D) is given in [5]. In many applications, one may know only a subset of all the hv-relationships. The subgraph of the known h- and v-relationships is called a (topological) constraints graph G′. The determination of all feasible dissections D′ which satisfy the given hv-relationships G′, i.e., $G' \subseteq G(D')$, is easier when there are fewer missing relationships, i.e., G(D′) - G′ is small. Thus it is important to "fill up" the constraint graph as much as possible by adding all h(i, j) and v(i, j) to G′ which are "logical" consequences (also called the implied constraints) of G′. An h(i, j) or v(i, j) is a *logical consequence* of G′ if every feasible dissection D′ contains that h(i, j) or v(i, j). The determination of the logical consequences by direct application of the inference rules is not a very effective method because of the indefinite nature of the inference rules. In the case where $G_h(D') \subseteq G'$, it is more efficient to first determine as much of T(D′) as possible from G′ and then determine the missing v-arcs by the inference rules, using T(D′) as a guide in the inferencing.

The four basic partitioning operations for defining a T_*-plan [3, 4] are illustrated in Fig. 1; also shown are the associated *structure trees* T(D) of the resulting T_*-plans, where the root nodes are labeled, respectively, as h, v, s, and S. A node with the label h is called an h-node, and similarly for the other labels. A T_*-plan is generated by repeated application of these four partitioning operations, starting with the initial rectangle R. Fig. 2(iii) shows the structure tree for the T_*-plan in Fig. 2(ii), except that the node which is shown labeled as "s/S" should be labeled "S". The *horizontal* and the *vertical* partitioning operations are called the h- and the v-operations. The s- and the S-operations, called the *left-spiral* and the *right-spiral* partitioning operations, creates five rectangles each from a single rectangle.

2. THE hv-GRAPH

An hv-graph is an acyclic directed graph (i.e., there is no directed cycle) each of whose arcs (i, j) is labeled with one of the two letters h and v. An arc (i, j) with the label h is called an h-arc, and is written as h(i, j); similarly we write v(i, j) for a v-arc. The *hv-graph* G(D) for a T-plan D is defined as follows [1, 3, 8]. There is one node in G(D) for each basic region of the dissection, and there is an arc h(i, j) from i to j if the basic regions r_i and r_j have a part of their vertical boundaries in common, with r_i to the left of that boundary and r_j to the right; an arc v(i, j) is defined similarly. The hv-graph G(D) is in a sense equivalent to (i.e., contains the same information as) the union of the horizontal and vertical channel graphs in [3, 7]. Shown in Figs. 3(i)-(iv) are the four *primitive* hv-graphs corresponding to the h-, v-, s-, and S-operations; the v-arcs are shown as solid lines and the h-arcs as broken lines. The graphs for the s- and S-operations are referred to as the s-graph and the S-graph, respectively. Associated with each T-plan one has four external regions N, S, W, and E as shown in Fig. 2(ii), where the regions N and S extend to infinity to both east and west directions. We do not normally include in G(D) the nodes corresponding to the external regions and the arcs to or from them. The h-arcs of G define the subgraph $G_h(D)$, called the *h-graph* of D; similarly, the v-arcs define the subgraph $G_v(D)$, called the *v-graph* of D. A horizontal wall (in short, an h-wall) in a T-plan D is a maximal horizontal line segment w [1]. An h-wall is written as w = <N(w), S(w)>, where N(w) is the list of all basic regions whose south edges together form the line w and S(w) is the list of all basic regions whose north edges together form the line w. Both the lists N(w) and S(w) are ordered in the left to right order. A vertical wall or v-wall is defined similarly and is written as w = <W(w), E(w)>. In Fig. 2(ii), w_1 = <(4, 6), (8)> is an h-wall and w_2 = <(1, 2), (3, 4, 8, 9)> is a v-wall. Corresponding to the external region W, we have the external v-wall, also referred to as external west-wall, e.g., <(W), (1, 2)> in Fig. 2(ii). Similarly, for the other external regions.

The hv-graph G(D) of a T-plan D has several important properties which are useful in the analysis of topological constraints of a design problem. We state some of these properties as inference rules in the next section. A node i is called an h-source (resp., h-sink) node if there is no h-arc to (resp., from) that node. We define similarly the v-source and the v-sink nodes. The h-source nodes correspond to the basic regions r_i which are adjacent to W and the h-sink nodes correspond to the basic regions r_j which are adjacent to E. Similarly, for the v-source and v-sink nodes. We use the terms 'node' and 'basic region' interchangeably. Also, the notations j and r_j are used interchangeably to refer either to a node in G(D) or the basic region r_j in D. A sequence of nodes $<x_0, x_1, x_2, ..., x_k>$, $k \geq 1$, where each pair of consecutive nodes is joined by an h-arc $h(x_i, x_{i+1})$ is called an *h-path* from x_0 to x_k. An h-path from x to y is denoted simply as h-path(x, y). We define a *v-path* analogously and a v-path from x to y is written, in short, as v-path(x, y). We say that y is to the *right* of x, or equivalently, x is to the *left* of y, if there is an h-path from x to y. Similarly, if there is a v-path(x, y), we say x is *above* y, or equivalently, y is *below* x [2]. It is easy to see that if there is an h-path from x to y, then there is no v-path from x to y or from y to x. Similarly, with h-path and v-path interchanged. We call this the *orthogonal* property of G(D). Another important property of G(D) is the *intransitive* property: if h(x, y) is an h-arc, then there is no other h-path from x to y; similarly for the v-arcs and v-paths.

3. INFERENCE RULES

The *inference rules* for determining the implied constraints from a constraint graph can be classified into two main categories: (1) the v-rules for determining the existence of v-arcs, and (2) the h-rules for determining the existence of h-arcs. We state below only the v-rules; the h-rules are similar. The rule (V_1) gives the existence of certain alternative sets of v-arcs, the rule (V_2) imposes a consistency condition among the selections made from the various alternative-sets given by the (V_1), and the rule (V_3) is a partial converse of the (V_1). The rule (V_3) is a consequence of the orthogonal property of G(D). The box-rule (B) states that certain combination of h-arcs and v-arcs must exists if certain other combination of them are known to be present. The nodes $<x_1, x_2, x_3, x_4>$ is said to form a *box* if there are h-path(x_1, x_2) and h-path(x_4, x_3), and there are v-path(x_1, x_4) and v-path(x_2, x_3) such that these paths have no common nodes except for the end points x_1, x_2, x_3, and x_4. In order to form a box, we require that at least three of the four nodes be distinct; for example, x_1 may be the same as x_2. (By the acyclic property of the hv-graph, we have $x_1 \neq x_3$ and $x_2 \neq x_4$.) Finally, the significance of the F-rule ('F' for five) is that it allows at most five arcs among any set of four nodes. (The planarity of G(D), being the dual of the dissection D considered as a planar graph, would allow six arcs among four nodes.) The rules given below, excluding the F-rule and the rules (V_3) and (H_3) (which follow from the box-rule and the acyclic property of $G_v(D)$) is minimal, in the sense that if an arc is derived by one rule, then one may not be able to derive the same arc by application of the remaining rules, in general. We do not know at this time if there are other minimal rule sets which contain fewer rules than the ones presented here and which have the same inference power (i.e., can infer the presence or absence of the same set of arcs).

The v-rules:

(V_1) Let H(x) = $\{x_i: h(x, x_i) \in G_h(D)\}$. Then there is an v-path $(x_1, x_2, ..., x_k)$ joining all nodes x_i in H(x) in some order. The same is true if H(x) = $\{x_i: h(x_i, x) \in G_h(D)\}$, set of end points of the h-arcs *to* node x.

If H(x) has k nodes, then the rule gives as many as k! possible alternative sets of v-arcs among the nodes H(x), each set consisting of (k−1) v-arcs. Because of the many alternatives given by this rule for a large k, it is considered a fairly 'week' rule.

(V_2) If $z \in H(x) \cap H(y)$, then the v-path connecting the nodes $H(x)$ (or $H(y)$) terminates at the node z and the v-path connecting the nodes $H(y)$ (resp., $H(x)$) starts at the node z. Here, both $H(x)$ and $H(y)$ are assumed to be the end points of arcs *from* x and *from* y, or the end points of arcs *to* x and *to* y.

(V_3) If there is an h-path from x to y, the v-arc $h(x, z)$, and a v-arc between y and z, then the v-arc $v(y, z)$ exists.

This rule selects the alternative $v(y, z)$ from the pair $v(y, z)$ and $v(z, y)$ under the given conditions. Similarly, if there is an h-path from x to y, the v-arc $v(z, x)$, and a v-arc between y and z, then the v-arc $v(z, y)$ exists.

The B-rule:

(B) If there are h-paths and v-paths connecting three nodes forming part of a box, then there exist a fourth node and the remaining h-path or v-path which form a complete box with those three nodes. (The fourth node may coincide with one of the three other nodes.)

The F-rule:

(F) For any set of four nodes, there are at most five arcs joining these nodes. The nodes $\{1, 2, 3, 4\}$ and the arcs $\{h(1, 2), h(3, 4), v(1, 3), v(2, 3), v(3, 4)\}$ constitutes an example of one such $G(D)$.

Example. The following example illustrates the application of the inference rules. Consider the constraint graph consisting of the nodes $\{1, 2, 3, 4, 5\}$, the h-arcs $G_h(D) = \{h(1, 4), h(2, 3), h(2, 5), h(3, 4)\}$ and the v-arc $v(1, 2)$. We determine the missing v-arcs of $G_v(D)$ as follows.

(i) Applying the rule (V_1) to the h-arcs $h(1, 4)$ and $h(3, 4)$ to node 4, we get one of $v(1, 3)$ and $v(3, 1)$ is in G. However, since $v(3, 1)$ creates the cycle $(1, 2, 3, 1)$ and G is acyclic, we conclude that $v(1, 3)$ is in G.

(ii) Applying the rule (V_1) to the h-arcs $h(2, 3)$ and $h(2, 5)$ from node 2, we get one of $v(3, 5)$ and $v(5, 3)$ is in G. However, if $v(5, 3)$ is in G, then there must be an h-path between 1 and 5 (due to the rule (H_1)). This being not the case, we get $v(3, 5)$ is in G.

(ii) Now apply the box-rule (B) with $x_1 = 3$, $x_2 = 4$, and $x_4 = 5$. Since there cannot be a v-arc from 4 to any of the nodes $\{1, 2, 3\}$, we conclude that $x_3 = x_4$ and $v(4, 5)$ is in G.

(iv) There is no other v-arc in G because any such arc would either create a cycle or violate the intransitive property of v-arcs. This completes the determination of $G(D)$, which is the hv-graph of the left-spiral.

If we were given $v(1, 3)$ instead of $v(1, 2)$, then applying the box-rule with $x_2 = 1$, $x_3 = 3$, and $x_4 = 2$, we would get $x_1 = x_2$ and $v(1, 2)$ is in G because that is the only way of having a v-path from 1 to 2. The remaining v-arcs could now be determined as before. On the other hand, if we assume that $v(2, 1)$ is in G instead of $v(1, 2)$, then the v-arcs determined now are exactly the reverses (opposite orientations) of those obtained before and the resulting G is the hv-graph of the right-spiral.

4. h-EQUIVALENCE OF BASIC REGIONS AND SUBREGIONS

We introduce here two fundamental concepts: h-equivalence and h-domination. The notion of h-equivalence explains why one may not be able to determine the tree $T(D)$ uniquely from $G_h(D)$. The notion of h-domination is needed in formulating the algorithm for determining $T(D)$, except for certain ambiguities. Two nodes x and y in $G(D)$ of a T-plan D are said to be h-equivalent if they are h-adjacent *from* the same set of nodes and are also h-adjacent *to* the same set of nodes. Put another way,

    (i)   x and y are not h-adjacent (i.e., there there is no h-arc between them),

    (ii)   for each node z, h(z, x) if and only if h(z, y), and

    (iii)   for each node z, h(x, z) if and only if h(y, z).

We write $x \equiv_h y$ if x and y are h-equivalent. If $x \equiv_h y$ and $y \equiv_h z$, then it is easy to see that x and z are not h-adjacent and $x \equiv_h z$. The reflexive ($x \equiv_h x$) and the symmetric ($x \equiv_h y$ implies $y \equiv_h x$) properties of the relationship $\equiv_h$ are also easily verified. Thus $\equiv_h$ is an equivalence relation. Let $[x]_h$ denote the equivalence class of x under $\equiv_h$. In terms of a T-plan, this means that there is a basic region i such that its east vertical side spans the west vertical side of each $y \in [x]_h$ (see Fig. 4(i)). Similarly, there exists a basic region j whose west vertical side spans the east vertical side of each $y \in [x]_h$. (Here, i may be the external region W and j may be external region E.) In particular, the union of the basic regions in $[x]_h$ form a sub-region. If we permute the positions of two or more basic regions in $[x]_h$, then the h-graph of the new T-plan is the same as $G_h(D)$, and thus one cannot uniquely determine from $G_h(D)$ the v-arcs among the basic regions in $[x]_h$. Another way that this non-uniqueness can persist is that there are two disjoint subregions R_1 and R_2 which play the role of two h-equivalent nodes or basic regions, and the following three conditions hold. In that case, we write, $R_1 \equiv_h R_2$ and say that R_1 and R_2 are h-equivalent. If both R_1 and R_2 are basic regions, then (i′)-(iii′) reduces to (i)-(iii).

    (i′)   There is no h-arc between a node in R_1 and a node in R_2,

    (ii′)   For each node $z \notin R_1 \cup R_2$, h(z, R_1) if and only if h(z, R_2), and

    (iii′) For each node $z \notin R_1 \cup R_2$, h(R_1, z) if and only if h(R_2, z).

Fig. 4(ii) illustrates such a situation. Here we can interchange the subregions R_1 and R_2 without affecting any of the h-relationships. The presence of equivalent regions mean that the ordering of the children of certain h-nodes in T(D) cannot be completely determined from $G_h(D)$. In the case of spiral partitions, the labeling convention for the five subregions created by the partition give the same h-arcs among them, and hence one cannot distinguish between the s- and S-partitions on the basis of $G_h(D)$.

5. h-DOMINATION BY v-WALLS

    An *unordered* wall $w = \langle L_1, L_2 \rangle$ is an ordinary wall except that L_1 and L_2 are now *sets* of basic regions, instead of being ordered lists. Thus, when viewed as an unordered wall, the wall v = <(1, 2), (3, 4, 8, 9)> is written as <{1, 2}, {3, 4, 8, 9}>. Let L(Q) denote the set of all nodes which are to the left of *some* node in $x \in Q$. Similarly, the set R(Q) is defined to be the set of all nodes which are to the *right* of each node $x \in Q$. If $w = \langle L_1, L_2 \rangle$ is an (ordered or unordered) v-wall, then by abuse of language, we write L(w) = L(L_2) and R(w) = R(L_1). Clearly, $L_1 \subseteq L(w)$ and $L_2 \subseteq R(w)$. We say that the v-wall w *h-dominates* a basic region j *from left* if each h-path from the external node W to the node j passes through one of the nodes in L_1. In terms of the T-plan D, this implies that the vertical line segment corresponding to the v-wall w completely covers the vertical span (as a subset of y-axis) of the basic region j (the converse is not true, however). The external west wall clearly h-dominates from left each basic region. A v-wall w is said to h-dominate from left a set of basic regions Q if it h-dominates from left each $j \in Q$. A v-wall w is said to h-dominate from left the v-wall $w' = \langle L'_1, L'_2 \rangle$ if w h-dominates from left the set of nodes in L'_1. The notion of h-domination from right by a v-wall is defined similarly. We write $w \leftarrow_h j$ and $w \leftarrow_h w'$, respectively, to denote the h-domination of j and w′ from left by w. Note that $w \leftarrow_h w'$ is not the same as $w' \rightarrow_h w$. We say that the v-wall w is to the left of w′ (or equivalently, w′ to the right of w) if for some $i \in L_2$ and $j \in L'_1$ there is an h-path from i to j. In terms of the T-plan D, this implies that the vertical line corresponding to w is to the left of that for w′ (the converse is not true, however). The above definitions of h-domination and a v-wall being to the left of another v-wall apply without change to the unordered v-walls as well. Note that if w_1 and w_2 are two v-walls which h-dominate a set of nodes Q from left, then either w_1 is to the left of w_2 or w_2 is to the left of w_1. Thus we may talk of the rightmost (leftmost) h-dominating v-wall of Q from left (right).

Input:	A set of basic regions Q and the h-graph $G_h(D)$ of a T-plan D.
Output:	The rightmost unordered v-wall w which h-dominates the set of basic regions Q from left.

Algorithm:

1. Add the external node W to the graph $G_h(D)$ and the h-arc (W, i) for each h-source node i in the given $G_h(D)$.

2. Choose a node $j \in Q$ and form the unordered v-wall $w = \langle L_1, L_2 \rangle$ where $j \in L_2$.

3. Remove each $i \in L_1$ which is not adjacent to some node (which may be different from j) in Q. Let L'_1 be the reduced L_1.

4. For each $i \in L'_1$, traverse the graph $G_h(D)$ in depth-first fashion starting from i. Delete an h-arc from $G_h(D)$ at the time of backtracking along that arc. (Thus an h-arc will be traversed for at most one starting node i.) Also, when the last h-arc to a node in Q is deleted, remove that node (which may be different from j) from Q.

5. If Q is non-empty, then add L'_1 to Q and go to Step 2; otherwise w is the required rightmost v-wall, and stop.

ALGORITHM 1. Algorithm for finding the rightmost unordered v-wall which h-dominates a set of nodes Q from left.

6. DETERMINATION OF T(D) FROM $G_h(D)$

Theorem 2. The h-graph $G_h(D)$ of a T_*-plan D determines its tree-representation T(D) uniquely, except for the following:

(a) The ordering of the children of the h-nodes.

(b) Distinguishing between the labels s and S for a spiral node. (The ordering of the children of each spiral node is uniquely determined.)

That Theorem 2 is the best possible can be seen by comparing T(D) and T(D'), where D is any T_*-plan and D' is obtained from D by the reflection along a horizontal mirror. (See [6] for a proof of Theorem 2.) We give below the algorithm for computing T(D), with the exceptions (a)-(b).

Input:	The h-graph $G_h(D)$ of a T_*-plan D.
Output:	The tree-representation T(D) of D, except for the ordering of the children of the h-nodes and distinguishing between the left- and right-spiral nodes.

Algorithm:

1. If $G_h(D)$ is not weakly connected (i.e., connected as an undirected graph), then create an h-node as the root of T(D). Label the weak components as $Q_1, Q_2, ..., Q_m$ in some order. Go to Step 7.

2. [$G_h(D)$ is weakly connected.] If $G_h(D)$ consists of a single node x, then T(D) has only one node x. Otherwise, find the unordered v-walls $w_j = \langle L_{j1}, L_{j2} \rangle$, $0 \leq j \leq m$, satisfying the following conditions:

   (i) $w_0 = \langle \{W\}, L_{02} \rangle$ is the external west wall and $w_m = \langle L_{m1}, \{E\} \rangle$ is the external east wall. Here, L_{02} is the set of h-source nodes in $G_h(D)$ and L_{m1} is the set of h-sink nodes.

(ii) w_{j+1} is the leftmost v-wall which h-dominates L_{j2} from right.

3.   If $m \geq 2$, then let $Q_j = R(w_{j-1}) \cap L(w_j)$, $1 \leq j \leq m$. Create a v-node as the root of T(D). Go to Step 7.

4. $[G_h(D)$ is weakly connected and $m = 1$.] Create the root of T(D) and label it "s/S", i.e., the root is either an s-node or an S-node. Choose an h-source node x, and find the right most v-wall $w \neq$ the external east wall which h-dominates x from right. Let Q = L(w).

5.   If w also h-dominates Q from right, then let $w_1 = w = <L_{11}, L_{12}>$, say. Find an h-source node $y \notin Q$ and let w' be the rightmost v-wall ($\neq$ external east wall) which h dominates y from right. Let w_2 be the leftmost v-wall which h-dominates w' from left ($\neq$ external west wall). If no such v-wall exists then take then set $w_2 = w'$. Let $m = 5$ and define the sets of basic regions Q_j, $1 \leq j \leq 5$, as follows. Go to Step 7.

$$Q_3 = R(w_1) \cap L(w_2)$$

$$Q_2 = L(w_1) \qquad\qquad Q_4 = R(w_2)$$

$$Q_1 = L(L_{21} - Q_3) \qquad Q_5 = R(L_{12} - Q_3).$$

6.   [The v-wall w does not h-dominate Q from right.] Find an h-sink node z to which there is an h-path from the node x. Reverse the direction of all h-arcs in $G_h(D)$, and go to Step 4 with x taken to be the node z.

7.   Apply the algorithm recursively to each non-terminal Q_j and make the resulting tree the jth subtree (from left) at the root.

ALGORITHM 2. Algorithm for determining T(D) from $G_h(D)$.

Example. The following example illustrates the computations performed by Algorithm 2 for the h-graph of the dissection shown in Fig 2. We write $v(Q_1, Q_2, ..., Q_m)$ to denote a v-node with child nodes which correspond to the subregions $Q_1, Q_2, ...,$ and Q_m. Similarly we write $h(\{Q_1, Q_2, ..., Q_m\})$ for h-nodes, and $s/S(Q_1, Q_2, Q_3, Q_4, Q_5)$ for s/S-nodes. Successive levels of the recursive applications of the algorithm are indicated by different levels of indentations.

Step 2. Weakly connected; m = 3.

$w_0 = <\{W\}, \{1, 2\}> \qquad\qquad w_1 = <\{1, 2\}, \{3, 4, 8, 9\}>$

$w_2 = <\{3, 5, 7, 9\}, \{10, 11\}> \qquad w_3 = <\{10, 11\}, \{E\}>$

Step 3. Compute the subregions Q_1, Q_2, and Q_3 as shown below, and create a v-node $v(Q_1, Q_2, Q_3)$.

$Q_1 = R(w_0) \cap L(w_1) = \{1, 2\} \qquad\qquad Q_3 = R(w_2) \cap L(w_3) = \{10, 11\}$

$Q_2 = R(w_1) \cap L(w_2) = \{3, 4, 5, 6, 7, 8, 9\}$

Step 7. Recursive application of the algorithm to $Q_1 = \{1, 2\}$.

Step 1. Not weakly connected; the h-weak components of $\{1, 2\}$ are new $Q_1 = \{1\}$ and $Q_2 = \{2\}$; m = 2. Create h-node $h(\{Q_1, Q_2\})$.

Step 7. Recursive application of the algorithm to the new Q_1 and Q_2 creates the terminal nodes 1 and 2 (by Step 2).

Step 7. Recursive application of the algorithm to $Q_2 = \{3, 4, 5, 6, 7, 8, 9\}$ will identify its h-weak components to be $\{3\}$, $\{4, 5, 6, 7, 8\}$ and $\{9\}$. We show below only the computations performed for Q = $\{4, 5, 6, 7, 8\}$.

Step 2. Weakly connected; m = 1.

$$w_0 = <\{W\}, \{4, 8\}> \qquad w_1 = <\{5, 7\}, \{E\}>.$$

Step 4. Create the s/S root node. Choose an h-source node, x = 4. We get

$$w = <\{4\}, \{5, 6\}>; Q = L(w) = \{4\}.$$

Step 5. Compute the subregions of the s/S-node. We have $w_1 = w = <\{4\}, \{5, 6\}>$ and let y = 8.

$$w' = <\{6, 8\}, \{7\}>, w_2 = w' \text{ and } m = 5.$$

$$Q_3 = R(w_1) \cap L(w_2) = \{6\}$$
$$Q_2 = L(w_1) = \{4\} \qquad Q_4 = R(w_2) = \{7\}$$
$$Q_1 = L(L_{21} - Q_3) = \{8\} \qquad Q_5 = R(L_{12} - Q_3) = \{5\}$$

Step 7. Recursive application of the algorithm to Q_1, Q_2, Q_3, Q_4, Q_5 creates the terminal nodes 4, 5, 6, 7 and 8 respectively (by Step 2).

Step 7. Recursive application of the algorithm to $Q_3 = \{10, 11\}$.

Step 2. Not weakly connected; the h-weak components of $\{10, 11\}$ are new $Q_1 = \{10\}$ and $Q_2 = \{11\}$; m = 2. Create h-node $h(\{Q_1, Q_2\})$.

Step 7. Recursive application of the algorithm to Q_1 and Q_2 creates the terminal nodes 10 and 11 (by Step 2).

References

[1]. Flemming, U., Wall representation of rectangular dissections and their use in automated space allocation, *Environment and Planning B*, 5(1978), pp. 215-232.

[2]. Flemming, U., Wall representations of rectangular dissections: additional results, *Environment and Planning B*, 7(1980), pp. 247-251.

[3]. Hassett, J. E., Automated layout in ASHLAP: an approach to the problem of "general" cell layout for VLSI, *Proceedings of 19th Design Automation Conference*, pp. 777-784, 1982.

[4]. Kundu, S., A new abstraction mechanism for space allocation problem in floor plan design, Tech. Rep. #86-021, Computer Sc. Dept., Louisiana State University.

[5]. Kundu S., Application of the subregion abstraction method in VLSI-layout and floor-plan design, Tech. Rep.#86-029, Computer Sc. Dept., Louisiana State University.

[6]. Kundu S. and Singh R., Spatial Reasoning in Rectangular Dissections - Part I, Tech. Rep.#87-019, Computer Sc. Dept., Louisiana State University.

[7]. Preas, B. T., Placement and routing for hierarchical integrated circuit layout, *Ph.D. Dissertation*, Dept. of Electrical Engineering, Stanford University, 1979.

[8]. Roth, J., Hashimshony, R., and Wachman, A., Turning a graph into a rectangular floor plan, *Building and Environment*, 17(1982), pp. 163-173.

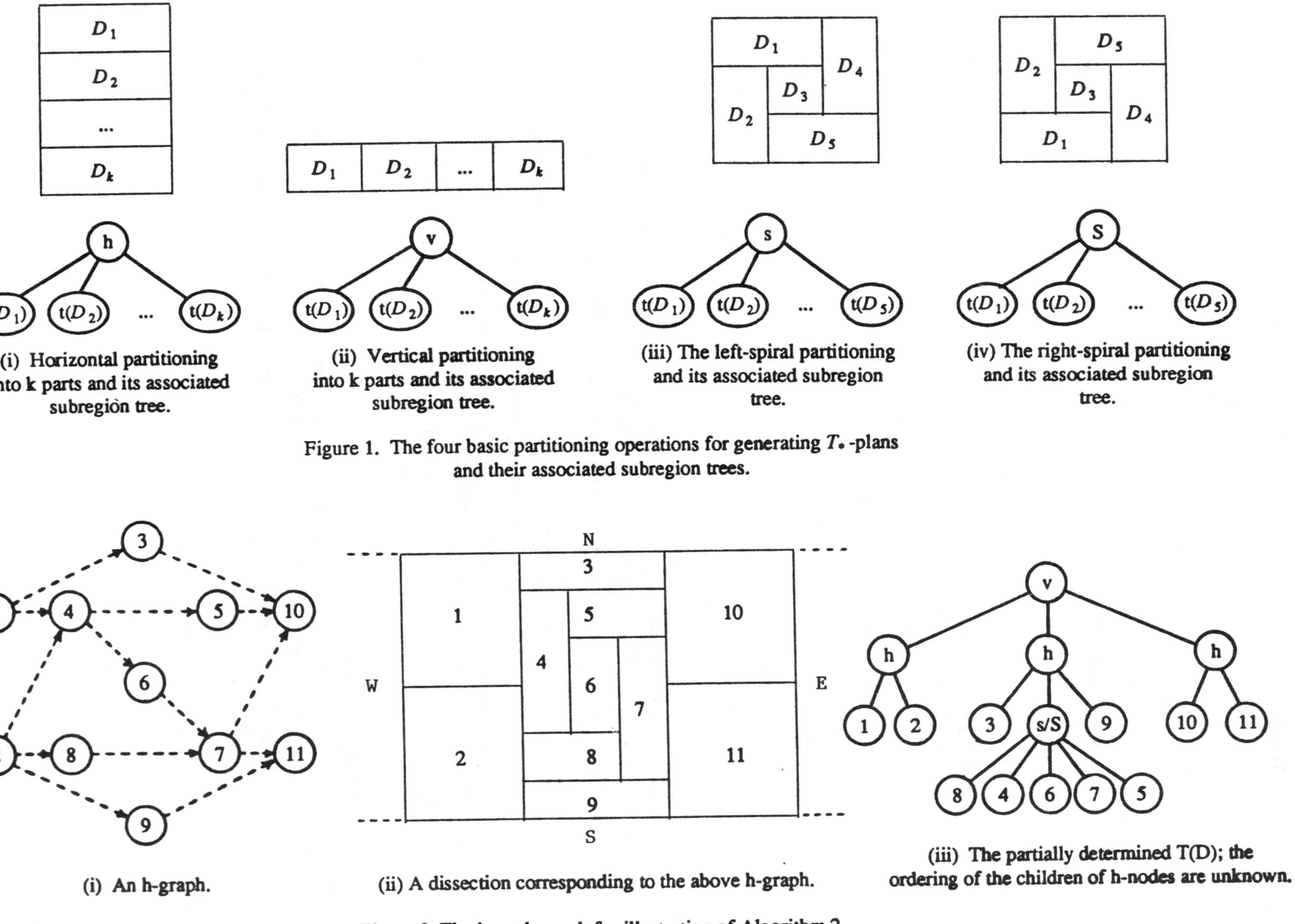

(i) Horizontal partitioning into k parts and its associated subregion tree.

(ii) Vertical partitioning into k parts and its associated subregion tree.

(iii) The left-spiral partitioning and its associated subregion tree.

(iv) The right-spiral partitioning and its associated subregion tree.

Figure 1. The four basic partitioning operations for generating T_*-plans and their associated subregion trees.

(i) An h-graph.

(ii) A dissection corresponding to the above h-graph.

(iii) The partially determined T(D); the ordering of the children of h-nodes are unknown.

Figure 2. The input h-graph for illustration of Algorithm 2.

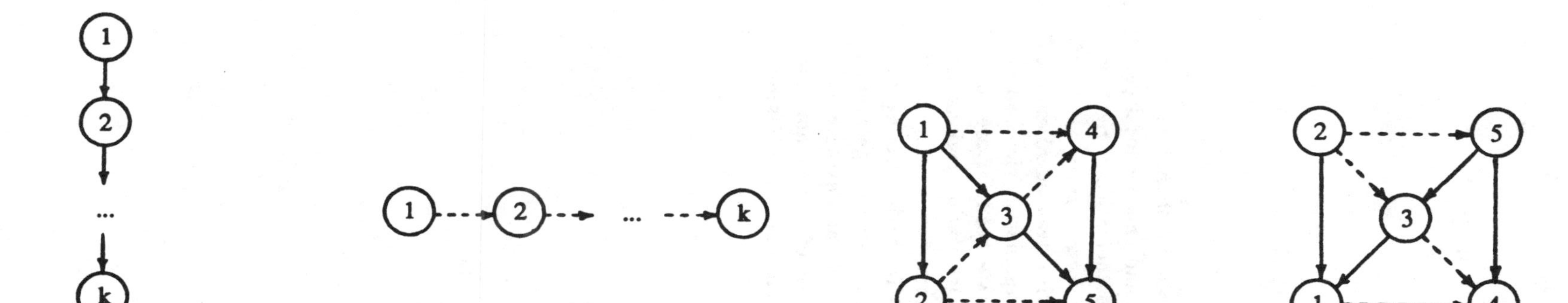

(i) The graph for the h-operation.   (ii) The graph for the v-operation.   (iii) The graph for the s-operation.   (iv) The graph for the S-operation.

Figure 3. The hv-graphs of the partitioning operations.

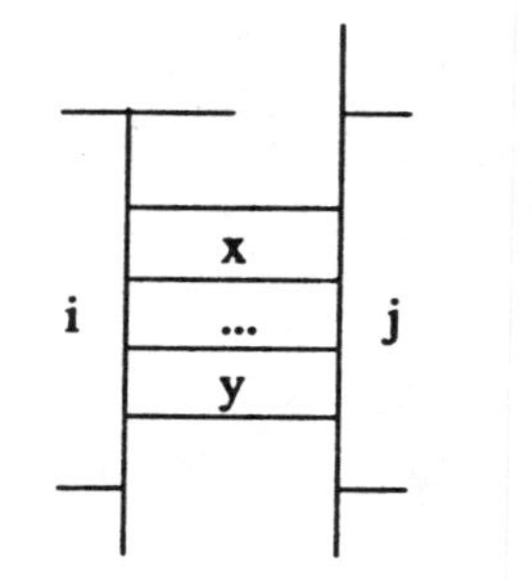

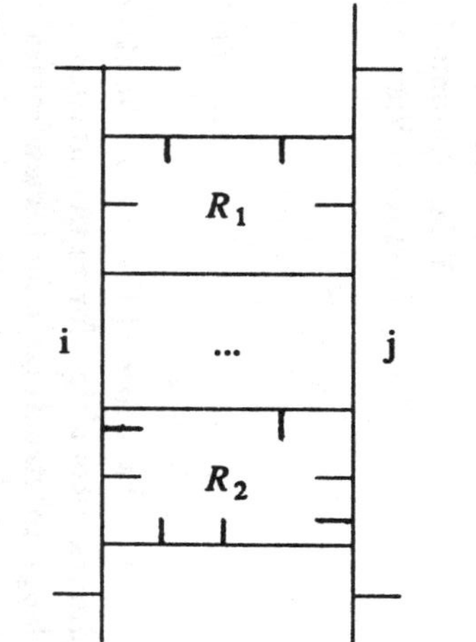

(i) Part of a T-plan where the basic regions x and y are h-equivalent. Here, i and j are two basic regions.

(ii) Part of a T-plan where the subregions R_1 and R_2 are h-equivalent. Here, i and j are two basic regions.

Figure 4.

VISUAL MEMORY STRUCTURE FOR A MOBILE ROBOT

Tod S. Levitt, Daryl T. Lawton, David M. Chelberg, Philip C. Nelson, John W. Dye

Advanced Decision Systems
201 San Antonio Circle, Suite 286
Mountain View, California 94040

ABSTRACT

This paper develops a formal theory for the structure of memory for a mobile robot that depends on visual landmark recognition for representation of environmental locations, and encodes local perceptual knowledge in structures called viewframes and orientation regions. Mathematically rigorous qualitative representations of places as visual events are developed in a uniform framework that smoothly integrates a qualitative version of the representation of space with traditional metric representations. Paths in the world are represented as sequences of sets of landmarks, viewframes, orientation boundary crossings, and other distinctive visual events. Approximate headings are computed between viewframes that have lines of sight to common landmarks. Orientation regions are range-free, topological descriptions of place that are rigorously abstracted from viewframes. They yield a coordinate-free model of visual landmark memory that can also be used for path planning and following. With this approach, a robot can use its visual memory to aid in predicting image events, to recognize regions it has passed through before, and to opportunistically observe and execute visually cued "shortcuts" when engaged in path planning and following. A simulation of this memory has been developed. The usefulness of the memory model is demonstrated within the simulation environment in path planning and following tasks based on visual memory.

VISUAL MEMORY STRUCTURE FOR A MOBILE ROBOT

INTRODUCTION

There are multiple purposes for a long term memory (LTM) for a mobile robot. These include representing places in the world the robot has passed through or has a priori knowledge of so that the LTM is useful for getting back to those places; facilitating visual re-acquisition of landmarks or other distinctive perceptual events so that the robot can perform recognition processes more efficiently and thus aid in determining its location relative to visual information stored in the LTM; responding to queries about spatial relational information between places and/or landmarks of interest; and formulating and updating map knowledge about the world.

These purposes levy requirements on an LTM that are much richer than those of a generic database. In essence, the LTM must be capable of responding to access functions that represent the queries: where am I, where are other places relative to me, and how do I get to other places from here?

We have developed a structure and processing for robotic visual memory and inference that fulfills these goals. It is based on a multi-level theory of spatial representation built around the observation and re-acquisition of distinctive visual events, i.e., landmarks. The representation provides the theoretical foundations for an LTM that includes coordinate free, topological representation of relative spatial location, yet smoothly integrates available metric knowledge of relative or absolute angles and distances. Rules and algorithms have been developed that, under the assumption of correct association of landmarks on re-acquisition (although not assuming landmarks are necessarily re-acquired) provably provide a robot with navigation and guidance capability. The ability to deduce or update a map of the environment, a posteriori, is a by-product of the inference process. In order to demonstrate our claims, we have built an LTM simulator (also called the qualitative navigation simulator) that provides a software laboratory for experimenting with the LTM and its relationship to path planning and execution.

Perhaps the key contribution of this work is the realization of true local coordinate systems, and a theory that makes them computationally useful to a mobile robot. Using local coordinate systems, which we call viewframes, a robot can navigate about its environment, determining its relative location in the world with essentially a constant error. In particular, there is no multiplicative accumulation of error in location that is the shortfall of all schemes that depend upon a global coordinate system for location.

In the following, we first present the requirements for the memory of a mobile robot, and then present an LTM architecture aimed at meeting these requirements. The LTM relationship to the perceptual parts of the vision system is then discussed. We present perceptual definitions of landmarks and requirements for vision system performance in re-acquisition of landmarks to support the proposed perception-based memory approach. Next we develop the mathematical theory of viewframes, boundaries and orientation regions. We then show how these qualitative, topological concepts interact with a priori metric map data. Inference for path planning over visual memory structures are presented in the following subsections. We finish LTM discussion with results from exercising the LTM and qualitative navigation simulator.

LTM REQUIREMENTS FOR A MOBILE ROBOT

Mobile robot operation under realistic cross-country field conditions gives rise to several requirements.

•LTM and access functions must be capable of representing and computing with large range and angular errors, and yet return answers that localize the robot sufficiently in the world to accomplish its tasks.

•The LTM must be organized so that sequences of visual events that correspond to observations on the (one-dimensional) path of the robot in the environment, can be recalled, predicted and robustly used for planning routes between places.

•The LTM must encode the spatial and visual relationships between landmarks and other observations so that they can be used to execute headings for navigation and guidance.

Many models of memory deal with relationships between sets of uniform elements (e.g. neuron models) [Fukushima-84], [Kanerva-84], and conceptual links between assemblies or patterns of elements [Goldschlager-84], [Kolodner-84]. This work tends to be motivated by neurobiological memory models [Gabriel et al.-86]. However, as Schacter [Schacter-86] points out, the import of biological research to date is on where memories occur, not on how they are structured, nor upon the principles that govern the complex mnemonic functions that characterize the use of memories.

On the other hand, research by cognitive psychologists [Kozlowski et al.-77], [Shepard-82], [Plyshyn-84] and zoologists [Schone-84] has clearly demonstrated that humans and animals record distinctive visual landmarks and use the structure inherent in local and temporal relationships between landmarks relative to observer paths of motion, in order to predict and identify places in the world, and to plan and execute paths between locations. Recent work that makes steps toward closing the gap between memory structure and neurobiology for spatial understanding and perception is presented in [Foreman et al.-87]. Even these preliminary advances strongly support the notions of landmark-based understanding of local environments. Furthermore, humans and animals perform navigation and guidance tasks quite reliably with extremely poor range estimates, and very coarse angular information.

In this work, we are primarily motivated by practical issues in mobile robotics, rather than biological or psychological modeling. However, most approaches to robotic visual memory have fallen short because of their reliance on global coordinate systems, requirement of absolute ranging to landmarks, and lack of accounting for available perceptual information [Brooks-87]. Furthermore, existing theories are largely concerned with the problem of measurement and do not centrally address issues of map or visual memory and the use of this memory for inference in vision-based navigation and guidance. Exceptions to this are the work of [Davis-86], [McDermott and Davis-84], and [Kuipers-78], [Kuipers-82], [Kuipers-85]. Davis addressed the problem of representation and assimilation of 2D geometric memory, but assumed an orthographic view of the world and did not consider navigation or guidance. McDermott and Davis developed an ad hoc mixture of vector and topological based route planning, but assumed a map, rather than vision derived world (in their assumptions of knowledge of boundaries and their shapes and spatial relationships), had no formal theory relating the multiple levels of representation, and consequently did not derive or implement results about path execution.

Kuipers has clearly defined the concept of "place" as a set of relative visual events, and has pioneered the development of computational models of spatial memory based on local sets of commonly visible landmarks and topological relationships between visual separated regions. His representations were proven efficacious by showing that they gave rise to workable techniques for navigation and guidance.

On the basis of this evidence, we postulate that a sighted mobile robot in outdoor environments should

- organize its visual memory about local coordinate systems of landmarks as the primary means of defining locations,

- account for the nature of visual events, and, in particular, use representations that allow for very poor range and angular measurements, while making full use of the extractable strong visual cues (e.g. occlusion) as primary data in visual memory representations,

- maintain memory structures that associate local landmark systems along paths of motion that the robot executed when it saw the landmarks,

- admit inference processes over visual memory that robustly perform navigation and guidance despite the poor quality of the quantitative data.

LTM ARCHITECTURE

The architecture for the LTM is pictured in Figure 1. LTM contains four databases: a priori terrain grids, a priori cultural feature networks such as roads and rivers, viewpaths, and landmarks. Landmarks are the distinctive visual events either observed at runtime or available from memory. These are chiefly pointers to schema in the perceptual structures database or schema network of the vision system the LTM is part of. Landmark data includes time of acquisition, viewframes it occurs in, pointers to map or grid data tying the landmark to absolute coordinate systems (if available), as well as perceptual data. Viewpaths are sequences of viewframes acquired while the robot was moving through its environment. They are the key structure of visual memory. Each viewframe points at the landmarks it records. Because the landmark and viewpath databases point at each other, all modules that use the LTM have access to both databases. Terrain grids and cultural feature networks constitute the a priori knowledge available to the LTM. They are used to make visual predictions on paths, and for a post-run processing for algorithms that use the LTM as input to creating and updating maps of the environment the robot has passed through.

Landmarks are the main interface to perceptual processes. Tracking of landmarks is tightly integrated with the viewframe making processes. Each landmark corresponds to structures in the perceptual structures database or to schema in STM. The interface to perceptual processes is maintained by the vision system.

Viewpath maintenance is the process that attempts to match the re-acquisition of landmarks to infer closeness of visual places in memory. Thus, when we re-acquire landmarks, our current viewpath is linked to existing ones in memory. This is the primary function that makes LTM useful for visual predictions and for path planning.

The spatial reasoning module computes relationships between objects in visual memory in response to tasks and queries from the vision system. Fundamental operations include planning headings between the current viewframe or orientation region and ones predicted in memory, path planning, and inference of global relationships between local coordinate systems.

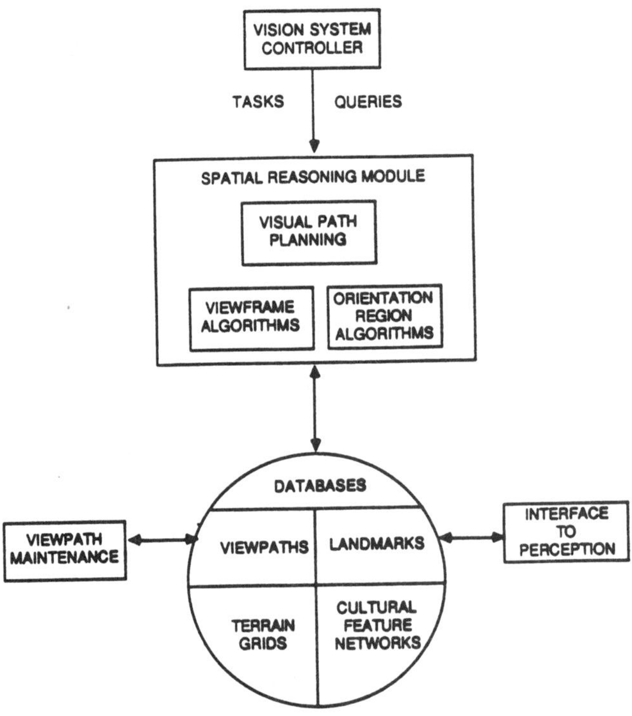

Figure 1: LTM - Architecture

LANDMARKS AND PERCEPTUAL EVENTS

The spatial representation we have developed was motivated to a large part by realistic assumptions concerning limitations on vehicle sensors and the capabilities of autonomous perceptual systems. A major constraint is the absolute uncertainty in the position of almost everything in the world, including vehicle position and the position of landmarks. This leads to basing the spatial representation on information that can be reliably extracted from single, but locally coupled views of the environment. We also have endeavored to represent landmarks at multiple levels of abstraction. These range from being a perceptual event, up to an explicit object in the world the levels reflect potential inadequate knowledge of world semantics. A key perceptual difficulty is recognizing the same landmark from very different points of view. In our representation, because it is based on locally established information, it doesn't matter if the same landmark is represented as different instances in different viewframes. When landmark matching across widely separated viewframes can be established, visually memory is significantly enriched, but the representation leads to a graceful degradation consistent with perceptual processing when this is not possible. The less powerful the perceptual system, the more fragmentary and localized spatial information becomes, but spatial memories can be formed nontheless.

Landmarks are distinctive and stable objects or perceptual events. One distinguishing dimension for landmarks is the extent to which they are perceptual events or instances of known types of objects. Perceptual processing can extract landmarks using distinctive image events that are unique in multiple fields of view and are stable during observer motion, but are not necessarily related to any type of modeled object. Landmarks that are an instance of an object model have default model-based information associated with them that can simplify and direct the accumulation of information as views of the landmark changes, especially due to model-based scale constraints. If a perceptually, but not model-based, landmark is not stable from different views, it will be represented multiple times as different landmarks. Another perceptual processing requirement for landmarks in the topological representation is to be able to extract and monitor specific qualitative singularities, such as co-linearity of landmarks, or an LPB crossing.

Monitoring the displacement of image features relative to a known axis of translation simplifies frame to frame matching, [Bolles and Baker - 85] [Lawton - 83], and provides basic information for determining how distant a landmark is, for how long a time it is visible, and when potential occlusions may occur. The classes of image transformations are constrained in these cases. Further, for the spatial representation we are building, it is not necessary to construct a precise depth map, but to track image events in terms of qualitative transformations such as occlusion/disocclusion, detail emergence/disappearance. For this, approximate, object-based matching along the translational flowpaths suffices. Depending on sensitivity of this computation, exact stabilization may not be required, and inertial estimates can drift over time.

TOPOLOGICAL LANDMARK REPRESENTATIONS

The notion of a geographic "place" is defined in terms of data about visible landmarks. A place, as a point on the surface of the ground, is defined by the landmarks and spatial relationships between landmarks that can be observed from a fixed point in space. More generally we can define a place as a region in space, in which a fixed set of landmarks can be observed from anywhere in the region, and relationships between them do not change in some appropriate qualitative sense. Data about places is stored in structures called viewframes.

Viewframes provide a definition of place in terms of relative angles and angular error between landmarks, and coarse estimates of the absolute range of the landmarks from our point of observation. Virtual axes between pairs of selected landmarks form a local coordinate system that can be used to localize the robot relative to all visible landmarks. These coordinate systems are truly local in that it is unnecessary to know anything about the absolute relationships between observed landmarks, or to relate the robot's current location to any past location the robot has passed through. Details are provided in [Levitt et al.-87].

If we drop the range information in viewframes, we are left with purely topological data. The basic concept is to note that if we draw a line between two (point) landmarks, and project that line onto the (possibly not flat) surface of the ground, then this line divides the earth into two distinct regions. If we can observe the landmarks, we can observe which side of this line we are on. The "virtual boundary" created by associating two observable landmarks together thus divides space over the region in which both landmarks are visible. We call these landmark-pair-boundaries (LPB's), and denote the LPB constructed from the landmarks L_1 and L_2 by $\text{LPB}(L_1, L_2)$.

LPB's give rise to a topological division of the ground surface into observable regions of localization, called orientation regions (ORs). Crossing boundaries between orientation regions leads to a qualitative sense of path planning based on perceptual information. However, there is topological information captured in the orientation region representation that distinguishs regions yet is invariant under large motions of the observing sensor. See [Levitt et al.-87] for details. Given a set of K landmarks, the set of all LPBs between them divides the ground into a set of disjoint orientation regions.

Under reasonable assumptions for cross-country scenarios, of the number of orientation regions implicit in a viewframe can be computed as:

number-of-orientation-regions

$$= (K^4)/8 - (3K^3)/4 + (23K^2)/8 - (13K)/4 + 1$$

The conjunction of LPB boundaries observed from our current location defines a symbolic description of visually distinguishable geographic regions. Any conjunction of LPB orientations that shares at least one LPB, but has the orientation reversed, must be in a different region of space. The localization sensitivity for ORs is pictured in Figure 2.

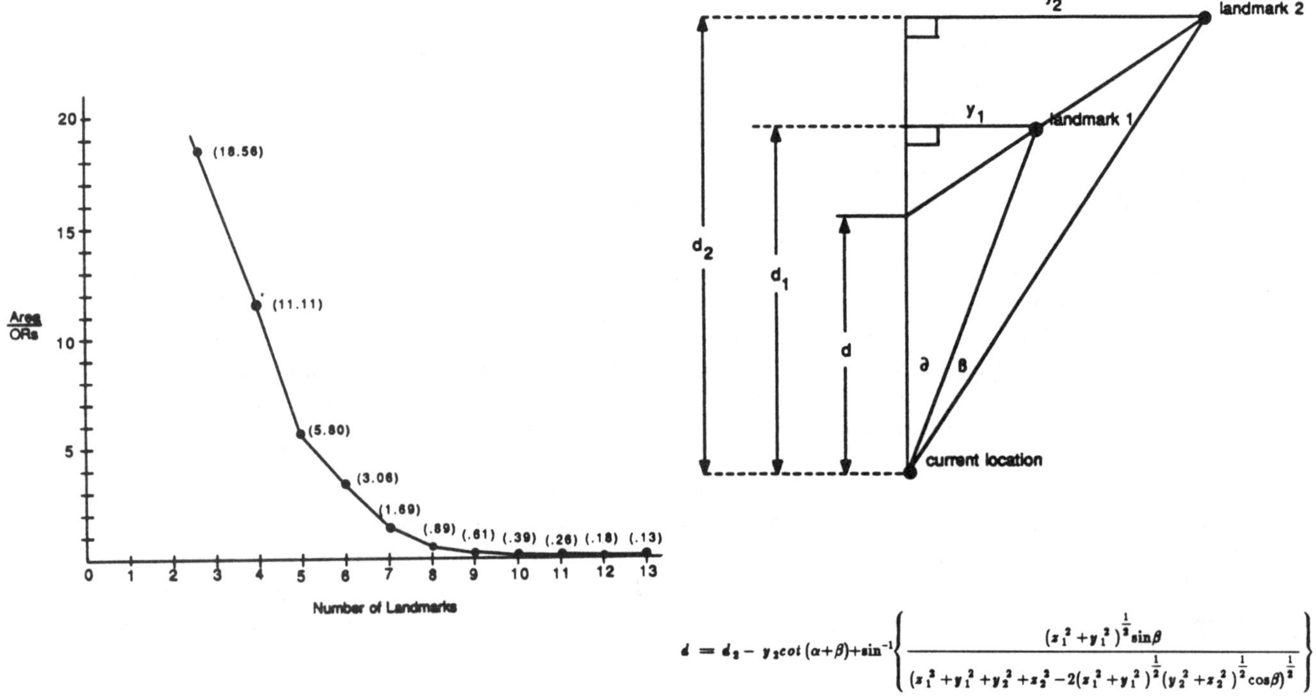

$$d = d_2 - y_2\cot(\alpha+\beta)+\sin^{-1}\left\{\frac{(x_1^2+y_1^2)^{\frac{1}{2}}\sin\beta}{(x_1^2+y_1^2+y_2^2+x_2^2-2(x_1^2+y_1^2)^{\frac{1}{2}}(y_2^2+x_2^2)^{\frac{1}{2}}\cos\beta)^{\frac{1}{2}}}\right\}$$

Figure 2:   Orientation Region
Localization Sensitivity

Figure 3:   Distance to LPB Crossing

HEADINGS INTEGRATING MEMORY WITH CURRENT OBSERVATIONS

Viewframe headings can be computed between two viewframes that share at least two landmarks (for 2D reasoning, three landmarks for 3D reasoning) in common. Thus we use our currently observed viewframe, and a memory of seeing a subset of the landmarks in the viewframe at some previous time and place, in order to compute an approximate heading back to the place we observed the landmarks from before. If the set of landmarks included in a viewframe destination are visible and we are close to our original point of observation, then it is straightforward (up to traversability of the intervening terrain) to perform a hill-climbing algorithm to bring the sensor to the point of observation where the viewframe was previously collected. This can be accomplished by dynamically computing a path based on control-feedback from the relative angles between the observed landmarks. However, if we are far enough away from our viewframe destination-goal, or if the goal is only to get to where a set of landmarks are all visible, then a control-feedback approach may fail (or at least be very tricky to develop) because we may have to cross LPB's to reach our destination-goal, and the relative angles between landmarks will vary non-monotonically, defeating hill-climbing.

An alternative approach is to formulate the viewframe localizations for each of the viewframes in the common local coordinate system defined by the two (or three) landmarks, and the sensor. We then have two regions expressed in the same coordinate system. Any affine linear transformation that maps one viewframe approximately onto the other may be taken as a heading. For example, we can translate the centroid of the first viewframe to the centroid of the second. This is the definition of viewframe heading transformation we use as a default. It defines a heading as a vector pointing between the viewframes, and supplies the vision system with an intuitive notion of "head thataway."

Orientation-headings are conjunctions of specifiers for crossing LPB's. An orientation-destination-goal is a conjunction of LPB crossing specifiers, with no more than one crossing specifier per LPB in the conjunction. The basic termination condition corresponding to an orientation-heading is that all crossings have occurred. Termination can also occur if it is impossible to proceed without re-crossing an already crossed LPB, or if none of the LPB's can be located. A typical desired behavior for choosing an orientation heading is to steer for the angular bisector between the pair of landmarks that are output from the production system. It can be shown that the path is a hyperbola, whose foci are the pair of landmarks.

The case when we are already on the goal side of an LPB requires more involved reasoning. We want to cross certain LPB's without crossing the ones we are already on the correct side of. Without (implicit or explicit) range information, we cannot tell which LPB we will cross first (on any heading). Using results from motion understanding we can estimate the time until we are perpendicular to a tracked landmark relative to our direction of (linear) motion. If we do such estimates for each land-mark in an LPB, we can recover the approximate distance to an LPB crossing as shown in Figure 3. Here, alpha and beta are observed angles, and d1, d2, y1, and y2 are estimated from motion processing ([Lawton-83]). The distance to the LPB, d, can be computed as shown in the figure. This allows us to reconstruct a map of the local environment and predict the appearance of viewframes from positions the robot has not yet visited.

THE STRUCTURE OF VISUAL MEMORY

A natural environmental representation based on viewframes recorded while following a path is given by two lists, one list of the ordered sequence of viewframes collected on the path, and another of the set of landmarks observed on the path. We call the viewframe list a viewpath. The landmark list acts as an index into the viewpath, each landmark pointing at the observations of itself in the viewframes. For efficiency, the landmark list can be formed as a database that can be accessed based on spatial and/or visual proximity. Visual proximity can be computed, for example, from an underlying elevation grid and a model of sensor and vision system resolution. See [Lawton et al.-87] for applications of this approach.

A dynamically acquirable environmental representation that merges the representations for viewpaths and orientation-paths consists of an ordered list interspersing viewframes, LPB crossings, and appearance and occlusion (or loss of resolution) of landmarks as well as recording the headings taken in the course of following the path over which the environmental map is being built. Thus we can integrate the representations required for viewframe and orientation region based reasoning with heading and landmark information to formulate an environmental representation that supports hybrid strategies for navigation and guidance. The representation is formed at runtime and consists of multiple interlocking lists of sequential, time ordered, lists of visual events that include those necessary for path planning and following algorithms. The top level loop for landmark-based path planning and following is to (1) determine a destination-goal, (2) compute and select a current heading, (3) execute the heading while building up an environmental representation. The destination-goals are typically determined recursively, implementing a recursive goal-decomposition approach to perceptual path planning. Details on use of the visual memory for qualitative path planning and inference are given in [Levitt et al.-87].

We have implemented a simulation environment for the LTM that supports dynamic simulated landmark acquisition scenarios, viewframe extraction, and execution. The LTM and qualitative navigation simulator supports a wide variety of capabilities at menu control. The simulator manipulates a priori grid and cultural feature data, allows the interactive specification of landmarks and vehicle locations, computes visibility of landmarks in 3D terrain data, calculates viewframe localizations relative to visible landmarks, as well as supporting a wide variety of color graphics and 2D/3D data conversions. The menu options divide into three major groups: viewframe creation, viewpath and visual memory creation, and plan generation and execution. Additional options are available in software, but not yet at menu level control. These include arbitrary settings of all simulation parameters, including robot step-size and range and angular uncertainty factors, orientation-region based path planning, the ability to add arbitrary feature displays on the terrain grid, and arbitrary manipulation of colors in displays.

<u>RESULTS</u>

To date, we have three types of results: sensitivity analysis for viewframe and orientation region localizations, including contrast against accumulated error for global coordinate system memory schemes; viewpath planning and execution; and orientation region planning and execution.

Figure 4(a-d) show the area of localization as the accuracy of range and angle estimates are varied. Figure 4(e) shows that the localization is very sensitive to the number of landmarks used, but not to the coarseness of the estimates. Figure 4(f) shows that the density of distribution of landmarks about the robot is critical to localization. In particular, a more uniform distribution guarantees approximate orthogonality of the pairwise localizations, ensuring a small region. Clustering the landmarks, for example, in front of the robot, allows a much larger localization, even with the same individual errors in range and angle. This argues for an omni-directional, or multiple sensor arrangement.

Qualitative path planning and execution is pictured in Figures 5(a-n).

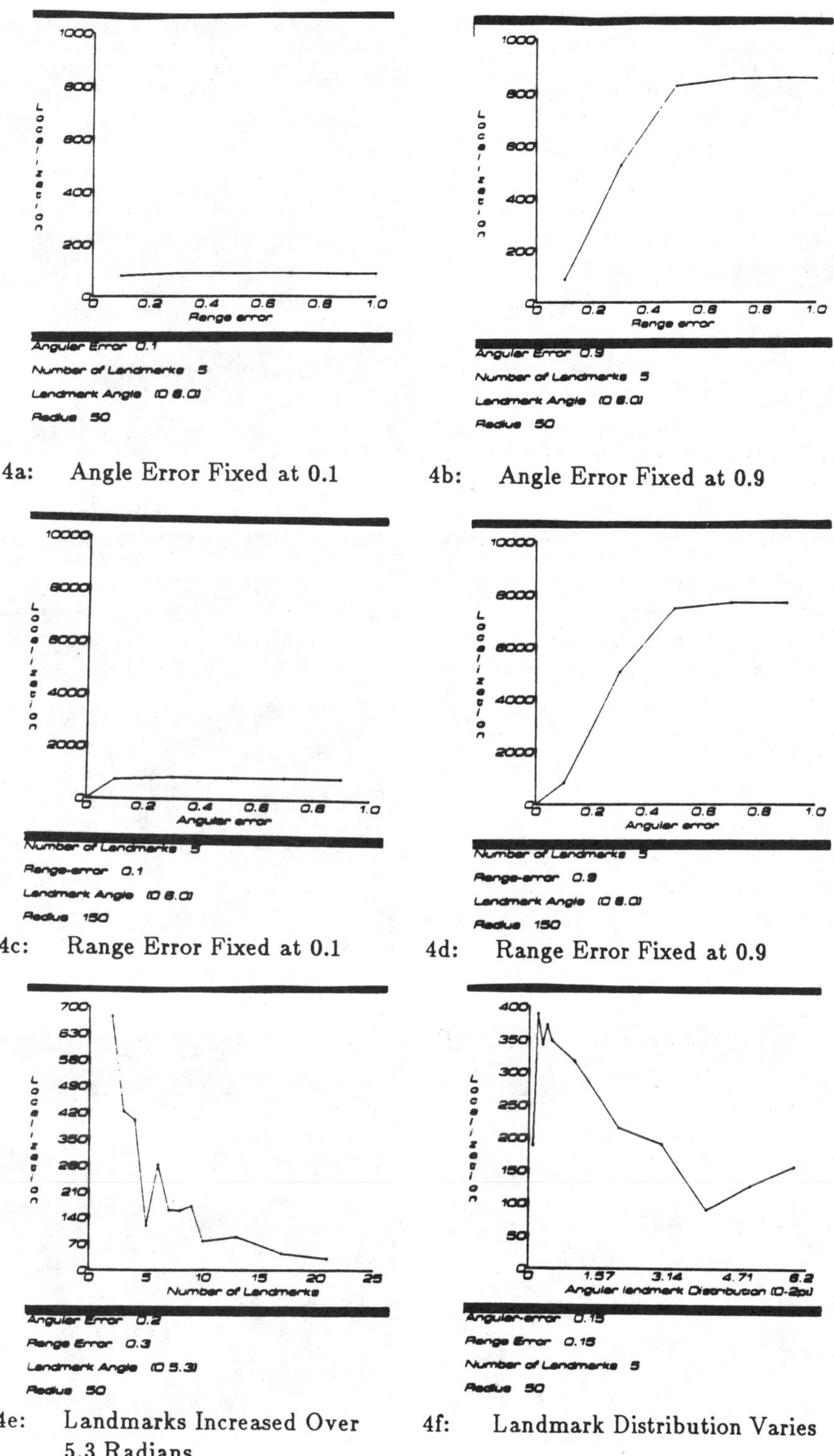

4a: Angle Error Fixed at 0.1

4b: Angle Error Fixed at 0.9

4c: Range Error Fixed at 0.1

4d: Range Error Fixed at 0.9

4e: Landmarks Increased Over
       5.3 Radians

4f: Landmark Distribution Varies

Figure 4: Viewframe Localization Sensitivity Graphs

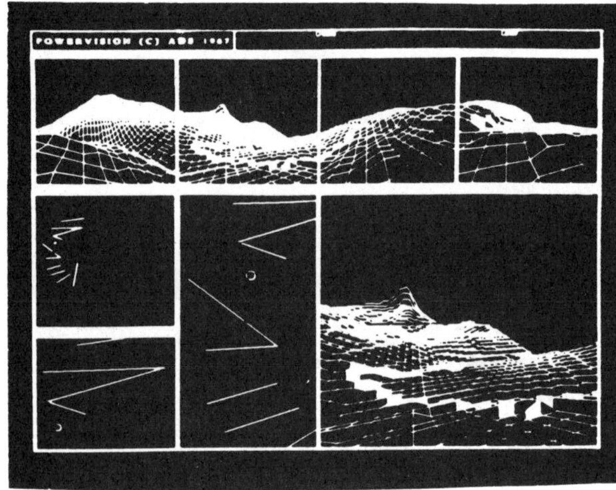

5a: Initial Qualitative Plan

5b: Viewframe at Initial Point

5c: First Re-Acquired Boundary
       LPB

5d: Initiation of Bisector
       Heading

5e: Heading at Landmark Due to
       Occlusion of LPB

5f: No LPB Sighted; Acquisition
       of Single Landmark Heading

Figure 5: Qualitative Path Planning and Execution

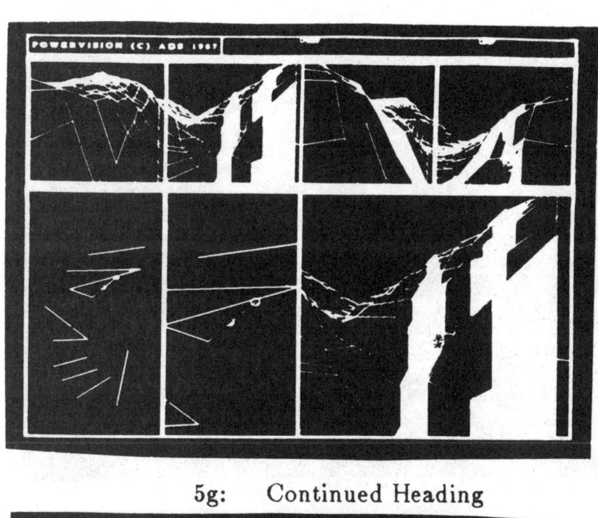

5g: Continued Heading

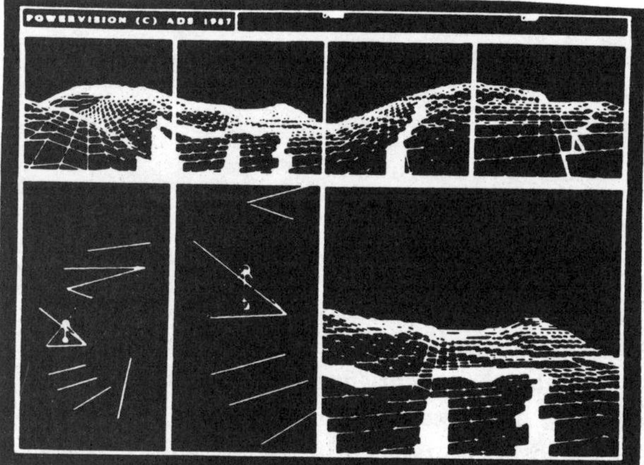

5i: Next LPB Acquisition

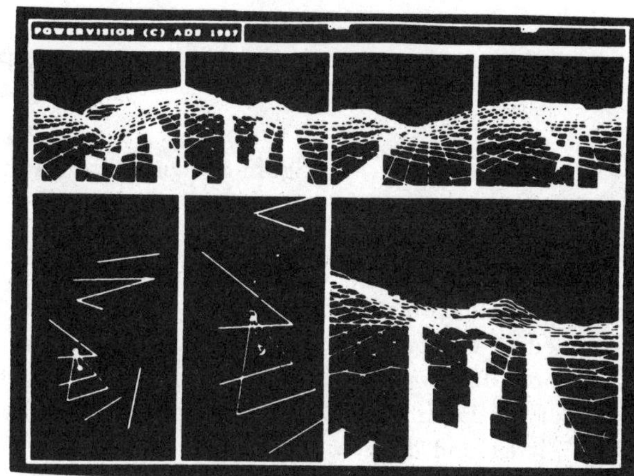

5j: Jumping Ahead Through
       a Visual Shortcut

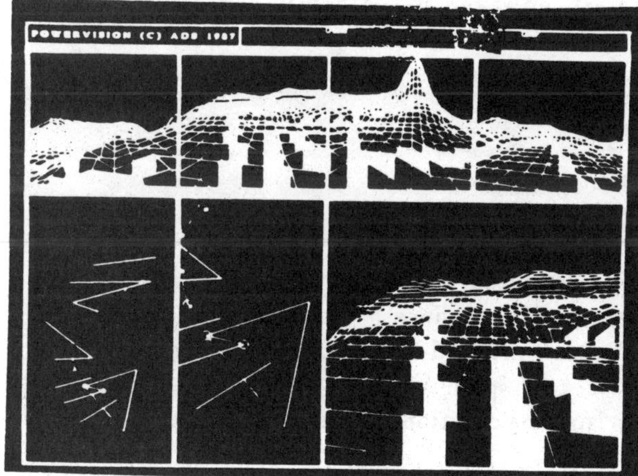

5k: Goal LPB First Sighted

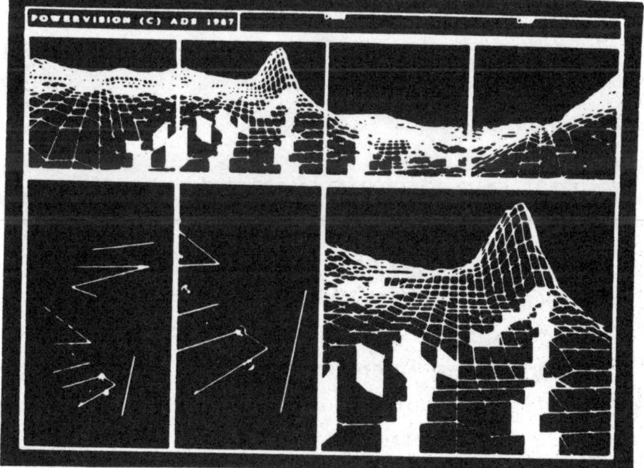

5l: Occlusion of Goal LPB and
       Reacquisition of Intermediate LPB

5h: Acquisition of Predicted LPB

Figure 5: Qualitative Path Planning and Execution

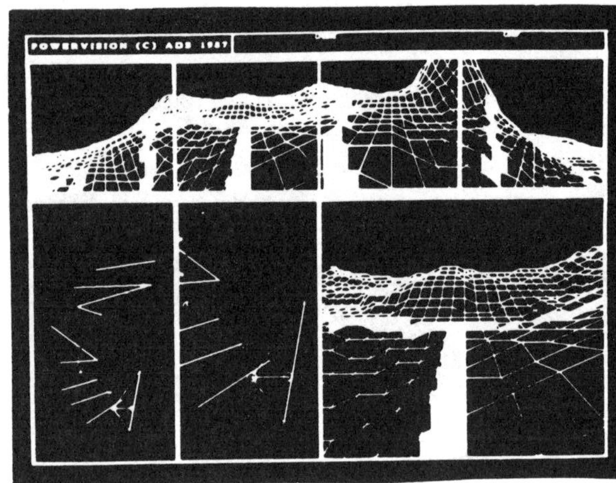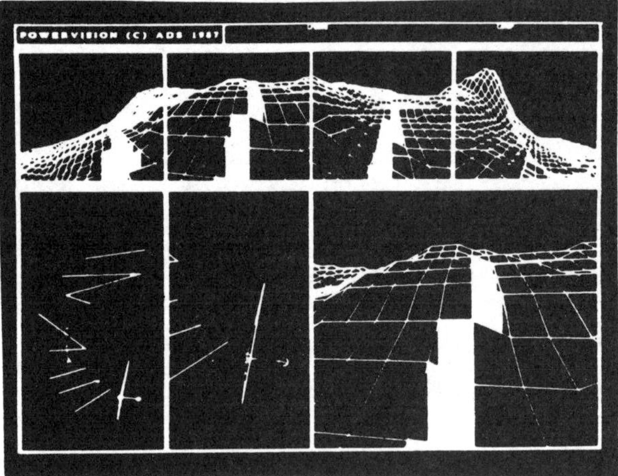

5m: Reacquisition of Goal LPB   5n: Goal Attainment

Figure 5: Qualitative Path Planning and Execution

In this simulation, the angle bisector heading, discussed in the section on orientation regions, was used as the heading determining the robot's path. For this purpose, lines of sight to landmarks were assumed to be completely accurate. Given landmark tracking, this is a reasonable assumption. Note that some dead-reckoning occurred, Figure 5(e), when the robot lost sight (due to occlusion) of one or both of the landmarks it was using to compute its heading. In the case when it lost just one, Figure 5(e-f), it headed directly toward the other; when both were lost, Figure 5(g), it dead-reckoned straight ahead (compass-heading) until one or more known landmarks became visible again. This is an instance of the heuristic to avoid re-crossing LPBs known to be on a path to the goal. Of course, backtracking strategies are possible. Of particular interest, however, is the non-monotonic reasoning displayed by the algorithm when it lost sight of the goal LPB, Figure 5(l), and automatically re-acquired a previous LPB based on matching from its currently visible set of landmarks against visual memory.

ISSUES AND FUTURE WORK IN SPATIAL REASONING

We have developed a rigorous theory for a LTM for a sighted, mobile robot. It is based upon a representation of spatial relationships between visual events that defines a computable realization of local coordinate systems, and smoothly integrates topological, interval-based, and metric information. The rule-based inference processes support opportunistic path planning and execution using visual memory and whatever data is currently available from visual recognition, range estimates and a priori map or other metric data.

Key on-going development tasks include:

- integration of the LTM band navigation and guidance capability with the vision system, and

- addition of a non-monotonic reasoning system that accounts for imperfect re-acquisition of landmarks.

Other tasks include representing and reasoning with extended landmarks, such as roads, rivers and ridges, and inference of shape and additional topological relationships such as region containment.

Acknowledgements

This document was prepared by Advanced Decision Systems (ADS) of Mountain View, California, under U.S. Government contract number DACA76-85-C-0005 for the U.S. Army Engineer Topographic Laboratories (ETL), Fort Belvoir, Virginia, and the Defense Advanced Research Projects Agency (DARPA), Arlington, Virginia. The authors wish to thank Nancy English for providing administration, coordination, and document preparation support.

References

[Bolles and Baker - 85] R. Bolles and H. Baker, "Epipolar-Plane Image Analysis: A Technique for Analyzing Motion Sequences," Proceedings for the Third Workshop on Computer Vision: Representation and Control, October 13-16, 1985, pp. 168-178.

[Brooks - 87] R. A. Brooks, "Visual Map Making for a Mobile Robot," in *Readings in Computer Vision*, M.A. Fischler and O. Firschein, eds., (Los Altos, California: Morgan Kaufmann, 1987). pp. 438-443.

[Davis - 86] E. Davis, "Representing and Acquiring Geographic Knowledge," Courant Institute of Mathematical Sciences, New York University, Morgan Kaufmann Publishers, Inc., 1986.

[Foreman et al. - 87] N. Foreman and R. Stevens, "Relationships Between the Superior Colliculus and Hippocampus: Neural and Behavioral Considerations," *Behavioral and Brain Sciences*, vol. 10, no. 1, March 1987, pp. 101-151.

[Fukushima - 84] K. Fukushima, "A Hierarchical Neural Network Model for Associative Memory," *Biological Cybernetics*, vol. 50, 1984, pp. 105-113.

[Gabriel, et al. - 86] M. Gabriel, S. P. Sparenborg and N. Stollar, "The Neurobiology of Memory," in *Mind and Brain: Dialogues in Cognitive Neuroscience*, J. E. LeDoux and W. Hirst, eds. (New York: Cambridge University Press, 1986), pp. 215-254.

[Goldschlager - 84] L. M. Goldschlager, "A Computational Theory of Higher Brain Function," Computer Science Department, Stanford University, California, April 1984.

[Kanerva - 84] P. Kanerva, "Self-Propagating Search: A Unified Theory of Memory," report No. CSLI-84-7, Center for the Study of Language and Information, Stanford University, Stanford, California, March 1984.

[Kolodner - 84] J. L. Kolodner, "Knowledge-Based Self-Organizing Memory for Events" in *Aritificial and Human Intelligence*, A. Elithorn and R. Banerji, eds. (New York: North-Holland, 1984), pp. 57-66.

[Kozlowski et al. - 77] L. T. Kozlowski and K. J. Bryant, "Sense of Direction, Spatial Orientation, and Cognitive Maps," *Journal of Experimental Psychology: Human Perception and Performance*, vol. 3, 1977, pp. 590-598.

[Kuipers - 82] B. J. Kuipers, "The 'Map in the Head' Metaphor," *Environment and Behavior*, vol. 14, no. 2, March 1982, pp. 202-220.

[Kuipers - 85] B. J. Kuipers, "The Map-Learning Critter," AITR85-17, Artificial Intelligence Laboratory, The University of Texas at Austin, Austin, Texas, December 1985.

[Kuipers - 78] B. J. Kuipers, "Modeling Spatial Knowledge," *Cognitive Science*, vol. 2, 1978, pp. 129-153.

[Lawton - 83] D. Lawton, "Processing Translational Motion Sequences", *Computer Vision, Graphics, and Image Processing*, vol. 22, 1983, pp. 116-144.

[Lawton et al. - 87] D. T. Lawton, T. S. Levitt, C. McConnell and J. Glicksman, "Terrain Models for an Autonomous Land Vehicle," *Proceedings DARPA Image Understanding Workshop*, (Los Altos: Morgan Kaufmann, February 1987).

[Levitt et al. - 87] T. S. Levitt, D. T. Lawton, D. M. Chelberg and P. C. Nelson, "Qualitative Navigation," *Proceedings DARPA Image Understanding Workshop*, (Los Altos: Morgan Kaufmann, February 1987).

[McDermott and Davis - 84] D. McDermott and E. Davis, "Planning Routes through Uncertain Territory," *Artificial Intelligence - An International Journal*, vol. 22, no. 2, March 1984, pp. 107-156.

[Pylyshyn - 84] Z. W. Pylyshyn, *Computation and Cognition: Toward a Foundation for Cognitive Science*, (Cambridge, Masschusetts: MIT Press, 1984).

[Schacter - 86] D. L. Schacter, "A Psychological View of the Neurobiology of Memory," in *Mind and Brain: Dialogues in Cognitive Neuroscience*, J. E. LeDoux and W. Hirst, eds. (New York: Cambridge University Press, 1986), pp. 265-272.

[Schone - 84] H. Schone, "Spatial Orientation - The Spatial Control of Behavior in Animals and Man," in *Princeton Series in Neurobiology and Behavior*, R. Capranica, P. Marler and N. Adler, eds., 1984.

[Shepard - 82] R. N. Shepard, and L. A. Cooper, L.A., *Mental Images and their Transformations*, MIT PRess, 1982.

MASK: AN OBJECT IDENTIFICATION ALGORITHM

Bijan Arbab
IBM Scientific Center, Los Angeles, CA 90025

ABSTRACT

An algorithm for identifying an object from a set of known objects is presented and justified. The novelty of this algorithm, called Mask, for object identification is in its use of three-dimensional data which has been obtained from projection of parallel laser light planes. The knowledge that laser light planes are parallel to each other allows automatic discovery of various constraints from the three-dimensional data. One constraint is based on colinearity between various points and another constraint on coplanarity between various segments of the three-dimensional data. These automatically derived constraints, then, are used by Mask in a tree search algorithm for object identification. Mask has been implemented in Prolog and sample applications to various objects are presented.

INTRODUCTION

Suppose a specimen object is selected from a set of **known** objects. It is assumed that all objects are polyhedral (possibly nonconvex). The specimen object may have up to six degrees of freedom relative to the sensors. How can a robot **recognize** the specimen object? Recognition in this context means (1) identifying the object as one, or none, in the set of known objects and (2) finding the exact location and orientation of the specimen object. The robot knows about an object if it has access to a polyhedral model of the object. A polyhedral model of an object consists of (1) a name for the object, (2) a list of edges, each described by starting and ending points, and (3) a list of faces, each described by the forming edges. This paper is a contribution, not to three-dimensional sensing, but to the process of using such data in object recognition. It differs from other approaches in that it discovers constraints from the three-dimensional data which are then applied in the tree searching process.

In order to recognize the specimen object, the robot will first generate a series of parallel laser light planes. One method to accomplished this is by using optical devices Mersch and Stubbs (1986). The distance between parallel planes can be specified as well. Once the parallel light planes are generated, the space curves which are formed as a result of the intersection of each light plane with the object can be extracted, see Echigo and Masahiko (1985), and Tsai (1985). Since we are working with polyhedral objects, each space curve is actually composed of a series of line segments. Thus, each space curve is reduced to a list of pairs of 3-D points which describe the starting and ending point of each line segment. Hereafter, this reduced list is referred to as the list-of-line-segments.

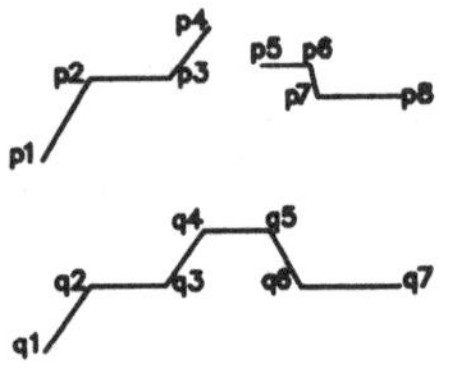

Figure 1.   Two different list-of-line-segments.

For example, in Figure 1 points p1 to p8 describe the first list-of-line-segments and all lie in one plane; similarly q1 to q7. After all, they were obtained from intersecting a light plane with the object. The line segments in a list-of-line-segments are not always connected. Discontinuities are due to occlusions. Thus, not every point in the list-of-line-segments corresponds to an edge of the object. Mask, however, requires that every point correspond to an object edge. To solve this problem which is caused by occlusions, the list-of-line-segments is further reduced to only those points that lie on an edge of the object. Hereafter, this reduced list is referred to as a light probe. Note that a light probe refers to a connected set of edge-points; not just projection of a light plane on an object. This reduction is possible and applied on the ground that a data-point in the list-of-line-segments lies on an edge of the object if and only if it is connected on both sides to other points. For example, in Figure 1 point p2 is an edge-point, however, points p4 and p5 might not correspond to edges of the object.

Mask takes as input, a collection of light probes and an **enhanced polyhedral model** of some object. The output consists of a set of object edge to edge-point assignments if the collection of light probes match the object model, otherwise, a failure is reported. This output can then be used to determine the object's exact location and orientation, see Silverman, Tsai and Lavin (1987). The set of object edge to edge-point assignments is also referred to as an interpretation Grimson and Lozano-Perez (1984).

The polyhedral model of an object is enhanced by precomputing (1) a table containing Min-Max distances between every pair of edges of the object, (2) a possible-next-edge-list for each edge of the object and (3) a table containing the angle between pairs of object faces. The Min-Max distance table is an idea taken from Grimson and Lozano-Perez (1984). A possible-next-edge-list for an edge Ei is simply a list of all the edges on the adjacent faces. Note that consecutive edge-points of a light probe would have to lie on edges of adjacent faces due to planar intersection of light with the object. The angle between faces of the object serve as yet another constraint that is used during the tree searching phase of Mask. These tables are precomputed and stored with the polyhedral model of every object.

Mask is composed of three phases which are described in the following three sections. In phase I, light probes are collected in various groups and certain conditions that hold between groups are discovered. Phase II assigns to each group of light probes a list of valid interpretations. These assignments are based on the Min-Max distance table and the possible-next-edge-list. Phase III propagates the conditions that were discovered by Phase I among the valid interpretations of each group as computed by phase II. As a result, a set of consistent interpretations is assigned to each group. Application of the algorithm to sample problems is then discussed.

PHASE I

The collection of light probes is first partitioned into various groups. Light probes correspond to the same group if and only if they come from adjacent parallel light planes that have intersected all the same edges of the specimen object. Thus, light probes are placed in the same group if and only if they satisfy two conditions. First, all the light probes in the same group must be of the same length. Light probes have the same length if they contain the same number of edge-points. Second, the corresponding points of all the light probes, in the same group, must be on the same edge of the object. This can be determined via a colinearity test.

The grouping of light probes, then, is done by selecting the first and second consecutive light probes of the same length and simply assuming that they correspond to the same edges of the object. The rest of the light probes, of the same length, which immediately follow the first two light probes can then be tested for colinearity on all the corresponding points. This technique for grouping light probes is correct on the grounds that the distance between parallel light planes is controllable and can be decreased, thus increasing the number of light planes, such that the smallest discontinuity in any of the known objects would not be skipped over. For an example of light probe grouping, see Figure 5 where light probes have been collected together in six groups labeled g1 to g6.

The presence of errors, introduced by various sensing devices, in the light probe data can cause the test for colinearity between three points to fail, when in fact the three points are colinear. Thus, the light probe grouping is not always unique. For example, in Figure 5 it is possible, due to errors, to collect light probes in group g3 into two or more smaller groups. Mask, however, is insensitive to the various groupings of the light probe. It suffices to find any one of the possible light probe groupings.

After the initial light probe grouping, two conditions that may hold between members of any two groups are discovered. These conditions will be used in the third phase of Mask as constraints in a tree search algorithm, as in Waltz (1973) and Huffman (1971).

The first condition holds between two groups gi and gj if for some N and M the Nth edge points of all light probes in gi are colinear with the Mth edge points of all light probes in gj. For example, in Figure 5 the second point of any light probe in group g2 is colinear with the second point of any light probe in group g1. In fact, they all lie on edge e2. The third point of any light probe in group g5 is colinear with the fourth point of any light probe in group g3. In fact, they all lie on edge e10. Note that here, colinearity between points of light probes in various groups does not always imply that the points must correspond to the same edge of the object. It could be that they correspond to two different object edges that happen to be colinear.

The second condition holds between two groups gi and gj if for some N and M the Nth line segment of all the light probes in gi is coplanar with the Mth line segment of all the light probes in gj. For example, in Figure 5 the first line segment of any light probe in group g1 is coplanar with the first line segment of any light probe in groups g2, g3 and g4. In fact, they all lie on the face which is composed of edges e1, e2, e3, e4 and e5. The second line segment of any light probe in group g5 is coplanar with the third line segment of any light probe in group g3 and g4, also with the second line segment of any group in g2 and g1. They all lie on the face which is composed of edges e2, e14, e10 and e15.

The presence of errors in the light probe data can cause the tests for colinearity and coplanarity that are employed to detect the above two conditions to fail. This failure implies that not all of the conditions between points and probe segments are detected in this phase. A complete list of the two conditions, however, is not a requirement. A partial list of the conditions will suffice. Errors in the light probe data do not play an important role in the next two phases, as the computations involved are symbolic.

PHASE II

The second phase of the algorithm starts out by picking from each group only two light probes, the first and last one. These are selected on heuristic bases only. This heuristic is based on the ground that Min-Max distances between edges of the object are more likely to occur around starting and ending points of edges. For each light probe a collection of valid interpretations is formed.

An interpretation for a light probe is a list of object-edge to data-point assignment. For example, (e1, e2, e15) is one possible interpretation for the light probe composed of the three points: (p1, p2, p3) and it assigns edge e1 to point p1, e2 to p2 and e15 to p3. An interpretation for a light probe is valid if and only if it satisfies two constraints.

The first constraint simply states that the actual distance between points Pj and Pk which has been obtained from the specimen object must be within the Min-Max distance that actually holds between edges Ej and Ek of the object. The second constraint applies on the grounds that (a) the light probe data does not contain any discontinuities and (b) it is impossible, in such a case, for a laser light plane to strike any face of the specimen object more than once. Thus, edges E1 to Ei can be assigned to points P1 to Pi of a light probe if and only if (1) the distance between Pj and Pk for $1 = < j < k = < i$ is bounded by the Min-Max distance between Ej and Ek and (2) an edge En can not be assigned to a point Pn if it belongs to a face that has already been assigned to a point Pm for $1 = < m < n = < i$. In short, consecutive edge-points of a light probe can be assigned only to adjacent faces.

With these two constraints in hand a tree search algorithm for a light probe is constructed. Every node in the tree corresponds to a point in the light probe. There is an arc emanating from each node for every object edge that can possibly be assigned to the node. The depth of this tree is equal to the length of the light probe. In Figure 2, a sample search tree for the first light probe of group g1 of model house object is shown. For example, the assignment of edge e1 to point p1 is not consistent with the assignment of edge e14 to point p2 on basis of the first constraint, i.e., the distance between points p1 and p2 is not within the Min and Max distances between edges e1 and e14. The assignment of edge e15 to point p1 is not consistent with the assignment of edge e15 to point p2 on the basis of the second constraint. A standard depth-first left-to-right backtrack tree search algorithm is then employed to propagate the constraints among the nodes of the tree. Only those interpretations that completely satisfy both constraints remain. These are the set of valid interpretations for a light probe.

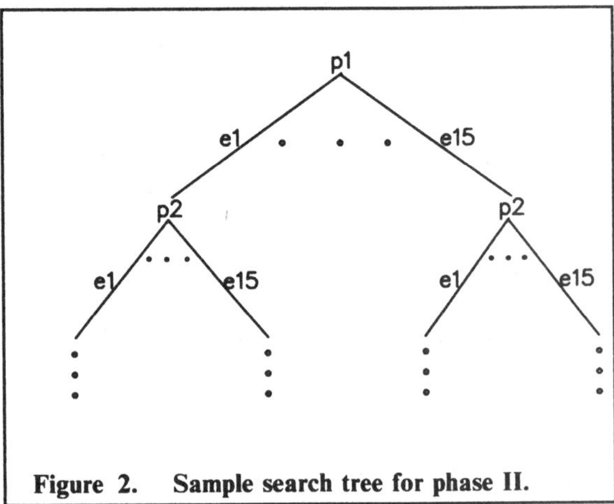

Figure 2.   Sample search tree for phase II.

Recall that the first and last light probes were selected from each group. The set of valid interpretations for each group, then, is formed by first taking the intersection of all valid interpretations for the first light probe with all valid interpretations for the last light probe. This is on the ground that both light probes correspond to the same group and thus must correspond to the same object edges. These interpretations of a group, that are common to all light probes within a group, are then subjected to three additional constraints. These constraints are explained below.

Figure 3 shows two light probes p1,p2,p3 and p4,p5,p6 where A is the angle between lines p1,p4 and p2,p5 and B is the angle between lines p2,p5 and p3,p6. The first constraint is applicable on the basis that the angle between edges assigned to p1,p4 and p2,p5 must be the same as A, up to errors. Similarly the angle between edges that are assigned to p2,p5 and p3,p6 must be the same as B, up to errors.

The second constraint is applicable on the basis that the distance between two probes from a group must be smaller than the length of the assigned edges. For example, the distance between points p1 and p4 must be smaller than the length of the edge that is being assigned to them. Note that according to the definition of edge-points, light probes within a group correspond to the same edges of the object.

The third constraint is applicable on the basis that the angle between the two planes formed by the points p1,p2,p4 and p3,p2,p6 must be equal to the angle between the two faces of the object which are being assigned to these points, up to errors. All of the above constraints help to reduce the number of valid interpretations of a group.

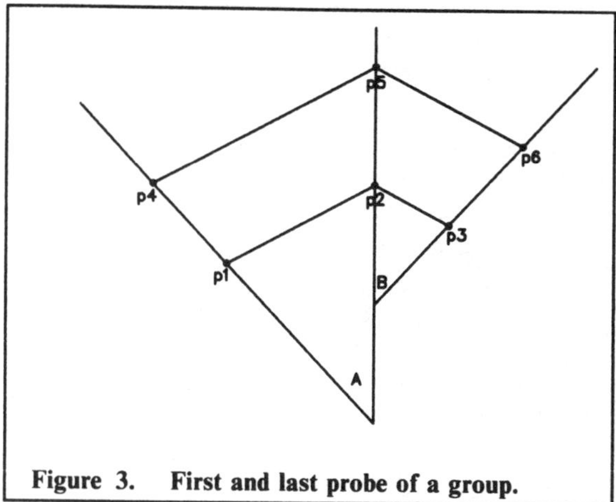

Figure 3.   First and last probe of a group.

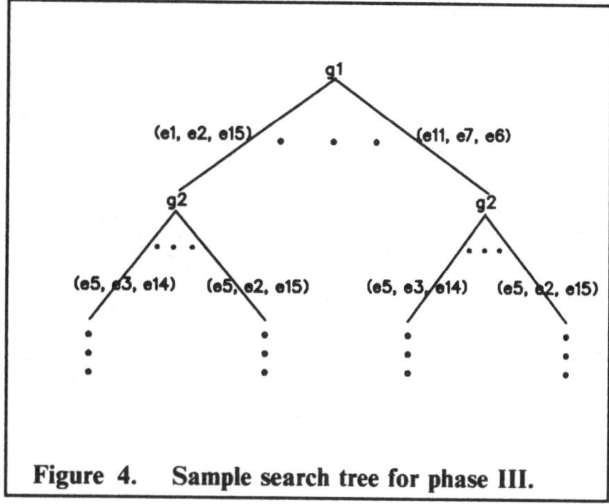

Figure 4.   Sample search tree for phase III.

PHASE III

A collection of valid interpretations for each group of light probes was constructed in the second phase. The size of this collection typically ranges from tens to hundreds for the objects experimented with so far. Recall that, in the first phase of the algorithm two conditions that could hold between various groups were extracted. They were: (1) colinearity between various light probe data points in different groups and (2) coplanarity between various light probe segments in different groups. In this phase, those conditions are employed as constraints and together with the Min-Max distance constraint, they form the backbone of another round of tree searches.

This time, a node of the tree corresponds to a group of light probes. There is an arc emanating from a node for every possible valid interpretation that can be assigned to the node. The depth of the tree is equal to the number of groups. In Figure 4, a sample search tree for the model house object is shown. For example, interpretation (e5, e3, e14) for group g2 is not consistent with interpretation (e1, e2, e15) for group g1 on the grounds of the first condition, i.e., edge e3 and e2 are not colinear. Interpretation (e5, e2, e15) for group g2 is not consistent with interpretation (e11, e7, e6) for group g1 on the grounds of the second condition, i.e., no line segment connecting e11 to e7 can be coplanar with a line segment connecting e5 to e2.

The Min-Max distance constraint is applicable to interpretations Ii and Ij for groups Gi and Gj. This is on the grounds that, for every light probe Pri in Gi and Prj in Gj the distance between every point of Pri and Prj must be within Min-Max distances of the corresponding edges in Ii and Ij. A standard depth-first left-to-right backtrack tree search algorithm is then employed to propagate the three constraints (the first and second condition plus the Min-Max distance constraint) among the nodes of the tree. Only those interpretations for each group that completely satisfy the three constraints are left behind. These are the set of consistent interpretations for each group. A group can have an empty set of consistent interpretations if light probe data from the specimen object does not correspond to the given object model.

APPLICATION

Application of Mask to a simple model house, shown in Figure 5, is described below. The edges of the object are labeled as e1 to e15. Intersection of some parallel light probes with the model house are shown. It is important to note that Figure 5 is showing the light probes and not the actual light planes that intersected the object. The distinction being that a light probe is obtained from the resulting intersection of the light planes according to the procedure specified in the introduction.

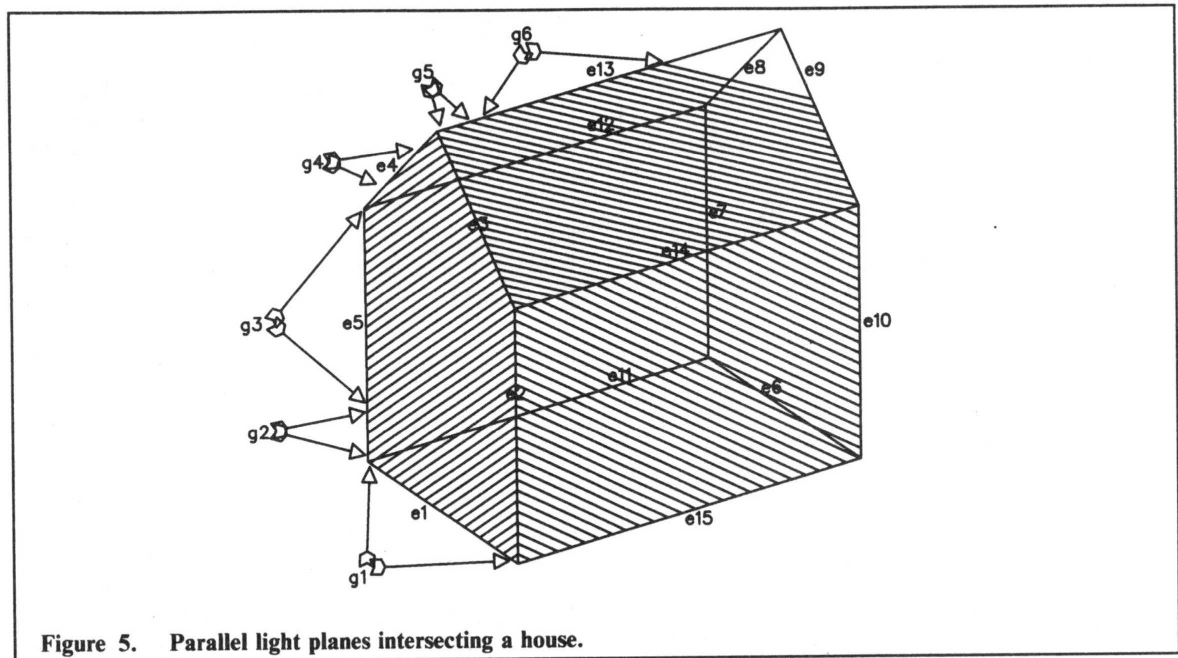

Figure 5.   Parallel light planes intersecting a house.

The data was obtained through simulation and some errors were artificially injected in the data. Each light probe has been classified by phase I of Mask as a member of some group. There are a total of six groups, labeled g1 to g6. There are 11 colinearity and 20 coplanarity relations that hold between light probe points and segments of various groups. Phase II of Mask finds 48, 84, 32, 120, 128 and 60 valid interpretations for groups g1 to g6. However, there are only 4 consistent interpretations that can be assigned to groups g1 through g6 and are discovered by phase III of Mask in approximately eight seconds on an IBM 3081.

Assignment of an interpretation to a group means that points of a light probe within that group can be assigned to edges in the interpretation list.   For example, ″g1 -- > (e1,e2,e15)″ means that first point of any light probe within group g1 can be assigned to edge e1, second point to e2 and the last point to e15.

Mask has found the solution, up to symmetry, of every problem to which it has been applied. It also reports a failure when light probe data from the specimen object does not match the model object.

ACKNOWLEDGEMENT

The author is grateful to Bernie Dimsdale, Hal Hichborn, Mark Lavin, Jim Moore, Eugene Paik and Gary Silverman for their discussions and comments on this work.   The author is also grateful to the anonymous referee whose comments resulted in a number of important clarifications.

```
Interpretation 1          Interpretation 2
g1 -- > (e1,e2,e15).      g1 -- > (e6,e7,e11).
g2 -- > (e5,e2,e15).      g2 -- > (e10,e7,e11).
g3 -- > (e5,e3,e14,e10).  g3 -- > (e10,e8,e12,e5).
g4 -- > (e4,e3,e14,e10).  g4 -- > (e9,e8,e12,e5).
g5 -- > (e13,e14,e10).    g5 -- > (e13,e12,e5).
g6 -- > (e13,e9).         g6 -- > (e13,e4).

Interpretation 3          Interpretation 4
g1 -- > (e1,e5,e11).      g1 -- > (e6,e10,e15).
g2 -- > (e2,e5,e11).      g2 -- > (e7,e10,e15).
g3 -- > (e2,e4,e12,e7).   g3 -- > (e7,e9,e14,e2).
g4 -- > (e3,e4,e12,e7).   g4 -- > (e8,e9,e14,e2).
g5 -- > (e13,e12,e7).     g5 -- > (e13,e14,e2).
g6 -- > (e13,e8).         g6 -- > (e13,e3).
```

Figure 6.   Set of consistent interpretations.

REFERENCES

1.   Arbab, B. ″Object Identification from Parallel Light Probes.″ IJCAI-87, Milano, Italy.

2.   Echigo, T. and Masahiko, Y. ″A Fast Method for Extraction of 3-D Information Using Multiple Stripes and Two Cameras.″

Proc. IJCAI-85, Los Angeles, California, 1985, pp. 1127-1130.

3. Gillet, M. "Description of the P.S.C. Prolog 1.2" IBM Paris Scientific Center Report, 1985.

4. Grimson, W. E. L. and Lozano-Perez, T. "Model-Based Recognition and Localization from Sparse Range or Tactile Data." The International Journal of Robotics Research, Vol. 3 No. 3, 1984, pp. 3-35.

5. Huffman, D. A. "Impossible Objects as Nonsense Sentences." Machine Intelligence 6 (Eds. Meltzer, B. and Michie, D.), 1971, pp. 295-323.

6. Inselberg, A. and Dimsdale, B. "Representing Muli-Dimensional Lines." IBM Los Angeles Scientific Center Report, submitted for publication.

7. Mersch, S. and Stubbs, J. "Projecting and Using Multiple Lines of Laser Light." Proc. Vision 86, Detroit, Michigan, 1986, pp. 613-625.

8. Silverman, G., Tsai, R. and Lavin, M. "Locating Polyhedral Objects from Edge Point Data." IJCAI-87, Milano, Italy, 1987.

9. Tsai, R. Y. "A Versatile Camera Calibration Technique for High Accuracy 3D Machine Vision Metrology using off-the-shelf TV cameras and Lenses." IBM T.J. Watson Research Report, RC 11413, 1985.

10. Waltz, D. L. "Shedding Light on Shadows." Progress in Vision and Robotics (Ed. Winston, P. H.), 1973, pp. 81-147.

Appendix A

A number of different examples are presented in this section. In each case Mask is presented with the 3-D light stripe data obtained from the simulator and asked if this data matches a particular model. For clarity, the intersection of light stripes with the actual object is presented first. The output of Mask, as it goes through various phases of the algorithm, is then presented. The grouping of light probes, as found by Mask, is also marked in each figure. It should be noted that not all light stripes get classified within various groups. This is primarily caused by errors in the light stripe data.

During phase I, Mask reports the number of different light probe groups found and the number of colinearity and coplanarity constraints between them. Phase II reports the number of interpretations found for the first and the last probe within each group and the number of interpretations in their intersection. The result of application of the three constraints, as explained in the section PHASE II above, to the interpretations of each group is then presented. Phase III reports the number of interpretations that are valid for all the groups, according to the colinearity, coplanarity and distance constraints. Each interpretation is then presented.

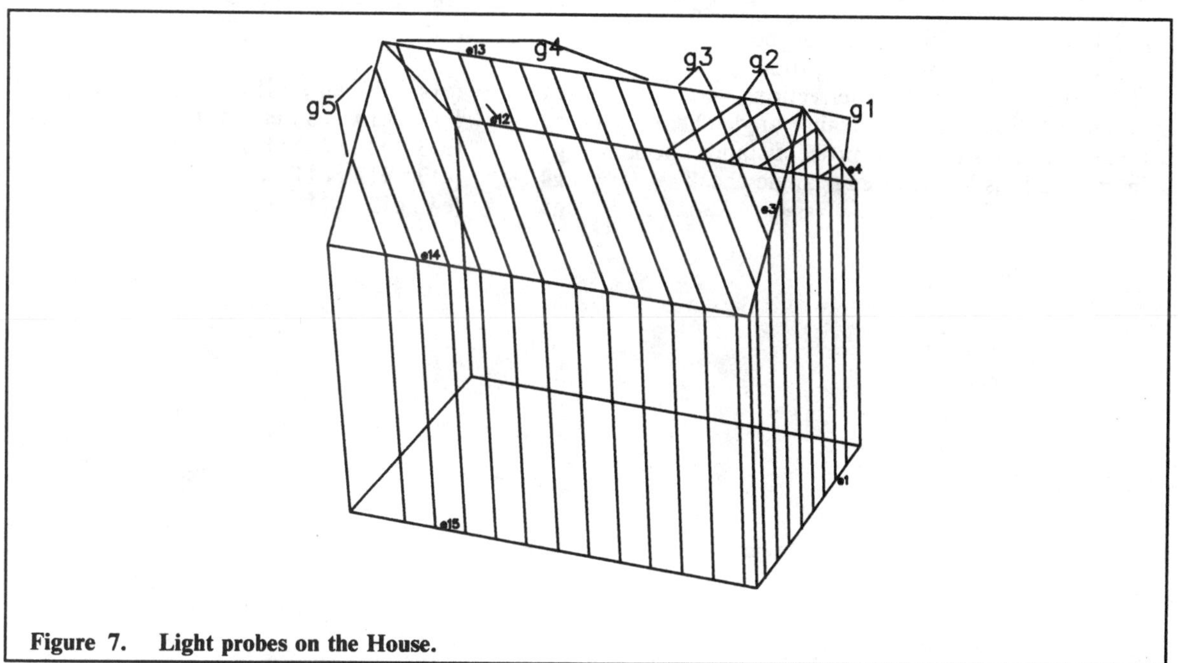

Figure 7.   Light probes on the House.

----------- Phase I ---------------

The light probe data divides into 5 different groups
There are 10 colinearity conditions
There are 11 coplanarity conditions

----------- Phase II --------------

-- > g1 < --
136 interpretations for the first probe
142 interpretations for the last probe
112 interpretations in the intersection
96 interpretations left after planar angle check
96 interpretations left after probe distance check
36 interpretations left after edge angle check

-- > g2 < --
132 interpretations for the first probe
148 interpretations for the last probe
120 interpretations in the intersection
84 interpretations left after planar angle check
84 interpretations left after probe distance check
12 interpretations left after edge angle check

-- > g3 < --
176 interpretations for the first probe
196 interpretations for the last probe
168 interpretations in the intersection
152 interpretations left after planar angle check
152 interpretations left after probe distance check
48 interpretations left after edge angle check

-- > g4 < --
204 interpretations for the first probe
204 interpretations for the last probe
204 interpretations in the intersection
22 interpretations left after planar angle check
10 interpretations left after probe distance check
2 interpretations left after edge angle check

-- > g5 < --
210 interpretations for the first probe
144 interpretations for the last probe
136 interpretations in the intersection
16 interpretations left after planar angle check
16 interpretations left after probe distance check
8 interpretations left after edge angle check

----------- Phase III --------------

Light probe data has 4 possible interpretations
for the object house

g1 -- > (e12 . e4 . e1 . nil) .
g2 -- > (e12 . e13 . e3 . e1 . nil) .
g3 -- > (e13 . e3 . e1 . nil) .
g4 -- > (e13 . e14 . e15 . nil) .
g5 -- > (e9 . e14 . e15 . nil) .

g1 -- > (e12 . e8 . e6 . nil) .
g2 -- > (e12 . e13 . e9 . e6 . nil) .
g3 -- > (e13 . e9 . e6 . nil) .
g4 -- > (e13 . e14 . e15 . nil) .
g5 -- > (e3 . e14 . e15 . nil) .

g1 -- > (e14 . e3 . e1 . nil) .
g2 -- > (e14 . e13 . e4 . e1 . nil) .
g3 -- > (e13 . e4 . e1 . nil) .
g4 -- > (e13 . e12 . e11 . nil) .
g5 -- > (e8 . e12 . e11 . nil) .

g1 -- > (e14 . e9 . e6 . nil) .
g2 -- > (e14 . e13 . e8 . e6 . nil) .
g3 -- > (e13 . e8 . e6 . nil) .
g4 -- > (e13 . e12 . e11 . nil) .
g5 -- > (e4 . e12 . e11 . nil) .

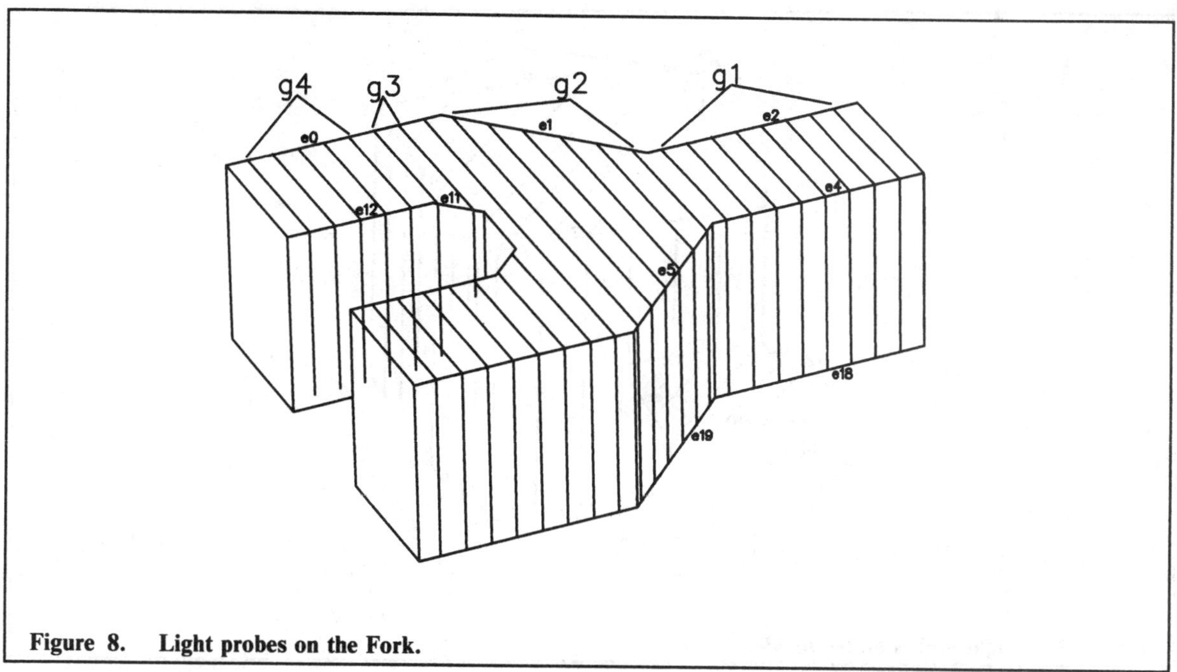

Figure 8.   Light probes on the Fork.

----------- Phase I ---------------

The light probe data divides into 4 different groups
There are 2 colinearity conditions
There are 6 coplanarity conditions

----------- Phase II --------------

--> g1 <--
1292 interpretations for the first probe
1292 interpretations for the last probe
1292 interpretations in the intersection
1232 interpretations left after planar angle check
204 interpretations left after probe distance check
16 interpretations left after edge angle check

--> g2 <--
1288 interpretations for the first probe
312 interpretations for the last probe
192 interpretations in the intersection
192 interpretations left after planar angle check
32 interpretations left after probe distance check
4 interpretations left after edge angle check

--> g3 <--
416 interpretations for the first probe
392 interpretations for the last probe
392 interpretations in the intersection
392 interpretations left after planar angle check
392 interpretations left after probe distance check
112 interpretations left after edge angle check

--> g4 <--
396 interpretations for the first probe

396 interpretations for the last probe
396 interpretations in the intersection
396 interpretations left after planar angle check
272 interpretations left after probe distance check
60 interpretations left after edge angle check

----------- Phase III --------------

Light probe data has 4 possible interpretations
for the object fork

```
g1 --> (e2 . e4 . e18 . nil) .
g2 --> (e1 . e5 . e19 . nil) .
g3 --> (e0 . e11 . nil) .
g4 --> (e0 . e12 . nil) .


g1 --> (e4 . e2 . e16 . nil) .
g2 --> (e5 . e1 . e15 . nil) .
g3 --> (e6 . e9 . nil) .
g4 --> (e6 . e8 . nil) .


g1 --> (e16 . e18 . e4 . nil) .
g2 --> (e15 . e19 . e5 . nil) .
g3 --> (e14 . e25 . nil) .
g4 --> (e14 . e26 . nil) .


g1 --> (e18 . e16 . e2 . nil) .
g2 --> (e19 . e15 . e1 . nil) .
g3 --> (e20 . e23 . nil) .
g4 --> (e20 . e22 . nil) .
```

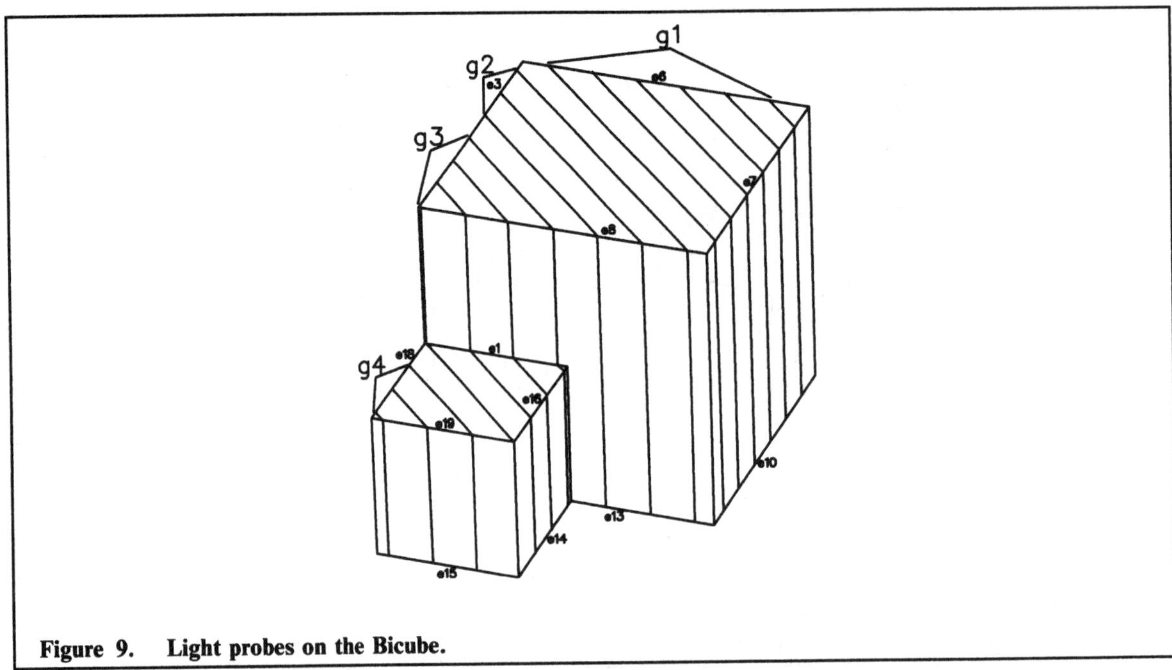

Figure 9.   Light probes on the Bicube.

---------- Phase I --------------

The light probe data divides into 4 different groups
There are 2 colinearity conditions
There are 5 coplanarity conditions

---------- Phase II --------------

-- > g1 < --
192 interpretations for the first probe
184 interpretations for the last probe
74 interpretations in the intersection
74 interpretations left after planar angle check
58 interpretations left after probe distance check
26 interpretations left after edge angle check

-- > g2 < --
184 interpretations for the first probe
194 interpretations for the last probe
102 interpretations in the intersection
102 interpretations left after planar angle check
102 interpretations left after probe distance check
46 interpretations left after edge angle check

-- > g3 < --
172 interpretations for the first probe
336 interpretations for the last probe
102 interpretations in the intersection
102 interpretations left after planar angle check
102 interpretations left after probe distance check
22 interpretations left after edge angle check

-- > g4 < --
212 interpretations for the first probe
212 interpretations for the last probe
212 interpretations in the intersection
212 interpretations left after planar angle check
212 interpretations left after probe distance check
64 interpretations left after edge angle check

---------- Phase III --------------

Light probe data has 2 possible interpretations
for the object bicube

g1 -- > (e6 . e7 . e10 . nil) .
g2 -- > (e3 . e8 . e13 . nil) .
g3 -- > (e3 . e8 . e1 . e16 . e14 . nil) .
g4 -- > (e18 . e19 . e15 . nil) .

g1 -- > (e9 . e7 . e3 . nil) .
g2 -- > (e10 . e11 . e4 . nil) .
g3 -- > (e10 . e11 . e0 . e16 . e18 . nil) .
g4 -- > (e14 . e17 . e20 . nil) .

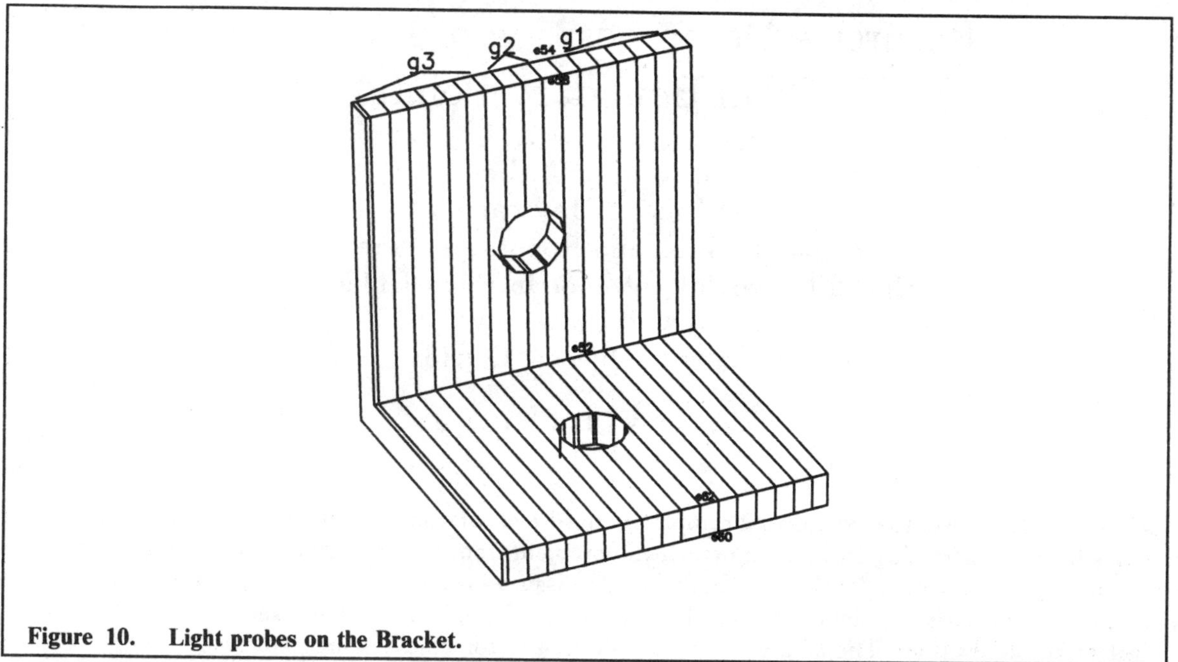

Figure 10.   Light probes on the Bracket.

----------- Phase I ---------------

The light probe data divides into 3 different groups
There are 9 colinearity conditions
There are 6 coplanarity conditions

----------- Phase II --------------

-- > g1 < --
310 interpretations for the first probe
310 interpretations for the last probe
310 interpretations in the intersection
310 interpretations left after planar angle check
126 interpretations left after probe distance check
2 interpretations left after edge angle check

-- > g2 < --
780 interpretations for the first probe
780 interpretations for the last probe
780 interpretations in the intersection
780 interpretations left after planar angle check
60 interpretations left after probe distance check
12 interpretations left after edge angle check

-- > g3 < --
310 interpretations for the first probe
310 interpretations for the last probe
310 interpretations in the intersection
310 interpretations left after planar angle check
126 interpretations left after probe distance check
2 interpretations left after edge angle check

----------- Phase III --------------

Light probe data has 2 possible interpretations
for the object bracket

g1 -- >   (e54 . e58 . e52 . e62 . e60 . nil) .
g2 -- >   (e54 . e58 . nil) .
g3 -- >   (e54 . e58 . e52 . e62 . e60 . nil) .

g1 -- >   (e60 . e62 . e52 . e58 . e54 . nil) .
g2 -- >   (e60 . e62 . nil) .
g3 -- >   (e60 . e62 . e52 . e58 . e54 . nil) .

Recursive Decomposition of Free-Space
From Boundary Points

Stéphane Aubry
Vincent Hayward
Computer Vision and Robotics Laboratory
McGill Research Centre for Intelligent Machines
McGill University
Montréal, Québec, Canada

July 31, 1987

Abstract Because of the exponential complexity nature of robotic path-planning and collision detection, there has been an increasing trend to approach the problem from a representational point of view as much as from an algorithmic one. This article addresses the issues involved in converting the information given by a collection of surface points, such as those made available from a range sensor, into a hierarchical volumetric decomposition. The aim of the representation is to achieve search efficiency, compactness and parallelism, while avoiding the creation of an arbitrary coordinate system such as is the case with the octree representation. We propose a paradigm for achieving such a goal, we show that surface connectivity is a key element of a valid representation and we present a method to obtain such a connectivity in optimal time.

Finally, we suggest that, because of topological considerations, the representation of free-space is often preferrable to the representation of obstacles.

1   Introduction

1.1   Path Planning

One of the most active areas of robotics research is that of path planning (Whitesides 1985, Hayward *et al.* 1987). Loosely stated, the **Findpath** problem consists of finding a collision-free path for all links of a three-dimensional manipulator through a space cluttered with a known set of obstacles. The problem's complexity is exponential in the number of links and polynomial in the geometrical resolution, rendering fully general and analytical solutions computationally intractable; See (Schwartz and Sharir 1983a,b) for such a solution. The aim of recent work has therefore been to devise efficient approximate techniques that can approach real-time performance, off-line information preprocessing being the key ingredient of most of these approaches.

Joint-space approaches, for example, map the known obstacles from their three-dimensional spatial coordinates to the n-dimensional space of robot configurations. The problem usually reduces to one of finding a path through a graph whose nodes are allowable configuration intervals (Lozano-Pérez and Wesley 1979,Lozano-Pérez 1983, Brooks and Lozano-Pérez 1983, Lozano-Pérez 1986). Unfortunately, such methods suffer from a combinatorial explosion for all but the simplest robots. Furthermore, the preprocessing computations are manipulator dependant and poorly accomodate dynamic changes in the environment.

Cartesian space approaches, in contrast, map the robot joints and links to the three-dimensional world in which they evolve. We note that these approaches often (but not always) lead to more heuristic solutions (Brooks 1983). In particular, one approach is to follow an iterative generate-test-and-update procedure whereby a planner module generates paths and incrementally updates them until one path gets accepted by a separate detection collision module. The computational load in such schemes mostly lies on the collision detector as the number of times the innermost geometrical interference detector is called a large number of times.

1.2   Collision Detection

Collision Detection is defined as the process by which a given path in cartesian space is checked for acceptability given a known set of obstacles. This check can be performed by checking for surface interferences only (Boyse 1979, Canny 1984, Cameron 1985). For example, assuming polyhedral links and obstacles and disregarding positioning singularities, Boyse showed that it suffices to check for edge-to-edge and edge-to-face contacts to detect all possible collisions. This type of algorithm requires that the geometrical data be given in the form of *boundaries* of both manipulator and obstacles.

Another method consists in checking whether or not a "shrunk" manipulator lies inside or outside the *volume* occupied by the obstacles. Using a shrunk manipulator is an artifact which allows us to simplify the computations. Rather than computing the volumetric inclusions, we shrink the volume occupied by the manipulator links down to their symmetric axes and grow the objects' volume by an equivalent amount. The symmetric axis is usually composed of planar regions, terminated by three-dimensional splines, themselves terminated by single dots. For such simple shapes, querying for inclusion inside the object can be reduced to trivial operations. We note that such an algorithm requires the data to be either converted to, or directly fed to the program as a volumetric representation. The next section elaborates on this point.

2   Representational Issues

As a result of the different approaches to the general problem of path planning and collision detection requiring different types of input data, there has been a increasing trend to approach the problem from a representational point of view as much as from an algorithmic one (Brooks 83, Hayward 86). The issue here is to find a suitable representation for the obstacles —and for the robot— which combines such properties as compactness, validity and ease of use. Solid modelling is the field of research which investigates the tradeoffs involved in the different schemes available. See Requicha (Requicha 1980) for a survey. We contend that recursive schemes are particularly suited to the purpose of fast collision detection as they allow to reduce the search space by zeroing in on the element on which to perform detection collision.

The most popular recursive scheme has thus far been the octree representation (Meagher 1982) and has led to some successful implementations. A clear disadvantage of the octree representation however is that it introduces an arbitrary set of coordinate axes and is hence very sensitive to even minute rotations and translations. Further, it uses a unique, arbitrary primitive, namely the cube, which is ill-suited to representing elongated objects. A desirable feature of a representation would be then to retain a recursive structure while allowing for a better correlation between the objects' intrinsic geometry and the shape and placements of the representational primitives. Such a representation would be invariant under rigid motions. To this effect, we propose to use a representation that defines a recursive decomposition of space into simple but versatile primitives.

2.1   Some Approaches to Intrinsic Decomposition of Space

The following is a review of hierarchical volumetric solid modelling schemes which fit the domain of the above discussion.

2.1.1   A Volume approach: Tetrahedra

Faugeras *et al.* (1984) give a decomposition algorithm based on a three-dimensional extension of a classical image processing algorithm (Ramer 1972). We briefly describe the algorithm below.

Ramer's algorithm in two dimensions   Given a closed two-dimensional curve given as an *ordered* list of discrete points, the algorithm works by recursively approximating the contour by triangles. At each level of the recursion, the triangle edges are "broken up" into new triangles whose vertices are the endpoints of the edge and the point on the curve farthest from the edge among those situated between the two edge endpoints. The algorithm works because we assume that the contour points are ordered along the contour. In general, this ordering is easy to define because a one-dimensional parameter such as the arc length defines a natural ordering between the points comprising the contour. Therefore, at each iteration we "assign" to the newly-created edges the list of points comprised between its endpoints. This list will serve as the pool of points among which to choose the third vertex of the triangle which the edge will spawn at the next iteration.

Faugeras *et al.*'s algorithm in three dimensions   A natural extension of Ramer's algorithm has been devised by Faugeras *et al.* (1984). Assuming the input data to be a set of three-dimensional points (such as those given by a series of range views), the algorithm can be extended in the following manner: edges are replaced by triangles and triangles are replaced by tetrahedra. In three dimensions, the tetrahedra are formed as faces are broken up and joined with the point farthest away from the face. The three points forming the original face, however, no longer enclose a set of points on which a natural ordering can be defined. That is, the algorithm only works provided we can allot the points as "belonging" to a given face of each newly-created tetrahedron. The connectivity graph of a non-intersecting surface being planar, any closed path on the surface points of the object forms two disconnected regions. In particular, any closed path through the three vertices of every triangular face splits the set of surface points into two complementary subsets, one of which is assigned to the face, the other to its complement. In order to find such a path however, we need to have a connectivity graph for all the surface points at the start of the tetrahedral decomposition phase of the algorithm. Although simple in appearance, such a connectivity graph is in general difficult to obtain from a set of discrete surface points. We delay the discussion on how to obtain such a graph until the next section.

The aim of Faugeras *et al.*'s algorithm was to obtain a polyhedral approximation of the surfaces of the objects rather than to build a model for use by a fast collision detector. We propose to adapt it for such a purpose.

2.1.2   A surface Approach: Prism Trees

Faugeras and Ponce (1985) introduced prism trees, whose construction actually make use of a variant of the above algorithm. Rather than being a generalisation of Ramer's algorithm, they are one of Ballard's Strip Trees (Ballard 1981). Although very general and versatile in nature, the prism tree representation suffers from its complexity and few researchers have so far adopted it.

2.2   Our Proposed Model

Following our earlier discussion on recursive decomposition of the space, we propose to use the three-dimensional simplex, the tetrahedron, as an adequate spatial primitive, and to build a tree of these simplices from a sample of object surface points. The manipulation of such a tree is simpler than is that of the prism tree and we show below that a judicious use of Faugeras *et al.*'s representation allows us to easily check for point inclusion.

2.2.1   The Label Tree

Because most obstacle-free space boundaries are not convex, the parent tetrahedra usually straddle those boundaries so that positive responses to the point inclusion queries are usually inconclusive since they only indicate inclusion in the convex hull of the object, rather than in the object itself (negative responses in all cases are). It is therefore necessary to label all inconclusive subtrees (corresponding to concave parts of the objects) as such.

Even though we assume no a priori knowledge of the sign of the curvature at the surface points, such a labelling of the subtrees is relatively easy to obtain as a byproduct of the tetrahedral construction process. At the start of the recursion, all nodes are assumed to be **valid** and **convex**. Suppose that at a given level of recursion of the construction, we are to break a face into a new tetrahedron. We can check if the point with respect to which the face is broken lies to the same side of that face as does the parent tetrahedron. If such is the case, we are dealing with a concave area and we must take two node labelling actions. We must first assign an *invalid* label to all ancestors of the newly created tetrahedron since those ancestors necessarily contain some free space. The *invalid* label is to be used as an indicator that a positive response to the inclusion query is not a sufficient test. One will then need to go down all *invalid* branches of the tree until *valid* branches are encountered before being able to make a decision.

In addition, a *concave* label must be assigned to the newly-created node to indicate that since the node is at least partially concave, inclusion in the tetrahedron indicates that the point is outside the object, rather than the opposite. Contrarily to the validity label, which propagates upwards, the concavity label propagates downwards to all children nodes. If the upper concave node is not fully concave (the general case), its children will eventually form convex areas. Again, two labelling actions need then be taken: labelling all parents as invalid and reversing the labelling of subsequent children to *convex*. In this fashion, it becomes possible to both know whether a positive node inclusion is conclusive and whether it indicates object inclusion or object exclusion.

2.2.2   The Tree of Convex Trees

We saw above that the non-convexity of real objects leads to complications in the design of a suitable representation. An alternative is then to represent the object as a collection of convex ones. A recent result (Kim 1987) shows that it is possible to do so in general by recursively decomposing the object into its convex hull and the convex hull of its convex hull difference. Every node along this tree can itself be represented as a tree of polyhedra which are all valid and convex. Point inclusion in the Convex Tree can be determined by descending down the tree nodes and verifying that the point belong to the convex hull of the object but not to any of its differences.

2.2.3   Searching the Connectivity Graph

As mentioned in the preceding section, the tetrahedral construction requires that a connectivity graph be available. Given any two points on the surface, Faugeras *et al.* choose as the optimal path joining them the one that remains closest to a particular bissector plane. The bissector plane generally bears no relation to the shape being approximated, and thus does not necessarily guarantee an optimal path in the shortest path sense. Therefore, we propose as an "optimal" path the one obtained by a hill-climbing method with euclidean distances as the metric.

3   Graph Construction

We mentioned above the need to obtain a connectivity graph for the surface points. Finding such a graph is not a trivial problem in the general case. Nonetheless, such a graph is often wrongly assumed to be known beforehand.

In the range image understanding literature, for example, local positional derivatives are frequently taken without consideration to how global information stemming from several views affects connectivity. As an example, consider the image created by a highly oblique planar surface. Very few surface points, very far apart from each other, cannot lead to the conclusion of the existence of such a surface unless information from other views is also available.

We review below some of the approaches available for the construction of the connectivity graph and present our proposed method.

3.1   Convex Objects: A Trivial Case

In the case of convex objects, the existence of a graph is *not* essential to the validity of the representation. Indeed, since the tetrahedrisation proceeds "from inside out", the allocation of surface points to their respective tetrahedral faces at every stage of the construction is simple: the decision can be unambiguously made on the basis of which side of the half-planes formed by the new faces the points lie.

3.2   Knowledge of convexity for each point

Boissonnat (1982) develops an algorithm for triangulating the surface of an object provided that a label is available at all surface points, indicating whether or not the surface is locally convex. Since a triangulation *is* a connectivity graph, the assumption is sufficient. This is not surprising if one considers the strong connection between connectivity and the ability to compute derivatives: the convexity boolean is given by the sign of the Gaussian curvature, a second derivative feature. Far from solving the problem then, our assumption only points to the existence of a "chicken and egg" problem.

3.3   An "Optimal" Method: The Delaunay Triangulation

Boissonnat (1985a,1985b) developed an elegant technique for computing the three-dimensional Delaunay triangulation of objects whose surface points are obtained from parallel, closed contour views. This is achieved by repeated two-dimensional triangulations and point projection operations, at great computational savings over a general-purpose three-dimensional Delaunay triangulation algorithm. However, we note that the restriction over the parallel organisation of the data may be undesirable in some cases, such as when exploring the environment with a wrist-mounted range sensor.

The Delaunay triangulation has many desirable properties. First, it is the most regular neighborhood graph that can be obtained from a set of points as it defines symmetrical and isotropic relationships between them. Second, it bears a close relation to the three-dimensional symmetric axis transform, with promising applications for object recognition. Lastly, it allows us to define a hierarchical object-centered representation for the object using a data structure called the Delaunay tree. Even though the representation introduces complex relationships between the nodes of the tree, it can be proven (Boissonnat and Teillaud 1985) that the expected tree height is $O(logN)$.

Despite these advantages, the three-dimensional Delaunay triangulation does not in general form a valid connectivity graph for the surface points. As an example, imagine the pattern formed by the surface points of an elongated slab. Since the Delaunay triangulation only considers euclidean distance relationships, it will tend to join points situated on either sides of the slab, since they are close to each other. This behavior is highly undesirable because the graph should "walk" along the object's surface, instead of cutting through it.

3.4   Contour Lines Sequences

Faugeras and Pauchon (1983) published an algorithm that ordered point sequences around a closed planar contour. This ordering in fact is a connectivity sub-graph for the surface points located in the plane of the contour. The graph joining the contours among themselves is then obtained using a planar contour triangulation algorithm (Keppel 1975).

A partial contour graph is incrementally built as the sensor rotates around the object. Adjacent pixels in each scan-line of each range image are assumed to be neighbours, unless the line-of-sight for a pixel of another image intersects the segment link joining the adjacent pixels. The major contribution of the approach is that the graph is constructed using the information provided by the sensor geometry, instead of from point proximity relationships or assumed surface properties. Because the range sensor reports the first intersection of the line-of-sight with the object, a strong clue as to its topological properties is provided that should not be overlooked. This clue is in fact the key to unambiguously building the surface graph without any external (and somewhat artificial) assumptions.

4   Our Proposed Model

We propose to further carry the idea of Faugeras and Pauchon's algorithm by doing away with the assumption that the points coming from different range views are organised along similar contour lines. The reasons for doing so are threefold. First, the original article illustrates examples in which the algorithm fails; heuristics are then used to detect those special cases. We will show below a fundamental improvement which allows us to deal with all cases in a uniform manner. Second, we mentioned above that parallel scanlines, or even non-intersecting ones, may not always be available in some sensor-to-environment configurations. Our algorithm relaxes this restriction. Third, although the scan-line approach as presented in the preceding subsection adequately solves the surface connectivity problem (a two-dimensional one) along the contour lines, it does resort to a euclidean metric in the orthogonal direction and hence retains a heuristic flavour.

We assume in the following that we have at our disposal an arbitrary number of range *images*, whose orientation in space is also arbitrary. Our purpose is to build a valid connectivity graph by resolving the different views together. Every range image defines a "frame". We define for now a frame as a point P in free-space, and a set of semi-inifinite rays passing through P such that the data points lie on those rays. The points are then the three-dimensional surface points acquired with the camera lens center at P. If we now project the points onto a plane cutting through all the rays, we can define a square matrix aligned along two non-collinear (although not necessarily orthogonal) vectors u, v and whose nodes are the projected points. The matrix coordinates define a metric which can be used to construct an initial connectivity graph of the points. This graph is valid in the sense that it only imbeds the connectivity as "seen" by the sensor and represents the best guess that can be made given the available information. The precondition for the validity of such an initial connectivity graph is that the set of points generated by the camera rays intersections form a convex envelope in the free space (Aubry and Hayward 1987). This condition is trivially satisfied in the case of an immobile camera lens center.

We are currently investigating whether a full two-dimensional triangulation (such as the Delaunay triangulation) is required or if sparser graphs such as the neighbourhood graph are sufficient to further yield an appealing tetrahedrisation.

In general however, the graph construction is implicitly performed by the range sensor apparatus since the most common way of acquiring the range data is through the use of planar sheets of light. These sheets usually define complete two-dimensional matrices of data points, with u, v being the sweep directions, and a natural graph is that given by the matrix four-neighbours. Note that the data points form a cone around P. See Figure 1.

The next challenge is to combine the graphs obtained from the different views. Because connectivity arcs and sensor lines-of-sight form arbitrary segments in three-dimensional space, they do not in general intersect, and Faugeras and Pauchon's method does not generalise to this case. Starting from the initial graph of a given frame, we propose to incrementally insert the points from the other views by testing for ray-to-cone intersections in the free-space. Namely, if the ray of the new data point pierces the polygon P_1 generated by the point P and all the data points with $u = u_1(v = v_1)$ but does not pierce the polygon P_2 generated by P and all the data points with $u = u_1 + n(v = v_1 + n)$, then we know that the given ray has crossed nothing but empty space up until a position somewhere between polygons P_1 and P_2 (See Figure 2). Since the polygons of constant u (constant v) define complete orderings on the data points, we can logarithmically determine which of the polygons are crossed by the new ray and which are not until we find a pair of adjacent polygons, only one of which is crossed by the ray. Alternately, if the ray either crosses no polygon or crosses both extrema polygons, then the data point is not to be inserted into the frame at hand and no further search need be performed.

By performing this search once along the u and once along the v direction, we can unambiguously "box in" the new data point and insert it into (i.e. establish its connectivity with) the previously acquired points. Figure 3 illustrates this process.

4.1   Complexity analysis

We assume for now that every point needs to be inserted into a frame and that there is a bounded number F of frames. Further, we note that a given point is to be inserted into one frame only. Supposing we know which frame the point is to be inserted into, we have to perform twice $O(logN)$ polygon intersections with the ray in order to find out between which polygons to insert the point.

Now, for every polygon that the ray associated with the point is to be tested against, we must perform $O(logN)$ operations. Indeed, for each polygon, there exists an implicit sorted triangulation of the polygon. The polygon triangles all have P as their first vertex and adjacent data points along the sorted direction of the polygon as their second and third vertices. See Figure 4. The intersection of a triangulated polygon with a three-dimensional ray is equivalent to the point-query problem in a two-dimensional polygon and can be performed in $O(logN)$ operations (Shamos and Preparata 1985).

Finally, we need to estimate the work required to find the frame into which the point is to be inserted. This can be done by testing only for the polygonal extrema of the frame and can therefore be done in $O(F*logN)$ time. Even though we cannot impose a bound on the number of frames of the data acquisition process, we can assume the number to be small relative to the total number of surface points. Indeed, F is bounded downwards by 2 (the cones of support of the convex hull of the object) but depends in practice on how we choose to position the sensor. Furthermore, not all frames are retained troughout the entire construction process since we can eliminate those which have all their points inserted into other frames (Aubry and Hayward 1987).

In summary, the worst-time complexity of the construction process is

$$2 * N * (F * (logN) + (logN) * (logN)) = N * (log^2 N)$$

5   Holes and Topological Considerations

The tetrahedral decomposition algorithm which is at the heart of our approach only works for objects of genus 0 (without holes). In addition, it is not suited to representing collections of disconnected objects. This rather unfortunate restriction led us to consider alternate ways of representing Space.

5.1   Free Space Versus Forbidden Space

Most of the work done in the solid modelling field has so far concerned itself with modelling *objects* rather than the free-space surrounding them. In fact, both approaches are equally valid since one space is by definition the complement of the other. The difference however lies in the topological shape of the spaces. Objects can both have holes and be disconnected. Free space, on the other hand, is always connected and does not usually contain holes.

The connectivity of free space relates to the impossibility for the manipulator to cross domain boundaries. Since we can safely assume that the beginning point of the Findpath problem is in the free space (!), the existence of holes within the object is irrelevant to the manipulator, and, from its point of view, the portion of free space in which it moves is the only one it needs be concerned about.

The absence of holes in the free space relates to a very simple observation: thanks to gravity, the obstacles are always regularly (surface-to-surface) connected to a boundary.

Hence, we can always model free space as a simple three-dimensional object without holes. Curiously, this simple observation has, to our knowledge, so far escaped the attention of researchers in the field.

5.2   The case in Outer Space

Robotics in space has recently attracted increasing attention. The absence of gravity in outer space implies that obstacles map as holes in the free space, and the conclusion of the preceding subsection does not hold. Two alternatives exist. The first one consists of creating an artificial cusp bridging the object and an arbitrary boundary of the free space, and to proceed with the tetrahedrisation as if the surface points of the cusp were part of the object. The approach may work but it introduces artificial artifacts not present in the original object. The second solution consists of slicing the entire space across every disconnected obstacle, so as to obtain several "free-spaces", each of which can be tetrahedrised as before. The major difficulty then is to merge the several trees into a meaningful, global representation.

6   Conclusions

We have proposed a recursive representation of the free space for use by a collision detection algorithm and investigated the connections with previous related work. We plan to implement the algorithm and to have preliminary results at the time of the conference.

7   References

Aubry, S. and Hayward, V. 1987, Recursive Decomposition of Free-Space From Boundary Points, McRCIM Technical Report, McGill University, Montréal, Canada (In preparation).

Ballard, D.H. 1981 (May), Strip Trees: A hierarchical representation for curves, *Comm. of the ACM Vol. 24, No 5*, 310–321.

Boissonnat, J.D. 1982, Representation of objects by triangulating points in 3-D space, *IEEE International Conference on Pattern Recognition*, 830–832.

Boissonnat, J.D. 1985a, Surface Reconstruction from planar cross-sections, *IEEE International Conference on Pattern Recognition*, 393–397.

Boissonnat, J.D 1985b, An automatic solid modeller for robotic applications, *Third International Symposium on Robots*, Paris, France.

Boyse, J. W. 1979. Interference detection among solids and surfaces. *Communications of the ACM*, Vol 22, No 1.

Brooks, R.A. 1983 (March/April), Solving the find-path problem by good representation of free space, *IEEE Trans. on Systems, Man and Cybernetics, V. SMC-13*, 190–197.

Brooks, R.A. and Lozano-Pérez, T. 1983 (August), A subdivision algorithm in configuration space for findpath with rotation, *Proc. Eight Int. Jt. Conf. on AI*, Karlsruhe, 799–806.

Cameron, S. 1985(March). A study of the clash detection problem in robotics. *IEEE Second Conference on Robotics and Automation*, St. Louis, Missouri. pp. 488–496.

Canny, J. 1984. Collision detection for moving polyhedra. AI Memo No 806, MIT, October 1984.

Faugeras, O.D. 1983, Measuring the shape of 3-D objects, *Proceedings of the Conference on Pattern Recognition and Image Processing*, 2–7.

Faugeras, O.D. and Ponce, J. 1983, Prism trees: A hierarchical representation for 3-D objects, *Proceedings of the International Joint Conference on Artificial Intelligence*, 982–988.

Faugeras, O.D., Hebert, M., Mussi, P., and Boissonnat, J.D. 1984, Polyhedral approximation of 3-D objects without holes,*Computer Vision, Graphics and Image Processing 25*, 169–183.

Hayward, V. 1986 (April 7–10), Fast collision detection scheme by recursive decomposition of a manipulator workspace, *IEEE Conference on Robotics and Automation*, San Francisco, CA, 1044–1049.

Hayward, V., Aubry, S., Jasiukajc, Z. 1987 (January). The use of 3D sensing techniques for on-line collision-free path planning. *Jet Propulsion Laboratory/NASA workshop on Space Robotics*. Pasadena, California.

Keppel, E. 1975 (January), Approximating complex surfaces by triangulation of contour lines, *IBM Journal of Research and Development*, 3–11.

Kim, Yong Se (April 17), A Convergent, unique convex decomposition of polyhedral objects, Technical Report, Design Division, Department of Mechanical Engineering, Stanford University.

Lozano-Péres,T. and Wesley, M.A. 1979 (January), An algorithm for planning collision-free paths among polyhedral obstacles, *Commun. Ass. Comput. Mach. Vol. ACM 22*, 560–570.

Lozano-Pérez, T. 1983 (January), Spatial planning: a configuration space approach, *IEEE Transactions on Computers, Vol. C-32*, 108–120.

Lozano-Pérez, T. 1986 (June). A simple motion planning algorithm for general robot manipulators. *Massachusetts Institute of Technology Artificial Intelligence Laboratory*, A. I. Memo 896.

Meagher, D.J. 1982, Geometric modelling using octree encoding, *Computer Graphics and Image Processing 19*, 129–147.

Ramer, U. 1972 (November), An iterative procedure for the polygonal approximation of plane curves, *Computer Graphics and Image Processing*, 244–256.

Requicha, A.A.G. 1980 (December), Representations of rigid solids: theory, methods and systems, *ACM Computing Surveys 12,4*, 437–464.

Schwartz, J.T. and Sharir, M. 1983a, On the piano movers' problem: I. The special case of rigid polygonal body moving amidst polygonal barriers, *Comm. pure Appl. Math Vol. XXXVI*, 345–398.

Schwartz, J.T. and Sharir, M. 1983b, On the piano movers' problem: II. General techniques for computing topological properties of real algebraic manifolds, *Adv. Appl. Math 4*, 298–351.

Shamos, M.I. and Preparata, F. 1985, Computational Geometry, Springer-Verlag.

Whitesides, S.W 1985, Computational geometry and motion planning, Toussaint G.T. (ed.), in *Computational Geometry*, 377–427.

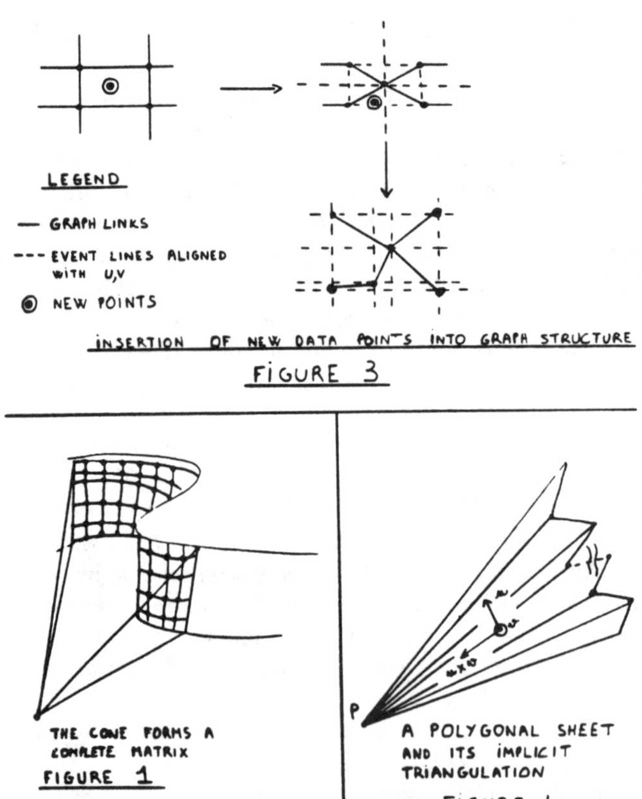

FIGURE 3

FIGURE 1

FIGURE 4

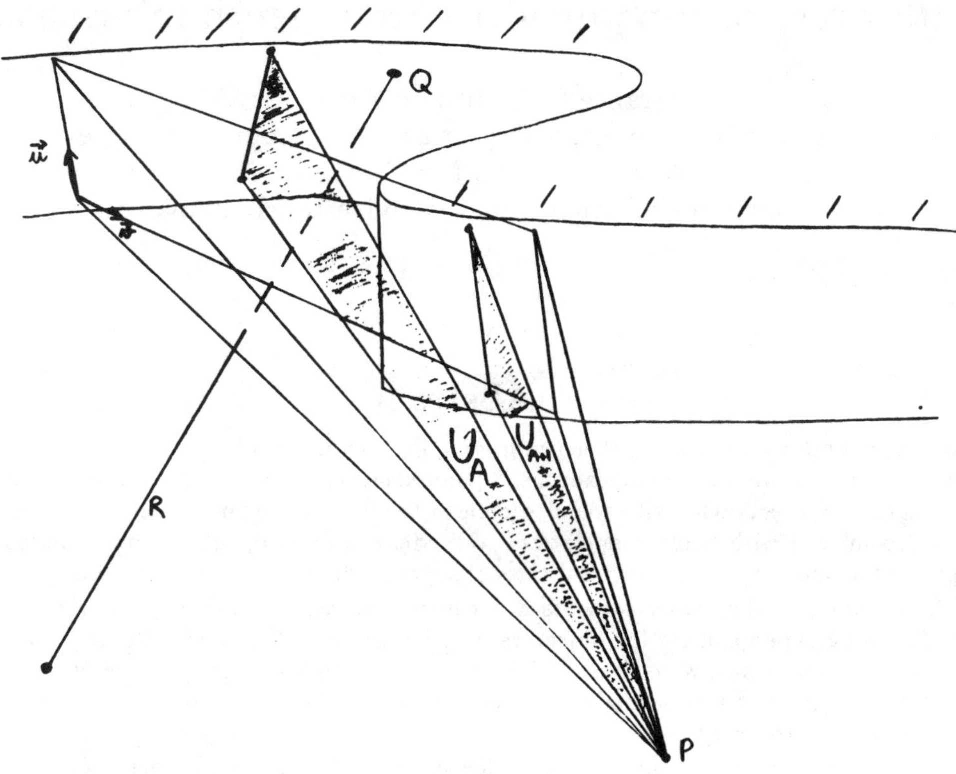

INSERTION OF DATA POINT Q INTO THE FRAME
GENERATED BY P. RAY R CROSSES POLYGON U_A
BUT DOES NOT CROSS POLYGON U_{A+1}

FIGURE 2

Recovery of superquadrics from depth information

Terrance E. Boult and Ari D. Gross
Columbia University Department of Computer Science
New York City, New York, 10027.
tboult@cs.columbia.edu, ari@sylvester.columbia.edu

Abstract

Superquadrics are a a class volumetric primitive which can model objects including rectangular solids with rounded corners, ellipsoids, octaheadrons, 8-pointed stars, hyperbolic sheets, and toroids with cross sections ranging from rectangles with rounded corners to elliptical regions. They can be stretched, bent, tapered and combined with boolean operations to model a wide range of objects. This paper discusses our progress at attempting to recover a subclass of superquadrics from 3D depth data.

The first section of this paper presents a mathematical definition of superquadrics. Some of the rationale for using superquadrics for object recognition is then discussed. Briefly, superquadrics are flexible enough to represent a wide class of objects, but are simple enough to be recovered from 3d data. Additionally, the surface and its normal surface both have well defined inside-out functions which provide a useful tool for their recovery.

The third section examines some of the difficulties to be encountered when modeling objects with superquadrics, or attempting to recover superquadrics from 3D data. These difficulties include the general problems of a non-orthogonal representation, difficulties of dealing with objects which are not exactly representable with CSG operations on the primitives, the need to recognize negative objects, certain numerical instabilities and some problems caused by using the inside-out function as an approximation of the distance of a point from the superquadric.

Our current system employs a nonlinear least square minimization technique on the inside-out function to recover the parameters. After discussing the details of the current system, the paper presents examples, using noisy synthetic data, where the system successfully uses multiple views to recover underlying superquadrics. Also presented are examples using range data, including the recovery of a negative superellipsiod.

Some pros and cons of our approach as well as few conclusions, and a discussion of our planned future work appear in the final section. The main result is that least square minimization using the inside-out function allows both positive and negative instances of superellipsoids to be recovered from depth data. A second preliminary result is that a single view of a superquadric may not be sufficient for reconstruction without additional assumptions.

Mathematical Definition of Superquadrics

Mathematically, superquadric solids are a spherical product of two superquadric curves. Superquadric curves are similar to traditional quadric curves except the terms in the definition are raised to parameterized exponents (not necessarily integers). For example, a superellipse (see [Gardiner-65]), is defined such that: $\left(\frac{x}{a}\right)^{\frac{2}{\epsilon}} + \left(\frac{y}{b}\right)^{\frac{2}{\epsilon}} = 1$. When ϵ, the *relative shape parameter* is 1, the curve describes an ellipse. As the relative shape parameter varies from 1 down to 0, the shape becomes progressively squarish; as it varies from 1 toward 2, the shape transforms from a ellipse to a diamond shaped bevel. When the parameter is greater than 2, the shape becomes pinched and as the parameter approaches infinity, the shape approaches a cross.

The result of the spherical product of two such curves is conveniently represented in a parametric form, e.g., a superquadric ellipsoid can be represented as (see figure 1):

$$\vec{s}(\eta,\omega) = \begin{bmatrix} a_1 \cdot \cos^{\epsilon_1} \eta \cdot \cos^{\epsilon_2} \omega \\ a_2 \cdot \cos^{\epsilon_1} \eta \cdot \sin^{\epsilon_2} \omega \\ a_3 \cdot \sin^{\epsilon_1} \eta \end{bmatrix}, \quad \begin{array}{l} -\frac{\pi}{2} \leq \eta \leq \frac{\pi}{2} \\ -\pi \leq \omega \leq \pi, \end{array} \quad \begin{array}{l} \text{for any fixed positive} a_1, \\ a_2, a_3, \epsilon_1, \text{ and } \epsilon_2. \end{array}$$

The parameters a_1, a_2, a_3 effect the size of the superellipsoid along the x, y and z respectively. The parameters ϵ_1 and ϵ_2 effect the relative shape of the superellipsoid in the latitudinal (xz) and longitudinal (xy) directions. When the 5 parameters are all unity, the superellipsoids define the unit sphere.

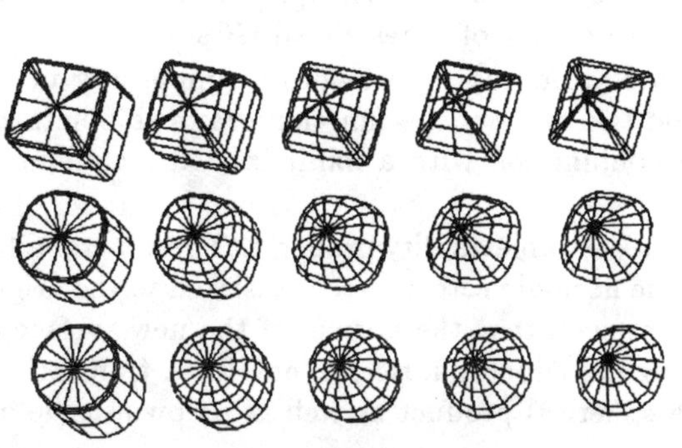

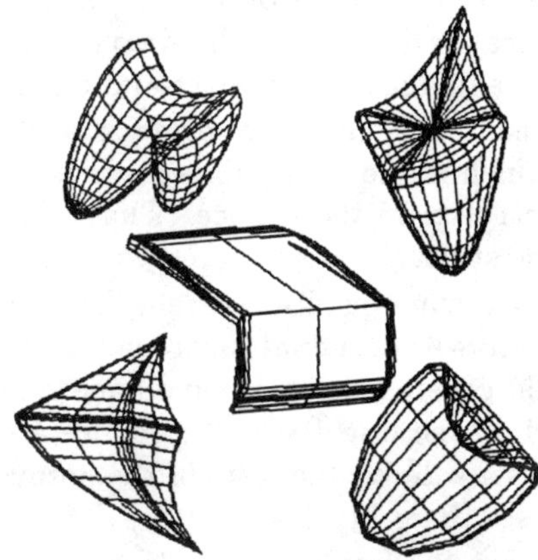

Figure 1: Superellipsoids with relative share parameter ϵ_1 having values .1, .5, 1, 1.5 and 2 (left to right), and ϵ_2 having values .1, .6 and 1 (top to bottom).

Figure 2: Examples of superquadrics deformed by bending and tapering

Superellipsoids have a well defined inside-out function:

$$f(x,y,z) = \left(\left(\frac{|x|}{a_1}\right)^{\frac{2}{\epsilon_2}} + \left(\frac{|y|}{a_2}\right)^{\frac{2}{\epsilon_2}}\right)^{\frac{\epsilon_2}{\epsilon_1}} + \left(\frac{|z|}{a_3}\right)^{\frac{2}{\epsilon_1}} \tag{1}$$

$$\text{where if} \begin{cases} f(x_0, y_0, z_0) = 1, & \text{then } x_0, y_0, z_0 \text{ is on the surface boundary,} \\ f(x_0, y_0, z_0) < 1, & \text{then } x_0, y_0, z_0 \text{ lies inside the surface boundary,} \\ f(x_0, y_0, z_0) > 1, & \text{then } x_0, y_0, z_0 \text{ lies outside the surface boundary.} \end{cases}$$

The absolute values are introduced to extend the inside-out function beyond the first octant.*

Superellipsoids (hereafter referred to as SEs) define the simplest of the superquadrics, and the only subclass which can model convex solids. One can also define superhyperboloids of one or two sheets and

---

*Alternatively, one could insure that fractional exponentiation was broken into two stages, squaring and then raising to the remaining fractional power.

supertoroids, see [Barr-81]. In addition to the variety of shapes defined by the basic superquadrics, Barr also discusses the application of angle-preserving transforms which allow translation, rotation, bending and twisting. With the addition of tapering and traditional boolean combination operations, superquadrics become a powerful modeling tool, see Figure 2.

Why use superquadric solids?

This section discusses some of the rational for using superquadrics for object recognition. In short, they are flexible enough to represent a wide class of objects, but are simple enough to be recovered from 3d data. Their inside-out function provides a useful tool for their recovery. In addition, they have a useful duality principle with their normal surface, which also has an inside-out function.

Traditional constructive solid modeling systems use boolean operations to combine primitives, such as, spheres, cylinders, and rectangular solids. By extending the primitive shapes to SEs, we allow the user to easily produce a continuum of forms, from spheres, to cuboids with rounded corners, to cubes, to diamond shapes. Such objects are difficult to model with traditional constructive solid geometry (hereafter CSG) systems. Making them primitives simplifies the job of the designer for any problem that contains objects with these properties.[†]

However, adding flexibility above that of a traditional CSG system is not the only reason to choose superquadrics. For added flexibility, one could make the primitives of the system Generalized Cylinders or Generalized Cones, as introduced in [Brooks-Binford-80]. The problem with GC's is that recovering them is a difficult process, partially because each GC may require hundreds of parameters to describe it.[‡] As in [Brooks-85] or [Rao-Nevatia-86], one generally has to greatly restrict the class of GCs allowed before one can reliably recover them. Superquadrics provide such a restriction, and in addition, provide mathematical properties (the inside-out function and normal surface duality principle) that will make the recovery of superquadrics simpler and more robust than the recovery of unrestricted GCs.

The inside-out function provides a useful tool for recovery, because it provides a simple way to determine which of the data points are inside the surface and the value of the function grows as points are moved farther from the surface. Thus it can be used in conjunction with a minimization technique to recover the surface.

Canonical superquadrics (except the supertoroids) have a desirable duality property. The superquadric normal vectors lie on a dual superquadric form; that is, if the normal vectors were translated to the origin, they would generate another superquadric of the same class such that the normal of the new surface (if translated to the origin) would produce a copy of the original superquadric (except for a translation). One can easily derive the form of the normal surface as a spherical product as well as its own inside-out function, see [Barr-81].

Note that the inside-out function for the surface normals may be used to find superquadrics fitting surface normal information as would be available from shape-from-X methods.

In summary, the authors are interested in recovering superquadrics because they are a flexible primitive for a CSG type system, but are simple enough to be recovered from 3d data. In addition, the surface and surface normals have easily computed inside-out functions.

Some Difficulties with Superquadrics

The difficulties of modeling with and recovering superquadrics can be divided into two classes: those difficulties common to any CSG based system and those difficulties particular to superquadrics. The former class includes general problems of non-orthogonality of the representation, difficulties of dealing with objects which are not exactly representable with CSG operations on the primitives, and the need

---

[†] A simple CAD system has been developed by A. Pentland, see [Pentland-86b] that combines SEs (constrained to only those that are convex solids) with CSG type operations plus bending and tapering. The easy with which people became accustomed to modeling with this system may be tied to their own internal representation of the objects. [Pentland-86a] presents arguments to assert motivate the use of superquadrics as modeling primitives by showing correspondences to human vocalization of object descriptions.

[‡] The number of parameters necessary to define a GC depends on the complexity of the cross-section function, the spine, and sweeping function. It is interesting to note that superellipsoids and supertoroids can be defined as a subclass of GC; e.g., SEs are those straight spined GC's with their cross-section and sweeping functions defined by superellipses. If the SEs are bent or tapered, these deformations are applied to the spine and sweeping function respectively.

to recognize negative objects. The latter class of difficulties includes certain numerical instabilities and particular types of parameter ambiguity. This section briefly discusses these difficulties.

One of the most difficult problems of any CSG system is the non-orthogonality of the representation. One can generate the same volume by a number of operations on primitive objects. This makes the matching of recovered objects with a database more difficult. Since the underlying objects are symmetric with respect to certain sequences of rotation, these rotations form a equivalence class which can be anticipated by the matching.

When the primitive objects are SEs some of the symmetries are nonintuitive. For example a cube with just slightly rounded corners can be represented as a SE with $\epsilon_1 = .01, \epsilon_2 = .01, a_1 = a_2 = a_3 = 1$ and also (after a rotation of $\frac{\pi}{4}$ around the z-axis) by one with $\epsilon_1 = .01, \epsilon_2 = 1.99, a_1 = a_2\sqrt{2}$, and $a_3 = 1$.** Other nonintuitive symmetries may also exist.

The two basic CSG operations are addition (set union) and subtraction (set difference). Thus if one is interested in recovering models created with boolean operations on superquadrics, one must be able to recognize them from partial boundaries, and also be able to recognize negative superquadrics as the result of a difference operation rather than a partial boundary of some other positive superquadric. Here again, a nonintuitive symmetry of SEs becomes apparent. Consider a small patch of strictly concave data. It can be modeled as a patch of a negative convex object or part of a positive concave (pinched) SE.

As with any CSG system, there are the difficulties of approximately representing objects. Two of the most difficult problems to solve are what level of detail needs to be preserved, and given that level, how does one allocate deviation from the actual object to different pieces of the construction. The importance of this became quite apparent as we attempted to reconstruct a soda-can from the utah range data, [utah-85]. The actual object (the can upside down) may, at one level of detail be modeled as just a cylinder. However, if a better model is desired, one can use a cylinder minus an ellipsoid. Finally more accurate models exist (because the small concave bevel which helps makes the can stable when stacked must also be modeled), e.g. a cylinder minus the ellipsoid plus a small section of a superhyperboloid of one sheet. Thus the level of accuracy chosen for the modeling can greatly effect the resultant model. As with the other problems mentioned in this section, the major impact of this difficulty is not really in the recovery phase, but becomes quite important when one attempts to match a recovered model (or part thereof) against some internal models.

A second, and more difficult problem in approximate modeling using superquadrics is how to measure "error of fit". The intuitive idea is simply to take $\sum_i [1 - f(x_i, y_i, z_i)]^2$ where f is the inside-out function. Unfortunately, this measure is *not* even proportionally related to the distance of the points from the surface. This problem is reminiscent of the problem of defining goodness of fit for conic filters, see [Turner-74], and in the future, these authors will be attempting to apply results from that work to the recovery of SEs. The problem of measuring error is exasperated as one attempts to apportion the error to individual data points, especially if there is any nonuniformity in data densities.

By examining the inside-out functions which define superquadrics[tt], one might expect to find problems of numerical instability because of the exponents ϵ_1 and ϵ_2. While these researchers have encountered some problem (most notably effects of roundoff errors and floating point overflows) when $\epsilon_1 \ll 1$ for reasonable values (say $> .1$), the instabilities encountered have not been insurmountable.

A final problem with the use of superquadrics as a modeling primitive is that they are often not well defined by a single view. This is especially a problem for the size parameters. An example of this is flat objects, for which information on a single face does not determine the objects size or rotation in the plane of the face. If the object is large enough one can incorporate multiple views (see the discussion below). However, if the flat object is just a patch of a negative object (e.g. the result of an intersection of a negative cube with another SE), one cannot get another view and recovery is difficult if not impossible without additional constraints. There are numerous ad hoc assumptions one can add to alleviate this problem, e.g., both [Bajcsy-Solina-87b] and [Pentland-86a] consider finding only the superquadric with the smallest volume. While this is rather ad hoc reasoning, the results are surprisingly good, see figure 10. This reformulation can also be rationalized because it makes the inside-out function a better approximation of the true distance of a point to the SE. Consider the square of the distance of a point $(r + k, r + k, r + k)$ from a sphere of radius r. The true distance is $3k^2$. At that point, the inside-out function has the value

---

**There are at least two ways to represent any SE which has $\epsilon_2 \neq 1$, which follows from the fact that except for rotation and scaling, an SE with $\epsilon_1 = \delta, \epsilon_2 = \gamma$ is equivalent to one with $\epsilon_1 = \delta, \epsilon_2 = 2 - \gamma$.

[tt] See [Barr-81] for those inside-out functions not presented here.

$3\frac{(k)^2}{r^2}$ which can (depending on r) be a gross underestimate of the distance for large objects. If only one view is available, the "error of fit" will decrease as the size of the object increases in the direction opposite the viewing direction. However, the distance of the surface to the data points may actually increase. Introducing the volume term into the inside-out function results in the value of $3r(k)^2$ which a overestimates the actual distance, but is still a better approximation than the standard inside-out function.

Our Current System

This section presents some of the details of our current system for the recovery of superquadrics from 3-D information. The basis of our system is the use of the inside-out function, see equation 1. Similar equations and constraints can be derived using the inside-out function of any of the superquadrics. Note that one of the advantages of minimizing the inside-out function is that it requires little extra effort to incorporate multiple views, assuming one knows the sensor position for each view (to convert points to a common coordinate system).

Given 3-D information about a SE in canonical position, one can use a nonlinear minimization technique to recover the 5 parameters needed to define it. Our system uses a Gauss-Newton iterative nonlinear least square minimization technique.[‡‡] That is, the system minimizes $\sum(1 - f(x,y,z))^2$ where the summation is over all known information points.

If the SE is not in canonical position, the system must also recover estimates of the translation and rotation necessary to put the information on the surface of a canonical SE. There are obviously many approaches to deal with the translation and rotation, the two most obvious are the use of a pair of transforms (one for translation and one for rotation) and the use of a homogeneous transform that combines both translation and rotation. Our system uses the first approach.

For the remainder of this section let $C_\theta = \cos\theta$ and $S_\theta = \sin\theta$. Thus given a canonical SE surface defined as $\vec{s} = \vec{s}(\eta,\omega)$ with an inside-out function $f = f(x,y,z)$, the translated and rotated SE solid $\vec{s}\,'$ is given by

$$\vec{s}\,' = R_\theta R_\eta R_\psi \vec{s} + \begin{bmatrix} t_x \\ t_y \\ t_z \end{bmatrix},$$

where θ, ψ, ϕ are the Euler angles expressing the rotation about the x, y, z axes respectively, $R_\theta R_\eta R_\psi$ are the rotation matrices about the x, y, z axes respectively and t_x, t_y, t_z are the translation in the $x, y,$ and z directions respectively.

Given the data for a general SE the system minimizes $\sum(1 - f'(x,y,z))^2$ where the summation is over all know information points[***], and where $f'(x,y,z) = f(x',y',z')$ and

$$\begin{bmatrix} x' \\ y' \\ z' \end{bmatrix} = \begin{bmatrix} C_\eta \cdot C_\psi & S_\theta \cdot S_\eta \cdot C_\psi - C_\theta \cdot S_\psi & C_\theta \cdot S_\eta \cdot C_\psi + S_\eta \cdot S_\psi \\ C_\eta \cdot S_\psi & S_\theta \cdot S_\eta \cdot S_\psi + C_\theta \cdot C_\psi & S_\theta \cdot S_\eta \cdot C_\psi - S_\theta \cdot S_\psi \\ -S_\eta & S_\theta \cdot C_\eta & C_\theta \cdot C_\eta \end{bmatrix} \begin{bmatrix} x - t_x \\ y - t_y \\ z - t_z \end{bmatrix}.$$

To employ the Gauss-Newton iteration, the system must compute the Jacobian of the transformation, and thus also needs the partial derivatives of $f'(x,y,z)$ with respect to the 11 parameters, (5 shape, 3 rotation and 3 translation), which were obtained symbolically.

The addition of bending is easily implemented as a simple angle preserving transform on a given axis before rotation and translation. Tapering is simply a linear scaling of the solid along some axis before the application of bending, translation or rotation. Thus in recovery, these transforms are applied first.

The initial implementation of the system recovered only the 5 shape parameters. Using synthetic data with up to 10% uniformly distributed noise, the system could start the minimization procedure from a canonical position (all 5 parameters $= 1$) and in most cases was still able to recover the underlying surface within the error of the data. Moreover, the convergence was generally quick, requiring < 15 iterations.

[‡‡] While it is often argued that the error in depth measurements is gaussian distributed in a direction parallel to the line of measurement, e.g., see [Bolle-Cooper-86], one cannot assume that the direction of measurement is constant for all data points. Thus in our system the use of least squares is an ad hoc assumption rather than an attempt to minimize the error of reconstruction with respect to noise in the data.

[***] One example presented introduced an extra factor of $a_1 a_2 a_3$ to make the inside-out function a better approximation to the true distance.

Next the system was extended to deal with translations in addition to the 5 shape parameters. Again the system was generally robust with respect to recovery of the underlying surface. The authors believe that this robustness is partially due to the fact that many of the symmetries which cause the general SEs to be nonorthogonal, require some amount of rotation.

When the system was extended to handle 11 parameters, things became more complicated. For most of the examples presented, even when presented with very poor estimates for starting values, the system was quickly able to find an SE that had low error. Unfortunately, the solutions proposed by the system often seemed to be nonintuitive. However, when examined closely, these solutions proved themselves to be reasonable interpretations of the data. For example, when presented with the range data (from the Utah range database, [utah-85]) for a coke can minus the concave portion of the bottom end, the system initially proposed a solution with error = .0078; the parameters were $\epsilon_1 = 2.0, \epsilon_2 = .88, a_1 = 1, a_2 = 1.3, a_3 = 19.59, t_x = -.19, t_y = -1.69$, and $t_z = -.834$.[*] These parameters describe an object that is beveled along its long axis, and rather round in the other direction. The length of the object is entirely incorrect but then it is being intersected with a negative ellipsoid, and the bottom is cut by a ground plane. When examined closely, the proposed object (when intersected with the other objects known to be in the scene) does seem to be a reasonable fit to the data, but still a cylinder seems intuitively to be a better fit. If forced to look for a cylindrical object, the system finds an SE with error .17.[†]

To help the system avoid local minima, Poisson noise was added to the residual[‡] The system also derived estimated bounds on the possible values for each parameter. These estimates were derived from knowledge of "sensor" and the data values. If during the minimization, any parameter attempts to stray beyond its allowed boundary, the system stochastically pushed it back toward its initial value.

Currently, the system obtaines initial estimates of the translation parameters from the centroids of the original data and derives bounds from sensor information and overall data (maximum variation in any data). However there are many problems with these estimates especially if the number of data points is small or if the system is only given a partial view of an object. These estimates are are obviously much better if multiple views of the object are available. The estimates also assume that the data is segmented, an assumption with which the authors feel particularly uncomfortable.

The system derives estimates of rotation angles and length scales from moments of inertia and bounds on the length parameters from sensor information and overall data. Because the moments of inertia require second order moments the estimates are plagued with more difficulties than the estimates of the translation parameters. The estimates of the both rotation and length scales are very poor if an object (after segmentation) is the result of boolean combinations.

A Few Examples from Our Current System

The first example in figure 3, is a synthetic SE with noisy synthetic data from multiple views. The actual parameters of the superquadric are $\epsilon_1 = 1.59, \epsilon_2 = .39, a_1 = 1, a_2 = 2, a_3 = 3, t_x = 1.5, t_y = 2.5, t_z = 3.5, \theta = .1, \eta = .1, \psi = .1$. The noise in the underlying object was uniformly distributed over the interval $[-.15, +.15]$ and then added to the z (depth) value of a point. The 1000 data points were randomly distributed on the surface before noise was added. The system recovered an SE with parameters $\epsilon_1 = 1.8, \epsilon_2 = .3, a_1 = 1, a_2 = 2, a_3 = 3.58, t_x = 1.49, t_y = 2.5, t_z = 3.47, \theta = .079, \eta = .09, \psi = .101$. The error of the reconstruction was .079. The system required 7 iterations from the initial values to find the solution.

Figure 4, is the recovery of the same synthetic SE as in example 1. However, this time this system was given 1000 data points from one view of the object. Under these condition the recovered parameters were: $\epsilon_1 = 2.09, \epsilon_2 = .67, a_1 = 1, a_2 = 1.94, a_3 = 3.36, t_x = 1.43, t_y = 2.53, t_z = 4.3, \theta = .075, \eta = .07, \psi = .08$. The error of the reconstruction was .169. Obviously the reconstruction from multiple views is superior.

Figure 5 shows the system recovering 5 parameters (i.e. an SE without translation or rotation) using only one view, and very sparse data. In figure 5 one can see the initial data (small dots) and recovered

---

[*] The error for all examples is defined to be the residual value $(\frac{1}{n} \sum_{i=1}^{i=n} [1 - f(x_i, y_i, z_i)]^2)^{.5}$ where f is the inside-out function of the superquadric. Note that this is not the same as the least square distance to the surface.

[†] This problem can be alleviated by multiplying by $a_1 a_2 a_3$ in the minimization, in which case the system converges to a reasonable cylinder. Oddly enough, the system converged to a can more readily if data from the negative ellipsoid was not removed.

[‡] This was suggested by A. Pentland.

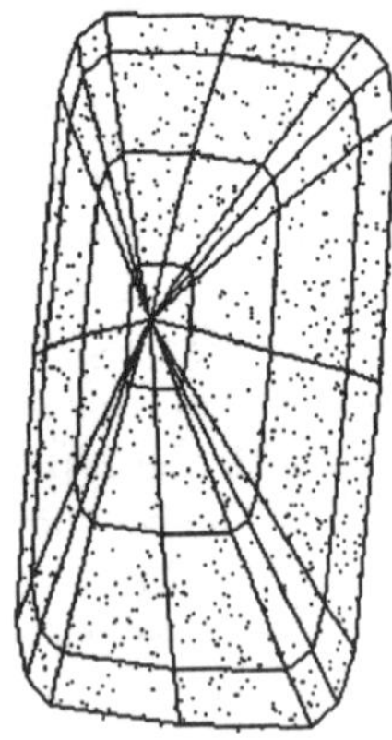

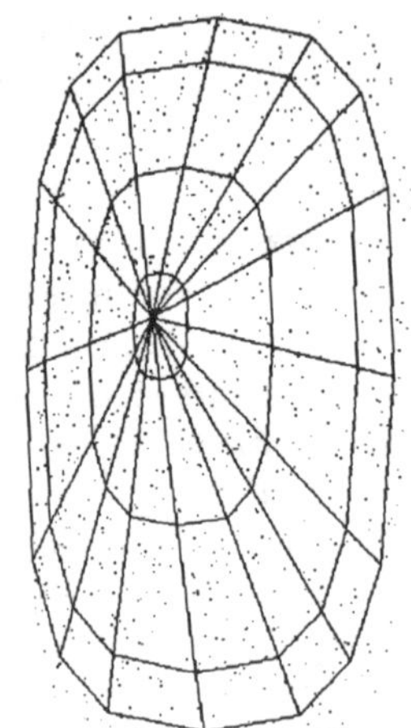

Figure 3: Example recovering 11 parameters using noisy synthetic data from multiple views

Figure 4: Example recovering 11 parameters using noisy synthetic data from single view

SE. The parameters of the initial data were: $\epsilon_1 = 1.234, \epsilon_2 = .2345, a_1 = 1.2, a_2 = 2.3, a_3 = 3.4$. The system was given only 32 data points which had uniform error in the range [-.17,+.17], and was able to reconstruct a SE with parameters $\epsilon_1 = 1.317, \epsilon_2 = .2745, a_1 = 1.222, a_2 = 2.333, a_3 = 3.53$ and an error of .178.

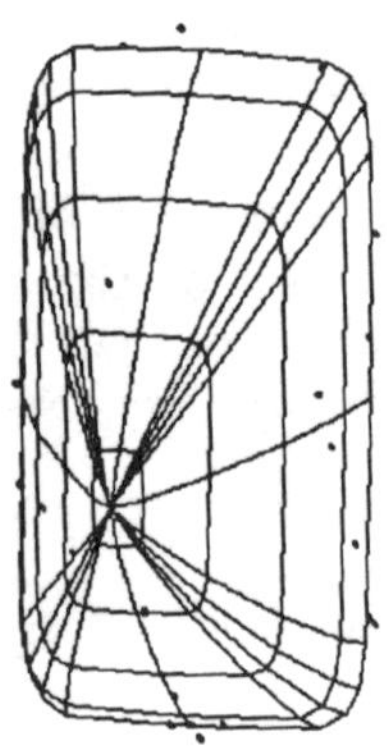

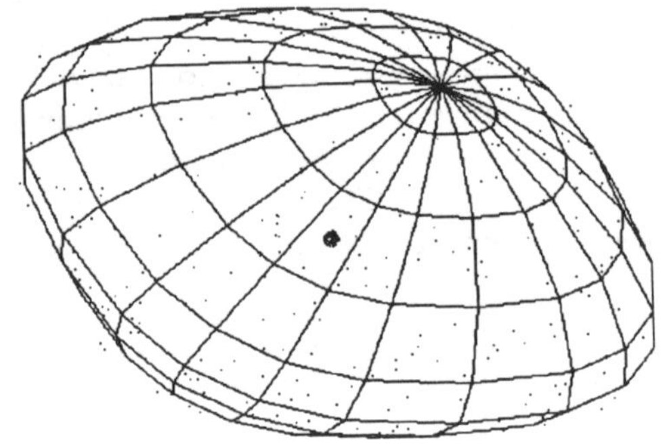

Figure 5: Recovery of 5 parameters from 32 noisy points

Figure 6: Synthetic example recovering 8 parameters with no initial estimates. Small dark circle is initial approximation.

As an example of the robustness of the algorithm, figure 6 shows an example of the system recovering 8 parameters using multiple views of synthetic data. Moreover, the system makes absolutely no calculated starting approximation to the parameters (i.e. starts the minimization with inital values that are independent of data). The figure shows the inital data (cloud of dots) computed solution (line figure) and the initial estimate (the small dark line figure). The actual parameters were: $\epsilon_1 = 1.39, \epsilon_2 = .795, a_1 = 50, a_2 = 35, a_3 = 25, t_x = 3, t_y = 2, t_z = 1, \theta = .9, \eta = .6, \psi = .6$. and the recovered parameters were $\epsilon_1 = 1.387, \epsilon_2 = .773, a_1 = 50.5, a_2 = 35, a_3 = 27.5, t_x = 3.011, t_y = 1.98, t_z = 1, \theta = .9, \eta = .6, \psi = .6$. One component of the initial data ($x, y,$ or z with equal likelihood) was perturbed by a random amount in the range [-2.5,2.5]. This noise was meant to simulate error in depth from multiple views.

The final three examples presented, show the fitting of actual range data from the Utah range database.

Figure 7 shows the elliptical indentation on the bottom of a soda can. The object which is defined by 590 data points. The system recovered the parameters $\epsilon_1 = 1.29, \epsilon_2 = .955, a_1 = .939, a_2 = .930, a_3 =$

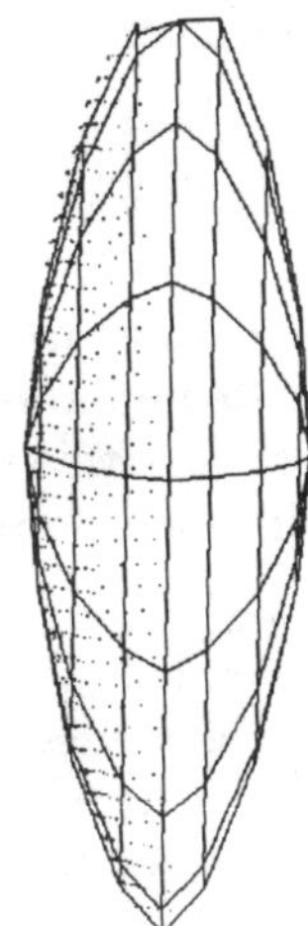

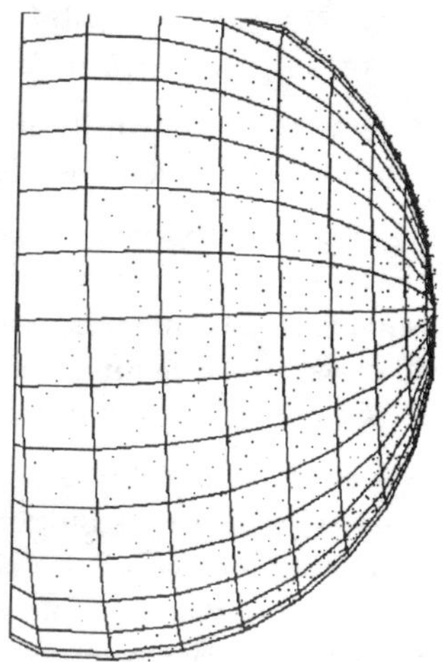

Figure 7: Reconstruction of a negative ellipsoid from real range data

Figure 8: Reconstructed sphere from actual range data

$.277, t_x = -.096, t_y = -1.55, t_z = 2.07, \theta = -.05, \eta = 0, \psi = 0.$ and the error was $.0293$.

Figure 8 shows a quasi-spherical object which is defined by 859 data points. The system recovered the parameters $\epsilon_1 = .994, \epsilon_2 = .951, a_1 = 1.19, a_2 = 1.13, a_3 = 1.13, t_x = .4729, t_y = 1.437, t_z = -1.457, \theta = -.05, \eta = -.04, \psi = 0$ and the error was $.021$.

Figure 9 shows the cylindrical portion of a soda can defined by 1645 data points. When using the above described estimations techniques, the system recovered the parameters $\epsilon_1 = 2.0, \epsilon_2 = .88, a_1 = 1, a_2 = 1.3, a_3 = 19.59, t_x = -.19, t_y = -1.69, t_z = -.834, \theta = -.04, \eta = .05, \psi = 0.0.$ and the error was $.0079$. When the inside-out function was modified to include an extra multiplicative factor of $a_1 a_2 a_3$, the result was the object in figure 10. Unfortunately, the residual errors cannot be compared.

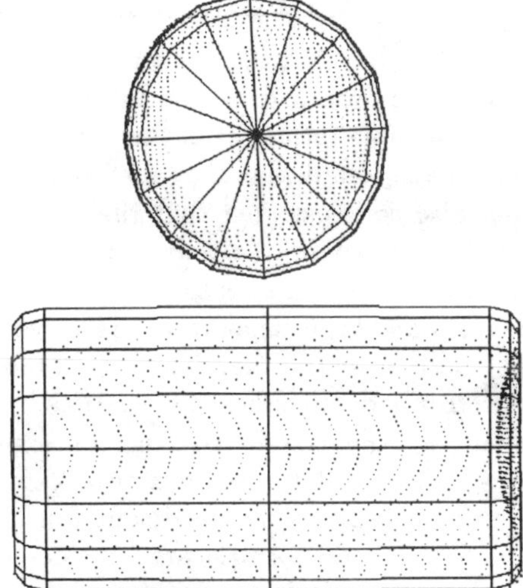

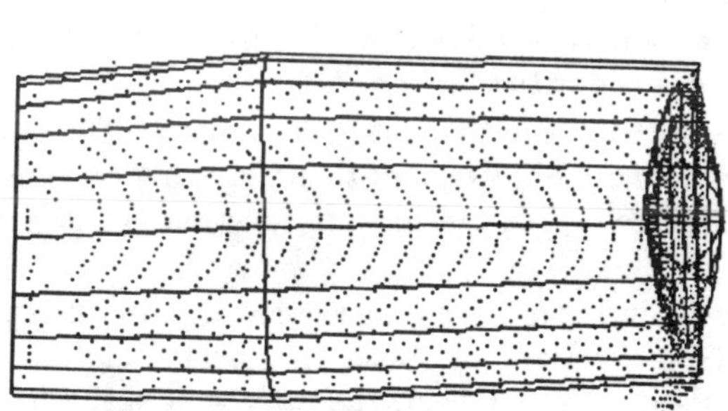

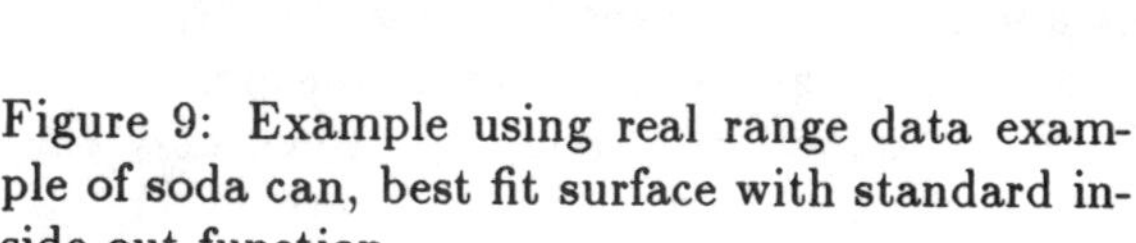

Figure 9: Example using real range data example of soda can, best fit surface with standard inside-out function.

Figure 10: Example using real range data example of soda can, best fit with inside-out function multiplied by $a_1 a_2 a_3$.

Advantages and Drawbacks of Our Approach

The approach has a number of advantages. This section presents them and discusses them with respect to the two other systems for recovery of SEs known to these authors. The other systems are described in [Pentland-86a], [Bajcsy-Solina-87a], and [Bajcsy-Solina-87b]. The advantages of our approach are:

+ The system has demonstrated the ability to recover negative superquadrics. This is particularly important if we wish to use SEs combined with boolean operations.

+ The system has shown itself to be quite robust, even for small data sets, if given good estimates of rotation and reasonable bounds on translation and size parameters.

± The system demonstrated (using synthetic data) that multiple views (i.e. data on more than one side of the SE) result in much better reconstruction. This turned out be be quite important because it helps remove some ambiguity about the size of the object. (The authors believe this approach is better than assuming minimal volume as in both [Bajcsy-Solina-87b] and [Pentland-86a]. Unfortunately, it is often difficult to obtain multiple views from known positions.)

± The system combines the advantages of a fast nonlinear estimation technique (Gauss-Newton least square) with a Poisson randomness to avoid local minima and the use of stochastic resets if parameters stray beyond their estimated bounds. If the bounds are correct, this helps the system to avoid some local minima. Unfortunately, if the bounds are incorrect, we have condemned the system to search in a space where no solution can exist.

- The system is based on the minimization of the inside-out function. Unfortunately, this function is not simply related to distance of a point to the surface. This leads to minima that are nonintuitive.

- If there are many more points on one portion of the surface than another, this surface will dominate the search because, as far as least squares minimization is concerned, the small number of points on other sides are "noise". This is partially alleviated by using multiple views of an object (assuming we can). Even then we may overly constrain the "top" as compared to the sides. (We share this problem with [Bajcsy-Solina-87b].)

- Currently, if the estimates of the parameters are poor, the system may converge to a point far from the true minima. This can be greatly alleviated by using data from multiple views which makes the estimates significantly more accurate.

Conclusions and Future Direction

This paper has shown that there is some promise in the use of a least square minimization of the inside-out function as an approach to recovering superquadrics from depth data, but the system is currently dependent on reasonable estimates of the moments of the object. Thus, our research investigated the use of multiple views and found that they greatly increase the reliability of the system.

This paper also demonstrated that the system can recognize negative superquadrics, an important consideration if we are going to attempt to segment scenes made with CSG operations.

In the near future, there are a number of extensions the authors plan to make to the system. The first is to include bending and tapering parameters so we can model more objects, and then begin experimenting with possible changes to the function to be minimized (currently the inside-out function) to give the system better error and convergence properties.

Future plans for the system also include extensions to incorporate surface derivative information. This will be accomplished by minimizing a sum with (some variant of) both the inside-out function and a differentiated form of the inside-out function. This is different from the approach suggested in [Bajcsy-Solina-87a] where normals are considered. Our approach has advantages over directly using surface normals because it is applicable when only one derivative can be accurately measured and if normals are available, they provide two pieces of derivative information. Conditions when only one derivative can be accurately measured arise on occluding contours of nearly "square" corners. While theoretically one knows the actual normal at the occluding contour, small errors in the measurement of the location of the contour can greatly affect the normal.

Of course one of the most important avenues for future research will be attacking the segmentation problem, our current plans are to attempt at least two approaches: pure growing of superquadrics from small data patches, and a skeletonization (to find axis) followed by both growing and splitting of superquadric solids.

Acknowledgements

This work was supported in part by Darpa Contract N00039-84-C-0165. The authors are grateful to Alex Pentland, Frank Solina and R. Bajcsy.

References

[Bajcsy-Solina-87a] R. Bajcsy and F. Solina. *Three dimensional object representation revisted.* Technical Report MS-CIS-87-19, GRASP LAB 99, University of Pennsylvania, March 1987.

[Bajcsy-Solina-87b] R. Bajcsy and F. Solina. Three dimensional object representation revisted. In *Proceedings of the IEEE Computer Society International Conference on Computer Vision*, pages 231–240, IEEE, June 1987.

[Barr-81] A. H. Barr. Superquadrics and angle preserving transformations. *IEEE Computer Graphics and Applications*, 1:11–23, January 1981.

[Bolle-Cooper-86] Rueud M. Bolle and D.B. Cooper. On optimally combining peices of information, with application to estimating 3-d complex-object position from range data. *PAMI*, ():, September 1986.

[Brooks-85] R.A. Brooks. Model based 3-d interpretation of 2-d images. In A. Pentland, editor, *From Pixels to Predicated*, Ablex Publishing Co., Norwood, N.J., 1985.

[Brooks-Binford-80] R.A. Brooks and T. O. Binford. Representing and reasoning about specific scenes. In *Proceedings of the DARPA Image Understanding Workshop*, pages 95–103, DARPA, April 1980.

[Gardiner-65] M. Gardiner. The superellipse: a curve that lies between the ellipse and the rectangle. *Scientific American*, September 1965.

[Pentland-86a] A. Pentland. *Recognition by Parts.* Technical Report 406, SRI International, December 1986.

[Pentland-86b] A. Pentland. Twoards an ideal 3-d cas system. In *Proceedings of the SPIE Conference on Machine Vision and the Man-Machine Interface*, SPIE, Janurary 1986. Order # 758-20.

[Rao-Nevatia-86] K. Rao and R. Nevatia. Generalized cone descriptions from sparse 3-d data. In *Proceedings of the IEEE Computer Society Conference on Computer Vision and Pattern Recognition*, pages 256–263, IEEE, 1986.

[Turner-74] K.J. Turner. *Computer perception of curved objects using a televesion camera.* PhD thesis, University of Edinburgh, 1974.

[utah-85] utah. *The University of Utah range database manual.* Technical Report , University of Utah, 1985.

3-D SCENE ANALYSIS
VIA FUSION OF LIGHT STRIPED IMAGE AND INTENSITY IMAGE †

Gongzhu Hu and George Stockman

Department of Computer Science
Michigan State University
E. Lansing, MI. 48824

ABSTRACT

A fusion scheme that uses both 3-D data and intensity information and generates a 2½D sketch-like representation is presented. 3-D surface data are collected from light striping and used for determining locations and rough shapes of objects. An intensity image of the same scene provides gradient (edges), contours, and shading information. The information obtained from the two sources complements each other to produce a more reliable scene representation. To study the intergration of the two channels of information and the relations between patches and contours, a set of inference rules and production system control is currently being used.

† This work was supported by the National Science Foundation under grant DCR-8600371

I. *INTRODUCTION*

Human visual perception is a multi-channel process. Visual information from many sources is processed in various neuro mechanisms, travels through different visual pathways, activates various visual functions, and then merges at the central cortex in a very sophisticated manner to produce a perceptual experience [1,2]. The sources may, for example, be intensity, texture, color, etc. for *form (shape)* perception; or binocular disparity, optical flow, gradient, etc. for *depth (spatial)* perception. The multi-channel processing in the human visual system suggests fusion of information from multiple channels in machine vision; for example, fusion of intensity and depth.

A fusion scheme that employs both 3-D surface data and a gray-scale image is presented, in which 3-D data are developed through structured lighting. 3-D surface data are important for object recognition, particularly for inferring object shapes and locations. Many 3-D sensing techniques have been successfully developed for that purpose [3]. A laser range finder is one device that can create a dense range image. Because this direct 3-D sensing method requires special laser equipment and processing of the range image itself is still complicated, some other 3-D sensing approaches have also been widely used in practice. Structured lighting is one of the approaches that we use, where the scene is illuminated with light that has a regular grid pattern.

In addition to providing 3-D surface data, structured lighting also provides rich information such as stripe texture that can be used to construct rough surface shapes. But, a critical weakness of this method is that we will not get any information at all from non-stripe areas. Some missing information can be obtained from a gray-scale image of the same scene. Information from the two channels is combined to generate an object representation that will be suitable for recognition (model matching, say).

Object representation consists of the following elements :

1. **surfaces**

    (a)   qualitative — type (planar, convex, concave, cylindrical, etc.),

    (b)   quantitative — boundary, 3-D location, orientation;

2. **edges**

    (a)   qualitative — type (extremum, blade, fold, mark, shadow),

    (b)   quantitative — location, length (in chain-code form);

3. **surface-surface relationships**

    (a)   occlusion,

    (b)   adjacency,

    (c)   belonging to same or different objects;

4. **surface-edge relationships**

    (a)   surface boundaries,

    (b)   surface marks,

    (c)   shadow edges,

    (d)   intersection (common border) of two surfaces.

In the representation, 1 and 3(a) are obtained from light striping; 2(b) is from the intensity image; other elements result from fusion of the two sources.

II. *INFORMATION FROM LIGHT STRIPING*

A standard slide projector projects a grid pattern onto the scene and produces light stripes on the object surfaces. The striped image taken by the camera is thresholded to generate a binary image in which pixels on bright stripes are one and other pixels are zero. 2-D processing on the binary image picks stripe intersection points and stripe end-points, which are the ones for which 3-D data will be computed. 3-D computation is carried out through triangulation; if stripes can be uniquely identified there will be a single 3-D point computed; otherwise each point will be associated with a set of possible 3-D solutions. To solve the "stripe identification" problem, a set of general constraints (both geometric and topological) is applied and propagated within and between stripe networks to filter out those 3-D solutions that fail the test. The 3-D solutions surviving the constraints are the results. The boundaries of each surface patch is computed from the 2-D stripe networks which give the initial segmentation possibilities. For details, see [4].

After 3-D data are computed at the grid points, a B-spline fitting followed by a curvature computation can be applied to determine surface shapes interior to the stripe networks [5]. Among the desirable curvatures are the two principle curvatures, which are the two eigenvalues of the Weingarten Map of the surface [6]. The corresponding eigenvectors give the two principle directions that are especially useful for determining the pose of cylindrical objects. Gaussian curvature is simply the product of the two principle curvatures. Local surface shape at a point is determined by the sign of the Gaussian curvature at the point. Then global shape is classified through clustering of the Gaussian curvatures at various points on the surface.

Another source for inferring rough surface shapes is 2-D stripe texture that almost always works in the first level shape classification (planar vs. non-planar), and is an appropriate method in distinguishing some regular curved surfaces; for example, spherical and cylindrical. See [7].

III. *LIGHT STRIPING vs. INTENSITY*

We have outlined the light striping approach for 3-D sensing. Besides providing locations of surface points in the 3-space, the sensed 3-D data have the following properties.

(1) They are sparse compared to dense data obtained using direct range sensors. Because of the sparseness, computational burden often inevitable in processing dense data is somewhat released.

(2) They are good representatives of the dense 3-D population, because they cover the major part of visible surface due to the way the feature points are created. The spatial relationships between the 3-D points are well defined in terms of the stripes that connect these points. Hence, a good surface fitting may be constructed based on these representative 3-D points.

(3) They are ambiguous in the sense that a surface patch may be at one of several locations in 3-space. But as far as surface shape is concerned, each of the several surface locations is equally workable. We can use any of them in inferring surface shape.

(4) They are only in the areas visible to both the projector (hence there are stripes) and the camera (hence stripes appear in image). For areas where no stripe appears, no information can be obtained.

Besides the weakness stated in (4) above, we have other problems in using structured lighting. On a smooth surface, the stripes would gradually fade out as the surface turns away from the projector. A stripe extraction procedure (brightness thresholding, say) will fail to pick up the fading tails of the stripes; but the tails, especially the end points of the tails, are indeed very important features for 3-D analysis. For the same reason that brightness of stripe pixels varies as the surface orientation varies from point to point, global brightness thresholding may result in broken stripes and fragmented stripe networks, which will introduce difficulties in later processing steps. There seems no way to get around these problems using only light striping and we ought to resort to other sources for the missing information. Fortunately, an intensity image of the same scene viewed at the same position and in the same direction is easily obtained by simply switching off the projector and switching on a light. From the intensity image, we can extract edges and contours, shading information, and textures, that complement what was missing in its striped counterpart. Since the two images are in registration, we will often talk about their overlay as if it was a single image.

The fusion idea is better illustrated by examples. In the right column of Figure 1, the gray-scale image of a block and its striped image are shown in (a) and (b), respectively. (c) is the result of a gradient operation on the gray-scale image followed by contour tracing and clean-up. The overlay of the contour map and striped regions is in (d). From the striped image alone, we can compute 3-D positions of the grid points, determine the rough surface shapes (planar in this case), and segment the image according to the stripe networks (two segments in the example). But it provides no information in the areas where light stripes are occluded, and no clues about whether the two surfaces belong to the same object. On the other hand, the gray-scale image may not catch discontinuities of surface normal (the concave edge is missing, for instance), and may have difficulties in segmenting surfaces. But it offers fine boundaries. In the example, the contour map suggests that the two striped surfaces belong to the same object because of well-connected outer boundaries. Also, the clear edge of the triangular-shaped surface is useful in breaking down the larger striped region into two sub-regions, which will be confirmed by the bending of the stripes. In the next section, we will find that this particular edge is a *fold*, and the two sub-regions are two surfaces meeting at the fold.

A second example of multiple objects (7 potatoes) is shown in the left column of Figure 1. Notice that the striped regions do not exactly agree with the contours, due to the continuous change of surface normal and stripe fading, but they provide a good preliminary segmentation, which is difficult to get from the intensities alone. A more accurate segmentation can be obtained by extending the striped regions with the gradient contours as boundary conditions.

Table 1 gives a comparison of the two information channels. A combination of the two channels will certainly facilitate the strengths of each and overcome some weaknesses.

Table 1. Comparison of two information channels

	Striped Image	Intensity Image
Information	gross surface shape, location, boundaries and segmentation; detect folds (crease edges) in surfaces and some blades & extrema	local surface albedo and orientation (under controlled illumination); little shadowing; fine boundaries and textures; can see into some of surfaces in shadow of projected light
Factored Out	albedo; fine texture	no direct 3-D info (no knowledge of projector)
Problems	shadows; occasional accidents; some ambiguity in 3-D solution; can miss illumination albedo discontinuities	segmentation into objects; difficult to get gross shape; can miss discontinuities of surface normal (folds)

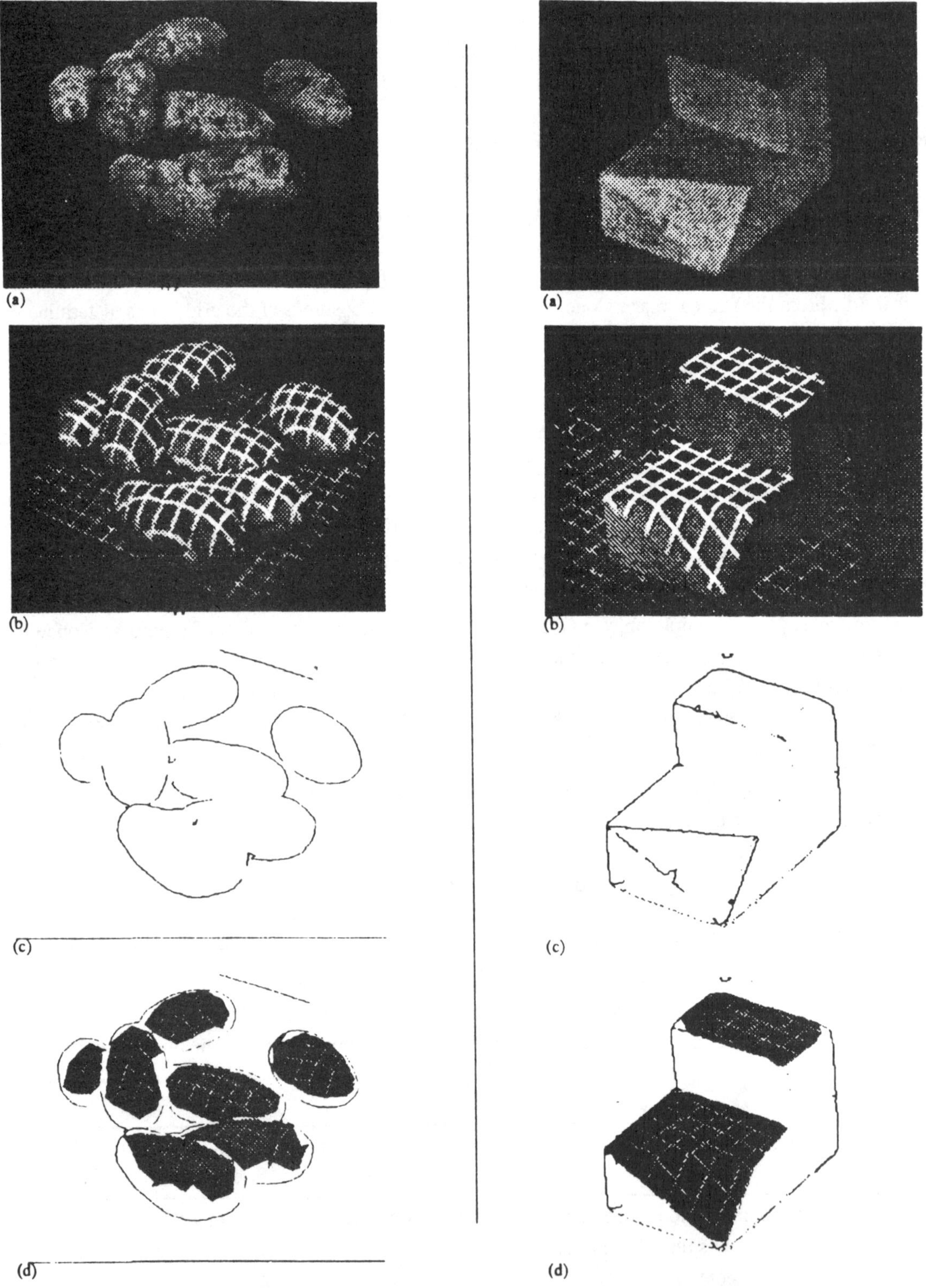

Figure 1.   (a) intensity images (b) striped images before thresholding (c) edge maps, and (d) overlay of edge map and striped regions

IV. *INFERENCE RULES FOR FUSION*

We have discussed the strengths and weaknesses of each of the two information channels. To fuse the two, we establish a set of inference rules that interprets the image contours and surface shapes at the vicinity of the contours.

There are five types of image contours as suggested in [8]:

extremum self-occlusion by a curved object, surface gradually turning away from the viewer, surface orientation perpendicular to the viewing direction at the contour.

blade two surfaces meet, just one visible; surface orientation discontinuous in 3-D and probably in 2½D across the contour.

fold two surfaces meet, both visible; surface orientation discontinuous.

shadow an abrupt change in illumination.

mark an abrupt change in reflectance.

For smooth surfaces, the surface shape at an occluding contour (extremum) can be determined by the "apparent" curvature, K_{app}, of the contour, which has the same deterministic characteristics as the intrinsic Gaussian curvature according to [9]. That is, convexities of the contour correspond to convex surface patches ($K_{app} > 0$), concavities to saddle-shaped surface patches ($K_{app} < 0$), inflections of contour ($K_{app} = 0$) to inflections of the surface. There are no exceptions to this rule.

The above apparent curvature theory is valid under the *smoothness* assumption. That is, for rigid objects the tangent plane must be defined for every point of the surface and moreover be a smooth function of position. In other words, the theory works only on one type of image contour — the *extremum*. There are contours of other types, e.g. *blades, folds, shadows*, and *marks*. For these contours, the apparent curvature theory does not apply. For example, Figure 2 shows the edges of a sculptured object, an orange and a block. If we know the circular contour at the left of the image is the boundary of a spherical object as it really is, we can label it convex according to the apparent curvature theory. But if the circular contour were a boundary of a disk, the surface at this boundary won't be convex any more; instead, it is a planar surface with a *blade* contour. To distinguish *extrema* from *blades*, we may use the shape from shading idea [10] that the intensity received is a function of the angle between the surface normal and the incident direction of the light source, if surfaces are Lambertion. Surface normal can be computed at every point of the surface using intensity information. But the shape from shading method requires very carefully set illumination and uniform surface characteristics (Lambertion, say). It may not be easily guaranteed in many cases. An alternative and easier way to decide the type of an image contour is via light stripes.

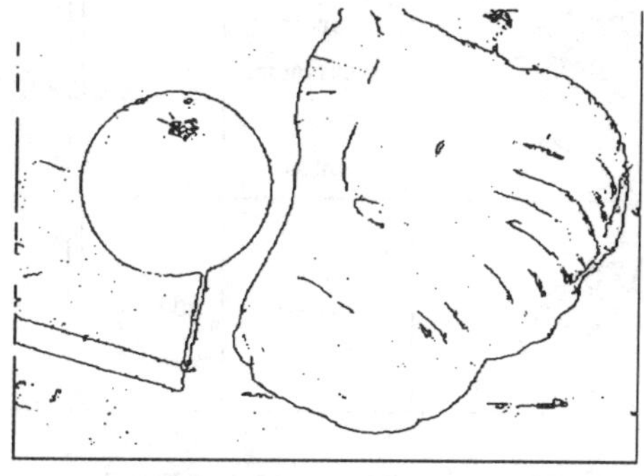

Figure 2. Edges of an orange, a sculpture and a block

As stated in section II, stripe networks and stripe texture, provide 3-D solutions for grid points, surface normals at these grid points, and rough surface shapes as well. Based on the computed rough shapes, we establish the following inference rules in interpreting contours under the *general position* assumption. The first rule is to determine if a contour is a *shadow* or not, while the remaining inference rules can be divided into two groups depending on whether there are striped regions on both sides of the contour or on only one side. See Figures 3 and 4 for examples where the rules are triggered.

example figure	stripe network	contour	surface type at contour	contour label
2a (knife) 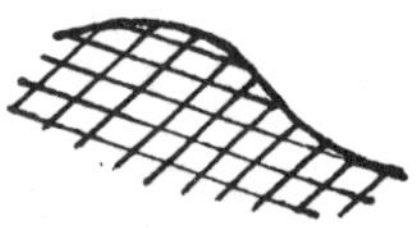	planar	all kinds	planar	blade
2b (step) 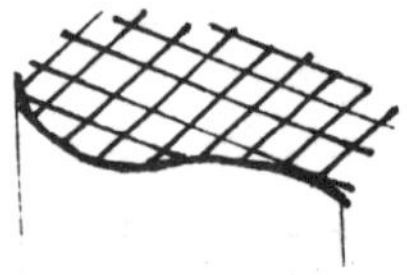	planar	all kinds	planar	fold
3 (can) 	convex	straight	cylindrical	extremum
4a (ball) 	convex, large change of normal	convex	convex	extremum
4b (can) 	convex, small change of normal	convex	convex	blade
5a (donut) 	convex, curvature towards contour	concave	saddle	extremum
5b (can) 	convex, no curvature towards contour	concave	convex	fold
6 (bowl) 	concave	all kinds	concave	blade or fold

Figure 3. Group-1 inference rules

example figure	stripe network	contour	surface type at contour	contour label
7 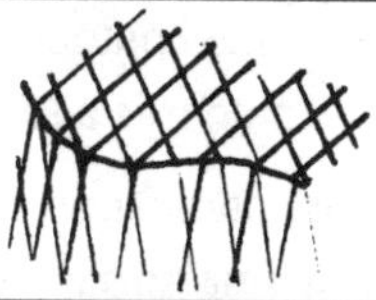	stripe continuous, normal change	all kinds	corner	fold
8a 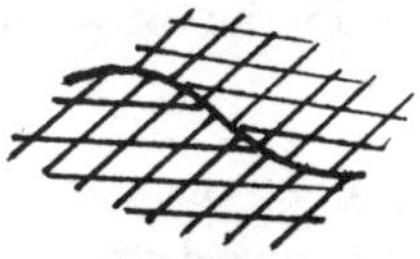	planar occluding	all kinds	planar	blade
8b 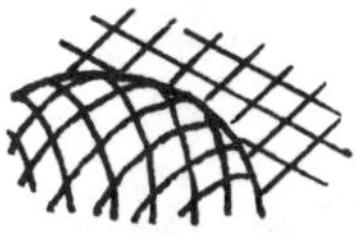	convex occluding	convex	convex	extremum
8c 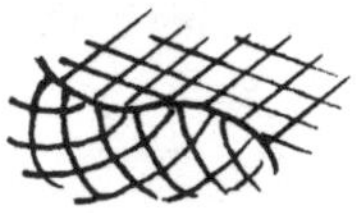	concave occluding	all kinds	concave	blade
9 	stripe continuous, normal same	all kinds	any kind	surface mark

Figure 4. Group-2 inference rules

(1) *Shadowing rule*: A contour is *shadow* if there is an object boundary that created the shadow in 3-space. This can be determined using the computed 3-D information from two stripe networks. A *shadow* excludes other labels being assigned to the contour.

   Group 1. Rules in this group apply to cases where only one side of a contour is a striped region. A contour is said to be convex if every chord drawn on it lies within the striped region.

(2) If a contour bordering a planar surface (indicated by straight stripes) represents a *fold* if there is evidence indicating an unstriped surface meeting at the contour, or a *blade* otherwise. This is because on a planar surface, the normal to the surface is a constant. At the contour, the normal has to be discontinuous from the visible striped plane to either the invisible surface of the object (blade case) or to the visible unstriped surface of the object (fold case).

(3) A convex surface patch bounded by a straight contour is *convex cylindrical* at the rim, the contour is an *extremum*.

(4) A convex surface patch bounded by a convex contour is *convex* at the rim, the contour is an *extremum* if there is a significant change of normal in the direction perpendicular to the contour, or a *blade* if the change of normal in that direction is small.

(5) A concave contour bounding a surface containing convex stripes is either a *fold* if an unstriped visible surface meets the contour; otherwise it is an *extremum* and the surface is *saddle-shaped*.

(6) A contour bounding a concave surface patch is a *blade* or a *fold*.

Group 2. Rules in this group apply to contours both sides of which are striped regions.

(7) If two regions meet at a contour, and the stripes continuously cross the contour (stripes are end-to-end connected at the contour) but the normals are discontinuous, then the contour is a *fold*.

(8) If two regions meet at a contour and the stripes are staggered from one region to the other, then one region is occluding the other. The contour is either a *blade* if the occluding surface is planar or concave, or an *extremum* if the occluding surface is convex. The occlusion relationship between the two surfaces may be determined by their computed locations in 3-space.

(9) If the stripes crossing a contour are continuous at the contour, and the changes of surface normal are small, then the contour is a *surface mark*. The two striped regions at the two sides of the contour belong to a same object surface.

V. *IMPLEMENTATION*

The implementation of the inference rules consists of a set of "if ... then" modules, each of which handles a particular group of contours. These modules form an "expert system" that controls the labeling process. The input and output are the following :

input :

    1). contours in some form (chain-code, say),

    2). surface patches, their types and boundaries;

output :

    1). labels associated with each contour (label can change along a single contour),

    2). surface types.

The labeling process is a contour-based procedure. It takes a contour at a time, segments the contour based on its adjacency relationships with the striped regions, and labels each segment of the contour according to the inference rules. The order of applying the rules is significant. For example, the *shadowing* rule (rule 1) is always applied first. Then it checks to what group the contour segment belongs — interior to a striped region, group-1, group-2, or stand-alone contour. In each group the inference rules are then applied in a specified order. As output, each contour segment may have one or more labels associated with it.

Multiple labels can be disambiguated using the knowledge about the spatial relationship between the camera and the projector. For example, if a contour in the image bounds the "upper" part of a planar surface, it indicates a *blade*, rather than ambiguous labels "blade or fold". The term "upper", as well as "lower", "above", "below" etc., are determined by the relationship between the camera coordinate system and the projector coordinate system. In addition a relaxation procedure based on the relationships between the image contours can also be used to sort out some multiple labels.

VI. *DISCUSSION*

An approach was discussed that combines information from structured lighting and intensity, puts labels on image contours, and make inferences about surface shapes. Each of the two channels provides important information; fusion of the two, along with the 3-D surface data, generates a 2½D sketch-like representation, which cannot be easily obtained using only one channel. The representation can be used later in model matching for final object recognition.

The inference rules described in section IV are not applicable to a contour if there is no striped region on either side of it, such as the contour at the lower border of a potato in Figure 1. To interpret these "stand-alone" contours, we need to look more closely into the shading information and some global relationships. There are some other information sources that may be useful, such as a second striped image taken by projecting a grid from a different angle (camera not moved), that may put stripes on the areas that were shadows before.

For future work, the fusion scheme can be related to Huffman-Clowes' line-drawing understanding [11,12], Waltz's relaxation labeling [13] and Kanade's origami world analysis [14] for object understanding. Not only will the fusion process be able to handle *perfect* line drawings, but also it allows imperfect contours (errors). In addition, both surface and edge information (rather than only "line drawings") available from fusion will be very useful in interpreting the scene. For example, for the block in Figure 1 it can be determined that all polygons indicate solid surfaces (solid block rather than open box) using the surface information obtained from light striping and shading information.

References

[1] Sekuler, R. and Blake, R. "Perception", *Alfred A. Knopf, Inc.*, 1985.

[2] Mishkin, M., Ungerleider, L. G. and Macko, K. A. "Object Vision and Spatial Vision : Two Cortical Pathways", *Trends in NeuroSciences*, 1983, 6, 414-417.

[3] Jarvis, R. A. "A Perspective on Range Finding Techniques for Computer Vision", *IEEE PAMI*, Vol. PAM-5, No.2, March 1983, 122-139.

[4] Stockman, G. and Hu, G. "3-D Surface Solution Using A Projected Grid", TR, #MSU-ENGR-85-024, CPS Department, MSU, 1985.

[5] Yang, H. S. and Kak, A. C. "Determinating of the Identity, Position and Orientation of the Topmost Object in a Pile", *CVGIP*, 36, 1986, 229-255.

[6] Millman, R. s. and Parker, G. D. "Elements of Differential Geometry", Prentice-Hall, Inc. 1977.

[7] Hu, G., Jain, A.K. and Stockman, G. "Shape from Light Stripe Texture", *CVPR'86*, Miami Beach, June 22-26, 1986, 412-414.

[8] Charniack, E. and McDermott, D. "Introduction to Artificial Intelligence", Addison-Wesley, 1985

[9] Koenderink, J. J. "What Does The Occluding Contour Tell Us About Solid Shape ?", *Perception*, Vol. 13, 1984, 321-330.

[10] Horn, B. K. "Obtaining Shape from Shading Information", in *The Psychology of Computer Vision* (P. H. Winston ed.), McGraw-Hill, 1985.

[11] Huffman, D. A. "Impossible Objects as Nonsense Sentences", in *Machine Intelligence* 6 (Meltzer, B. and Michie, D. Eds.), Edinburgh University Press, Edinburgh, 1971.

[12] Clowes, M. B. "On Seeing Things", *Artificial Intelligence* 2(1), 1971, 79-116.

[13] Waltz, D. I. "Generating Semantic Description from Drawings of Polyhedral Scenes with Shadows", in *The Psychology of Computer Vision* (Winston, P., Ed.), McGraw-Hill, NY. 1975

[14] Kanade, T. "A Theory of Origami World", *Artificial Intelligence* 13(1), 1980, 279-311.

A Process-Grammar for Representing Shape

MICHAEL LEYTON
Department of Psychology, Busch Campus,
Rutgers University, New Brunswick, NJ 08903

ABSTRACT

The shape of an entity, such as an embryo, tumor, or cloud, is often used infer processes that have acted upon, and determined, the entity. We develop formal inference rules by which the curvature extrema of a shape can be used to infer the precise trajectories of processes that have created the shape. A formal grammar is also elaborated by which, given two views of the same entity at two developmental stages, the scientist can infer the processes that acted in between the two stages.

1. INTRODUCTION.

Scientists in many disciplines, such as astrophysics, developmental biology, medicine, geography, meteorology, etc., use the shape of an entity, such as an embryo, tumor, or cloud, to infer processes that have acted upon the entity. This paper presents a set of inference rules by which the curvature extrema of a shape can be used to infer the significant processes that have determined the shape. A formal grammar is also developed by which a scientist, who has two views of an entity at two developmental stages, can infer the processes that produced the second stage from the first.

2. THE INFERENCE OF HISTORY FROM A SINGLE SHAPE

In this section, two simple inference rules are presented by which the curvature extrema of an *individual* shape can be used to infer significant processes that have acted upon that shape. We will assume, throughout the paper, that the input to the rules are shapes represented in the form of smooth planar outlines. However, in Leyton (1987c), we show that an equivalent analysis is applicable to three-dimensional input.

2.1. FIRST RULE: Curvature Extrema → Symmetry Axes

Central to the development of our process inference rules will be the use of a symmetry analysis. It is important, to observe, however, that, given two segments of a curve, a straight reflectional symmetry axis might only rarely exist. Nevertheless, it may be possible to define symmetry in a *differential* sense. Consider the two bold curves c_1 and c_2, in Fig 1a. Although there is no mirror that reflects one curve onto the other, a mirror along line QO reflects the *tangent line*, at A, onto the *tangent line*, at B.

It turns out that the existence of such a symmetry is equivalent to the existence of a circle that is tangential at both A and B. (The mirror will contain the circle center O.) Now drag the circle along the two curves, while always maintaining the double-touching property. As in Leyton (1987b), one can define a *differential symmetry axis* to be the trajectory of some *mid-point* associated with the circle.

For example: The *Symmetric Axis Transform (SAT)* of Blum (1973) defines the symmetry axis to be the locus of circle-centers O. This will give some curved axis running between the two curves c_1 and c_2. Again, the *Smooth Local Symmetry (SLS)* of Brady (1983) defines the symmetry axis to be the locus of chord midpoints P. (In the present case, this will produce a slightly different axis from the SAT.) Alternatively, we have proposed (in Leyton, 1987c) a new symmetry analysis in which the symmetry axis is the trajectory of the midpoint Q of the arc AB, as the circle moves. As shown in Leyton (1987c), this analysis has remarkably different properties from the other two analyses and these properties make the analysis particularly appropriate for the inference of processes. Because of its appropriateness to process-inference, the new analysis will be called *Process-Inferring Symmetry Analysis (PISA)*. Several examples of the application of PISA will be seen later.

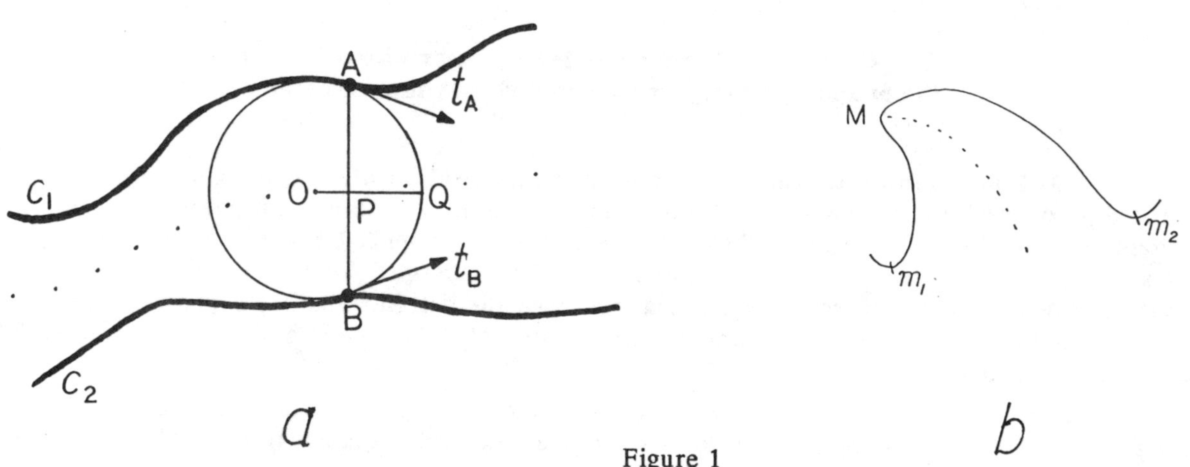

Figure 1

With the concept of a differential symmetry analysis, it becomes possible to state a theorem that is the basis of the entire paper. The theorem, which was proposed and proved in Leyton (1987b), relates the symmetry structure of a smooth planar curve to the curvature extrema.

SYMMETRY-CURVATURE DUALITY THEOREM (Leyton, 1987b): *Any segment of a smooth planar curve, bounded by two consecutive curvature extrema of the same type (either both maxima or both minima) has a unique differential symmetry axis (under SAT, SLS, or PISA) and this axis terminates at the curvature extremum of the opposite type (minimum or maximum, respectively).*

An illustration of the theorem is given in Fig 1b. Consider the two points labeled m^-, in the figure. They are two consecutive extrema of the same type (i.e. they bend in the same direction relative to the curve). The theorem states that, under any of the alternative differential symmetry analyses, there is one and only one symmetry axis. Furthermore, as predicted by the theorem, this axis terminates at the extremum M^+, of the opposite type (this extremum bends in the opposite direction).

We shall regard the theorem as our first inference rule, thus: The rule assigns, to each extremum, a unique symmetry axis that terminates at that extremum.

2.2. SECOND RULE: Symmetry Axes $\rightarrow$ Processes

The importance of symmetry to process-inference is given by the following crucial principle which was proposed and extensively corroborated in Leyton (1984, 1985, 1986a, 1986b, 1986c, 1987a, 1987d), in shape perception as well as motion perception.

INTERACTION PRINCIPLE (Leyton, 1984): *The symmetry axes of a perceptual organization are interpreted as the principal directions along which processes are most likely to act or have acted.*

Besides the extensive empirical data in support of this principle, the principle can be justified using the following three-stage argument: (1) Invariant lines are interpreted as principal directions of action. (2) If a transformation, acting on an organization is one in which symmetry axes become invariant lines (eigenspaces) under the transformation, then the transformation will tend to preserve the symmetries; i.e. be *structure-preserving* on the organization. (3) Transformations that are most structure-preserving tend to be understood as most likely.

The Interaction Principle is our second inference rule: The rule takes a symmetry axis, and interprets it as the record of a process.

2.3. Curvature Extrema $\rightarrow$ Processes

The two inference rules given above, the Symmetry-Curvature Duality Theorem and the Interaction Principle, can be locked together yielding this conclusion:

**Each curvature extremum implies a process whose trace is
the unique symmetry axis associated with that extremum.**

We shall now show that the two inference rules yield highly appropriate process-analyses. Richards, Koenderink & Hoffman (1985) have provided drawings of all possible shapes that have eight extrema or less. In Fig 2, we have taken all these drawings and applied our two inference rules. The lines with arrows represent the process-records inferred by our rules. That is, the lines are the directions of growth, indentation, squashing, etc, along which the deformations are supposed to have happened. Observe that the process-records correspond strongly with one's intuition as to the way the shapes were formed.

For later purposes, we have placed, on each shape in Fig 2, letters denoting the curvature extrema, as follows: M and m denote a local maximum and local minimum respectively, and + and −

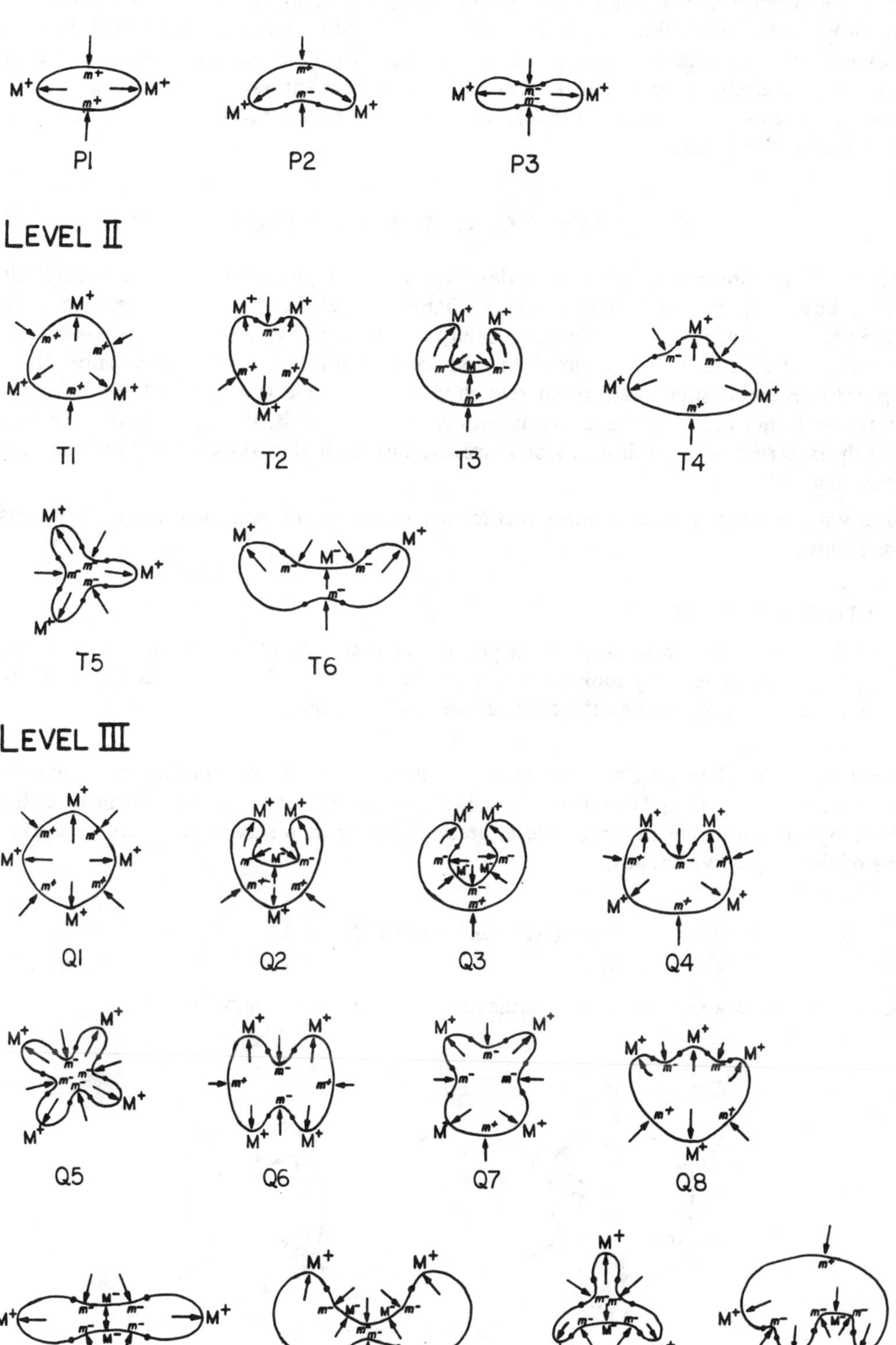

Figure 2

denote positive and negative curvature respectively. Thus there are four types of extrema: M^+, m^-, m^+, and M^-. Furthermore, Fig 2 is stratified into levels according to the *number* of extrema of each shape. The only three levels that can exist, with up to eight extrema, are: Level I, shapes with 4 extrema; Level II, shapes with 6 extrema; Level III, shapes with 8 extrema. Finally, we should note that the symmetry analysis, used in Fig 2, was PISA, the new analysis introduced in Leyton (1987c). This is because, as shown in Leyton (1987c), the SAT and SLS cannot correctly infer squashing and indentation, whereas PISA can.

3. THE INFERENCE OF INTERVENING HISTORY

In section 2, we presented inference rules that assign a process-history to a *single* shape. It is often the case however, that the scientist has available *two* views of an object at two developmental stages. Under these conditions, the scientist usually attempts to infer the processes that produced the second stage from the first. It is this problem that we now attempt to formalize and solve. We shall develop a *process-grammar* such that, given two shapes, one shape is expressed as the *extrapolation* of processes inferred in the other by the above inference rules. That is, the operations of the grammar are specified purely in terms of modifications at extrema, but such that these modifications correspond to process-*extrapolations*.

Physically natural extrapolations have two forms, *continuations* and *bifurcations*. We consider these two types as follows:

CONTINUATION OPERATIONS

Observe first that the continuation of a process at a M^+ or m^- extremum does not change the extremum type, as can be seen by looking at any of the M^+ and m^- extrema in Fig 2. However, continuation at a m^+ or M^- does change the type, as we shall now see:

(1) **Continuation at m$^+$** (labeled **Cm$^+$**) yields m^-, as is illustrated by continuing the upward m^+ process at the bottom of shape T1 (Fig 3) and thus obtaining shape T2 (Fig 3). This form of extrapolation is fully specified by the following re-write rule expressed purely in terms of the curvature extrema along the bottoms of the respective shapes:

$$Cm^+ : m^+ \rightarrow Om^-O$$

(where each 0 represents a curvature zero, indicated by a dot on the curve in T2).

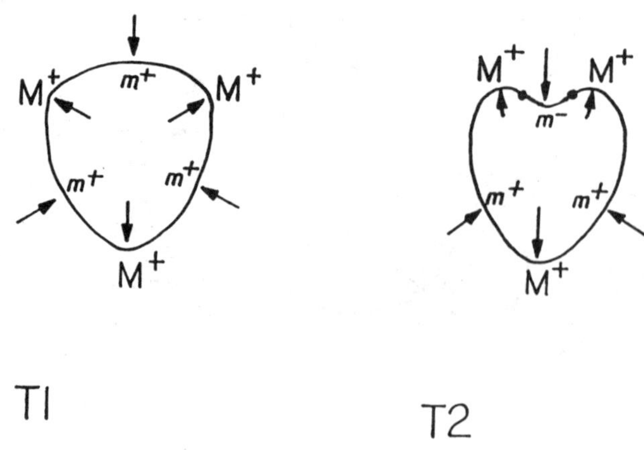

Figure 3

(2) **Continuation at M⁻** (labeled **CM⁻**) yields M^+, as is illustrated by continuing the upward M^- process in shape T3 (Fig 4) and thus obtaining the top protruding M^+ process in T4 (Fig 4). The rule is specified as:

$$CM^- : M^- \rightarrow OM^+O$$

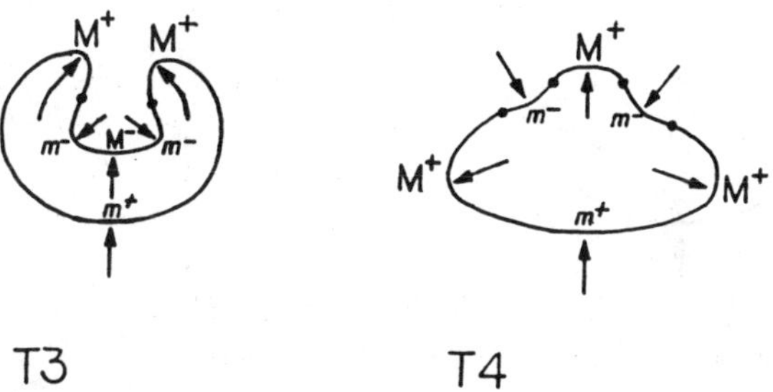

Figure 4

BIFURCATION OPERATIONS

We have seen above that only two non-trivial continuation operations can exist at extrema. We shall now see that only four non-trivial bifurcation operations can exist.

One can consider a bifurcation to have the effect of taking an extremum (maximum or minimum) and pulling it apart into two copies of itself. Between the copies, an extremum of the opposite type (minimum or maximum, respectively) is unavoidably introduced. In the smallest such non-trivial change, the introduced extremum has the same sign as the splitting extremum. Logically, there are four such primitive bifurcations, as follows. All other bifurcations are derivable from these together with the above two continuation operations.

(3) **Bifurcation at M⁺** (labeled **BM⁺**) must logically be given by the re-write rule

$$BM^+ : M^+ \rightarrow M^+m^+M^+$$

An illustration is the following. Consider the protruding process at the top of T4 (in Fig 5). If the process bifurcates, one branch goes to the left and the other to the right. The resulting shape is Q6 in Fig 5.

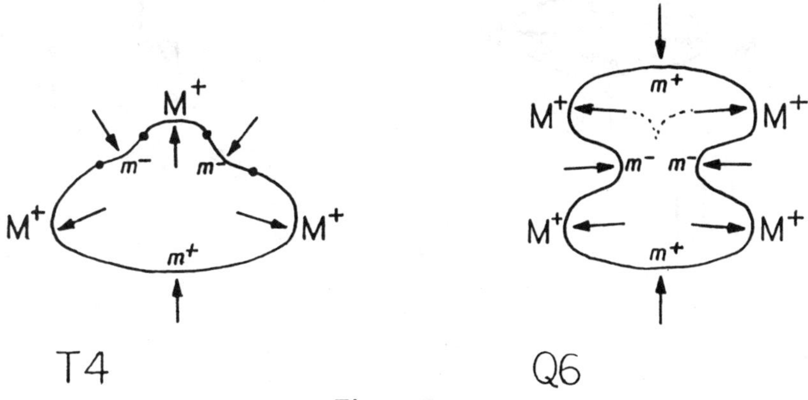

Figure 5

(4) Bifurcation at m⁻ (labeled **Bm⁻**) must logically be given by the re-write rule

$$Bm^- : m^- \rightarrow m^- M^- m^-$$

An illustration is the following. Consider the indenting process at the top of P2 (in Fig 6). If the process bifurcates, one branch goes to the left and the other to the right. The resulting shape is T3 (in Fig 6).

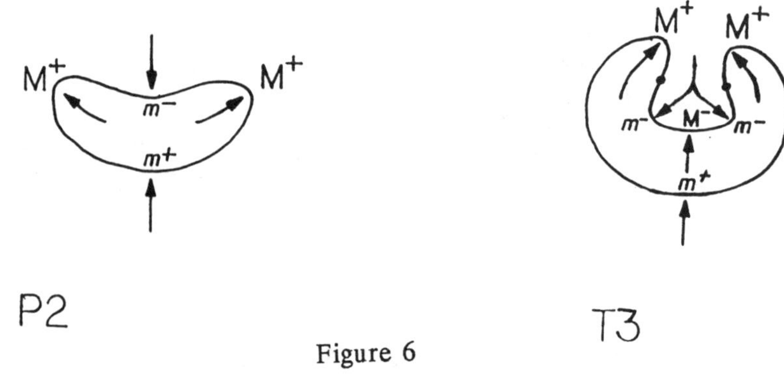

Figure 6

(5) Bifurcation at m⁺ (labeled **Bm⁺**) must logically be given by the re-write rule

$$Bm^+ : m^+ \rightarrow m^+ M^+ m^+$$

and is simply the introduction of a protrusion. An illustration is the transition from P1 to T1 (in Fig 7); i.e. a protrusion has been introduced at the top of T1.

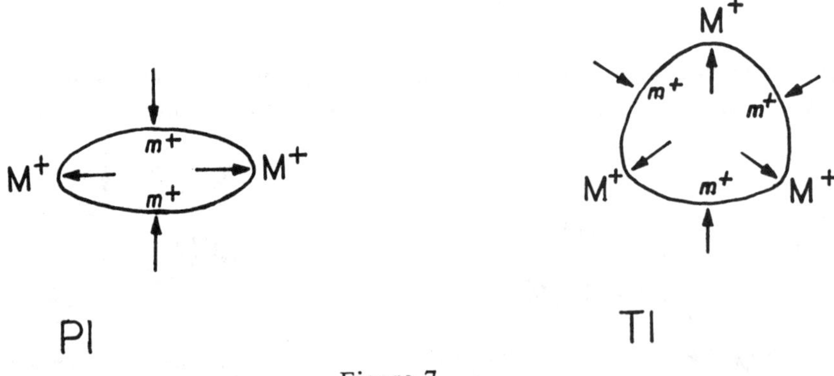

Figure 7

(6) **Bifurcation at M⁻ (labeled BM⁻)** must logically be given by the re-write rule

$$BM^- : M^- \rightarrow M^- m^- M^-$$

and is simply the introduction of an indentation. An illustration is the transition from T3 to Q3 (in Fig 8); i.e. an extra indentation has been introduced in the bottom of the lagoon in Q3.

Figure 8

4. ILLUSTRATION

We have found that a grammar of only six operations generates all process extrapolations. Let us illustrate the intuitive power of the grammar to yield intervening process-history. Consider two arbitrary shapes, for example, the pair shown in Fig 9. The assumption is that the two shapes are two stages in the development of the same object; e.g. a tumor, cloud, island, embryo, etc. Using a blurring heuristic, described in Leyton (1987c), one can identify the intervening succession of *shape-outlines*. We shall suppose that the succession is T6 → T5 → Q7 → Q5, as shown in Fig 10.

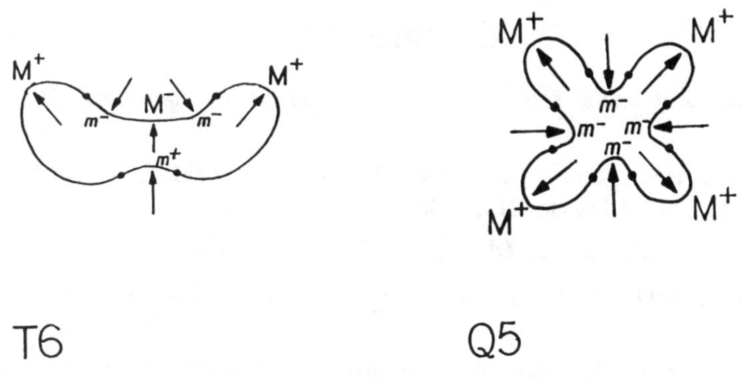

Figure 9

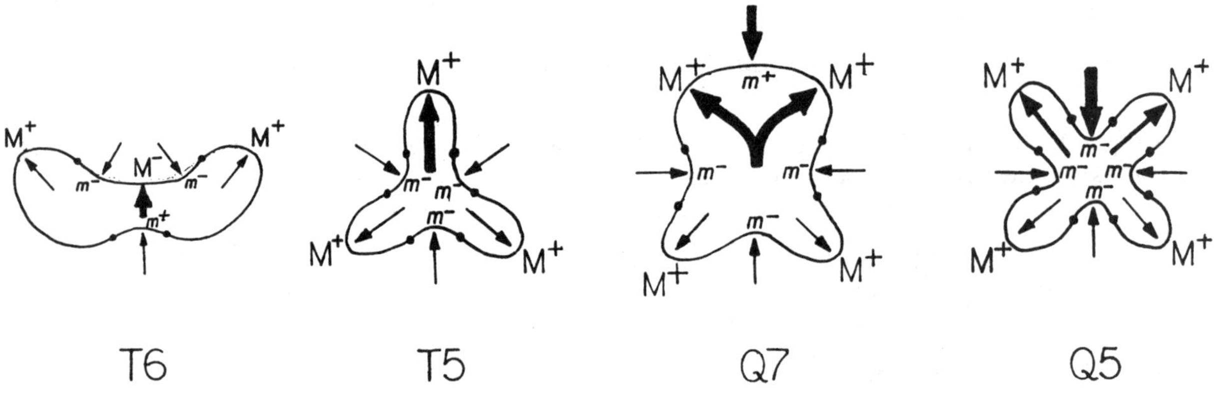

Figure 10

However, a succession of outlines is not a process-explanation. One requires the *grammar* to provide the intervening process-history. The grammar does this by the successive transformation of process-diagrams. In particular, for Fig 9, the grammar generates the successive process-structures by the sequence of operations, $CM^- * BM^+ * Cm^+$.

This operation-sequence is the *process-explanation* for the intervening development. Under this explanation, one particular process turns out to be crucial to the entire development. It is the internal process represented by the bold upward arrow in the first shape of Fig 10 (the arrow terminating at M^-). The entire intervening history is the successive transformation of this process, as follows: Firstly, the process continues upward and creates the protrusion in the second shape of Fig 10. Secondly, the process bifurcates, creating the lobe in the third shape of Fig 10. In this shape, a downward squashing process has also been introduced from above. Finally, this new downward process continues, creating the top indentation shown in the fourth shape of Fig 10.

ACKNOWLEDGEMENTS

The research was supported by NSF grant IST-8418164 to Harvard; and by NSF grant IST-8312240 and AFOSR grant F49620-83-C-0135 to MIT.

REFERENCES

Blum, H. Biological shape and visual science (part 1). *Journal of Theoretical Biology, 38,* (1973) 205-287.

Brady, M. Criteria for Representations of Shape. In A. Rosenfeld & J. Beck (Eds.), *Human and Machine Vision.* Erlbaum, Hillsdale, NJ. 1983

Leyton, M. Perceptual organization as nested control. *Biological Cybernetics, 51,* (1984) 141-153

Leyton, M. Generative systems of analyzers. *Computer Vision, Graphics and Image Processing, 31,* (1985) 201-241

Leyton, M. Principles of information structure common to six levels of the human cognitive system. *Information Sciences, 38,* (1986a) 1-120. Entire journal issue.

Leyton, M. A theory of information structure I: General principles. *Journal of Mathematical Psychology, 30,* (1986b) 103-160

Leyton, M. A theory of information structure, II: A theory of perceptual organization, *Journal of Mathematical Psychology, 30,* (1986c) 257-305

Leyton, M. Nested structures of control: An intuitive view. *Computer Vision, Graphics, and Image Processing, 37,* (1987a) 20-53

Leyton, M. Symmetry-curvature duality. *Computer Vision, Graphics, and Image Processing, 38,* (1987b) 327-341

Leyton, M. A Process-Grammar for Shape. *Artificial Intelligence,* (1987c) In press.

Leyton, M. A Limitation Theorem for the Differential Prototypification of Shape. *Journal of Mathematical Psychology,* (1987d) In press.

Richards, W., J.J. Koenderink, and D.D. Hoffman, Inferring 3D shapes from 2D silhouettes. *Submitted for publication.* Previous version appeared as AI. Memo # 840, MIT, 1985

FIGURING OUT MOST PLAUSIBLE INTERPRETATION FROM SPATIAL CONSTRAINTS

Toyoaki Nishida, Atsushi Yamada and Shuji Doshita
Department of Information Science
Kyoto University
Sakyo-ku, Kyoto 606
Japan
netaddress: nishida%doshita.kuis.kyoto-u.junet%japan@cs.net.relay

ABSTRACT

This paper describes a spatial component being developed in an ongoing research project called the Integrated Spatial Description Understanding project. The aim of this project is to eatablish a method for reconstructing spatial configuration from given natural language descriptions. In this paper, we concentrate on a particular class of spatial relations, namely positional relations on a two-dimensional space. We will also assume objects to be sizeless.

A theoretical device we present in this paper is called the *potential model*. The potential model provides a means for accumulating from fragmentary information. It is possible to derive (possibly more than one) maximally plausible interpretation from a chunk of information accumulated in the potential model. When new information is given, the potential model is modefied so that that new information is taken into account. As a result, the interpretations with maximal plausibility may change. A program called SPRINT (SPatial Reasoner for INTegrated understanding) reflecting our theory is in the way of construction.

1   Introduction

This paper describes a spatial component being developed in an ongoing research project called the Integrated Spatial Description Understanding project. The aim of this project is to eatablish a method for reconstructing spatial configuration from given natural language descriptions.

The problem we want to handle in this research is vagueness. Vagueness plays an important role in our communication in that it allows us to transfer partial information. Suppose a situation in which a boy is looking around for his toy. Even if we cannot tell exactly where it was if we know it was somewhere around my desk, we can transfer him this partial information by telling that his toy is *around* my desk. It would be nice if we can communicate with our robot in the same way.

The problem of vagueness has not been studied widely in spatial reasoning[2,3,4,5]. Work by Drew McDermott and Ernie Davis is among few exceptions. They addressed the vagueness of spatial concept and they introduced a theoretical device called *fuzz box*[1]. A fuzz box denotes a region in which a given object may possibly exist. Possiblility of the existence is uniformly positive in a fuzz box, and zero outside the box.

This formulation has a couple of drawbacks. First, the shape of the region must be rectangular. Second, Davis had to have the boundary of fuzz box sharp, due to computational reasons.

Thus their approach has a significant difficulty in modeling various spatial concepts. For example, the meaning of *aroundness* is hard to represent with fuzz box, since it is still hard to draw an exact boundary to distinguish the region which is around something from that that is not.

In order to solve these problems, we propose the *potential model*. The potential model employs both continuous and discontinuous functions to represent spatial relations, so that the probability changes either continuously or discontinously, depending on the nature of a given constraint. Currently, we are concentrating on a particular class of spatial relations, namely positional relations on a two-dimensional space, although the potential model is more general. We assume objects to be sizeless.

A program called SPRINT (SPatial Reasoner for INTegrated understanding) reflecting our theory is in the way of construction.

2   The Potential Model

At the center of potential model is a *potential* function, which gives a value indicating the cost for accepting the relation to hold among a given set of arguments. The lower is the value provided by a potential function, the more plausible is the corresponding relation. We

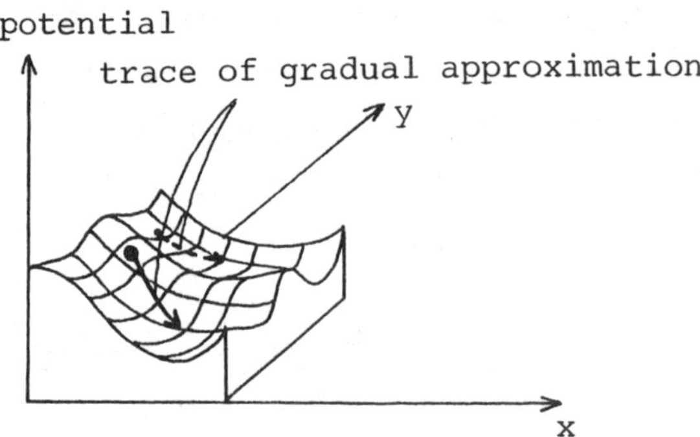

Figure 1: Potential model and gradual approximation.

allow the value of potential functions to range from 0 to $+\infty$. A potential function may give a minimal value for more than one combination of arguments. Such case may be taken as an existence of ambiguity.

A primitive potential function is defined for each spatial relation. A potential function for overall situation is constructed by adding primitive potential functions for spatial relations involved.

When a potential function is formulated from a given set of information, the system will seek for a combination of arguments which may miminize the value of potential function. We use a gradual approximation method to obtain an approximate solution. Starting from an appropriate combination of arguments, the system changes the current set of values by a small amount proportional to a virtual force obtained by differentiating the potential function. This process will be repeated until the magnitude of virtual force becomes less than a certain threshold. Figure 1 illustrates those idea.

Unfortunately, this algorithm may not find a position which makes a given potential function minimam. When there is more than one minimal solution, the algorithm will terminate with a location appropriately near one of them. Which minimal solution is chosen depends on the initial set of arguments. We assume there exists some heuristic which predicts a sufficiently good initial values and the above approximation process works rather as an adjustment than as a means for finding solution.

2.1   The Spring Model

We use an imaginary, virtual mechanical spring between constrained objects to represent constraint on distance. If the distance between the two objects is equal to the natural length of the spring, the relative position is most plausible. The more extended or compressed the spring, the more (virtual) force is required to maintain the position, corresponding to the interpretation being less plausible.

An integration of the force needed either to extend or compress the spring is called an elastic potential. The spring model, subclass of the potential model, takes an elastic potential as a potential function. Let the positions of two objects connected by a spring of natural length L and elastic constant K be (x_0, y_0) and (x_1, y_1), respectively. Then the potential is given by the following formula:

$$P(x_0, y_0, x_1, y_1) = \frac{K(\sqrt{(x_1 - x_0)^2 + (y_1 - y_0)^2} - L)^2}{2}.$$

2.2 Inhibited Region and Inhibited Half Plane

Unlike other primitive potential functions introduced so far, inhibited region and half plane pose a discontinuous constraint on the possible region of position. By inhibited region and half plane we mean a certain region and half plane is inhibited for an object to enter, respectively. Inhibited regions and half planes are not global in the sense that each is defined only for some particular object. Inhibited region is less basic concept because it can be represented by a logical combination of inhibited half plane.

An inhibited half-plane is characterized by its directed boundary line. A directed boundary line in turn is characterized by the orientation θ (measured counter-clockwise from the orientation of x-axis) and a location (X, Y) of a point (referred to as a *characteristic point*) on it. The inhibited half plane is the right hand side of the directed boundary.

2.3 Directional Potential

Suppose we want to represent a constraint that an object B is to the direction θ of another object A (measured counter-clockwise). Let the position of A and B be (x_0, y_0) and (x_1, y_1), respectively. We use the following potential function to represent the constraint:

$$P(x_0, y_0, x_1, y_1) = \frac{K_1(-(x_1 - x_0)\sin\theta + (y_1 - y_0)\cos\theta)^2 + K_2}{(x_1 - x_0)\cos\theta + (y_1 - y_0)\sin\theta + 1/\delta}$$

When viewed horizontally from A, this function represents a hyperbola. If this function is cut vertically to the intended direction, this represent a parabola (upside down). See figure 2 for the shape of this function. Note that the notion of direction defined here denotes that in everyday life, which is not very rigid.

Since the value of the potential function defined above P jumps from positive (infinite) to negative (infinite) if one proceeds for the $-\theta$ direction.

We add inhibited half planes in the $-\theta$ direction, so that it is impossible to put the object in this region.

"B is to the direction θ from A."

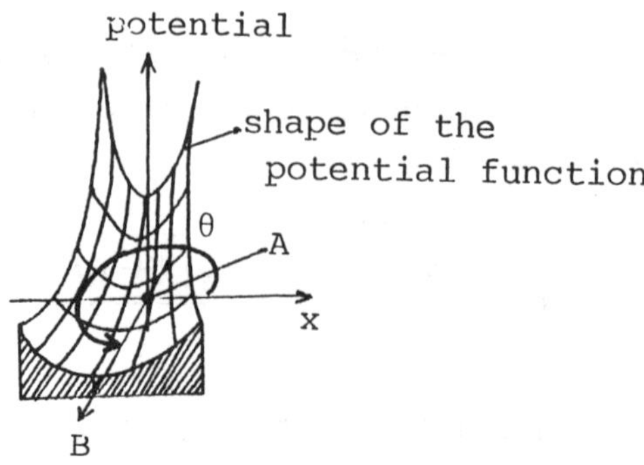

Figure 2: Directional potential.

3   A Method of Gradual Approximation

A maximally plausible position is obtained by revising a tentative solution repeatedly.
The move $\Delta = (\Delta_x, \Delta_y)$ at each step is given as follows:

$$\Delta = (\Delta_x, \Delta_y) = K \cdot (\partial P/\partial x, \partial P/\partial y), \qquad \text{where } K \text{ is a positive constant.}$$

This basic move may be complicated by taking inhibited regions into account. The following
two subsections explain how it is done.

3.1   Pushing Objects out of Inhibited Half Plane

We do not assume that our initial placement heuristic is clever enough to place objects so
that every constraints are satisfied; it is rather hard when a lot of constraints are given.
An algorithm for escaping from inhibited half plane is applied when the initial placement
heuristic placed an object within an inhibited half plane. If such a situation is detected, the
algorithm defined below will push the object out of an inhibited half plane in five steps. At
this time, any influences from other constraints are taken into account. Thus, the move
$d = (d_x, d_y)$ of the object at each step is the sum of $d_V = (d_{V_x}, d_{V_y})$ (a component vertical
to the boundary) and $d_P = (d_{P_x}, d_{P_y})$ (a component in parallel to the boundary). Suppose
the initial position of an object is (x_0, y_0), then each of which is defined as follows:

$$d_{V_x} = -L \sin \theta / 5$$

$$d_{V_y} = L \cos \theta / 5$$

where, $L = |(x_0 - Y) \sin \theta - (y_0 - Y) \cos \theta|$ represents the distance from the initial position to
the boundary of the inhibited half plane. Note that the inhibited half plane is characterized

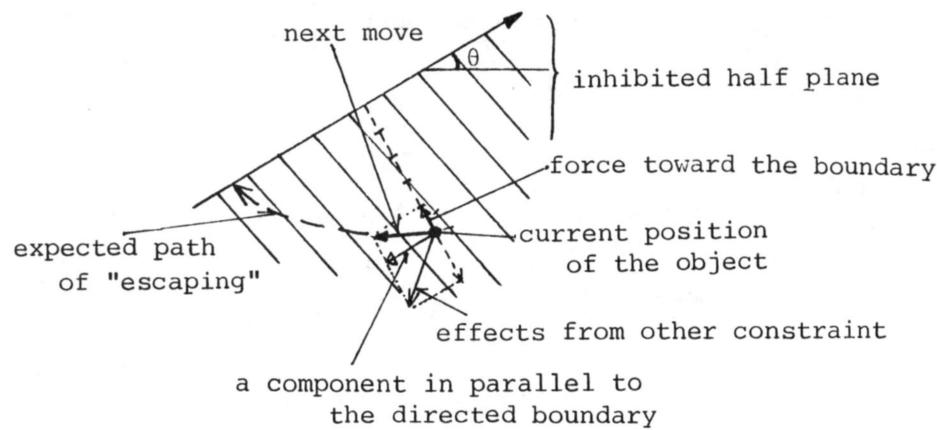

Figure 3: Pushing an object out of an inhibited region.

by its directed boundary with a characteristic point (X, Y) and the orientation θ.

$$d_{P_x} = C(f_x \cos^2\theta + f_y \sin\theta \cos\theta)$$

$$d_{P_y} = C(f_x \sin\theta \cos\theta + f_y \sin^2\theta)$$

where, C is a positive constant, and $f = (f_x, f_y)$ is a virtual force from other constraints. Figure 3 illustrates how this works.

The above process is repeated for each inhibited half plane violated, so that the object is pushed out ofeach inhibited half plane, one at a time.

3.2 Avoiding to Push Objects into Inhibited Half Plane

Once an object has been put out of an inhibited half plane, one must want it not to have it re-enter the same inhibited half plane. However, the gradual approximation algorithm may try to push the object there again. An algorithm described in this section watches out for such situation. If it detects, it will recourse the gradual move.

Suppose an inhibited half plane is characterized by θ and (X, Y) on the boundary. Suppose also that the next position suggested by the gradual approximation algorithm is (x, y). If

$$L = x \sin\theta - y \cos\theta - X \sin\theta + Y \cos\theta > 0,$$

then, the next position will be forced into the inhibited half plane. In such a case, the move is modified and the new destination becomes:

$$(x', y') = (x - (1 + \epsilon)L \sin\theta, y + (1 + \epsilon)L \cos\theta)$$

where, ϵ is a positive infinitesimal.

See figure 4.

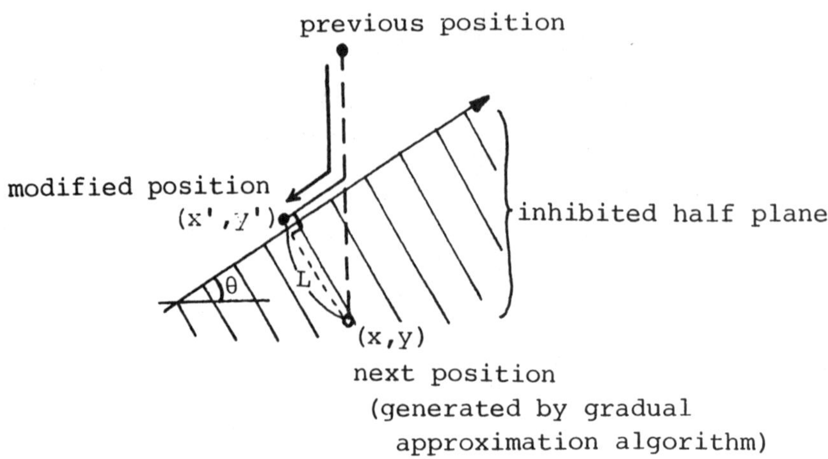

Figure 4: An algorithm for avoiding to push an object into an inhibited half plane.

3.3   Dependency

It would require a great amount of computation, if the position of all objects have to be determined at once. Fortunately, human-human communication is not so nasty as this is the case; natural language sentences contain many cues which help the hearer understand the input. For example, in normal conversations, the utterance

> Ginkakuji (temple) is to the east of Kyoto University

is given in the context in which the speaker has already given the position of *Kyoto University*, or s/he can safely assume the hearer knows that fact. If such a sue is carefully recognized, the amount of computation must be significantly reduced.

Dependency is one such cue. By dependency we mean a partial order accoering to which position of objects are determined. SPRINT is designed so that it can take advantage of it. Instead of computing everything at once, the spatial reasoner can determine the position of objects one by one. An object whose position does not depend on any other objects is chosen as the origin of local coordinate. SPRINT determines the temporary position of objects from the root of the dependency network. The position of an object will be determined if the position of all of its predecessors is determined. Figure 5 shows how SPRINT does this.

This algorithm has three problems:

1. the total plausibility may not be maximal.

2. in the worst case, the above may result in contradiction.

3. objects may be underconstrained.

given text:
    (1)Hieizan-Mt. is to the north of Kyoto-Eki(station).
    (2)Kyoto University is between the Hieizan-Mt. and Kyoto-Eki.
    (3)Ginkakuji(temple) is to the east of Kyoto University.

dependency:

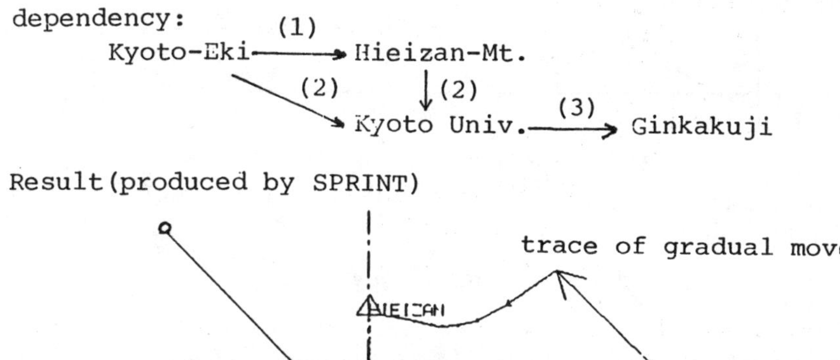

Result(produced by SPRINT)

Figure 5: Positioning using dependency.

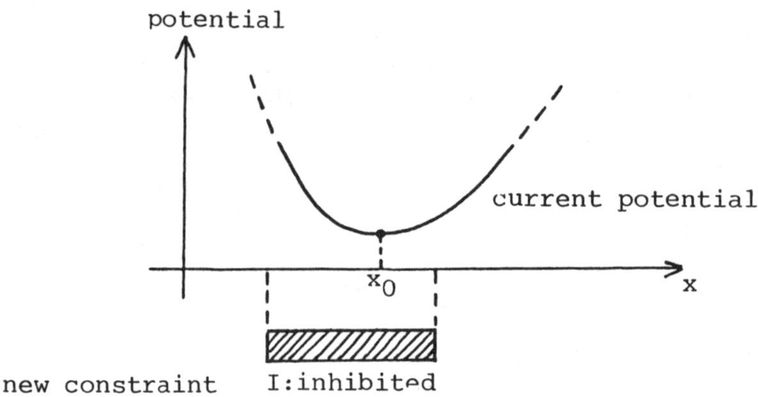

Figure 6: An inconsistency.

Currently, we compromise with the first problem. More adequate solution may be to have an adjustment stage after initial configulation of objects are obtained. The second problem will be addressed in the next subsection. The third remains as a future problem.

3.4   Resolving Contradiction

Adding new information may result in inconsistency. In order to focus an attention to this problem, let us temporalily restrict the spatial coordinate as one-dimensional. Suppose an object is given a maximally plausible position x_0. Suppose also that a new inhibited region (interval I in a one dimensional world) is given as a new constraint. See figure 6. Then the position of the object is recomputed so as to take this new constraint into account. If the interval I accidentally involves x_0, then the algorithm mentioned in section 3.1 is applied, and the object may be moved to x_1. This is the situation in which the object tends to move to the position x_0 but cannot due to the inhibited half space. In this case, the parent node in the dependency is tried to move in the reverse direction to resolve this situation.

A situation is worse than the above if the inhibited region (or interval) is too wide to fit in a space. This problem rises especially when we take size into account. Suppose the position of two objects A and B are already given maximally plausible positions x_0 and $x_1(x_0 < x_1)$, respectively. Suppose now the third object C with width being wider than $x_1 - x_0$ is declared to exist between A and B. This causes a failure because there is no space to place C.

The solution to this problem comprises in two stages. First, the reason of the failure is analyzed. Then, parents of the current objects are moved gradually so that the inconsistency can be removed. Figure 7 illustrates how this works.

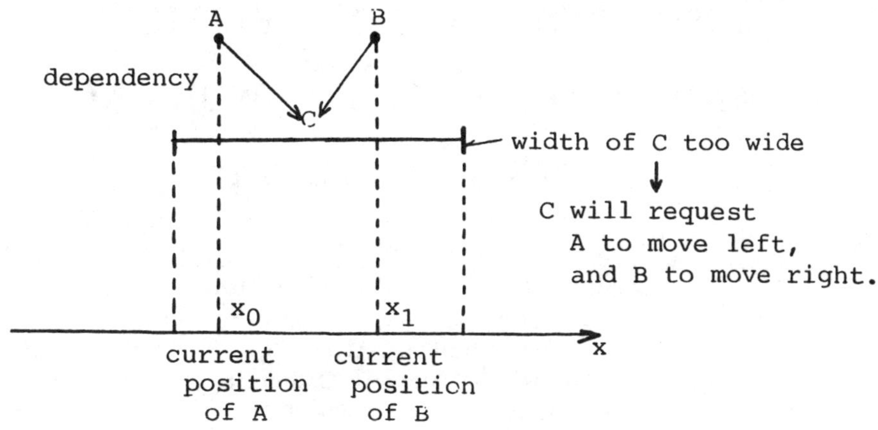

Figure 7: Resolving contradiction.

4   Concluding Remarks

The area of spatial reasoning contains lots of hard issues, only a fragment of which has been addressed in this paper. A couple of major problems related to this work are as follows:

- A systematic method should be developed to determine actual values of the model.

- Although the current program is forced to figure out most plausible configuration from given information, there do exist cases in which things are so underconstrained that figuring out temporary configuration is useless or rather harmful.

References

[1] Davis, E., Organizing Spatial Knowledge, Research Report 193, Yale University, January, 1981.

[2] Kuipers, B., Modeling Spatial Knowledge, *Cognitive Science 2(2)*, 1978.

[3] Lavin, M. A., *Computer Analysis of Scenes from a Moving Viewing Point*, PhD Thesis, Massachusetts Institute of Technology, 1977.

[4] Novak Jr., G. S., Representations of Knowledge in a Program for Sloving Physics Problems, *Proc. IJCAI-77*, 1977.

[5] Waltz, D. L., Towards a Detailed Model of Processing for Language Describing the Physical World, *Proc. IJCAI-81*, 1-6, 1981.

ISSUES IN SHAPE DESCRIPTION AND AN APPROACH FOR WORKING WITH SPARSE DATA[1]

Kashipati Rao, R. Nevatia and G. Medioni,
Institute for Robotics and Intelligent Systems,
Powell Hall 204, MC-0273,
University of Southern California,
Los Angeles, CA-90089.

ABSTRACT

We discuss the issues and problems in shape description in vision. We spell out our criteria for shape description and then examine various schemes for it. We study the problems of shape description especially in the context of sparse, imperfect 3-D data, such as that obtained from stereo. We then present our approach to shape description as an example to solve the shape problem, and show a specimen result on real data.

[1] This research is supported by the Defense Advanced Research Projects Agency under contract number F33615-84-K-1404, monitored by the Air Force Wright Aeronautical Laboratories, Darpa Order No. 3119.

1   Introduction

Shape description is a problem of fundamental importance in vision in man and machine [1, 2, 3]. That it is an important component of the human visual system is evinced by the fact that we humans are capable of recognizing an object by merely having its shape description. Shape is somehow intrinsic to an object and is quite independent of lighting intensity or color. Also, we find that shape description is an important component of machine vision, especially indoor robotics vision. It is useful for such tasks as recognition, inspection, grasping and manipulation, and reasoning and planning in assembly (see [4, 5], for example).

This paper is based on some work we have described earlier [6]. However, here we provide a broader perspective, give our approach as an example and present results on real data. We focus on the issues and problems in shape analysis. The salient features of this paper are: *first*, we give a detailed discussion on the issues involved in the choice of a shape representation. We describe some schemes for shape description and examine their merits and demerits. *Second*, we explain the problems and difficulties in obtaining shape descriptions from sparse 3-D data. *Third*, we present our approach to illustrate a possible solution to the shape problem. We give one specimen result on real data (for lack of space) and conclude by indicating future directions of our research in shape understanding.

2   Choice of shape representation

2.1   Criteria for shape representation

What are the criteria for good shape representation? The shape representation scheme should be robust to the normal changes in viewing conditions like rotation, perspective, scale, illumination etc. It should be *stable*, that is, small changes in shape should not cause radical changes in the description. The representation should be *rich*, meaning that it should be information preserving. This is important so that partially visible objects can still be identified. The representation should have *local support*, meaning that it can be locally computed. This is important for dealing with occlusion and for performing detailed inspection. Occlusion of parts of the object should result in partial descriptions that are invariant for the parts that are visible. These criteria suggest *segmented, hierarchical* descriptions. The representation should allow for easy matching for recognition of an object from its shape. It should also be such that it is possible to recreate a shape close to the original object. Articulation of parts (i.e., relative movement of parts) should cause a change in only the relationships of the parts. The representation should be descriptive and *natural* so that we can, not only find similarities with stored models but also differences from them. This ability would be useful if our system were to be capable of learning from new objects and scenes. The shape representation scheme should also be natural in the sense that it should be easily developable by a human. The shape representation scheme should be *accessible* [7], that is, it should be computable relatively efficiently by some process.

2.2   Schemes for shape representation

2.2.1   Non-segmented descriptions

Here the attempt is to describe the object globally, without segmenting it into its component parts. As the object is described as whole, these methods are sometimes called *holistic* descriptions. Examples of such representation schemes are below:

(1) Extended Gaussian Images [8]:
In this representation the surface orientation at each point is represented on the unit sphere. In the discrete case it is an *orientation histogram* in three-space. The representation is rich (information preserving) but is unstable and global. We therefore do not consider it appropriate for shape description in general.

(2) Generalized Hough Transform [9]:
This is also a global method and is closely related to the template matching idea. The shape of the object

has to be known *a priori*. It is rich, but is again unstable and being global, very poor with respect to occlusion. This too is inappropriate for shape description.

There are other shape descriptions methods based on Fourier transform and moments. These also suffer from the problems mentioned above.

2.2.2   Segmented descriptions

Here the idea is to describe the object in parts (and relationship between parts). These methods are therefore local and are good at handling occlusion. Examples of these representation methods are:

(1) Surface patches:
Surface patches may be obtained by analyzing the 3-D data in terms of curvature properties. Examples of work on this are in [10, 11, 12]. These representations are rich, local and stable but they are viewer-centered and they only represent the visible part of objects. They are, therefore, good for objects that are essentially surfaces, such as a metal sheet, or for a relatively smooth, "featureless" surfaces such as a piece of paper or a turbine blade. Segmented surface descriptions are also useful as a first step for generating generalized cone descriptions (see [13]).

(2) Superquadrics [14, 15]:
The idea here is to model the world as a composition of parts. The modeling primitive may be thought of as a "lump of clay", which may be deformed and shaped, and is intended to correspond to the notion of a part. While the superquadrics are good for graphics and CAD, they may not be useful for vision because it is not clear how to extract their parameters from an image. Also, their parameters are *unstable*.

(3) 3-D SAT and SLS:
Nackman [16] has developed a 3-D generalization of Blum's symmetric axis transform (SAT). In 3-D the axis of the object is a surface rather than a curve got by using maximal spheres rather than maximal circles. Although the 3-D SAT is a rich description, it still suffers from the problem the 2-D SAT faced. The SAT has problems at sharp corners, for example those of a cube or a cuboid. Also, sometimes the axis may not lie in the part of the body whose axis is being found. As in 2-D the SAT is extremely sensitive to changes in the object surface. The SAT requires complete knowledge of the object being viewed and will not work well with partial views. It is also non-intuitive in 3-D.

Brady and Asada [17] have developed the smoothed local symmetries (SLS) representation similar to the SAT and the generalized cones (see below). It emphasizes the smoothness of the axis of the representation. It is rich, local and stable, but like the SAT generalizes to a surface in 3-D. This makes it undesirable for shape representation in 3-D.

(4) Generalized Cones:
Generalized cones were introduced by Binford as useful volume descriptions for 3-D objects [18]. A tutorial description may be found in [1]. A Generalized Cone or a Generalized Cylinder (GC) may be defined as consisting of an arbitrary planar shape called a *cross-section*, swept along an arbitrary 3-D curve called an *axis*. In general, the size and even the shape of the cross-section may change along the axis; the rule describing the change is called the *sweep rule* or the *cross-section function*. Although the axis, cross-section and the sweeping-rule could be arbitrary analytic functions, in practice only simple functions are used. Typically, the axis is straight or circular, the sweep rule is constant or linear and the cross-section is rectangular or circular.

The precise restrictions for a GC have been different for various researchers; e.g. some do not allow the cross-section shape to change. Shafer and Kanade have developed a terminology for describing the variants of a generalized cone [19]; we shall follow this terminology where appropriate. In this terminology a *linear* cone has a linear cross-section function, a *straight* cone has a straight axis, and a *homogeneous* cone has an invariant cross-section shape. Some examples of generalized cone classes are shown in figure 1. It may be noted that figure 1 (a) subsumes all the generalized cones (except one with a circular spine, shown in part (c) of figure) used as primitives by Brooks in his fairly general *ACRONYM* system [20][2]. We may thus conclude that the Linear Straight Homogeneous Generalized Cones form a fairly large class

---

[2]Note that the generalized cone at the bottom right in part (a) of the figure has an irregular cross-section, and the cross-section is more general than that handled by the *ACRONYM* system.

of objects.

The GC representation is rich and has local support. Using the functions discussed above we can describe all points on the generalized cone (except at sharp bends, see [21]). Thus the representation is information-preserving, and is therefore rich. At each point on the axis we can define a local coordinate system using the tangent, normal and binormal of differential geometry [22]. The GC is naturally amenable to a segmented, hierarchical representation. For example, the hierarchical decomposition of the human figure in terms of generalized cones. The GC representation is natural for complex objects that can be represented as assembly of simpler objects, each of which is better described as a GC. The junctions between the simpler objects may described as joints [21]. For complex objects that articulate, the GCs are again natural because all that the articulation means is a local change in the relationship between parts at the joints [21]. The GC description is invariant to rotation, scale changes, perspective or change in illumination.

Because of the above properties, the generalized cone representation has deservedly received considerable attention in the vision community. Agin [23] used GCs to describe objects from dense range data. Nevatia and Binford [21] used the boundaries derived from 3-D range data; the method would apply to 2-D boundaries also, but in either case requires that boundaries be complete and that the objects be viewed from a "side view" with the ends of the GCs not visible. Marr describes another method for determining axes, also from complete boundaries [24], though it is unclear if this method was actually implemented and tested. Brooks deals with imperfect data in his *ACRONYM* system [20], but he requires rather detailed knowledge of the object being viewed (very specific models and constraints), and some knowledge of the viewing position. The predicted features of the models are matched to the image features.

However, there are some difficulties with the GC representation. They are difficult to compute. They are not appropriate if we are looking for very fine details in the object. Also, as the GC description is not unique for an object, ad hoc rules may have to be used to choose a description. (See section 3 for more details on problems in computing shape descriptions.)

Besides these representation schemes, there are others, more popular, in CAD. They are: boundary representation, pure primitive instance schemes, spatial occupancy enumeration, cell decomposition (eg: oct-trees) and constructive solid geometry. These methods are really better for display purposes as in computer graphics rather than for computer vision. Details of these schemes may be found in [25, 26, 27]. (Recently, another description scheme using variational calculus was developed [28]. Again, it seems to be more useful for graphics rather than for vision.)

3   Why is the problem so hard?

To obtain *volumetric* shape of objects in a scene, we must first segment it, *i.e.*, resolve the so-called "figure-ground" problem and describe the objects in terms of some chosen representation. The segmentation problem is particularly difficult if only 2-D information is utilized. The problem is simplified considerably if complete and accurate 3-D information of visible surfaces (sometimes called $2\frac{1}{2}$-D data) is available. We assume that our low-level descriptions consist of sparse 3-D data, as might be generated by a stereo system for example. In stereo, information is available only at the intensity discontinuities, typically at the object boundaries, surface discontinuities and surface markings. We do not assume that the 3-D data is available everywhere on the boundary, i.e., we must reason with incomplete, and imperfect data. (We are tempted to call such data as being $2\frac{1}{4}$-D.)

An example of a typical "simple" scene we wish to analyze is shown in figure 2 (the labelling of boundaries is explained later, in section 4). We assume that the 3-D positions of the boundaries in the figure are known, but no information is available for the other points. The boundaries may also be broken up, as shown in the figure. Humans have no difficulty interpreting the scene (even without 3-D data — and despite the fragmentation), but the breaks may *acutely* complicate machine analysis. This paper is concerned with computing appropriate *volumetric* shape descriptions from such scenes.

It may seem that such scenes are rather straight-forward to analyze and that many of the techniques in computer vision should apply. However, a careful analysis indicates this to be not the case. The best understood domain is that of polyhedral objects, for example see [29, 30]. However, in this work, complete and perfect line-drawings of polyhedra without any markings or shadows are essential. In recent work [31], methods have been developed that apply to non-polyhedral scenes, but they also assume perfect line-drawings. The usual approach to cope with the imperfections in the low-level descriptions is to assume that the specific objects to be viewed, and even their approximate orientations, are known *a priori*, and then segmentation is performed by fitting the models to the low-level descriptions. The various systems differ in the specificity with which the object models must be known. For example, the system of Bolles and Horaud [32] solves for the orientation and position of objects, but the objects being viewed are *known* to be cylindrical castings. Also, the authors use *dense* range data and only the physical discontinuities are perceived (no surface markings). The system of Grimson and Lozano-Perez [33] recognizes objects by making measurements of features in the scene and comparing with a database of models but without explicitly understanding the shape of the objects in the scene.

It is our belief that none of these systems (both the non-GC-based and the GC-based systems mentioned in section 2) would be able to analyze the seemingly simple scene shown in figure 2 and that the nature of the data in that scene is typical of what we may expect in a practical system. In practice, the methods that give range data give information that is sparse and imperfect. In feature-based stereo, for example, it is possible to obtain range data for only the non-homogeneous parts of the image. Thus, for smooth objects, we may be able to get this information at object boundaries only and there too, we might have missing information. Even with the use of an active range-finder, the data is still likely to be imperfect due to color of the object or poor reflectivity properties of its surface.

In the next section we shall explain an approach to shape description, as an example to illustrate the issues and problems discussed earlier.

4 Approaches to shape description: an example

One approach to deriving shape descriptions from sparse data is to first build a dense surface by interpolation, e.g., see [34, 35]. However, interpolation requires knowledge of the object boundaries, that is, the solution of the segmentation problem itself. Also, interpolation schemes perform poorly if the data is not spread *throughout* the region being interpolated in and has erroneous points. Moreover, a surface description scheme is not essential if our ultimate objective is a volume-based, object-centered description. (Also, a surface description can always be obtained from a volume description.) We have therefore adopted the *more direct* volume-based approach, and we have used the generalized cone as our shape primitive because of its good properties as explained in section 2. These two approaches, in the perspective of vision research in general, are summarized in figure 3.

A scene with objects describable as GCs may be labelled as shown in figure 2. By "axial contour generator" or acg we mean that part of the occluding boundary of the GC that is along its length. By terminators of a GC we simply mean its ends. A scene may also have surface marks and missing information as shown in figure 2.

The general approach in this shape description method is based on the *hypothesize and verify* paradigm. That is, hypothesize a description of shape using one piece of evidence and verify using another piece. The pieces of evidence we shall use are the axial contour generators and terminators mentioned above.

To hypothesize and verify we shall use some properties of GCs. The general properties we shall use are:

In-betweenness/extremity: The terminator boundary lies completely within the axial contour generators. In other words, the axial contour generators are the extremities of the object.

Tangency: The axial contour generator is tangential to the terminator boundary both in 3-D and in 2-D.

The other properties that we use are those specific to the particular class of GCs we consider. The first class of GCs we study is the Linear Straight Homogeneous Generalized Cone (LSHGC) [19]). For these, *the axial contour generators are planar from any view* (from Shafer and Kanade [19]). In the concluding section we briefly mention the specific properties of a more general class of GCs.

A block diagram of the system is given in figure 4. A brief description is given in this paragraph, more details can be found in [6]. The input to the system is a sparse set of 3-D line segments, made available by lower-level programs. After preliminary processing (finding relationship between lines, finding junctions), we search for GCs. The methods used are: axial contour generator directed method and terminator directed method. The axial contour generator directed method finds a pair of candidate axial contour generators (acgs) first. These are long segments and, for LSHGCs, the pair has to be coplanar too. Then the method verifies the hypothesis by finding corresponding terminators. This is done by tracing a contour between the acgs while satisfying the "in-betweenness" and tangency properties. On the other hand, the terminator directed method finds candidate terminators first by finding maximal, coplanar, convex sets, ordering them and finding the corners of the sets. It then verifies the hypothesis of a GC by finding the corresponding acgs using the tangency and in-betweenness (extremity) properties and, for LSHGCs, the coplanarity property too. The different descriptions generated are then rated based on the following heuristic criteria: long, parallel acgs preferred, closed, planar (and if possible circular) terminators preferred, two parallel terminators preferred etc. The best disjoint descriptions are then extracted and described in terms of the cross-section function, the axis and the cross-section of the GC.

The above system was tested on a large number of synthetic scenes [6] and scenes from both passive and active ranging devices [13]. Special problems in working with real data like difficulty in tracing 3-D contours and difficulty in finding planes due to jaggedness in depth were discussed in [13]. Here we shall suffice it by showing an example on real data from a segment-based stereo system [36]. Figure 5 shows two objects with occlusion. We display the stereo pair of images, the segments extracted and the stereo output in two projections. Note, that the stereo data is very jagged. The output of our program is shown, with the cross-sections output as circles, due to the jaggedness of the data in depth. In this example, we have 60 segments and there are potentially $\binom{60}{2} = 1770$ possible acg-pairs. Of these the program explores 105 cases and finds two objects: a combination with acgs 54 & 41 and corresponding terminators, and another with acgs 35 & 24 and corresponding terminators. Other combinations are also found, like one with acgs 41 & 24 but are eliminated because they have segments belonging to combinations with higher ratings. The program takes about 15 minutes to run on this scene. Note that no special and extra techniques have yet been developed to handle occlusion other than the ones mentioned in [6].

5 Conclusions

We laid out our criteria for shape representation and examined various schemes for it. We next looked at problems in shape computation. Having looked at representation schemes and problems in shape computation, we illustrated, as an example, an approach to solving the shape description problem (from sparse 3-D data, such as that obtained from stereo). We demonstrated the working of a system using the above approach on real data with Linear Straight Homogeneous Generalized Cones and some occlusion.

We are currently working on shape description of more complex generalized cones, where the axis need not be straight and the cross-section function need not be linear. For these more complex objects, we expect that, in addition to in-betweenness and tangency, the axial contour generators will be smooth and piecewise coplanar. We also expect to use symmetry properties of these shapes more strongly.

References

[1] R. Nevatia. *Machine Perception*. Prentice Hall, 1982.

[2] J. M. Brady. *Computer Vision*. North-Holland, 1981.

[3] D. Marr. *Vision*. W. H. Freeman and Company, 1982.

[4] C. R. Rosen. *Machine Vision and Robotics: Industrial Requirements*. Technical Report Technical Note 174, Stanford Research Institute, Menlo Park, California, 1978.

[5] G. J. Agin. Computer vision systems for inspection and assembly. *Computer*, 13(5):11–20, 1980.

[6] Kashipati Rao and R. Nevatia. Generalized cone descriptions from sparse 3-d data. In *Proceedings of Computer Vision and Pattern Recognition Conference*, pages 256–263, June 1986.

[7] D. Marr and K. Nishihara. Representation and recognition of the spatial organization of three dimensional shapes. In *Proceedings of the Royal Society of London*, pages 269–294, 1978.

[8] B. K. P. Horn. Extended gaussian images. *Proceedings of the IEEE*, 72(12):1671–1686, December 1984.

[9] D. H. Ballard. Generalizing the hough transform to detect arbitrary shapes. *Pattern Recognition*, 13(2):111–122, 1981.

[10] T. J. Fan, G. Medioni, and R. Nevatia. Description of surfaces from range data using curvature properties. In *Proceedings of Computer Vision and Pattern Recognition Conference*, pages 86–91, June 1986.

[11] J. Ponce and M. Brady. Toward a surface primal sketch. In *Proceedings of the IEEE International Conference on Robotics and Automation*, pages 420–425, St. Louis, Mo., March 25-28 1985.

[12] P. J. Besl and R. C. Jain. Segmentation through symbolic surface descriptions. In *Proceedings of Computer Vision and Pattern Recognition Conference*, pages 77–85, June 1986.

[13] Kashipati Rao and R. Nevatia. From sparse 3-d data directly to volumetric shape descriptions. In *Proceedings of the DARPA Image Understanding Workshop*, pages 360–369, February 1987.

[14] A. P. Pentland. Perceptual organization and the representation of natural form. *Artificial Intelligence*, 28:293–331, 1986.

[15] R. Bajcsy and F. Solina. Three dimensional object representation revisited. In *First International Conference on Computer Vision*, pages 231–240, June 1987.

[16] L. R. Nackman and S. M. Pizer. Three-dimensional shape description using the symmetric axis transform 1: theory. *IEEE Transactions on Pattern Analysis and Machine Intelligence*, PAMI-7(2):187–201, March 1985.

[17] M. Brady and H. Asada. *Smoothed Local Symmetries and their Implementation*. Technical Report Memo 757, Massachusetts Institute of Technology Artificial Intelligence Laboratory, Cambridge, Mass., February 1984.

[18] T. O. Binford. Visual perception by computer. In *IEEE Conference on Systems and Controls*, Miami, December 1971. Unpublished talk.

[19] S. A. Shafer and T. Kanade. *The Theory of Straight Homogeneous Generalized Cylinders and A Taxonomy of Generalized Cylinders*. Technical Report CMU-CS-83-105, Carnegie-Mellon University, January 1983.

[20] R.A. Brooks. *Symbolic Reasoning among 3-D Models and 2-D images*. Technical Report AIM-343, Stanford Artificial Intelligence Laboratory, June 1981.

[21] R. Nevatia and T.O. Binford. Description and recognition of complex-curved objects. *Artificial Intelligence*, 8:77–98, 1977.

[22] M. Lipschutz. *Differential Geometry*. McGraw-Hill, 1969.

[23] G. J. Agin. *Representation and Description of Curved Objects*. PhD thesis, Stanford University, October 1972.

[24] D. Marr. Analysis of occluding contour. In *Proceedings of the Royal Society of London*, pages 441–475, 1977.

[25] A. A. G. Requicha. Representations for rigid solids: theory, methods, and systems. *Computing Surveys*, 12(4):437–464, 1980.

[26] D. Ballard and C. Brown. *Computer Vision*. Prentice Hall, 1982.

[27] M. E. Mortenson. *Geometric Modeling*. John Wiley and Sons, 1985.

[28] D. Terzopoulos, A. Witkin, and M. Kass. Symmetry-seeking models for 3-d object reconstruction. In *First International Conference on Computer Vision*, pages 269–276, June 1987.

[29] D. L. Waltz. *Generating Semantic descriptions from drawings of scenes with shadows.* Technical Report AI-TR-271, Massachusetts Institute of Technology Artificial Intelligence Laboratory, Cambridge, Mass., November 1972.

[30] A. Mackworth. Interpreting pictures of polyhedral scenes. *Artificial Intelligence*, 4:121–137, 1973.

[31] J. Malik. *Interpreting Line Drawings of Curved Objects.* PhD thesis, Stanford University, Stanford, California, 1985.

[32] R.C. Bolles and P. Horaud. 3DPO: A Three-Dimensional Part Orientation System. *The International Journal of Robotics Research*, 5(3):3–26, 1986.

[33] W.E.L. Grimson and T. Lozano-Perez. Model-based recognition and localization from sparse range and tactile data. *The International Journal of Robotics Research*, 3(3):3–35, 1984.

[34] W.E.L. Grimson. *From Images to Surfaces: A Computational Study of the Human Early Visual System.* MIT Press, 1981.

[35] D. Terzopoulos. *Multiresolution Computation of Visible-Surface Representations.* PhD thesis, Massachusetts Institute of Technology, Departments of Computer Science and Electrical Engineering, January 1984.

[36] Gerard Medioni and Ramakant Nevatia. Segment-based stereo matching. *Computer Vision, Graphics, and Image Processing*, 31:2–18, 1985.

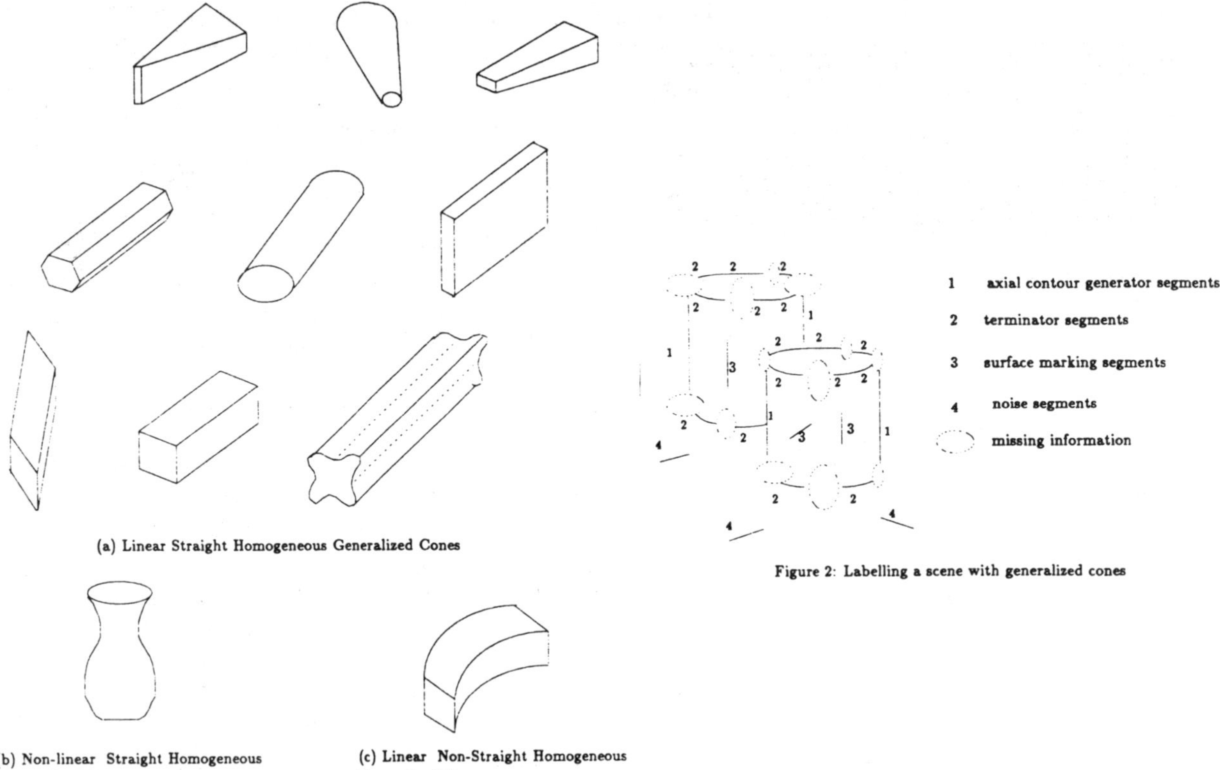

(a) Linear Straight Homogeneous Generalized Cones

(b) Non-linear Straight Homogeneous
Generalized Cone

(c) Linear Non-Straight Homogeneous
Generalized Cone

Figure 1: Some examples of generalized cone classes. All examples in (a) except the bottom right and (c) are taken from Brooks [1981] to illustrate a point. See text.

Figure 2: Labelling a scene with generalized cones

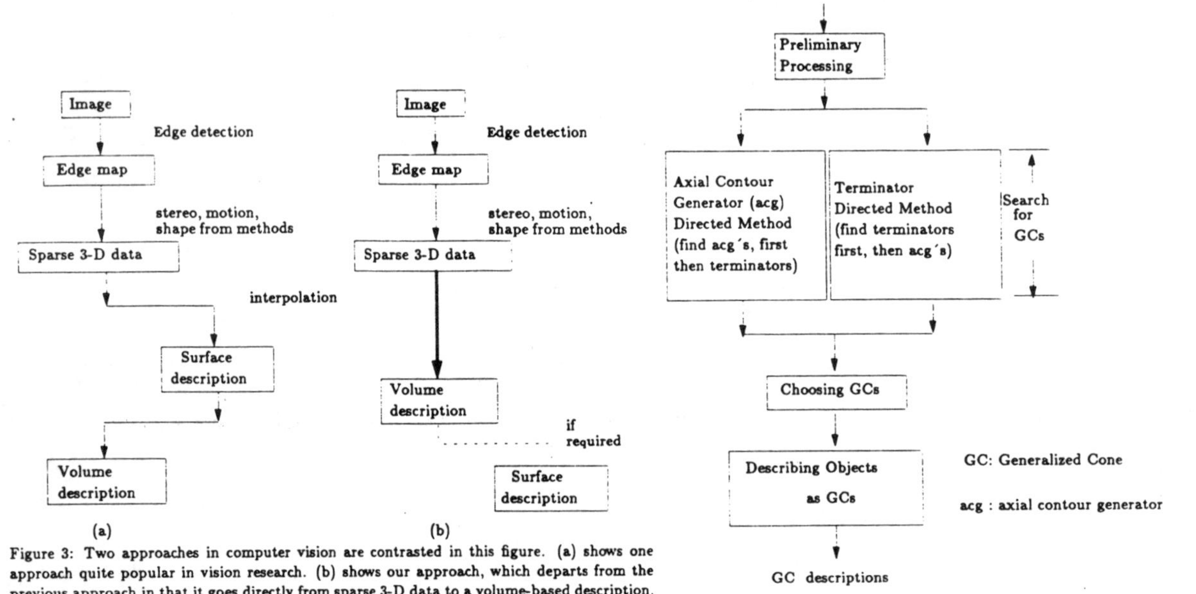

Figure 3: Two approaches in computer vision are contrasted in this figure. (a) shows one approach quite popular in vision research. (b) shows our approach, which departs from the previous approach in that it goes directly from sparse 3-D data to a volume-based description. Note, we do not go through the intermediate surface description stage.

Figure 4: Block diagram of the system

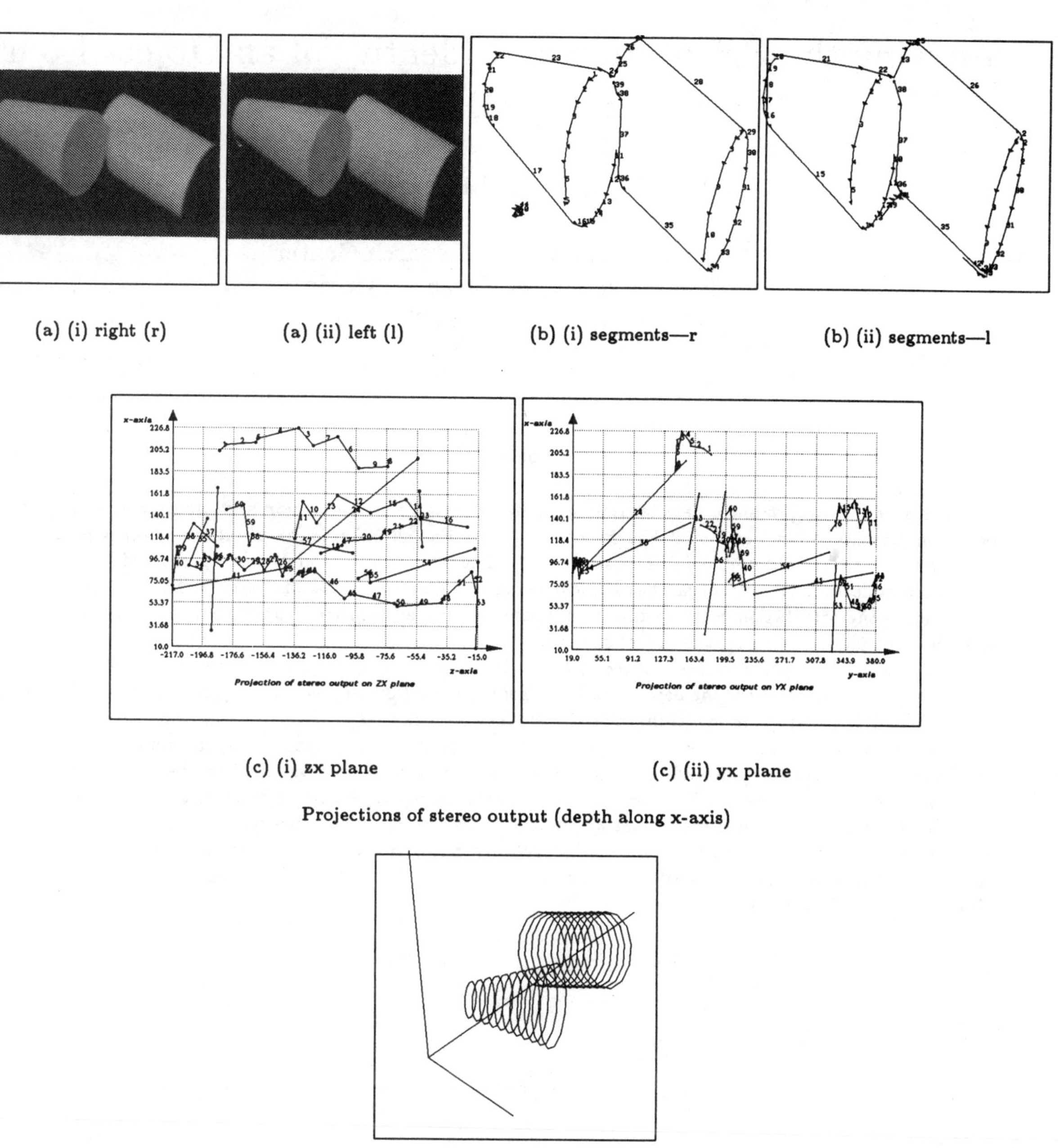

Figure 5: Data of two objects with occlusion from stereopsis and output of our system

Resolving the Orientation and Identity of an Object from Range Data

B. C. Vemuri and J.K. Aggarwal *

Computer and Vision Research Center
The University of Texas at Austin
Austin, Tx 78712

Abstract

In this paper, we present a new technique for determining the orientation and identity of an object based on matching object and model surface descriptions. *Partial information about the object is provided in the form of range data acquired from a single view.* The objects and models are represented by regions that are a collection of surface patches homogeneous in curvature-based properties. The technique for determining the orientation requires that correspondence be established exactly, between one point on the object surface and one on the model surface.

Given exactly one point on the surface of the unknown view of an object and the corresponding point on the surface of the model of the object, the principal vectors (if unique) can be used to determine the 3-D rotation required to bring the model into the same orientation as that of the object. In order to determine this one point correspondence, we first extract curves of constant principal curvature from the surfaces (corresponding to regions possessing the same sign of the principal curvatures) of the model and the unknown view of an object. *Then, the problem of establishing a one point correspondence between the object and the model is equivalent to that of finding the one point correspondence between curves of same constant principal curvature on the object and model surfaces.* The local maxima in the curvature of these curves are utilized as a means to establish the one point correspondence. We present the ideas discussed above in a formal framework.

---

*This work was supported in part by the Air Force Office of Scientific Research under Contract F49620-85-K-0007 and in part by National Science Foundation under Contract DCR8517583.

1   Introduction

Recognizing objects and determining their orientation in 3 space in an important problem in computer vision with applications in robotics. The specific problem we consider in this paper is to identify an unknown view of an object as an instance of the model of the object and determine its orientation in 3 space relative to the model. Partial information about the object is provided in the form of range data acquired from a single view.

Given an object description obtained from a scene and a model description stored in a data base, several techniques have been proposed in literature for matching these descriptions to achieve the goal of recognition [1]-[12]. In this paper we discuss a new scheme for determining the orientation and identity of an object, that is based on matching the surface descriptions of the object with a model. The objects and models are represented by regions that are a collection of surface patches homogeneous in curvature-based properties [13],[14]. The technique for determining the orientation requires that correspondence be established exactly, between one point on the object surface and one on the model surface. Establishing this correspondence invariably involves a search in two dimensions, since the surfaces are parameterized by two parameters. We reduce the it dimensionality of this search by establishing the point correspondence between curves of constant principal curvature, extracted from regions on the object and model possessing same sign of principal curvatures. Once the single point correspondence is specified, closed form solutions are given for determining the orientation of the unknown view of the object in 3 space with respect to the model.

An informal description of the technique employed for resolving the orientation and identity of the object is given below. It is well documented in differential geometry literature that, there exist two distinct orthogonal vectors, corresponding to the minimum and maximum normal curvatures respectively, at any point on a variable Gaussian curvature surface. These orthogonal directions are referred to as the principal directions. *Thus, given exactly one point on the surface of the unknown view of an object and the corresponding point on the surface of the model of the object, the principal vectors are used to determine the 3-D rotation required to bring the model into the same orientation as that of the object.*

In order to determine this one point correspondence, we first extract curves of constant principal curvature from the surfaces (possessing the same sign of the principal curvature) of the model and the unknown view of an object. *Then, the problem of establishing a one point correspondence between the object and the model is equivalent to that of finding the one point correspondence between curves of same constant principal curvature on the object and model surfaces.* We suggest a simple way to achieve the point correspondence between these curves. The technique involves direct comparison of the local maxima in the curvature of these curves. In case of multiple choices for a given point, the ambiguity is resolved by utilizing the distance information between the points of local maxima. One could utilize a more sophisticated method of matching these curves, such as the least squares method suggested in Schwartz [15]. The ideas discussed above are presented in a mathematical framework in the next two sections.

This paper is organized as follows : in section 2 we define the problem precisely, and give the derivations for determining the attitude of the object in three space with respect to the model. Section 3 depicts the implementation results. Section 4 contains conclusions.

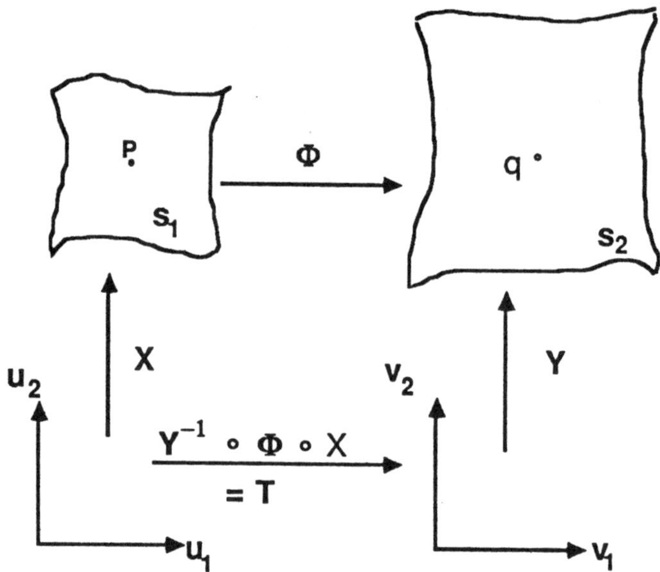

Figure 1: Parameterizations of S_1 and S_2

2   On Resolving the Orientation and Identity

The specific problem addressed in this paper is formulated as follows: **Formulation** : Given the surface descriptions of the unknown view and the model of an object, denoted by S_1 and S_2 respectively such that $S_1 \subset S_2$ i.e., the unknown view is contained in or generated from the model.

1. Find $S_v \subset S_2$ such that S_v matches S_1

2. Find $\phi : S_1 \Rightarrow S_v$, where ϕ is a rigid motion in $\Re^3$

where S_v is said to match S_1, if the principal curvatures at corresponding points on S_v and S_1 are identical.

Let $X(u_\alpha)$ and $Y(v_\alpha)$, $\alpha = 1, 2$ be the parametric representations at a point $p \in S_1$ and a corresponding point $q \in S_2$ with u_α and v_α as parameters respectively. Figure 1 depicts the parameterizations and is referred to as a commutative diagram. *If the neighborhoods of points $p \in S_1$ and $q \in S_2$ can be parameterized using a common set of parameters, then the transformation between the two parameter spaces takes a simple form as will be shown subsequently. We can then use the commutative diagram in figure 1 to compute the rigid motion ϕ.* So, the question that remains to be answered is, how to define such a parameterization? The rest of this section will be devoted to answering this question and determining the rigid motion ϕ. We now recall some definitions and a theorem from differential geometry of surfaces embedded in $\Re^3$ [16], which will allow us to define special parameterizations at p and q of S_1 and S_2 respectively, to be used subsequently.

Definition: Let C be a regular curve [16] on a surface S passing through a point $p \in S$, k the normal curvature of C at p, and $cos\theta = <n, N>$, where n is the normal vector to C and N is the normal vector to S at p. The number $k_n = kcos\theta$ is called the normal curvature of $C \subset S$ at p (see figure 2).

Definition: The maximum normal curvature k_1 and the minimum normal curvature k_2 at $p \in S$ are called the principal curvatures at p; the corresponding directions are called principal directions at p.

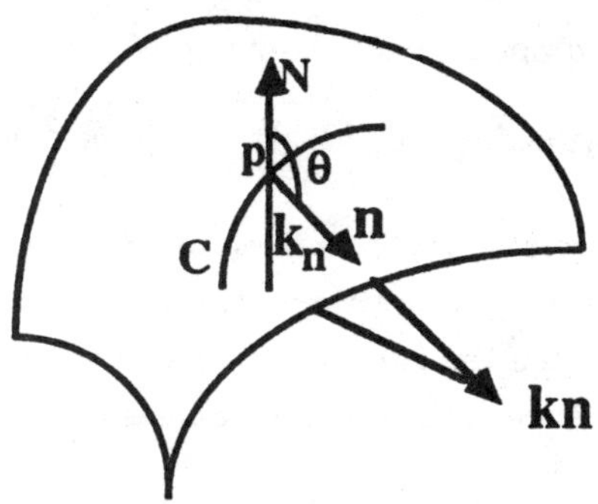

Figure 2: Normal Curvature at a Point on a Curve of a Surface

Definition: If at a point $p \in S$ $k_1 = k_2$, then p is called an umbilical point of S; in particular, the planar points $(k_1 = k_2 = 0)$ are umbilical points.

All the points of a sphere and a plane are umbilical points. A nonumbilical point is one at which the principal curvatures and therefore the principal directions are distinct.

Definition: If a regular connected curve [16] C on S is such that for all $p \in C$ the tangent line of C is a principal direction at p, then C is said to be a line of curvature of S.

Theorem 1 *Let p be a nonumbilical point of a surface S. Then it is possible to parametrize a neighborhood of p in such a way that the coordinate curves of this parametrization are the lines of curvature of S.*

Let $X(u_\alpha)$ and $Y(v_\alpha)$ be the parameterizations in the neighborhoods of $p \in S_1$ and $q \in S_2$ such that the coordinate curves of parameterization are the lines of curvature. Consider a regular curve $X(t) = X(u_\alpha(t)), \alpha = 1, 2$ on the surface S_1 and define its length $\ell_1(t)$ by the integral

$$\ell_1(t) = \int_0^t \sqrt{(X'(\sigma))^2} d\sigma \tag{1}$$

Since $X'(t) = \sum_{\alpha=1}^2 X(u_\alpha) du_\alpha/dt$, it follows that

$$d\ell_1^2 = X' \bullet X' = E_1 (du_1)^2 + 2F_1 du_1 du_2 + G_1 (du_2)^2 \tag{2}$$

where E_1, F_1 and G_1 are the coefficients of the first fundamental form of S_1 at the point under consideration. The right hand side of equation 2 is called square of the line element or alternatively the first fundamental form. In a similar manner, we can define the square of a line element on S_2 given by

$$d\ell_2^2 = E_2 (dv_1)^2 + 2F_2 dv_1 dv_2 + G_2 (dv_2)^2 \tag{3}$$

Using the invariance property of line elements to rigid motion, the line elements on S_1 and S_2 at corresponding points in the corresponding directions must be equal. Let point $p \in S_1$ correspond to point $q \in S_2$.

Then the line elements at p and q must be equal, giving us

$$E_1 (du_1)^2 + 2F_1 du_1 du_2 + G_1 (du_2)^2 = E_2 (dv_1)^2 + 2F_2 dv_1 dv_2 + G_2 (dv_2)^2 \qquad (4)$$

One *consistent choice of corresponding directions* on S_1 and S_2 at corresponding points p and q for equation 4 to be valid is the *principal directions*. In order to equate line elements on S_1 and S_2 as in equation 4, the relationship between the two parameterizations u_α and v_α, $\alpha = 1, 2$ should be determined. Since the parameters u_α and v_α were chosen to be the lines of curvature at $p \in S_1$ and $q \in S_2$ respectively,

$$[v_\alpha] = T [u_\alpha] \qquad (5)$$

Where T is a transformation, whose form is discussed in the following proposition.

Proposition 1 *Given a non-umbilical point $p \in S_1$ and the corresponding point $q \in S_2$, $X(u_\alpha)$ and $Y(v_\alpha)$, $\alpha = 1, 2$, the parameterizations in the neighborhood of p and q respectively, such that the lines of curvature are the coordinate curves of parameterization. Then, the transformation $T : u_\alpha \mapsto v_\alpha$ between the parameter spaces is a dilation.*

Proof : Notice that it suffices to answer the question: what transformation T would preserve the principal directions locally ? Since the principal directions at a non umbilical point are unique, the only transformation that can locally preserve these directions must be the one in which v_1 is a function of u_1 only, and v_2 is a function of u_2 only. Which implies that T is a diagonal matrix. Since $p \in S_1$ has been identified with $q \in S_2$, it is possible to choose the aforementioned functions to be linear i.e.,

$$T = \begin{bmatrix} a & 0 \\ 0 & b \end{bmatrix} \qquad (6)$$

Where a and b are scaling constants in the parametric directions respectively.

$$\begin{bmatrix} v_1 \\ v_2 \end{bmatrix} = \begin{bmatrix} a & 0 \\ 0 & b \end{bmatrix} \begin{bmatrix} u_1 \\ u_2 \end{bmatrix} \qquad (7)$$

We now proceed to determine the scale factors a and b by invoking the invariance property of a line element to rigid motion.

$$dv_1 = a\, du_1 \qquad (8)$$

$$dv_2 = b\, du_2 \qquad (9)$$

Substituting equations 8 and 9 into equation 4 we have

$$a^2 E_2 (du_1)^2 + 2ab F_2 du_1 du_2 + G_2 b^2 (du_2)^2 = E_1 (du_1)^2 + 2F_1 du_1 du_2 + G_1 (du_2)^2 \qquad (10)$$

Since the parameterizations (u_1, u_2) and (v_1, v_2) were chosen to be the lines of curvature and since they have the special property of being an orthogonal family of curves on a surface, we have $F_1 = F_2 = 0$. Therefore, substituting into equation 10 we get

$$a^2 E_2 (du_1)^2 + b^2 G_2 (du_2)^2 = E_1 (du_1)^2 + G_1 (du_2)^2 \qquad (11)$$

Equating coefficients of like terms

$$a^2 E_2 = E_1 \Rightarrow a = \pm\sqrt{E_1/E_2} \tag{12}$$

$$b^2 G_2 = G_1 \Rightarrow b = \pm\sqrt{G_1/G_2} \tag{13}$$

Thus, determining the transformation T between the parameter spaces u_α and v_α, $\alpha = 1, 2$. Therefore we have shown that knowing one point correspondence between S_1 and S_2, T can be determined and is seen to be a dilation. $\square$

We will now consider the case of constant mean curvature surfaces without going into the proof. For constant mean curvature surfaces, the transformation $T : u_\alpha \mapsto v_\alpha$, $\alpha = 1, 2$ is composed of a scaling and a rotation. Since, the principal directions are not uniquely determined for constant mean curvature surfaces, any two orthogonal directions can be taken as the principal directions. Therefore, in general the choice of these principal direction pairs at $p \in S_1$ and $q \in S_2$ will differ by a rotation. In addition to the rotation, a scaling is introduced in each parametric direction as discussed in proposition 1. The transformation T can be determined in a manner similar to that shown in proposition 1, except in this case it is required to have two points on S_1 correspond to two points on S_2.

Once the transformation $T : u_\alpha \mapsto v_\alpha, \alpha = 1, 2$ is determined , the commutative diagram in Figure 1 can be used to determine the rigid motion ϕ,

$$T \;=\; Y^{-1} \circ \phi \circ X \tag{14}$$

$$\phi \;=\; Y \circ T \circ X^{-1} \tag{15}$$

In the next section we will consider the problem of determining the one point correspondence for *variable mean curvature* surfaces, given the surface descriptions obtained from dense range maps.

2.1   Determining The One Point Correspondence

The one point correspondence problem is a global problem and will invariably involve some kind of a search. The search space is in general large and consists of all possible points on the model surfaces, which are possible candidates for a match for a given point on the unknown view. In order to limit the search space, by reducing the dimensionality of the search, we will introduce certain geometric constraints, which must be satisfied by a candidate solution.

To establish the one point correspondence between the unknown view of an object and its model, certain prominent features of unknown view and the model must be extracted. Since, the surfaces $S_v \subset S_2$ and S_1 differ by a rigid motion, and rigid motion is a special isometry, the necessary and sufficient conditions for two surfaces to be isometric can be utilized to derive similar conditions for this special case of isometry.

It can shown that the *iff* conditions for two surfaces to differ by this special isometry (rigid motion) are (see [17])

$$k_1(u_\alpha) = k_1'(v_\alpha) \tag{16}$$

where k_1 and k_1' denote the maximum principal curvatures on S_1 and S_v respectively. Similarly,

$$k_2(u_\alpha) = k_2'(v_\alpha) \tag{17}$$

k_2 and k'_2 denote the minimum principal curvatures on S_1 and S_v respectively.

Thus, if the two surfaces S_1 and S_v satisfy the above *iff* conditions then, curves defined by $k_1(u_\alpha) = a$ correspond to $k'_1(v_\alpha) = a$ and similarly $k_2(u_\alpha) = b$ correspond to $k'_2(v_\alpha) = b$. Since $S_v \subset S_2$, we can determine the constant curvature curves of S_2 and then try to establish the one point correspondence between curves of same constant curvatures on S_1 and S_2. The search space can be further reduced by selecting local maxima of the curvature k of the curve on the surface (see figure 2). The local maxima of a curve $k_1(u_\alpha) = a$ on S_1 should correspond with local maxima of the corresponding curve $k'_1(v_\alpha) = a$ on S_2. The correspondence between local maxima can be obtained by a direct comparison. In the case of ambiguity arising from multiple choice of point correspondences on S_2 for a given point on S_1, further constraints involving other intrinsic features eg: relative position of the local maxima can be imposed. Once a possible choice for the correspondence is made, the rigid motion ϕ can be computed as discussed earlier, and may be applied to the unknown view of the object for verification purposes.

3   Implementation Results

In this section, we present the implementation results obtained for one object, a toy rabbit. The range data for the object was obtained using a laser range finder [18].

Figure 3a is the range image of a toy rabbit. Figure 3b depicts the curvature-based region classification of the toy rabbit. In this example we have elliptic (bright) and hyperbolic (dark) regions as indicated. Constant principal curvature curves for the positive curvature regions on the toy rabbit are depicted in figure 3c. Curves of same constant principal curvature belonging to regions of same curvature-based classification were chosen from the unknown view and the model for establishing the one point correspondence. The rotational axis R_a and the rotational angle θ used in generating the unknown view are

$$R_a = [0.707, \ 0.707, \ 0.0]$$
$$\theta = 90^o$$

The estimated rotational axis $\hat{R}_a$ and rotational angle $\hat{\theta}$ are

$$\hat{R}_a = [0.711, \ 0.702, \ 0.0001]$$
$$\hat{\theta} = 86.6107^o$$

The error in estimated rotational axis and angle can be attributed to the process of extracting constant principal curvature curves, which involved quantization of the principal curvatures and then using spline approximations to represent the curves.

Throughout this paper, we have limited our attention to the case where the unknown view of the object was compared to its model. To cary out recognition between several objects, it is necessary to compare the unknown view with several object models. To eliminate extraneous candidate models, region type and region adjacency information that are made available in the region representation [13], can be utilized. In the case of multiple choices of models, the rigid motion required to register the model and the unknown view can be computed and ambiguous choices can be eliminated based on error in registration computed at a select set of points (points of local maxima in curvature on curves of constant principal curvature).

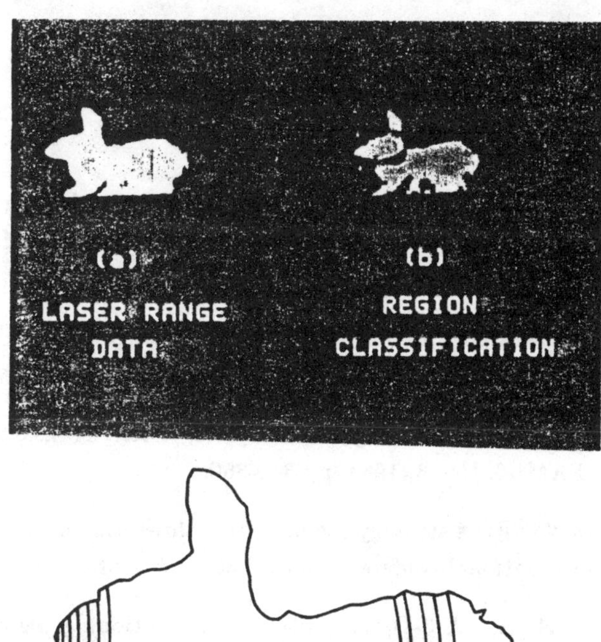

Figure 3: (a) Unknown view of toy rabbit(b) Elliptic and Hyperbolic regions on the rabbit (c) Constant principal curvature (k_2) curves

4   Conclusions

In this paper we have described a new technique for resolving the orientation and identity of objects from dense range maps. The objects and models are represented by regions that are a collection of surface patches homogeneous in curvature-based properties. A salient feature of our method is that, exactly one point correspondence between the object and its model is required to determine the orientation of the object in three space relative to the model. Also our method can easily distinguish between similar objects, but of different sizes. This is because the computed registration when applied to the model for verification would yield high error due to size differences between the object and the model. However, the above claim needs to be verified experimentally.

The techniques introduced in this paper were tested on data obtained using a laser ranging system. The objects depicted in the examples are of reasonable complexity and the results obtained seem encouraging.

5   References

1. R. Nevatia and T. O. Binford, "Description and recognition of curved objects," Artificial Intelligence, Vol. 8, No. 1, 1977, pp.77-98.

2. D. R. Smith and T. Kanade, "Autonomous scene description with range imagery," DARPA Proceedings of the Image Understanding Workshop (New Orleans), Science Applications, Mclean, Va., 1984, pp.282-290.

3. B. Boyter and J. K. Aggarwal, "Recognition of Polyhedra from range data," IEEE Expert, Vol. 1, No. 1, Spring 1986, pp. 47-59.

4. B. Bhanu, "Representation and shape matching of 3-D objects," IEEE Transactions on Pattern Analysis and Machine Intelligence, PAMI-6, No. 3, 1984, pp.340-350.

5. P. Horoud and R. C. Bolles, "3DPO's strategy for matching three-dimensional objects in range data," IEEE Proceedings of the international conference on robotics, Atlanta, Ga., March 1984, pp.78-85.

6. O. D. Faugeras, and M. Herbert, "A 3-D recognition and positioning algorithm using geometrical matching between primitive surfaces," in Proceedings of 7th International Joint Conference on Artificial Intelligence, Vancouver, B. C., 1983, pp. 996-1002.

7. K. Ikeuchi, "Determining the attitude of object from needle map using extended Gaussian image," AIM-714, Massachusetts Institute of Technology, Cambridge, massachusetts, 1983.

8. M. Oshima, and Y. Shirai, "Object recognition using three-dimensional information," IEEE transactions on Pattern Analysis and Machine Intelligence, Vol. PAMI-5, July 1983, pp. 353-361.

9. P. Besl, and R. Jain, "Three-dimensional object recognition," ACM Computing Surveys, Vol. 17, No. 1, March 1985.

10. F. P. Ferrie, and M. D. Levine, "piecing together the 3-D shape of moving objects: An overview," Proceedings of the Computer Vision and Pattern Recognition Conference, San francisco, California, June 1985, pp. 574-584.

11. R. M. Bolle and D. B. Cooper, "On optimally combining pieces of information, with application to estimating 3-D complex object position from range data," IEEE Transaction on Pattern Analysis and Machine Intelligence, Vol. PAMI-8, No. 5, 1986, pp.619-638.

12. W. E. L. Grimson, and T. LoZano-P'erez, "Model-based recognition and localization from sparse range and tactile data," The International Journal of Robotics Research, Vol.3, No.5, Fall 1984, pp.3-35.

13. B. C. Vemuri, A. Mitiche and J. K. Aggarwal, "Curvature-based representation of objects from range data," Image and Vision Computing, Vol. 4, No. 2, may 1986, pp.107-114.

14. B. C. Vemuri, and J. K. Aggarwal, "3-D model construction from multiple views using range and intensity data," in Proceedings of the Computer Vision and Pattern Recognition Conference, Miami, June 1986, pp. 435-437.

15. J. T. Schwartz and M. Sharir, "Identification of partially obscured objects in two and three dimensions by matching characteristic curves," Robotics Report 46, Robotics Activity, New York University, 1985.

16. M. P. Do Carmo, *Differential Geometry of Curves and Surfaces*, Prentice-Hall, Inc., Englewood Cliffs, New Jersey, 1976.

17. J. A. Thorpe, *Elementary Topics in Differential Geometry*, Springer-Verlag, NY 1979.

18. White Scanner 100A manual, Technical Arts Corporation, Seattle, WA, USA (1984).

Eye Movements and Visual Cognition

Dana H. Ballard
Computer Science Department, University of Rochester

Abstract

One aspect of primate intelligence is the ability to coordinate eye movements in the process of solving complex tasks. Primate eye movements have been studied in several disciplines but little work has been directed toward a computational theory that shows how the eye *movements* can confer specific advantages that can be used in problem-solving behaviors. This paper outlines some elements of such a theory.

1. Introduction

As animals, we move in relatively fixed environments, but we also have to deal with other moving objects, animate and inanimate. Although we must function in the presence of different kinds of motion, our visual system works best when the imaged part of the world does not move. Thus we have several mechanisms that program eye movements with a common purpose: to stabilize the image on the retina. The purpose of this paper is to show that these simple observations have profound implications for the structure and function of our visual system.

At first, the ability to make different kinds of programmed eye movements might seem to complicate a computational model, but in fact, the converse is true. The ability to make eye movements actually simplifies the information-gathering process of the eye. The intent of this short paper is to show the extent of these simplifications in two principal areas.

1. *Low-level computation of visual features.* The use of programmed eye movements provides additional constraints that allow the computation of optic flow and relative depth in a way that is much simpler than can be done with a passive system. Also, certain mathematical approximations are valid near the fovea and this can lead to simplified analysis of fixated targets.

2. *Spatial Relationships.* The solution to many visual tasks involves computing spatial relationships between objects. We show how this computation can be facilitated with active vision. Also, visual tasks can involve the computation of information at only a few areas of the image that each subtend a very small visual angle. We show how an active visual system can use internal data structures to compute the required movements and thus obtain the requisite information. The key observation is that the sequentiality of eye movements can be used to encode spatial relations economically.

In a longer version of this paper [Ballard 1987] we provide a primer on primate vision and also explore two additional areas where eye movements provide leverage:

3. *Calibration of Visual Dimensions.* Conventional vision systems depend on an independent measure of ground truth regarding the analytical form of constraints and length scales. Systems currently being built have shown that actually obtaining such accuracy is difficult. We argue that current work in learning algorithms can be used in an active vision system to keep the system in calibration to the required accuracy. An active vision system can learn the desired visuo-motor relationships in the process of trying to make the required movement.

4. *Solving the indexing problem with visual search.* A number of psychological experiments have shown that humans use a predominantly parallel lookup strategy to identify objects from visual features. Using a formal model of this process, we show why the introduction of some sequential searching, such as that which would be available to a system with active vision, helps to make this strategy work.

A recent paper by [Aloimonos et al. 1987] complements the work herein by showing that knowledge of camera motion can stabilize a wide range of computations in early vision. Our work is directed to the more cognitive aspects of visual processing. Specifically, the view is advanced that vision is best understood in the context of its information-gathering purpose. This view forces the question: what information is the vision system gathering at any instant? The answer is that the visual data is analyzed in a mode that is heavily dependent on context, and that usually only a portion of the image must be analyzed. Our manifesto is that:

The parsing of the intrinsic image is minimal with respect to the goals.   (1.1)

To some extent this view was held by vision researchers before Marr's influence (e.g., [Freuder 1975]). However, the mistake made at the time was to vastly underestimate the amount of vision hardware necessary. This was changed by two papers [Barrow and Tennenbaum 1978; Marr 1978] that have led to the elucidation of the constraints and algorithms necessary for "early vision," focusing on pre-attentive data structures of intrinsic images that can be computed with minimal context. One impact of this work and that in visual imagery in neurobiology has been to revive notions of an image in the head and programs to account for visual stability in terms of image-like data structures. This paper forces a reevaluation of the extent to which static visual stability can be maintained. Our view is that visual stability is the product of the function of an active eye movement system, which can parse the image quickly enough to satisfy the viewer's goals. To put it another way: visual stability is the side effect of being able to answer questions about the world in a timely manner using stability as a working hypothesis.

One should not interpret the above to mean that the kinds of massively parallel computations that build up a preliminary description of the world are not necessary. It is just that at some point this strategy breaks down since the number of alternate hypotheses about the world that need to be represented becomes too large. At this point some temporary (dynamic) data structure to represent scene invariants must be built and the availability of neural hardware that allows sequential processing with modifiable data structures is necessary. In this case, some minimization principal must be linked to control the amount of work done and that is the intent of (1.1). Given this position, eye movements are a natural mechanism.

In analyzing the importance of eye movements, one problem is that any mechanism that we propose that is handled by eye movements could, in principle, be handled by neural "software." In fact, some of the mechanisms that we consider have been previously described in terms of neural software. For example, Ullman's visual routines, such as area filling and contour following [1984], can be carried out by software or eye movements. Other examples obviously must use software such as Kosslyn's mental imagery demonstrations [Kosslyn 1980], Just and Carpenter's demonstration of sequential transformation in problem solving [Just and Carpenter 1987] and Shepard's mental rotations [Shepard and Cooper 1982]. However, the genesis of all of these examples may have been the physical movements of the eyes. The main argument for the primacy of eye movements is weak, but is that of shared implementation. Given that eye movements were in place to serve other functions, the extension of their use to handle spatial relationships may be more natural than that which could have plausibly been shared by the neural circuitry.

In the face of all the potential advantages of programmed eye movements, one might wonder why such a system was not considered earlier. There are several reasons. One is the popular belief that humans can analyze images without eye movements. The extent to which this is true has not been demonstrated and, in any case, we argue that eye movements make matters simpler. Another is the myth of simulation: why bother to build an eye movement system when one can simulate its properties with graphics software? Although current 3D rendering has made enormous advances, it is still very costly to generate real-time images. In contrast, the technology for building an eye movement system has recently changed to make a system with the desired performance characteristics very economical. At Rochester, a collaborative effort by researchers in computer science and mechanical engineering has led to the construction of the Robot Eyes system shown in Figure 1. This system was inspired by earlier work at the University of Pennsylvania by R. Bajczy [1985].

2. Foveal Mathematics and Kinetic Depth

An active vision system will typically have better resolution near the origin in a region termed the fovea. A feature of the fovea is that special mathematical approximations hold there because terms vanish owing to the fact that the retinal coordinates (x, y) are approximately zero. This section shows an example of how these constraints can be used to solve the problem of *kinetic depth*. The key point is that almost all of the computations of low-level vision are facilitated by programmed eye movements. The kinetic depth calculation is meant to be representative of the kinds of simplifications that are possible.

Kinetic depth is the sensation of visual depth that one gets when moving the head while fixating a target. Objects in front of the fixation point appear to move in the opposite direction to the motion while objects behind the fixation point move in the same direction. The apparent velocity is proportional to the distance from the fixation point. Figure 2 shows this relationship.

The ability to fixate a point is an example of a *programmed movement* that the eyes can make. It has the effect of choosing an instantaneous origin at $(0, 0, Z_0)$ about which the system is rotating. The analysis assumes an instrumented binocular system so that the point Z_0 can be easily obtained from the vergence geometry as:

$$Z_0 = b \sin \phi / \cos (\theta + \phi) \tag{3.1}$$

Let us use standard projection equations $x = -fX/Z$, $y = -fY/Z$. Differentiating these provides the relationship between the velocity of a point in 3D (V_X, V_Y, V_Z) and optic flow (u, v):

$$-Zu = fV_X + xV_Z \tag{3.2}$$
$$-Zv = fV_Y + yV_Z$$

Now make the foveal approximation: assume that V_X and V_Y are roughly comparable or greater than V_Z and that $f >> x, y$. Then:

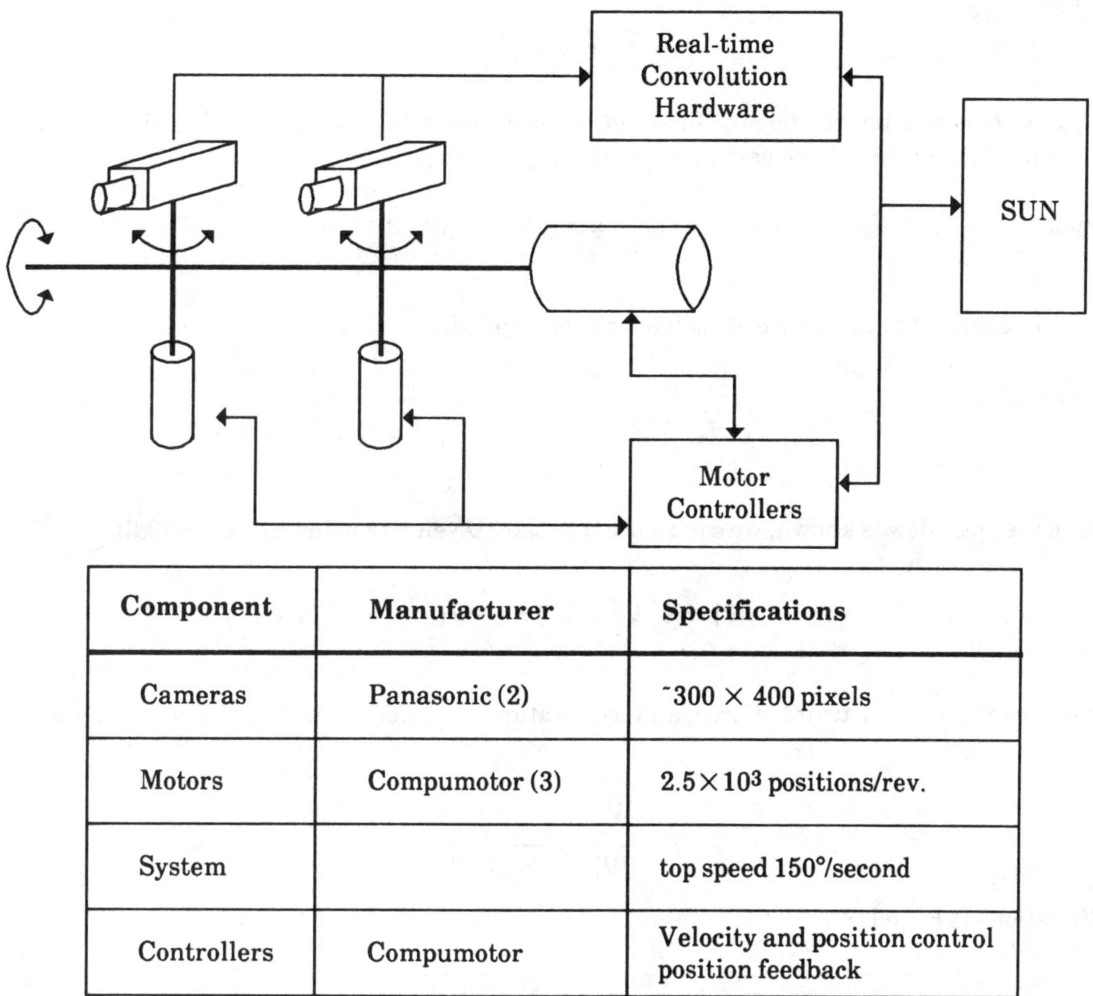

Component	Manufacturer	Specifications
Cameras	Panasonic (2)	⁻300 × 400 pixels
Motors	Compumotor (3)	2.5×10^3 positions/rev.
System		top speed 150°/second
Controllers	Compumotor	Velocity and position control position feedback

Figure 1 The Rochester Robot Eyes eye movement system has three degrees of freedom. Each camera can move independently in yaw but is are yoked to the others in pitch.

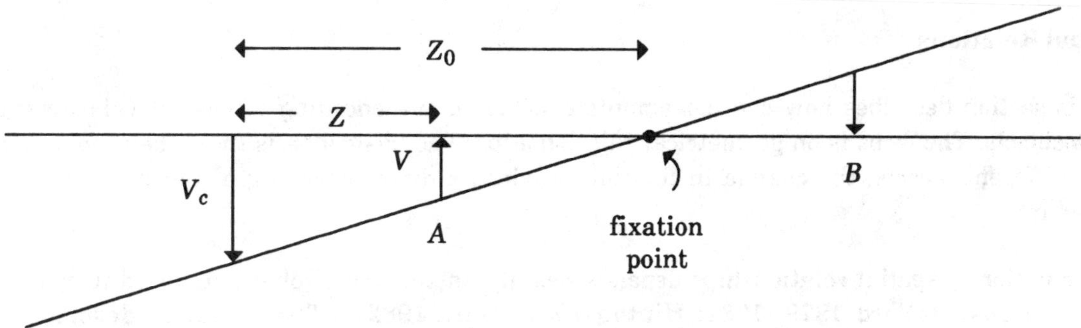

Figure 2 Kinetic depth obtained by making head motions with respect to a fixation point. Points in front of the fixation point (A) appear to move in the opposite direction to the commanded motion V_c, whereas points behind (B) appear to move in the same direction.

$$\frac{u}{v} \approx \frac{V_X}{V_Y} \tag{3.3}$$

where $f(x, y, t)$ is the image itensity function; then differential analysis yields the well-known aperture equation in terms of the partial derivatives f_x, f_y, and f_t.

$$f_x u + f_y v + f_t = 0 \tag{3.4}$$

Equations (3.3) and (3.4) can be used to solve for foveal optic flow:

$$v = -f_t / (f_x(\frac{V_X}{V_Y}) + f_y), \quad u = +f_t / (f_x + (\frac{V_Y}{V_X})f_y) \tag{3.5}$$

Once the optic flow is known, we can relate it to the 3D velocity using Equation (3.2):

$$|V| = \sqrt{(V_x^2 + V_y^2)} = \frac{Z}{f}\sqrt{(u^2 + v^2)} \tag{3.6}$$

Now from the original constraint of programmed rotation, if we additionally assume that V_Z is small, then:

$$\frac{|V_c|}{|V|} = \frac{|Z_o|}{|Z_o - Z|} \tag{3.7}$$

From Equations (3.6) and (3.7):

$$Z = Z_0 (1 + \frac{Z_o \sqrt{(u^2 + v^2)}}{V_c f})^{-1} \tag{3.8}$$

The crucial approximation neglected the second terms in (3.2) to derive (3.3) and (3.6). The result shows that the depth, Z, can be calculated by knowing the flow vector (u,v) and the fixation point Z_0.

3. Spatial Relations

This section describes how eye movements can aid in the encoding of spatial relationships between objects. The focus is on geometrical relationships. The basic idea is that when *sequentially* fixating different objects, the change in fixation provides a direct encoding of the desired spatial relationship.

Our notion of spatial relationships depends heavily on the use of object-centered frames and transformations [Ballard 1979, 1981; Hinton 1981; Marr 1982]. The model is described in connectionist terms in Figure 3. The crucial notion of object invariance is that an object preserves its identity even though its retinal image may change due to object or observer motion. For this reason it is parsimonious to divide the internal representation of an object into a view-independent part and a view-variant part. The view independent part describes the object in an object-centered frame. The

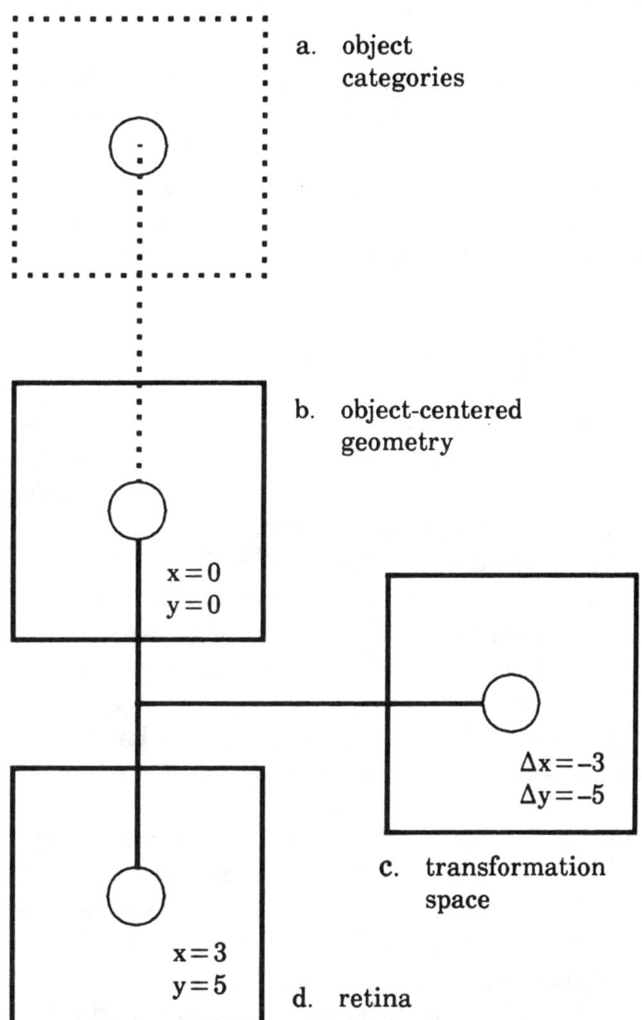

Figure 3 Model of object-centered representation of visual data after [Hinton 1981]. Object tokens (a) are related to their geometrical descriptions (b), which are coupled to retinotopic descriptions (d) explicitly via transformations (c). Object feature tokens (dotted lines) have locations but these are described with respect to object-centered coordinates. The task in vision is to relate retinocentric coordinates to object-centered coordinates. One way to do this is to use transformation units and explicitly represent the relationship as a triple (X_0, T_x, X_R) where $X_0 = T_x X_R$.

view variant part describes the transformation necessary to map the retinotopic description into object centered coordinates. This model was originally proposed by [Hinton 1981] based on [Ballard 1979; 1981]. However, its implications in terms of the sequentiality of eye movements have so far not been considered.

For simplicity, the discussion will be limited to 2D, with only translations possible. The techniques discussed will extend to 3D, rotation, and scale, but for the moment such extensions will only confuse the main issue.

194   Ballard

3.1 Foveation

With the restrictions, the transform space becomes an elegant model of foveation, as shown by Figure 4. Suppose there was a focus of attention process that could, by focusing on the object-centered "C," selectively activate the triple (C_O, T_C, C_R). Then T_C^{-1} describes how to move the eyes so as to foveate C_R. Furthermore, the impact of the new image on the transformation space can be anticipated since for every object X, its transformation T_X is changed by $T_X^{-1}T_C$. If the *actual motor command* were to trigger the updating process, it would explain why the world appears to jump when the eyeball is suddenly pushed.

3.2 Encoding Spatial Relations

We now turn to the issue of remembering the locations of objects. This has been tackled previously by [Feldman 1985; Haber 1985; Hinton 1981; Zipser 1984]. Hinton proposes a two-level system, as depicted in Figure 5. However, the details of its implementation are vague. The problem arises in considering its use. The relationships between the scene frame and object frame cannot be predetermined and thus, in our application, these relationships (defined by dashed lines in Figure 5) must be dynamically allocated. Furthermore, accomplishing this is tricky: to handle multiple objects, some kind of attentional mechanism must indicate the construction of links. Figure 5 does illustrate a principle for saving spatial relations, however. Suppose that the scene frame has the same status as the object frame and that they contain object geometries for objects A and B respectively. The relationship between the two objects A and B, T_{AB}, is precisely what one would like to save instead of either T_A or T_B. The reason is that it is invariant with respect to changes in the viewer's position.

In our scheme the attentional mechanism is linked to eye movements. Furthermore, this allows the object-centered frame to be shared so that no scene frame is necessary. To see how such a strategy could work, consult Figure 6. Suppose we are looking at an object A and would like to remember its location. The transformation units for currently visible objects provides a basis for remembering location. Any of them can potentially be used, but those associated with large objects are likely to be the most helpful since they will be in view for the largest changes in the viewer position. If object B is selected, a dynamic link can be activated. The mechanisms for accomplishing this are discussed in [Feldman 1984; Ballard 1986]. One remaining problem is that of distinguishing T_{AB} from T_{BA}. One way of doing this is to incorporate temporal delays in synapses. Using this strategy, the activation sequence specifies which is activated: A→B activates T_{AB}, and vice versa.

One difference between Hinton's original proposal and the one described herein is the way integration over eye movements is handled in the case of orthoscopic perception. If the segments of a figure such as an octagon are displayed sequentially with sufficient rapidity, human subjects have no difficulty guessing the figure's identity, even though the individual parts are never visible at the same time. Hinton argues that the integration takes place in the scene frame. We argue that it takes place in the retinotopic frame using the mechanism of Section 3.1.

This is similar to the Norton and Stark scanpaths proposal [1971] but the neural implementation hints that functions other than the original scanning sequence are very plausible. For example, given T_{AB}, one can create T_{BA}. Furthermore, given a network of such transformations, the transformation between any two objects is readily computable as long as there is a directed path between them, e.g. $T_{AB}, T_{BC}, T_{CD} \vdash T_{AD}$.

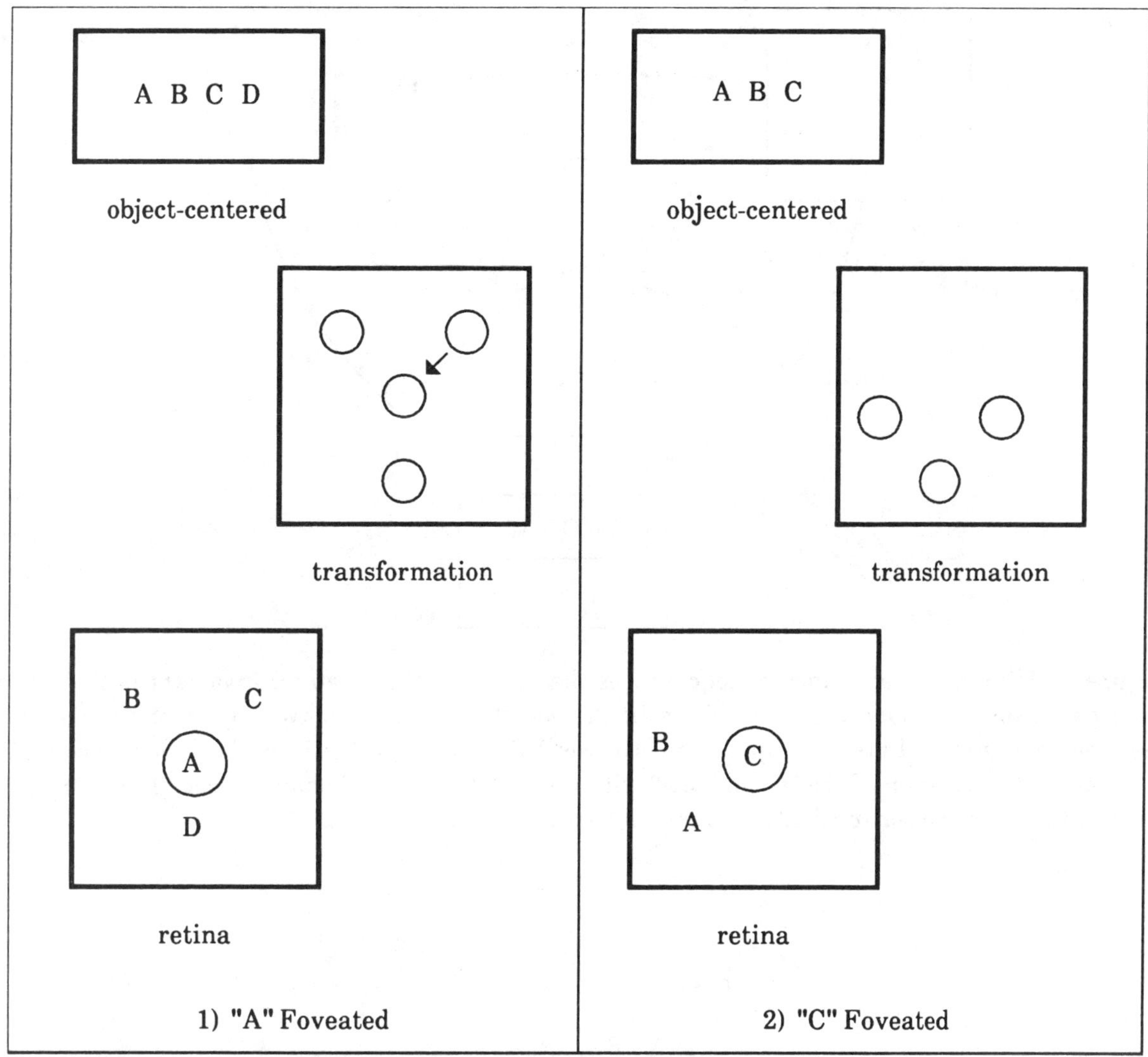

Figure 4 The transform unit for "C" describes how to move the retina so "C" is foveated

3.3 Are Topological Relationships Pre-Categorical?

A difficult question in vision is to draw the line between what is pre-categorical, that is, does not depend on the image segmentation, and what is post-categorical. This section argues that the computation of topological relationships must be post-categorical. The reason is that if they were not, the task of computing them would have to deal with too many alternatives. To see this, suppose a scene is composed of x parts and that the combination of these into objects has not been determined. If all combinations of parts are allowed, there there are potentially 2^x objects. Allowing only binary-valued relations between objects, such as ABOVE, LEFT-OF, etc., would mean that there are potentially $(2^x)^2$ instances of each relationship. Given R relations, the number of potential relationships is:

$$R(2^x)^2$$

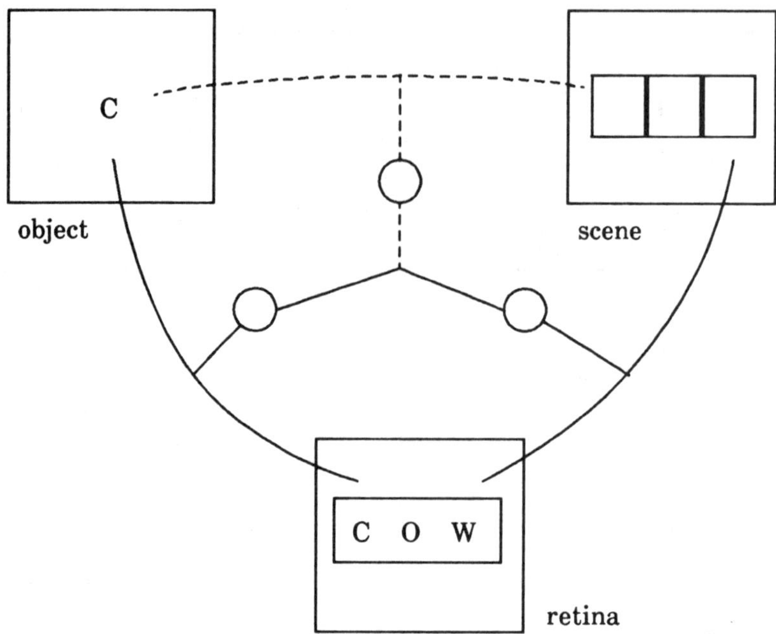

Figure 5 Hinton's three frame model captures the idea that the essential invariant is that which describes transformations between objects in the world. It builds on two copies of the circuitry described in Figure 3. In the example there is a "word shape" object that is used for the scene and the invariant is the position of the "C" in "cow" with respect to the word shape object. In general, the invariant transformation (dashed lines) cannot be precomputed.

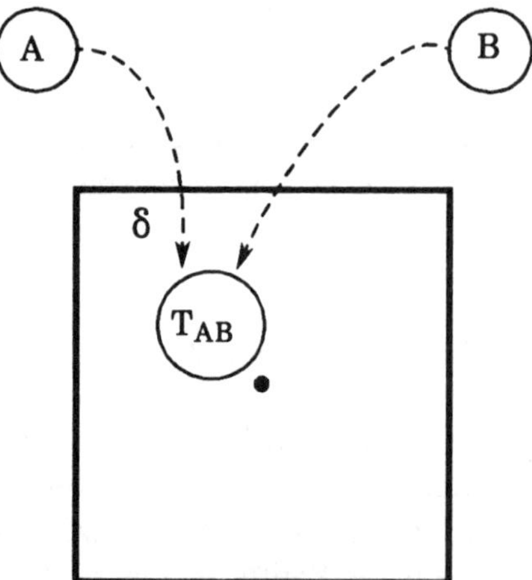

Figure 6   Remembering object locations. The sequence AB, created by looking at A then B or thinking about A then B, will activate T_{AB}.

From this, one can see the value of using segmentation rules to eliminate possibilities as the critical variable is the number of parts. For ten parts per scene and ten relations the number of instances is

10^7. But for 100 parts, the number of instances is 10^{31}. Thus unless one can group the parts of a scene to eliminate many possibilities, the preattentive computation of relationships seems unlikely.

The previous section showed that, provided one is willing to compute slowly (sequentially), spatial relationships can be handled easily with eye movements. In addition, certain of these measurements can be converted to topological relationships easily with the foveation mechanism. For example, to establish LEFT-OF(A, B):

> foveate (A);
> if sign(T_B) > 0 then LEFT-OF(A, B) (*)
> else RIGHT-OF(A, B)

Furthermore, knowing the relationship between ourselves and another observer T allows the relationship to be reported from the latter's perspective. So instead of the above, to establish the relationship from the other observer's perspective, simply substitute TT_B for T_B in (*).

3.4 Hand-Eye Coordination

In this section we consider the interaction of the visual system with the motor system in a hand-eye coordination problem. Figure 7 shows the basic circuitry for the task of grasping a hexagonal nut with a wrench. The method of establishing invariant relationships between visualized objects has been discussed earlier, so emphasis is placed on the additional mechanisms needed for the grasping task.

A very important point, made in [Ballard and Hartman 1986], is that in the object-centered frame it is plausible to learn a set of desired relationships between different prototypes. For the grasping task it is plausible that $T_{desired}$ could be stored. Thus the work that has to be done in establishing the desired relationship is simply the difference between the current relationship and the desired relationship. Thus:

$$T_{comm} = (T_W^{-1} T_N)^{-1} T_{desired}$$

In the figure, consistent with earlier notation, T_W is the transformation of the wrench such that $W_0 = T_W W_R$ and T_N is the transformation of the nut such that $N_0 = T_N N_R$. Thus the invariant $T_W^{-1} T_N$ describes the relationship of the wrench with respect to the nut, and can be established with eye movements, as described earlier.

Another independent source of the relationship between wrench and nut is available from proprioception. This is depicted in the lower part of Figure 7. These two sources can be combined as shown. One way of doing this is simply to weight the two sources, i.e.,

$$T_a = \alpha \, T_{av} + \beta \, T_{ap}$$

where $\alpha + \beta = 1$, v = visual, p = proprioception, and $T_a = (T_W^{-1} T_N)^{-1}$.

In summary, following [Jeannerod 1987], our proposal is that there are two independent systems for measuring spatial relationships. The main difference between the proposal here and that of Jeannerod is that here the transformations are computed in object-centered coordinates as opposed to body-centered coordinates. The most useful of the two systems uses eye movements to build up a

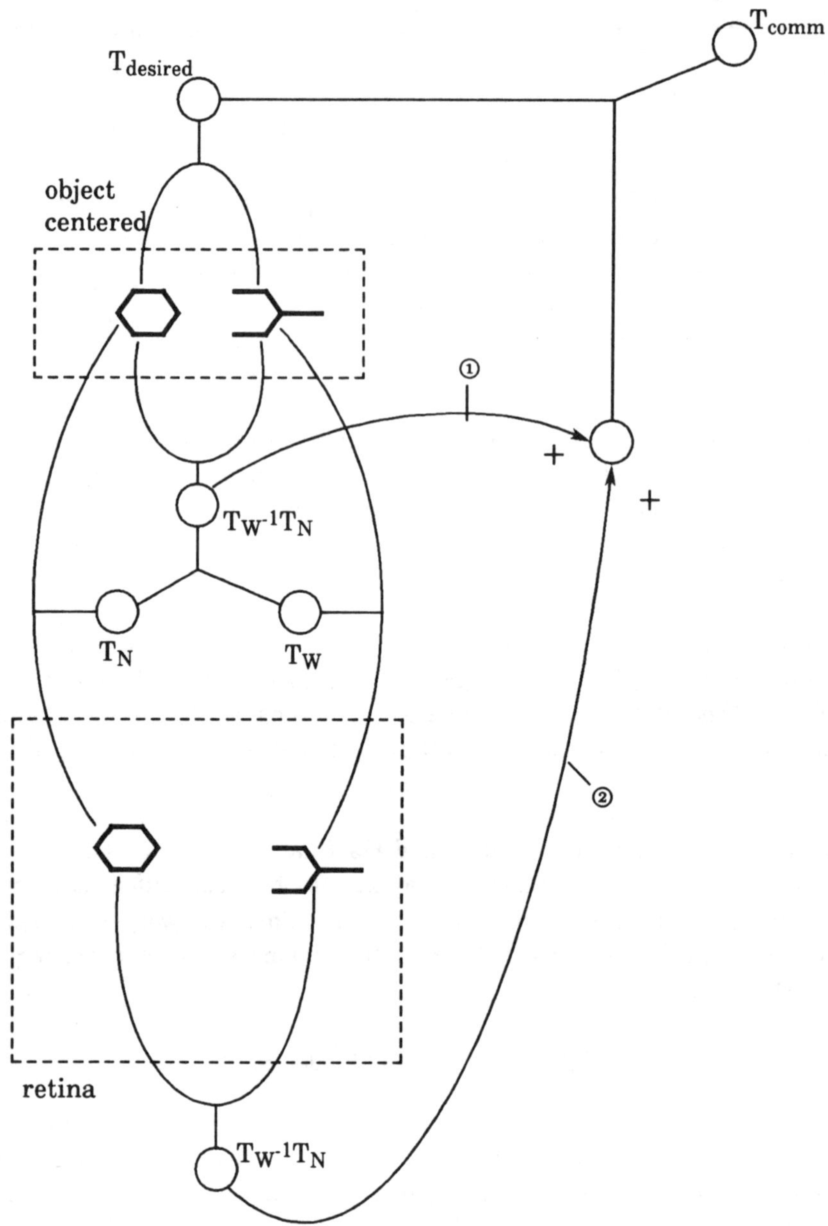

Figure 7 Two independent ways of computing spatial relationships between objects. (1) The difference between object-centered transformations provides the desired invariant. This can be computed by eye movements, as described in Section 3.2. (2) For parts of the body that are interconnected, the same transformation can be computed by using proprioceptive information.

spatial map. However for hand-eye coordination there is a proprioceptive system that uses the gaze vector as part of a transformational chain relating the eyes to the hand.

4. Conclusions

This paper attempts to show that programmed eye movements play a pivotal role in the *computations* that are performed in the process of seeing. These computations occur at many levels of analysis:

1. Since the mathematics is simpler near the origin, the constraints about the world are special in the region of the fovea. The main technical point was that programmed eye movements can be used to reduce the degrees of freedom in a given computation and thus lead to simple solutions. For example, the computations for kinetic depth could be done in constant time.

2. Eye movements are a necessary part of the goal-directed analysis of the world. Object-centered models are part of a feature network (the "what" channel), and transformations are part of a spatial map (the "where" channel).The main technical point is that the sequentiality of eye movements solves a crucial problem in storing spatial relationships. In a parallel circuitry is has proven very difficult to distinguish ArB from BrA where r is some relationship between concepts A and B. Eye movements resolve this temporally. Thus if A is activated before B, the relationship ArB is encoded and vice versa. This is easy to implement using neural delays.

3. An equally important point is that there are actually *two* ways of getting coordinate information for visuo-motor behavior. One way is to establish the relative change that has to be made using only visual information. Another way uses proprioceptive information. The latter has the disadvantage of being restricted to transformations between connected parts of the body. The two system model clears up confusions that may have resulted from trying to model visuo-motor coordinaton and visual stability with a single system.

Eye movements have often been regarded as a nuisance by experimenters in psychology and neuroscience and as an unnecessary complicating factor in computational vision. However, the computational advantages summarized above suggest that they play a central role in any complete model of primate vision.

References

Aloimonos, J., I. Weiss and A. Bandopadhay, "Active vision," *ICCV*, London, 1987.

Anderson, R.A., "The role of posterior parietal cortex in spatial perception and visual-motor integration," in *Handbook of Physiology*, in press, 1987.

Bajcsy, R., 2nd Workshop on Computer Vision, Bel Air, MI, 1985.

Ballard, D.H., "Cortical connections and parallel processing: Structure and function," *The Behavioral and Brain Sciences 9*, 1, 67-120, 1986.

Ballard, D.H., "Eye movements and visual cognition," TR 218, Computer Science Dept., U. Rochester, August 1987.

Ballard, D.H., "Interpolation coding: A representation for numbers in neural models," TR 175, Computer Science Dept., U. Rochester, 1986.

Ballard, D.H., "Generalizing the Hough transform to arbitrary shapes," *Proc.*, Int'l. Conf. on Computer Vision and Pattern Recognition, 1981.

Ballard, D.H., "Generalizing the Hough transform to arbitrary shapes," TR 55, Computer Science Dept., Univ. Rochester, 1979.

Ballard, D.H. and L. Hartman, "Task frames: Primitives for sensory-motor coordination," *CVGIP 36*, 1986.

Bandopadhay, A., "A computational study of rigid motion," Ph.D. Dissertation, Computer Science Dept., Univ. Rochester, 1987.

Bandopadhay, A. and D.H. Ballard, "Active navigation: Egomotion perception by the tracking observer," to appear, *Canadian J. of Artificial Intelligence*, 1987.

Barrow, H.G. and J.M. Tenenbaum, "Recovering intrinsic scene characteristics from images," in *Computer Vision Systems*, Hanson, A.R. and E.M. Riseman (eds.), Academic Press, 1978.

Bower, T.G.R., *Development in Infancy*, second edition, W.H. Freeman and Co., 1982.

Bronson, G.W., *The Scanning Patterns of Human Infants: Implications for Visual Learning*, Ablex Publishing Corp., 1982.

Feldman, J.A., "Four frames suffice: A provisional model of vision and space," *The Behavioral and Brain Sciences 8*, 265-289, 1985.

Feldman, J.A., "Dynamic connections in neural networks," *Biological Cybernetics 46*, 27-39, 1982.

Freuder, E.C., "A computer system for visual recognition using active knowledge," Ph.D. Dissertation, Lab. for Artificial Intelligence, M.I.T., 1975.

Haber, R.N., "Toward a theory of the perceived spatial layout of scenes," *Computer Vision, Graphics and Image Processing 31*, 3, September 1985.

Hartman, L., personal communication.

Haith, M.M., *Rules that Babies Look By, Lawrence Erlbaum Associates*, 1980.

Hinton, G.E., "Learning distributed representations of concepts," *Proc.*, 8th Ann. Conf. of Cognitive Science Soc., Amherst, MA, August 1986.

Hinton, G.E., "Shape representation in parallel systems," *Proc.*, 7th IJCAI, Vancouver, B.C., 1088-1096, August 1981.

Jeannerod, M., presentation, Comput'l. Neuroscience Conf., Carmel, CA, June 1987.

Just, M.A. and P.A. Carpenter, "Cognitive coordinate systems: Accounts of mental rotation and individual differences in spatial ability," *Psych. Rev. 92*, 1987.

Kiel, F.C., *Semantic and Conceptual Development: An Ontological Perspective*, Harvard University Press, 1979.

Kosslyn, S.M., "Seeing and imagining in the cerebral hemispheres: A computational Approach, *Psych. Rev. 94*, 2, 148-175, 1987.

Kosslyn, S.M., *Image and Mind*, Harvard University Press, 1980.

Marr, D.C., *Vision*, W. H. Freeman and Co., 1982.

Marr, D.C. and H.K. Nishihara, "Representation and recognition of the spatial organization of three-dimensional shapes," *Proceedings, Royal Soc. Lond. B 200*, 269-294, 1978.

Mishkin, M., "A memory system in the monkey," *Philos. Trans. Royal Soc. Lond. B 298*, 85-95, 1982.

Mishkin, M., L.G. Ungerleider and K.A. Macko, "Object vision and spatial vision: Two cortical pathways," *Trends in NeuroSciences, 6*, 414-417, 1983.

Norton, D. and L. Stark, "Scan paths in eye movements during pattern perception," *Science 171*, 308-311, 1971.

Rayner, K., "What guides a reader's eye movements?" *Vision Res. 16*, 829-837, 1976.

Shepard, R.N. and L.A. Cooper, *Mental Images and Their Transformations*, MIT Press, 1982.

Van Essen, D., "Functional organization of primate visual cortex," in *Cerebral Cortex*, Vol. 3, A. Peters and E.G. Jones (eds.), Plenum Press, 1985.

Van Essen, D.C. and J.H.R. Maunsell, "Hierarchical organization and functional streams in visual cortex," *Trends in NeuroSciences, 6*, 370-375, 1983.

Wurtz, R.H. and W.T. Newsome, "Divergent signals encoded by neurons in extrastriate areas MT and MST during smooth pursuit eye movements, *Soc. Neurosci. Abs. 11*, 1246, 1985.

Yarbus, A.L., *Eye Movements and Vision*, Plenum Press, 1967.

Zipser, D., "A computational model of hippocampus place-fields," ICS report 8405, Institute for Cognitive Science, Univ. Calif., San Diego, 1984.

A GEOMETRIC APPROACH TO MULTISENSOR FUSION AND SPATIAL REASONING

Su-shing Chen
Department of Computer Science
University of North Carolina
Charlotte, North Carolina 28223

ABSTRACT

In this paper, a geometric approach to multisensor fusion and spatial reasoning is presented. There are three parts of this paper. The *first* part is concerned with a spherical sensory model. Its spherical data structure provides an efficient and unified representation scheme for multisensor fusion, navigation, motor control, and spatial reasoning. This model is independent of different sensor types. Images of different sensors located at the origin may be integrated in the same model to enhance image understanding and object recognition capabilities. It is also useful to integration of temporal images on the same image sphere. This is a sensor-family-based spherical representation scheme. There is also an object-based spherical representation scheme which is centered at the centroid of an object. Integration of multiple image frames of the object over the sphere provides complete surface information of the object. There is a spatial correspondence between these two representation schemes. The *second* part deals with some efficient algorithms of navigation, using the spherical data structure locally at each point of a path. This illustrates how to combine this spherical sensory model with navigation and motor control which is a special topic of the field of spatial reasoning. The *third* part is concerned with spatial reasoning. It is explained why the spherical data structure - spherical octree, is an efficient representation scheme in spatial reasoning. Spatial relationships, such as "Object A lies above object B", "Object A_1 lies to the left of object B_1", "Object A_2 is between objects B_2 and C_2", "Object A_3 is included in object B_3", "Object A_4 intersects object B_4", may be represented easily by the elevation angle θ and the azimuth angle ϕ, with the help of the depth (radial) value ρ. The collection of objects is defined as compact and closed sets in an universe in the 3-D world space. The Hausdorff distance between two objects is defined so that nearness and convergence of objects are represented. Two topologies are defined on the space of objects. These concepts will be further extended to random sets for treating uncertainty in multisensor fusion and spatial reasoning.

In [1]-[14], a spherical perceptual model and its computational aspects have been investigated. Earlier researchers on the spherical model include Gibson, Clocksin, Loomis and Nakayama. This model and its spherical data structure provide a single data structure for sensory processing, motor control, navigation and spatial reasoning. This is very convenient to applications that require a sensory feedback control system. This simplification leads to feasiblity of real-time processing and supplies certain human cognitive capabilities in robotics. A more complete and rigorous account of this approach will be published in [12].

MULTISENSOR FUSION

The main question of multisensor fusion is to integrate many numerical and spatial sensory data so that useful information about an object or a scene may be obtained. Our approach is to gather 3-D spatial information by partial visible surface reconstruction from each sensory data. The integration is performed in the spherical model into a single set of spatial data of the object or the scene.

The spherical perspective eliminates several limitations of the flat perspective model, such as distorted images under wide viewing angles and vanishing points; and supplies a mechanism to integrate temporal (or dynamic) sensory data on a single image sphere. While the orthographic model represents viewing at infinity, the spherical perspective model represents viewing at any finite point in the world space. If we move the viewer to infinity, the sequence of spherical perspective models converges to the orthographic model. The spherical model is to use the unit sphere as the image sphere on which all image data received by sensor arrays located at the origin are represented. One significant improvement over the flat model is that we may represent sensory data of not only 360 degrees but also the whole spherical solid angle around the sensor array. The unit sphere is parametrized by two parameters - the elevation angle θ and the azimuth angle ϕ. The image point in the image plane under the flat perspective is related to the spherical image point under the spherical perspective by a simple nonlinear transformation which maps the image plane into the image sphere. Geometrically, the image plane at $(0,0,1)$ is the tangent plane to the image sphere at the north pole $(0,0,1)$. By a rotation, any image plane at an arbitrary direction can be transformed on the image plane at the north pole. Thus a full field-of-view can be obtained by rotating a sensor at the origin or building a spherical sensor array.

In the spherical spatial coordinates (ρ,θ,ϕ), the radial value (depth value) ρ depends on the angles (θ,ϕ). Surface geometry and reconstruction in spherical coordinates have been investigated in terms of the radial value ρ and its partial derivatives ρ_1, ρ_2, with respect to θ and ϕ [14]. In [13], quantities ρ/ρ_1 and ρ/ρ_2 are related to spherical optical flow fields of images. Knowing an initial radial value ρ_0 (we can measure this value from known landmark), we may reconstruct the visible surface from observables. Normally, smooth surface reconstruction requires intensive computation. For real world applications, we combine this reconstruction method with the spherical octree structure. That is, we may discretize the reconstruction scheme in the framework of octree structure which has an inherent hierarchical structure of multiple resolutions. For details, see [12].

The spherical octree structure (see Figure 1) is a generalization of the rectangular octree structure which is made for the orthographic model. This data structure divides a solid sector or the whole spherical shell in the world space into eight octants. There is the intial radial distance (inner radius) from the viewing position which limits the universe to a solid sector or the whole spherical shell. Each octant is again divided into eight octants. This recursive scheme provides a fine structure of the universe. This spherical data structure is rotation invariant in the sense that we do not have to recalculate the whole tree under any rotation completely.

Multisensor families may be homogeneous or heterogeneous of different types and kinds (sonar, radar, optical, thermal,·and laser ranger) [7]. Multisensor fusion is classified into two categories - static and dynamic. Furthermore, in both cases, there are two possibilities: a single sensor family at one position or a distributed system of sensor families at separate positions. In the static case, both the sensor families and the environment are static. Dynamic multisensor fusion deals with situations that sensor families and/or the environment may be in motion. Dynamic multisensor fusion is temporal for it integrates sensory data over time. The spherical model is useful for dynamic fusion, because we may integrate temporal images on the same sphere at each viewing position (See Figure 2).

First, visible surfaces from various sensory data of a static sensor family which may have different sensor kinds at a position are reconstructed. We refer to [7],[12] for details. We have considered sensory data fusion of (1) range and shading

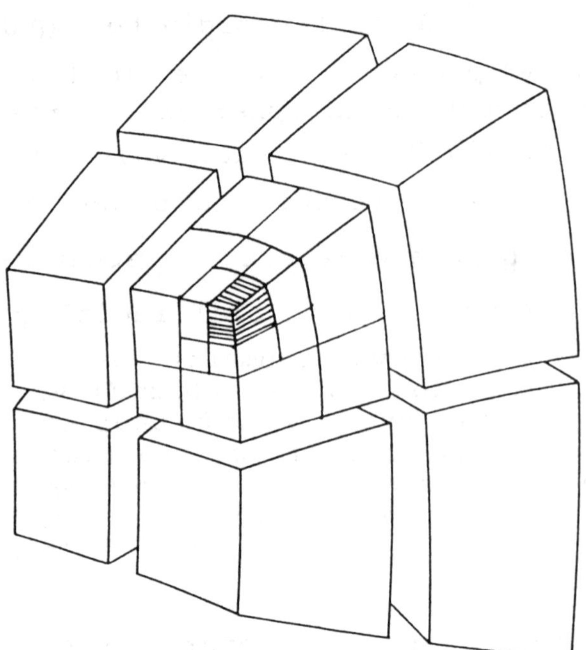

Figure 1 Spherical Octree

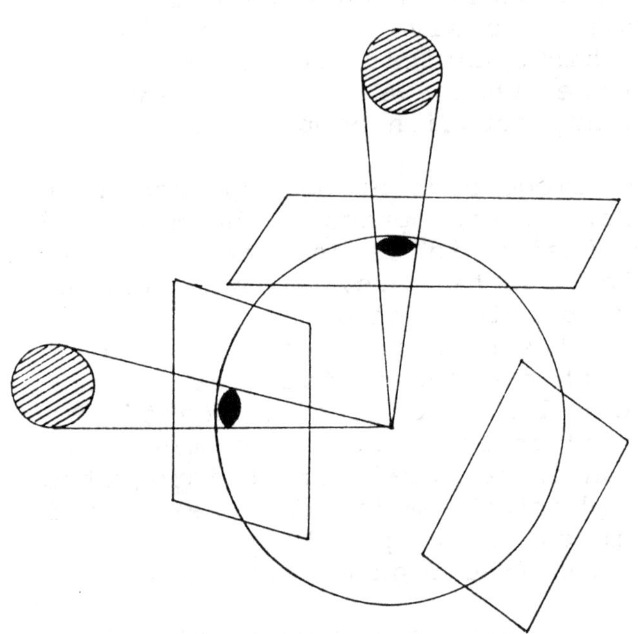

Figure 2 Temporal Fusion

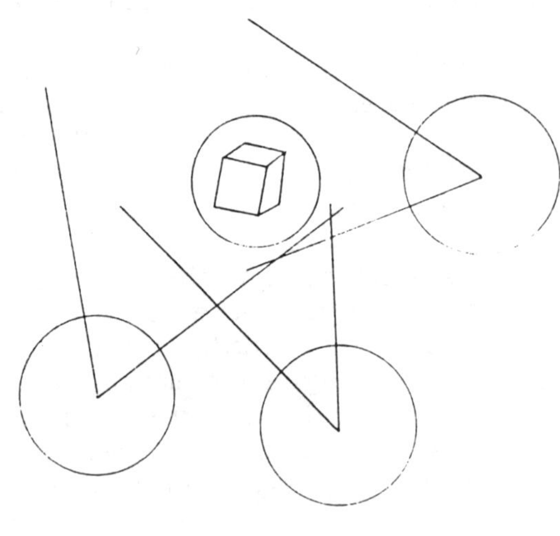

Figure 3 Multiframe Views
         and Object-based
         Representation

data, (2) multiframe shading data (this case may also be considered as dynamic sensory data fusion of a moving sensor probing a scene; see Figure 3), (3) thermal and shading data, and (4) radar and shading data. These data fusions lead to other combinations of data fusion.

There are three possibilities of dynamic multisensor fusion: (1) static sensors and dynamic scene, (2) dynamic sensors and static scene, and (3) dynamic sensors and dynamic scene. There are spatial interrelationships among these possibilities. Here, we consider only the simpler case of one sensory family in dynamic multisensor fusion. If one sensor family and one object are moving with motions $M_1(t)$ and $M_2(t)$, all three possiblities are equivalent by using compositions of $M_2^{-1}(t)$ and $M_1(t)$. So, we may assume that the sensory family is static and the scene is dynamic, without loss of generality. The sensory family is placed at the origin and multisensor fusion is performed on the unit sphere. This is the sensor-family-based spherical representation scheme. The equivalence mentioned above also establishes a correspondence (see Figure 3) between the sensor-family-based and the object-based representation schemes.

NAVIGATION AND COLLISION AVOIDANCE

Navigation and collision avoidance may be considered as a subarea of spatial reasoning. As a mobile robot moves along a planned path, its multisensor system is constructing a local map of the surrounding which is not completely known to the robot. The spherical multisensor system of the robot supports a full field-of-view and creates a complete local map. This system detects obstacles that are unknown to the global path planner. While the robot moves along a path, the global map is updated continuously. During the updating, new alternative paths may be discovered and known alternative may be checked for feasibility.

If the robot reaches a deadend or is trapped in a complex maze, the updated map is very useful to retreat the robot to a position where it can move along an alternative path. The spherical vision system sees all 360 degrees (in a 2-D map) around the robot so that it can easily find a suitable direction to retreat. In existing visual systems, only a limited field-of-view is used. Thus, overhead is significant to integrate local maps at different positions. One must keep track of what angles have scanned and what remains to be scanned.

Navigation is concerned with finding free pathways and choosing a suitable one for the next period of motion. We assume that the planned path is polygonal. Free pathways are represented by clear sectors which span angles of varying degrees at the origin (the robot) between obstacles or landmarks. They are maximal in the sense that they are not contained in any larger sector satisfying the same conditions. At each position on the path, there is a spherical octree (or circular quadtree) structure representing obstacles and free pathways. If the diameter of a robot is D, we use a cone with the disk of diameter D as its base to estimate whether a free pathway is suitable for the planned path. The robot finds a suitable free pathway whose clear sector intersects with the planned path and looks for a direction in the sector of the next period of motion. If there is no suitable free pathway intersecting the planned path, a detour is necessary and then an effort is made to return to the planned path. We describe here the "walk around" algorithm which performs the detour and looks for the planned path. This algorithm will also navigate the robot to walk around any nonconvex obstacle, such as a cul-de-sac (Figure 4). Moreover, it will navigate the robot to walk around a maze, although the orbit may not be the shortest. The robot will be able to leave the maze by using the spherical local map. If returning to the planned path is impossible (the global map will be used here), the robot has to replan the path by using stored information about the environment which has been collected along the path.

   Walk-Around Algorithm (See Figure 5) Following the planned path, the robot may find an obstacle intersecting the path which should be avoided. The following algorithm will guide the robot to move around the obstacle provided that the planned path is not completely blocked off (thus replanning is not necessary).

(1) Find a suitable free pathway nearest to the planned path.
(2) Find a sector whose base has diameter D+d (a small quantity) which is tangent to the obstacle.
(3) Use its bisector as orientation of the next period of motion.
(4) This process is repeated finitely many times.

It can be proved that the robot will reach other side of the obstacle and will intersect the planned path again if the robot continuously walks around a connected obstacle. For a dense configuration of obstacles (Figure 6), this algorithm may not work well. For example, the robot may get into a cluster of many obstacles. Instead of moving in this cluster, a better approach is to avoid this cluster completely. First we enclose it by a larger connected region which is considered as an obstacle. Then we apply the "walk-around" algorithm to this enclosure. Now the question is to decide when to enclose several obstacles. Clearly, a larger enclosure will imply a longer detour. We should find the minimal enclosure so that there is a suitable free pathway tangent to the enclosure.

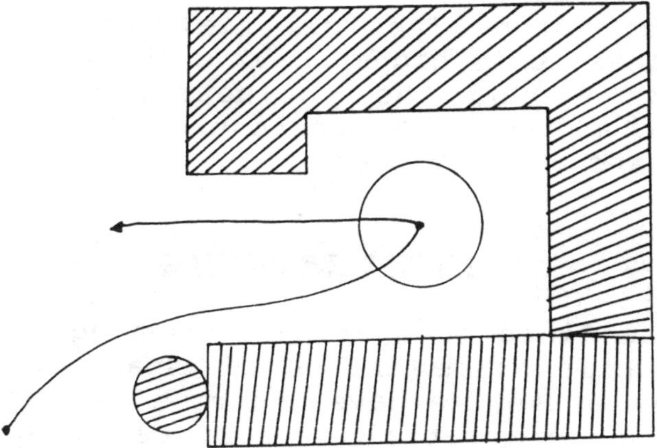

Figure 4 Turn Around in a Cul-de-sac

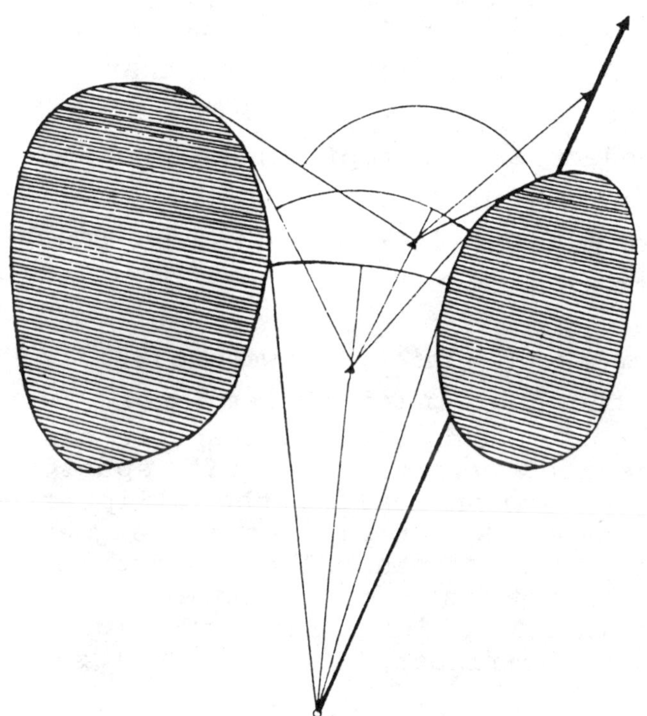

Figure 5   The Walk-around
           Algorithm

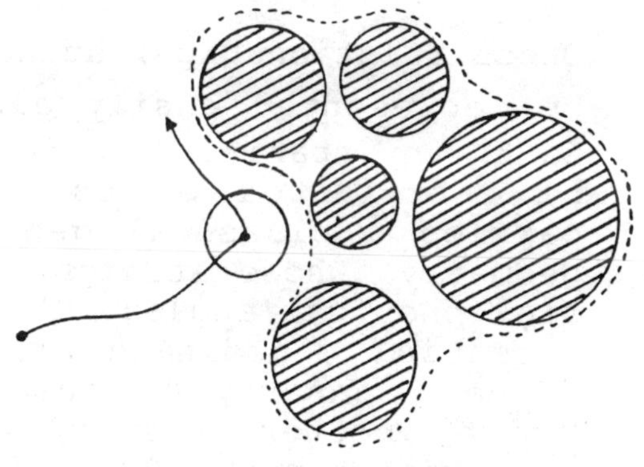

Figure 6   A Dense Cluster
           of Obstacles

The spherical multisensor system is more useful than the flat multisensor system. The full field-of-view does not miss any obstacle unless it is hidden behind observed obstacles. When the robot walks around the enclosure, more obstacles are observed and are added to the enclosure. Thus the enclosure is dynamically updated and enlarged.

SPATIAL REASONING

The general field of spatial reasoning is concerned with reasoning and decision making about spatial information and knowledge. In the above, we have described a spherical model and its representation of spatial sensory data. Spatial knowledge and reasoning concerning sensory data are representable in this model. The spherical octree structure is an efficient representation scheme. The elevation and azimuth angles θ and ϕ describe spatial relationships from the viewing position. We illustrate this point by the following examples:

(1) "Object A lies above object B" is represented by "The elevation angle interval of A lies above that of B".
(2) "Object A_1 lies to the left of object B_1" is represented by "The azimuth angle interval of A_1 lies to the left of that of B_1".
(3) "Object A_2 is included in object B_2" is represented by "The solid angle of A_2 is contained in that of B_2".
(4) "Object A_3 intersects with object B_3" is represented by "The solid angle of A_3 intersects with that of B_3".

Other relationships, such as complement, union, betweenness, may be represented easily also by the coordinate system (θ, ϕ). In fact, any spatial relationships observed on the image sphere can be represented by this coordinate system. The unit sphere carries a classical geometric structure, called the elliptic geometry, whose straight lines are the great circles and angles are spherical angles. The radial value (depth value) is another essential coordinate axis. It is not easy to be observed by visual sensors, because it coincides with lines of sight. However, other sensors, such as range-finder, will be ideal for such measurements.

The spherical octree structure subdivides the universe into a fine structure recursively. The "atomic" structure of spatial objects is given by spherical sectors at a certain level of resolution of the hierarchy. Thus, spatial objects are represented by sets which are unions of "atom"s. Nevertheless, not all spatial objects are 3-D with smooth bounding surfaces .

In our convention, spatial objects include (0-D) points, (1-D) curves,and (2-D) surfaces. They may be even sets of quite strange nature, such as fractal sets. In general, we require them to be compact and closed sets, and the collection of them to be a compact family in the topology of sets. See below for definitions.

In order to have the right framework for spatial reasoning, we consider the space (collection) $\mathbf{S}=\mathbf{S}(E)$ of all spatial objects in an "universe" E which occupies a part of the 3-D world (Euclidean) space. We shall define a topology on $\mathbf{S}$ so that spatial relationships of nearness and convergence may be expressed in terms of this topology. We like to choose the topology which will be suitable also for probabilistic use in our uncertainty study. The "universe" E inherits the subspace topology of the Euclidean topology. With respect to this topology of E, spatial objects are closed as well as compact sets. First, we study a larger space $\mathbf{F}=\mathbf{F}(E)$ of all closed sets in E. Using intersection logics in $\mathbf{F}$, we define two classes of closed sets:

$$\mathbf{F}_B = \{ F:F \ \varepsilon \ \mathbf{F}, \ F \cap B \neq \varnothing \} \text{ (closed sets hitting B)},$$

$$\mathbf{F}^B = \{ F:F \ \varepsilon \ \mathbf{F}, \ F \cap B = \varnothing \} \text{ (closed sets disjoint of B)},$$

for any subset B in E. Let $\mathbf{G} = \mathbf{G}(E)$ and $\mathbf{K} = \mathbf{K}(E)$ denote the space of open sets and the space of compact sets respectively. There are two particular classes $\mathbf{F}_G$, $G \ \varepsilon \ \mathbf{G}$, and $\mathbf{F}^K$, $K \ \varepsilon \ \mathbf{K}$. The topology generated by the above two classes on $\mathbf{F}$ is compact, Hausdorff and separable. (All the nice properties of topology!) We give $\mathbf{S}$ the subspace topology of the topology of $\mathbf{F}$. In $\mathbf{S}$, nearness and convergence are defined by the topology in $\mathbf{F}$.

The topology of E is defined by the Euclidean distance d. Compact, open and closed sets are defined by this metric topology. For any point x in E and nonempty $F \ \varepsilon \ \mathbf{F}$, $d(x,F) = \inf\{d(x,y), \ y \ \varepsilon F\}$, and $d(x,\varnothing\}=\infty$. It is known that a sequence $\{F_n\}$ converges in $\mathbf{F}$ if and only if for any x in E the sequence $\{d(x,F_n)\}$ converges in the usual sense (with respect to nonnegative real numbers). The convergence concept is a rigorous way to define nearness between two sets. It provides also a formal representation scheme for fine tasks in robotics. For example in robotic navigation, we want to find a sequence $\{F_n\}$ from an initial state F_0 to a goal state F_∞.

On the space $\mathbf{K}\backslash\{\varnothing\}$, the Hausdorff distance $\rho(K,K')$ of two compact sets K and K' is defined as

$$\rho(K,K') = \max\{ \sup_{x \varepsilon K} d(x,K'), \ \sup_{x' \varepsilon K'} d(x',K') \}.$$

The Hausdorff distance defines also a topology on $\mathbf{K}\backslash\{\emptyset\}$ which is finer than the topology on $\mathbf{F}$ in general. However, they coincide on the collection of spatial objects which belong to both $\mathbf{K}$ and $\mathbf{F}$. Therefore, we may talk about how far or near two objects are from each other in these topologies. Also, we may talk about the convergence of a sequence of spatial objects to a limiting spatial object with respect to the Hausdorff distance.

<u>REFERENCES</u>

1. S. Chen. Image processing by incomplete knowledge, Proc. IEEE Workshop on Languages for Automation: Cognitive Aspects in Information Processing, Palma de Mallorca, 1985.
2. S. Chen. An intelligent computer vision system. International Journal of Intelligent Systems, Vol. 1, 1986.
3. S. Chen and M. Penna. Shape and correspondence, Proc. SPIE – Advances in Intelligent Robotics System Symposium, Cambridge MA, 1986.
4. S. Chen and M. Penna. Motion analysis of deformable objects, <u>Advances in Computer Vision and Image Processing</u>, Vol. 3, JAL Press, Ed. T. Huang, 1987.
5. S. Chen. Spherical data structure and visual feedback for robotic control, Proc. IEEE First Annual Workshop on Intelligent Control, Troy NY, 1985.
6. M. Penna and S. Chen. Shape-from-shading using multiple light sources, International Journal of Intelligent Systems, Vol. 1, 1986.
7. S. Chen. Multisensor fusion and navigation of mobile robots, <u>Special Issue on Robotic Navigation</u>, International Journal of Intelligent Systems, Vol. 2, 1987.
8. S. Chen. Image reconstruction from zero-crossings, Proc. IJCAI-87, Milano, 1987.
9. S. Chen. Real-time visual processing and robotic navigation, Proc. International Conference on Intelligent Control, Philadelphia, 1987.
10. S. Chen. A two-dimensional solution to the problem of zero-crossings and spatiotemporal interpolation in computer and human vision, Proc. IEEE International Conference on Computer Vision, London, 1987.
11. S. Chen. Neural networks and computer vision, Proc. IEEE First Annual International Conference on Neural Networks, San Diego, 1987.
12. S. Chen. Spatial reasoning, <u>Encyclopedia of Computer Science and Technology</u>, Marcel Dekker, Ed. Kent and Williams, to appear.
13. S. Chen and M. Penna, Spherical perspective approach to optical flow, Proc. SPIE Cambridge Symposium on Optical and Optoelectronic Eng., Advances in Intelligent Robotics Systems, Cambridge, 1987.
14. M. Penna and S. Chen. Spherical analysis in computer vision and image understanding, to appear.

A SENSORY INPUT SYSTEM FOR AUTONOMOUS MOBILE ROBOTS

J. Patrick Bixler
Department of Computer Science
Virginia Tech
Blacksburg, VA 24061

David P. Miller
Department of Computer Science
Virginia Tech
Blacksburg, VA 24061

ABSTRACT

In order to accomplish navigation in an unfamiliar world a robot must be able to build and update its own world map continuously and in real time. This paper proposes a sensory input system based on the fusion of simple low-resolution vision with directed high-resolution sonar. The basic idea is to use a simple vision system to locate the direction in which an obstacle lies, and then use an ultra-sonic rangefinder to determine the depth of the object and to gain clues about its shape. By fusing two simple systems we attempt to exploit the strengths of each while maintaining an acceptable computational cost. An idealized example is given and we discuss the possibilities and some of the problems.

INTRODUCTION

Given an accurate map of the world, an autonomous mobile robot can plan a navigation route between any two points in its domain. One method for accomplishing this task is to use an incremental route-planning strategy [21]. Using the most current version of its map, the robot computes the next few waypoints to traverse. Then, as it moves, the robot senses the surroundings and verifies or updates its world map. Repeating this process, the robot eventually achieves its destination. Although the question of which is the best planning paradigm remains very much open, all such systems require substantial knowledge about the surrounding world. This research focuses on the problem of creating a reasonably accurate wire-frame map of an unfamiliar world.

Because the robot is assumed to be in unfamiliar surroundings, the navigation system must be able to obtain information about the physical world from the robot itself in real time. This implies some kind of sensory data processing system, capable of both collecting and interpreting information, be mounted on the robot platform. A number of different sensory systems could be used including touch sensors, rangefinders, and vision systems [17,18]. Tactile sensors are apparently not useful in this situation because of their short range and limited targetability. Such sensors necessarily interfere with the surrounding world and would also severely limit the speed of the robot.   Ultrasonic rangefinders also have limited targetability, but have a significant range and do not interfere with surrounding objects. Although substantial time is required to re-target these sensors [15], they represent an excellent method for measuring the distance to an object. Computer vision has been studied extensively and is now sufficiently developed to be of some practical use. Low level vision operations such as image enhancement, feature detection, and limited pattern recognition can be implemented in hardware making real time systems possible. While automatic interpretation of images falls far short of what humans are capable of, at least the mechanics of visual systems are reasonably well understood [11].

Whatever sensory system is used must be capable of determining, and then processing, that information which is relevant to the current goals of the robot. For example, recognizing which portion of the image represents objects that are sufficiently in the distance or not in the path of travel can allow time to be spent analyzing more immediate obstacles. The system must also be able to differentiate quickly between a shadow, which can be passed through and therefore ignored, and actual objects which cannot. Obviously, because the robot is moving, the time to detect obstacles must be short enough to allow the robot to change course. The system should be able to provide a boundary within which the object is absolutely certain to lie and a probability map, such as in [19], on the chances of actually encountering an obstacle.

There are also several other issues common to sensing and object recognition that are not necessarily of immediate concern in this application. For example, objects do not have to be described in great detail. In most cases, only a rough estimate of shape, or the projection onto the plane of the floor, and a fairly accurate estimate of location is needed. Secondly, because the robot is moving, the system need not be restricted to a single view. Rather, it can give a partial or preliminary description first and then complete and verify that description based on subsequent views [4]. It might also be possible to process some information off line. That is, whenever the robot comes to a situation that is relatively simple and unchanging (a long straight hallway, for example) some effort could be directed toward refining its total map based on previous stored views of other parts of the world.

The robot platform used for this research is Real World Interface's *Vectrobot* robot base. The robot is modified with a two degree of freedom pan and tilt platform upon which is mounted a high-resolution sonar, see Figure 1. A low resolution (128 by 128 pixels) RAM camera is also mounted on top of the robot on the single degree of freedom rotary platform. The camera will therefore be able to pan the horizon in a complete circle, and the sonar can be pointed at any small area within the camera's field of view.

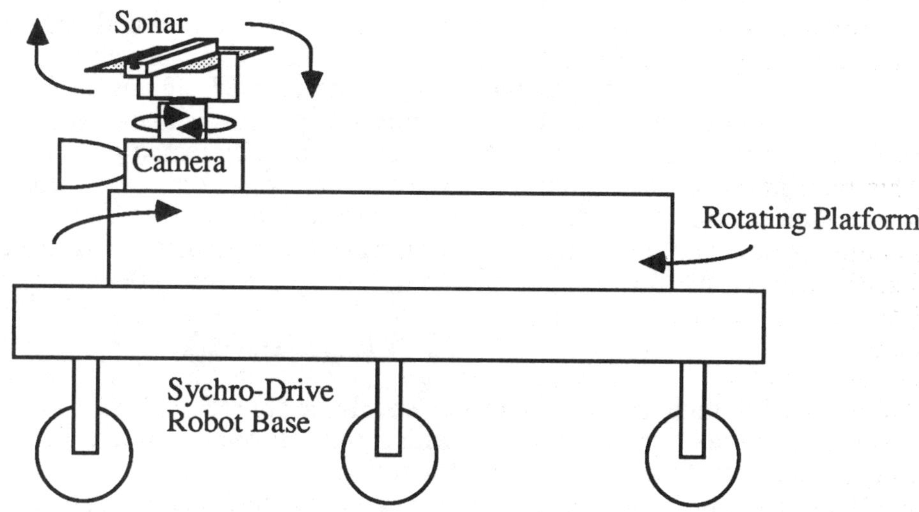

Figure 1. Sensor system mounted on robot platform.

THE VISION SYSTEM

A total reliance on vision for detecting obstacles can suffer from high computational expense and difficulties interpreting the scene. A single view of a scene rarely leads to a single consistent interpretation [6,10,23]. For example, when one object partially obscures another, there are certain edges for which it is impossible to tell whether they belong to one or both of the objects. Basically, some cue about depth is needed. Such a cue could be obtained from the use of two cameras making up a stereo vision system similar to the human visual system [12]. If one assumes that the robot is always capable of moving at least a small amount at any time, a single camera can supply the two required views [9,20]. In addition to having to solve the correspondence problem, however, stereo vision systems typically require substantial computation to locate objects accurately.

The approach taken here is to make the vision system be responsible only for giving a fairly accurate estimate of the direction in which the object lies. Once the object has been detected, the rangefinder can be directed to a small sample of points on or near the object. The depth information thus obtained can then be used to compute or confirm the exact location. As an example, suppose the robot is to cross the floor of a room on which a collection of obstacles has been randomly placed. Since the robot travels on the floor, the logical thing to do is to keep an eye on the floor and map the boundaries of clear floor space. This implies that the vision system be capable of quickly locating the edges that represent the intersection of each object with the floor. Once the robot knows the exact location of these edges it can essentially build polygonal columns around the obstacles and subsequently plan its route.

To this end the vision system will be required to produce an edge image of the current scene. There are a substantial number of edge detection algorithms described in the literature with many of them surveyed in [1] and [7]. Many are tuned to be most effective on a specific type of scene and it may well be that the sensory system maintain a catalog of techniques and attempt to use the most appropriate one for the current environment. In most cases one of the simpler gradient schemes, such as the cross difference or a Sobel operator will be the best choice.

Because of real time constraints and the fact that we need only find edges, a low-resolution (128 by 128 pixels) camera will be used. If we are able to localize the area of interest, however, a higher resolution image could be used. In any case, once the edge pixels have been identified they must be linked together to form actual edge segments. Here again there is a choice of techniques, such as a local similarity test, a global Hough transform, or perhaps a fast tracking algorithm. The edges that represent the intersection of the floor with an obstacle are the most important ones and must be found first. We will also investigate the feasibility of simply growing the region of the floor in order to detect these edges quickly.

THE SONAR SYSTEM

In an ideal, static situation the robot should be able to make up a depth map of the world by carefully scanning in all directions with some sort of rangefinder [8]. Unfortunately, this approach is impractical or inefficient for several reasons. First, such scans take time. The rangefinder must be scanned in a wide arc centered about the current heading. If a complete map is to be made, then several scans at varying elevations are necessary. In addition to the time required simply to move the sensor, taking the readings themselves requires noticeable time. The problem is severe when one considers the fact that the robot is supposed to be moving, and is compounded if the environment is dynamic. Finally, both ultrasonic and laser rangefinders suffer problems of range limitations and reflections; relying on range information exclusivley is seldom sufficiently accurate.

Once an edge has been detected by the vision system, however, the sonar can be used to obtain depth information at a small sample of points along that edge. The sonar that we use consists of a narrow beam, high frequency transducer/receiver. The high frequency (compared with the 25kHz Polaroid sonar rangefinders often used in robotics research) has several advantages: greater accuracy, narrow beam (no side lobes), lower incident angle reflection, and a slightly reduced range that will tend to reduce echos. The sonar is mounted as close to the camera as possible in order to minimize the error in targeting. Once the x- and y-coordinates of a point in the image plane are known, the sonar can be fired in that direction. The resulting distance measurements then determine the location of the point in world coordinates.

To increase the confidence that an edge in the image actually represents a straight edge in the scene, several points along that edge will be measured. If the resulting world points are collinear, then it would be reasonable to assume that the edge was formed by the intesection of two planes. If not, the edge can be approximated by a sequence of vectors to some abritrarily prescribed tolerance. For edges that are known to be on the floor, the default assumption will be that the intersecting plane is a vertical wall. When several edges intersect in the image, test points along those edges will be further checked to see if they are coplanar. If so, the plane segment bounded by the edges under consideration will be added to the world map. Although this will necessarily lead to some errors, it is a reasonable first approximation. Subsequent views by the sensory system can be used to produce increasingly accurate mappings.

A variant of this approach to mapping three-dimensional space is to use the above technique to produce the first approximation. Then determine the location of some point in the interior of that polygon and triangulate the polygon based on that point. Successive refinements would eventually lead to a fairly accurate polyhedral representation of the robot's domain.

The primary role of the sonar is to determine the distance to a given point in the robot's world. The return signal, however, contains information that may be of value. If the sonar's return signal is sampled at a high enough rate and the curve is normalized, then some comparison and interpretation may be possible. As an example, consider the sample two-dimensional obstacles and their corresponding return signals shown in Figure 2. The smooth continuous nature of the first curve indicates that the obstacle is probably also smooth and possibly flat. The other two curves have corners in them corresponding in some way to the corners in the obstacles. Note that the second part of curve (c) is lower than the first part. This corresponds to the protruding corner in the obstacle. In curve (b) the second part is higher than the first part indicating that the obstacle is probably concave. Although it is not clear exactly how to interpret the curves, there is at least the potential for distinguishing some obstacles based on the shapes of their curves [16].

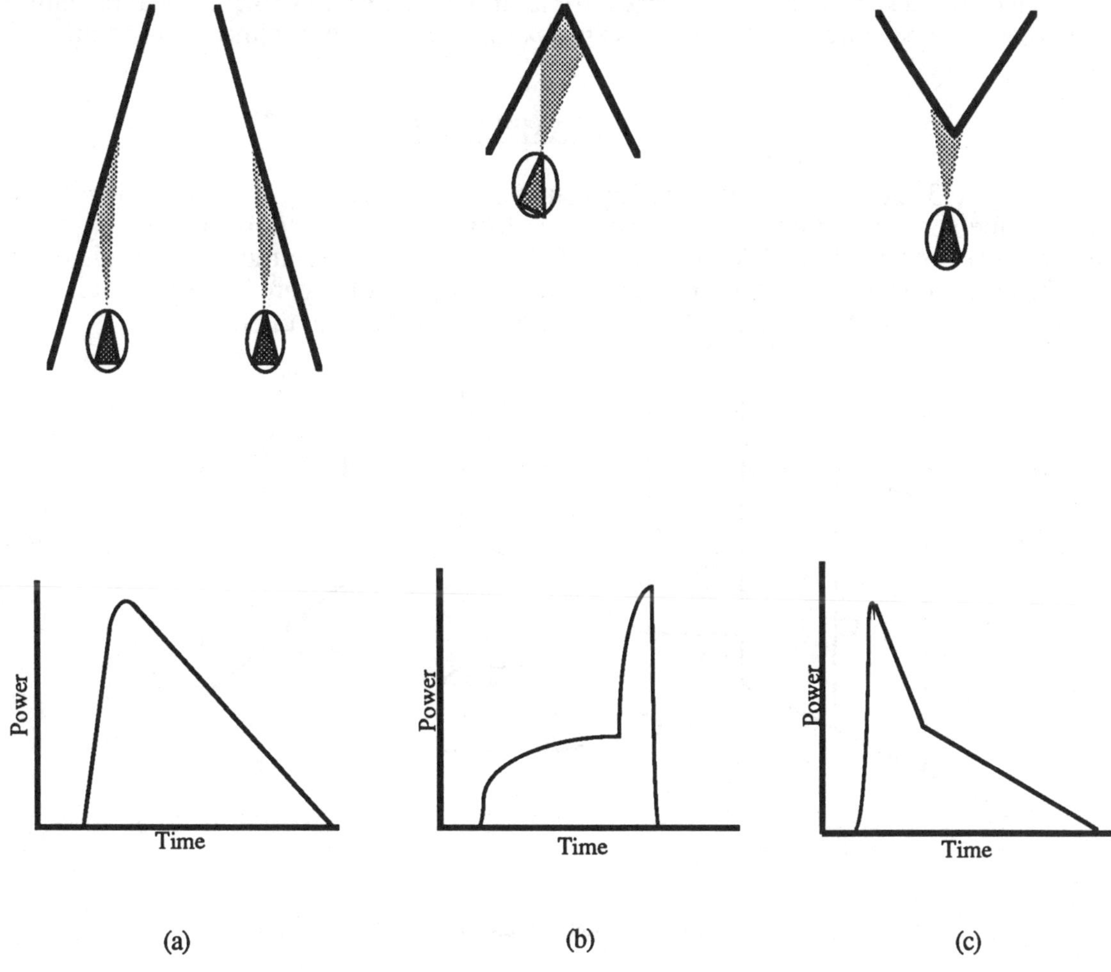

Figure 2. Sample 2-dimensional obstacles and return signals

An application of this is to distinguish edges caused by shadows from those representing actual objects. Relying solely on vision it is difficult, if possible at all, to make such distinctions. However, looking at the return signals improves the likelyhood of correctly disambiguating the two cases. In the case of the shadow edge, the return signal should be smooth, whereas an actual surface edge should return a signal with some shape in it, such as a bump or a step.

Once the edges have been located in world coordinates, a high level representation of the edges can be formed and from this the beginnings of a 3-dimensional wire-frame grid map of the world can be constructed [2]. A grid map will be used rather than a more detailed object map such as the Mercator [4,5] or Spam systems [13]. While a Mercator map provides more information, much of its strength derives from the sensory system providing object identification information, in addition to position information. The Mercator system uses information about an object's color, texture, and other physical properties in order to make inferences about hidden and partially obscured obstacles. While such information is unquestionably useful, it is at this point too expensive to gather and compute for guiding a real-time robot. Also, there currently is no reliable theory for representing an object map where objects can move, appear, and disappear through time. The grid map used here will be updated with every view. Because the approximate position of the robot will be known through dead reckoning, the search space for assimilating new information will be quite small. An object will be represented only as its approximate shape and last known position.

A SAMPLE SCENE

Figure 3 shows a simple scene consisting of a main hallway with several side hallways and a cube-shaped obstacle on the floor. The obstacle casts a shadow due to a light source in the hallway to the right. For the sake of illustration, we assume that the vision system produces an edge image that is a reasonable approximation of Figure 3. The robot is instructed to navigate to a position somewhere down the second hallway to the right.

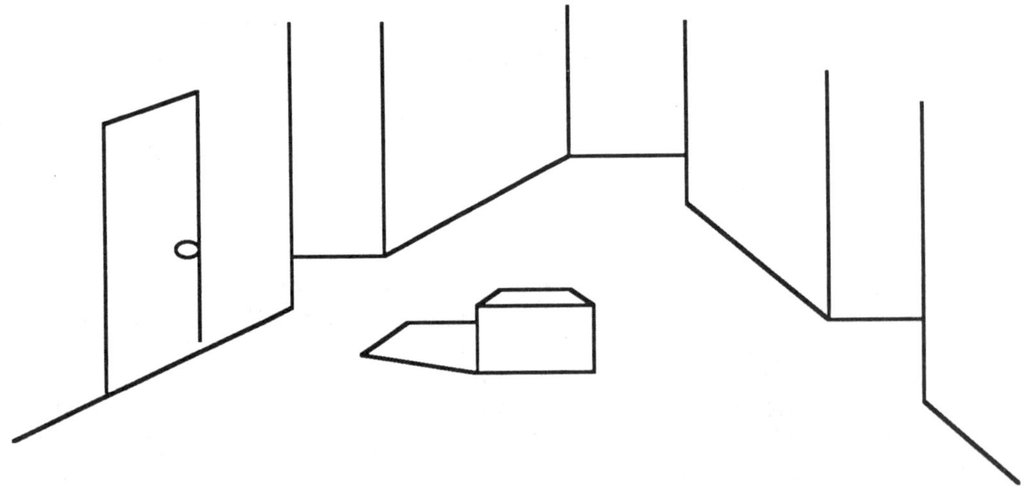

Figure 3.   A sample hallway scene with obstacle.

The edges that lie in the floor and are in the immediate vicinity of the robot are measured first and the default assumption that they represent vertical walls is verified. Next, the edges that are associated with the shadow are considered and are all found to be flush with the floor. This indicates that they do not represent part of the obstacle and they can essentially be ignored. The edges of the door frame to the left are then evaluated and found to be in the plane of the left wall, also indicating no obstacle. The robot now knows what clearance is available to either side of the obstacle and can plan its route. As it proceeds around the obstacle it continues to refine its map of the obstacle and verifies the exact location of the side hallways.

CONCLUSIONS

Several similar projects have previously been reported in the literature. Some have relied primarily on vision-based sensory systems [18,24], while others have tried to use only rangefinders [3,14,19]. Our approach differs in that it has each sensor perform only a very simple task, and attempts to produce the necessary information through the combination of the two.

To be sure, there are still many difficulties that must be overcome. The quality of the edge detection efforts is a primary concern. Detecting edges in a restricted domain with good lighting and where all obstacles are made up of simple polyhedra may be manageable, but it may be quite difficult in a more natural setting with irregular, curved shapes and multiple shadows. Shadows may also conceal an obstacle altogether: if the vision system does not detect an edge, the sonar will not know to look for an object.

Even though the sonar will be required to scan relatively few points, those points may not be near each other. The time needed simply to retarget the sonar may be significant, and the accuracy with which the sonar can be aimed must be very carefully controlled. A certain minimum error due to the fact that the camera and the transducer are offset slightly must be able to be tolerated.

In order to get any useful information from the curve of the return signal, the rate at which the signal is sampled must be sufficiently high. In some cases the signal will not be spread out enough to return much more that a short blip. Even when the curves are well formed and reasonably long they are by no means unique. It is easy to exhibit examples of two distinct obstacles that produce the same reflection. This ambiguity is further aggravated by secondary reflections and by the uncertainty about the reflectance properties of the obstacles' surface.

All computations must be performed quickly enough to allow the robot to update its world map at a reasonable rate, and of course, all computations must be adjusted to allow for the motion of the robot itself. One final difficulty is the correlation between what the robot thinks should be there and what it actually sees. When the robot takes a subsequent view and finds an edge in a different than expected location, it must be able to determine if it has found a new edge or if it should correct the location of a previous edge. The problem of matching polyhedra from different views is extremely difficult even when the parameters are well-known [4].

We have performed a number of simulations of the sonar on 2-dimensional obstacles and are in the process of developing a 3-dimensional version of the simulator. The actual sonar device has been designed and is in the final stages of being built. Concurrent experiments are planned involving both the device and the simulator, and preliminary work on testing various edge detection algorithms on low-resolution images is also underway.

<u>REFERENCES</u>

1. Abdou, I.E. "Quantatative design and evaluation of enhancement thresholding edge detectors." *IEEE Proceedings*, 67 pp 753-763, (1979).

2. Bixler, J.P. and J.P. Sanford. "Finding straight lines and curves in engineering line drawings." *Technical Report TR-87-12* , Virginia Tech Department of Computer Science, (1987).

3. Crowley, J.L. "Dynamic world modeling for an intelligent mobile robot using rotating ultra-sonic ranging device." *Proceedings of the 1985 International Conference on Robotics and Automation,* pp 128-135, IEEE, St. Louis, MO. (March 1985).

4. Davis, E. *Representing and acquiring geographic knowledge.* Morgan Kaufman, (1986).

5. Davis, E. "The Mercator representation of spatial knowledge." *Proc. IJCAI*, 8, pp 295-301, IJCAI (1983).

6. Guzman, A. "The decomposition of a visual scene into three dimensional bodies." *Proc. FJCC*, pp 291-301, Fall Joint Computer Conference, (1968).

7. Hildreth, E.C. "Edge detection." *Technical Report 858*, MIT AI Laboratory, (1985).

8. Letovsky, S. "Interpreting range data for a mobile robot." *Proceedings of the Fifth National Conference of the Canadian Society for Computational Studies of Intelligence,* pp 70-72, CSCSI, London, Ontario (May 1984).

9. Longuet-Higgins, H.C. and K. Prazdny. "The interpretation of a moving retinal image." *Proceedings of the Royal Sociecty of London*, pp 385-397, (1985).

10. Mackworth, A.K. "Interpreting pictures of polyhedral scenes." *Artificial Intelligence*, 4, pp 121-137, (1973).

11. Marr, D. Vision, W.H. Freeman, (1982).

12. Marr, D. and T. Poggio. "A computational theory of human stereo vision." *Proceedings of the Royal Society*, Series B, 204, pp 301-328, (1979).

13. McDermott, D.V. and E. Davis. "Planning routes through uncertain territory." *Artificial Intelligence*, 22, pp 107-156, (1984).

14. Miller, D.P. "A spatial representation system for mobile robots." *Proceedings of the 1985 International Conference on Robotics and Automation*, pp 122-127, IEEE, St. Louis, MO. (March 1985).

15. Miller, D.P. "Scheduling robot sensors for multisensory tasks." *Proceedings of the 1986 Robots West Conference*, SME, Long Beach, CA. (September 1986).

16. Miller, D.P. and J.P. Bixler. "A taxonomy of obstacles as seen by an ultrasonic rangefinder." *Proceedings of the 1987 IEEE Conference on Systems, Man, and Cybernetics,* IEEE, Alexandria, VA. (October 1987).

17. Moravec, H.P. "Obstacle avoidance and navigation in the real world by a seeing robot rover." PhD Thesis, Stanford University, (September 1980).

18. Moravec, H.P. "Visual mapping by a robot rover." *Proceedings of the International Joint Conference on Artificial Intelligence*, pp 598-600, IJCAI, (1979).

19. Moravec, H.P. and A. Elfes. "High resolution maps from wide angle sonar." *Proceedings of the 1985 International Conference on Robotics and Automation*, pp 116-121, IEEE, St. Louis, MO. (March 1985).

20. Roach, J.W. and J.K. Aggarwal. "Determining the movement of objects from a sequence of images." *IEEE Trans. on PAMI*, 6, pp 554-562, (1980).

21. Slack, M.G. and D.P. Miller. "Route planning in a four dimensional environment." *Proceedings of the 1987 Workshop on Tele-Robotics*, JPL, Pasadena, CA. (January 1987).

22. Ullman, S. *The interpretation of visual motion*, MIT Press, (1979).

23. Waltz, D. "Understanding line drawings of scenes with shadows." in *The Psychology of Computer Vision*, Patrick Winston, ed., McGraw-Hill, (1975).

24. Waxman, A.M., J. LeMoigne and B. Srinivasan. "Visual navigation of roadways." *Proceedings of the 1985 International Conference on Robotics and Automation*, pp 116-121, IEEE, St. Louis, MO. (March 1985).

AN INTRODUCTION AND ANALYSIS OF A STRAIGHT LINE PATH ALGORITHM FOR USE IN BINARY DOMAINS

Douglas Walter J. Chubb
U.S. Army Center for Signals Warfare
Vint Hill Farms Station
Warrenton, VA 22186-5100

ABSTRACT

Since 1984 the U.S. Army Center for Signals Warfare (CSW) has been involved in the development of an artificial intelligence based information fusion system. A research issue of particular importance to this effort has been the development of a fully automated, robust, and domain independent *spatial problem solver* (SPS). An important function within the SPS is the ability to accurately generate paths from one point to another within a binary spatial representation. Several binary domain path development algorithms currently exist. However, these algorithms possess limitations which have made them less than optimal for use within the SPS. Collectively, these algorithm limitations include:

1. *a priori* assumptions must be made about the *types of permissable obstacle structures* present within the spatial representation, and,
2. the algorithm does not develop a *complete path solution* for a given problem.

A *complete path solution* is defined to be the *maximal set of compliant paths*, where a path B is defined to be *compliant* if and only if B is everywhere compliant with the path-generating heuristics and there exists no other path description B', and a point-to-point path-connected linear transformation F, such that F[B'] = B where F is the identity function for points X and Y.   In 1985, CSW developed a new path development algorithm called a *Straight Line Path Algorithm* (SLPA). The SLPA does not possess any of the limitations mentioned herein. The purpose of this paper is to introduce the SLPA and to analyze its performance by comparing the SLPA to that of the most general path development algorithm currently being used, the A* heuristic search algorithm (AHSA). This paper describes both algorithms in detail and compares their path development performance and efficiency when developing a path solution for a canonical set of binary domain occluding obstacles. Execution time inequality expressions, which compare the execution time of the SLPA to the execution time of the AHSA, are developed for each canonical occluding obstacle example. Finally, modeling techniques are used to develop a probability value for each execution time inequality expression and its associated geometry.

INTRODUCTION

For the past two years the U.S. Army Center for Signals Warfare (CSW) has been actively involved in the development of an artificial intelligence based information fusion system. This system is being developed to provide accurate, automated assistance to the Army Division Level Intelligence Officer (G2) during the preparation of an tactical situation assessment [Chubb 1984, 1986]. A research issue of particular importance to this effort has been the development of a fully automated, robust, and domain independent *spatial problem solver* (SPS). The SPS generates solutions to spatial problems which arise during the G2's preparation of the tactical situation assessment. Spatial problems measure the creditability of the G2's hypothesized enemy tactic. Enemy tactics involving movement or mobility require that the SPS be capable of quickly generating a variety of alternative paths from one point to another within the modeled spatial representation. A detailed analysis of the SPS *path development algorithm*, which generates these paths, is the subject of this paper.

The spatial representation used by the SPS during the problem solving process is a binary spatial representation. Given some spatial domain, assume that there exists a corresponding raster formatted digital spatial representation D. Further assume that D has been binary decomposed [Chubb, 1986] into an NxM array where each element of D has been assigned a value of either 0 or 1. This binary decomposition of D represents the contextual state of D for some actor action during some short period of time. One important actor action is called *path development:* the actor planned movement from some starting point X ε D to some target point Y ε D. The following definitions are required for a discussion of the SPS path development algorithm.

DEFINITIONS

1. Define a *path, p(X,Y)*, in binary spatial representation D to be a minimal, finite set of 8-connected 0-element points in D which path connect 0-element point X ε D to 0-element point Y ε D. Note that since p(X,Y) is a finite set, p(X,Y) can not contain any path connected loops.

2. Define the *length of a path, lp(X,Y)*, to be the rank of p(X,Y).

3. Define *8N(X)* to be the *8-neighborhood set of elements about point X*. Likewise, define 4N(X) to be the *4-neighborhood set of elements about point X*. Note that if X and Y are 0-elements in D where either X $=$ Y or X ε 8N(Y), then p(X,Y) $= \emptyset$, and lp(X,Y) $= 0$.

4. Define the *distance, d(X,Y)*, between points X , Y ε D, to be the standard Euclidean distance metric: $((x1-x2)^2 + (y1-y2)^2)^{1/2}$ where X and Y have the form X $= (x1,y1)$ and Y $= (x2,y2)$.

5. Assume X,Y are 0-element points in D such that X $\neq$ Y. Define a *Straight Line Path, slp(X,Y)*, between X and Y to be the p(X,Y) such that for all Z ε p(X,Y), Z satisfies a function with form Y $= mX + b$.

6. Define an **obstacle, O_j,** in binary decomposed D to be a non-empty set of 4-connected 1-elements in D.

7. Assume X,Y are 0-element points in D such that X ≠ Y and X not in 8N(Y). Let slf(X,Y) be the set of *all* points (0-element and 1-element) in D which satisfy the function Y = mX + b. Define obstacle Oj to be an **occluding obstacle** in D to slp(X,Y) iff slf(X,Y) contains a 1-element point Z, where Z ε bl(Oj), the boundary list of Oj.

The following lemma may be easily proved.

Lemma 1:   Let X and Y be 0-element points in D such that X ≠ Y and X not in 8N(Y). If slp(X,Y) does not exist, then there exists at least one occluding obstacle, OB, in D with 1-element point K ε OB such that K satisfies the function Y = mX + b.

8. Assume points X and Y are 0-element points in D such that X ≠ Y and X not in 8N(Y). Let OB be an occluding obstacle to X and Y and bl(OB) the boundary list of OB.   Define the set op(X,Y) = (slf(X,Y) ∩ bl(OB)). Call set **op(X, Y)** the **set of obstacle points** for points X and Y and region OB.

9. Let X and Y be 0-element points in D such that X ≠ Y and X not in 8N(Y).   Let OB be an occluding obstacle to X and Y and op(X,Y) non-empty. Define the **set of closest obstacle points**, **cop(X, Y)**, to be a subset of op(X,Y) such that if point K ε cop(X,Y), then K = min d(X,K) for all K ε op(X,Y).

The following lemma may be proved.

Lemma 2: Assume points X and Y are 0-element points in D such that X ≠ Y and X not in 8N(Y). If OB is an occluding obstacle to X and Y, then cop(X,Y) contains a single, uniquely defined point K ε bl(OB).

10. Assume points X and Y are 0-element points in D such that X ≠ Y and X not in 8N(Y).   Define the **closest adherent point, cap(X, Y)**, to be a member of the adherent list of occluding obstacle OB, where cap(X,Y) ε {slf(X,Y) ∩ 8N(cop(X,Y))}.

BINARY DOMAIN PATH DEVELOPMENT ALGORITHMS

Several binary domain path development algorithms exist. The most popular include the *A* heuristic search* algorithm (AHSA) [Nilsson]; a variant of the A*, the *polygon vertices algorithm (Dijkstra's algorithm)* [Lozano-Pe'rez]; the *boundary following algorithm* [Rosenfeld]; and a variant form, the *thinning algorithm* [Fink].   Although each of these algorithms has definite applications, they each possess one or more limitations which have made them less than optimal for use within the SPS. Collectively, these algorithm limitations include:

1) *a priori* assumptions must be made about the *types of permissable obstacle structures* present in D, and,

2) the algorithm does not develop a *complete path solution* for a given problem.

We define a **path solution** , or simply the **solution**, to be a set of sets where each subset represents a unique path-connected description of a path from some start point, X, to target point, Y. A path description B from X to Y is defined to be *compliant* if and only if B is everywhere compliant with the path-generating heuristics and there exists no other path description B', and point-to-point path-connected linear transformation F, such that F(B') = B where F is the identity function for points X and Y. We define a **complete path solution** to be the *maximal set of compliant path descriptions.*

Since obstacle shape may vary in time, *a priori* assumptions made about the structure of obstacles present within D is ill founded. Likewise, for CSW applications, the path problem is frequently couched as a hypothetical question, where additional constraints to path development are only considered once a tentative path solution has been developed. For example, the problem may be to see if it is possible to construct **any** path from X to Y under some very general set of conditions. The basis for this type of problem might be to investigate possible constraints which may develop in time. Under these conditions, a "best" path solution is impossible to develop and is conceptually devoid of meaning since "best" as a concept can not be sufficiently defined *a priori.* In 1984 CSW began the development of a path development algorithm which would not require *a priori* notions about obstacle structure for path development, which would be capable of producing a complete path solution, and which would be **efficient** to use. This research culminated in the development a new path development algorithm for use in binary domains called the *straight line path algorithm (SLPA).* This paper will introduce the SLPA and analyze its general performance and efficiency by comparing the performance of the SLPA to that of the most general path development algorithm currently being used: the A* heuristic search algorithm (AHSA).

The AHSA is an *admissable algorithm*; it is guaranteed to find a shortest "best" path, if such a path exists and can be defined. The SLPA is **not** an admissable path development algorithm; it is, however, capable of generating a *complete path solution.* The AHSA is a very inefficient type of path development algorithm and provides a **"worst case"** efficiency benchmark for comparing other path development algorithms. Since an implemented algorithm's efficiency is dependent upon a variety of factors, such as computer word size and the language used to implement the algorithm, the efficiency of these algorithms will be measured independent of these factors by comparing the **size** of the search space constructed by each algorithm while developing a path from point X to point Y. Path solution results will be analyzed and compared using a canonical set of occluding obstacle geometries.

COMPARATIVE ANALYSIS OF THE AHSA AND THE SLPA

We begin the comparative analysis of the AHSA and the SLPA with a brief description of the AHSA.

THE A* HEURISTIC SEARCH ALGORITHM

The AHSA [Nilsson] path development consists of rank ordering the elements of the AHSA search space using the heuristic cost function $g(N) + h(N)$ where $g(N) = lp(X,N)$, and $h(N) = d(N,Y)$, for each N in the search space. If point N is the search space minimal cost point then every 0-element point $W \varepsilon 8N(N)$ is added to the search space, with appropriate path linkages assigned between the "parent" point N and each W "son". The process repeats until Y becomes a member of the AHSA search space. As each point N is "expanded" it is identified with a tag and is not examined again for path development. The resulting AHSA search space becomes a directed graph with graph nodes represented by points in the search space and directed links between nodes represented by the W ε 8N(N) relationship. With W ε 8N(N), we are guaranteed that the developed path is appropriately path-connected. Path development begins with X = N. Assuming a path solution exists, the unique sequence of linked search tree nodes from points Y to X is the AHSA best-first path solution.

THE STRAIGHT LINE PATH ALGORITHM

The SLPA is similar to the AHSA in that both are search algorithms which rely upon heuristics to aid in the development of a search tree. The SLPA *implicitly* makes use of the slp(X,Y) heuristic, similar to that used by the AHSA, to first develop a sub-optimal, non-admissable set of paths. This set of paths is then reprocessed, using a min d(X,Y) heuristic, in an attempt to minimize path length. These two path development strategies are called respectively *PASS-1* and *PASS-2*. An optional, user-prompted third pass of path development processing called *PASS-3* is also described.

The PASS-1 Algorithm

PASS-1 recursively develops a set of sub-optimal possible paths from X to Y where X , Y ε D. *PASS-1*'s only strategy is to repeatedly attempt to develop a slp(W,Y), where W is a terminal node in the SLPA search tree. If this strategy is not possible, it is assumed that an occluding obstacle has been encountered and two subpaths are generated at the cap(X,Y) point . Each sub-path point is appropriately stored in the SLPA stacks: A-Stack, where point-to-point path movement about obstacles is stored; and B-Stack, where slp(X,Y) path movement points are stored. *PASS-1* recursively processes A-Stack and B-Stack data until both stack pop instructions return nil. The stack pop functions are atypical and are defined as follows:

pop(A-Stack):   return the last A-Stack point Z such that slp(Z,Y) does NOT exist and Z not a member of path(Q,K) where Q , K ε B-Stack; else return nil.
pop(B-Stack):   return the last B-Stack point Z such that there exists at least one untagged obstacle adherent list point W such that W ε 8N(Z); else return nil.

Points used during path development are tagged and may not be used again. A path-flag is used to indicate that at least one successful path was developed from X to Y. A detailed pseudo-code description of *PASS-1* is given in [Chubb, 1987].

The PASS-2 Algorithm

PASS-2 processes *PASS-1* stack data by attempting to reduce the path length of each of the paths developed by *PASS-1*. *PASS-2* uses two functions to accomplish this path optimization: *describe*, and *choice*. The *describe* function produces, upon demand, an ordered list of points (not necessarily path-connected) in D which describe a possible path from X to Y. *Describe* constructs possible paths by concatenating appropriate piece-wise path descriptions into a single list. Path pieces are chosen using a local path-connected criteria for the branching points and by the *choice* function. The *choice* function interprets and represents the *PASS-1* A-Stack/B-Stack data as a directed graph where nodes represent branching points, ie., B-Stack datum, and arcs represent path connections, ie., either slp(Z,K) or A-Stack data about obstacles. As an example, consider figure 1. The branch points in this example are: X, A, B, B', C, C', D, D', and Y. The straight-line path pieces are: slp(X,A), slp(B,C), slp(B'C'), slp(D,Y), and slp(D',Y). The point-wise path connected path pieces are: (A,B), (A,B'), (C,D), (C,C') and (C',D'). An equivalent directed graph representation of these path points and path connected pieces is shown in figure 2.

An example of a possible locally developed (*PASS-1*) path from points X to Y in D, as produced by function *describe*, is as follows:

$$describe \;\rightarrow\; [(slp(X,A),(A,B),slp(B,C),(C,D),slp(D,Y)].$$

Other possible path descriptions from X to Y follow immediately from an examination of figure 2. Note that multiple path solutions are developed by *PASS-1*, *choice*, et al. *PASS-2* optimizes (shortens) each path by attempting to develop new branch points, ie., as stored in B-Stack, within each *PASS-1* path. The process consists of examining the difference in path length between the path developed by the describe function between points W,Q in that path and a slp(W,Q), if it exists. This process continues piece-wise until the end of the *describe* path is encountered.

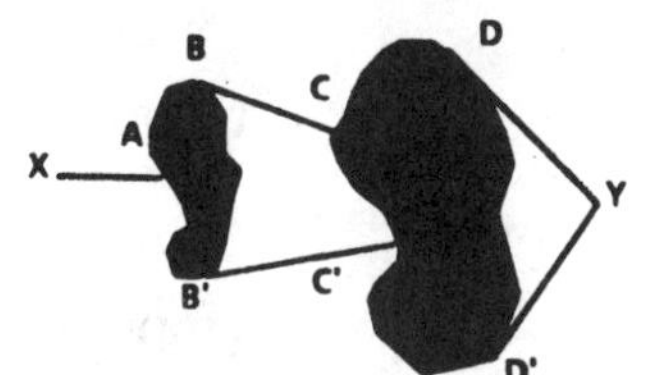

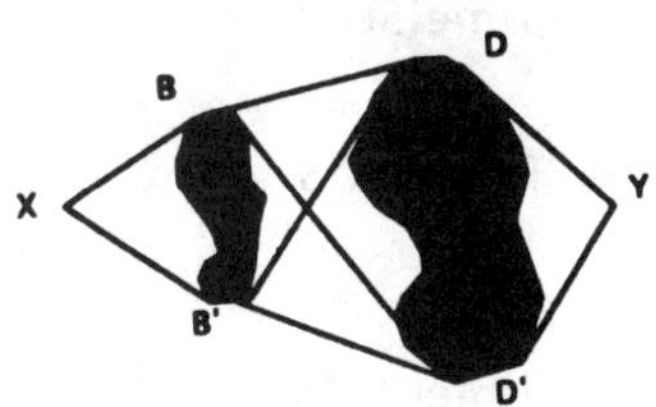

FIGURE 1. PASS-1 Paths   **FIGURE 2. PASS-1 Graph Representation**   **FIGURE 3. PASS-2 Paths**

PASS-2 improvements are not guaranteed to result in an optimal path. Some reduction in path length can occasionally be made by using an additional, and generally expensive, level of processing called *PASS-3*. *PASS-3* attempts to introduce a shorter version of the *PASS-2* results by creating new branching points about obstacles not encountered during *PASS-1*. The use of *PASS-3* is user controlled. A detailed pseudo-code description of *PASS-2* and *PASS-3* is given in [Chubb, 1987].   Figure 3 illustrates the results of *PASS-2* path development processing using figure 1 *PASS-1* path data. Note that *four paths* are illustrated from points X to Y: path X to B to D to Y, path X to B' to D' to Y, path X to B to D' to Y, and path X to B' to D to Y.

DEVELOPMENT OF THE AHSA TIME EXPRESSION

In general, the total time required to execute the AHSA may be expressed as a function of the sum of the number of search tree terminal nodes searched per processing recursion, ie., the finite sum of RTS recursions, where lp(X,Y) < RTS. The maximum number of terminal nodes searched , SS, which is required to develop p(X,Y) for the AHSA is developed at the RTSth recursion and can be expressed as,

$$SS = p_1 - 1 + p_2 - 1 + \ldots + p_{(RTS-1)} - 1 + p_{(RTS)}. \tag{1.1}$$

where SS = the (max) rank of the search space,

RTS = the number of recursions necessary to develop p(X,Y),

and p_j = rank of the jth neighborhood expansion of untagged elements in D,
          where $1 \leq p_j \leq 8$, for $j = 1,...,$RTS.

For the worst possible case, $p_i = 5$ for all $i = 1,...,$RTS. It can be shown [Chubb, 1987] that,

$$\textit{(Worst-Case)}\ \text{Time(AHSA)} = H*[\text{RTS}*\text{SS} - (\text{RTS-1})*4 - (\text{RTS-2})*4 - .... -4]$$
$$= H*[\text{RTS}*\text{SS} - 4*\text{RTS} + 4*(\text{RTS-1})!]$$
$$= H*[\text{RTS}*(\text{SS-4}) + 4*(\text{RTS-1})!]. \tag{1.2}$$

DEVELOPMENT OF THE SLPA TIME EXPRESSION

The SLPA execution time equation has the following form:

$$\text{Time(SLPA)} = \text{Time(PASS-1)} + \text{Time(PASS-2)}$$

where, $\text{Time(PASS-1)} = \sum_{j=1}^{z} \text{RTS}_j\, H_{min} + B_j\, H_{max},$ $\tag{1.3}$

and $\text{Time(PASS-2)} = \sum_{j=1}^{z} \text{RTS}_j + B_j\, *\text{Irt}_j\, *H_{max},$ $\tag{1.4}$

and H_{max} = the average time required to compute slp(Q,W), d(X,Y), and lp(X,Y),
          H_{min} = the time needed for the slp(Q,W) function to fail within the 8N(Q) of Q,
          Irt_j = real number > 1.0, which accounts for the number of iterations
                   required to $\overline{\text{optimize}}$ the jth path, $j = 1,...,z,$
          B_j = the number of B-Stack nodes used to construct the jth path, $j = 1,...,z,$
          RTS_j = the number of A-Stack nodes used to construct the jth path, $j = 1,...,z,$
and z = total number of trial paths developed by SLPA.

It can be shown [Chubb, 1987] that,

$$\textit{Worst-Case}\ \text{Time (SLPA)}\ \text{may be approximated as:}\ \approx \sum_{j=1}^{2N} [(N*\text{SS}_j + \text{RTS}_j)*H_{min}]. \tag{1.5}$$

where N = the number of occluding obstacles and SS_j = the set of points tested by slp(X,Y) for all X,Y in RTS_j and B_j. $\text{RTS}_j = $ lp(X,Y)$_j$ which was developed during *PASS-1*. It can be shown that for most paths $\text{SS}_j >> \text{RTS}_j, j = 1,...,z.$

Equations (1.2) and (1.5) demonstrate that AHSA and SLPA execution times are principally a function of variables RTS and SS. We now develop specific values for these variables as a function of the canonical set of possible occluding obstacles.

THE AHSA AND SLPA TIME COMPARISON EXPRESSIONS

Assume N is the number of occluding obstacles and S_t, $t = 1,2,3$, is an occluding obstacle boundary geometry which presents itself between branching point Z in slp(Z,Y) and point Y, the target. Four types of obstacle boundary geometries may be present: CASE 1: no occluding obstacle present; CASE 2: planar surface present (figure 4,5) ; CASE 3:concave surface present, (figure 6); or CASE 4: convex surface present (figures 7-10). It can be shown (by consideration of all the possible 1-element geometries potentially present in 8N(W), where W is a 1-element boundary element of some occluding obstacle) that any obstacle boundary surface may be closely approximated by a linear combination of these three surface types. For the purposes of this discussion we will assume, without loss of generality, that for each cap(Z,Y) that the type of surface geometry is fixed for all obstacle points which are elements of 8N(cap(Z,Y)). Each canonical geometry has been analyzed and time inequality statements developed comparing Time(SLPA) to Time(AHSA). However, because of limitations on the length of this paper, only the inequality equations are listed herein. A detailed mathematical derivation and evaluation may be found in [Chubb, 1987].

CASE 1 : N = 0, It can be shown that Time(SLPA) < Time(ASHA).

CASE 2a: N = 1. Normal Planar Obstacle Surface (see figure 4).
It can be shown that Time(AHSA) > Time(SLPA).

CASE 2b: Non-Normal Planar Surface (see figure 5)
Assume occluding obstacle planar surface [A,B] is not normal to slp(X,Y) with point H = cap(X,Y); and points A ≠ H ≠ B and angle YHB = θ , where $90 > \theta > 0$.
Then Time (AHSA) > Time(SLPA) whenever,

1) $6*d(X,H)^2 + (7-Z)*d(X,H)*d(H,B) + 2*(H,B)^2$ > 0 where we assume d(A,B) = Z*d(H,B)

2) $6*W + 2/W + 7 > Z$ where we also assume $\sin \theta \approx 1.0$.

3) $6*d(X,H)^2 + 7*d(X,H)*d(H,B) + d(H,B)^2 > d(A,B)$ where we assume $\varepsilon \approx 0$ and $\theta \approx 0$ and $d(H,B) = d(H,Y)*\cos\theta \approx d(H.Y)$.

4) $d(A,B) + d(A,H)*d(X,H) + d(B,Y) < [d(B,Y)^2 + 3*d(X,H) + 2*d(B,Y)]*[d(B,Y)^2 + 2*d(X,H) + d(B,Y)]$ where we assume ξ large and $d(H,Y) << d(H,B)$.

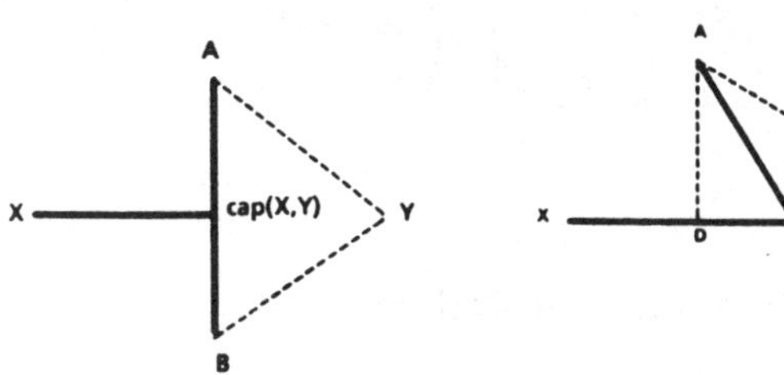

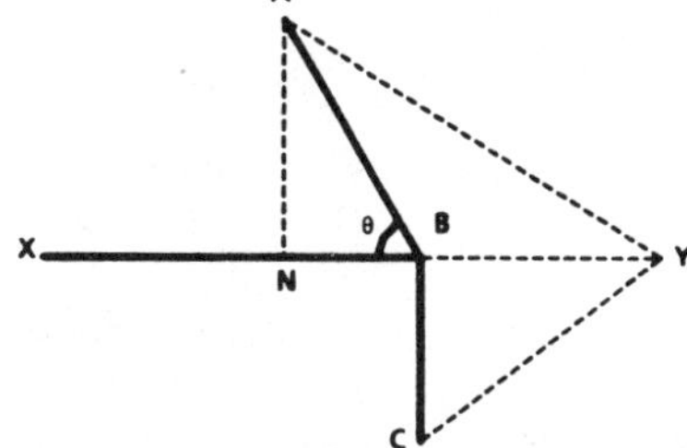

FIGURE 4. Normal Surface   FIGURE 5. Non-Normal Surface   FIGURE 6. Concave Surface

CASE 3: Concave Obstacle Surface (see figure 6)
Assume angle ABX = θ where $0 < \theta < 90$, angle XBC normal to slp(X,Y).

Then Time(AHSA) > Time(SLPA) whenever,

$$d(X,B)^{-1}*[d(B,C) + 3*[d(A,Y)2 + d(X,B)2 + 2*d(X,B)*d(A,Y) + d(B,C)*(d(X,B))]] - d(B,C) > d(A,B),$$

CASE 4: Convex Obstacle Surface (see figure 7)
We assume that angle ABX = 90 and 90 < angle XBC < 180.

CASE 4a: (see figure 8)
We assume d(A,Y) = d(Y, C') < d(Y,C). Then, Time(AHSA) > Time(SLPA) whenever,

$$d(A,Y) >> d(X,B) \text{ and } d(B,C) < 3*d(A,Y)2 + 6*d(A,Y),$$

CASE 4b: (figure 9) Assume d(A,Y) > d(Y,C) .
CASE 4b-1: Assume d(A,Y) > d(Y,C) and d(B,Y) > d(B,C).
Then Time(AHSA) > Time2(SLPA) whenever:

$$4/d(X,B)]*[d(X,B) + d(B,C) + d(C,Y)]2 + d(C,Y)*[d(X,B) + d(B,C)]] > d(A,B).$$

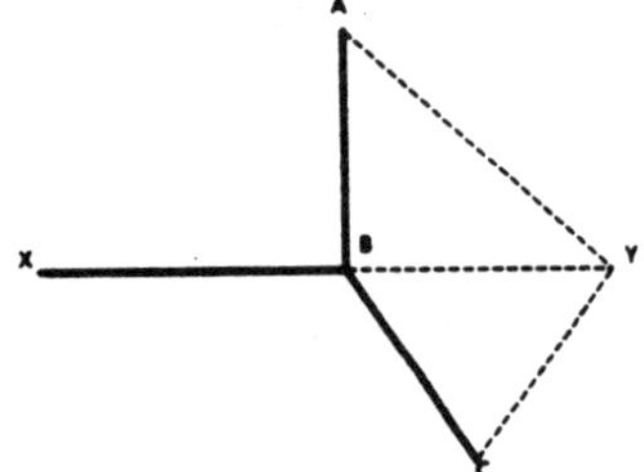

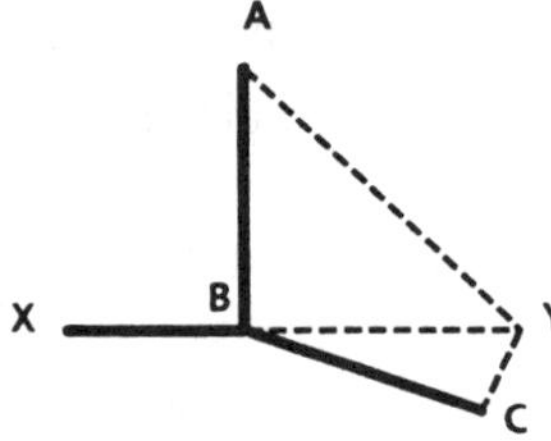

FIGURE 7. Convex Surface   FIGURE 8. Convex, CASE 4a   FIGURE 9. Convex, CASE 4b

CASE 4b-2: (figure 10A)
Assume the following: d(A,Y) > d(Y,C), d(B,Y) < d(B,C), and d(Y,C) < d(B,Y).
Then Time(AHSA) < Time(SLPA) whenever,

$$[2/d(X,B)]*[3*d(Y,C)2 + 2*d(X,B)2 + d(B,C)2 + 6*d(X,B)*d(Y,C) + 4*d(X,B)*d(B,C) + Z*[5*d(X,B) + 5*d(Y,C) + 4*d(B,C)]] \leq d(A,B).$$

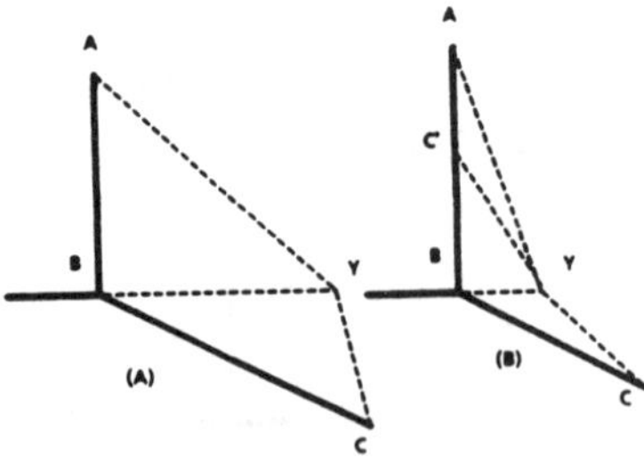

FIGURE 10(a,b). Convex Surface, CASE 4b(2-3).

CASE 4b-3: (figure 10B)
Assume d(A,Y) > d(Y,C), d(B,Y) < d(B,C), and d(Y,C) > d(B,Y).
Then Time(AHSA) > Time(SLPA) whenever,

$$[2/d(X,B)][4d(Y,C)2 + 2d(X,B)2 + d(B,C)2 + 4d(X,B)d(B,C) + 7d(X,B)d(Y,C) + 6d(B,C)d(Y,C)] > d(A,B).$$

CONCLUSIONS

We have shown that if no occluding obstacles are present, Time(AHSA) > Time(SLPA). In addition, an execution time inequality expression for SLPA and AHSA has been developed for each canonical occluding obstacle. The inequality equations are parameterized in terms of the various distances (eg., d(X,A)) considered within each topological case summary expression and the relative positions of start point X and target point Y. The likelihood that a particular inequality equation is true or false, given some occluding obstacle geometry, is defined by the *probability* that geometric conditions exist within D which, when parameterized and substituted into the inequality equation, would either support or refute the equation's initial hypothesis, eg., that Time(SLPA) < Time(AHSA). A probability value was computed for each case/sub-case summary inequality equation using standard simulation techniques. Modeling results are given in [Chubb,1987]. In general, Time(SLPA) < Time(AHSA) for most cases except when the length of the additional path(s) computed by SLPA became disproportionally long (≈40x) as compared to the AHSA path. The likelihood that model conditions such as these would be realistically found in nature is obviously unknown. However, regardless of the spatial domain being considered, the SLPA always produces a *complete path solution* set whereas the AHSA produces a single, potentially non-optimal, path solution. For the CSW tactical battlefield domain and other such spatial domains where an *a priori* "best" strategy path development description is neither practical nor possible, this feature alone may represent sufficient rationale to make use of the SLPA.

References

D. Chubb. A Primitive Driven Artificial Intelligence Threat Model. Proceedings of the 1984 U.S. Army Science Conference, West Point, N.Y. (1984)

D. Chubb. A Spatial Problem Solver and Its Associated Spatial Representation. Geographic Information Systems in Government, Vol 2, B. Opitz, Editor. A. Deepak Publishing, Hampton, Virginia, pp. 815-836 (1986)

D. Chubb. Introduction and Analysis of a Straight Line Path Algorithm for Use in Binary Domains. Center for Signals Warfare Technical Report, VHFS, Warrenton, Virginia, (1987)

P. Fink, J. Lusth & H. Mullaney. Automated Mission Planning in an Autonomous Underwater Vehicle. In Proceedings, U.S. Army Research Office, Workshop on Future Directions in Artificial Intelligence, June 17-19, Washington, D.C., pp.153-162 (1986)

T. Lozano-Pe'rez & N. Wesley. An Algorithm for Planning Collision-Free Paths Among Polyhedral Obstacles, CACM, Vol 22, October, pp. 560-570 (1979)

N. Nilsson. Principles of Artificial Intelligence. Tioga Publishing Company, Palo Alto, California, pp. 72-94 (1980)

A. Rosenfeld. Connectivity in Digital Pictures. J. ACM, Vol 17, Jan. (1970)

EFFICIENT NAVIGATION THROUGH DYNAMIC DOMAINS

David P. Miller   **Marc G. Slack**

Department of Computer Science

Virginia Tech

Blacksburg, VA 24061

ABSTRACT

In this paper we present a message passing algorithm for planning routes and navigating through dynamic domains. The spatial representation of the world (in 2D) is provided by a rectilinear grid. This system models dynamic aspects of the world as time-dependent functions on the states of individual nodes in the grid. Route and navigation planning are performed by a spreading search of legal paths through the grid. This is performed in an efficient manner through the use of a hierarchy of grids at different levels of detail, and through the exploitation of the natural parallelism of the problem. The representation and algorithms trivially generalize to three, and more, dimensions. An implementation of this system is also discussed.

1 - INTRODUCTION

The ability to represent and plan movements through space is necessary for any autonomous mobile robot. Mechanical error and uncertainty make it impractical to maneuver a robot through a series of complex tasks strictly by dead-reckoning. In almost all applications, dead-reckoning is also of limited use because it ignores the possibility of change in the world. Despite its obvious importance, until recently, most issues involved with navigation through dynamic domains have been ignored.

There have been many systems devised for robot navigation through static domains. Topological graphs [Laumond83], [Chatila85] have been used for guiding route planning through a loosely connected set of convex polygons representing free-space areas in an indoor environment. Regions mapped with traversable conduits [McDermott84] have been used successfully for large scale navigation in uncertain environments. Representation of the exteriors of obstacles as the edges of a highly connected graph was used by Davis, allowing detailed knowledge of the environment and its accompanying uncertainty to be captured [Davis86].

Other representations have been used for capturing movement or navigational details necessary for a robot to plan its activites. Configuration space [Lozano-Perez83] provides a computationally tractable approach to calculating the practical steps for moving a robot from one position to another. Using Voronoi diagrams and representations of free space, movements in three-dimensions have been calculated to maintain a robot the maximal possible distance from any obstacle [Brooks82]. Similar methods, when combined with an analysis of the robot's sensors, can calculate a path that is both relatively safe and easy to navigate [Miller85].

All of the systems described above have several shortcomings in addition to being limited to static domains. None of the systems takes into account the quality of the surface upon which the robot travels, relying on the surface being either traversable or not. Many of the systems described above also tend to look at the world at a single level of detail. This causes inefficiencies when the world contains large features that could block the robot's travel. Also, most of the systems above provide navigation clues along with the calculated route; thus they depend on the robot relying on dead-reckoning in order to follow the planned path.

In addition to being able to function in a dynamic world, a robot should be able to reason about dynamic processes and how they may affect it. For example, if a robot knows the local train schedule and needs to get to the other side of the train tracks, then it should use that information when planning to get to the other side. If the robot has information predicting that a long freight train will be coming just before it can reach the tracks, then given the choice between a short path that involves crossing the train tracks, and a slightly longer plan to go under the tracks, the robot should choose the latter plan. Similarly, if the robot's task is to rob a train, then the ability to plot a path that will allow the robot to jump onto the moving train is necessary.

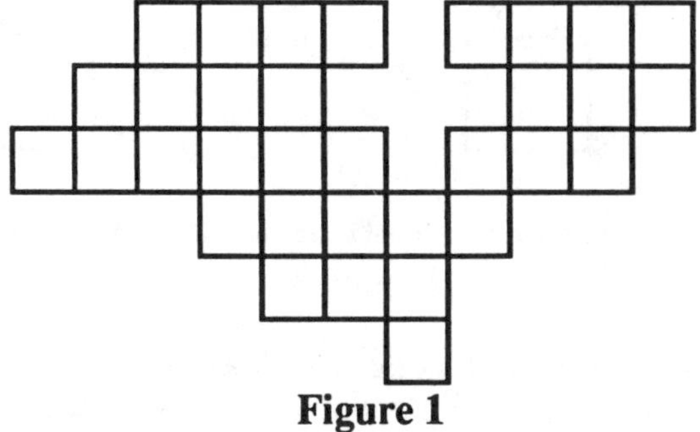

Figure 1

Below, we briefly review one of our recent systems [Slack87] that overcomes most of these shortcomings. Unfortunately, that system had a serious shortcoming of its own – when executed on traditional computer architectures its algorithm is computationally intractable. Another problem with that system was its inability to represent space at a sufficient level of detail for finding some paths. This paper will also describe some of the alterations to that system that we have devised to make it a practical dynamic domain route planning system. These include both hierarchical and overlapping extensions to the spatial representation.

2 - REPRESENTING SPACE AND FINDING PATHS

We use a grid-like representation of space (in two dimensions). Grids have been used successfully for modeling well-defined maps, and as a framework for building maps from sensory data [Moravec85]. We make up our grids through the spatial concatenation of nodes – each representing a small square area. In general, we use hypercubes as our nodes where the dimension of the hypercube is equal to the dimensions of space we are representing.   The collective area occupied by the nodes is called "space", while the remainder of existence is referred to as "void". For example, Figure 1 shows an arbitrary two-dimensional space constructed from the spatial concatenation of square shaped nodes. In general, the size of a node will be of at least sufficient size to contain the robot.

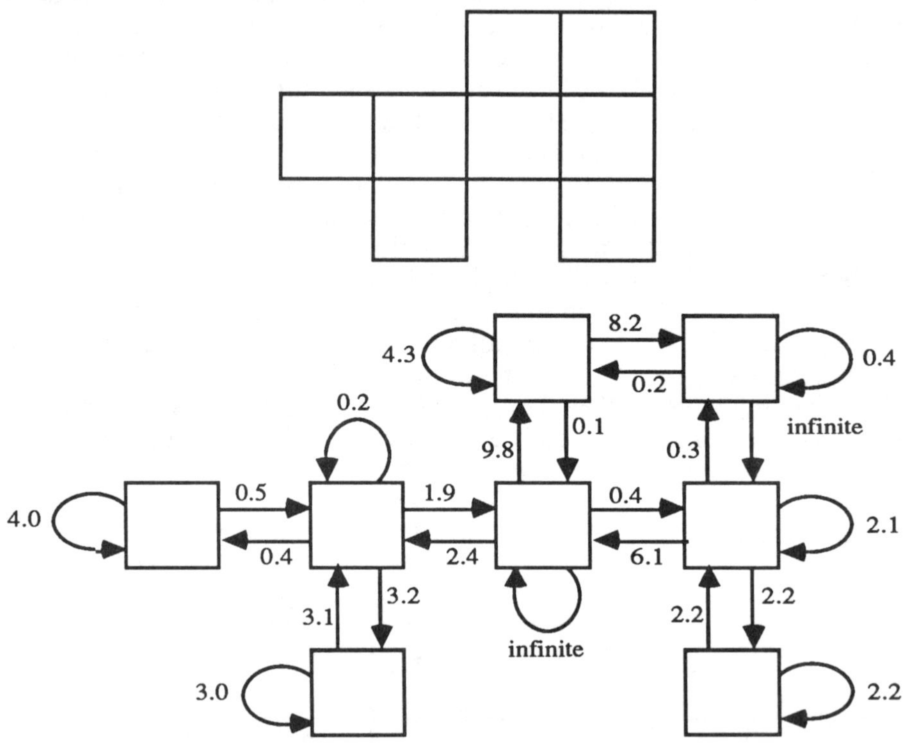

A given two dimensional space and its associated links

Figure 2

The relationship between adjoining nodes (such as the ability to move from one node to another) is represented by unidirectional links between each of the nodes (see Figure 2). The ability to stay in one place is expressed as a link from a node to itself. Associated with each of the links is a cost. The cost is used to represent such things as: Whether the surface between the two nodes is continuous, a downgrade, directly below, or if a node represents a safe place to stop. The function of the links is to provide a communication path over which messages can be sent. A node can have up to $2n$ communication links with its neighboring nodes and one to itself.

For example, consider the links that are associated with the two-dimensional space shown in Figure 2. In the figure it can be seen how the nodes constituting the edge of space have fewer connecting links then the nodes that are oriented in the middle of the space, farthest from the void. Each of the unidirectional links has a cost associated with it in the range of 0.0 to infinity. These costs may either be fixed or time-dependent functions. Consider Clyde the commuter: he may plan different paths to the office depending on the time of day (e.g. the freeways are always backed up from 7am to 9am and 4pm to 6pm Monday through Friday so take the back streets if going to or from the office at these times). In general the links will be used to represent the relative cost for a robot to make a transition from one node to another.

Areas where no nodes exist, or where communications links have infinite cost are representations of obstacles in the real world. Therefore, a connected sequence of nodes represent a path through space from the source node to the destination. In [Slack87] we used a two phase spreading activation algorithm (See Figures 3 and 4). Messages are passed from a node to all its neighbors (and itself) in a recursive manner until a message of acceptable cost reaches the destination node.

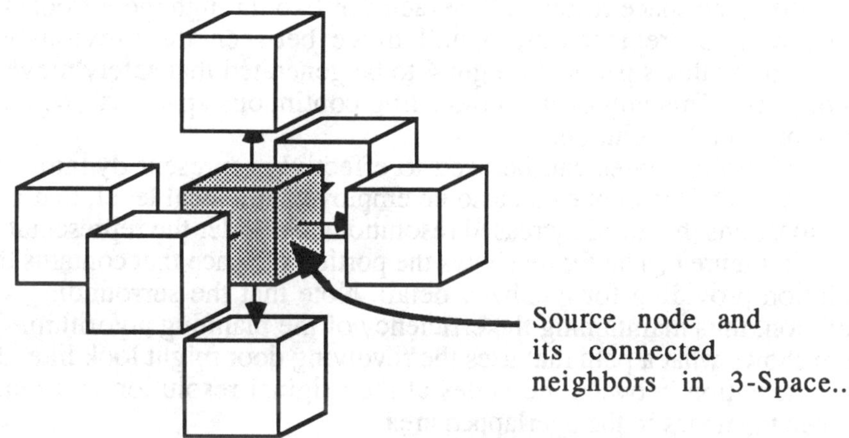

Phase 1: Creating the initial message set.
One message is created for each of the
source nodes connected neighbors.

Figure 3

The nodes themselves can also have information attached to them. This information represents navigational cues. For example, all the nodes surrounding an obvious landmark can have the appropriate notation. When a message passes through a node marked with a navigational cue (during the search process) navigation information (based on the direction of the message) is added to the message. Thus a message could contain a notation that tells the robot "at this point in the route the Washington Monument should be directly on your left". These navigational landmarks may also be time-dependent functions which will tell the robot not only whether it is on the right path, but if it is going at the pre-planned pace.

The algorithm and representation described above map very well onto a fine-grained SIMD architecture with sufficient processors to assign one to each of the nodes in the spatial representation. On such a computer, paths may be computed in $O(N)$ time where N is the length of the path. However, on a single processor machine (or a SIMD machine of inadequate size) the complexity quickly rises to at least $O(M^d)$, where d is the number of dimensions in space and M is the size (in unit nodes) of a dimension.

3 - IMPROVING RESOLUTION THROUGH OVERLAPPING NODES

Unfortunately there are some problems with the use of a discretized representation of space. The most significant occurs because object representation is an all or nothing deal. That is, if an object occupies only a small portion of a node, than that node is still considered to be occupied and impassable. An example of this problem is depicted in the two-dimensional space of Figure 5. The figure shows a simple *2x2* space containing two physical objects. Also indicated are the robots position **R** and the desired destination location **D**. The objective is to move the robot from the top left corner of the space to the bottom right corner. Using the standard object representation space the two objects block both of the possible paths that lead to the destination. Clearly, any reasonable representation of space that is to be of value must provide a representation of free space that allows for the generation of paths that move the robot in between the two objects. To accomplish this, our model uses overlapping nodes to more accurately represent the space around an object. The second part of the example figure shows the same space resolved by a factor of two through the introduction of five new nodes. Each new node representing a half move between the previously existing nodes. The modification allows paths of length 4 to be generated that safely move the robot between the two objects. This approach to modeling continuous space can be extended to any desired degree of spatial resolution.

Overlapping nodes can be used to effectivly represent dynamic objects at any desired resolution. The technique can also be employed at a local level, that is resolving the space in those locations that need increased resolution. Consider the representation of a revolving door shown in Figure 6. The figure shows the portion of space that contains the door at an increased resolution providing for localized detail. Note that the surrounding space is at the original resolution, thus maintaining the efficiency of the planning algorithm. The second half of the figure shows what a path that uses the revolving door might look like. It assumes that there is a unit transition between the nodes at the original resolution and thus a half unit transition between the nodes in the overlapped area.

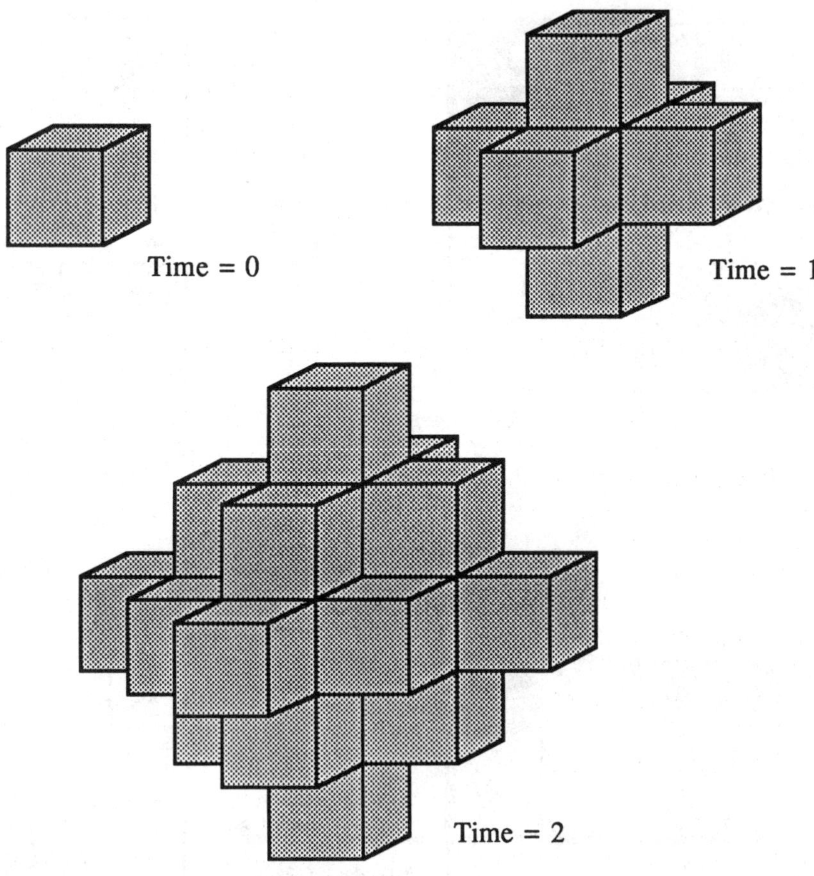

Phase 2: Spreading message activity in some 3-space
Figure 4

4 - A HIERARCHICAL APPROACH TO REPRESENTATION

The previous section discussed the additional complexities to the basic search algorithm that result if detail smaller than the robot size is needed. Fortunately, no such complications appear if the nodes size is made considerably larger than that of the robot.

To improve the efficiency and performance time of the path planning algorithm, we now represent space at several different levels of detail (see Figure 7). The lower the level, the larger the space represented by each node. At level 0, each node is made of sufficient size so that a path through those nodes may be quickly calculated using our spreading activation algorithm. At representation levels where the nodes are larger than the robot the message passing algorithm passes along probabilities of a successful path in addition to the paths cost. In other words, a large node has some representation of the probability that the robot could succesfully pass through that space [Moravec87], and into the space represented by its neighbor nodes (see figure 8).   In levels of representation where the node size is larger than the robot, occupation of a node by an object is not a binary function. That is the occupation of a node is expressed as a probability.

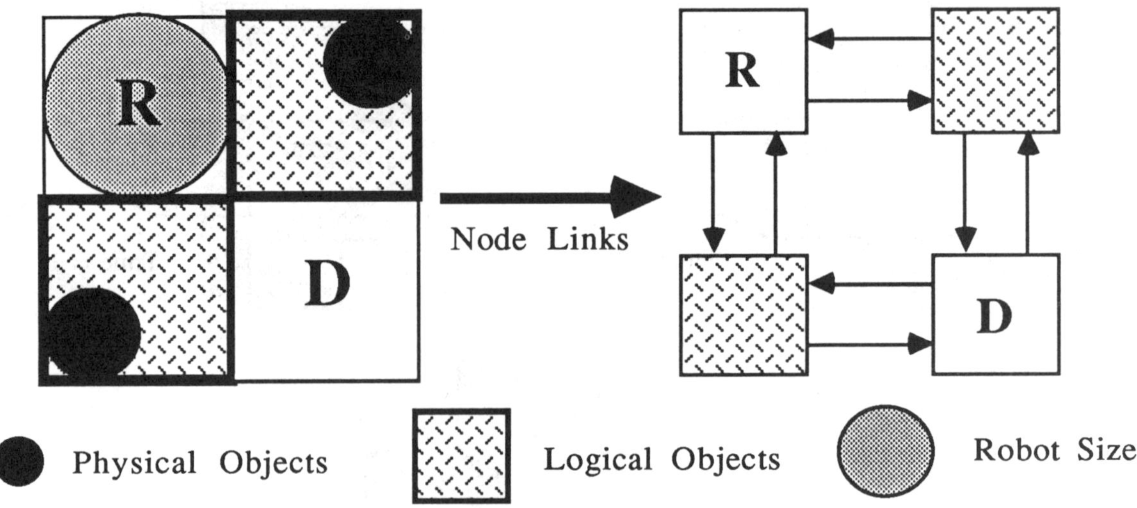

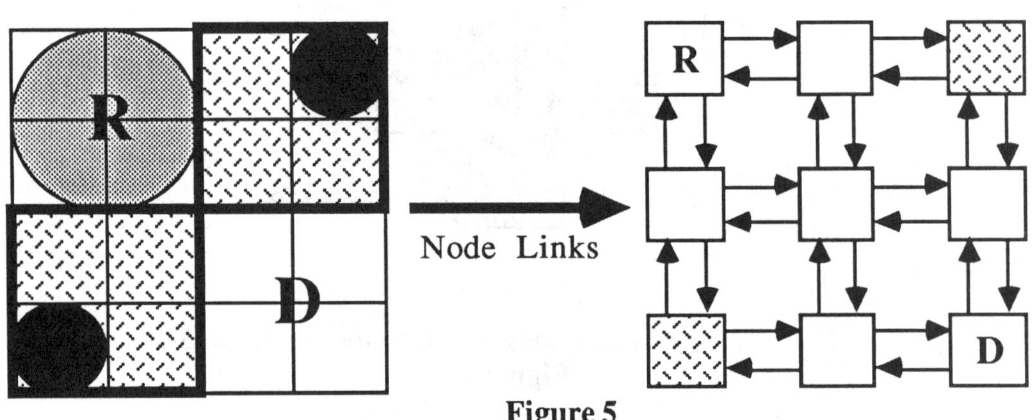

Figure 5

5 - PUTTING IT ALL TOGETHER

The hierarchical approach to spatial representation and the overlapping of nodes, to get a higher resolution of detail, give a new overall structure to the path planning algorithm. When planning is first started the message passing algorithm in Section 2 is used over level 0 of the representation. This produces a crude path that contains the probabilities of being able to successfully traverse each node in the path. If the probability for traversing a node is 1 then the node must represent a section of space that is completely devoid of obstacles. Traversal through such a node need be planned at no further detail. Nodes with a traversal probability of less than 1 possibly should be looked at the next higher level of detail. Whether this is done or not depends on the desired certainty that the path is valid (i.e. it is possible that a node with probabilty less than 1 cannot be traversed in the necessary way to get the robot into the next node; to ensure that the entire path is valid, each section of the path must be broken down to the level where no obstacles occurs in the examined chunks of space). Such a breakdown must also occur until a node contains no dynamic objects, or is at the most detailed level of the hierarchy.

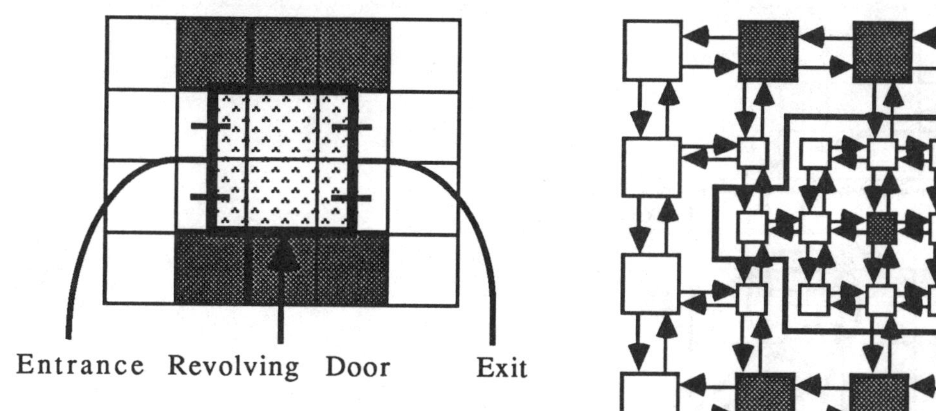

Nodes involved in the representation of the revolving door are resolved by a factor of two.

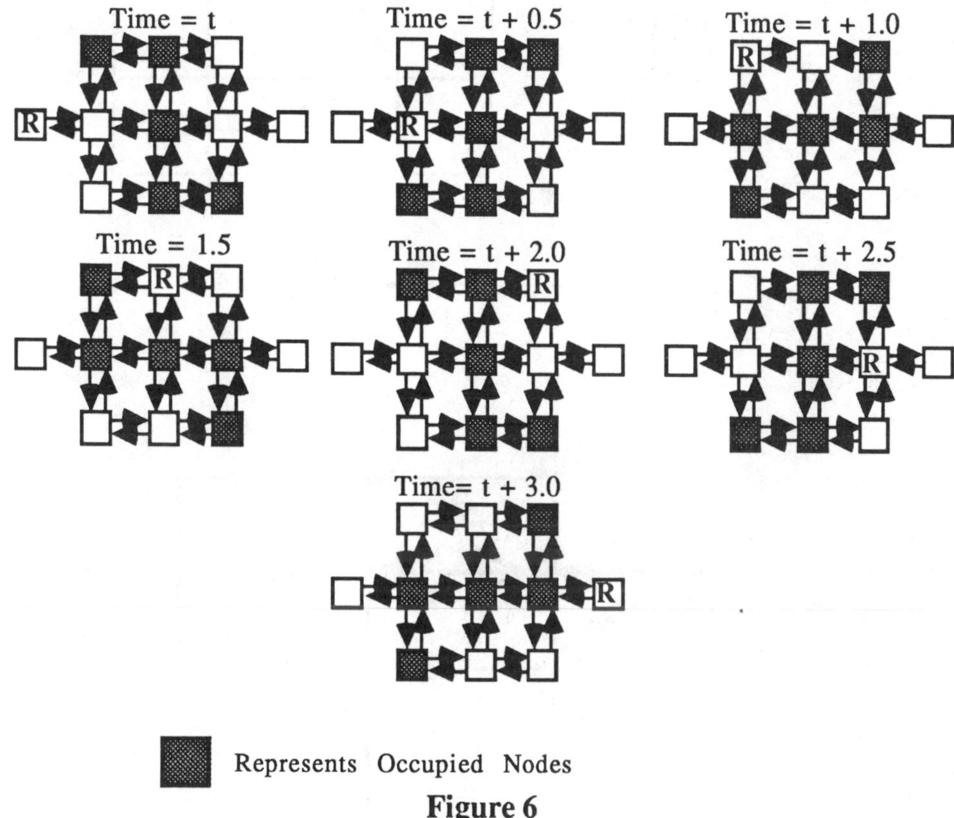

Represents Occupied Nodes

Figure 6

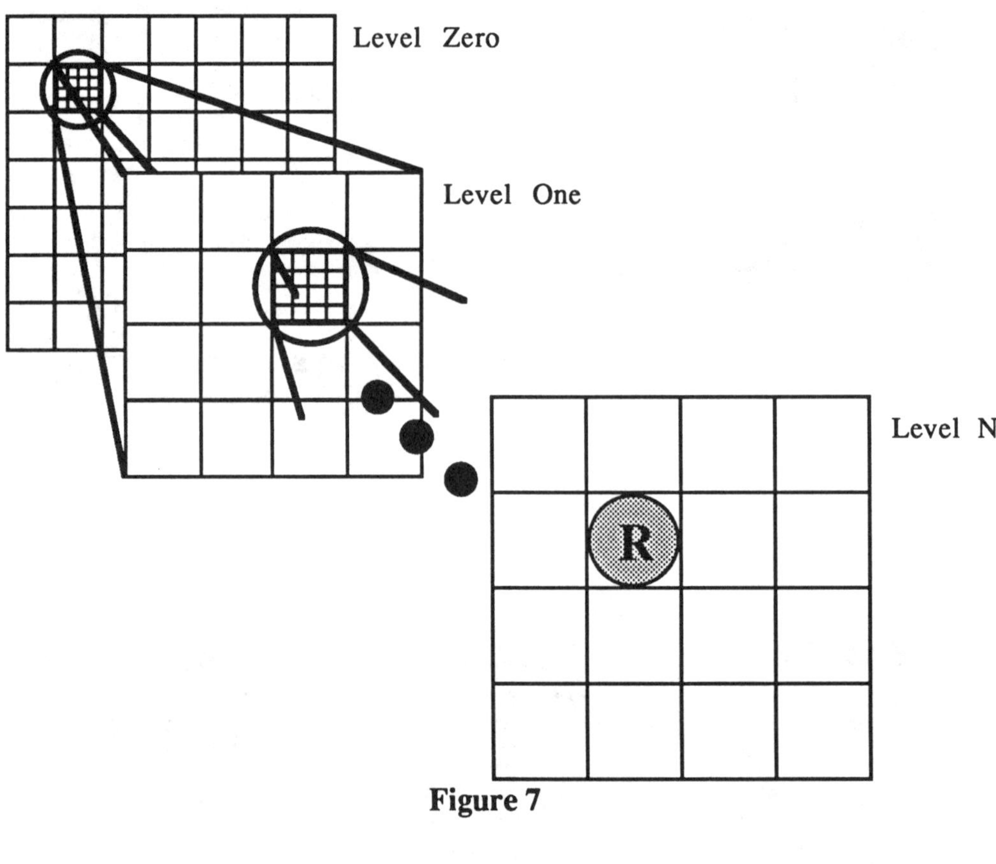

Figure 7

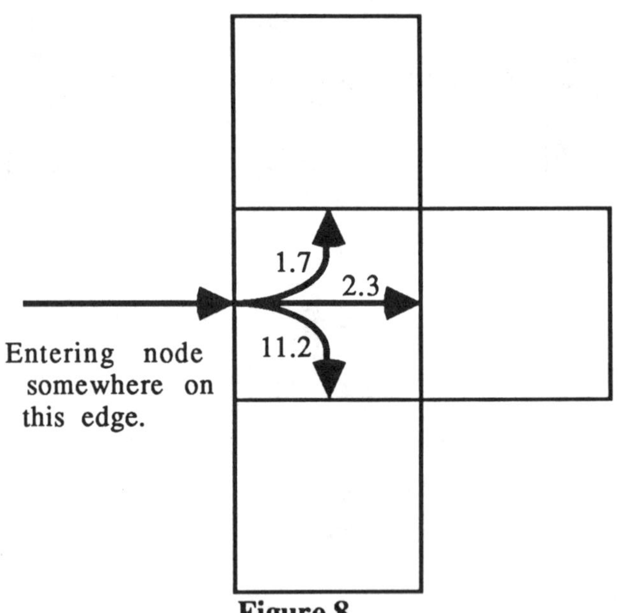

Figure 8

By putting the spatial representation into a hierarchy of detail levels we have reduced the complexity of finding paths by an exponential factor. By using overlapping representations to get finer levels of detail we effectively add additional virtual levels to the hierarchy. This allows the system to quickly get to whatever level of detail is necessary for the successful navigation of that space.

The navigation cues for a route may be incorporated into the resulting plan by passing the cues through algorithm attached to the appropriate messages. At different levels of the detail hierarchy the navigation messages will have varying levels of detail (e.g., you should be able to see an oak tree; you should pass under an oak tree; the trunk of an oak tree should be within two feet of you on your left) In this way the routes contain not only the paths the robot should take, but information to help the robot verify that it is on that path.

In domains with unpredictable dynamic objects the system is operated in an incremental fashion. But rather than repeating the entire path planning for each step, the crude path is refined and detailed planning is performed with the latest information in the robots immediate surroundings. Thus, at any one step the system only examines a small section of the entire space in any detail.

Bibliography

[Brooks82] Brooks, R. A., Solving the find path problem by a good representation of free space, in *Proceedings of AAAI 82*, AAAI, pp. 381-386, 1982.

[Chatila85] Chatila, R., Position referencing and consistent world modeling for mobile robots, in *Proceedings of the International Conference on Robotics and Automation*, IEEE, pp. 138-145, 1985.

[Davis86] Davis, E., *Representing and acquiring geographic knowledge*, Morgan Kaufman, 1986.

[Laumond83] Laumond, J. P., model structuring and concept recognition: Two aspects of learning for a mobile robot, in *Proceedings of the 8th IJCAI*, IJCAI, pp. 839-841, 1983.

[Lozano-Perez83] Lozano-Perez, T., Spatial planning: a configuration space approach, *IEEE transactions on computing*, c'32, pp. 681-698, 1983.

[McDermott84] McDermott, D. V., Davis, E., Planning routes through uncertain territory, *Artificial intelligence*, v22, pp. 107-156, 1984.

[Miller85] Miller, D. P., A spatial representation system for mobile robots, in *Proceedings of the International Conference on Robotics and Automation*, IEEE, pp. 122-127, 1985.

[Moravec85] Moravec, H. P., Elfes, A. E., High Resolution Maps from Wide Angle Sonar, in *Proceedings of the International Conference on Robotics and Automation*, IEEE, pp. 116-121, 1985.

[Moravec87] Moravec, H. P., Certainty Grids for Mobile Robots, in *Proceedings of the Workshop on Space Tele-Robotics*, JPL Pasadena California 1987.

[Slack87] Slack, M. G., Miller D. P., Route Planning in a Four Dimensional Environment, in *Proceedings of the Workshop on Space Tele-Robotics*, JPL Pasadena California 1987.

THE MANAGEMENT OF SPATIAL INFORMATION IN A MOBILE ROBOT

Thomas M. Strat and Grahame B. Smith

Artificial Intelligence Center
SRI International
333 Ravenswood Avenue
Menlo Park, California 94025

Abstract

In this paper we describe an architecture that has been designed to fulfill the information requirements of autonomous systems. It includes features from many technologies, including blackboard architectures [2], relational and spatial databases, uncertain reasoning, epistemic logic [5], computer graphics, and knowledge bases. While the system we describe is not a complete cognitive model for an autonomous system, it is an open-ended architecture that can be used as the basis for building incrementally an autonomous system that displays competent performance in a natural environment. This paper describes our Core Knowledge System architecture, focusing on the spatial and relational organization and on its implications for integrating information from multiple sources. Further details of other aspects of the system are reported elsewhere [10].

The approach is essentially based on the notion of a system that exists in the world and persists over time, thereby raising the possibility of reasoning within a dynamic world and learning from experience. Its design as a community of intelligent processes allows for incremental increases in functionality as well as for modular development of islands of expertise. Its ability to perform uncertain reasoning and to store multiple opinions allows information to be integrated in a sensible fashion.

In short, its goal is to serve as the central information manager within a community of specialized experts. The availability of an integrated knowledge database should thus encourage the development of new algorithms for perception that make use of centrally available stored knowledge and the opinions of other modules that possess relevant expertise.

[0]The work reported herein was supported by the Defense Advanced Research Projects Agency under Contract DACA76-85-C-0004.

1   Introduction

Much of the current work in image understanding is motivated by the desire to provide autonomous systems with a means for perceiving their environment. These goals have compelled researchers to expand the set of techniques that have traditionally been used in image interpretation. While present-day successes have relied on image feature recognition and model-based approaches [1] [4], the next generation will require sophisticated reasoning processes and adaptable architectures to achieve the competence that autonomous systems must have.

As an example of the type of system we envision, consider the problem of designing a robot to guard a farmer's storage shed in a sparsely populated area. Such a system would be expected to detect intruders (and perhaps impede them), to discriminate between humans and deer, to function in all seasons and under varying lighting conditions, to discover fires in the vicinity, and so on. It may or may not be mobile, and it may or may not be working alone. The perceptual abilities that are needed to achieve an operational understanding of the environment exceed the limits of current technology, although some ongoing work is directed toward achieving these goals [3] [7]. There is substantial interest within the research community in developing autonomous land vehicles; some impressive results have already been demonstrated. However, the adaptability and competence of these systems must be improved substantially if the goals of these projects are to be met. The designers of autonomous underwater vehicles and aircraft face similar challenges. While the focus of effort, the level of difficulty, and range of capabilities among these projects vary, they are inherently similar to the storage shed surveillance system.

What are the common requirements of these autonomous systems that underlie the development of new approaches to their design?

- First, each has a fundamental need to perceive its environment and images (or image-like data) are likely to be the primary sensory modality. The medium may not necessarily be visual data—underwater vehicles, for example, may rely primarily on sonar imagery, while airborne vehicles may make the best use of radar images of various sorts. Whatever the source of data, each of these systems needs to perform image understanding, match image data with stored expectations, and build a model of its surroundings incrementally.

- Second, each system is expected to operate in the natural world, unmodified by artificial guides to navigation, recognition, or interpretation. These environments are largely unstructured, and consequently, highly complex. Traditional model-based approaches to image understanding are not sufficient. Highly adaptable procedures that utilize novel representations of natural form are called for.

- Third, the environment these systems operate in is dynamic—indeed, in many ways. The mobility of the robot itself is only one source of change. Other objects will be moving as well— aircraft, deer, clouds, leaves on trees, etc. Still other kinds of change will be present, such as leaves changing color, trees growing, sands shifting on the ocean bottom, and fires burning.

- Fourth, the processing that must be carried out for perception, planning, and execution monitoring must be knowledge-intensive. The tasks that confront autonomous systems in natural environments are too unpredictable for modules with limited reasoning capabilities. Domain-specific knowledge must be encoded and made available for use in nearly all stages of computational processing.

- Fifth, information will be available from a variety of sources. An autonomous system will almost certainly have access to a suite of sensors that can provide information regarding

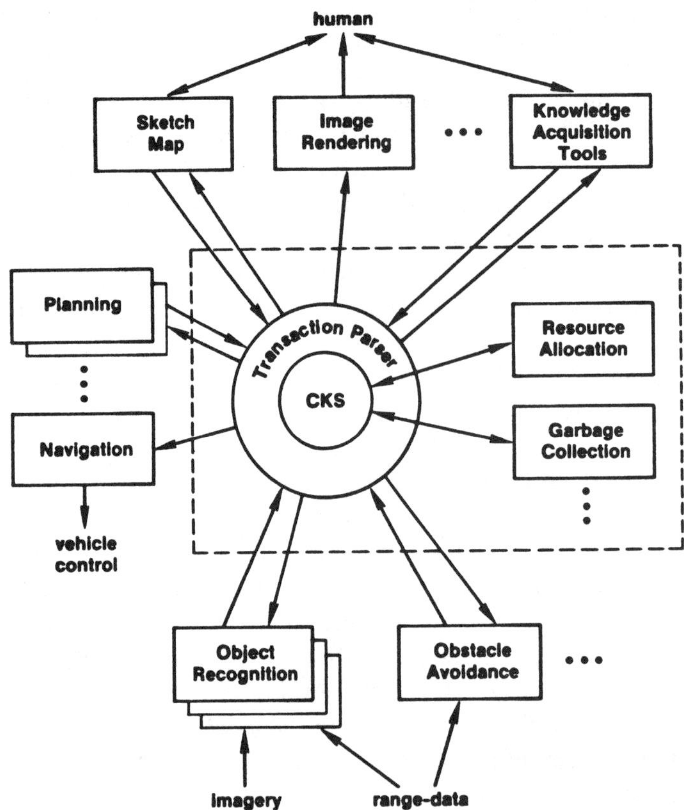

Figure 1: Architecture of an Autonomous Vehicle Designed around the Core Knowledge System.

various characterstics of the surroundings. Further information will be available from preparatory instructions, from the experience gained during the system's own operation, and perhaps from other robots. This wealth of data must be integrated if the system is to be effective. The integration of information is crucial to successful operation in natural environments. Available information will be imperfect; superior integration techniques can mitigate the adverse effects of individual imperfections. The insensitivity to noise typically enjoyed by model-based recognition techniques can be achieved by integrating newly acquired information with stored models. Fusion of redundant information from multiple sources can help reduce uncertainty about the state of the world. Information integration also fills in gaps that would be present if available information were not combined. All these factors contribute to improved perception based upon imperfect information.

- Finally, the fact that autonomous systems must respond to the environment in a timely fashion places a special emphasis on identifying the most critical tasks and finding efficient algorithms for solving them. This real-time requirement cannot be ignored.

2   Overview of the Design

In this paper we describe a knowledge system that has been designed to support the requirements outlined above in order to form a world model that will ultimately be used by an autonomous system to plan and execute its tasks. The overall architecture of our Core Knowledge System (CKS) can be viewed as a *community* of interacting *processes*, each with its own limited goals and expertise, but all of which cooperate to achieve the higher goals of the system. The various processes may represent sensors, interpreters, controllers, user-interface drivers, planners, or any other information processor that can be envisioned. Each process can be both a producer and a consumer of information. Information is shared among modules by allowing them to read data stored by other processes and to update that information. Each module updates information continually and asynchronously on the basis of sensor readings, deductions, renderings, or other interpretations that it makes. Figure 1 portrays the interrelationship between the CKS and the various processes that can be expected to be present in an autonomous vehicle.

The CKS includes a global knowledge database through which information is shared. Access to this database is provided by means of spatial and semantic indices that arise naturally in the domain of autonomous vehicles. The indexing structures are associated with the need to retrieve information that is grouped appropriately for the task of navigation in the three-dimensional world. A *spatial directory* that forms subsets of the data according to spatial location and a *semantic directory* that forms subsets of the data according to object class are the principal indexing schemes used to organize the storage and retrieval of data tokens.

In particular, data tokens are stored according to three-dimensional position in the world and can be retrieved either by absolute location or by their positioning relative to other known objects. For retrieval purposes, the location of an object is represented by its bounding polyhedron. In addition to the spatial description, each data token is assigned one or more *semantic labels* that classify the entity according to properties of interest in the domain. Complex database queries can be formulated through logical combinations of simpler queries based upon convex polyhedral spatial descriptions and semantic labels.

A system that views processes as individual experts, which may make conflicting interpretations of the data, must have a policy to determine what is stored in the database. For example, if two processes arrive at different determinations of the height of a particular tree, which opinion should be stored: the last one given, that of the process with more expertise, or the average of the two? There is no "correct" way to determine a single value. Traditionally, information integration is accomplished as the data are being inserted into the database; the data that are retained are presumed to be free of conflict. Within the CKS, all processes are considered equal and only their *opinions* are stored. This approach reflects the view that conclusions are not only a function of the data used, but also of the knowledge sources that provide those data and of the anticipated use of the conclusion. The user of the information should have the opportunity to interpret it based upon knowledge of both its content and its source. Information in the data store can be modified only by the process that furnished it, although other processes can cast their opinions as well.

Data tokens are stored as frames consisting of a number of slots. From an external perspective, each slot has a single value. Viewed internally, however, a separate value is maintained for each process that offers an opinion. When retrieving a slot's value, one specifies the method desired for combining all opinions that have already been provided for that slot. This approach makes it possible to integrate multiple opinions in a manner that is suited to the task at hand. For example, if a robot wants to guarantee that its camera will have an unobstructed view over a fence, it should use the opinion that has the greatest value for the HEIGHT slot. On the other hand, if its goal is to keep all the cows in a confined area, it should be interested in the smallest value of HEIGHT.

3   Organization of Spatial Information

The spatial directory organizes the data tokens into groups determined by spatial location. Because an autonomous vehicle may roam about in an extensive environment, we need a representation of the world that can deal with its spatial extent. In addition, the representation must be efficient in indexing data when the data are distributed nonuniformly over the environment. Data will need to be accessed at various levels of resolution, depending on the task at hand. Route planning, for example, needs lower-resolution data than does landmark identification or obstacle avoidance.

3.1   Spatial Directory

The world is three-dimensional, but most objects of interest are restricted to a two-dimensional surface embedded in this world. Although there are many reasons for choosing a two-dimensional index, such as latitude and longitude, and then representing the third dimension as a data value, we prefer a three-dimensional index. Our selection was motivated by the advantage such an index affords in encoding spatial relations within the directory, generating visibility information, and employing this architecture in spatial domains in which movement is not restricted to a two-dimensional surface (such as for underwater vehicles).

The spatial directory is organized as an *octree* [6] [9]. Each node in the tree represents a volume in space (a *voxel*) that can be subdivided into eight smaller volumes, as needed. This multiresolution data structure allows for the representation of position at a range of granularities. When a data token is stored in the spatial directory, a pointer to that token is placed in a voxel that contains the object. For economy of representation, in noncritical parts of the world one may choose to place pointers to data tokens in coarse-grained volumes, while the part of the world in which the vehicle is active can be subdivided into finely partitioned volumes.

Because the voxels are shaped uniformly , we must address the problem of indexing objects whose shape does not match this partitioning of space. Generally, it is easy to place stationary compact objects within a voxel that can contain them completely, but objects like linear structures, surfaces, and moving objects require alternative approaches. A linear structure like a road, river, telephone wire, or fence is stored as a single data token, but pointers are placed in all the voxels through which the structure passes. The smallest-sized voxels that are appropriate are used; for example, the voxel size for a road will be determined by the road width so as to provide assurance that the road "fits" within the voxel. The same approach is taken with other extended objects, such as a surface or the track of a moving object: a single data token has pointers to it from the set of voxels through which the surface or track passes.

An advantage of a multiresolution spatial directory is the ease with which approximate location can be represented. An object is placed in a voxel that is large enough to contain the full range of its possible locations. Object location may be approximate because of image-processing errors when objects are being detected in imagery, or because a sensor's exact calibration is unknown. Data pertaining to an object can be added to the database before its position is known; when better locational information becomes available, the directory can be updated by moving the data to a smaller volume. A background process whose task is to move each object to its most precise location within the directory (when processing resources are available) accomplishes the directory update, thereby attaining retrieval efficiency. Hence, all data can be directly inserted into one directory, whether their locations are known accurately or only approximately.

3.2   Retrieval

Having all data whose position is known or uncertain within one directory structure allows the CKS to respond easily to data retrieval requests that seek "all objects that are within a certain volume in space," as well as "all objects that could possibly be within that particular volume of space." Clearly, in the task domain of an autonomous vehicle, knowing what *might be* ahead and what *is* ahead is essential for competent navigation and obstacle avoidance. For example, a landmark recognition process needs to know what objects are definitely in some volume, while an obstacle avoidance process is interested in all objects that are possibly in front of the vehicle. In terms of the spatial directory, "within a volume" maps to the subtree of voxels below (finer than) the voxel containing the volume, while "possibly within a volume" corresponds to the octree nodes above (coarser than) that voxel.

When data can be retrieved on the basis of their locations, retrievals on the basis of spatial relations are also possible. The spatial directory implicitly encodes the spatial relationships between tokens stored in the database. As objects are moved or their spatial positions refined, these spatial relations are maintained without additional processing. New objects entered into the database inherently express their spatial relationships with previously entered data. In a mobile robot domain, we expect to retrieve tokens on the basis of relative position—objects to the right of the road, trees casting shadows on the road, and so on. Having an indexing structure that matches the world structure permits this without the overhead that would be introduced by alternative schemes, such as a relational database.

4   Organization of Semantic Information

A primary feature of the CKS is a capability for characterizing and retrieving information in accordance with the semantic content of that information. In this regard, the CKS plays two roles within the context of an autonomous community of processes. First, it provides a common *vocabulary* so that each process can share information with all its counterparts without concern for the specifics of their implementations. Second, it contains a knowledge base that is used to provide a degree of understanding of the terms in its vocabulary. Access to this knowledge is gained either implicitly (as when the CKS attempts to evaluate a query) or explicitly (to give user processes access to that knowledge base). The net result is that the CKS can function alternatively as a knowledge base, as a database, or as a knowledgeable database in its domain of discourse.

4.1   The Vocabulary

The vocabulary is a set of terms that has been constructed by examining the communication requirements of processes operating in the ordinary outdoor environment. It is intended to be the primary means of communication among processes and thus comprises their common vocabulary. The meaning of each term is intended to be that which is suggested by the word(s) used; of course, communication can occur only to the extent that the processes using the terms agree on the meaning. We make no attempt to define any of the vocabulary terms completely—such a task is generally impossible. Instead we stipulate certain relations to hold among these terms, thus creating a partial definition that the agents can use as a basis for communication. In actuality, their relation to English words serves a strictly mnemonic purpose.

Data tokens are given meaning by a user process through the assignment of a *semantic description*. From a syntactic standpoint, a semantic description is simply an unordered list of vocabulary terms. It is interpreted as meaning that each term in the list represents a true property of the token. For example, the semantic description (LARGE POST RED) is tantamount to stating that the data token denotes something that is large and red and is a post. A formal treatment of the semantics of such "semantic descriptions" is described elsewhere [10].

The allowable set of semantic descriptions is restricted to include only those terms listed in the vocabulary. The challenge here is not to provide unlimited flexibility in the language, but rather to identify a moderately sized set of properties that are sufficient for interprocess communication in the domain of interest. If the properties chosen are not adequate, the vocabulary should be modified; such inadequacy does not imply a fundamental limitation of the database design. The majority of terms in the vocabulary have been chosen on the basis of their value in fostering communication about sensing and navigation in a natural outdoor environment. Some additional terms have been included for the purpose of exploring the limitations of the representation. It is expected that the vocabulary will evolve as domain requirements become more fully understood.

4.2   Semantic Relationships

The semantic relations among vocabulary words are explicitly described by axioms encoded in a semantic network. These formulas are domain-specific and are carefully selected to enable the types of inference necessary for meaningful communication among the independent processes of an autonomous vehicle. They are represented as a collection of machine-readable graph structures. In particular, the semantic-network fragment

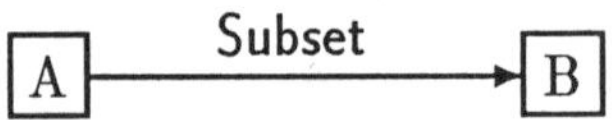

encodes the sentence $(\forall x)[A(x) \rightarrow B(x)]$, while

encodes $\neg(\exists x)[C(x) \wedge D(x)]$.

These two arcs allow the specification of all possible set relationships. As with the choice of vocabulary terms, design of the semantic network requires that careful consideration be given to the autonomous vehicle's domain and the anticipated applications of the CKS. As a result, we do not expect that the network in its current form will be the final choice for use on an autonomous vehicle. Instead we anticipate a continual process of revision as experiments with sensory and navigational processes are conducted. An example of a small portion of the semantic network is given in Figure 2.

A third type of arc is also included in the network. Specifically, the semantic network fragment

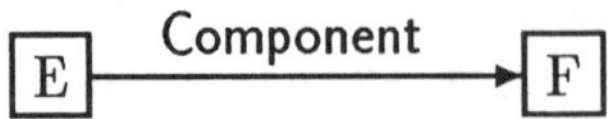

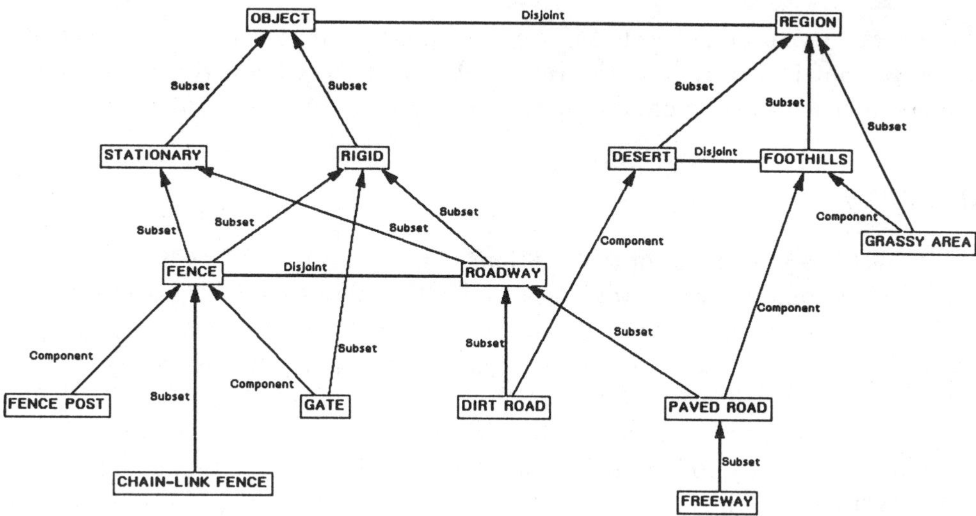

Figure 2: A Portion of the Semantic Network Used in the Semantic Directory.

encodes the knowledge that E *typically* contains F as one of its components. For example, a car usually has a wheel as a component and a desert typically has cacti. It is important to recognize that we have not chosen to represent absolute component relationships—such strong statements are truly rare in the outdoor world. For example, we would not want to state that all cars have wheels, because a car without wheels is still a car. Instead, the notion of typical containment seems more useful, even if not as clearly defined.

4.3   The Semantic Directory

The spatial directory provides an indexing scheme that matches the spatial nature of the data in the task domain, whereas the semantic directory provides an indexing scheme that matches the semantic nature of the data in that domain.

Each node of the semantic network is associated with a vocabulary term and has pointers to all the data tokens in the database that have been labeled with this term. The nodes of the semantic network can be accessed directly by the vocabulary term thus comprising a directory to data tokens on the basis of the semantic label. Although we view the semantic directory as a graph structure and display the semantic network as a graph, the implementation uses hash tables for speed of access. When tokens are added to the database or when a token's description acquires additional labels, the semantic directory is updated accordingly.

Data tokens are attached to the most specific network nodes possible. If, for example, a token has been labeled by a process as being a PAVED-ROAD, it is attached only to the semantic network node for PAVED-ROAD, even though all PAVED-ROADs are known to be ROADWAYs. This approach was adopted to save storage space as well as to provide a straightforward implementation of retrieval requests to return "all objects that are PAVED-ROADs," as opposed to "all objects that might be PAVED-ROADs." The second descriptor includes objects in the more general class ROADWAY as well as those labeled PAVED-ROAD. Data tokens that represent paved roads are found attached to the lattice nodes that form a tree rooted at the node labeled PAVED-ROAD, whereas roadways that *might be* paved are found attached to the nodes of the lattice *above* the node labeled PAVED-ROAD. This arrangement parallels the mechanisms used in the spatial directory to find objects that are at a particular location, as distinct from those that *might* be at that location. It is the responsibility of the CKS access routines to retrieve the appropriate tokens from the database by means of the semantic network.

5   Summary

The CKS database is a storehouse of the *opinions* of many agents. It is not a database of facts. This design gives it some unusual properties that allow it to function as a central repository of information for a community of processes. Furthermore, the fact that much of the research in database designs is inapplicable has spurred us to develop a new technology for the storage and retrieval of multiple opinions.

The community-of-processes architecture adopted for the CKS requires that processes be able to communicate their opinions to one another and to do so without undue interference from processes with competing views. The formalization and use of an opinion base in lieu of a database give rise to the following important features:

- The ability to store information that is *inconsistent.*

- The ability to *integrate* multiple opinions and to adapt that integration to the intended use of the information.

- The ability to *separate* one source's opinions from another's.

These goals have been achieved while retaining an ability to incorporate general knowledge that is universally accepted as being true. An opinion base appears to us to be a better model of the way humans store information than a conventional database of facts.

The Core Knowledge System provides a rich infrastructure for building autonomous systems. Its major features are the following:

Representation of both knowledge and data– The CKS is a true knowledge-based database. It has the ability to perform inferences from stored knowledge as well as the ability to infer information from newly acquired data. It retains the virtues of database systems in providing for rapid retrieval based upon selected indices and in being a system that persists over time, well beyond the extent of a single execution.

Spatial orientation– Autonomous vehicles operate in the physical world. It is vital, therefore, that a vehicle's information manager possess the ability to represent the three-dimensional world in a natural way. The spatial directory, designed as a volume-based octree, provides the CKS database with a spatial orientation.

Multiple opinions– The need for representations of uncertainty as well as procedures for combining multiple pieces of evidence has been demonstrated by the many techniques and systems developed for this purpose. The CKS recognizes this need by providing a mechanism for maintaining multiple, conflicting opinions within its database. This approach affords the opportunity to integrate information according to the demands of the present situation, and also affords the option of forgoing integration altogether when it would be irrelevant to the task at hand.

Mixed-initiative control– Borrowing from the technology of blackboard systems, the CKS is organized as a community of asynchronous processes that communicate by sharing a common database. Additional flexibility of control is attained both through implementation of a complete demon facility and through metalevel control processes that oversee the operation of the community.

Centralized database– Communication between computational processes is fostered by having all shared information in a common database. Centralization has the additional benefit of enabling a single display or user interface tool to access all the data. Thus a tool that is constructed for a particular purpose is immediately available for use with data supplied by any source. Such a capability is conducive to rapid development and facilitates conversion to new domains.

Admittedly, none of these features is especially new. What makes the CKS novel, however, is the integration of all these features in a single, coherent system that allows the implementor of an autonomous vehicle to take advantage of whatever capability is required for his task. It is our contention that the availablility of a core knowledge system will encourage the development of new algorithms that utilize stored knowledge for the task of image understanding, in particular, and for autonomous vehicle control, in general.

References

[1] Barrow, H. G., *et. al.*, "HAWKEYE: An Interactive Aid for Cartography and Photo Interpretation," Proceedings of the DARPA Image Understanding Workshop, Palo Alto, California, pp. 111-127, October 1977.

[2] Erman, Lee D., Frederick Hayes-Roth, Victor R. Lesser, and D. Raj Reddy, The Hearsay-II Speech Understanding System: Integrating Knowledge to Resolve Uncertainty, *Computing Surveys*, Vol. 12, pp 213-253, June 1980.

[3] Lawton, Daryl T., *et. al.*, "Environmental Modeling and Recognition for an Autonomous Land Vehicle," Proceedings of the DARPA Image Understanding Workshop, Vol. 1, Los Angeles, California, pp. 107-121, February 1987.

[4] Mackworth, A., and Havens, W., "Representing Knowledge of the Visual World," IEEE Computer, Vol. 16, pp. 90–98, 1983.

[5] Moore, Robert C., and Hendrix, Gary G., "Computational Models of Belief and the Semantics of Belief Sentences," SRI Artificial Intelligence Center Technical Note 187, SRI International, Menlo Park, California, June 1979.

[6] Samet, Hanan, The Quadtree and Related Hierarchical Data Structures, *Computing Surveys*, Vol. 16, pp 187–260, June 1984.

[7] Shafer, S., Stentz, A., and Thorpe, C., "An Architecture for Sensor Fusion in a Mobile Robot," in IEEE International Conference on Robotics and Automation, 1986.

[8] Smith, Grahame B., and Strat, Thomas M., "Information Management in a Sensor-based Autonomous System," Proceedings of the DARPA Image Understanding Workshop, Vol. 1, Los Angeles, California, pp. 170-177, February 1987.

[9] Srihari, Sargur N., Representation of Three-Dimensional Digital Images, *Computing Surveys*, Vol. 13, pp 399—424, December 1981.

[10] Strat, Thomas M., and Smith, Grahame B., "The Core Knowledge System," SRI Artificial Intelligence Center, Internal Report A007, SRI International, Menlo Park, California, May 1987.

3-D CURVE MATCHING

Eyal Kishon and Haim Wolfson[*]
Robotics Research Laboratory
Computer Science Department
Courant Institute of Mathematical Sciences
New York University

ABSTRACT

An algorithm to find the longest common subcurve of two 3-D curves is presented.

The curves are represented by sequences of local, rotationally and translationally invariant shape signatures. Then these signature sequences are compared using the 'geometric hashing' technique, and a number of long 'candidate' matching subsequences is obtained. The subcurves corresponding to the above mentioned subsequences are then matched, and their 'best' relative rotation and translation is discovered, where the quality of match is evaluated in the L_2 metric. The longest matching subcurve with a good L_2 fit is chosen to be the final solution.

This algorithm is of average complexity O(n) where n is the number of the sample points on the two curves. Applications to part assembly and object recognition problems are discussed. Experimental results are included.

[*]Work on this paper was supported by Office of Naval Research Grant N00014-82-K-0381 and National Science Foundation Grant No. NSF-DCR-83-20085.

1   Introduction

1.1   Object Recognition

Object recognition is a major task in robotic vision. In a factory environment one is usually faced with the restricted problem of model based object recognition, since we expect the robot to see only a certain subset of factory tools and manufactured parts. Under this assumption we have to solve two major problems which are interrelated. The first is the *'model acquisition'*, or *'data-base formation'* problem. The second is the actual *'object recognition'* problem, which will use a previously prepared data-base. The model descriptions used must be rich enough for recognition purposes; however, we would like them be terse to enable an efficient recognition process. An efficient object recognition algorithm is apt to rely on a favorable model description.

Existing object recognition systems (see [BJ85], [CD86]) use either 2-D or 3-D models. 3-D descriptions have the advantage of allowing a full description of a 3-D model from an unconstrained viewpoint. In an industrial application we can usually expect to be in a position to obtain this description. Other sensory information may be available as well. Since a natural description of a 3-D object is by its bounding surfaces, much prior work concentrates on object recognition using surface information (see the surveys cited above). However, a reliable surface description requires a large amount of data. Handling this data, even using efficient algorithms, is likely to make recognition time consuming.

Use of surfaces for object description may be motivated by an implicit concern for object reconstruction. In order to reconstruct a 3-D object, it is sufficient to know all its bounding surfaces. However, the object recognition problem is really more restricted. All we need, is to decide to which one of the models taken from a data-base, which is usually not very big, it fits best. However, the object itself can be observed from an arbitrary viewpoint and may be partially occluded. For this reason we have to describe the objects in a way which can distinguish them given an unknown viewpoint and partial occlusion. We believe that the curve based techniques described below provide a rich enough description for these purposes, and also allow efficient handling (almost real time). Various sorts of curves on 3-D objects can be used for this. These may be curves of occlusion (i.e. object boundaries), curves of intersection between neighbouring surfaces, lines of maximal local curvature, and artificially painted curves. Of course, there are surfaces on which there are almost no significant curves. In such cases surface information is essential.

1.2   Related Work

Our work exploits efficient curve matching algorithms which were developed for the 2-D recognition problem. In this simpler situation objects are uniquely defined by their boundary curves, hence the use of curves for object description is very natural. In order to recognize a partially occluded curve as belonging to a specific model in a 2-D situation, we need an algorithm which finds the best possible match between a curve and its proper subcurve. An algorithm due to Schwartz and Sharir (see [SS 87]), first implemented in the 2-D case, has proved to be very robust, as indicated by its successful application in visual assembly of a 200-piece jigsaw puzzle (see [WSKL 87]). This algorithm has been implemented for the 3-D case as well ([BSSS 86]), and also extended to the case in which several subcurves have to be matched simultaneously against the same curve ([K 86]). However, this algorithm requires knowledge of the exact starting point and endpoint of the observed subcurve. Such information is not always available in composite overlapping scenes of objects. When it is not, a more general curve matching algorithm is required, namely, we have to solve the following problem :

given two curves, find the longest matching subcurve which appears in both curves.

Several algorithms that solve this problem for the 2-D case were proposed in [W 86]. The idea of that paper is to transform 2-D curves into strings of local, rotationally and translationally invariant shape signatures, apply efficient string matching techniques to discover starting points and endpoints of long matching subcurves, and then match these subcurves using the Schwartz-Sharir curve matching algorithm. The approach to the 3-D curve matching problem described in this paper is quite similar. Again we transform the curves into sequences of local, rotationally and translationally invariant shape signatures. These signatures are actually k-tuples based on k signatures taken at different resolutions. Then we apply a geometric hashing technique to find candidate long matching subcurves. Finally, we choose just one of the several candidates by using the 3-D version of the Schwartz-Sharir algorithm, which also computes the transformation which has to be applied to this curve in order to align it with the other along their longest matching subpart.

The geometric hashing technique (so called, 'footprint' method) for curve matching that we generalize was first proposed in [KSSS 87] and later improved in [HW]. We use this later version of the technique. One of the major advantages of this technique is that it makes it possible to match an observed curve against a large data-base of other curves in average time linear in the number of sample points of the observed curve. Thus it enables us to tackle the more general recognition problem :

given a database of model curves, and an observed curve, find the model curve in the database with the longest matching subcurve with the observed curve.

Another significant advantage of this technique is its straightforward parallelism.

1.3   Practical Implementation

At this stage in our work we have restricted our experiments to matching of curve pairs. This has other applications besides the object recognition problem. One such application is the problem of reassembly of broken objects. For example we have assembled the fractured 3-D object in Figure 1 by matching the boundary curves of the different pieces. Another possible application is to obtain a full description of a 3-D curve from a small number of overlapping partial views (curve reconstruction). Suppose, more specifically, that we are given two images (including depth information) of the same object from different viewpoints, so that the scenes overlap. We would like to merge the information obtained from both images into one consistent model. The obvious way to merge the curve information is by joining the appropriate curves along their longest matching subcurve. This technique will enable us to build a description of an object model, based on its

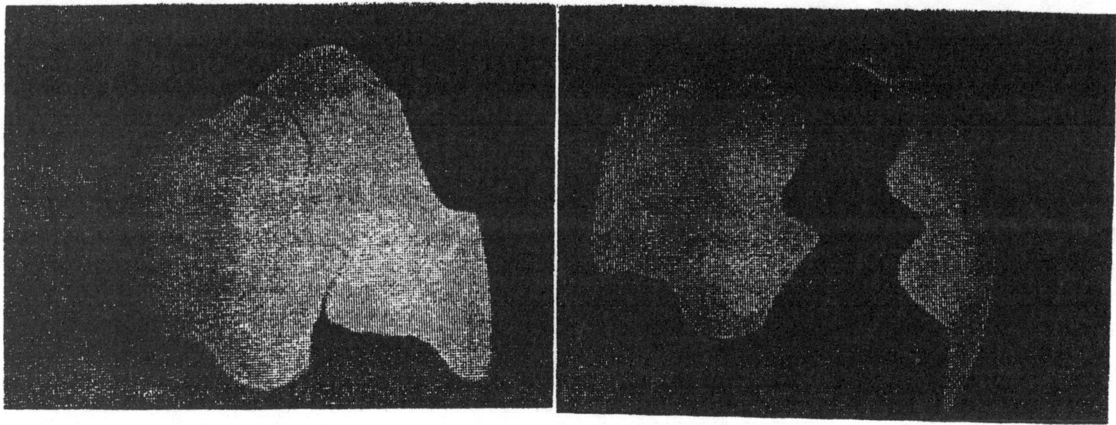

Figure 1: a) two pieces of a plastic ball. b) the two pieces assembled together.

curves, by taking pictures from a small number of viewpoints.

1.4   Organization

This paper is organized as follows. Section 2 describes the shape signatures we have experimented with. Section 3 describes our geometric hashing algorithm. Section 4 presents experimental results. In section 5 we suggest some directions for future research.

2   Shape Signatures

2.1   Signature Properties

In this section we describe the curve signatures which are used in our matching algorithm. The signatures are used to compare relatively short segments of the curves to each other, hence we require them to be

i) local,

ii) translationally and rotationally invariant,

iii) stable, in the sense that small changes in the curve induce
      small effects (or no effect at all) on the associated signatures,

a further desirable, but less essential, property is :

iv) an approximation to an observed curve can be reconstructed
      from its signature sequence.

Although reconstruction is not essential for the recognition problem, we desire a weaker property which is important for successful recognition, namely, separation, to wit :

iv') essentially different local curve segments will create different
      signatures.

It is well known from Differential Geometry that smooth curves can be uniquely reconstructed within a rigid motion (i.e rotation and translation) using three geometric invariants, which are arc length s, curvature $\kappa(s)$ and torsion $\tau(s)$ as a function of s (see, for example, [D 76] or [S 69]). For ideal differentiable curves curvature and torsion are therefore suitable candidates for curve signatures. However, our applications must deal with noisy polygonal representations of curves, making it impossible to compute curvature and torsion either accurately, or at every point of a curve. This introduces a problem of numerical stability. Curvature is essentially a second order derivative, and torsion involves even higher order derivatives. It is known that computations of (approximated) derivatives of noisy data are numerically unreliable. Hence we have decided not to use (an approximation to) torsion in our experimental signature.

Given this decision we have experimented with two signature schemes, which can best be explained using the following notation. We represent a point on a curve C by the vector $X(s) = (x(s), y(s), z(s))$, where s is the arclength. Since our curves are sampled, curves are represented by a sequence of sample points $(X_i, i = 1, ..., n)$.

2.2   Curvature Based Signatures

The first signature we experimented with was based on curvature alone. The curvature of an arc $X(s)$ ($\alpha \leq s \leq \beta$) can be defined as the length of the curve traced out by the normalized tangent $t(s) = \frac{dX/ds}{\|dX/ds\|}$ on the unit sphere (the so called Gaussian sphere) as s varies over the arc (see [S 69] p.54).

Thus, calculation of approximate local curvature can be accomplished as follows:

1. take equally spaced (by arclength) sample points $(X_i(s); i = 1, ..., n)$ on the curve;

2. at each sample point compute an approximate tangent vector at this point $T_i = X_{i+1} - X_{i-1}, i = 2, ..., n-1$;

3. normalize the tangents: $t_i = \frac{T_i}{\|T_i\|}$; (This gives us points on the Gaussian sphere.)

4. compute the distance between successive normalized tangents : $\kappa_i = \|t_i - t_{i-1}\|, i = 3, ..., n-1$; (This gives approximation of the geodesic distance between the normalized tangents on the Gaussian sphere .)

It is clear that this signature, although only an approximation to local curvature, satisfies properties (i)-(iii), emphasized above. To improve separation we define our signature to be a k-tuple (in our experiments k=5) of local curvatures defined as just explained. In the actual computation we apply a multi-resolution approach, so that the relevant sample points for our local curvature measurements are taken at successively increasing distances, namely, the signature vector at point i is defined as

$$\mathcal{S}_i = (\kappa_{i,1}, \kappa_{i,2}, ..., \kappa_{i,k}),$$

where $\kappa_{i,j}$ $(j = 1, ..., k)$ is generated as explained above using the tangent approximation $T_{i,j} = X_{i+j} - X_{i-j}$; $i = k + 1, ..., n - k$; $j = 1, ..., k$.

At each sample point on the curve we therefore get a k-dimensional vector (k-signature) representing the multi-resolution curvature measurements.

2.3 Tangent Magnitude Based Signatures

As noted above, a problem of numerical stability arises when derivatives of noisy data are computed. The previous paragraph describes a signature which is based on an approximation of a second order derivative. Obviously a signature based on a first order derivative should be more stable. This leads as to consider a second signature, based on the norm of the tangent vector at a curve point, namely $\|X'(s)\|$. To approximate this signature at a sample point X_i we simply take the Euclidean norm of the difference vector $T_i = X_{i+1} - X_{i-1}$. Here again we compute k-signatures (in our experiment again k=5) using the multi-resolution approach analogous to the previously explained example. The thereby formed signature is obviously local, and translationally and rotationally invariant. Our experiments show this second signature to be more efficient than the curvature based signature, probably because of its greater computational robustness.

It is obvious that our signature sequences cannot describe a curve uniquely. However, as will be seen from the description of the matching algorithm in the next section, we only use these signatures in the first stage of the algorithm to filter out unsuitable candidates for matching. The reduced number of candidates that survive this filtering procedure are then matched by the robust 3-D matching algorithm due to Schwartz and Sharir, which takes into account all 3-D information about given sample points.

3   The Matching Algorithm

In this section we describe the matching algorithm applied in our experiments and the geometric hashing used. This technique was introduced for the 2-D case in [KSSS 87], and later improved in [HW]. The approach of [HW] is well tailored for partial curve matching and is used in our 3-D experiments. This method can be applied to the problem of matching one curve against another (*two-curve matching*), as well as to the problem of matching an observed curve against a large data-base of model curves. Although the purpose of our experiment was two-curve matching, we describe the algorithm in general terms to emphasize that it is suitable for use in the general object recognition problem (see discussion in the Introduction).

The algorithm consists of two major steps. The first one is a preprocessing step which is applied to the data base of model curves. The complexity of this step is linear in the total number of sample points of the curves in the data base. This step is executed off-line before actual matching is attempted. The second step, matching proper, uses the data prepared by the first step and can be executed in time which, on the average, is linearly dependent on the number of sample points on the observed curve, thus achieving matching in time almost independent on the size and number of curves in the data-base.

3.1   Preprocessing

All the curves in the data-base are processed as follows. The curve is sampled and shape signature values are computed at each sample point, using the signature generation process described in the previous section. Note again that this produces k-tuples of signatures representing local, rotationally and translationally invariant characteristics of the curve (so called, *'footprints'*). For each such k-signature we record the *curve number and the sample point number* at which this signature was generated. This data is held in a hash-table, whos entries are k-dimensional vectors. (Of course, vector coordinates must be properly quantized to make the number of entries finite.) Successive signatures along the curve have a natural order defined by the way the curve is traced. Preprocessing time is linearly dependent on the total of sample points on the data-base curves. New curves added to the data-base can be processed independently without recomputing the hash-table (except when we must re-hash).

3.2   Matching

In the matching stage an observed curve is sampled and k-signatures are computed at the sampling points. For each such signature we check the appropriate entry in the hash-table, and for every pair of (*model curve number, sample point number*), appearing there we add a vote for this model curve and the relative shift between the model curve and the observed curve. For example, if a signature, which was computed at the i'th sample point on the observed curve, appeared on model curves k_1 and k_2 at sample points j_1 and j_2 respectively, we add votes to model curve k_1 with relative shift $i - j_1$ and model curve k_2 with relative shift $i - j_2$. Obviously, long matching subcurves will cause a large number of signature coincidences between the appropriate curves. However, we look for *consistent coincidences*, which are singled out by identical relative shifts between signature sequences. (Because the signature coordinates are truncated we make the check described not only for the appropriate entry but also for its $3^k - 1$ immediate neighbours.)

At the end of this process we determine which *(model curve,shift)* pairs got the most votes, and for every such pair determine approximate starting and endpoints of match between the signature sequence of the observed curve and the signature sequence of the model curve under the appropriate shift. This is done by aligning the signature sequences for the candidate according to the appropriate shift and finding the longest consecutive matching subsequence (allowing minor mismatches). Given these subsequences we find the actual subcurves to which they correspond and then apply the robust Schwartz-Sharir matching algorithm (see [SS 87]), which is of complexity $O(nlogn)$ (n-number of sample points on the longer curve), but reduces to complexity $O(n)$ in our case. The Schwartz-Sharir algorithm produces the rotation and translation parameters needed to match one curve to the other and also a L_2 goodness of fit score between the curves along the matching subcurve. Given this rotation and translation, we can align both curves and re-determine their longest matching subcurve in true 3-D coordinates. Combining the evidence on the length of fit and score we decide which of the candidate pairs *(model curve, shift)* obtained from the geometric hashing process represents the correct match. As mentioned above, signature sequence hashing is only used to filter out inappropriate candidates, and the few remaining 'strong' candidates are distinguished using the 3-D subcurve matching algorithm due to Schwartz and Sharir.

3.3   Summary of Algorithm Steps

To summarize our algorithm :

A) We represent model curves by sequences of characteristic signatures which are local, translationally and rotationally invariant, and have satisfactory separation properties. We hash these signatures into a table which stores all pairs *(curve number, sample point number)* for every signature.

B) Given an observed curve we compute its signature sequence and find the pairs *(curve number, relative shift)* which obtained the most coincidence votes. For each such candidate pair we align the signature sequences according to the appropriate shift and find the longest consecutive matching subsequence (allowing minor mismatches). Candidates which have long enough consecutive matching subsequences are passed to the next step.

C) For each subsequence passed from *Step B*, we go back to the original curves and match the two subcurves which correspond to these subsequences using the Schwartz-Sharir subcurve matching algorithm, thus determining the desired translation and rotation of one curve with respect to the other, and the goodness of the proposed fit. We discard candidate matches with 'poor' fit.

D) For each candidate match from the previous step, we rotate and translate the curves as the match specifies, and redetermine the longest matching subcurves of the two curves, given this rotation and translation. This subcurve is found by simply checking the (x,y,z) coordinates of corresponding points on the curves and demanding that the distance between the points should be less than a certain threshold value ϵ. This final check works with points on the curves themselves, and not with the (less accurate) signature sequence values at these points; hence it is quite robust.

E) The result giving the longest matching subcurve (allowing minor mismatches) with a good L_2 fit is chosen as the final solution.

3.4   Complexity Analysis and the Weighted Signature Approach

The algorithm that we have described is on the average linear in the number of sample points on the observed curve, and the computational cost is relatively independent of the number of points on the model curves in the data-base. (As noted previously in matching of two curves we have only one model curve, hence the hash table records only the indices of the sample points where a given signature appears.)

This method can be improved by introducing *weighted* signatures. Specifically, since for typical curves not all the signatures will have an equal probability of occurrence, it seems undesirable to give an equal weight to every 'hit', but to

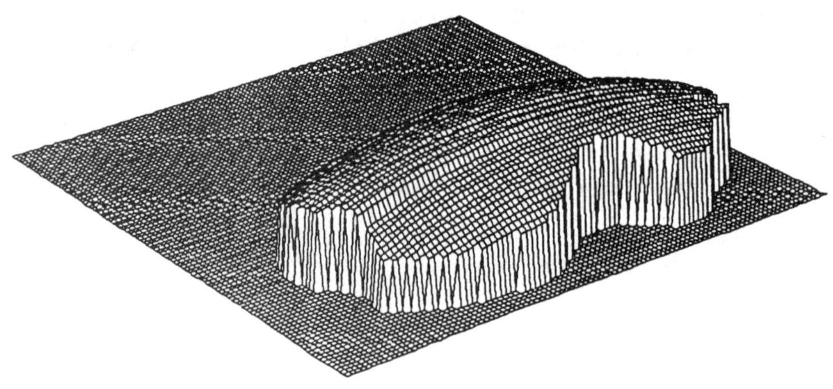

Figure 2: range image of a piece

weight coincidence of 'rare' signatures. The actual probability of occurrence of each individual signature can be estimated by the number of its occurrences in the data-base, which naturally can serve as a statistical sample for this data. Such a weighted signature approach can also improve the efficiency of our algorithm by making it linear instead of linear on the average. This can be done by assigning zero weight to very frequent (more than a certain predefined constant threshold K) signatures thereby eliminating the need to process hash-table entries representing many candidates; such entries require much computer time but contribute only a small amount of information to the matching process.

A major potential advantage of the algorithm presented is its high inherent parallelism. Since all the signatures can be processed independently, parallel implementation of both the *Preprocessing* and *Matching* parts of the algorithm is straightforward; moreover, it' should be quite easy to build a special device for this implementing it at very high speed.

4   Experimental Results

A series of experiments was carried out to test and evaluate the performance of the matching algorithm with real 3-D data. Pieces of a plastic ball were chosen as experimental objects. Piecewise linear approximations to the boundary curves of these pieces were extracted from the range data obtained with a *Technical Arts Corporation* laser rangefinder. The 3-D curves of the different pieces were matched against each other in order to find how these pieces should be assembled together (see a typical example in Fig 1).

4.1   Data Acquisition

To match 3-D objects by our method 3-D coordinates of points lying on curves along the object are needed; hence we acquire range information. Range data can be gathered in many ways (see [BJ 85] for a survey of range gathering techniques). In our application we used a plane of light, laser based range sensor [WS 83]. (See Figure 2 for a perspective view of the range image of one of the pieces.) The range data obtained is fairly accurate, so no initial smoothing or averaging of raw range

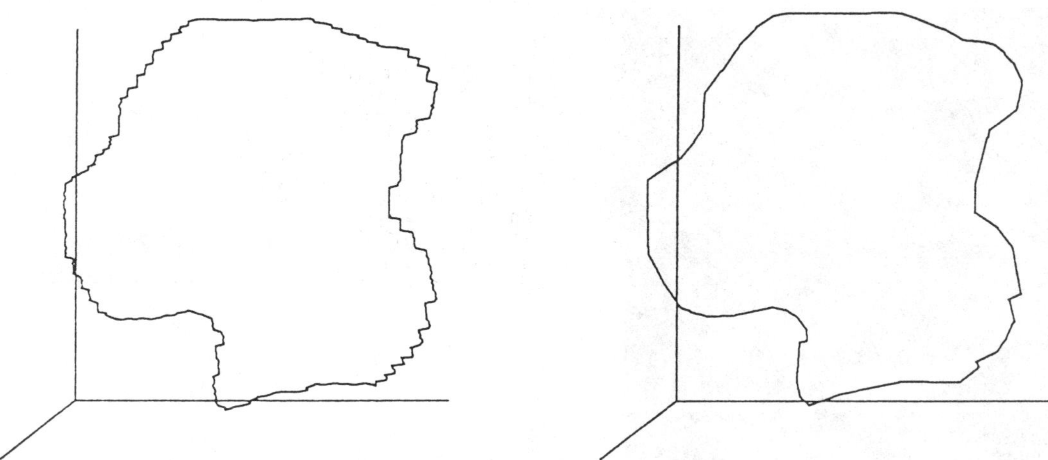

Figure 3: a) the original curve. b) the curve smoothed with epsilon 0.1

data before edge extraction is necessary. Boundary edges of the plastic pieces used are well defined by large discontinuities in the range data, allowing a simple gradient based edge detection operator to extract the boundary edges of the pieces. The next step is to walk around each boundary in the range image and connect all edge fragments into one curve, while registering the 3-D coordinates of the points lying along the curve.

4.2   Processing of 3-D curves

Figure 3 shows the 3-D curve extracted from the piece of Figure 2. Although no smoothing or averaging were applied to the data, the Z-coordinate of this 3-D curve is quite smooth. Nevertheless the XY projection of this curve is not perfectly smooth because of discretization errors. A pixel in the camera has a finite extent, and so a pixel on the edge of an object would receive light not only from the portion of the pixel that is on the object, but also from the portion of the pixel that covers the background. As a result, some pixels on the boundary of an object will be considered as part of the object, while other pixels will be considered as background, and so the the boundary of an object (even a smooth object) will be noisy. Our algorithm uses the arc length of a curve in an important way; this forces us to smooth before going on. However, since only the XY projection of the 3-D curve is noisy, we only want to smooth this 2-D projection of the curve. Hence we use the Z coordinates of the original 3-D curve and the smoothed 2-D curve to reconstruct a smoothed version of the 3-D curve. Two issues arise in the smoothing process: the length of the resulting smoothed curve should be insensitive to random noise in the original curve (because of the parametrization by arc length), and should preserve local curvatures as much as possible (so as not to distort the local signature that we use in the algorithm).

2-D smoothing of a curve is achieved by surrounding the original curve by a 'belt' whose width is an estimated noise parameter ϵ. and then finding the shortest polygonal path in the resulting 'belt'. (A detailed description of this technique is found in [SS 87].) Figure 3 shows the raw 3-D curve of a piece, and its smoothed version.

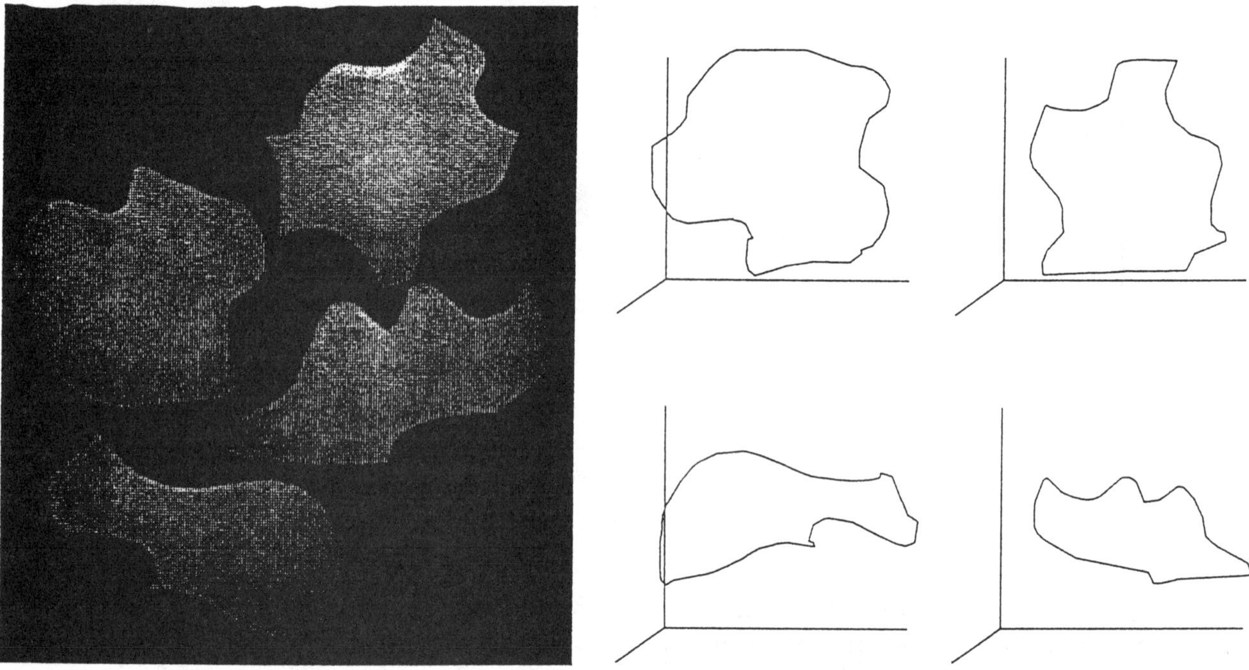

Figure 4: a) four pieces of the plastic ball. b) the boundary curves of the
pieces.

4.3   Matching results

Fig 4 shows four different pieces of the plastic ball, and Fig 5 shows the results of
matching individual pieces of the ball and finding the best subcurve match. Notice
that the subcurves blend smoothly in the match, so that the boundaries of the
subcurves to be matched cannot be distinguished by any sharply defined features.

The number of points used to represent the smoothed curves is about 100, and
since the matching algorithm is linear on the average, running time for a typical
match was less than 1 second on a MicroVax.

5   Future Research

The matching algorithm presented in this article can serve as a key ingredient in a
number of important robotic vision tasks. Applications and extensions with which
we intend to deal are as follows:

1) Extension of the partial curve matching technique to a global technique for re-
assembling broken objects.

2) Definition and extraction of significant *'characteristic'* curves on a 3-D object.

3) Systematic study of 3-D object models based on *'characteristic'* curves.

4) Construction of curve based models of 3-D object using views acquired from
a small number of viewpoints. The matching algorithm can be applied here to

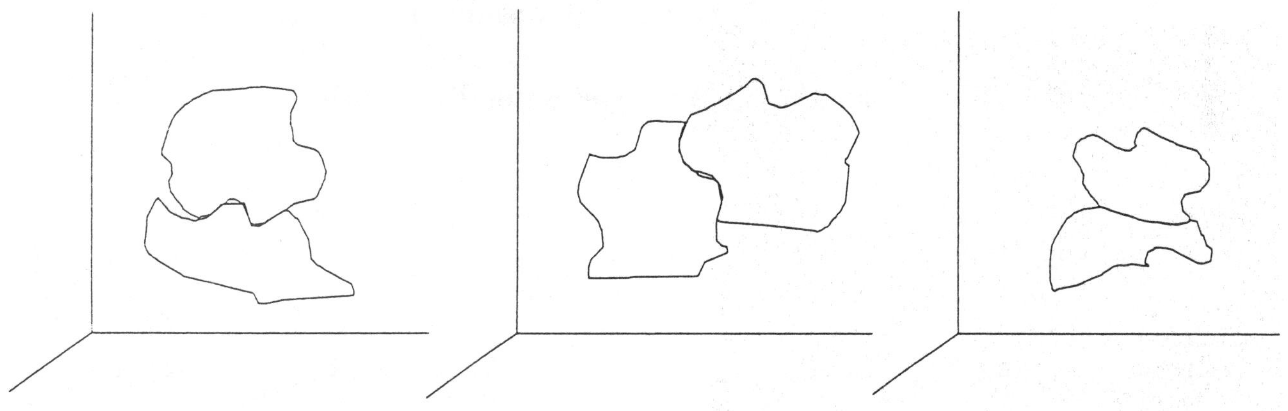

Figure 5: matching results.

assemble such models.

Bibliography

[*B*81] C.M.Brown, Some Mathematical and Representational Aspects of Solid Modeling, *IEEE Trans. on PAMI-3,4*, July, 1981.

[*BB*82] D.H.Ballard and C.M.Brown, *Computer Vision*, Prentice Hall, 1982.

[*BJ*85] P.J.Besl and R.C.Jain, "Three-Dimensional Object Recognition", *ACM Computing Surveys*, March, 1985.

[*BS*86] C.M. Bastuscheck, and J.T. Schwartz, "Experimental Implementations of a Ratio Image Depth Sensor", *Techniques for 3-D Machine Perception*, A. Rosenfeld, Ed. North Holland, 1986.

[*BSSS*86] C.M. Bastuscheck, E. Schonberg, J.T. Schwartz, and M. Sharir, "Object Recognition by 3-Dimensional Curve Matching", *Int. J. of Intelligent systems, Vol.1, No.2*, 1986.

[*CD*86] R.T.Chin and C.R.Dyer, "Model-Based Recognition in Robot Vision", *ACM Computing Surveys, Vol.18, No.1*, March, 1986.

[*D*76] M.P. Do Carmo, *Differential Geometry of Curves and Surfaces*, Prentice Hall, 1976.

[*HW*] J.W. Hong, and H.Wolfson, "On Footprints", *in preparation*.

[*K*86] E.Kishon, "Simultaneous Matching of Curves in Three Dimensions", *Robotics Report No. 91, Computer Science Div., Courant Inst. of Math., NYU*, Nov. 1986.

[*KSSS*87] A. Kalvin, E. Schonberg, J.T. Schwartz, and M.Sharir, "Two Dimensional, Model Based, Boundary Matching Using Footprints", *Int. J. of Robotics Research, Vol.5, No.4*, 1987.

[*S*69] J.J. Stoker, *Differential Geometry* , Wiley-Interscience, 1969.

[*SS*87] J.T. Schwartz, and M. Sharir, "Identification ot Partially Obscured Objects in Two or Three Dimensions by Matching of Noisy Characteristic Curves", *Int. J. of Robotics Research, Vol.6, No.2*, 1987.

[*W*86] H. Wolfson, "On Curve Matching", *Robotics Report No. 86, Computer Science Div., Courant Inst. of Math., NYU*, 1986.

[*WSKL*87] H.Wolfson, E.Schonberg, A.Kalvin, Y.Lamdan, "Solving Jigsaw Puzzles by Computer", *to appear in the volume " Approaches to Intelligent Decision Support" in the series " Annals of Operations Research"*, 1987.

[*WS*83] "White Scanner 100A User's Manual", *Technical Arts Corp., Seattle* , 1983.

Spatial Reasoning, Sensor Repositioning and

Disambiguation in 3D Model Based Recognition

Michael Magee   *†
Artificial Intelligence Laboratory
Computer Science Department
P.O. Box 3682
University of Wyoming
Laramie, Wyoming   82071

Mitchell Nathan   *
Department of Psychology
Campus Box 345
University of Colorado
Boulder, Colorado   80309

Abstract

A method for recognizing three-dimensional objects for which there are ambiguous interpretations is presented. The fundamental approach embodies model based knowledge as well as observed data to reason about where useful (disambiguating) features may be located. For cases in which a large number of feature correspondences can be established, the spatial reasoning system computes an optimal new viewpoint from which to observe the object such that a disambiguating feature can be seen. For cases involving fewer feature correspondences, new viewpoints are sought by finding the maximal intersection of all unseen quadratic three-dimensional half-spaces. The system is shown to operate well for synthetic range scenes involving both curved and planar surfaces. Work is proceeding to apply the method to actual laser range images.

This research was supported by the
* Advanced Automation Technology Section of Martin Marietta Denver Aerospace and
† National Science Foundation Grant DCR-8602555.

Introduction

Within the problem domain of computer vision, considerable research has been devoted to image understanding and recognition. One of the earliest topologically based methods was that of [Waltz, 1975]. This classic work built upon the polyhedral junction labelling scheme of Huffman and Clowes and was able to interpret the three-dimensional topology of projected two-dimensional line segments using either a tree search or junction filtering algorithm. The edge labelling scheme did not facilitate processing scenes with curved surfaces or with thin (paper-like) structures, however. Subsequent research by [Kanade, 1982] demonstrates how the labelling scheme can be extended to handle folded paper objects. Additional extensions were made by [Sugihara and Shirai, 1977] who employ junction dictionaries that include curved as well as linear features. The capabilities of these studies are constrained by the very nature of the representation, however, since only edge topologies are deemed to be significant.

ACRONYM [Brooks, 1981] is a more flexible system that attempts to describe an image as a picture graph. Once the picture graph has been computed, it interprets the image by trying to find subgraph isomorphisms between the picture graph description and graphs of known or anticipated objects. This method contrasts with a more syntactically directed approach in which picture grammars define proper structural relationships [Fu, 1982] [Rosenfeld, 1979].

A common theme of most image understanding systems is that ambiguities can arise in the recognition process due to inadequate or incomplete observed data. It is not unusual for a feature which could be used to disambiguate two or more candidate models to be unobserved because it is occluded by other portions of the observed object. Figure 1 provides a simple illustration of such a case. The observed data provides only two quadrilaterals connected by a common linear edge. Such data could arise as the result of viewing either a wedge, a rectangular solid or a stair-step shaped object. Structurally, there is no way in which an image understanding system (or a human for that matter) can categorically identify which of the three alternatives is correct. Therefore, additional structural information is required. The fundamental approach that should be taken is to seek a disambiguating feature in an intelligent manner by repositioning the data gathering sensor so that a new view can be processed. Such repositioning should then reveal (1) a triangle in the case of the wedge, (2) a rectangle in the case of the rectangular solid or (3) an L-shaped polygon in the case of the stair step.

In the discussions that follow, it is shown that disambiguating features may be based either on edges or surfaces. Surfaces prove to be exceptionally useful since their extraction is generally based on large numbers of range values. Examples for objects involving both curved quadratic as well as planar surfaces are provided.

System Assumptions

The image understanding and spatial reasoning system (IUSRS) that has been developed assumes that basic three-dimensional features and spatial relationships between these features have been extracted from laser range data in a manner

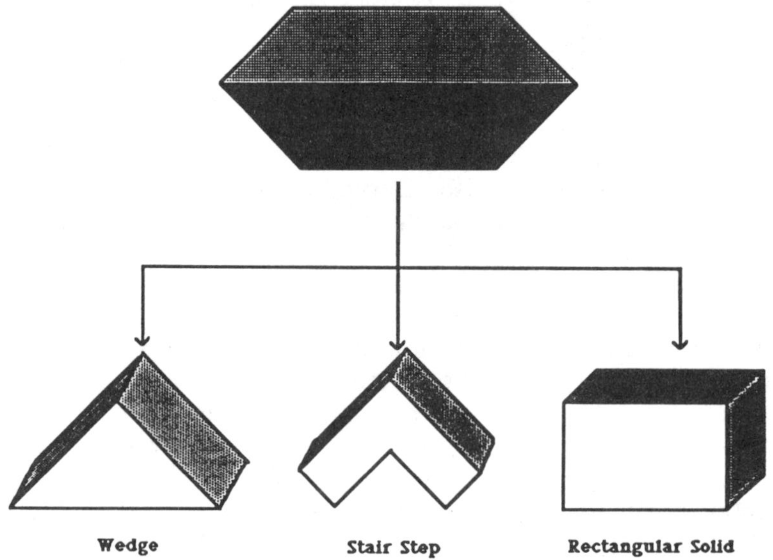

Figure 1

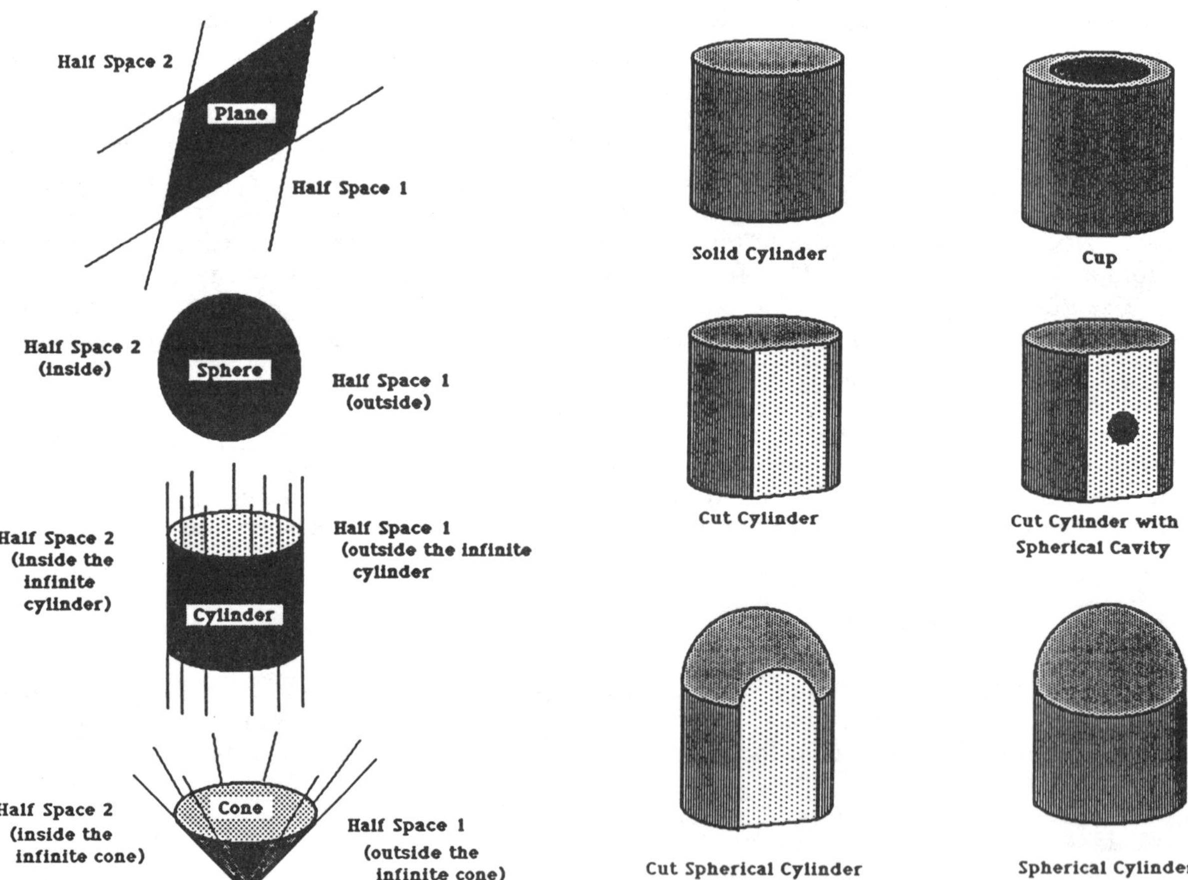

Half Spaces for Typical Quadratic Surfaces

Figure 2

Test Objects Involving Various Quadratic Surfaces

Figure 3

analogous to that described by [Lin and Wee, 1985]. The most important features and relationships include:

a. surface geometries - planar, cylindrical, spherical, etc.
b. surface types - concave, convex, etc.
c. edge geometries - line, circle, ellipse, etc.
d. edge types - concave, convex, inflection, occluding, etc.
e. surface meetings (common edges)
f. three-dimensional (quadratic) surface equations
g. the three-dimensional coordinates of important features - e.g. edge junctions, centers of circles, etc.

Of these factors, the first five types of qualitative information (a-e) have proven to be the most useful in the image understanding (recognition) process. The quantified three-dimensional data (f and g) are of greatest utility when there is not sufficient information to make an unambiguous statement regarding the identity of a viewed object. They become particularly useful when invisible features can be hypothesized on the other side of occluding edges. IUSRS can reason about where these features should appear using both hypothesized feature locations and half-space intersections.

Predicate Logic Based Recognition

The IUSRS represents both known models and observed data as sets of logical assertions. Foremost among these are:

a. (surface_geometry s1 geometry)
   means surface s1 has a certain surface geometry. Geometry can be planar, cylindrical, spherical, conic, etc.

b. (surface_type   s1 type)
   means surface s1 has a curvature type. Type generally indicates whether the surface, when observed, is concave or convex. For example, both the inside and outside curved surfaces of a cup are cylindrical (indicated by the surface_geometry predicate). The types of these surfaces, however, are different. The inside surface type is concave whereas the outside surface type is convex.

c. (surfaces_meet   s1 s2)
   indicates that two surfaces, s1 and s2, have a common set of edge pixels.

d. (edge_geometry   s1 s2 edge_name edge_geometry)
   states that the edge between surfaces s1 and s2 (with name edge_name) has a particular edge geometry (e.g. line, circle, ellipse, etc.)

e. (edge_type   s1 s2 edge_name edge_type)
   specifies that the edge is a certain type (e.g. convex, concave, occluding, inflection). The type is based on the way that the two bounding surfaces join.

f. (edge_points   p1 p2 edge_name)
    represents the fact that the edge extends from point p1 to point p2.

g. (quadratic_equation s1 (A B C D E F G H I J))
    specifies that the quadratic equation for surface s1 is
    $$AX^2 + BY^2 + CZ^2 + DXY + EXZ + FYZ + GX + HY + IZ + J = 0$$

h. (3D_feature_coordinate feature_type feature_name (x y z))
    means that the feature whose name is feature_name and whose type is
    feature_type is located at (x y z) in three-dimensions. Typical feature types are
    points where three or more surfaces meet or characteristic points of curved
    edges or surfaces (e.g. the centers of circles or spheres).

Each model for which the system has knowledge is represented as a complete set
of assertions analogous to the foregoing descriptors. This **viewpoint
independent** representation for models is the basis for matching partial
descriptors of **viewpoint dependent** assertions derived from observed data. In
order to perform this match, however, the viewpoint dependent assertions must be
transformed so that they are viewpoint independent in nature.

The viewpoint dependent to viewpoint independent transformation seeks to
satisfy two primary objectives. The first of these is to get rid of any "artifactual
edges" that arise due to viewer perspective. The best example of such an artifactual
edge are the two occluding edges that one would see at the sides of a right cylinder.
Because a cylinder has no lines in its model descriptor, these artifacts must be
discarded when transforming viewpoint dependent data. Since IUSRS has high
level knowledge that each of these edges is (a) occluding, (b) in a cylindrical
surface and (c) in no other visible surface, it can conclude that such an edge is an
artifact. The second heuristic that is used in the transformation is to note that any
remaining occluding edge is actually convex, since only convex edges can produce
occluding edges when viewed.

Once the viewpoint dependent to viewpoint independent transformation is
complete, a clause representing all of the transformed knowledge is generated.
This clause is simply the 'and' of all the transformed assertions, in which free
variables have been substituted for features for which uniqueness is enforced.
This means that the object will be recognized if and only if one of the model
descriptors can be used as the basis to instantiate all of the topological, geometric
and spatial relationships in a consistent manner. Alternatively stated, there must
be a unidirectional subgraph isomorphism between the observed data and the
selected model.

It is this ability to determine this subgraph isomorphism that gives the system
its considerable power. Embedded in the instantiation lists are

1. correspondences between visible features and model features,
2. correspondences between occluded features (e.g. surfaces) and model features,
3. knowledge that can be used to infer features that may have been missed by the
    feature extraction routines,
4. knowledge that can be used to disambiguate candidate models if the viewed data
    is consistent with more than one model.

A more complete discussion of these issues is given in [Magee and Nathan, 1987].

Disambiguation of Model Candidates Using Multiple Views

Occasionally, a case will arise such that a useful disambiguating feature is not visible, perhaps due to occlusion. When this occurs, the system must reason (1) which feature would be distinguish between the candidate models and (2) where (in three-dimensions) the anticipated feature should exist and how the sensor should be repositioned in order to see it. To find the disambiguating feature, IUSRS performs **model differencing**. That is to say, the features in the assertions for each candidate model are variabilized and tested to see if they can be instantiated in the other candidate models. If a feature cannot be instantiated in the other candidate models, it is called a "disambiguating feature" because of its uniqueness among features for the remaining candidates. If the disambiguating feature is not visible in the observed data, it is sought by requesting a sensor repositioning. This repositioning is driven by an expectation that the feature is at a position relative to visible (instantiated) features in the observed data.

Once the sensor is repositioned, the recognition process is initiated again, but with a refined set of candidates (namely those in the list of ambiguous models). If the disambiguating feature is found in the new view, the recognition process terminates, otherwise it continues by seeking a new view.

Model Based Sensor Repositioning

Repositioning of the sensor based on correspondences established between observed data and models is founded on being able to transform observed feature points to their corresponding locations in a current model under consideration. The foundation for this method is that if at least four (4) three-dimensional correspondences can be established, a 4 X 4 matrix T can be computed that represents the spatial transformation between the model and the observed data. This transformation represents the product of three rotational transformations (in X, Y and Z) and a translation.

Formally stated, if
$m = [x_m \ y_m \ z_m \ 1]$ is a homogeneously represented point in the model and
$v = [x_v \ y_v \ z_v \ 1]$ is a homogeneously represented point in the viewed data
corresponding to model point m then

T is the 4 X 4 transformation matrix that minimizes (in the least squares sense) the error between all correspondence pairs of points in the viewed data and the transformed model.

A detailed description of the method may be found in [Magee and Aggarwal, 1986].

Once the transformation matrix has been computed and the location of the disambiguating feature (in the model) has been hypothesized, its transformed position is computed by applying T to the coordinate of the disambiguating feature. The sensor is then repositioned along the line of sight defined by the transformed centroid of the object and the point representing the disambiguating feature.

Data   Driven   Sensor   Repositioning

In some cases there may not be four feature points that can be used to define the previously described transformation.   For example, a right solid cylinder has only two feature points (the centers of the circles at the top and bottom).   Thus, model based repositioning is not useful in these cases since the 4 X 4 transformation matrix cannot be computed.

It is possible, however, to hypothesize a new useful viewpoint based on geometric half-spaces.   This method relies on the fact that there are equations describing surfaces in the knowledge base.   Using these equations, it is possible to determine "which side" of each surface the sensor is currently on (see Figure 2). By combining knowledge about these half-spaces, the system can suggest a three-dimensional region (the intersection of unseen half-spaces) that should be examined next.   The actual position is currently determined by a spiraling algorithm on a Gaussian sphere.   When a coordinate is found that maximizes the number unseen half-spaces, it is chosen as the new location for the sensor.

The algorithm for half-space reasoning is straightforward but general for any quadratic surface.   If the evaluation of the quadratic formula

$$AX^2 + BY^2 + CZ^2 + DXY + EXZ + FYZ + GX + HY + IZ + J$$

at the two points (x_1, y_1, z_1) and (x_2, y_2, z_2) are of different signs, then those points are on opposite sides of the surface described by that formula.   The half-space reasoning system evaluates each of the quadratic formulae for the observed surfaces, given the current viewpoint.   Then potential viewpoints are generated by spiraling around the surface of a virtual sphere that surrounds the object.   At each generated coordinate, the sign of the quadratic formula is determined and the number of half-space deviations is computed.   If this number is equal to the maximum number of possible half-space deviations (= the number of visible surfaces) the procedure terminates.   Otherwise, the a position is found for which the number of deviations is maximized relative to other positions.

Results

For the examples that follow, six curved objects and various polyhedra were considered.   Typical views of the curved objects are shown in Figure 3.   This data set is designed primarily to show the flexibility of the representation as well as to illustrate the operation of assertion transformation, candidate disambiguation and sensor repositioning.   There are no particular biasses in the data or models toward any particular types of objects except that their surfaces should be characterizable within the quadratic domain.

For the first case considered, Figure 4a shows an initial view of a "cut cylinder with spherical cavity" which may be ambiguously interpreted as that model or simply as a cut cylinder.   Figures 4b and 4c illustrate subsets of viewpoint dependent and viewpoint independent assetions that are derived from this viewpoint.   Clearly there is at least one visible feature that is inconsistent with each of the model candidates solid cylinder, cup, cut_sphere_cylinder and spherical cylinder.   However, the visible features are all consistent with known features for a cut cylinder and a cut cylinder with spherical cavity.

The spatial reasoning system must therefore determine which feature(s) could disambiguate these models if it could be seen.   Its conclusion, based on differencing the features for these two models is that it should seek the spherical cavity.   It does this by establishing a correspondence between four points in the observed data

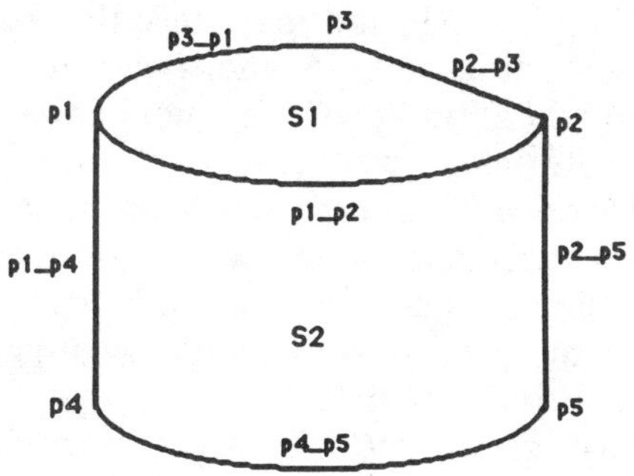

First Viewpoint of the Cut_Cylinder_with_Spherical Cavity

Figure 4a

```
(vi_surface_type $s2 convex)
(vi_surface_geometry $s2 circular)
(vi_edge_geometry $S2 $p1_p2 circle)
(vi_edge_type $S2 $p1_p2 convex)
(vi_surfaces_meet $S1 $S2)
```

Examples of Viewpoint Independent Features

Note the removal of predicates involving artifactual edge
p1_p4 and the replacement of features with free ($) variables.

Figure 4c

Examples of Viewpoint Dependent Features for Figure 4a

```
(surface_type S2 convex)
(surface_geometry S2 circular)
(edge_geometry S1 S2 p1_p2 circle)
(edge_type S1 S2 p1_p2 convex)
(edge_geometry S2 background p1_p4 line)
(edge_type s2 background p1_p4 occluding)
(quadratic_equation s2 (1 1 0 0 0 0 0 0 0 -1))
(surfaces_meet s1 s2)
(angle_between s1 s2 0)
```

Figure 4b

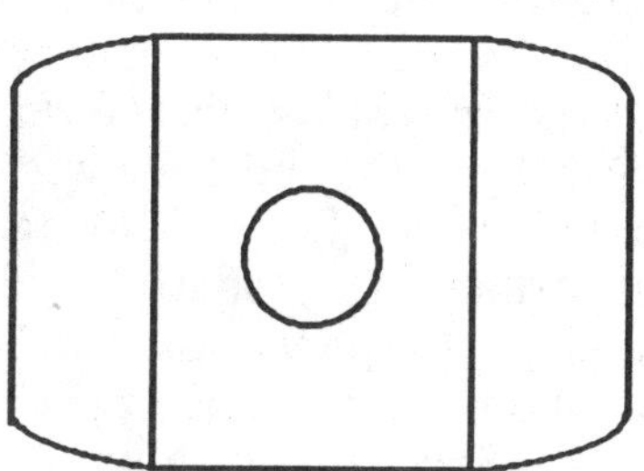

Second View of the Cut_Cylinder_with_Spherical_Cavity

Figure 4d

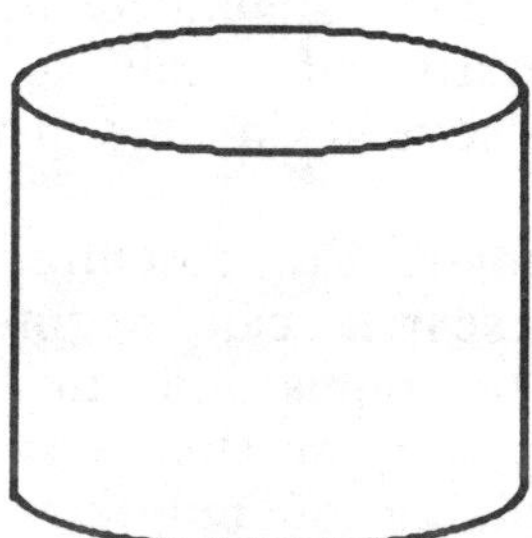

First View of an Inverted Cup (above and to the side)

Figure 5a

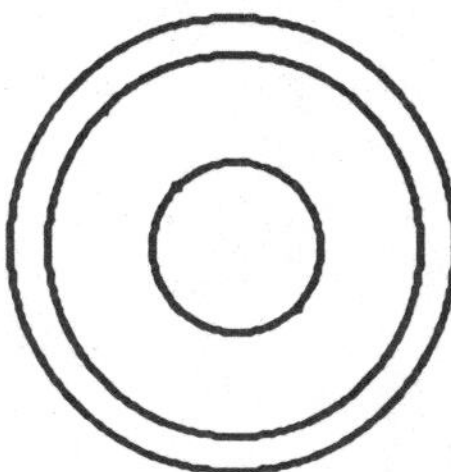

Second View of an Inverted Cup (from below)

Figure 5b

(which are p2, p3, the center of the circle whose arc joins p1 and p2, and the center of the circular arc between p4 and p5) and analogous point sets in the two models. This correspondence is actually a byproduct of the theorem proving mechanism in which free variables in the object descriptor are instantiated with model features. A new viewpoint is then proposed to reposition the sensor and a new view is taken. In this particular case, the proposed viewpoint lies along a line which joins the geometric center of the object and the center of the sought feature (the spherical cavity). Figure 4d illustrates the new view. Based on this new view, the object is unequivocally recognized as a cut cylinder with spherical cavity.

Now, in the preceding case, there is a relatively good set of three-dimensional information upon which to base repositioning of the sensor. This is because there are at least four non-coplanar points of correspondence that exist between the observed data features and the models. Other cases are not as straightforward, however. Consider the inverted cup of Figure 5a, for example. This case is similar to the previous one except that the initial view is so devoid of information rich features that its descriptor matches several candidate models. The disambiguating feature that is sought is that of a cylindrical concave surface (the inside of a cup) which is found in the next view. An important difference is that the new viewpoint in this case is hypothesized using half-space logic since there are not four feature coordinates that the spatial reasoning system can use for optimal sensor repositioning. That is to say, a location in three dimensions is sought that maximizes the number of previously unencountered half-spaces relative to the initial view. Specifically, this produces a location below the upper planar surface and inside the visible (outer convex) cylindrical surface.

Future Directions and Goals

The most immediate goal of continuing this research is to apply the methods to actual laser range data. To date, only simulated data have been used. The laser range data base from the University of Utah has been obtained and work is proceeding to apply the methods described in this paper to several of the objects in that data base.

With respect to longer term goals, the essential mathematical and logical tools have been developed such that research can begin on the problem of automated model generation. The ability to reposition the sensor based on data driven expectations has been described in the section on half-spaces. The problem that must now be attacked is the combining of multiple views once repositioning of the sensor has been achieved.

References

[Brooks, 1982]
R. Brooks, "Acronym", in *The Handbook of Artificial Intelligence (Volume III)* , P.R. Cohen and E.A. Feigenbaum (editors), Wm. Kaufmann, 1982, pp. 313-321].

[Fu, 1982]
K.S. Fu, *Syntactic Pattern Recognition and Applications*, Prentice-Hall, 1982.

[Jackins and Tanimoto, 1980]
C.L. Jackins and S.L. Tanimoto, "Oct-Trees and their use in representing Three-Dimensional Objects", *Computer Graphics and Image Processing*, Volume 14, Number 3, November, 1980, pp. 249-270.

[Kanade, 1982]
T. Kanade, "The Origami World and Shape Recovery", in *The Handbook of Artificial Intelligence (Volume III)* , P.R. Cohen and E.A. Feigenbaum (editors), Wm. Kaufmann, 1982, pp. 183-194.

[Lin and Wee, 1985]
"Shape Detection Using Range Data", *Proceedings of the International Conference on Robotics and Automation*, St. Louis, Missouri, March, 1985, pp. 34-39.

[Magee and Aggarwal, 1986]
M.Magee and J.K. Aggarwal, "Determining Motion Parameters Using Intensity Guided Range Sensing", *International Journal of Pattern Recognition,* Volume 19, Number 2, March, 1986, pp. 169-180].

[Magee and Nathan, 1987]
"A Viewpoint Independent Modelling Approach to Object Recognition", *Jounal of Robotics and Automation*, to appear.

[Rosenfeld, 1979]
A. Rosenfeld, *Picture Languages: Formal Models for Picture Recognition* , Academic Press, 1979.

[Sugihara and Shirai, 1977]
K. Sugihara and Y. Shirai, "Range Data Understanding Guided by a Junction Dictionary", *Proceedings of the Fifth International Joint Conference on Artificial Intelligence*, 1977, p. 706.

[Waltz, 1975]
D. Waltz, "Understanding Line Drawings of Scnes with Shadows", in *The Psychology of Computer Vision*, P.H. Winston (editor), McGraw-Hill 1975.

AN APPROACH TO THE FUSION OF
MULTIPLE SHAPE FROM TEXTURE ALGORITHMS

Mark L. Moerdler and John R. Kender[1]

Department of Computer Science
Columbia University
New York, N.Y. 10027

ABSTRACT

This paper describes an approach that intelligently integrates several conflicting and/or corroborating shape-from-texture methods in a single system that derives the orientation of surfaces and aids in their separation and segmentation. The system uses a new data structure, the *augmented texels*, each of which combines multiple constraints on orientation in a compact notation for a single surface patch. The augmented texels initially store weighted orientation constraints that are generated by the system's several independent shape-from-texture components. These texture components, which run autonomously and may run in parallel, derive constraints by any currently existing shape-from-texture approaches, e.g., shape-from-uniform-texel-spacing. For each surface patch the related *augmented texel* then combines the potentially inconsistent orientation data, using a hough transform-like method on a tesselated gaussian sphere, resulting in an estimate of the most likely orientation for the patch. When more than one orientation is derived as "most likely", the system re-analyzes the results to remove the conflicts. Finally, the system defines which patches are part of the same surface, simplifing surface reconstruction.

This knowledge fusion approach is illustrated by a system that integrates information from two shape-from-texture methods: shape-from-uniform-texel-spacing and shape-from-uniform-texel-size. The system is demonstrated on camera images of artificial and natural textures including images containing more than one surface.

---

[1]This research was supported in part by ARPA grant #N00039-84-C-0165, by a NSF Presidential Young Investigator Award, and by Faculty Development Awards from AT&T, Ford Motor Co., and Digital Equipment Corporation.

INTRODUCTION

This paper proposes a new approach to the problem of deriving the orientation and segmentation of surfaces based on **multiple** independent textual cues. The generality of this approach is due to the interaction between textural cues, thus allowing it to extract shape information from a wider range of textured surfaces than any individual method. The method, as diagrammed in figure 1, consists of three major phases: the calculation of orientation constraints and the generation of *texel patches*[2], the consolidation of constraints into a "most likely" orientation per patch, and finally the reconstruction of the surface.

During the first phase, the different shape-from-texture components generate texel patches and *augmented texels*. Each augmented texel consists of the 2-D description of a texel patch and a list of weighted constraints on its orientation. The orientation constraints for each patch are potentially inconsistent or potentially incorrect because the shape-from methods are applied to noisy images, locally based, and derive constraints without a priori knowledge of the type of texture or number of surfaces.

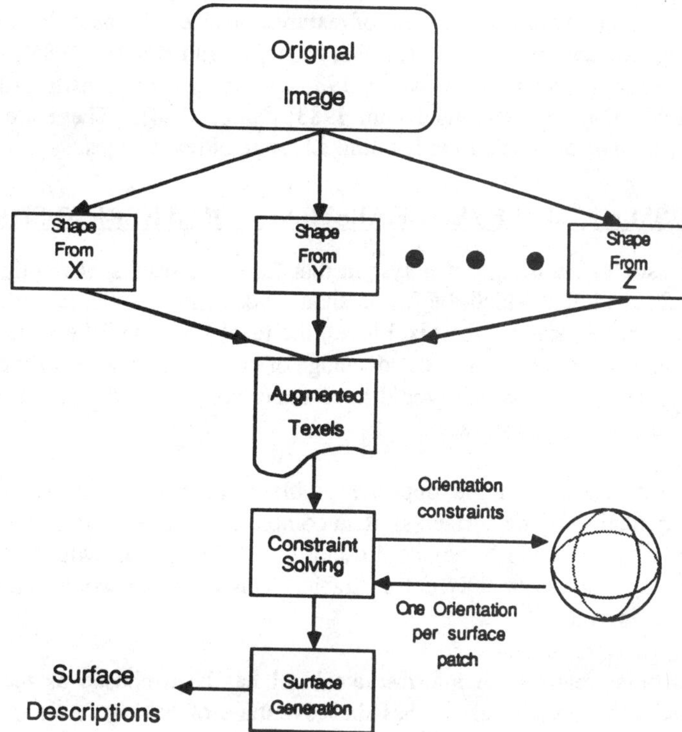

Figure 1:   Integrating multiple shape-from methods

In the second phase, all the orientation constraints for each augmented texel are consolidated into a single "most likely" orientation by a Hough-like transformation on a tesselated gaussian sphere. During this phase the system will also merge together all augmented texels that cover the same area of the image. This is necessary because some of the shape-from components define "texel" similarly, thus the constraints generated should be merged and a single orientation generated for the surface patch. In those instances in which multiple "most likely" orientation are found, the system re-analyzes the texel's constraints and checks their validity as measured in relationship to other texels. This allows it to prune out some of the constraints and possibly remove one or more of the "most likely" orientations resulting in a single orientation. This is a type of symbolic segmentation where segmenting is applied to the "intrinsic image" of surface orientation.

---

[2]A *texel patch* is a 2-D description of a subimage that contains one or more textural elements. The number of elements that compose a patch is dependent on the shape-from-texture algorithm.

Finally, the system re-analyzes the orientation constraints to determine which augmented texels are part of the same constraint family and groups them together. In effect, this segments the image into regions of similar orientation. The surface can then be reconstructed from these surface patches.

The robustness of this approach is illustrated by a system that fuses the orientation constraints of two existing shape-from methods: shape-from-uniform-texel-spacing (Moerdler and Kender, 1985), and shape-from-uniform-texel-size (Ohta et. al., 1981). These two methods generate orientation constraints for different overlapping classes of textures.

HISTORICAL BACKGROUND

Current methods to derive shape-from-texture are based on measuring a distortion that occurs when a textured surface is viewed under perspective.[3] This perspective distortion is imaged as a change in some aspect of the texture. In order to simplify the recovery of the orientation parameters from this distortion, researchers have imposed limitations on the applicable class of textured surfaces. Some of the limiting assumptions include uniform texel spacing (Kender, 1980; Kender, 1983; Moerdler and Kender, 1985), uniform texel size (Ikeuchi, 1980; Ohta et. al., 1981; Aloimonos and Swain, 1985), uniform texel density (Aloimonos, 1986), and texel isotropy (Witkin, 1980; Davis, Janos and Dunn, 1983; Dunn, 1984). These are strong limitations causing methods based on them to be appliable to only a limited range of real images.

CHOOSING THE LEVEL OF ABSTRACTION WHERE FUSION OCCURS

An important issue in the design of a system that fuses the results of multiple knowledge sources is to decide the level of abstraction at which the fusion should occur. In the integration of many shape-from-texture methods that are three major levels : the pixel level, the texel level, and the surface level. Fusing orientation constraints at the pixel level has the major disadvantage of creating a data explosion since most images have in excess of 100,000 pixels each of which would have many constraints that need to be fused and then would require the fusion of the pixels into surfaces.

The surface level has almost the opposite problem. In order to consider orientation constraints as constraints on the orientation of the surface(s), data compression occurs and some data is lost. It also requires assumptions about the surfaces which may be difficult to justify, e.g., knowledge of the number of surfaces in the image. This information is normally not available. This approach would have great difficulty separating overlapping transparent surfaces.

For these and other reasons, an intermediate level has been chosen as the level at which orientation constraints are fused - the texel level. It has the advantage of having fewer elements than the pixel level (hundreds as compared to hundreds of thousands) without requiring additional a priori information about the surfaces.

DESIGN METHODOLOGY

The generation of orientation constraints from perspective distortion is performed using one or more image texels. The orientation constraints can be considered as local, defining the orientation of individual surface patches (called *texel patches*[4]) each of which covers a texel or group of texels. This definition allows a simple extension to the existing shape-from methods beyond their current limitation of planer surfaces or simple non planer surfaces based on a single textural cue. The problem can then be considered as one of intelligently

---

[3]Under the assumption that natural texture does not mimic projective effects nor does it cancel those effects out.

[4]Texel patches are defined by how each method utilizes the texels. Some methods (e.g. uniform texel size) use a measured change between two texels; in this case the texels patches are the texels themselves. Other methods (e.g. uniform texel density) use a change between two areas of the image , in this case the texel patches are these predefined areas.

fusing the orientation constraints per patch.[5]

The process of fusing orientation constraints and generating surfaces can be broken down into the following three phases:

1. The creation of texel patches and multiple orientation constraints for each patch.

2. The unification of the orientation constraints per patch into a "most likely" orientation.

3. The formation of surfaces from the texel patches.

Each of the remaining subsections of this chapter describes one of these phases.

SURFACE PATCH AND ORIENTATION CONSTRAINT GENERATION

The first phase of the system consisting of several shape-from-texture components which generate augmented texels. Each augmented texel consisting of a texel patch, orientation constraints for the texel patch, and an assurity weighting per constraint. The orientation constraints are stored in the augmented texel as vanishing points which are mathematically equivalent to a class of other orientation notations (e.g. pan and tilt constraints) (Shafer, Kanade and Kender, 1983). Moreover, they are simple to generate and compact to store.

The assurity weighting is defined separately for each shape-from method and is based upon the intrinsic error of the method. For example, shape-from-uniform-texel-spacing's assurity weighting is a function of the total distance between the texel patches used to generate that constraint. A low assurity value is given when the inter-texel distance is small (1 texel distance) because under these conditions a small digitization error causes a large orientation error. Above the threshold the assurity weighting is set high (6) and then starts to decrease as the inter-texel distance increases. Mathematically, given the radius of the texel, *radius*, and the inter-texel distance, *distance*, the assurity weighting W is :

$$W = 6 \times radius/distance$$

The decreasing assurity occurs because once the inter-texel distance grows too large the local surface is no longer approximated by a plane and the orientation error grows. This further acts to make the constraints group locally rather than globally which is valid since texels that are part of the same surface are normally located close together.[6]

MOST LIKELY ORIENTATION GENERATION

Once the orientation constraints have been generated for each augmented texel, the next step consists of unifying the constraints into one orientation per augmented texel. The major difficulty in deriving this "most likely" orientation is that the constraints are errorful, inconsistent, and potentially incorrect. A simple and computationally feasible, solution to this is to use a Gaussian Sphere which maps the orientation constraints to points on the sphere (Shafer, Kanade and Kender, 1983). A single vanishing point circumscribes a great circle on the Gaussian Sphere; two different constraints generate two great circles that overlap at two points uniquely defining the orientation of both the visible and invisible sides of the surface patch.

The Gaussian sphere is approximated within the system by the hierarchical tesselated Gaussian Sphere based on triangular shaped faces called trixels (See figure 2) (Fekete and Davis, 1984; Korn and Dyer, 1986). The top level of the hierarchy is the twenty face icosahedron. At each level, other than the lowest level of the hierarchy, each trixel has four children which more closely approximate the curvature of the spherical surface

---

[5]Ikeuchi (Ikeuchi, 1980) and Aloimonos (Aloimonos and Swain, 1985) attempt a similar extension that use constraint propagation and relaxation to derive a single orientation per surface patch. These approaches were further limited by the use of only a single shape-from-texture method.

[6]The only exception occurs when a surface is overlapped by another transparent surface and the texels are interspersed.

than their parent. This hierarchical methodology allows the user to specify the accuracy to which the orientation can be calculated by defining the number of levels of tesselation that are created.

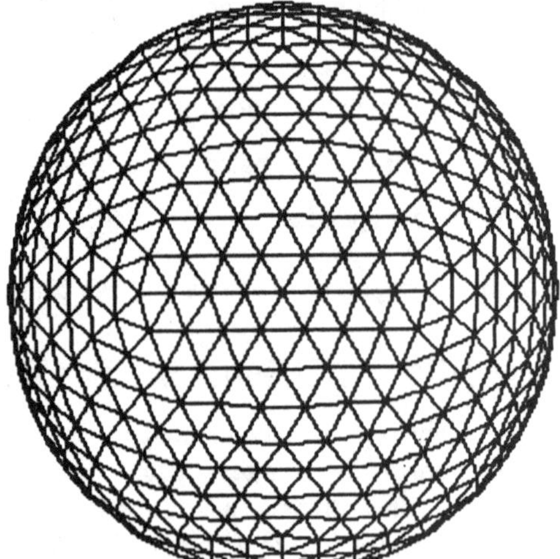

Figure 2:   The Trixelated Gaussian Sphere

The system generates the "most likely" orientation for each texel patch by accumulating the evidence from all the orientation constraints (generated in phase one) for the patch. For each constraint, it initially visits the twenty top level trixels , determines whether the great circle falls on the trixel and if the result is positive, visits the children. At each lowest level trixel through which the great circle travels, the likelihood value of the trixel is incremented by the constraint's weight. The hierarchical nature of this approach limits the number of trixels that need to be visited.

Once all of the constraints for a texel patch have been considered, a peak finding program smears the likelihood values at the lowest level trixels. Currently, this is done heuristically: the smeared value of each leaf is equal to its accumulated value plus 1/2 the value of its neighbors plus 1/4 the value of all its neighbor's neighbors that are not a neighbor of the leaf. This is a rough approximation to a gaussian blur. The "most likely" orientation is defined to be the trixel with the largest smeared value.

This method does not assure that under all circumstances a single "most likely" orientation will be derived. When more than one "most likely" orientation is derived for a patch the system performs a Waltz type filtering. It computes the "most likely" orientation for the remaining augmented texels and then re-analyzes the orientation constraints for each texel that does not have a single "most likely" orientation. For each unsolved texel patch the system considers all of the patch's constraints and removes any constraints that do not correctly define the "most likely" orientation of another texel patch. Once this constraint pruning has occurred the system recomputes the "most likely" orientation for the patch. This reanalysis does not assure a single "most likely" orientation either, but it does aid in simplifying and deriving a single "most likely" orientation for the largest number of surface patches.

DERIVING OF SURFACE SEGMENTATION INFORMATION

The final phase of the system generates surfaces from the individual augmented texels. This is done by re-analyzing the orientation constraints generated by the shape-from methods in order to determine which augmented texels are part of the same surface. In doing this the surface generation is also performing a first approximation of surface separation and segmentation.

The re-analysis consists of iterating through each Augmented Texel, considering all its orientation constraints and determining which constraints aided in defining the "most likely" orientation for the texel patch as described in phase two. If an orientation constraint correctly determined the orientation of all the texels that were used in generating the constraint then these augmented texels are considered as part of the same surface.

Once it is determined which augmented texels are part of the same surface, the surfaces can be generated by a simple surface generation algorithm. The surfaces could then be defined as the best fit approximation that contains all the related texel patches. This approach allows both the generation and the separation of surfaces that are connected or overlapping.

TEST DOMAIN

The knowledge fusion approach outlined in the previous section has been implemented in a test system that contains two shape-from-texture methods, shape-from-uniform-texel-spacing (Moerdler and Kender, 1985), and shape-from-uniform-texel-size (Ohta et. al., 1981). Each of the methods is based on a different textural characteristic that allows the generation of orientation constraints and also limits the applicability of the approach.

Shape-form-uniform-texel-spacing derives orientation constraints based on the assumption that the texels can be of arbitrary shape but are equally spaced, while shape-from-uniform-texel-size is based on the unrelated criteria that the spacing between texels can be arbitrary and the size of all of the texels is equivalent but unknown.

In shape-from-uniform-texel-size if the distance from the center of mass of texel T_1 to texel T_2 (see figure 3) is defined as D then the distance from the center of texel T_2 to a point on the vanishing line can be written as :

$$F_2 = D \times S_2^{1/3} / (S_1^{1/3} - S_2^{1/3})$$

In shape-from-uniform-texel-spacing the calculations are similar. Given any two texels T_1 and T_2 (see figure 4) whose inter-texel distance is defined as D, if the distance from T_1 to a mid-texel T_3 is equal to L and the distance from T_2 to the same mid-texel T_3 is equal to R, the distance from texel T_1 to a vanishing point is given by :

$$X = [D + (R \times D)] / [L-R]$$

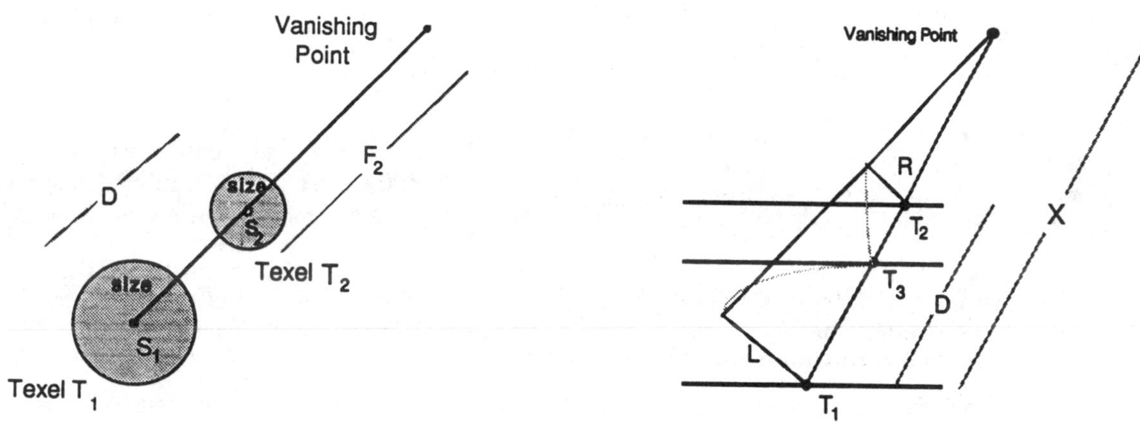

Figure 3: The calculation of shape-from-uniform-texel-size   **Figure 4:** A geometrical representation of back-projecting.

Under certain conditions either method may generate incorrect constraints which the system has effectively ignored. On textures that are solvable by both methods the methods cooperate and correctly define the textured surface(s) in the image. Some images are not solvable by either method by itself but can be correctly defined by the interaction of the cues.

EXPERIMENTAL RESULTS

The system has been tested over a range of both synthetic and natural textured surfaces, and shows robustness and generality. Three examples are given on real, noisy images that demonstrate the cooperation and competition among the shape-from methods.

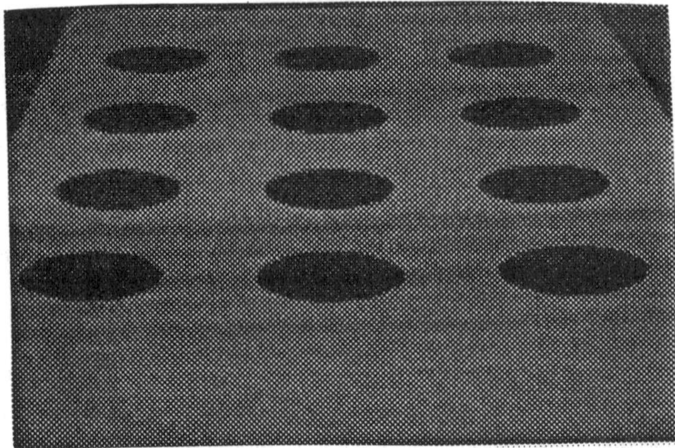

Figure 5:   Surface textured with evenly spaced evenly sized circles

The first image, figure 5, shows a real image of a man-made texture consisting of equally spaced, equally sized circles. The system finds fifteen texels: the twelve texels on the surface, plus three noise texels located in the background. It is able to generate both the correct p and q values for each of the twelve surface texels (see figure 6 for the positions of the texels and figure 7 for the individual p and q values.). In figure 8 the orientations of the texel patches are displayed as needle-like surface normal vectors.

The system is also able to segmented the image into multiple surfaces, one of which contains only the twelve correct surface texels while the shadow and noise texels are each individually marked as part of separate surfaces.

The second example consists of an image containing 2 surfaces which are covered with a total of seventeen nickels (see figure 9), eight from one surface and nine from the other. This is a truly difficult image containing a number of real world problems that would be unsolvable by a less robust approach which include:

1. The nickels, in the image, are raised slightly above the surface creating slight shadows. These shadows are considered by the threshold based blob finding algorithm as part of the texels, thus generating incorrect sizes for the blobs which in turn can cause the shape-from-uniform-texel-size algorithm to generate skewed results.

2. The nickels are shiny and reflect the lighting. This can cause parts of a texel to be considered as background pixels causing the method to ignore pixels that should be part of texels.

3. To add to these imaging difficulties are the more general problems that arise because there is more than one surface and the system has no knowledge about the placement of surfaces. Further compounding this problem is the fact that some of the texels of the different surfaces are closer to each other than they are to other texels of their surfaces (e.g. texel 7 and texel 8 in figure 9).

Considering these potential problems the system responses admirably. It can compute an orientation within the measurement error for fifteen of the seventeen texels (see figure 10). For the other two texels it is unable to decide which of three orientation to choose. One of which orientations is within the measurement error. The inability caused by excessive shadows around these texels.

The system is able to group the texels correctly, with texels zero through seven as part of one surface and

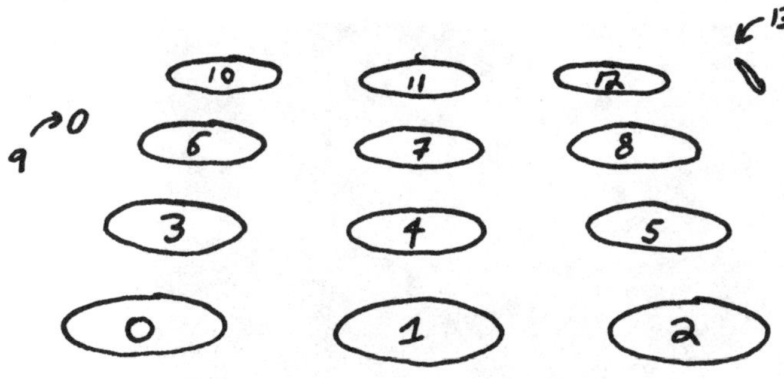

Figure 6: The numbering of texels for the circles texture

all of the remaining texels as part of the second surface.

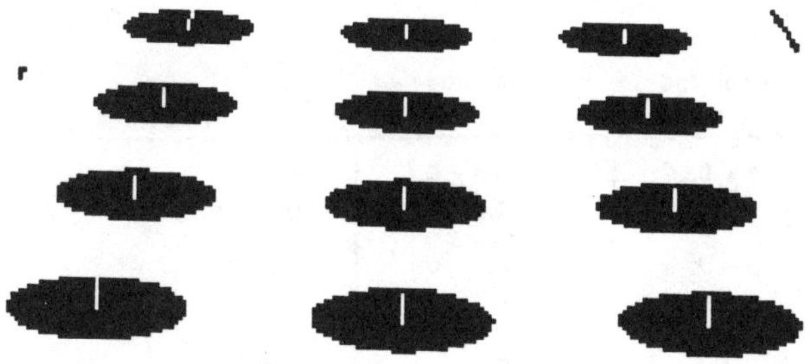

Texel Numbers	Measured p & q	Actual p & q	Error
0 to 8	p = 3.0 q = 0.0	p = 3.0 q = 0.0	0° 0°
9	p=11.0 q=6.7	Shadow Texel	
10 to 12	p = 3.0 q = 0.0	p = 3.0 q = 0.0	0° 0°
13	p=11.0 q=6.7	Shadow Texel	

Figure 7: Surface normals for the surface textured with circles   **Figure 8:** Orientation values for the surface textured with circles

The camera images that were used in the experimental results (see section 5) contain both noise and shadows which are in many cases effectively ignored by the system. The system treats shadows as potential surface texels (see texels 9 and 13 in figure 5) and uses them to compute orientation constraints. Since many texels are used in generating the orientation for each individual texel the effect of shadow texels on the generation of the correct orientation for the "real" texels (for example texel nine and texel thirteen in figure 6) is minimized[7].

---

[7]Even under the conditions where many shadow texels are found they do not effect the computed orientation of surface texels so long as the placement of the shadow texels does not mimic perspective distortion.

Figure 9:   An image of a surface covered with coins

Texel #	calculated p & q	Measured p & q	Error in degrees
0,2	p = 0.00 q = 4.38	p = 0.0 ± 0.4 q = 4.9 ± 0.4	p = 0 q = 1.3
1,3,4,5	p = 0.18 q = 4.38	p = 0.0 ± 0.4 q = 4.9 ± 0.4	p = 10.2 q = 1.3
6	p = 0.10 q = 4.60	p = 0.0 ± 0.4 q = 4.9 ± 0.4	p = 5.7 q = 1.3
7	p = 0.08 q = 3.78	p = 0.0 ± 0.4 q = 4.9 ± 0.4	p = 4.6 q = 3.3
8,10,14	p = 0.51 q = 0.70	p = 0.5 ± 0.4 q = 0.8 ± 0.4	p = 0.5 q = 3.7
9,12	p = 0.50 q = 0.68	p = 0.5 ± 0.4 q = 0.8 ± 0.4	p = 0.0 q = 0.8
13,15	p = 0.49 q = 0.74	p = 0.5 ± 0.4 q = 0.8 ± 0.4	p = 0.0 q = 1.5

Figure 10:   The numbering of the coin texels found   **Figure 11:**   Orientation values

THE EFFECTS OF NOISE

Noise can create texels, and change the shape, size, or position of texels. If noise generated texels are sufficiently small then they are ignored in the texel finding components of the shape-from methods. When they are large, they are treated in much the same way as shadow texels and, as described above, do not effect the orientation of the surface texel patches. Noise can also change the shape or size of a texel and thus cause any specific shape from method to generate incorrect constraints (for example a few extra pixels added to a texel will cause the shape-from-uniform-texel-size method to generate false results while these additional texels will have little or no effect on the results generated by the shape-from-uniform-texel-spacing method). These effects are thus minimized in the system by the combination of multiple shape-from methods and the smearing method which helps lessen the effects of noise.

CONCLUSION AND FUTURE RESEARCH

This paper describes a system that can fuse the results of a number of shape-from-texture methodologies to generate surface segments and their orientations. The system has been tested using two existing shape-from methods: shape-from-uniform-texel-spacing and shape-from-uniform-texel-size and has shown the ability, under noisy conditions, to recover surface orientation and suggest surface segmentation.

The robustness of the system has been exercised using images that contain multiple surfaces, surfaces that are solvable by either method alone, finally by surfaces that are solvable by using only both methods together.

Future enhancements to the system would include the addition of other shape-from-texture modules, the investigation of other means of fusing information (such as object model approaches), and optimization of the method, especially in a parallel processing environment.

ACKNOWLEDGEMENT

I would like to acknowledge Terrence Boult for providing both his time and helpful suggestions that have improved this work.

References

John Aloimonos. *Detection of Surface Orientation and Motion from Texture: 1. The Case of Planes.* Computer Vision Patttern Recognition, 1986.

John Aloimonos and Michael J. Swain. *Shape from Texture.* IJCAI, 1985.

Larry S. Davis, Lubvik Janos, and Stanley M. Dunn. Efficient Recovery of Shape from Texture. *IEEE Transactions on Pattern Analysis and Machine Intelligence,* September 1983, *PAMI-5, (5),* 485-492.

Stanley M. Dunn, Larry S. Davis, and Hannu A. Hakalahti. *Experiments in Recovering Surface Orientation from Texture.* Technical Report CAR-TR-61, University of Maryland Center For Automation Research, May 1984.

Gyorgy Fekete and Larry S. Davis. Property Spheres: A New Representation For 3-D Object Recognition. *Proceedings of the Workshop on Computer Vision Representation and Control,* 1984, , 192 - 201.

James J. Gibson. *Perception of the Visual World.*
Riverside Press, 1950.

Katsushi Ikeuchi. Shape from Regular Patterns (an Example from Constraint Propagation in Vision). *Proceedings of the Internation Conference on Pattern Recognition,* December 1980, , 1032-1039.

John R. Kender. *Shape from Texture.* PhD thesis, C.M.U., 1980.

John R. Kender. Surface Constraints from Linear Extents. *Proceedings of the National Conference on Artificial Intelligence,* March 1983.

Matthew R. Korn and Charles R. Dyer. *3-D Multiview Object Representation for Model-Based Object Recognition.* Technical Report RC 11760, IBM T.J. Watson Research Center, March 1986.

Mark L. Moerdler and John R. Kender. *Surface Orientation and Segmentation from Perspective Views of Parallel-Line Textures.* Technical Report, Columbia University, 1985.

Mark L. Moerdler and John R. Kender. *An Integrated System That Unifies Multiple Shape From Texture Algorithms.* AAAI, 1987.

Yu-ichi Ohta, Kiyoshi Maenobu, and Toshiyuki Sakai. *Obtaining Suface Orientation from Texels under Perspective Projection.* IJCAI, 1981.

Steven A. Shafer and Takeo Kanade and John R. Kender. Gradient Space under Orthography and Perspective. *Computer Vision, Graphics and Image Processing,* 1983, *(24),* 182-199.

Kent A. Stevens. *Surface Perception from Local Analysis of Texture and Contour.* PhD thesis, Massachusetts Institute of Technology, 1979.

Andrew P. Witkin. Recovering Surface Shape from Orientation and Texture. In Michael Brady (Eds.), *Computer Vision,* North-Holland Publishing Company, 1980.

LOCATING POLYHEDRAL OBJECTS FROM EDGE POINT DATA

Roger Tsai
IBM T.J. Watson Research Center
Yorktown Heights, NY 10598

Gary Silverman
IBM Scientific Center
Los Angeles, CA 90025

Mark Lavin
IBM T.J. Watson Research Center
Yorktown Heights, NY 10598

ABSTRACT

A method is presented to locate a general polyhedron in space with six degrees of freedom. A light stripe sensor is assumed to be capable of providing three-dimensional data points on known edges of the polyhedron to within a known accuracy. A representation is found for all the ways three line segments of fixed length can fall between the edges of a polyhedron. This representation, called an edge interval, is used in a tree search to find the location of each data point to within an interval on the edge. The final location of the object is determined by a one-dimensional line search. The method is illustrated with simulated data from a unit tetrahedron and results from a computer implementation are presented. The tree search takes a negligible amount of time and the one-dimensional line search takes a small additional increment.

INTRODUCTION

The general problem is to determine the identity and location of a part in 3-D space to within a known error in real time. Gordon and Seering '87 describe a method which uses light stripes between known edges of a polyhedral object. When three light stripes intersect a right corner, they are able to locate the object in negligible time. Bolles and Horaud '86 "concentrate on edges because they contain more information than surface patches and are relatively easy to detect in range data," page 8. Grimson and Lozano-Perez '84 use points on a known face and an estimate of the surface normal at each point to locate the object. On page 9, they suggest that if a point is on an edge of an object, "the recognition process is greatly simplified."

The problem treated in this paper is to locate a general polyhedral object with six degrees of freedom using data from a light stripe sensor. We assume that the light stripes locate 3-D data points on edges of the object to within a known error. Call each of these data points an **edge point**. Research is currently underway to develop effective sensors for this kind of application, see Tsai '85, Gordon and Seering '87 and Bolles and Horaud '86. There is a further assumption that each edge point is on a known edge of the object. This may occur in an application such as in Gordon and Seering '87, where the geometric relation between the sensor and the object has been specified in advance or as in Arbab '87, where the edge points are identified with an edge via an interpretation method.

In the next section the main results are provided on how the ends of a line segment of fixed length may intersect two edges of an object in 3-D space. The Edge Interval Tree section shows how the edge intervals may be propagated as constraints in a tree search to find the location of each edge point to within an interval on the edge. The section on Locating The Object shows how to locate the object within error by a one-dimensional line search.

EDGE INTERVALS

Consider a line segment of fixed length, d, whose end points are known to intersect each of two edges, e_0 and e_1, see Figure 1. Now add an orientation to each line, so that a minus $(-)$ and a plus $(+)$ direction is defined along the line. **Edge intervals** are defined as a pair of intervals, one interval on each line, with the following property. As the point of intersection on the first line moves in a monotonic direction from beginning to end of the first interval, the point of intersection on the second line moves in a monotonic direction on the second interval. These intervals are mutually exclusive and include all possible intersections of the line segment with the two edges.

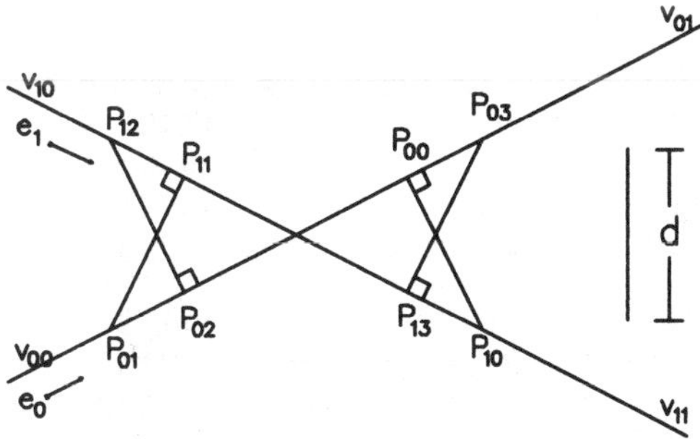

Figure 1. Monotonic edge intervals on two edges.

To describe the edge intervals introduce vertices v_{00}, v_{01} which define a finite edge e_0 in Figure 1 and a positive direction on e_0. Define a parameterization of a point along the edge using a convex combination of the vertices,

$$(1) \qquad P_0(\alpha_0) = (1 - \alpha_0)v_{00} + \alpha_0 v_{01},$$

so that,

$$(2) \qquad P_0(0) = v_{00}$$

$$(3) \qquad P_0(1) = v_{01}.$$

Similar vertices and parameterization are defined for edge e_1.

Consider the line segment $\overline{P_{00}, P_{10}}$ of length d. This line segment is constructed to be perpendicular to edge e_0. As one end of the line segment moves from P_{00} to P_{01} on edge e_0, the other end moves from P_{10} to P_{11} on edge e_1. One end of the line segment is moving along e_0 in the negative direction and the other end is moving along e_1 in the negative direction. At $\overline{P_{01}, P_{11}}$ a sense of direction must change. This is because at P_{11} the line segment is perpendicular to edge e_1. It is impossible to continue moving in the negative direction on both edges and still maintain contact. Therefore, as the line segment moves from $\overline{P_{01}, P_{11}}$ to $\overline{P_{02}, P_{12}}$ the sense of direction along e_0 must change from $-$ to $+$. Similarly, from $\overline{P_{02}, P_{12}}$ to $\overline{P_{03}, P_{13}}$ the senses are $+$, $+$. Finally, from $\overline{P_{03}, P_{13}}$ returning to $\overline{P_{00}, P_{10}}$ the senses are $-, +$. To convince yourself, cut out the line and re-trace this path on Figure 1.

To calculate values of α_0 and α_1 that correspond to edge intervals, the orthogonality condition

$$(4) \qquad (P_0(\alpha_0) - P_1(\alpha_1)) \bullet (v_{01} - v_{00}) = 0$$

and the distance condition

$$(5) \qquad \|P_0(\alpha_0) - P_1(\alpha_1)\| = d$$

must be satisfied.

Equations (4) and (5) may be reduced to a standard quadratic equation in α_0. The solution is the following equations for α_0 and α_1, where a_1, b_1, c_1, g_1, g_2 and g_3 are dependent only on the edge vertices and the distance. The derivation of these equations is included in Appendix A.

$$(6) \qquad \alpha_0 = \frac{-b_1 \mp \sqrt{b_1^2 - 4a_1c_1}}{2a_1}$$

$$(7) \qquad \alpha_1 = \frac{g_1\alpha_0 + g_2}{g_3}$$

Cases where equations (6) and (7) are degenerate are classified as follows. If the distance, d, is shorter than the minimum distance between the edges, then the discriminant term in (6) is negative. If the edges are orthogonal, the discriminant in (6) is equal to zero. If the edges are parallel, the term a_1 in (6) equals zero and the edge intervals are illustrated in Figure 2. In all of these cases, degenerate or non-degenerate, it is possible to compute the edge intervals by solving simple quadratic equations.

This is a complete representation of edge intervals along edges e_0 and e_1, and although Figure 1 and Figure 2 are planar, this representation extends immediately to arbitrary edges in 3-D space. Errors in the edge point data will cause error in the final location of the object. For the parallel case shown in Figure 2 if the distance, d, is within sensor error of the distance between the edges, edge interval calculation may fail.

THE EDGE INTERVAL TREE

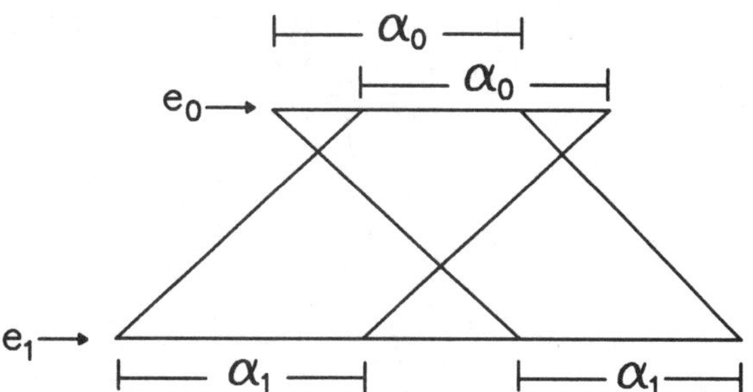

Figure 2. Edge intervals on parallel edges.

The edge interval tree has three levels: 0th level, 1st level and 2nd level, one for each edge point. A node at the *ith* level represents an interval on e_i. There is an arc emanating to the next level for each edge interval. The monotonic character of the edge intervals enables an edge interval tree search for a set of three **valid intervals,** one on each edge. The valid intervals are subsets of the respective edge intervals. A set of valid intervals contains all sets of values $\{\alpha_0^*, \alpha_1^*, \alpha_2^*\}$ such that; if each edge point is located at the value of α_i^* on its respective edge, then the three mutual distances are consistent with the sensor data to within error. This is a location where the edge point data fit the object.

Valid intervals are determined by propagating the edge intervals from e_0 to e_1 to e_2 and back to e_0. The monotonic property of the edge intervals implies there is a continuous, monotonic mapping from any point α_i within the edge interval on e_i, which with d_{ij}, maps to a unique point α_j on e_j. Let this mapping and its inverse be denoted by the transfer functions,

$$(8) \qquad\qquad \alpha_j = T_{ij}(\alpha_i)$$

and

$$(9) \qquad\qquad \alpha_i = T_{ji}(\alpha_j).$$

The transfer function T_{ij} is the location of a point on an edge at a given distance from a point on another edge, where both points are expressed parametrically as in (1).

The equation for T can be derived by solving

$$(10) \qquad\qquad \|P_i(\alpha_i) - P_j(\alpha_j)\| = d_{ij}$$

for (8) or (9). This leads to a quadratic equation

$$(11) \qquad\qquad \alpha_j = T_{ij}^{\mp}(\alpha_i) = \frac{-b_2(\alpha_i) \mp \sqrt{b_2(\alpha_i)^2 - 4a_2(\alpha_i)c_2(\alpha_i)}}{2a_2(\alpha_i)}$$

where a_2, b_2, c_2 are functions of α_i, see Appendix B for details. This quadratic equation is nondegenerate for any α_i in the edge interval on e_i. The function $T_{ij}^{\mp}$ indicates there are two points on e_j at a given distance from α_i, one each for the plus and minus root in (11). At any node in the edge interval tree search the correct sign in (11) is determined by the edge interval on e_j. In the discussion below, let T denote a specific transfer function where the sign is determined by the edge interval being propagated.

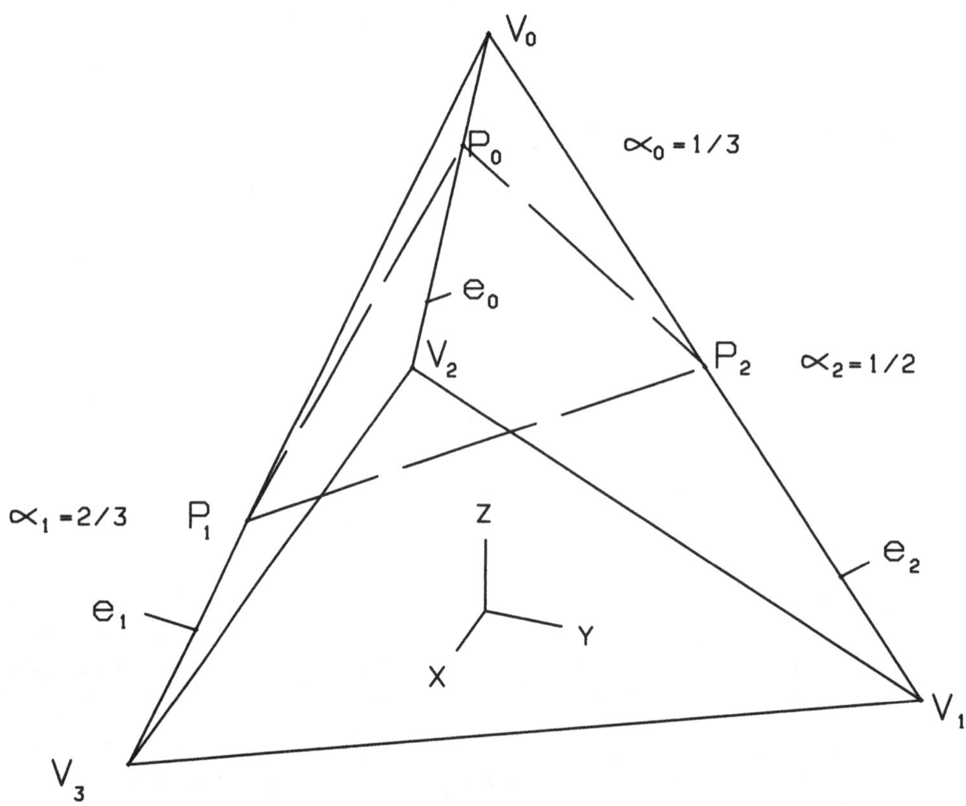

Figure 3.   Simulated light stripe on unit tetrahedron.

Searching the Edge Interval Tree

A unit tetrahedron is illustrated in Figure 3. Three edges, e_0, e_1 and e_2, are cut by a simulated light stripe. Three edge points, P_0, P_1, P_2, are known to within a given sensor error. The three mutual distances between edge points may be computed, d_{01}, d_{12} and d_{20}. A model of the object provides the vertices for each edge in some canonical location. The edge intervals for the the first two unit tetrahedron edge pairs are displayed in Figure 4 and Figure 5. This example will be used to illustrate the tree search.

The tree is propagated by intersecting intervals on common edges and transferring the resulting intervals to the next edge with (11). Pruning occurs when the intersected interval is empty. The propagation and pruning steps for the tree differ at each level. Figure 6 shows the edge interval constraint propagation from edge interval E_{01}^0 in Figure 4 to E_{12}^1 in Figure 5. In Figure 6 the unit tetrahedron has been "unfolded" along e_1 to make a planar figure illustrating the edge interval tree search.

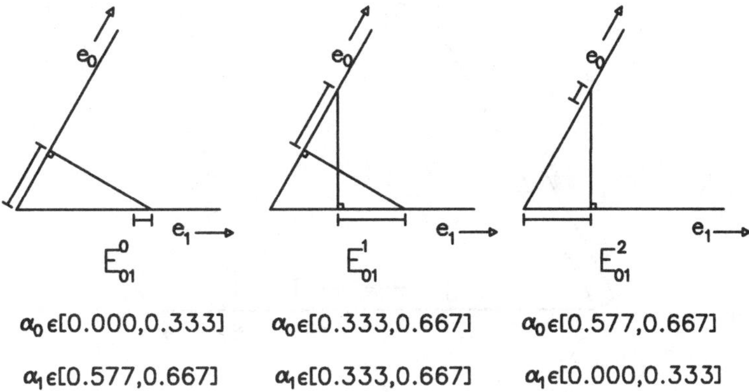

Figure 4.   Edge intervals on edges 0 and 1 of unit tetrahedron.

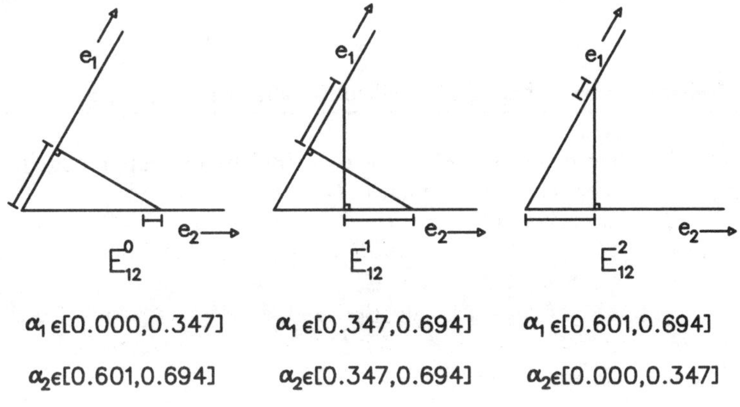

Figure 5.   Edge intervals on edges 1 and 2 of unit tetrahedron.

The 0th level: This level propagates intervals on e_0 to intervals on e_1 using the edge intervals. Let this interval be noted by $I_1 = [\alpha_1^l, \alpha_1^u]$. In Figure 6, I_1 is actually the edge interval E_{01}^0 on e_1, $\alpha_1 \in [0.577, 0.667]$.

The 1st level: This level propagates intervals on e_1 to intervals on e_2 using d_{12}. For the edge intervals from e_1 to e_2, intersect the interval on e_1 with I_1, the interval passed in from the 0th level. Let this intersected interval be noted by $H_1 = [\beta_1^l, \beta_1^u]$. If H_1 is empty, then the tree is pruned at this point. In Figure 6, this results in I_1 being intersected with E_{12}^1. Here $H_1 = I_1$ because $I_1 \subset E_{12}^1$.

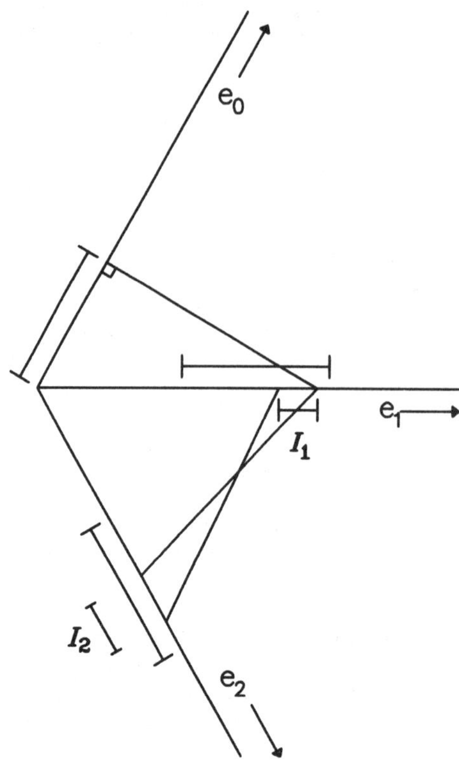

Figure 6.   Edge interval constraint propagation on unit tetrahedron.

If H_1 is equal to E_{12} then propagate H_1 to e_2 by using the respective edge interval. If not, propagate H_1 to e_2 using the transfer function T. That is $I_2 = [\alpha_2^l, \alpha_2^u]$ where,

$$(12) \qquad \alpha_2^l = T_{12}(\beta_1^l),$$

$$(13) \qquad \alpha_2^u = T_{12}(\beta_1^u).$$

This is illustrated in Figure 6, where $I_2 = [0.500, 0.622]$.

The 2nd level: This level propagates intervals on e_2 back to intervals on e_0 using d_{20}. The propagation and pruning steps at level 1 are repeated at level 2 using the edge intervals from e_2 to e_0 and the distance, d_{20}. The result is an interval, $H_0 = [\beta_0^l, \beta_0^u]$, on e_0. Now propagate H_0 to e_1 to e_2 and back to e_0 to obtain another interval $I_0 = [\alpha_0^l, \alpha_0^u]$. That is,

$$(14) \qquad \alpha_0^l = T_{20}(T_{12}(T_{01}(\beta_0^l)))$$

and

$$(15) \qquad \alpha_0^u = T_{20}(T_{12}(T_{01}(\beta_0^u))).$$

Errors in the sensor data may cause localizations to be missed unless both intervals are increased. Let V_0 be the intersection of the increased intervals, H_0 and I_0. If V_0 is empty the tree may be pruned at this point. Any non-empty interval, V_0, is a valid interval. This final pruning step is possible because the line segments d_{20} and d_{01} must intersect e_0 at the same point, P_0, to within error.

LOCATING THE OBJECT

If the solution is known to lie in $V_0 = [\alpha_0^l, \alpha_0^u]$ a one-dimensional line search for a fixed point to within error, of the function,

$$(16) \qquad \beta_0 = T_{20}(T_{12}(T_{01}(\alpha_0)))$$

will find all solutions within the valid interval. The line search is required because while all three distances are maintained by (16), both starting and ending points of intersection on e_0 must be the same to within error.

The object localization problem is solved by locating the edge point, P_i, at α_i^* on each edge, e_i, for $i = 0, 1, 2$. Once a particular triple $(\alpha_0^*, \alpha_1^*, \alpha_2^*)$, is known a transformation to within error from model space to image space may be computed to fit the object.

A program has been written implementing the ideas presented here and it has been tested on the unit tetrahedron data. The edge interval calculation involves only a few quadratic equations to solve and takes negligible time. The edge interval tree search requires a few comparisons and some evaluations of (11) per node. This too takes only a very small amount of time. Any edge interval tree with three levels has a maximum of 84 nodes, because the maximum number of branches at any node is four. The edge interval tree search for the unit tetrahedron has to examine only 15 out of the possible 84 nodes. The rest are pruned from the tree. Experience with the current program indicates a few seconds of execution time on the IBM RT PC programmed in C. This includes line search of two valid intervals. It should be possible to substantially improve upon this.

ACKNOWLEDGMENTS

We would like to thank Bob Cypher of the University of Washington and our colleagues, Bijan Arbab, Fernando Vicuna and Jim Moore for many helpful discussions. The authors are also grateful to the referee whose comments resulted in a number of important clarifications.

REFERENCES

1.   Arbab. B. "Object Identification by Parallel Light Stripes." In Proc. IJCAI-87. Milano, Italy, August 1987.

2.   Bolles R.C. and P. Horaud, "3DPO: A Three-Dimensional Part Orientation System." The International Journal of Robotics Research, 5:3 (1986) 3-26.

3.   Gordon, S.J. and W.P. Seering, "Locating Polyhedral Features from Sparse Light Stripe Data." In Proc. IEEE International Conference on Robotics and Automation, Raleigh, NC, April, 1987, pp. 801-806.

4.   Grimson, W.E.L. and T. Lozano-Perez, "Model-Based Recognition and Localization from Sparse Range or Tactile Data." The International Journal of Robotics Research, 3:3 (1984) 3-35.

5.   Silverman, G. J., R. Tsai and M. Lavin, "Locating Polyhedral Objects from Edge Point Data." In Proc. IJCAI-87. Milano, Italy, August 1987.

6.   Tsai, R.Y. 1985 "A Versatile Camera Calibration Technique for High Accuracy 3-D Machine Vision Metrology using off-the-shelf TV Cameras and Lenses," IBM T.J. Watson Research Report RC 11413, Yorktown Heights, NY, September 1985.

Appendix A. Edge Interval Equations

In this Appendix the derivation of the edge interval equations in (6) and (7) is provided. Let two edges, e_0 and e_1, have vertices v_{00}, v_{01} and v_{10}, v_{11}, respectively, so that,

$(A.1)$
$$v_{00} = (x_{00}, y_{00}, z_{00}),$$

$(A.2)$
$$v_{01} = (x_{01}, y_{01}, z_{01}),$$

$(A.3)$
$$v_{10} = (x_{10}, y_{10}, z_{10}),$$

$(A.4)$
$$v_{11} = (x_{11}, y_{11}, z_{11}),$$

and let

$(A.5)$
$$\Delta x_0 = x_{01} - x_{00}, \ \Delta y_0 = y_{01} - y_{00}, \ \Delta z_0 = z_{01} - z_{00},$$

$(A.6)$
$$\Delta x_1 = x_{11} - x_{10}, \ \Delta y_1 = y_{11} - y_{10}, \ \Delta z_1 = z_{11} - z_{10},$$

$(A.7)$
$$\Delta x_2 = x_{10} - x_{00}, \ \Delta y_2 = y_{10} - y_{00}, \ \Delta z_2 = z_{10} - z_{00}.$$

Then construct an edge point parameterization on each edge as in (1) so that,

$(A.8)$
$$P_0(\alpha_0) = (1 - \alpha_0)v_{00} + \alpha_0 v_{01},$$

and

$(A.9)$
$$P_1(\alpha_1) = (1 - \alpha_1)v_{10} + \alpha_1 v_{11}.$$

Now expand the orthogonality condition, (4),

$(A.10)$
$$((1 - \alpha_0)x_{00} + \alpha_0 x_{01} - ((1 - \alpha_1)x_{10} + \alpha_1 x_{11}))(x_{01} - x_{00}) +$$
$$((1 - \alpha_0)y_{00} + \alpha_0 y_{01} - ((1 - \alpha_1)y_{10} + \alpha_1 y_{11}))(y_{01} - y_{00}) +$$
$$((1 - \alpha_0)z_{00} + \alpha_0 z_{01} - ((1 - \alpha_1)z_{10} + \alpha_1 z_{11}))(z_{01} - z_{00}) = 0.$$

Let

$(A.11)$
$$g_1 = (\Delta x_0)^2 + (\Delta y_0)^2 + (\Delta z_0)^2,$$

$(A.12)$
$$g_2 = - (\Delta x_0 \Delta x_2 + \Delta y_0 \Delta y_2 + \Delta z_0 \Delta z_2),$$

$(A.13)$
$$g_3 = \Delta x_0 \Delta x_1 + \Delta y_0 \Delta y_1 + \Delta z_0 \Delta z_1.$$

Then simple manipulation of $(A.10)$ shows that,

$(A.14)$
$$\alpha_1 = \frac{g_1 \alpha_0 + g_2}{g_3},$$

which completes the derivation of (7).

Now use the distance equation (5) to eliminate α_1 in $(A.14)$. Squaring both sides of (5) gives,

$(A.15)$
$$((1 - \alpha_0)x_{00} + \alpha_0 x_{01} - ((1 - \alpha_1)x_{10} + \alpha_1 x_{11}))^2 +$$
$$((1 - \alpha_0)y_{00} + \alpha_0 y_{01} - ((1 - \alpha_1)y_{10} + \alpha_1 y_{11}))^2 +$$
$$((1 - \alpha_0)z_{00} + \alpha_0 z_{01} - ((1 - \alpha_1)z_{10} + \alpha_1 z_{11}))^2 = d^2.$$

Now let,

$$(A.16) \qquad g_4 = g_3 \Delta x_0 - g_1 \Delta x_1,$$

$$(A.17) \qquad g_5 = g_3 \Delta y_0 - g_1 \Delta y_1,$$

$$(A.18) \qquad g_6 = g_3 \Delta z_0 - g_1 \Delta z_1,$$

$$(A.19) \qquad g_7 = g_3 \Delta x_2 + g_2 \Delta x_1,$$

$$(A.20) \qquad g_8 = g_3 \Delta y_2 + g_2 \Delta y_1,$$

$$(A.21) \qquad g_9 = g_3 \Delta z_2 + g_2 \Delta z_1,$$

By substituting $(A.16)$ through $(A.21)$ into the expansion of $(A.15)$ the quadratic coefficients of (6) are obtained,

$$(A.22) \qquad a_1 = (g_4)^2 + (g_5)^2 + (g_6)^2,$$

$$(A.23) \qquad b_1 = -2(g_4 g_7 + g_5 g_8 + g_6 g_9),$$

$$(A.24) \qquad c_1 = (g_7)^2 + (g_8)^2 + (g_9)^2 - (g_3)^2 d^2,$$

so that,

$$(A.25) \qquad \alpha_0 = \frac{-b_1 \mp \sqrt{b_1^2 - 4 a_1 c_1}}{2 a_1}$$

and α_1 is available from $(A.14)$.

Appendix B. Transfer Functions

In this Appendix the derivation of the transfer function $T_{ij}^{\mp}$, in (11) is provided. For simplicity, let us set $i = 0, j = 1$. Any other values for i and j follow immediately. The notation developed in $(A.1)$ through $(A.9)$ from Appendix A will be retained.

Note that (5) represents the distance constraint between a point on e_0 and a point on e_1, expressed as a function of α_0 and α_1, respectively. To derive (11) we merely solve for α_1 in terms of α_0. To begin, rewrite the distance condition, (5), as follows,

$(B.1)$
$$(\alpha_0 \Delta x_0 - \alpha_1 \Delta x_1 - \Delta x_2)^2 +$$
$$(\alpha_0 \Delta y_0 - \alpha_1 \Delta y_1 - \Delta y_2)^2 +$$
$$(\alpha_0 \Delta z_0 - \alpha_1 \Delta z_1 - \Delta z_2)^2 = d^2.$$

Now square the indicated terms in $(B.1)$ and sum. Separate the three orders of coefficients of α_1 as functions of α_0, so that the following parametric quadratic results,

$(B.2)$
$$a_2(\alpha_0)\alpha_1^2 + b_2(\alpha_0)\alpha_1 + c_2(\alpha_0) = 0,$$

where,

$(B.3)$
$$a_2(\alpha_0) = (\Delta x_1)^2 + (\Delta y_1)^2 + (\Delta z_1)^2,$$

$(B.4)$
$$b_2(\alpha_0) = \alpha_0(-2(\Delta x_0 \Delta x_1 + \Delta y_0 \Delta y_1 + \Delta z_0 \Delta z_1)) +$$
$$(2(\Delta x_1 \Delta x_2 + \Delta y_1 \Delta y_2 + \Delta z_1 \Delta z_2)),$$

$(B.5)$
$$c_2(\alpha_0) = \alpha_0^2((\Delta x_0)^2 + (\Delta y_0)^2 + (\Delta z_0)^2) -$$
$$\alpha_0(2(\Delta x_0 \Delta x_2 + \Delta y_0 \Delta y_2 + \Delta z_0 \Delta z_2)) +$$
$$(\Delta x_2)^2 + (\Delta y_2)^2 + (\Delta z_2)^2 - d^2.$$

Equations $(B.3),(B.4),(B.5)$ are the parametric coefficients in (11).

Mathematical Tools for Representing Uncertainty in Perception

James L. Crowley
Fano Ramparany

LIFIA (IMAG)
Institut National Polytechnique de Grenoble
46 Avenue Félix-Viallet
38031 Grenoble
France

ABSTRACT

This paper presents a set of mathematical tools for representing and manipulating spatial uncertainty. A mathematical basis for uncertainty is proposed and this basis is used to develop operations for matching uncertain values, for combining uncertain estimates and for projecting uncertainties with non-linear transformations.

The use of uncertainty is illustrated with the problem of representing perceptual information with parametric primitives. A generalization for parametric primitives is presented in which each attribute is represented by an estimate and an uncertainty. The utility of this approach is then illustrated with the problem of matching line segments. The article concludes with a discussion of a variety of other domains where these techniques may be applied.

1 Introduction

Matching is ubiquitous in perception. However, matching real world data poses a serious problem. Data that should match exactly always seem to differ by a small amount. The typical response is to match two values within a tolerance. But what tolerance? Usually it is the programmer who decides based on his experience. The result can be a myriad of hidden "constants" for which even the programmer may not be able to provide a justification.

If we represent measurements by a best estimate and the precision of the estimate, the precision replaces the tolerances used in matching. In principal, as more observations are obtained, the precisions may be combined to dynamically adjust the matching tolerance. However, this requires techniques for representing and manipulating precision. Equally important, techniques are required for propagating precision as the original measurements are combined into more abstract primitives.

The problem of choosing a matching tolerance is not simply a problem of accommodating noise. It is a problem of representing the limits in precision of the basic measuring devices. This paper proposes techniques which permit the precision of measurements to be explicitly represented and to be propagated through multiple levels of abstraction. This problem is commonly known as the problem of representing and manipulating spatial uncertainty.

1.1 The Problem: Representing Spatial Uncertainty

Spatial uncertainty defines an interval within which an estimate is believed to exist. The two dominant operations on uncertainty are combination and inclusion. In one dimension, uncertainty may be easily represented as an interval, with both combination and inclusion defined by intersection. In two or more dimensions, however, the region of uncertainty must have a geometric form, and this poses a difficult problem. If uncertainty is represented by polygonal regions, the combination of regions with unconstrained orientations soon creates a very large number of sides. If the region is represented by a circle, its size is always larger than the "worst-case"; in particular, highly directional uncertainties with different orientations can not be effectively combined or exploited. An elliptical tolerance region is natural, except that no simple mathematics exists for representing the intersection of two ellipses by a third ellipse.

A solution to this problem is provided by a technique from statistics: The representation of a distribution of values by a set of parameters. In particular, the normal distribution, which represents a population by its first and second moments, provides a mathematical bases for representing and manipulating spatial uncertainty.

Although the normal distribution is generally associated with a statistical behavior of random processes it is not necessary to adopt a statistical interpretation. The normal distribution may serve equally well as the basis for a calculus of the limits of certainty. It provides simple mathematical techniques for combining uncertainties, for testing for inclusion, and for transforming uncertainties.

1.2 Previous Work

The problem of spatial uncertainty is well known in the natural sciences. A classic example is provided by the Heisenberg uncertainty principal which describes a limit to the ability to simultaneously measure the position and velocity of an atomic particle. The mathematical basis for the techniques presented below have been developed within the field of statistics [Berger 80] and are basic to such neighboring domains as statistical pattern recognition [Nilsson 65] and Control Theory [Sage-Melsa 73].

Interest in the representation and manipulation of spatial uncertainty has been encouraged recently by work in the area of position estimation for a mobile robot, as well as the development of system for combining shape measurements from different sources and different points of view. The problem is clearly evident in the system for combining sparse tactile data described by Grimson and Lozano-Pérez [Grimson-Pérez 84]. The problem appears in a different form in a system for dynamic world modeling for a mobile robot using ultrasound [Crowley 85]. It is also discussed in the context of position estimation in a paper by Chatila and Laumond [Chatila 84]. Brooks has recently explored the use of circular tolerance regions [Brooks 84] for a mobile robot. The use of techniques from statistics has been encouraged by Cheeseman [Cheeseman-Smith 86]. This approach has been further developed in papers by [Faugeras et.al. 86] and [Durrant-Whyte 87].

The techniques described below have been developed as part of a system for dynamically modeling the geometry of a 3-D scene in terms of parametric primitives for corners, contours and surface patches [Crowley 86]. In developing this system it was found that combining data from different sensors and different points of view required techniques for explicitly representing and combining uncertainty in multiple dimensions.

2 Mathematical Tools for Modeling Uncertainty

In this section we review the definition of the multivariate normal distribution. We then define three useful operations for manipulating uncertainties.

2.1 The Multi-Variate Normal Distribution

A mathematical basis for manipulating uncertainty may be defined using the multi-variate normal (or Gaussian) distribution. In one dimension, this distribution is the well known "Bell-shaped curve" represented by a mean, m, and standard deviation, s. The parameters m and s may be determined by calculating the first and second moments from a population of samples. However, it is not necessary that these parameters be derived from a sample population. Mean and variance can be used to represent an estimated value and a symmetric tolerance interval. While this representation is marginally useful in one dimension, it becomes extremely useful for parameters in two or more dimensions.

The normal distribution is easily generalized to N dimensions to form the multi-variate normal distribution. In N dimensions, the distribution predicts the probability of obtaining a particular vector, X, given a mean vector, μ, and covariance matrix, Λ.

$$g(X) = \frac{1}{\sqrt{2\pi}^n \det(\Lambda)^{\frac{1}{2}}} \, Exp\{-\frac{1}{2}(X-\mu)^T \Lambda^{-1} (X-\mu)\}$$

In the statistical interpretation, μ is a vector of mean values for each component of X. The covariance, Λ, is an N by N matrix of covariances between components of X. If the mean vector is interpreted as an estimate for a parameter, then the covariance may be used to define an ellipsoidal uncertainty region for the estimate, where the axes of the ellipsoid are defined by the eigenvalues of Λ. Such a representation for uncertainty permits the mathematical definition of operations for determining the similarity of two parametric representations, the combining parametric representations, and the non-linear transformation of uncertainties.

2.2 Uncertainty in Parametric Primitives

Most vision and perception systems quickly convert raw data to a more abstract "parametric" representation. The classical example in vision is the use of edge-lines and intersections to describe an image. The generalized cylinder [Agin 76] of Agin and Binford is an example of a more complex 3-D parametric primitive.

Whether explicitly represented or not, any expression of measurements with a parametric representation involves an uncertainty tolerance. In the case of fitting line segments, the uncertainty is usually expressed as the maximum allowable perpendicular distance at which an edge point may contribute to the formation of an edge-line [Duda-Hart 73]. Given the proper mathematical tools, the uncertainty can be measured from the precision of the measuring instrument (e.g. the pixel size) and propagated to more abstract primitives.

Let S be a parametric primitive, composed of N attributes, where each attribute may itself be a single value or a vector. Each attribute, i, is represented by an estimated value, P_i., and an uncertainty, Λ. While it is not necessary that the attributes be independent, redundant attributes may result in unnecessary calculations.

2.3 Matching Parametric Primitives: Functions "NormDist" and "Similar"

A common operation in perception is the comparison of two primitives to determine if they represent the same physical entity. However, perceived quantities are never exactly equal; they must be compared with respect to a tolerance. Using a covariance to represent uncertainty makes possible normalize the distance between two vectors by the uncertainty with which the values are known. The covariance can be used to define a multi-dimensional elliptical "acceptance" tolerance based on precisions propagated directly from perceptions. This acceptance tolerance is based on a distance normalized by uncertainty.

Suppose that we have a vector, P_m, with uncertainty, Λ. The distance to a second vector, P_o, normalized by the uncertainty is given by:

$$\text{NormDist}(\,P_o,\,P_m,\,\Lambda\,) = (P_m - P_o)^T\,\Lambda^{-1}\,(\,P_m - P_o)$$

If the vector P_o has uncertainty Λ_o, and vector P_m has uncertainty Λ_m independant of Λ_o then it is possible to define a joint uncertainty distribution, Λ_{om}, for the distance $|\,P_m - P_o\,|$ as the sum of the two distributions Λ_o and Λ_m.

$$\Lambda_{om} = \Lambda_o + \Lambda_m$$

This joint uncertainty is equivalent to the convolution of the two uncertainty distributions. This can be shown by converting the distributions to Fourier Transform domain and considering their product. Thus the normalized distance between two attributes, P_m and P_o may be computed by $\text{NormDist}(\,P_o,P_m,\,\Lambda_o + \Lambda_m\,)$.

Normalized distance provides a measure of the similarity of attributes. This value of this measure may be exploited in matching primitives. Alternatively, the normalized distance may simply be compared to a confidence threshold to determine if two attributes may potentially correspond. This comparison may be formalised by the function Similar. For a 90% confidence, the normalized distance must be less than or equal to 4. Thus Similar is defined:

$$\text{Similar}(\,P_o,\,P_m,\,\Lambda\,) = \begin{cases} \text{True} & \text{if } \text{NormDist}\,(\,P_o,\,P_m,\,\Lambda\,) \leq 4 \\ \text{False} & \text{otherwise} \end{cases}$$

If the attributes are one dimensional, then SIMILAR may be simplified to Similar_1D:

$$\text{Similar\_1D}(P_o, P_m, \sigma) = \begin{cases} \text{True} & \text{if } \text{ABS}(P_m - P_o) \leq 2\sigma \\ \text{False} & \text{otherwise} \end{cases}$$

As before, if both attributes have an uncertainty then a symmetric similarity measure may be obtained by using the sum of the uncertainties as the matching tolerance.

Given the function Similar, two parametric primitives, S_o and S_m, may be said to "match" if a specified subset of their attributes are similar. A typical use for Similar is to determine which observed primitives can correspond to a projected model primitive. The function Similar does not guarantee a unique match from a set of matches. It guarantees only the "feasibility" of a match. A further test must be used to select the most desirable match. This test may be based on individual properties of the primitives (such as length) or on properties of groups of matches, such the maximal cliques algorithm [Bolles 82], or rigid transformations [Faugeras-Hebert 83].

2.4 Refining Parametric Primitives: Function "MERGE"

In a dynamic scene modeling system, a scene is described by a set of parametric primitives. Such primitives may be based on observations as well as knowledge about the scene. In such a system, the attributes of the primitives are refined by observations.

Given a match between a model primitive S_m and an observed primitive, S_o, it is possible to reduce the uncertainty associated with the attributes of the model primitive. This reduction may be formalised by the function "MERGE", which produces a new estimate and uncertainty for each attribute (P_n, Λ_n) from a pair of matching attributes (P_m, Λ_m) and (P_o, Λ_o).

$$(P_n, \Lambda_n) = \text{MERGE}(P_m, \Lambda_m, P_o, \Lambda_o)$$

where the new estimate and uncertainty may be calculated by

$$\Lambda_n = [\Lambda_m^{-1} + \Lambda_o^{-1}]^{-1}$$

and

$$P_n = \Lambda_n [\Lambda_m^{-1} P_m + \Lambda_o^{-1} P_o].$$

This operation requires 2 additions, 3 multiplications and 5 matrix inversions. The merge operation is equivalent to a Kalman Filter [Cheeseman-Smith 86], which requires 4 additions and 3 multiplications but only one inversion. In the Kalman formulation, merge is defined using a gain, **K**.

$$K = \Lambda_m [\Lambda_m + \Lambda_o]^{-1}$$

The new estimate and its uncertainty, (P_n, Λ_n), are then calculated by :

$$\Lambda_n = \Lambda_m - K \Lambda_m{}^T$$

and

$$P_n = P_m + K \left[P_o - P_m \right]$$

The attributes (P_m, Λ_m) and (P_o, Λ_o) must be independent, or else the resulting estimate and reduction in uncertainty will be false.

2.5 Transforming Uncertainty

There are many situations in which attributes of parametric primitives are related by transformations. If the transformation is linear then it may be described by a Matrix, F. Let M be an estimated attribute vector and O be an observed attribute vector such that.

$$M = F O$$

The uncertainty of the observation, Λ_O, may be related to the uncertainty Λ_M, by

$$\Lambda_M = F \Lambda_O F^T .$$

Note that it is not necessary that O and M be in the same basis space. They may even have a different number of dimensions. If the transformation, F, is not linear than it is necessary to approximate F with a linear approximation. This may accomplished with the aid of a Jacobian of F, calculated using a Taylor series expansion about an estimated value provided by O. The Jacobian of $F(O)$ is the vector of derivatives of $F(O)$ with respect to each component of M.

$$J_f = \partial F(O)/\partial O$$

In the case of a non-linear F, the covariances are related by

$$\Lambda_M = J_F \Lambda_O J_F{}^T .$$

2.6 Constraining Uncertainty: The Generalized Kalman Filter

In many perceptual situations an observation provides a constraint which has fewer dimensions than the uncertainty which we wish to constrain. In this case, the "extended Kalman filter" provides a very elegant mechanism for applying the constraint to the uncertainty [Faugeras et. al. 86]. To apply the extended Kalman FIlter, we must relate our observation, say O, to the estimated attribute vector, M, by some function, F.

$$M = F(O).$$

The Jacobian J_F, is then used to relate the uncertainty of the observation to the uncertainty of the estimate to produce a new estimate of the uncertainty, Λ_n.

$$\Lambda_n = [\Lambda_m{}^{-1} + J_F{}^T \Lambda_O{}^{-1} J_F]^{-1}$$

and

$$P_n = \Lambda_n \left[\Lambda_m{}^{-1} P_m + J_F{}^T \Lambda_O{}^{-1} J_F P_o \right].$$

Alternatively, the extended Kalman Gain may be computed by:

$$K = \Lambda_m^{-1} J_F^T (J_F \Lambda_m J_F^T + \Lambda_O)^{-1}.$$

The new estimate and its uncertainty are then provided by:

$$P_n = P_m + K (O - J_F P_m)$$

with uncertainty:

$$\Lambda_n = (I - K J_F) \Lambda_m.$$

3 Example: Matching of Parametric Line Segments

The mathematical tools for representing uncertainty developed in the previous section are useful for a variety of problems that occur in perception. The application of these techniques to the representation and matching of point structures, such as 2-D junctions or 3-D corners, is relatively obvious. It is less obvious how these techniques may be applied to geometric primitives that have a finite spatial extent such as line segments, contours or planar patches. This section illustrates such a case by describing the representation and matching of line segments using an explicit representation of uncertainty. Section four discusses other domains of application.

The algorithm presented below was originally developed for dynamic modeling of the limits of free space for a mobile robot [Crowley 85] using a rotating ultrasound. The same techniques have recently been adapted to tracking edge lines during camera movements, and for determining the correspondence of 3-D contours for dynamic scene analysis.

The classic parametric representation expresses an edge line as two end points, say (P_1, P_2). However, this representation is not convenient for matching. A more convenient parametric representation is obtained from the center point, P_M, the angle, θ, and the half-length, L. This representation permits a test for the correspondence of line segments as a series of three very simple attribute tests for similar orientation, colinearity and overlap, using function SIMILAR.

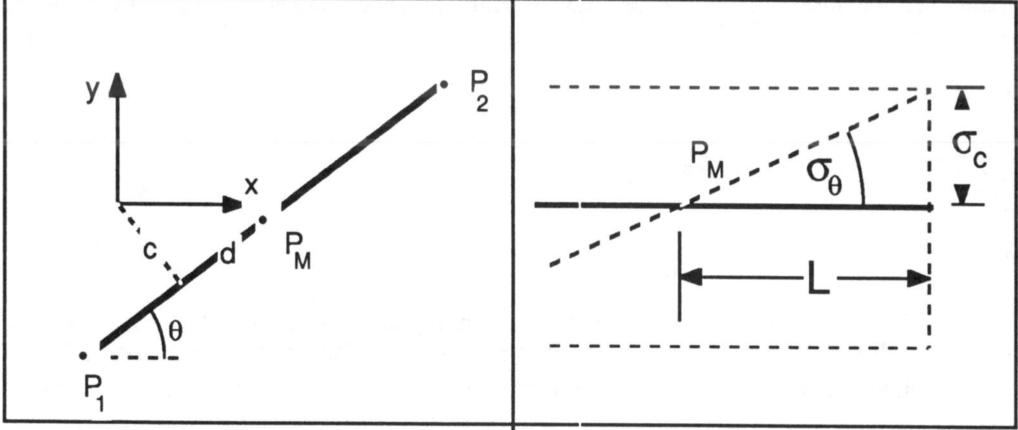

Figure 1. A Parametric Representation for a 2-D Edge-Line. The left illustrates the parameters (c, θ, d). The right illustrates the uncertainties (σ_c, σ_θ, L).

Orientation, colinearity and overlap may be tested more rapidly if line segments are already expressed in parameters which correspond to these values. Such a representation is obtained if the centerpoint of the line segment is rotated about the origin by the orientation of the line segment. The result is an expression of the center point in terms of (d, c) where c is the perpendicular distance to the origin, and d is the distance along the edge line from the perpendicular intercept to the the center point of the segment, as illustrated in figure 1. Notice that the pair (θ, c) is equivalent to the parameters of the line equation $Ax + By + C = 0$, where $A = Sin(\theta)$, $B = -Cos(\theta)$ and $C = -c$.

The parameter d specifies the displacement along the line to P_m, while the length L serves to delimit a segment of the line centered at P_m. The parameters c and θ have uncertainties represented by the standard deviations σ_c and σ_θ. The length, L, serves as the uncertainty for the displacement, d. Given the end points, P_1 and P_2, the representation is computed from the center point, (x_m, y_m), and the vector between end points, $(\Delta x, \Delta y)$.

$$(x_m, y_m) = (P_1 + P_2)/2 \qquad (\Delta x, \Delta y) = P_1 - P_2$$

then

$$\theta = Tan^{-1}(\Delta y/\Delta x)$$
$$d = x_m Cos(\theta) + y_m Sin(\theta)$$
$$c = -x_m Sin(\theta) + y_m Cos(\theta)$$

The uncertainty perpendicular to the line, σ_c, may be determined during line extraction as the perpendicular distance to the furthest point (x_i, y_i) admitted to the line.

$$\sigma_c = Max\{ A x_i + B y_i + C \}$$

The half length, L, is half the distance between the end points of the line.

$$L = ([\Delta x^2 + \Delta y^2]^{1/2})/2$$

The uncertainty in orientation, σ_θ, may be determined from the uncertainties (σ_c, L) by the relation:

$$\sigma_\theta = (\partial(Tan^{-1}(\sigma_c/ L))/\partial \sigma_c) [Tan^{-1}(\sigma_c/ L)]$$

For $\sigma_c/ L << 1$ This may be approximated by:

$$\sigma_\theta = Tan^{-1}(\sigma_c/ L)$$

To illustrate the advantage of this representation in matching, suppose we have an image expressed in edge lines, $L_i(k)$, in this representation, and we project a model onto this image. Given a model edge line, L_m, we wish to know which image edge line(s) might correspond. The correspondence between edge lines consists of a simple set of attribute tests using the function SIMILAR, as embodied in the function CORRESPOND [Crowley 85].

CORRESPOND(L_i, L_m : LineSegments)
BEGIN

```
         IF  Similar_1D(L_i.θ,  L_m.θ,  (L_i. σ_θ + L_m.σ_θ) )  THEN

         IF  Similar_1D (L_i.d,  L_m.d,  (L_i. σ_d + L_m.σ_d ) )  THEN

         IF  Similar_1D (L_i.c,  L_m.c,  (L_i. L + L_m. L) )  THEN
                    RETURN(TRUE);
END;
```

4 Example Application Domains

The tools developed in section 2 are very useful in a number of domains. In this section we discuss their application to problems in the domains of locomotion, dynamic scene modeling and pattern matching.

4.1 Localisation of a Mobile Platform

The explicit representation of uncertainty in position is very useful in the navigation of a mobile robot. Such uncertainty is used to determine the tolerance which the robot must maintain to avoid collisions with surfaces in its environment. Such an uncertainty is also useful for matching perceptual information taken from different viewing position.

The location of a mobile robot is typically expressed as a position, (x,y) with a 2 by 2 uncertainty Λ_p, and orientation, θ, with an uncertainty σ_θ. As the robot moves, its estimated location is maintained from internal sensors such as wheel encoders. At the same time a model of the sources of uncertainty can be used to increase the uncertainties in location. Typical sources of uncertainty include drift (due to uneven weight distribution) and wheel-slippage.

To reduce the uncertainty in location, the robot must observe the distance and direction to a known landmark. One technique involves placing beacons at known locations. Other techniques involve observing visual landmarks during the displacement. In either case, function SIMILAR may be used to discover the correspondance between the observed and known (beacon or landmark) location. The function MERGE is used to correct the estimated position and reduce the uncertainty in location.

4.2 Dynamic Scene Analysis and Data Fusion

In order to act within an unpredictable environment, a robotic system must be able to dynamically maintain a model of the geometry of the local limits to free space. Such a model is ideally maintained by integrating data from multiple sources and from multiple viewing positions. The integration of such data is facilitated by a parametric representation that explicitly represents the uncertainty of each parameter. A family of such primitives is described in [Crowley 86]. Maintaining the model involves determining the correspondence of observed primitives with model primitives. Such correspondence may be accomplished using function SIMILAR are illustrated in section 3. Updating the attributes of model primitives may be accomplished with function MERGE.

4.3 Learning Structural Descriptions of Patterns.

Structural descriptions of pattern classes, in both 2-D and 3-D, may be represented by a network of parametric primitives, in which position and orientation are defined in a local "pattern" coordinated system. The variability in position, orientation, and other parameters may be described by a explicit representation of uncertainty within the primitives. Such a system has been developed for learning and matching 2-D patterns using both edge lines and scale space primitives [Crowley-Sanderson 86].

5 Conclusion

This paper has presented a mathematical representation for spatial uncertainty based on the multi-variate normal distribution. Three important mathematical operations have been defined using this representation:

similarity, merging, and non-linear transformation. The use of this representation has been been illustrated with parametric primitives. To illustrate the advantage of this representation, an efficient technique for matching 2-D line segments was presented. The explicit representation of uncertainty replaces arbitrary fixed tolerances with dynamically maintained tolerances, and simplifies matching operations in perception, locomotion and manipulation.

Bibliography

[**Agin 76**]   Agin G. J. and T. O. Binford, "Computer Description of Curved Objects", IEEE Trans. on Computers, C-25(4), April 1976.

[**Berger 85**] Berger J. O, _Statisical Decisions_, Springer Verlag, 1985

[**Bolles 82**] Bolles, R. C. and R. A. Cain, "Recognizing and Locating Partially Visible Objects: The Local Feature Focus Method ", Int. Journal of Robotics Research, 1 (3) 1982.

[**Brooks 84**] Brooks, R., "Aspects of Mobile Visual Map Making", Proceedings Second ISRR, Kyoto, Japan, 1984.

[**Chatila 85**] Chatila, R. and J. P. Laumond, "Position Referencing and Consistent World Modeling for Mobile Robots", Proc of the 2nd IEEE Conference on Robotics and Automation, St. Louis, March 1985.

[**Crowley 85**] Crowley, J. L. "Navigation for an Intelligent Mobile Robot", IEEE Journal on Robotics and Automation, 1 (1), March 1985.

[**Crowley 86**] Crowley, J. L., "Representation and Maintenance of a Composite Surface Model", IEEE Int. Conf. on Robotics and Automation, San Francisco, April 1986.

[**Crowley-Coutaz 86**] Crowley, J. L. et J. C. Coutaz, "Navigation et Modèlisation pour un Robot Mobile", Technique et Science Informatique, Universités de Grenoble, Octobre, 1986.

[**Crowley-Sanderson 86**] "Multiple Resolution Representation and Probabilistic Matching of 2-D Gray-Scale Shape", IEEE Transactions on PAMI, PAMI 9 (1), January, 1987.

[**Cheeseman-Smith 86**] Cheeseman, P. and R. C. Smith, "On the Representation and Estimation of Spatial Uncertainty", Technical Report (Draft), SRI International, 1986.

[**Duda and Hart 73**] Duda, R. O. and P. E. Hart, "Pattern Classification and Scene Analysis", Wiley, N. Y. 1973.

[**Durrant-Whyte 87**] Durrant-Whyte, H. F., "Consistent Integration and Propagation of Disparate Sensor Observations", To appear in _Int. Journal of Robotics Research_, 1987,

[**Faugeras and Hebert 83**] Faugeras, O. D. and M. Hebert, "A 3-D Recognition and Postioning Algorithm using Geometrical Matching between Primitive Surfaces", Proc. of Eighth IJCAI, Aug, 1983.

[**Faugeras, et. al.**] Faugeras, O. D. , N. Ayache, and B. Faverjon, "Building Visual Maps by Combining Noisey Stereo Measurements", IEEE Int. Conf. on Robotics and Automation, San Francisco, April 1986

[**Grimson and Lozano-Pérez 84**] Grimson, W. E. L. and T. Lozano-Pérez, "Model Based Recognition and Localization from Sparse Range and Tactile Data", _Int. Jour. of Robotics Research_, 3 (3), Fall 1984.

[**Melsa-Sage 73**] Melsa, J. L. and A. P. Sage, _An Introduction to Probability and Stochastic Processes_, Prentice Hall, 1973.

[**Nilsson 65**] Nilsson, N., "Learning Machines: Foundations of Trainable Pattern Classifying Systems", McGraw Hill, New York, 1965.

SENSOR MODELS AND MULTI-SENSOR INTEGRATION*

Hugh F. Durrant-Whyte
Department of Engineering Science
University of Oxford
Oxford, U.K.

Abstract

A multi-sensor robot system comprises many diverse sources of information. The sensors of these systems take observations of a variety of disparate geometric features. The measurements supplied by the sensors are uncertain, partial, occasionally spurious or incorrect and often geographically or geometrically incomparable with other sensor views. It is the goal of the robot system to coordinate these sensors, direct them to view areas of interest, and to integrate the resulting observations into a consistent consensus view of the environment which can subsequently be used to plan and guide the execution of tasks.

We maintain that the key to the efficient fusion of disparate sensory information is to provide a purposeful description of the robots environment and to develop an effective model of sensor capabilities. We model the world as a collection of uncertain geometric objects, and describe each sensor by its ability to extract descriptions of these objects from the environment. A sensor model has three components; an observation model which describes a sensors measurement characteristics, a dependency model which describes a sensors dependence on information from other sources, and a state model which describes how a sensors observations are affected by it's location and internal state. Each model is represented as a probability distribution on observed geometric objects. This provides a powerful mechanism with which to manipulate, transform and integrate uncertain sensor observations. We show that these sensor models can deal effectively with cooperative, competitive and complimentary interactions between different disparate information sources.

---

*This material is based on work supported by the National Science Foundation under Grants DMC-84-11879 and DMC-85-12838, and conducted while the author was at the University of Pennsylvania. Any opinions, findings, and conclusions or recommendations expressed in this publication are those of the author and do not necessarily reflect the views of the National Science Foundation.

1   Introduction

Recent years have seen an increasing interest in the development of multi-sensor systems [5]. This interest stems from a realization of the fundamental limitations on any attempt at building descriptions of the environment based on a single source of information. Single sensory systems are only ever capable of supplying partial information and are consequently limited in their ability to resolve interpret unknown or partially unknown environments. If robot systems are ever to achieve a degree of intelligence and autonomy, they must be capable of using many different sensors in an active and dynamic manner; to resolve single sensor ambiguity, to discover and interpret their environment.

In order to make efficient use of sensory information, it is important to model the environment and sensors in a manner which explicitly accounts for the inherent uncertainty encountered in robot operation. We will model all geometric features in the environment by functions $\mathbf{g}(\mathbf{x}, \mathbf{p}) = \mathbf{0}$. Each function defines a family of features, parameterized by the vector $\mathbf{p}$. Our environment model characterizes each feature by a probability density function $f_g(\mathbf{p})$ on this parameter vector [2]. We will consider sensors in terms of their ability to extract these uncertain descriptions of the environment geometry. The manipulation and transformation of uncertain geometric observations provides a basis for the communication of information between different sensor systems and allows the development of techniques to compare and combine disparate observations.

We will develop a team-theoretic model of sensor abilities in terms of an information structure. The purpose of a sensor model is to represent the ability of a sensor to extract descriptions of the environment in terms of a prior world model. Sensor models should provide a *quantative* ability to analyze sensor performance, and allow the development of robust decision procedures for integrating sensor information. The advantage of having a model of sensor performance is that capabilities can be estimated à priori, spurious information can be readily identified, and sensor strategies developed in line with information requirements. In a multi-sensor system, these models can also be used to enhance cooperation between disparate sensory cues and to encourage distribution of sensing and problem solving tasks.

2   Sensor Models

We can divide a sensor model into three parts; an *observation* model, a *dependency* model, and a *state* model. An observation model is essentially a static description of sensor performance, it describes the dependence of observations on the state of the environment. For example, if a camera is taking pictures or images of the environment, a static model would describe the ability of the camera to extract edges or surfaces from the image, in terms of locations or feature parameters, together with some measure of their uncertainty. A dependency model describes the relation between the observations or actions of different sensors. For example, the observations made by a tactile probe may depend on the prior observations supplied by a vision system, or an edge detector may provide a segmentation algorithm with a first estimate of region boundaries. A state model describes the dependence of a sensors observations on the location or physical state of a sensing device. For example, a mobile camera platform, may be able to change it's location (viewpoint) or the focus of it's lens to provide different observation characteristics. A description of the dependency of observations on sensor state would enable the development of sensor strategies.

Sensor information is inherently dynamic; observations provided by one sensory cue cannot be considered in isolation from the observations and actions of other sensors. Different sensors may provide quite disparate capabilities, which when considered together are *complementary*. If we have a number of sensors that provide essentially the same information for the purpose of reducing uncertainty and allowing redundant operation, we are likely to have information that is *competitive*, or in disagreement. When two or more sensory cues depend on each other for guidance, then these information sources must *cooperate* to provide observations.

We will develop a probabilistic model of sensor capability in terms of an *information structure*. We consider a multi-sensor system as a team, each observing the environment and making local decisions, each contributing to the consensus view of the world, and cooperating to achieve some common goal. The information structure of a team describes the observations and decisions made by the team members, how they are related, and how they depend on the organization and operation of the team.

2.1   Information Structure

The ith team member is described by an *information structure* η_i. This structure is a model of sensor capabilities. An information structure is defined by the relation between observations, state and decisions;

Definition: The *information structure* of the ith sensor or team member ($i = 1, \cdots, n$) is a function η_i which describes the observations $\mathbf{z}_i$ made by a sensor in terms of it's physical state $\mathbf{x}_i$, available prior information about the state of the environment $\mathbf{p}_i \in P_i$, and the other sensors or team members actions $\mathbf{a}_j \in A_j$, $j = 1, \cdots, n$. So that: $\mathbf{z}_i = \eta_i(\mathbf{x}_i, \mathbf{p}_i, \mathbf{a}_1, \cdots, \mathbf{a}_{i-1}, \mathbf{a}_{i+1}, \cdots, \mathbf{a}_n)$
$\square$

We are primarily interested in teams of observers, where the action $\mathbf{a}_i$ of each sensor is to make an estimate of some geometric feature $\mathbf{a}_i \in P$ in the environment. By relating the actions of each sensor or team member to it's observations through a decision function $\delta_i(\mathbf{z}_i) \mapsto \mathbf{a}_i$. This allows us to consider the information structure as a transformation of observations to observations; the observations $\mathbf{z}_i$ are random vectors and η_i is a stochastic function transforming the decisions $\delta_j(\cdot) \in P_j$, the prior information $\mathbf{p}_i \in P_i$ and the sensor state $\mathbf{x}_i$ into elements of P.

This transformation of observations between different sensors or team members suggests that we describe each decision function in terms of a distribution function, so that

$$f(\mathbf{z}_i) \quad = \quad f\big(\eta_i(\mathbf{x}_i, \mathbf{p}, \delta_1(\mathbf{z}_1), \cdots, \delta_{i-1}(\mathbf{z}_{i-1}), \delta_{i+1}(\mathbf{z}_{i+1}), \cdots, \delta_n(\mathbf{z}_n))\big)$$

$$= \quad f_{\eta_i}(\mathbf{x}_i, \mathbf{p}, \delta_1(\mathbf{z}_1), \cdots, \delta_{i-1}(\mathbf{z}_{i-1}), \delta_{i+1}(\mathbf{z}_{i+1}), \cdots, \delta_n(\mathbf{z}_n))$$

This representation of the information structure has a number of advantages: The description of observations is now dimensionless so we can manipulate this function using standard probabilistic techniques and apply the tools of uncertain geometry [3] to the communication of information between different sensory cues. This allows us to develop decision procedures capable of using many disparate sources of information. Another important advantage of describing the information structure in terms of a probability distribution function is that the variables (prior information, state and other sensor decisions) can be separated from each other by expanding f_{η_i} as a series of conditional probability distributions. This in turn allows us to decouple the three types of sensor model, $(\eta^p, \eta^\delta,$ and $\eta^x)$ from each other. Let $\overline{\delta}_i = (\delta_1, \cdots, \delta_{i-1}, \delta_{i+1}, \cdots, \delta_n)$ then;

$$f(\mathbf{z}_i) = f_{\eta_i}(\mathbf{x}_i, \mathbf{p}_i, \overline{\delta}_i) = f_{\eta_i}(\mathbf{x}_i \mid \mathbf{p}_i, \overline{\delta}_i) f_{\eta_i}(\mathbf{p}_i \mid \overline{\delta}_i) f_{\eta_i}(\overline{\delta}_i) = f_x(\eta_i^x) f_p(\eta_i^p) f_\delta(\eta_i^\delta)$$

The state model $f_x(\eta_i^x)$ now describes the dependence of a sensors observations on its location and internal state *given* any prior information and all other sensor opinions. The observation model $f_p(\eta_i^p)$ describes the dependence of sensor measurements on the state of the environment *given* all other sensor decisions. The dependence model $f_\delta(\eta_i^\delta)$ describes the prior information supplied by the other sensors in the system. The product of these three models describes the observations made by the sensor.

2.2   Observation models

Consider a sensor taking observations of a geometric feature, an instance of a given family parameterized by the vector $\mathbf{p}$. We can model this observation as a conditional probability distribution $f_g(\mathbf{z} \mid \mathbf{p})$ that describes the likelyhood of feature observation given all prior information about $\mathbf{p}$. This distribution is our observation model; $f_g(\mathbf{z} \mid \mathbf{p}) \equiv f_p(\eta^p)$. The exact form of $f(\cdot \mid \mathbf{p})$ will depend on many physical factors. It is unlikely that we can obtain an exact description of the probabilistic character of observations in all but the simplest of cases. It may in fact be undesirable to use an exact model even if it were available because of its likely computational complexity, and its inability to model non-noise errors such as software failures or algorithmic misclassifications. We propose to use an approximation that describes the observations by some nominal distribution together with an unknown likelyhood of errors or mistakes. These distributions are termed *gross error models* [8], and have the general form:

$$P_\epsilon(F_0) = \{F \mid F = (1 - \epsilon)F_0 + \epsilon H, \quad H \in M\} \tag{1}$$

These models are described by a set of distributions F which are composed of some nominal distribution F_0 together with a small fraction ϵ of a second probability measure H. This second measure is often assumed unknown and acts to contaminate the nominal distribution with unexpected observations. Statistically the purpose of the contamination is to flatten the tails of the observation distributions and force resulting decision procedures to be robust with respect to possible outlying measurements. This model results in decision procedures which cluster observations and trim outliers from consideration in the integration process [3]. If the nominal model has finite moments, then this clustering process converges to a Gaussian observation model.

2.3   Dependency Models

Consider the dependence of the ith sensor or team members information structure as described by the dependence model: $\eta_i^\delta(\overline{\delta}_i) = \eta_i^\delta(\delta_1(z_1), \cdots, \delta_{i-1}(z_{i-1}), \delta_{i+1}(z_{i+1}), \cdots, \delta_n(z_n))$. We will interpret this dependency model as a distribution function, describing the information provided to the ith sensor by all other sensors as a prior probability of feature observation:

$$f_i(\eta_i^\delta(\overline{\delta}_i)) = f_\delta(\overline{\delta}_i(z_1, \cdots, z_{i-1}, z_{i+1}, \cdots, z_n)) = f_\delta(\overline{\delta}_i) \tag{2}$$

This interpretation makes statistical sense as the joint feature density is found by multiplying the conditional observation model $f_i(z \mid p) = f_p(p \mid \overline{\delta}_i)$ by the prior information $f_i(p) = f_\delta(\overline{\delta}_i)$, so that following Bayes-rule: $f_i(z, p) = f_i(z \mid p)f_i(p) = f_p(p \mid \overline{\delta}_i)f_\delta(\overline{\delta}_i) = f_\eta(\eta_i(p, \overline{\delta}_i))$. This interpretation is also intuitively appealing as it is the observations made by other sensors, communicated to the ith sensor, that provide the initial prior information.

The interpretation of the dependency model as a probability distribution allows us to expand $f_\delta(\cdot)$ as a series of conditional distributions describing the effect of each individual sensor on the ith sensors prior information. For example, if the numeric order of decision making is also the natural precedence then;

$$\begin{aligned} f_\delta(\overline{\delta}_i) = f_\delta^i(\delta_1, \cdots, \delta_n) &= f_\delta^i(\delta_1 \mid \delta_2, \cdots, \delta_n)f_\delta^i(\delta_2 \mid \delta_3, \cdots, \delta_n) \cdots f_\delta^i(\delta_n) \\ &= f(\eta_1^i(\delta_1) \mid \eta_1^\delta(\delta_2, \cdots, \delta_n)) \cdots f(\eta_n^i(\delta_n)) \end{aligned}$$

Each term $f_\delta^i(\delta_j \mid \delta_k) = f(\eta_j^i(\delta_j) \mid \eta_j^\delta(\delta_k))$ describes the information contributed by the jth sensor to the ith sensors prior information, given that the information provided by the kth sensor is already known. The transformation affected by $\eta_j^i(\delta_j)$ takes the jth sensor observation and interprets it in terms of observations made by the ith sensor; $\eta_j^i(\cdot) \in P_i$.

This decomposition by conditionals can, in general, be written in any appropriate order. If there is a natural precedence order in which sensors take observations, then an expansion in that order is appropriate. For example, if the decision δ_j only depends on information provided by the $(j-1)^{th}$ sensor, then the ith dependence model can be represented by;

$$f_\delta^i(\delta_1, \cdots, \delta_{i-1}) = f_\delta^i(\delta_{i-1} \mid \delta_{i-2}) \cdots f_\delta^i(\delta_2 \mid \delta_1)f_\delta^i(\delta_1) \tag{3}$$

describing a Markovian chain of decision makers as shown in Figure 1.

The use of conditional probability distributions in this way induces a *network* structure of relations between different sensors and cues. This network is a constraint exposing description of sensor capabilities: Each arc in the network describes a dependence between sensor observations, represented by a constraining transformation and implemented by the propagation of prior information between sensors.

To fix these ideas, consider the simple (non-recursive) example of a vision system (1), seeking to find planer surfaces, using a two-resolution edge detector (2,3) and a region-growing algorithm (4), described by $f_1^\delta(\delta_2, \delta_3, \delta_4) = f_1^\delta(\delta_4 \mid \delta_3)f_1^\delta(\delta_3 \mid \delta_2)f_1^\delta(\delta_2)$

The high resolution edge detector receives information from the lower resolution edge finder described by the information structure $f_1^\delta(\delta_2)$. In this case the lower resolution detector is just used to provide preliminary estimates for use by the fine edge detector; ie prior information. The region-grower uses the information provided by the fine edge detector to localize possible surfaces. The information structure $f_4^\delta(\delta_3, \delta_2)$ describes the transformation of edges in to surface representations, and $f_1^\delta(\delta_4 \mid \delta_3)$ describes

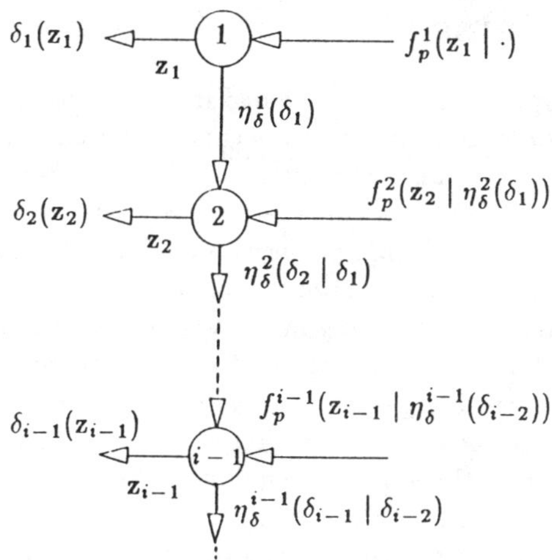

Figure 1: The Markovian team decision network

the observations provided by the region grower. The final result or estimate of surfaces can be found by combining the outputs from both the edge detectors $f_1^\delta(\delta_2, \delta_3)$ and the region-growing algorithm $f_1^\delta(\delta_4 \mid \delta_3)$.

2.4 State Models

We will describe the dependence of sensor observations on it's location and state by a state model η_i^x. This model acts as a "view-modifier" on the other sources of information supplied to the sensor; a function that transforms the prior information and observation model to the current viewpoint of the sensor. This is best interpreted as a probability distribution function $f_x(\mathbf{x}_i \mid \mathbf{p}_i, \overline{\delta}_i)$ which describes the posterior likelihood of feature observation in terms of a state vector $\mathbf{x}_i$, given the prior information provided by other sensors. This density function can be considered as a transformation that modifies the observed model $f_p(\mathbf{p}_i \mid \overline{\delta}_i)$ and the prior information provided by other sensors $f_\delta(\overline{\delta}_i)$ to account for sensor state. The transformation is just a product of distribution functions:

$$f_i(\mathbf{z}_i) = f_x(\mathbf{x}_i \mid \mathbf{p}_i, \overline{\delta}_i) \cdot \left[f_p(\mathbf{p}_i \mid \overline{\delta}_i) f_\delta(\overline{\delta}_i) \right] \tag{4}$$

There are two related parts to this description of a state model; the dependency of observation uncertainty on sensor state, and the transformation of prior world information to the current sensor location to determine if a feature is in view. Both of these considerations involve a process of transforming feature descriptions between coordinate systems.

Consider a mobile sensor located arbitrarily in space by the vector $\mathbf{x} = [x, y, z, \phi, \theta, \psi]^T$, observing a given feature $\mathbf{g}(\mathbf{x}, \mathbf{p}) = 0$ parameterized by the vector $\mathbf{p}$. Suppose that the observations made by this sensor when in a fixed location can be described by a Gaussian distribution $\mathbf{z}_i \sim N(\hat{\mathbf{p}}, \Lambda_p)$. This is our observation model. When a Gaussian feature is transformed between coordinate systems as $\mathbf{p}_j = {}^j\mathbf{h}_i(\mathbf{p}_i)$, the mean vector follows the usual laws of geometry, $\hat{\mathbf{p}}_j = {}^j\mathbf{h}_i(\hat{\mathbf{p}}_i)$ and with ${}^j\mathbf{J}_i = \frac{\partial {}^j\mathbf{h}_i}{\partial \mathbf{p}_i}$, the variance matrix is transformed by ${}^j\Lambda_p = {}^j\mathbf{J}_i(\mathbf{x}){}^i\Lambda_p{}^j\mathbf{J}_i^T(\mathbf{x})$ This transform can be interpreted as a change in sensor location resulting in a change in feature observation. In this case, the observation model will be state dependent; $\mathbf{z}_i \sim N({}^j\mathbf{h}_i(\hat{\mathbf{p}}_i), \mathbf{J}\Lambda_p\mathbf{J}^T) \sim N(\hat{\mathbf{p}}_j, \Lambda_p(\mathbf{x}))$, describing how the uncertainty and perspective in feature observation are affected by the location of the sensor. Now suppose that we have some prior information about a feature to be observed, either from a prior world model or from observations made by other sensors, described again as $\mathbf{g}(\mathbf{x}, \mathbf{p}) = 0$, with $\mathbf{p} \sim N(\hat{\mathbf{p}}, \Lambda_p)$. Neglecting the possibility of occlusion[1], this information can be transformed into the coordinate system of the sensor through the relation $\mathbf{p}' = \mathbf{h}(\mathbf{p})$. This transformation is described by the state model $f_x(\mathbf{x} \mid \cdot)$ and implemented by the equations relating the mean and variance in different coordinate systems. This allows us to describe the prior information available to a sensor in terms of the features it may actually view.

---

[1] The problem of occlusion can be accounted for using standard computer graphics techniques for deciding if a surface is in view from a particular location.

3   Multi-Sensor Systems

We will describe a multi-sensor system as a *team* of decision makers. Each sensor of this team will be considered as an individual decision maker; taking observations, making local decisions and implementing it's own actions. Together, the sensors must coordinate their activities, guide each other to view areas of interest, and ultimately come to some team-consensus view of the environment. The characteristics of a team structure capture many of the desirable properties of a multi-sensor system: Team members can make local decisions based on a team goal, providing a means of delegating observation tasks and actions. Team members can help each other by exchanging information unattainable to individual members, thus providing the team with a more complete description of events. Team members can disagree with each other as to what is being observed; resolving differences of opinion can supply a mechanism for validating each others operation. The most important observation about a team is that the coordinated activities of the members is more effective than the sum of their individual actions.

We are primarily interested in teams of observers; sensors making observations of the state of the environment. In this case individual team members can be considered as Bayesian estimators. The team decision is to come to a consensus view of the observed state of nature. The static team of estimators is often called a Multi-Bayesian system [9]. A multi-Bayesian team works by considering the likelihood function $f_i(\cdot \mid \mathbf{p})$ of each team member as the (normalized) utility of individual observers. Then the team utility is considered to be the joint posterior distribution function $F(\mathbf{p} \mid \mathbf{z}_1, \cdots, \mathbf{z}_n)$ after each sensor i has made the observation $\mathbf{z}_i$.

3.1   Multi-Bayesian Systems

Before developing the general multi-Bayesian system, it is helpful to study the simpler case of two scaler homogeneous observers. Consider two team members, each observing the same scalar variable $p \in P$ (feature in the environment), with observation density $f_i(\cdot \mid p)$, $i = 1, 2$. Suppose each observer takes a single observation z_i, considered independent and derived from a Gaussian distribution with mean $\hat{p}$ and variance σ_i^2. The goal of this team is to come to some consensus estimate of state $\overline{p} \in P$, based on the two observations z_1 and z_2. In the multi-Bayesian system, each team members individual utility function is given by the posterior likelihood; $f(p \mid z_i) \sim N(\hat{p}, \sigma_i^2)$. The team utility function is given by the joint posterior likelihood; $F(p \mid z_1, z_2) = f_1(p \mid z_1) f_2(p \mid z_2)$. A team member will be considered *individually* rational if it chooses the estimate $\overline{p} \in P$ which maximizes it's local posterior density;

$$\overline{p} = \arg \max_{p \in P} f_i(p \mid z_i) \qquad i = 1, 2. \tag{5}$$

The team itself will be considered group-rational if together the team members choose the estimate $\overline{p} \in P$ which maximizes the joint posterior density;

$$\overline{p} = \arg \max_{p \in P} F(p \mid z_1, z_2) = \arg \max_{p \in P} f_1(p \mid z_1) f_2(p \mid z_2) \tag{6}$$

In the first case, described by Equation 5, the estimate will just be the unique mode of the (Gaussian) posterior likelihood function; exactly as for an unbiased Bayes estimator. However, in the second case, described by Equation 6, two possible results can be obtained; either $F(p \mid z_1, z_2)$ has a unique mode and satisfies

$$\max_{p \in P} F(p \mid z_1, z_2) \geq \max_{p \in P} f_i(p \mid z_i); \qquad i = 1, 2, \tag{7}$$

or $F(p \mid z_1, z_2)$ is bimodal, the inequality in Equation 7 will be reversed, and no unique group-rational consensus estimate will exist.

We will consider our two-member team to be antagonistic in the following sense: Each team member can either agree with a team estimate $\overline{p}_t$ and be subject to the team utility $F(\mathbf{p} = \overline{p}_t \mid z_i, \cdot)$, or choose it's own estimate $\overline{p}_i$ and be subject to an individual utility $f_i(\mathbf{p} = \overline{p}_t \mid z_i)$. A rational team member will maximizes utility by choosing to either agree or disagree with the team consensus: If a team members observation does not satisfies Equation 7, then it will not cooperate with the team estimate.

Whether or not the individual team members will arrive at a consensus team estimate will depend on some measure of how much they disagree $|z_1 - z_2|$. If z_1 and z_2 are "close enough" then the posterior

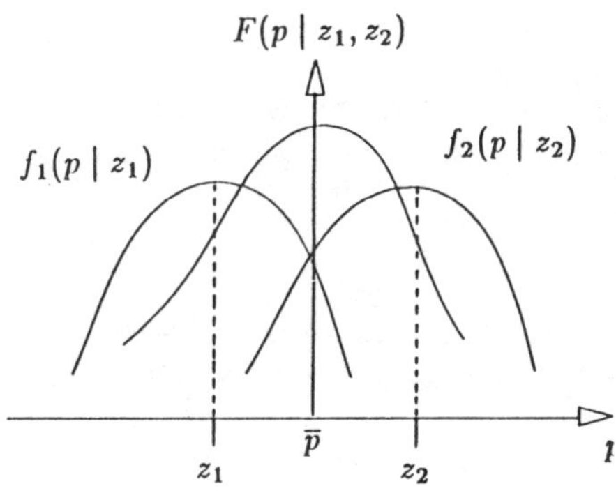

Figure 2: Two Bayesian observers with joint posterior likelihood indicating agreement.

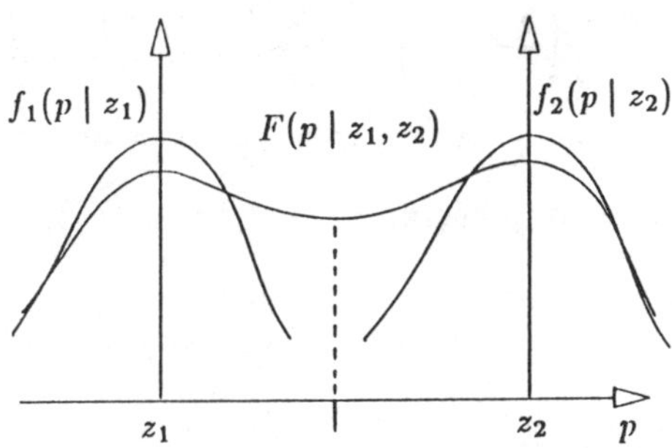

Figure 3: Two Bayesian observers with joint posterior likelihood indicating disagreement.

density $F(p \mid z_1, z_2)$ will be unimodal and satisfy Equation 7, with the consensus estimate given by Equation 6 (Figure 2). As $|z_1 - z_2|$ increases, $F(p \mid z_1, z_2)$ becomes flatter and eventually bimodal (Figure 3). At this point, the joint density will not satisfy Equation 7, no consensus team decision will be reached, and the members individual estimates will satisfy Equation 5.

We will now generalize this two-Bayesian system to a team of n Bayesians all taking different observations of geometric features in the environment. As before, we will define the preference order on team decisions to be the joint posterior density function $F(\mathbf{p} \mid \cdot)$. If the sensors are considered to make independent observations, then this can be written as;

$$F(\mathbf{p} \mid \delta_1(\mathbf{z}_1), \cdots, \delta_n(\mathbf{z}_n)) = \prod_{i=1}^{n} f_i(\mathbf{p} \mid \delta_i(\mathbf{z}_i)) \qquad (8)$$

Following similar arguments to those of the two-Bayesian system, the observations $\mathbf{z}_i$ will only provide a consensus estimate for $\mathbf{p}$ if $F(\mathbf{p} \mid \cdot)$ is convex in all it's arguments. To determine convexity, we need only ensure that the Hessian of F is positive semi-definite. It can be shown [4] that a consensus value of $\mathbf{p}$ which satisfies this also satisfies

$$\left[\sum_{i=1}^{n} \mathbf{\Lambda}_i^{-1} (\mathbf{p} - \delta_i(\mathbf{z}_i)) \right]^T \left[\sum_{i=1}^{n} \mathbf{\Lambda}_i^{-1} \right]^{-1} \left[\sum_{i=1}^{n} \mathbf{\Lambda}_i^{-1} (\mathbf{p} - \delta_i(\mathbf{z}_i)) \right] \leq 1 \qquad (9)$$

If it exists, the consensus parameter estimate $\hat{\mathbf{p}}$ that maximizes Equation 8 and minimizes the left side

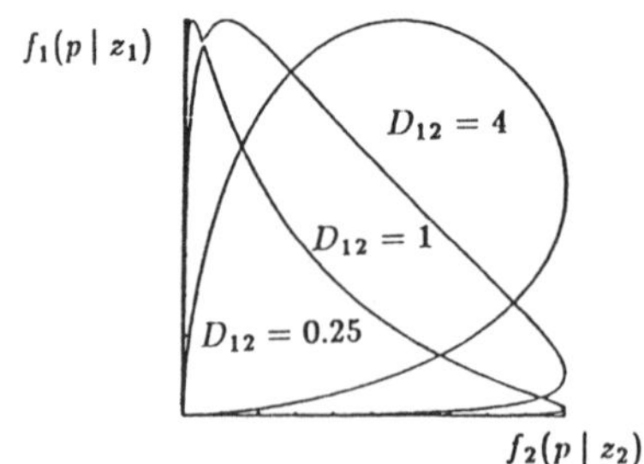

Figure 4: The space of preferences for a two-Bayesian team

of Equation 9, is given by the modified Kalman minimum-variance estimate;

$$\hat{p} = \left[\sum_{i=1}^{n} \mathbf{A}_i^{-1} \right]^{-1} \left[\sum_{i=1}^{n} \mathbf{A}_i^{-1} \delta_i(\mathbf{z}_i) \right] \tag{10}$$

It is useful to interpret Equation 9 in terms of the set of posterior density functions;

$$\mathbf{f}(\mathbf{p}) = [f_1(\mathbf{p} \mid \delta_1(\mathbf{z}_1)), \cdots, f_2(\mathbf{p} \mid \delta_1(\mathbf{z}_n))]^T$$

We will call this set $\mathbf{f}(\mathbf{p}) \subseteq \Re^n$ the opinion space of the n-sensor team. This is an n-dimensional space with basis axis corresponding to individual sensor preferences f_i,(Figure 4 is a two-sensor example of this space). The set $\mathbf{f}(\mathbf{p})$ describes an $n - 1$ dimensional surface in this space, parameterized by $\mathbf{p}$ and enclosing a volume $v(\mathbf{z}_1, \cdots, \mathbf{z}_n) \in \Re^n$. A consensus of *all* sensors requires that this volume be convex along each axis. The consensus value lies on the surface enclosing this volume. If $v \in \Re^n$ is concave along the jth axis then the jth sensor observation will be unable to agree with other sensor opinions; it's individual maximum likelihood estimate is preferred to the team decision. Thus if the volume v is concave in one or more directions f_i, then coalitions supporting different decisions will be formed.

3.2   Hypothesis Generation

The hypotheses $\{\mathbf{p}_i\}$ generated by each sensor from it's observations can be interpreted in terms of partial hypotheses $\{\mathbf{p}\}$ of some underlying global geometric environment description $\mathbf{g}(\mathbf{x}, \mathbf{p}) = 0$, $\mathbf{p} \in P$. The fact that individual sensor hypotheses $\mathbf{p}_i$ can only ever supply partial estimates of the global geometry $\mathbf{p}$, is a primary motivation for the use of many sources of sensory information. The partial hypotheses on global geometry provided by the sensors provides a means of comparing and combing different sensor views.

Consider a single sensor taking observations $\{\mathbf{z}_i\}$ of a particular type of feature in the environment $\mathbf{g}_i(\mathbf{x}, \mathbf{p}_i) = 0$. Each sensor observation is described through the observation model $f_i^p = f_i(\mathbf{z}_i \mid \mathbf{p}_i)$. The features described by $\{\mathbf{p}_i\}$ are considered to be related to some underlying global geometric description $\mathbf{g}(\mathbf{x}, \mathbf{p}) = 0$ through the transformation $\{\mathbf{p}_i\} = \mathbf{h}_i(\mathbf{p})$; $\mathbf{p}_i \in P_i$, $\mathbf{p} \in P$. This is a stochastic transformation of one type of geometry to another. The forward transformation $\mathbf{h}_i(\cdot)$ is usually well-defined, and if we have some prior information about $\mathbf{p}$, $\mathbf{h}_i$ can be used to obtain prior feature information. However, in general no prior information will be available. In this case we must use the inverse transform to generate hypotheses about the underlying geometry: $\mathbf{p} = \mathbf{h}_i^{-1}(\mathbf{p}_i)$. The inverse transform is usually indeterminant; a single estimate $\mathbf{p}_i$, insufficient to generate a complete hypotheses $\mathbf{p}$.

Consider now a multi-sensor system comprising n sensors $S_1, \cdots, S_n$, each taking a set of geometric observations $\{\mathbf{z}_i\}$ of geometric features $\{\mathbf{p}_i\}$ in the environment (Figure 5). From these observations, each sensor can make individual estimates $\delta_i(\mathbf{z}_i) \in P_i$ of possible features of a particular type, resulting in

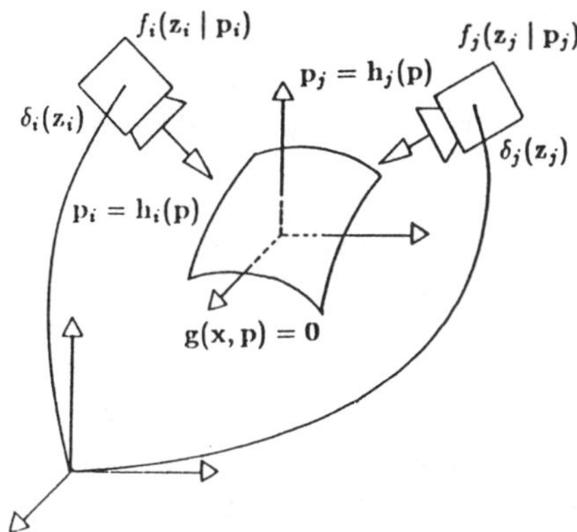

Figure 5: Two sensors observing different features of a common geometric object

a set of feature hypotheses; $\{p'_i\} = \{\delta_i(z_{i,1}), \cdots, \delta_i(z_{i,1})\} = \{p'_{i,1}, \cdots, p'_{i,1}\}$ We will consider the posterior distribution $f(p_i \mid z_i)$ as the preference order induced by the observations z_i on possible hypotheses p_i. With this identification, we can consider the estimates p'_i as modeled by a Gaussian $p'_{i,j} \sim N(p_{i,j}, \Lambda_{i,j})$. To transform these feature hypotheses on some underlying geometry, we need to apply the transformation $h^{-1}(\cdot)$ to the set $\{p'_i\}$. If the elements of this hypotheses set are considered Gaussian, we can approximate this transform by a transformation of mean and variance, so that for each $\delta_i(z_i)$, we have;

$$\hat{p}' = h_i^{-1}[p'_i] = h_i^{-1}[\delta(z_i)], \qquad \Lambda_p^{-1} = \left(\frac{\partial h_i^{-1}}{\partial p_i}\right) \Lambda_i^{-1} \left(\frac{\partial h_i^{-1}}{\partial p_i}\right)^T \tag{11}$$

Thus by transforming each feature hypothesis, we can obtain from each sensor S_i a set of hypotheses $\{p\}_i$ on the underlying environment geometry, each of which can be described by a mean and variance. The information matrix Λ_p^{-1} will be singular, no information in one or more degrees of freedom, because the transform $h_i^{-1}(\cdot)$ is indeterminant. This provides for the feature hypotheses p'_i to generate only partial estimates of the underlying geometry.

We now have a means of generating partial hypotheses of the environment geometry, regardless of the existence of prior information, in a language common to all sensors. It remains now to compare verify and combine these partial estimates to provide a complete description of the underlying environment geometry. We will formulate this problem in terms of a multi-Bayesian team, verifying individual sensor hypotheses by comparing their contribution to some global environment description.

Consider the preference placed on environment descriptions p by each sensors partial estimates p' as the posterior density; $f_i(p \mid p') = f_i(p \mid h_i^{-1}[\delta_i(z_i)])$, $i = 1, \cdots, n$. This preference ordering represents an *individual* sensors preferred contribution to a team consensus. We will define the *team* preference ordering as the joint posterior density on all contributions;

$$F(p \mid h_1^{-1}[\delta_1(z_1)], \cdots, h_n^{-1}[\delta_n(z_n)]) = \prod_{i=1}^{n} f_i(p \mid h_i^{-1}[\delta_i(z_i)]) \tag{12}$$

We will seek consensus values of p which make $F(p \mid \cdot)$ convex. The hypotheses generated from different sensor observations will be associated with many different values of p. Rather than comparing all of these hypotheses in one opinion pool, it makes sense to compare different estimates pair-wise, recursively clustering hypotheses into groups, one associated with each value of p.

From Equation 9, the pair-wise comparison of two hypotheses $h_i^{-1}[\delta_i(z_i)]$ and $h_j^{-1}[\delta_j(z_j)]$, requires that we can find a consensus hypotheses p which satisfies;

$$\bar{p} = \left[\Lambda_i^{-1} + \Lambda_j^{-1}\right]^{-1} \left[\Lambda_i^{-1} h_i^{-1}[\delta_i(z_i)] + \Lambda_j^{-1} h_j^{-1}[\delta_j(z_j)]\right] \tag{13}$$

Thus for two sensors to agree on a hypothesis, there interpretations must satisfy:

$$\left(\mathbf{h}_i^{-1}[\delta_i(\mathbf{z}_i)] - \mathbf{h}_j^{-1}[\delta_j(\mathbf{z}_j)]\right)\left(\Lambda_i + \Lambda_j\right)^{-1}\left(\mathbf{h}_i^{-1}[\delta_i(\mathbf{z}_i)] - \mathbf{h}_j^{-1}[\delta_j(\mathbf{z}_j)]\right)^T \leq 1 \tag{14}$$

Note that the transformation of observations is often only partial, so that the sensor may have invariant (or indifferent) opinion preference to certain degrees of freedom of the team hypothesis.

3.3 Sensor Control

The state of the sensor $\mathbf{x}$, describing the location $\mathbf{T}_s(\mathbf{x})$, modifies the observation model as; $\mathbf{z}_i \sim N\left(\mathbf{h}(\mathbf{p},\mathbf{x}), \mathbf{J}_s(\mathbf{x})\Lambda_z\mathbf{J}_s^T(\mathbf{x})\right)$ This describes the dependence of feature observation on sensor state as a transformation of geometry $\mathbf{h}(\mathbf{p},\mathbf{x})$ and variance $\mathbf{J}_s(\mathbf{x})\Lambda_z\mathbf{J}_s^T(\mathbf{x})$. Using the triangular constraint relation between base coordinates, sensor location and feature description, the modified variance in estimated object location Λ_p, can be found in terms of the observation variance Λ_z and sensor location variance Λ_s as $\Lambda_p = \Lambda_s(\mathbf{x}) + \mathbf{J}_s(\mathbf{x})\Lambda_z\mathbf{J}_s^T(\mathbf{x})$ To gain the maximum information from an observation, we must find the sensor location $\mathbf{T}_s(\mathbf{x})$ that will minimize the elements of Λ_p (in some sense), subject to the constraints on feasible viewpoints. We make the simplifying assumption that the sensor can be located with constant variance Λ_s and that it takes observations with variance proportional to its absolute distance $|\mathbf{p}_z|$ from the object of interest: $\Lambda_z = \Lambda|\mathbf{p}_z|$. In this case any minimization of Λ_p is dependent only on $\mathbf{J}_s\Lambda_z\mathbf{J}_s^T|\mathbf{p}_z|$. If we intend to use a sensor that provides only partial information (a mobile ultrasonic ranger for example), then the minimization of variance should be considered as the maximization of the information equation:

$$\Sigma' = \mathbf{J}_s^{-T}\Sigma_z\mathbf{J}_s^{-1} \quad , \qquad \Sigma = \Lambda^{-1} \tag{15}$$

Maximization of a matrix quantity is not strictly defined. Generaly, a sensor strategy will attempt to maximize some weighted sum of the elements of Σ'. If our sensor takes only partial observations, then we may wish to take a sequence of observations that successively maximize specific elements, localizing and resolving information in each degree of freedom independently. If however our sensor can obtain relatively dense information, maximizing the trace elements may be more appropriate.

References

1. J.O. Berger, "Statistical Decisions", (second edition), 1985, Springer Verlag.

2. H.F. Durrant-Whyte, "Uncertain Geometry in Robotics", Proc. IEEE Int. Conf. Robotics and Automation, 1986, p1464., To appear IEEE J. Robotics and Automation, 1987.

3. H.F. Durrant-Whyte "Consistent Integration and Propagation of Disparate Sensor Observations", Int. Journal of Robotics Research", Vol 6, no 3, 1987.

4. H.F. Durrant-Whyte, "Integration, Coordination, and Control of Multi-Sensor Robot Systems", Kluwer Academic Publishers, Boston, 1987.

5. T.C. Henderson, et.al, "Workshop on Multisensor Integration" University of Utah Tech. Report UUCS-87-006.

6. Y.C. Ho, K.C. Chu, "Team Decision Theory and Information Structures in Optimal Control", IEEE Trans. Automatic Control, 1972, vol 17, p15.

7. P.J. Huber, "Robust Statistics", John Wiley, 1981.

8. J. Marshak, R. Radnor, "The Economic Theory of Teams", 1972, Yale University Press.

9. S. Weerahandi, J.V. Zidek, "Elements of Multi-Baysian Decision Theory", The Annals of Statistics, vol 11, p1032, 1983.

Searching for Information

Greg Hager and Max Mintz
Department of Computer and Information Science
University of Pennsylvania
Philadelphia, PA 19104-6389

Abstract

We consider the problem of constructing an intelligent, active sensor. Such a sensor is able to choose the number and placement of views needed to gather requested information while contending with noise processes, quantization and limitations of sensor scope. We outline an organization for an intelligent sensing system based on a statistical sensor model. A data structure similar to Koenderink and van Doorn's aspect graphs is developed as a local representation for information about the environment. Using ideas from decision theory, we formalize the tradeoff between the value of information and the cost of information.

We then state the basic expression for the optimal sensing strategy. This equation is generally not solvable in closed form. We simplify the problem by decoupling the choice of sample size from the choice of viewpoint. This allows the computation of the information value of various viewpoints with regard to the task at hand. We then show how game-theoretic techniques can be used to solve the problem of choosing a set of sensor views to maximize the information content of a sensor estimate. We discuss extensions of this work to multiple sensors, and the problem of intelligent search for information.

1   Introduction and Overview

This paper addresses the problem of sensor utilization and coordination in the context of robotic systems. Robotic systems are task-oriented, goal-driven systems which direct sensors to gain the information needed to accomplish grasping, movement, and manipulation tasks. They require more of sensors than the ability to recognize objects; they need information such as size, position and orientation. Often this information is required to be within certain tolerances and to be supplied within strict time limits. Sensors must be flexible and intelligent to adapt to these changing information needs.

We feel that there are two aspects to designing a robotic system: selecting an architecture or organization of components, *and* prescribing the behavior of those components. In [4], we have described an experimental system architecture similar to that found in [13] (left half of Figure 1). In this architecture, the world model is a dynamically maintained representation of the robot's environment. The integrator is responsible for combining new sensor information with prior information so as to maintain a consistent world model. The supervisor is responsible for using the information present in the world model to drive the system toward its current goal.

We are focusing on system goals which are states of information – that is, the supervisor is deploying the system to achieve a certain level of knowledge about the environment. In order to achieve this goal, it must contend with the three basic sources of uncertainty in sensor data: statistical uncertainty due to random noise processes in the sensing device, non-statistical uncertainties modeling quantization or mechanical backlash, and incompleteness or underdeterminedness due to limited sensor scope. This requires the ability to combine observations across sensors, space and time into a single statement about the world – the *sensor fusion* problem.

A significant amount of the intelligence necessary for refining information can be embedded into the sensor itself. The right half of Figure 1 shows the basic components of an intelligent sensor. Data from the sensor is processed, then sent to an estimation procedure which fuses it into a consistent estimate based on models of the sensor noise characteristics. Sensor control software is responsible for choosing sensor views and adjusting sensor and processing parameters. In order to facilitate this process, a copy of the local world model is kept in the sensor. The purpose of this local copy is to represent the information in the global world model in a manner useful to this particular sensor. The projector is responsible for transforming information from the global model into the local representation.

In a previous paper [7], we discussed the problem of sensor estimation. In this paper, we will present and discuss our methods for solving the sensor utilization problem. In brief, our approach is based on modeling sensors as noisy information sources. Extraction and fusion of sensor information is a problem in estimation theory [1]. The control of a noisy information source for the best performance of an estimation procedure will be considered as a problem in experimental design [1,2].

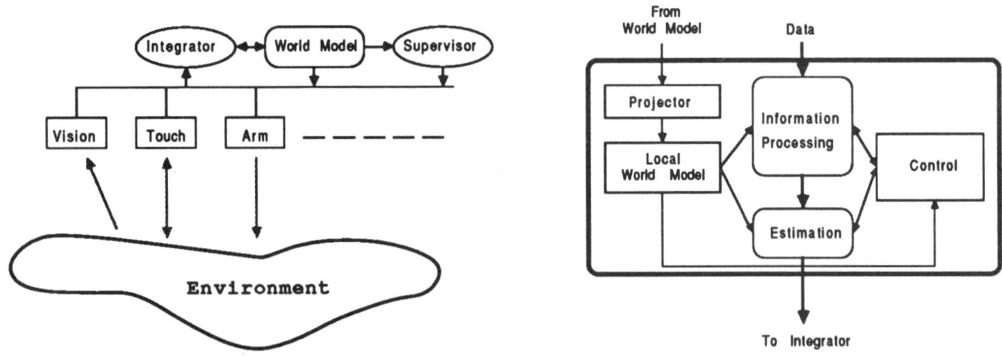

Figure 1: On the left, a robotic system with several sensing/manipulation components, an integrator which adds information to the world model, and a supervisor which manages the system. On the right is an intelligent sensor with a local world model, processing software, an estimation procedure, and control software.

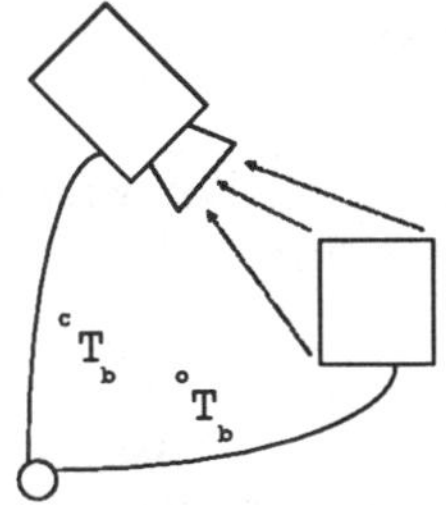

Figure 2: A camera is used to determine the position and orientation of a polygonal object.

2 Problem Formulation

We will address the utilization problem from a formal point of view using decision-theoretic techniques. Decision theory allows us to weigh the *value* of information against the *costs* of getting that information. In our formulation, we will allow the system using the sensor to specify the value of the information, and build procedures which allow the sensor to decide how much work to put into gathering that information, and how to distribute that work over time and space.

2.1 Sensor Models

A sensor takes observations of the environment as described by some transformation contaminated by noise. Both the transfer function and the observation noise can be influenced by control parameters. Thus, we can formalize a controllable measurement device subject to additive noise as a mathematical system of the following general form:

$$z_i = H(u_i, p) + V(u_i, p) \tag{1}$$

where H is k-dimensional, u_i is an m-dimensional control vector from a set $\mathcal{U}$, and $p \in \mathcal{P}$ is the s-dimensional quantity we are attempting to estimate. We observe z_i, a function of both u_i and p contaminated by additive noise $V(\cdot, \cdot)$ of dimension k. In general, the distribution of V will be a function of our control vector and the parameter of interest. Our problem is to optimize, by choice of some sequence $\underline{u} = [u_1, u_2, \ldots, u_n] \in \mathcal{U}^n$, the performance of an estimation procedure $\delta_n(\cdot)$ estimating p from $\underline{z} = [z_1, z_2, \ldots, z_n]$.

For example, consider estimating the position of an object using a stereo camera as illustrated in Figure 2. For ease of exposition, we will only consider the 2-D case using orthogonal projection. In this case, the sensor can by modeled by the combined transformation from object coordinates to camera coordinates.

$$^c T_o(p, u) = {}^c T_b(u) {}^o T_b(p)^{-1} \tag{2}$$

Let $^o f_i = {}^o [x_i, y_i, 0, 1]^T$ denote a homogeneous feature position in object coordinates, and let $^c z_i = {}^c [x_i, y_i, 0, 1]^T$ represent an observation of f_i in camera coordinates. The vector p we are estimating is $p = [x_o, y_o, \alpha_o]^T$ of an object. Our control vector, $u = [x_c, y_c, \alpha_c]$, corresponds to the choice of camera position. The utilization problem is essentially a choice of how to move the camera about the object (which lies within some region of uncertainty) so as to achieve the best final estimate of position.

2.2 The Cost of Information

A sensing strategy is to be evaluated relative to its expected utility. This utility can be thought of in two parts: the performance of the estimation procedure for that choice of strategy, and the cost of implementing that strategy. This can be expressed as

$$l(p, \hat{p}, n, \underline{u}) = l^d(p, \hat{p}) + c(n, \underline{u}) \tag{3}$$

where l^d represents the loss attributed to the estimation procedure δ, and c represents the cost of taking n samples via the sensor strategy $\underline{u}$.

In earlier reports [3,4,5,6], we discuss how interaction with a sensor can be handled using four element requests within a message-based framework. The first element is some indication of the type of information to seek and initial bounds on the parameters. The desired quality of this information is expressed by a tolerance, ϵ. A better estimate can always be gained by using more samples, but at a higher cost. A priority, w, encodes a time/accuracy tradeoff for the requested information. Finally, a query will contain a hard time constraint, t, which should not be violated. The choice of an uncertainty region, ϵ, suggests that an appropriate evaluation of the value of an estimate $\hat{p}$ is the *0-w loss*.*

$$l^d(p, \delta_n(\underline{z})) = \begin{cases} 0, & \text{if } \|\delta_n(\underline{z}) - p\| < \epsilon; \\ w, & \text{otherwise} \end{cases} \tag{4}$$

By taking expectations of Equation 3, we can compute the *risk function* of an estimation procedure δ_n as

$$r(p, n, \underline{u}_n, \delta_n) = E_{\underline{z}_n|p,\underline{u}_n} \left[l^d(p, \delta_n(\underline{z}_n)) + c(n, \underline{u}_n) \right] = r^d(p, \delta_n) + c(n, \underline{u}_n) \tag{5}$$

It is easy to show that, under a $0 - w$ loss, $r^d(p, \delta_n) = w P(\|\delta_n(\underline{z}) - p\| > \epsilon \,|\, p)$. In other words, the risk function associated with the procedure $\delta_n(\cdot)$ is the weighted probability of the estimated value falling outside the specified tolerance. In cases where we have a distribution on p we can take expectations of r^d and compute the *Bayes risk* of an estimate. In other cases, we will assume the p falls within a known set, and consider the minimax risk.

Once a sensor performs a sensing task, the results returned should indicate the degree to which the set task was found to be achievable. The *most* information a sensor could return would be the posterior distribution on the parameters. However, in general it may not be feasible to compute this distribution. Instead we shall return the risk of the estimate since it is usually simple to compute, and it indicates the value of the returned information. In summary, a sensor request consists of a triple $\langle \epsilon, t, w \rangle$, and sensor results take the form of a pair $\langle \hat{p}, P(\|\hat{p} - p\| > \epsilon \,|\, \underline{z}) \rangle$.

2.3   Prior Knowledge About the World

Just as solving the statistical signal-processing problem requires prior models of the sensor, solving the limited aspect problem depends on having prior knowledge about the sensor environment. In general there are certain regularities that can be exploited to choose a new viewpoint. For example, in a polygonal world sensing an edge indicates the presence of vertices somewhere along that edge. If vertices are "good" points, then a reasonable strategy is to follow the edge till it leads to a vertex.

In this paper, we will assume that we are looking at a known object, and we are attempting to discern some information about that object (*e.g.* position). In this case, we can compute a "map" of vantage points from which specific sensor cues are visible. This is, in essence, the same notion as Koenderink and van Doorn's *aspect graphs* [9]. Aspect graphs encode the relationship between various characteristic views of an object. Formally, they can be thought of as a mapping, $f(o, p, u)$, which, given an object o, a spatial position p, and a viewpoint u, returns the set of features visible from that vantage.

Our representation differs from aspect graphs in that we need geometric information about the spatial extent of the area from which a feature is visible. Kender and Freudenstein discuss the derivation and use of a such a representation from the viewpoint of object recognition [8], and note that this structure would be useful for selecting sensor views. They also review several existing techniques for representing the spatial extent of aspect graphs. In our implementation, we use a finite element technique to find regions, and a simple representation of space using four extreme points of a region.

---

*It is important to realize that δ_n may have been *derived* from very different criteria, *i.e.*, the mean square error criterion. Now, *given* δ_n, we are evaluating it relative to the 0-w loss.

3   Solving the Utilization Problem

The statistical sensor model requires that we have an estimation procedure for a (possibly non-linear) measurement system which also supplies the risk associated with its estimate. In a previous paper [7], we discussed the derivation and evaluation of three estimation procedures for nonlinear measurement systems. We found that quasi-linearization techniques such as the extended Kalman filter do not always have a reliable performance or risk calculations. However, we were able to show that appropriate modifications to this technique have acceptable performance, and we developed other approximation techniques which also work as reliable estimators with calculable risk.

Our next question is whether the performance of an estimation procedure is substantially influenced by the choice of sensing strategy; and if so, how to efficiently pick a strategy. To answer, we will consider techniques studied in the field of experimental design [1,2,15].

3.1   Experimental Design

Experiment design is concerned with the problem of maximizing the information gained from an experiment under cost constraints. This essentially involves two decisions: the choice of the number of observations, and the choice of experimental parameters. The former deals with choosing *a priori* the number of observations to take (referred to as the *batch size*), or deriving a criterion (referred to as a *stopping rule*) to judge when sufficient data has been taken. Batch rules are mathematically easier to derive, but can often take more or fewer observations than optimal. Conversely, sequential rules, while mathematically more complicated, can be much more efficient in practice.

Optimizing experimental parameters has been studied extensively in the context of linear regression under Gaussian noise [2]. Several different criterion, including the determinant, trace, and maximum eigenvalues of the variance-covariance matrix, have been documented [15]. Within the control literature, Müller and Weber [12] consider the problem of finding the measurement system design maximizing a suitable norm of the observability or controllability of a system linear in both state and control. The norms they discuss are the trace, determinant, an maximum eigenvalue of the observability matrix. Mehra [11] combines and extends these results to include time-varying systems and randomized designs.

Let s represent the cost of taking one sample, let e represent the cost of computing an estimate and selecting a control sequence, and suppose that the cost of changing from control u_i to u_{i+1} is t_{i+1}. Furthermore, let $\pi_i \in \Pi$ indicate the information known about p at stage i. For example, in a Bayesian setting, Π could be a set of priors on $\mathcal{P}$. Alternatively, Π could be a set of pairs consisting of a member of $2^{\mathcal{P}}$ and the probability of the true parameter falling in that set. Presumably, intermediate decisions using δ update prior information and allow better selection of strategy. Let μ represent this updating transformation. We can now define the risk J of a plan for sensor utilization:

$$J(p,\underline{u}_n,\pi_i,n) = \min_n\{\min_{u_n}[J(p,\underline{u}_{n+1},\pi_i,n+1)] + s + t_{i+1}, E\left[J(p,\underline{u}_n,\mu(\delta(\underline{z}_n)),n)\right] + e, r^d(p,\delta_n)\} \quad (6)$$

where the expectation is taken with respect to the distribution of z conditioned on p and $\underline{u}_n$. This recurrence expresses the fact that the measurement system can take another observation from another viewpoint, update the prior information about the parameters based on observations, or stop sampling and return a final decision. Quite often, updating is done at every step so that the second term of the minimization disappears. The problem then reduces to finding the optimal set of control points from which to sample. Even this minimization is often intractable since it must be carried out over an unbounded sequence. A significant amount of theoretical work in experimental design has been devoted to the study of finite horizon approximations to this expression.

In the cited Linear-Quadratic-Gaussian problems (in which the noise is independent of u and p), there is no need of intermediate decisions as the choice of strategy and sample size is independent of p. In this case, closed form solutions often exist and can be computed offline before the task is even begun. However, in general solutions become too complex to calculate or implement in realtime. Since they often depend on p, selecting a new viewpoint will have to be done online – concurrent with estimation. Rather than attempt to directly derive and implement a solution, we will consider how to decouple the problem and efficiently pick viewpoints.

3.2 Decoupling Batch Size and View Selection

We do not have an infinite horizon problem – the sensor request supplies a finite time bound. Since the time to take and process a sample is known, the time bound can be thought of as fixing the maximum possible number of observations. Consequently, we can in effect think of minimizing risk over a limited number of samples. Also, the complexity of the problem grows quickly with the number of control points. The form of Equation 6 is such that we must choose a viewpoint for every sample. Since the time to plan and change sensor configurations is, in robotics applications, typically substantially longer than the time to take new samples, it makes sense to "decouple" the choice of view from the choice of sample size. The system should spend its time taking data, not deciding where to go for another another view.

Therefore, instead of choosing a viewpoint for each sample, we note that, for the current viewing position, call it u_0, there is an optimal number of samples, n^* which minimizes the Bayes risk of the estimate based on that view. That is,

$$n^* = \arg \min_n E_p \, r(p, n, \underline{u_0}, \delta_n) \quad n \le \frac{t}{s} \tag{7}$$

This number also fixes a time boundary – after those samples have been taken, if no better (in terms of risk) viewpoint has been found, an estimate will be returned. Note that, in the case of backlash or quantization, there is presumably no advantage to taking more than one estimate. In this case, the time bound becomes the time to process an observation.

Using the time-cost per sample, s, we can discount the time for the current batch from the maximum allotted time, t. That is, $t_l = t - n^* s$ is the time remaining after sampling from this view. The new time limit yields a bound on how far the sensor can travel and thereby restricts the region of space from which a new view could be taken. Also, if the time required to reach a point p in space is t_p , we know what the maximum number of samples that could be taken from that point is given by $n_p = (t_l - t_p)/s$.

Finally, rather than consider each point in space singly, we group them according to the regions in the aspect graph and use a pessimistic estimate of the time to reach that region of space. By this method, we have a conservative estimate of the maximum number of samples that could be taken from that region. We now consider minimizing the Bayes risk over the number of samples taken in the new region. If u_p is the view under consideration, we have

$$\min_n E_p \, r(p, n, \underline{u_n}, \delta_n) \quad n^* \le n \le n_p \tag{8}$$

where $u_i = u_0$ if $i \le n^*$ and $u_i = u_p$ otherwise. If the minima occurs at an n larger than n^*, there is an expected gain from moving to this region, and we label the region with the computed minimum risk. By considering all accessible regions, we have labeled each region of the aspect graph with a number representing its information content given the current state of affairs.

3.3 Evaluating Views

How should the sensor decide whether to move and where to go? If we have strong distributional information about the parameter, it makes sense to use a Bayesian approach – choose the view which maximizes expected information. We have argued that knowing the exact form of the distribution is infeasible in general, so we will instead assume that the parameter of interest falls within a known set and that we have a "map" of the information values associated with regions of space accessible by the sensor. These values may come from risk evaluations as we have outlined in the previous section, or could be any other measure of the value of information, $e.g.$ the area of an uncertainty set.

As a first approximation, the most conservative approach to the problem would be to look at the maximum possible risk associated with a point in space, and choose the point with the minimum risk. However, this

Figure 3: Two two-dimensional games. Each square represents a region of space, and the number represents its associated risk.

approach disregards a number of geometrical constraints. For instance, consider the two situations depicted in Figure 3. Where should the sensor move in each case, and which scenario is better if we know little or nothing (distributionally) about the parameter? For instance, if the latitude in $\theta = [\theta_1, \theta_2]$ is large enough, then any choice of u will lead to a possibility of incurring a large penalty. If the uncertainty set of θ is slightly larger then one of the square regions, then note that, in the left game, the value of both the lower middle square and the right middle square have a worst case risk of 5, though the right middle square is clearly a better choice. By varying the geometry of the regions, we can come up with even more drastic examples demonstrating that this simplistic approach is not very discriminating and often too conservative.

Here, we will make no distributional assumptions about the parameter and demonstrate that a direct game-theoretic (minimax) approach yields a more reasonable solution.[†] For reasonable uncertainty in θ, we can illustrate optimal minimax solutions to this navigation problem. Since we do not by any means have a complete solution, we shall proceed informally and omit any proofs of optimality.

Consider a scalar game defined as:

Game 1

$$K(x) = \begin{cases} 0, & |x| < 1; \\ c_1, & x \le -1; \\ c_2, & x \ge 1 \end{cases}$$

We will consider $K(u + \theta)$ with $u \in [-1, 1]$ $\theta \in [-d, d]$.

First, we note that if $c_1 < 0 < c_2$, then the obvious strategy is $u = -1$ and $\theta = d$. Given this, a few comments on generality are in order. First, if $c_1 < 0$ and $c_2 < 0$, then we can consider the dual game in which u is the maximizer, θ is the minimizer, and the kernel is multiplied by -1. Thus, both c_1 and c_2 may be taken to be positive. Second, since kernels are invariant with respect to affine transformations, we can always consider the game rooted at the origin, the value of c_1 to be 1, and the width of the 0 portion of the kernel to be 2. Finally, we need only consider the case in which $c_2 > c_1$ since the game is symmetric about the origin. To be completely general, u should take on values in a parameterized set, but this complicates the case analysis, and does not substantially affect the basic solution.

In reality, we generally cannot guarantee a specific choice of u. More realistically, u represents an element of an associated tolerance set. For example, we can consider the choice of u to determine the distribution of a random variable $u' \sim U(u - \epsilon, u + \epsilon)$. This changes the kernel to one of the form:

[†]The method outlined above has provably higher risk than minimax, with equality in certain cases.

Game 2

$$K^*(x) = \begin{cases} 1, & x < -1-\epsilon; \\ \frac{1}{2\epsilon}(|x|-1+\epsilon), & -1-\epsilon < x < -1+\epsilon; \\ 0, & |x| < 1-\epsilon; \\ \frac{c}{2\epsilon}(x-1+\epsilon), & 1-\epsilon < x < 1+\epsilon; \\ c, & x > 1+\epsilon \end{cases}$$

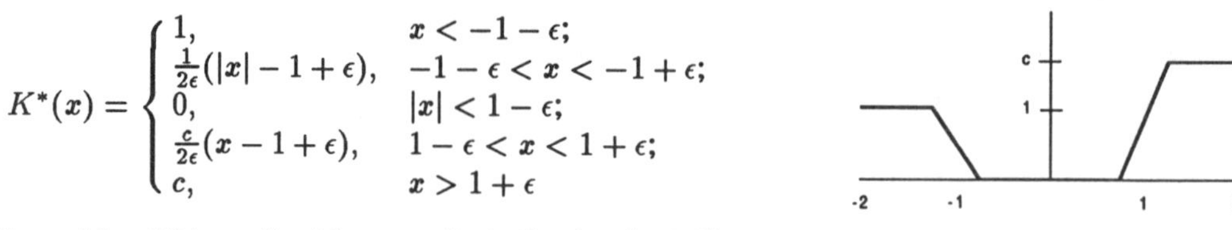

We will consider $K^*(u+\theta)$ with $u \in [-1,1]$ $\theta \in [-d,d]$ $c \geq 1$.

Initially, if it is known that $d < 1 - \epsilon$, then the optimal strategy is clearly $u = 0$. Of course, the payoff is also 0. Once d exceeds this bound, there is a possibility of incurring the loss assigned to one of the tails or the kernel. Since we have no distributional information, the worst case distribution is one in which θ only takes the values $\pm d$. The optimal strategy from $d = 1 - \epsilon$ to $d = 2 - \epsilon$ is to choose $u = -(d-1+\epsilon)$ for $c/c+1$ of the trials, and $u = (d-1+\epsilon)$ for the remaining trials. This has the effect of guaranteeing that either $K^*(u+d)$ or $K^*(u-d)$ is 0. From $2 - \epsilon$ to $1 + \frac{2\epsilon}{c} - \epsilon$, u has no way of avoiding the tails and goes between 1 and -1. As d increases further, the probability of u going to -1 increases until finally it stays at -1 continuously.

The solution to the scalar problem gives us sufficient power to address the two-dimensional problems presented above. In the first problem, note that each row reduces to the same game after scaling and translating. Hence, each row has the same solution. Given this solution, we can calculate the payoff in each of the rows and use that as the specification of the game across the columns. Thus, the solution only requires the consideration of two independent scalar games. The solution to the second game is similar except that the symmetry is about the line $y = x$.

3.4   Using Partial Information

If we have strong prior knowledge about θ in terms of a distribution, we should certainly use that information in deriving a decision rule for sensor placement. The game-theoretic solution can be thought of as first deriving a *worst-case* distribution over the parameters, and then optimizing the decision (minimizing Bayes risk) relative to this worst case situation. In the example above, if θ is characterized by a distribution exhibiting reasonably low second moments, then the choice of u will tend to stay close to the estimate of θ. The game-theoretic solution will be sub-optimal in this case, since it assumes a distribution on θ which places mass at the endpoints.

Since, in many cases, the exact distribution on θ will not be known analytically, a Bayesian solution to the utilization problem may require extensive numerical techniques. Conversely, the game-theoretic version, though conservative, appears to yield reasonably computational, closed-form solutions. These solutions would be enhanced if we could somehow make use of any statistical information about θ. In particular, our estimation procedures produce confidence intervals. These intervals can be thought of as constraints on the actual distribution of θ – namely that a certain amount of probability mass *must* be located within a given interval. As it turns out, we *can* use this information in a game-theoretic solution. The exact method of doing this is known as Γ-minimax decision theory [1, Chap. 4, Sec. 7.6]. This approach lies between game-theory and Bayesian decision-theory by in that it places constraints on what the worst case prior can look like. If nothing is known about the prior, Γ-minimax is equivalent to standard minimax. If the prior is known, it is equivalent to the Bayesian approach. We are currently investigating the use of Γ-minimax procedures in this problem.

4   Extensions and Discussion

4.1   Fusion and Coordination

It is often the case that two sensors working in concert would be more efficient than one. For example, consider the case of estimating distance and orientation using a laser ranging device and a tactile sensor. While it is certainly the case that both sensors, after taking enough observations, could determine both distance and orientation, we would expect that the laser scanner would be good at determining distance, and the tactile sensor would be good at getting surface orientations.

In general, we need to decide when and how a particular sensing task should be shared between sensing systems. When two more sensors are involved in a sensing task, there is the added factor of *communication cost*. For a sensor team to be completely aware of all data and actions taken, each observation and control adjustment would have to be broadcast to all other team members. In general this is not feasible, resulting in a partitioning of information within the system. Therefore, deciding when and how to distribute a sensor problem should be based on the degree of coupling needed among sensor systems. In a tightly coupled problem, the communication overhead and degradation of estimation and navigation due to the partitioning of information may outweigh the gains from multiple sensors.

We believe that we can measure the gains from distributing a sensing problem, and derive methods for carrying out the coordination of sensor systems using *team theory* as a formal framework [6,10]. Team theory extends decision theory to groups of decision-makers, and thereby allows the formal treatment of communication and coordination. The application of team theory will require some extensions to the estimation methods we are currently using. Since the decision-makers are working on a coupled problem, they each must be able to use the information the other produces. In essence, they must be able to estimate using the parameters they are observing, and use a Γ-minimax procedure based on the collaberating sensor's messages for the remaining parameters. If this is possible, the sensors can be modeled as separate information sources using independent local control and communicating partial estimates. We can then look at the expected risk of a combined estimate vs. the risk of independent estimates and make a decision as to whether one or both sensors should be applied to the problem.

4.2   Searching for Information

The information in the world model and general information about the environment is also to be applied at the task level. For example, knowledge of gravity dictates that, in locating a dropped object, the floor near where the object was lost is a good initial guess for its location. In essence, this is the same sort of process as in the intelligent sensor. Using current information, and prior information about the environment, the system should gather more information. This in turn allows a better choice of further strategies, and so on. This "bootstrapping" of information is the basis for any information gathering activity.

The difference between an intelligent sensor and a sensor coordinator is that intelligent action at the task level requires the *interpretation* of information at the proper level of abstraction so that other information about the behavior and structure of the world can be applied to constrain the search. This, in turn, postulates the existence of a data/rule/knowledge base of information, and techniques to apply this information to a task. What is an appropriate model for the process of search, and what are possible implementation techniques for this model? While we do not have an answer, we can suggest that the process search is, as we have suggested, similar, to feedback control. We believe we can formalize the dynamics of the world model and view the process of search as a reaction to the current belief about the world in manner similar to situated automata [14]. Solving this problem will allow robotic systems to maintain *incomplete* world models which are dynamically updated based on current information needs.

5   Conclusions

We have presented a natural and powerful decision-theoretic framework for discussing sensor estimation, control, fusion, and coordination. The framework fits very naturally with the system design that we outlined at the beginning of this paper. At this point, we do not have complete solutions to the sensor utilization problem, but we have informally presented some preliminary results which illustrate the general methods. These solutions have been implemented in simulation, and are currently being implemented in an existing system.

To this point, we have dealt with reducing uncertainty at the sensor level using very specific prior information about the scene under observation. In general we may not know what we are looking at or from what vantage.

In this case, the task of estimation will be different. For example, in identifying an object, prior information about the class of objects is often used. If the goal was to map out space, certain regularities about shape and space could be used as prior information. For example, the fact that, in a polygonal world, vertices are connected by edges. We hope to explore these cases.

We have also discussed possible extensions of this paradigm, and its relationship to search. We believe that these techniques, which allow a system to maintain an incomplete world model and dynamically gather information, will substantially increase the power of robotic and sensory systems.

Acknowledgements

This work was supported in part by NSF/DCR 8410771, NSF DMC-8411879 and DMC-12838, US Air Force F49620-85-K-0018, US Air Force F33615-83-C-3000, US Air Force F33615-86-C-3610, DARPA/ONR, ARMY/DAAG-29-84-K-0061, NSF-CER DCR82-19196 A02, NIH NS-10939-11 as part of the Cerebrovascular Research Center, by DEC Corp., and LORD Corp.

References

[1] J. O. Berger. *Statistical Decision Theory and Bayesian Analysis*. Springer-Verlag, New York, 1985.

[2] V. Fedorov. *Theory of Optimal Experiments*. Academic Press, New York, 1972. Translated from Russian.

[3] G. Hager. *Active Reduction of Uncertainty in Multi-Sensor Systems*. Technical Report MS-CIS-86-76, University of Pennsylvania, Philadelphia, PA, September 1986. Author's Dissertation Proposal.

[4] G. Hager. *An Agent Specification Language*. Technical Report MS-CIS-87-08, University of Pennsylvania, Philadelphia, PA, February 1987.

[5] G. Hager. *Information Maps for Active Sensor Control*. Technical Report MS-CIS-87-07, University of Pennsylvania, Philadelphia, PA, February 1987.

[6] G. Hager and H. Durrant-Whyte. Information and multi-sensor coordination. In *Proceedings of the 1986 AAAI Workshop on Uncertainty*, pages 99–108, Philadelphia, PA, August 1986. A revised version appears as Univ. of Penn report MS-CIS-86-68.

[7] G. Hager and M. Mintz. *Estimation Procedures for Robust Sensor Control*. Technical Report MS-CIS-87-09, University of Pennsylvania, Philadelphia, PA, February 1987.

[8] J. Kender and D. Freudenstein. What is a "degenerate" view? In *Proceedings of the DARPA Image Understanding Workshop*, pages 589–598, February 1987.

[9] J. Koenderink and A. van Doorn. The internal representation of solid shape with respect to vision. *Biological Cybernetics*, 32:211–216, 1979.

[10] J. Marschak and R. Radner. *Economic Theory of Teams*. Yale University Press, New Haven, 1972.

[11] R. K. Mehra. Optimal measurement policies and sensor designs for state and parameter estimation. March 1974. presented at the Milwaukee Symposium on Automatic Controls.

[12] P. Müller and H. Weber. Analysis and optimization of certain qualities of controllability and observability for linear dynamical systems. *Automatica*, 8:237–246, 1972.

[13] R. Paul, H. Durrant-Whyte, and M. Mintz. A robust, distributed multi-sensor robot control system. In *Proc. Third Int. Symposium of Robotic Research*, Gouvieaux, France, 1985.

[14] S. Rosenschein. *Formal Theories of Knowledge in AI and Robotics*. Technical Report 362, SRI International, Menlo Park, CA., September 1985.

[15] S. Silvey. *Optimal Design*. Chapman and Hall, New York, 1980.

LOW LEVEL INFORMATION FUSION: MULTISENSOR SCENE SEGMENTATION USING LEARNING AUTOMATA

James S. Duncan[†,*] , Gene R. Gindi[†,*] and Kumpati S. Narendra[*]
Departments of *Electrical Engineering and †Diagnostic Radiology
Division of Imaging Science
Yale University, New Haven, CT 06510

ABSTRACT

An optimization approach to scene segmentation in noisy environments by simultaneously utilizing registered images obtained from 2 disparate imaging sensors is presented. More specifically, segmentation is performed in this dual stochastic environment according to an objective function - based algorithm, modified to include the ability to switch between the sensors' data in order to obtain an optimal result. In the simple case of a unimodal objective function, such as could be obtained when segmenting a single object from its background, the task is thus to learn the most efficient way to climb a hill (segment an object or region) by using the information from two noisy impressions of the shape of that hill. The proposed algorithm uses a hierarchy of learning automata to first choose which impression (i.e. which sensor's image) of the hill should be used for climbing in a particular part of the underlying scene and secondly in which direction the system should move within that particular domain to most efficiently find the entire object. Three key assumptions are made about the segmentation problem: (1) all points in an object or region of interest are contiguous, (2) the segmentation problem is necessarily sequential and (3) it is desirable to perform the segmentation in the minimal number of search steps possible.

Preliminary investigations have proceeded using a simple version of this situation where the two sensors' images, obtained while viewing the same static object, are presumed to generate hills that have exactly complimentary spatial noise when measured according to a similarity metric. In other words, in the spatial regions where one sensor's image is noisy according to the metric, the other sensor's image produces a less noisy (or even crisp) result and vice versa. This situation is initially even further simplified to consider segmenting a one-dimensional noisy scene into 2 regions. Simulations using idealized hills have been run and results will be shown using basic fixed structure Tsetlin learning automata as the elements in the hierarchy. The environment rewards the automata hierarchy when positive upward hill climbing occurs while using one set of data (impression of the hill) and after considering a number of steps (attempts to climb). If insufficient upward hill-climbing progress is made after these same number of steps, the automata are penalized, which in turn causes the system to consider switching to the other set of data, in this case the second version of the hill (i.e. the second sensor's data).

INTRODUCTION

The combining of relevant information from multiple sensor sources is a topic of interest in the computer vision research community. Much of the current work has considered the fusion of information at higher descriptive levels, i.e. where pertinent low level information has already been separately extracted from each sensor and fusion algorithms look for a single consistent interpretation [1,2] or generate high level hypotheses about the scene [3,4]. The approach taken here assumes that in certain situations, registered image information from multiple sensors may be synergistically integrated to perform the operations required to gather lower-level information into meaningful groupings. Thus, information fusion is performed during the segmentation stage of the vision system. The underlying scene will be optimally segmented according to a particular metric using multisensor information.

The two image segmentation options of boundary finding or region growing are often case as optimization problems (see, for example, [3] and [14]). Low level information can be grouped according to a homogeneity criteria that is incorporated in an objective function. Thus, edge elements of like-direction and close spatial position could be linked into a boundary or pixels with similar gray level values and spatial proximity could be grouped into a single region. Low level elements (edge points, texture elements, pixels, etc.) are included or excluded in a boundary or region as long as they meet the homogeneity criteria and boundary formation or region growing terminates when no more elements may be added. This terminating point can be viewed as the top of a hill, a global maximum where the complete segmentation has been achieved according to the particular metric used. The segmentation is optimally achieved when the maximum is reached as efficiently as possible (i.e. via the shortest path or by considering the fewest number of candidate points). The case of interest here is when prior information about the regions is not given, i.e. the algorithm must find or learn the optimal segmentation in an unsupervised manner. For the work presented here, the objective functions are designed to be unimodal. Of course, it is possible to have an objective function which contains many local maxima, and future work will consider this issue with regards to the multisensor segmentation problem.

Arriving at an optimal segmentation may be difficult due to spatial uncertainty in the image. Physical and electronic noise sources inherent in many imaging systems can easily confuse the image segmentation algorithms. Boundary or region elements may not be included when they should have been and/or non-boundary or non-region points may be wrongly included due to scene noise. In such noisy environments it may be advantageous to use an additional sensor to view the scene in order to assist in object segmentation. The hope is that the second sensor would be less noisy in the sub-regions where the first one is very noisy and vice versa. Even if this happens in only some percentage of the sub-regions, a two-sensor segmentation should be helpful. With this extra information, however the optimization problem becomes more involved. There are now two versions of the underlying hill that may be climbed. The hill climbing algorithm must not only decide which direction and how far to move in that direction, but which version of the hill to choose in order to move towards convergence. With regards to the segmentation problem at hand, the analog is that the algorithm must decide which and how many boundary points or region elements to include or exclude on a given step in the boundary finding or region growing process, and which sensor's image to use in order to evaluate the candidate points. Because of the large amount of low-level elements to evaluate, the number of steps needed for the algorithm to converge to a single segmented region or set of segmented regions is of concern. Thus, the algorithm must learn the most expedient way to arrive at the optimal segmentation according to a given metric.

Some examples of environments where complimentary sensors may be useful are 1) the use of both visible light and infrared sensors to detect objects when bright reflections and/or thermal currents partially obscure the object in one sensor but not the other (e.g. blob finding from visible and FLIR images [12]) or 2) in medical problems where two imaging modalities might have complimentary properties when viewing certain structures. One medical example might be the complimentary use of x-ray computed tomography (usually better for viewing bone) and Magnetic Resonance Imaging (usually better for viewing soft tissue). Virtually any situation where a robot is maneuvering through a changing environment with unexpected signal and noise properties could potentially benefit from the integrated sensor approach discussed here.

In addition to alternating between sensors, it may be desirable to alternate between segmentation approaches (ie, region growing vs. line finding) using a single sensor's images (e.g., [14]) in order to achieve an optimal segmentation according to a particular metric. A hierarchy of decisions must thus be made with regard to which sensor should be used, which segmentation approach should be used and what are the appropriate moves to be made within a given approach. Thus, a key issue with regard to approaches to optimal segmentation (as well as the optimal use of segmented information) is with regard to the control of the information flow . One approach to this problem (using only region-based information) is presented below.

The above segmentation problem formulation has discussed the need for an iterative hill-climbing algorithm to operate in a stochastic environment. The solution proposed in this paper is a hierarchy of learning automata in the form of those suggested by Tsetlin [5]. Such computational elements have been suggested for use in computer vision and pattern recognition tasks by others. Bartos's [6] work considered statistical pattern recognition problems and was an attempt to replace supervised learning procedures with a learning procedure which uses stochastic search. Thatachar and Sastry[7] provided a new look at the relaxation labeling algorithm previously developed by Rosenfeld, Hummel and Zucker [8]. Their approach was aimed at improving the convergence properties of this algorithm. This work complements these efforts and is intended to show the use of learning automata at the early levels of vision systems. Although the initial implementations consider only deterministic automata, it is intended to ultimately investigate the use of stochastic learning automata schemes.

LEARNING AUTOMATA AND HILL CLIMBING USING MULTIPLE HILLS

LEARNING AUTOMATA

For a complete discussion of types of learning models using automata, the reader is referred to [9]. The P-model, fixed-structure learning automaton will be briefly described here, since a hierarchy of these will be used in our segmentation algorithm. A learning automaton contains an automaton and an environment (A, E) coupled together as shown in Figure 1. The automaton is most completely described as a quintuple $(\phi, \alpha, \beta, F, G)$ as shown in figure 1.

Since F and G are both deterministic mappings, the automata to be used here are referred to as deterministic automata. The use of stochastic automata (where either F or G is stochastic) is being considered for future efforts. The basic operation of the deterministic automaton shown in figure 1 may be simply described as follows. An initial state $\phi(0)$, is given or assumed, and since there is a one-to-one correspondence between states and actions in this simple automaton, action $\alpha(0)$ is taken. The environment receives this action and responds either negatively (penalty, $\beta = 1$) or positively (reward, $\beta = 0$). Now the automaton receives the environment's response, β, and uses this and its current state to determine the next state via the mapping. Since the automata used need only take 1 of two actions, as is described below, the state transition function takes on values such that a reward leaves the automaton in its present state and a penalty causes it to change state. The operations described are performed recursively, obtaining a state and action sequence for any given input sequence. It is key to note that the state and action at any given n depends only on the state and input at the previous (n - 1)st instant. This Markovian property is a key consideration for proving convergence and in deciphering expedience [9].

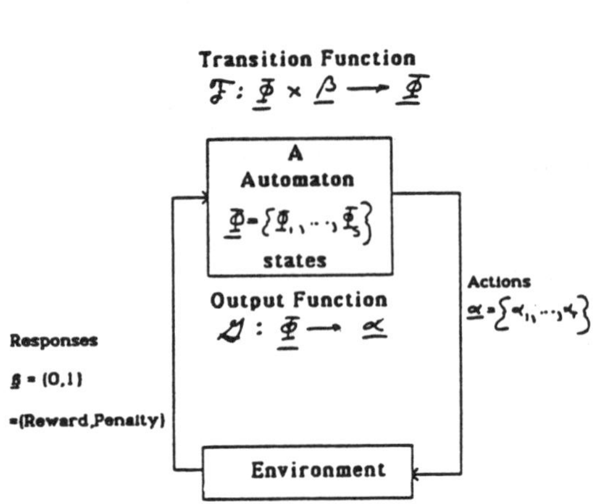

Figure 1. A fixed structure, P-model, deterministic learning automaton.

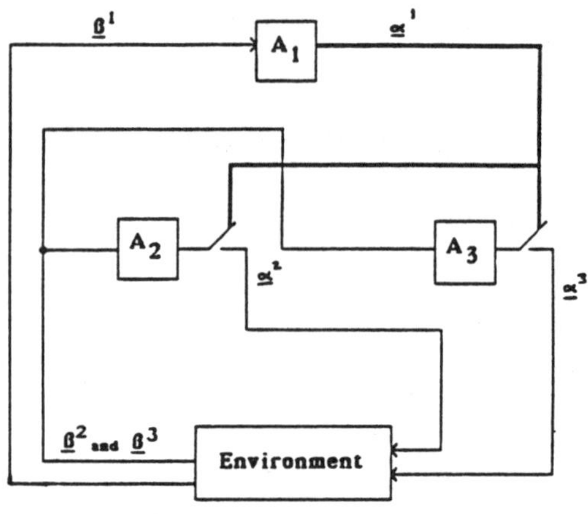

Figure 2. A hierarchy of learning automata with one (A1) acting as an overseer or coordinator. Note: α_i and β_i refer to the action and response sets of automaton i, respectively.

HILL CLIMBING USING MULTIPLE IMPRESSIONS OF THE HILL AND A HIERARCHY OF LEARNING AUTOMATA

Hierarchies and/or teams of automata have been suggested by several authors [6,7,11]. Modification of a specific scheme suggested by Wheeler and Narendra [11] is presented here for this multisensor segmentation task for reasons which will become clear below. This simple hierarchy is shown in Figure 2. Note that all three automata are interacting with the same environment. Thus, it is implicitly assumed for the problem at hand that although there are two versions of the underlying hill that can be used for climbing, these are part of a single underlying environment.

Automata A2 and A3 in figure 2 yield actions which cause climbing movements on version 1 (sensor 1's impression) or version 2 (sensor 2's impression) of the underlying hill. The actions are simply $\{\alpha_1^2, \alpha_2^2\}$ = {move left on version 1, move right on version 1} and $\{\alpha_1^3, \alpha_2^3\}$ = {move left on version 2 , move right on version 2} for A2 and A3 respectively. It is important to keep in mind that the 2 versions of the hill are precisely registered, such that if climbing stops at a point in one hill version, it can be picked up at exactly that point in the other version. A single response, $\beta = \{0,1\}$, is sent as input to both automata, rewarding or penalizing the last hill climbing action. Consideration is being given also to separating the responses from both versions of the hill. This would create a slightly altered configuration and would allow for climbing to proceed simultaneously in each version of the hill for a fixed number of steps, which may be advantageous.

Automata A1 acts as an overseer or coordinator in the proposed system as seen in Figure 2. It's actions are to decide whether A2 or A3 should be used at a particular step in the iterative process, which effectively decides which version of the underlying hill should be used for climbing. It should be clear that the environment is considered to be both the data from which measurements are made and the measurements themselves, which determine responses to all automata. Thus, $\{\alpha_1^1, \alpha_2^1\}$ = {allow climbing on version 1, allow climbing on version 2}. The response to automata A1, denoted $\beta^1 = \{0,1\}$ is determined from a weighted sum (in the simplest case an average) of the last k steps of climbing on a given version of the hill according to a simple gradient metric (measured between the last move and the next proposed move). If climbing is proceeding in an upward direction, A1 is rewarded ($\beta^1 = 0$), and allows continued climbing on the current hill version (i.e., continues to choose A2 or A3). If there is downward movement, or oscillatory movement on a particular version of the hill, A1 is penalized for its current action, causing the automaton to change actions (i.e., switch from A2 to A3 or vice versa). The meaning of hill-climbing according to an example region growing segmentation metric will be described below. Two important aspects of learning automata theory are the assurance of convergence of the scheme and the number of steps taken for convergence. The proposed hierarchical, deterministic scheme must be fully investigated with regard to these properties, but there is reason to expect the expediency of convergence to be dependent on the amount of noise present in each version of the hill. Convergence itself is predictable, as it has been shown for the very similar coordinator hierarchical scheme suggested by Wheeler and Narendra [11] that 2-action automata that start with equal probabilities will converge to the largest equilibrium.

SEGMENTATION IN ONE-DIMENSIONAL MULTISENSOR IMAGES

This section presents results on experiments using the automata hierarchy to segment one-dimensional (1-D) images (signals) where 2 approximately complimentary noisy versions of the scene exist. These experiments represent initial work on using the proposed scheme to optimally segment 2 regions separated by a single boundary. For the simulations, a form of region-based segmentation is used. Data from the entire frame (or region of interest) is considered at once, although updates are made by considering only local data. The goal of the algorithm is to mark the spatial (or temporal, if a time-varying signal is assumed, instead of a spatially-varying 1-D image) point at which on one side of the point there are only pixels from one region and the other side there are only pixels from a second region. Obviously, because the signal is 1-D and all points are contiguous, this problem could be solved in many different ways, including forms of gray level thresholding. However, a generalized solution is sought that basically extends to two dimensions. In addition, because the images will be corrupted with unknown (but complimentary) noise, the segmentation process is nontrivial. Finally, it is desired to solve the problem as an optimization task, in hopes of generalizing the automata-based solution to other forms of low level vision. By requiring an optimal segmentation according to a particular metric, precise termination criteria can be defined for iterative algorithms. This is not the case when less rigorously designed segmentation algorithms (see examples in [10]) are utilized. However, the development of an optimal 2-D region growing algorithm is nontrivial due to the large number of possible combinations of local regions which must be considered. An exhaustive search through all of these combinations is computationally extensive, and this burden is worsened as terms are added to the region growing metric. As outlined by Levine and Nazif [14], at least 2 terms are required to evaluate region-based segmentations in real time (i.e. without referring to a known or desired region delineation). First, the uniformity of a feature over a region must be considered and is inversely proportional to the variance of the values of that feature evaluated at every pixel inside that region. Secondly, contrast between adjacent candidate regions must be considered. This is usually computed on the basis of the average values of features in adjacent regions. For the initial development work described here, only the contrast metric based on a variance feature is used.

The 1-D segmentation problem is thus cast in the following manner. First, an evaluation function is defined by comparing the variance of the image on either side of a candidate region delineating point. As mentioned above, the variances are computed over the entire image. Thus, for a candidate delineating point x, the evaluation or merit function is:

$$
\begin{aligned}
J(x) &= \sigma_1^2(x) - \sigma_2^2(x) \\
&= \sum_{i=1}^{x} \left(\frac{f(i) - \mu_1}{x} \right)^2 - \sum_{i=x+1}^{n} \left(\frac{f(i) - \mu_2}{n - x} \right)^2
\end{aligned}
$$

where

$x =$ the position in the image

$f(x) =$ the gray level value at position x

$n =$ the total number of positions

$\mu_1, \mu_2 =$ the gray value means to the left and right of x

It is desired to drive this function to the point where the variances agree by iteratively changing the position of x. This optimal point x^* thus must be iteratively learned in an unsupervised manner from the data according to the variance metric. This optimal point represents the point in the image that separates, segments or delineates 2 differing contiguous regions. Although x can take on any position value in the image (i.e., $x \epsilon \{1, \ldots, n\}$) the variances do not need to be entirely recomputed at each step. By remembering the variances from the last iteration, only changes in these numbers must be computed.

Iterative updating is carried out using deterministic automata and a form of stochastic approximation according to Kiefer and Wolfowitz [13]. In this approach, updating proceeds according to

$$
\begin{aligned}
x(k+1) &= x(k) + \nu(k)\nabla J \\
&= x(k) + \frac{1}{k} \left(J[x(k+1)] - J[x(k-1)] \right)
\end{aligned}
$$

where

$k =$ step number

$x(k) =$ the position of the candidate delineating point at iteration k

For any 1 hill, the automaton is used to determine the direction of the next move (left or right) in order to obtain a new trial segmentation point. The amount of points moved in one direction or the other is determined by the gradient, $J[x(k+1)] - J[x(k-1)]$, weighted by one over the number of moves already made. This method guarantees convergence to the proper maximum of the variance-based evaluation function, even in the presence of zero mean noise.

Figure 3(a) shows a noisy one-dimensional image where the noise has been created by the amplification of points selected in the range between 0 and 1 according to a uniformly distributed random number generator and added to or subtracted from an underlying image. Notice that the noise gets alternately higher and lower in adjacent spatial regions (these regions are smaller than the regions to be segmented). Figure 4(a) represents a simulation of the hill that might be created by the variance metric if the single automaton system were initialized to $x(0) =$ the leftmost point in the image and moves only to the right were permitted. In other words, this is a simulated scan of the hill formed by the variance metric. Thus, without knowing which are the correct moves (e.g. all right moves if start at left or vice versa), it is the job of the automata to find the top of the hill in the most efficient manner possible, by considering only left/right moves. In these figures, there are 100 possible positions (moves off the ends are reset) and the peak of the hill has a value of 100 and occurs at position 50. Figure 5 shows the results of a single automaton-based algorithm attempting to move to the top of this hill after starting at the leftmost point in the image. Based solely on these left/right moves, it is obvious that the automaton can swiftly maneuver through clean regions on the hill (in the image) and may take a while to get around noisy regions, while deciding the final segmentation point. Nonetheless, the single automata scheme segments the 1-D image (climbs to the top of the hill in figure 4(a)) shown in figure 3(a) in 67 steps.

Figure 3(b) shows a second image (signal), which has spatial noise that is exactly complementary to the noise shown in the signal of figure 3(a). This is intended to represent an ideal multisensor imaging situation. In this case, wherever a larger amount of noise is present in figure 3(a) a smaller amount is present in figure 3(b). The simulated hill scanned to the right according to the variance metric used in this section is shown in figure 4(b). Notice its complimentary noise properties with regards to the hill of figure 4(a). The hierarchical deterministic automata scheme shown in figure 2 is used to find the top of the underlying hill by considering both hills. Automata A2 and A3 in figure 2 make the left/right moves up the hill in 4(a) or the hill in 4(b) respectively according to the variance metric shown earlier. However, automata A1 decides which hill version will be used at a particular step. After every 10 moves (heuristically set due to total points) on a particular hill, the average upward progress is determined. If the average movement is upward to within some threshold (which will eventually also be learned) new trial segmentation points are found using the same version of the hill (i.e. the same sensor's signal). If the average movement is more than slightly downward, the environment penalizes automata A1 in figure 2, causing it to switch states and consider the second version of the hill (i.e. second sensor's data), starting at the last (registered) point in the first version. Figure 6 shows the results of climbing to the maximum point in the underlying hill due to the variance metric by considering 2 complimentary hills. This point (and thus the segmentation of the underlying scene) is now achieved in 57 steps. Note that the peak value differs slightly from the single hill climbing case due to noise at the top of the second hill, but there is a marked reduction in the number of steps required when using 2 complimentary hills instead of one. Thus, the multisensor algorithm will efficiently utilize complimentarily noisy data to find the maximum of a particular metric. This should be helpful even in non-ideal noise cases where only some regions are less noisy.

It is intended to use stochastic automata in further experiments to probabilistically still consider moves in noisy regions. Also, it may be desirable to vary the number of moves considered in the average before A1 switches to alternate sensor information. This is due to the fact that larger moves of the candidate boundary points through the spatial regions are made in the earlier iterative stages. This alteration of the original scheme is currently being investigated.

<u>EXTENSION TO 2-D REGION SEGMENTATION</u>

The unsupervised approach to segmentation proposed in the section above is limited to one-dimensional images where there are two contiguous regions with only 1 separating point between them. Ultimately, it is desired to extend this approach to a two-dimensional case where there is a single object with many delineating points separating it from the background, imaged by 2 sensors with complementary spatial noise. Such a case is shown pictorially in figure 7. However, this extension is not so straightforward. Making optimal moves in a 2-D space in order to optimize a variance - based objective function is difficult. The 1-D work above is thus extended in the following 2-stage manner.

1-D IMAGES WITH TWO BOUNDARIES

First, the 1-D case where an object in the 1-D image rises up from the background and then falls again must be considered, i.e. when 2 delineating borders are present. The 2 sensor images are still present and complementary spatial noise is again assumed, as shown in figure 8(a and b), but the objective function must consider the variances in 3 different regions: the two possible background regions (σ_1^2 and σ_3^2) and the possible object region (σ_2^2). Thus, the J(x) term from above now becomes

$$J(x) = [\sigma_2^2(x) - (\sigma_1^2(x) + \sigma_3^2(x))].$$

Iterative updating can now proceed in the same manner on either hill for any given position of the 2 points chosen as the region delineating points (θ_1 or θ_2) at a given iteration. In other words, at a particular step, a variance gradient (using all 3 variances) is computed to see if upward hill climbing is proceeding.

The learning algorithm is implemented using the automata hierarchy shown in figure 9. The search for an optimal segmentation is carried out in three levels. At the lowest level, the automata (A3, A4, A6, A7) simply decide to move a particular boundary (leftmost (θ_1) or rightmost (θ_2) to the left or to the right. The intermediate automata (A3 and A5) decide which boundary point should be considered for moving in order to optimize the variance objective function. Finally the top level automaton (A1) simply chooses whether to use data from sensor 1 or sensor 2. An important part of the switchover process as dictated by A1, is that the algorithm, via the environment, maintains the points already included in a region segmented according to the first sensor's data. In other words, the partially segmented scene is the starting point from which pixels will be considered in the second sensor. This is a somewhat tricky undertaking however, since the homogeneity properties of the regions from sensor 1's image may not carry over to sensor 2's image. Thus, the variances in sensor 2's image are recomputed based on sensor 1's partial segmentation and will be the basis for the start of the continuation of segmentation in sensor 2's version of the hill. This effort to maintain continuity is important and other options are being investigated, as well.

2-D OBJECT/BACKGROUND SEGMENTATION

The second stage of development will further extend the 1-D, two boundary case described above to consider the full 2-D object/background/noise case shown in figure 7. The approach considers only convex objects initially (unlike figure 7). Raster lines in the image are segmented one at a time using a modified version of the hierarchy of figure 9 to learn the delineating points (θ_1 and θ_2) on each line that optimally separate the object from the background. The modification is that an extra term is added to the objective function for each line that considers smoothness between delineating points (separately considering θ_1's and θ_2's) found on consecutive scan lines. The delineating points from the last scan line are also used to initialize the search on the next line if the process were performed serially. Performing this two dimensional segmentation on a line by line basis in parallel would obviously be more efficient and pleasing. The search is still carried out by switching betwen the two sensors' data on a line by line basis, however. This raster scan approach is an alternative to a multidirectional simultaneous search of the multisensor registered images for an optimal segmenting boundary. Although this approach is being investigated, it appears to be much more computationally cumbersome. The current approach is also being extended to include segmentation of multiple objects and concave objects from background in noisy, multisensor environments.

SUMMARY

An optimization approach to scene segmentation in noisy environments using multiple sensors and learning automata has been presented. It is claimed that if segmentation may be viewed as a hill-climbing optimization problem according to an objective function, then segmentation using two sensors may be viewed as an attempt to optimally use two impressions of an underlying hill to climb that hill. It has been shown that these two impressions might be used most advantageously when the hill impressions have complimentary noise characteristics. Simulations have been performed in one dimension in order to show feasibility. The results show that a hierarchical automata scheme climbs an ideal underlying hill with relatively few wasted moves when using 2 noisy, but complimentary environments. A basic outline was presented to extend the one dimensional problem to two-dimensional object/background segmentation. The approach discussed here will efficiently arrive at a optimal segmentation result, felt to be more predictable than many other (more ad hoc) segmentation techniques previously proposed. One area of future work is the consideration of the problems associated with efficient multi-directional optimal search in 2 dimensions. In addition, it is hoped that the usefulness of this paradigm will be shown by considering additional application areas, such as optimization approaches to boundary finding in noisy environments from edge vectors or optical flow matching in noisy environments. It is predicted that teams of deterministic, and eventually stochastic, automata could be assigned to many low level optimization tasks in parallel in a vision system. Multiple isolated object segmentation is an obvious first application.

REFERENCES

[1] A.M. Nazif and M.D. Levine, "Low Level Segmentation: An Expert System," Tech. Report TR-83-4, Dept. of Electrical Engineering, McGill University April, 1983.

[2] R.R. Kohler, "Integrating Non-Semantic Knowledge Into Image Segmentation Processes," COINS Tech. Report 84-04, Univ. of Massachusetts, March, 1984.

[3] R.Belknap, E.Riseman and A. Hanson, "The Information Fusion Problem and Rule-Based Hypotheses Applied to Complex Aggregations of Image Events," Proc. of the Conf. on Computer Vision and Pattern Recognition, IEEE Press, Miami Beach, Florida. June, 1986. Pp. 227-234.

[4] R. Bajcsy and M. Tevakoli, "Computer Recognition of Roads from Satellite Pictures," IEEE Transactions on Systems, Man and Cybernetics, SMC - 6, September, 1976, Pp. 623-637.

[5] M.L. Tsetlin, Automaton Theory and Modeling Biological Systems. New York: Academic, 1973.

[6] A.G. Barto and P. Anandan, "Pattern Recognizing Stochastic Learning Automata," IEEE Trans. on Systems, Man and Cybernetics, VOL. SMC-15, No. 3, May/June, 1985. Pp. 360-375.

[7] M. Thatachar and P.S. Sastry, "Relaxation Labeling with Learning Automata," IEEE Trans. on Pattern Analysis and Machine Intelligence, VOL. PAMI-8, No. 2, March, 1986. Pp. 256-268.

[8] A. Rosenfeld, R. Hummel and S. Zucker, "Scene Labeling by Relaxation Operations," IEEE Trans. on Pattern Analysis and Machine Intelligence, VOL. PAMI-5, June, 1976. Pp. 420-433.

[9] K.S. Narendra and M.A.L. Thatachar, "Learning Automata - A Survey," IEEE Trans. on Systems, Man and Cybernetics, VOL. SMC-4, July, 1974. Pp. 323-334.

[10] D. Ballard and D. Brown, Computer Vision, Prentice Hall, Englewood Cliffs, N.J., 1982.

[11] R.M. Wheeler, "Decentralized Learning in Games and Finite Markov Chains," Ph.D. Dissertation, Dept. of Electrical Engineering, Yale University. May, 1985.

[12] M. Schneier, "Using Pyramids to Define Local Thresholds for Blob Detection," IEEE Trans. on Pattern Analysis and Machine Intelligence, VOL. PAMI-5, No. 3, May, 1981. Pp. 345-349.

[13] J. Kiefer and J. Wolfowitz, "Stochastic Estimation of the Maximum of a Regression Function," Annals of Mathematical Statistics, VOL. 23, 1952, Pp. 462-466.

[14] M.D. Levine and A.M. Nazif, "Dynamic Measurement of Computer Generated Image Segmentations," IEEE Trans. on Pattern Analysis and Machine Intelligence, Vol. PAMI-7, No.2, March, 1985. Pp.155-164.

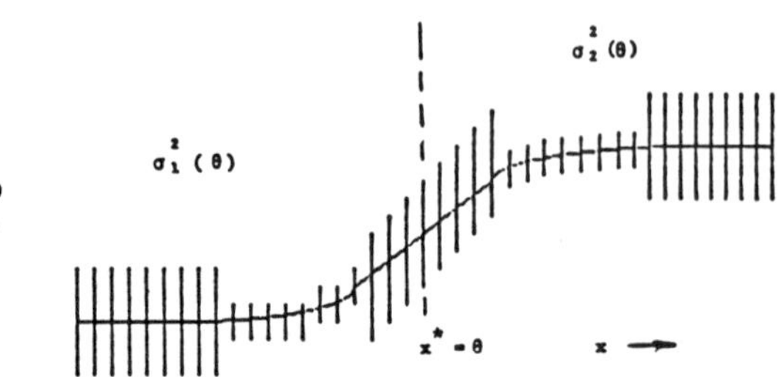

Figure 3(a). Image 1: A 1-D image with alternating regions of noise magnitude. All noise is uniform and zero mean. The ratio of the difference in magnitude between very noisy and less noisy regions is 4:1. The lines on the image only show the range of the noise; the effect on the objective function is better indicated in figure 4(a).

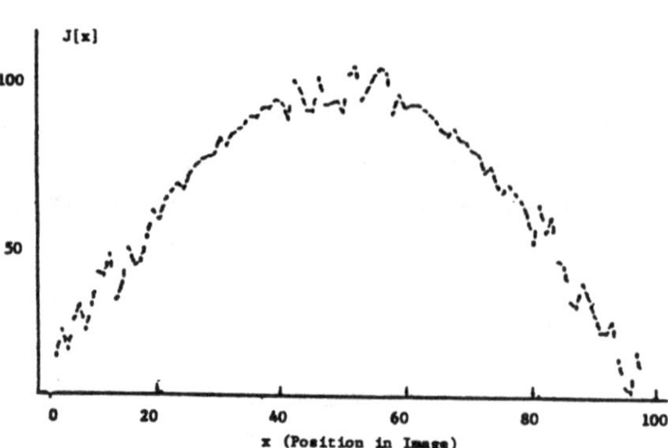

Figure 4(a). Value of the variance objective function versus position in image 1. Note alternating noise magnitude after every 20 image points.

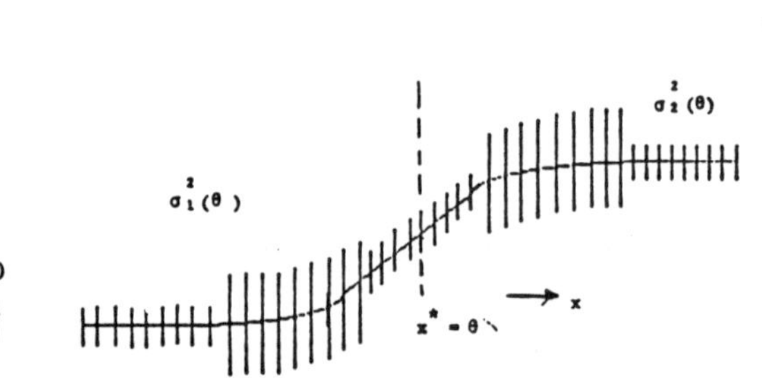

Figure 3(b). Image 2: A 1-D image with alternating regions of noise magnitude. The magnitude of the noise in each spatial region is complementary to that of the same registered region in figure 3(a). The effect of noise on the objective function is shown in figure 4(b).

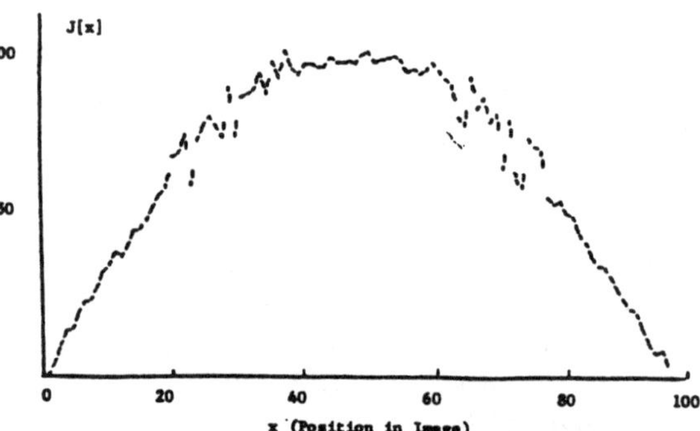

Figure 4(b). Value of the variance objective function versus position in image 2. Note that the noise magnitude alternates after every 20 pixels and is complementary to that of image 1's objective function shown in figure 4(a).

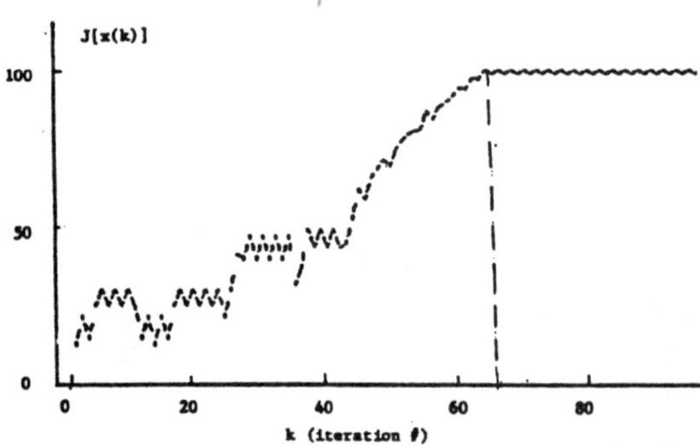

Figure 5. Single sensor hill climbing. Level reached in underlying hill ((100 - level) = distance from maximum) versus iteration number using a single automaton and image 1 (fig. 3) only.

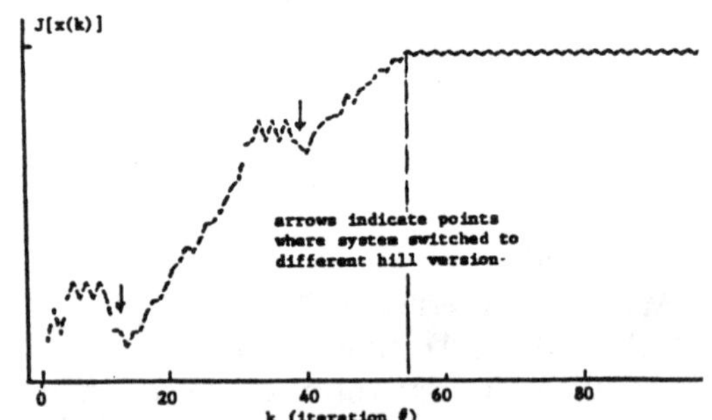

Figure 6. Multiple sensor hill climbing. Level reached in underlying hill versus iteration number using automata scheme of figure 2 and data from both image 1 and image 2 (figs. 3 and 4).

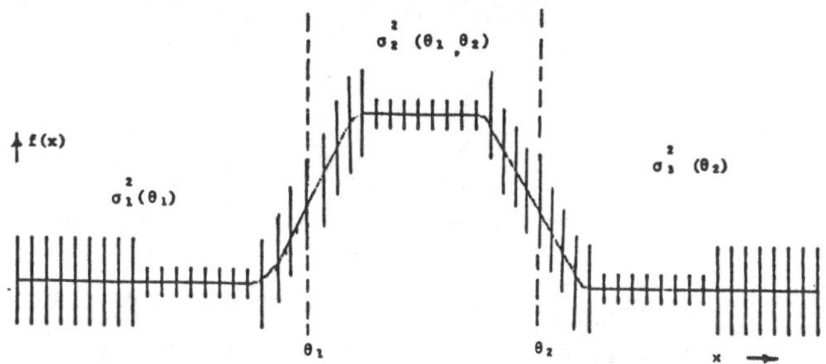

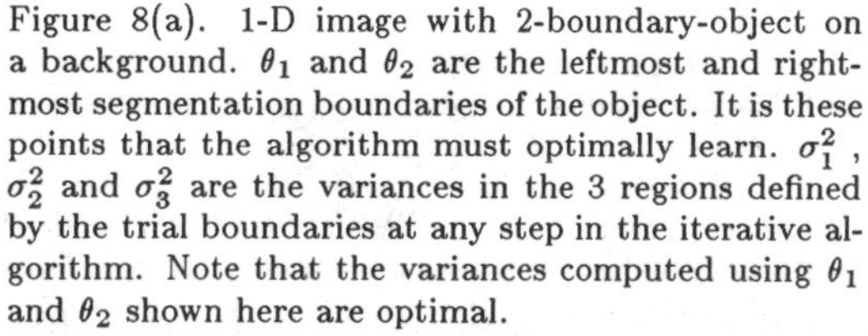

Figure 8(a). 1-D image with 2-boundary-object on a background. θ_1 and θ_2 are the leftmost and rightmost segmentation boundaries of the object. It is these points that the algorithm must optimally learn. σ_1^2, σ_2^2 and σ_3^2 are the variances in the 3 regions defined by the trial boundaries at any step in the iterative algorithm. Note that the variances computed using θ_1 and θ_2 shown here are optimal.

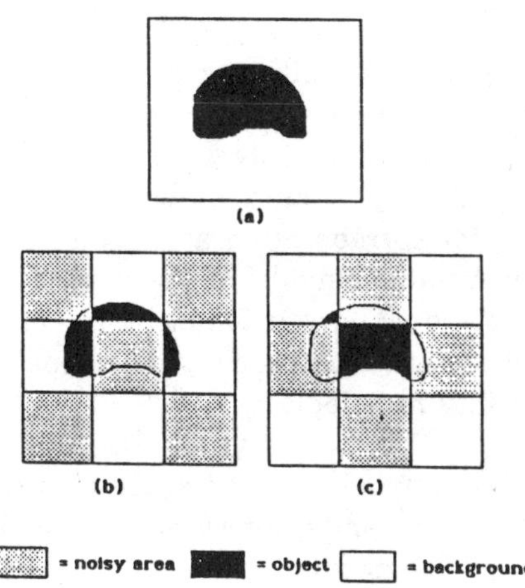

Figure 7. Idealized multisensor 2-D images ((b) and (c)) of the same underlying scene (a).

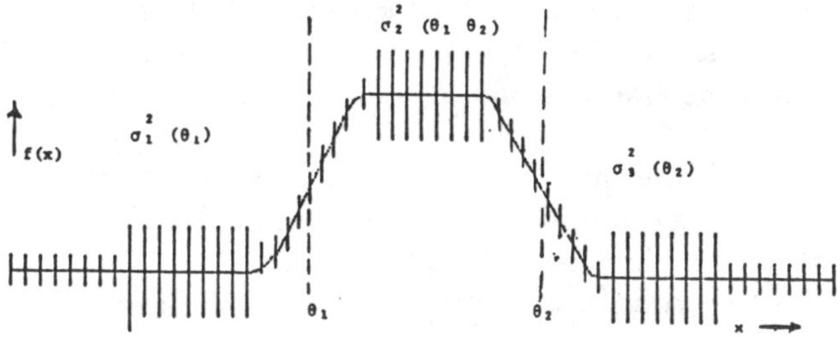

Figure 8(b). A second 1-D image viewing the same underlying scene as in figure 8(a), but with complementary spatial noise properties.

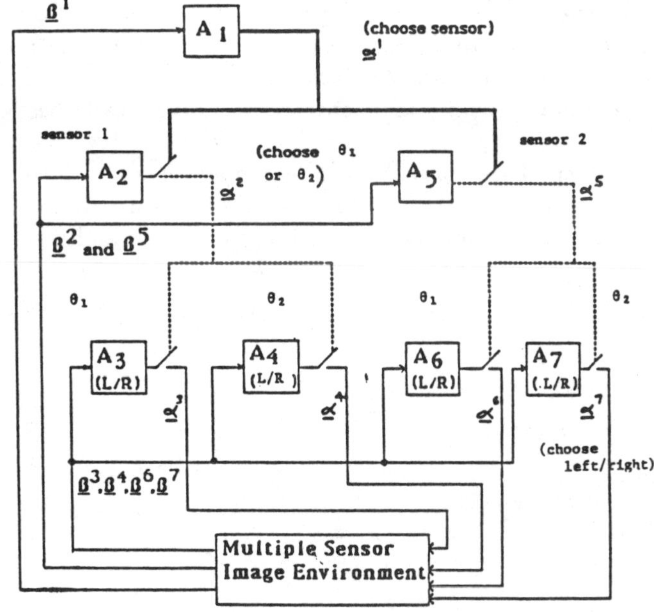

Figure 9. A hierarchy of learning automata for multisensor segmentation of 1-D images with a single 2-boundary-point object on a background.

SHAPE DETERMINATION FROM INCOMPLETE AND NOISY MULTISENSOR IMAGERY

James S. Duncan[*,†] and Lawrence H. Staib[*]
Departments of [*]Electrical Engineering and [†]Diagnostic Radiology
Division of Imaging Science
Yale University, New Haven, CT 06510

ABSTRACT

The problem of fusing image-derived information from sensors with differing noise and imaging properties is examined. Our goal is to delineate an object from a scene based on a consensus of the incomplete and uncertain information the images have provided about the object. After an initial examination of the images separately, a consensus is achieved by identifying areas of disagreement from the separately generated high level descriptions, then searching for corroboration at a lower level. In this way, the sensors confirm and complement each other. A probabilistic model of the range of object boundary shape is assumed known, but the actual position of the boundary is found by the proposed analysis. Possible applications include object recognition problems in robot vision and aerospace from multi-spectral data and organ characterization from multi-modality radiology.

Processing proceeds from a discrete semantic representation, for model-based analysis of general shape to a continuous representation, for detailed shape characterization and comparison. Uncertainty is tracked probabilistically, using the principle of maximum entropy. The maximum entropy solution is the most conservative estimate of the probabilities given the known constraints. This method of tracking evidence is preferable to methods such as Dempster-Shafer because it allows for the combination of dependent information.

A trial contour is formed from the edge segments using the most probable labelings. The shapes of the contours derived by the two sensors are compared and the regions of discrepancy cause adjustments to the model, which is reapplied to the segment data. This process is repeated in order to consider alternate segments which could decrease the disagreement. By only allowing changes that increase the degree of match, we guarantee stability and convergence to the locally best consensus.

The maximum entropy-based probabilistic reasoning system is currently operational, along with the lower level parts of the image analysis scheme and the curve analysis. The algorithm is being tested on simulated contours and dual modality medical imagery of human hearts.

INTRODUCTION

MULTISENSOR IMAGE ANALYSIS

The work discussed here is aimed at integrating multisensor image information in order to merge individual sensor-derived object shape descriptions into a consensus description. Several approaches to multisensor integration have been proposed, ranging from integrating the information sources at the low level processing stage to generating high level shape and object hypotheses from the sensors' separately formed scene descriptions [2]. The data fusion work that will be discussed here will separately process low level information from two sensors, compare this information at higher levels of processing, and iteratively modify the system's probabilistic constraints on the low level information in order to seek a consensus opinion about the underlying scene.

A discrete semantic representation is useful for the model-based analysis because it allows for the application of an approximate or probabilistic model specifying the general shape expected. The detailed quantitative shape analysis is needed for intersensor comparison and for the final shape description. Thus, once this model correspondence is established, a continuous representation is derived to facilitate further processing.

This further processing will initially take the form of a more detailed level of model matching. Thus, the discrete semantic representations of a model and the image-derived information will be used to bring the two into rough correspondence, possibly isolating a class of object models to which an image-derived contour could be matched, whereas the shape curves formed from the multisensor consensus object boundaries will be used to isolate a particular version of an object within a general class. The use of boundary shape descriptors for object identification is certainly not without precedent. For example, Persoon and Fu [7] have used Fourier shape descriptors to identify printed characters and machine parts from segmented images and Young [8] and others have used local tangential measures for analysis of cell pathology.

CONSIDERATION OF UNCERTAINTY

The information content of noisy imagery will, in general, be incomplete and uncertain (hence the need for multiple sensors). Objects will often be occluded or obscured and thus can only be known to some degree of confidence. This inherent uncertainty will be tracked with a probabilistic methodology. The uncertainty is propagated to the high levels of the system and indicates the system's confidence in it's combined output. Many non-probabilistic methods for handling uncertainty have been considered recently, such as fuzzy sets, confidence factors and Dempster-Shafer theory. These techniques lack the strong mathematical basis and interpretability of probability theory. In addition, dependent evidence is not treated. The work proposed here will incorporate an approach to uncertainty based on the principle of maximum entropy or least commitment.

Maximum entropy has been considered as a means of tracking probabilistic evidence [4,6]. It does not require the assumption of independent evidence, as does traditional Bayesian updating and most non-probabilistic techniques [3]. The maximum entropy method used here calculates the most conservative, or unbiased, estimate of the probabilities given constraints on the probability space, or event group, taken from the model and the data. The use of this approach here is attractive for considering uncertainty at two levels, first making initial anatomical assignments to grouped low level information (i.e. edge segments) and secondly combining information from various segments to provide a consistent contextual result for a group of segments.

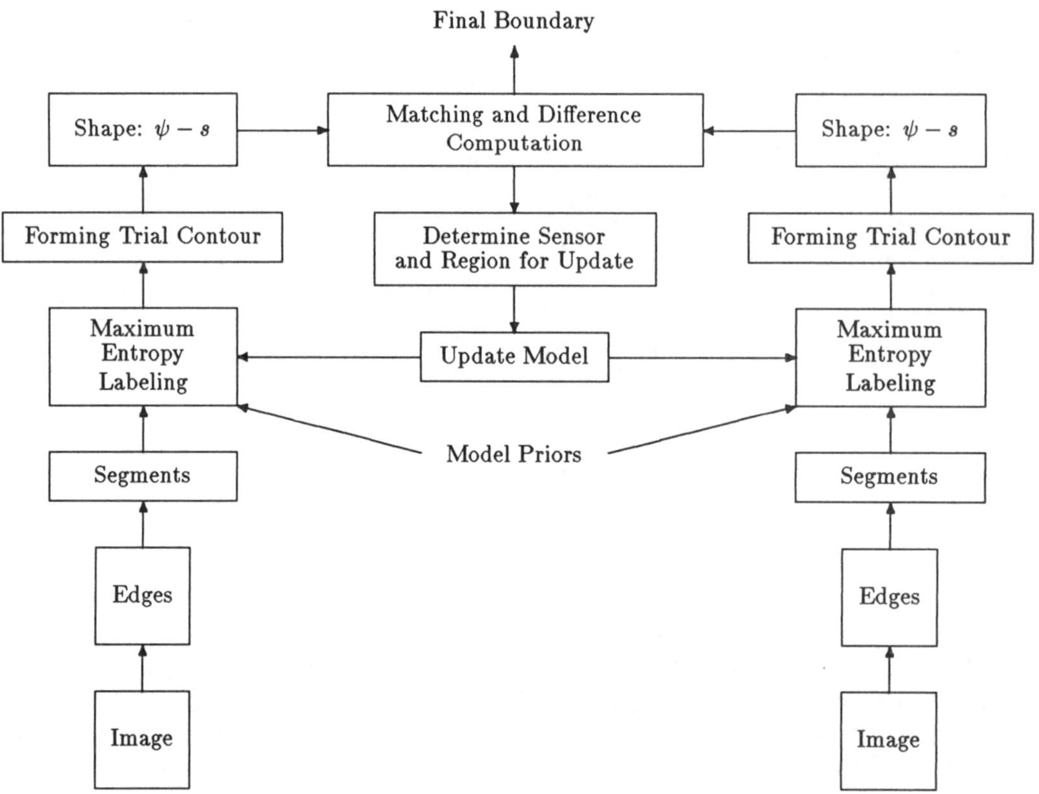

Figure 1: System Block Diagram

SYSTEM OVERVIEW

The system block diagram is shown in figure 1. This represents a complete strategy for integrated, geometrically-based multisensor shape analysis. Note that at the low and intermediate levels of the system, identical processing operations are performed on each sensor's image. As can be seen, an important feature of this system is the presence of a feedback loop between the upper and lower levels of the system. This feedback is intended to drive the analysis toward obtaining a consensus interpretation of shape from multiple sensors. Each of the system modules is described in more detail below, with emphasis placed on the approach to reasoning from uncertainty.

PRELIMINARY ANALYSIS

EDGE FINDING

At the lowest level of the system, image feature information will be extracted from the images using local neighborhood gradient convolution operators to find magnitudes and directions of gray level gradients in the image. The decision to use this type of operator was made in conjunction with the overall planned approach to boundary finding. Briefly, the strength of discontinuities are found in two orthogonal directions and from this information, the magnitude and direction of each edge vector is easily computed. Depending on the size of the convolution operators (typically 3x3 or 5x5), several edge vectors may be produced across a given edge region. In the context of this system it is worthwhile to thin the vectors in a region down to a single maximum edge vector for the eventual purpose of boundary tracking. These edge finding processes are the same as those used in [5].

BOUNDARY GROUPING

Second level algorithms are aimed at grouping or linking homogenous lower level information so that these groupings may be symbolically and quantitatively described in preparation for the higher level reasoning strategies. An edge linking approach used in earlier work[5] was modified and used here to obtain and describe the curve segments.

Edge elements are associated (linked) into segments based on their adjacency and closeness of orientation. Segments are followed until there is no possible continuation or until there is a branch. Segments are broken at branches to avoid possibly confounding the object with noise. A segment is also broken if it exceeds a maximum length limit. The limit is imposed to ensure that individual segments most likely correspond to only one model region. The edge image is scanned until all edge elements are linked or are identified as outliers and discarded due to their separation from others. The linked lists of edge points are taken to contain all of the evidence regarding the presence or absence of a boundary that can be found from the particular image from a particular sensor. Thus, any higher level decisions about shape will be made primarily considering this partial boundary evidence.

SHAPE REASONING

MAXIMUM ENTROPY PROBABILISTIC LABELING

The degree of confidence in the partial and uncertain image-derived information is tracked with subjective probabilities using the principle of maximum entropy. We will use it to solve the problem of labeling the edge segments according to our model for the object. For each sensor, each piece of segmental evidence is considered first separately and then together with other segments to determine the likelihood of it being labeled as a part of the boundary, according to an initial model of what the regions of the boundary should look like. The constraints derived from this model constitute the system's prior bias on the analysis. The desirable neutral prior of the general form of the object is chosen, and is created by incorporating the statistical distributions of a range of ideal objects boundary data into discrete mathematical constraints with regards to the direction and relative position of boundary regions that make up the object.

The distribution of probabilistic confidence to the different labeling possibilities for each edge segment is done in two stages. This separation of stages is done in order to limit the size of the event groups and thus the corresponding computational burden. In order to update the labeling probabilities of an edge segment based on new information, the principle of maximum entropy is applied, in conjunction with the constraints arising from the data and the model, to the event group corresponding to the edge under consideration. At the first stage, shown in figure 2(a), the event group consists of the following events: $\mathcal{E}$ is the edge segment to be updated, P_x is the x-position of the segment, P_y is the y-position of the segment, D is the direction of the segment, I is the node representing the presence of the image derived information P_x, P_y and D. This event group forms an initial estimate of the probabilities based only on the low level information.

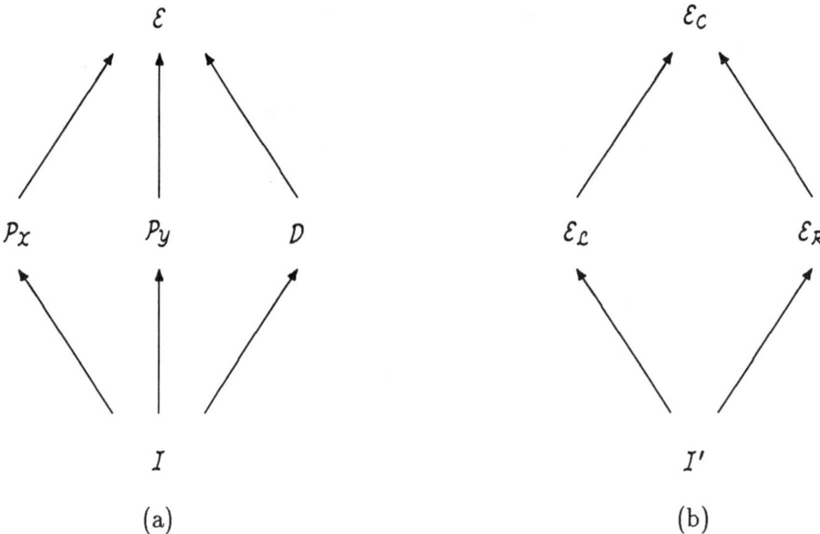

Figure 2: Event groups for labeling

The second stage, shown in figure 2(b), is formed to incorporate contextual information into the label probabilities for each edge segment by including the edge segments nearest to the edge in question. Thus, the events in the group are: $\mathcal{E}_C$ is the edge segment to be updated, $\mathcal{E}_L, \mathcal{E}_R$ are neighboring segments, I' is the node representing the presence of the image derived information used for $\mathcal{E}_L$ and $\mathcal{E}_R$.

We will now follow the mathematics for the second stage in detail. The first stage is solved in a corresponding way using the same methodology. $\mathcal{E}_C$, $\mathcal{E}_L$ and $\mathcal{E}_R$ have possible values ranging over the number of segments in the object model (i.e. O_1 = apex, O_2 = posterior, ...). We also include a noise segment in the object model to account for segments which do not belong to the actual boundary. I' is either true or false (i.e. 1 or 0). This defines the events in our probability space, designated $P_{i,j,k,l}$. We now constrain certain marginal and conditional probabilities defined on the space, all of which are expressable as partial sums. First, the probability space must be normalized by making the probability of the certain event equal to 1:

$$P(S) = 1 \qquad \text{or} \qquad \sum_{i,j,k,l} P_{i,j,k,l} = 1$$

The labeling probabilities for edge segment $\mathcal{E}_C$ derived from low level information are known from the first stage, and thus impose a constraint on the space:

$$P(\mathcal{E}_C = O_i) = A_i \qquad \text{or} \qquad \sum_{j,k,l} P_{i,j,k,l} = A_i$$

The labeling probabilities for edge segments $\mathcal{E}_L$ and $\mathcal{E}_R$ derived from low level information are also known from the first stage. These are conditioned off I' to allow for the updating of $\mathcal{E}_C$ based on this information.

$$P(\mathcal{E}_L = O_j | I' = 1) = B_j \qquad \text{or} \qquad \frac{\sum_{i,k} P_{i,j,k,1}}{\sum_{i,j,k} P_{i,j,k,1}} = B_j$$

$$P(\mathcal{E}_\mathcal{R} = O_k | I' = 1) = C_k \qquad \text{or} \qquad \frac{\sum_{i,j} P_{i,j,k,1}}{\sum_{i,j,k} P_{i,j,k,1}} = C_k$$

The likelihood of particular adjacencies of segments as imposed by the model further constrains the space.

$$P(\mathcal{E}_\mathcal{C} = O_i | \mathcal{E}_\mathcal{L} = O_j) = D_{i,j} \qquad \text{or} \qquad \frac{\sum_{k,l} P_{i,j,k,l}}{\sum_{i,k,l} P_{i,j,k,l}} = D_{i,j}$$

$$P(\mathcal{E}_\mathcal{C} = O_i | \mathcal{E}_\mathcal{R} = O_k) = E_{i,k} \qquad \text{or} \qquad \frac{\sum_{j,l} P_{i,j,k,l}}{\sum_{i,j,l} P_{i,j,k,l}} = E_{i,k}$$

In order to determine the most conservative values for the probability space consistent with the constraints, we must maximize the entropy, H, over the possible $P_{i,j,k,l}$ values where:

$$H = -\sum_{i,j,k,l} P_{i,j,k,l} \log P_{i,j,k,l}$$

This constrained optimization can be solved using Lagrange multipliers by first forming the function H' that incorporates the constraints as follows:

$$H' = H + \sum_{i=1}^{m} \lambda_i \phi_i$$

where the ϕ's are the constraints written to equal zero and the λ's are constants to be determined, along with the values of $P_{i,j,k,l}$ at the extreme point. The derivative of H' with respect to each $P_{i,j,k,l}$ is set to zero. This set of equations, along with the original constraints, is solved, thus determining the probability space. In our case, H' will have the form (showing only the first few terms):

$$H' = -\sum_{i,j,k,l} P_{i,j,k,l} \log P_{i,j,k,l} + \lambda \left(1 - \sum_{i,j,k,l} P_{i,j,k,l} \right) +$$
$$\lambda_{a2} \left(\sum_{j,k,l} P_{i,j,k,l} - A_2 \right) + \lambda_{b4} \left(B_4 \sum_{i,j,k} P_{i,j,k,1} - \sum_{i,k} P_{i,4,k,1} \right) + \cdots$$

The derivative equations will have different terms, depending on the index of P, as shown.

$$0 = \frac{\partial H'}{\partial P_{w,x,y,z}} = -\log P_{w,x,y,z} - 1 - \lambda + \underbrace{\lambda_{a2}}_{\text{if } w=2} + \underbrace{\lambda_{b4} B_4}_{\text{if } z=1} - \underbrace{\lambda_{b4}}_{\text{if } z=1 \text{ and } x=4} + \cdots$$

This gives:

$$P_{w,x,y,z} = \exp\left(1 + \lambda - \underbrace{\lambda_{a2}}_{\text{if } w=2} - \underbrace{\lambda_{b4} B_4}_{\text{if } z=1} + \underbrace{\lambda_{b4}}_{\text{if } z=1 \text{ and } x=4} + \cdots \right)$$

Using the substitutions $e^{-(\lambda+1)} = \alpha_0$, $e^{\lambda_{a2}} = \alpha_{a2}$, and $e^{\lambda_{b4}} = \alpha_{b4}$ we get:

$$P_{w,x,y,z} = \alpha_0 \underbrace{\alpha_{a2}}_{\text{if } w=2} \underbrace{\alpha_{b4}^{B_4}}_{\text{if } z=1} \underbrace{\alpha_{b4}^{-1}}_{\text{if } z=1 \text{ and } x=4} \cdots$$

Since we can now express $P_{i,j,k,l}$, and thus the original constraints, in terms of the α's, we have an equation for each α. This set of simultaneous equations is then solved using standard techniques. Since the original entropy function is strictly concave upwards and the constraints are linear, the extremum is unique and global. The updated label probabilities for segment $\mathcal{E}_C$ is then determined by calculating $P(\mathcal{E}_C = O_i \mid I' = 1)$ from the newly derived expression for $P_{i,j,k,l}$ in terms of the α's. The low-level stage, along with parts of the high level stage, have been run on simulated edge segment data.

FORMING TRIAL CONTOURS

The labelled segments are now combined into a trial contour. A search is performed separately for each sensor to find the best boundary from the possible segments. The criteria for boundary goodness are high probabilities for the segment label of the appropriate region, low cumulative curvature, and small gap distances between segments. Since the criteria involve only local relationships, the search may be performed using dynamic programming. The search starts at a particular label and proceeds, changing to the next label when the current best partial boundary ends with a segment labeled with the succeeding label. The search terminates when the appropriately labeled segments form a closed path or a segment with a predetermined termination labeling is found. The result of the dynamic programming process is a contour with gaps between segments. These gaps are closed by linearly interpolating from surrounding segments. This procedure can possibly cause discontinuities in the curvature, but these are lessened by smoothing the entire curve in preparation for further analysis.

SHAPE ANALYSIS

The measurement of shape is a much addressed problem in computer vision and image understanding [1]. To characterize the contour, we need a local, tractable measure of shape that also carries sufficient surrounding point information. The $\psi - s$ curve, as discussed in [1], provides such a representation. In this representation, ψ is the angle made between a fixed line and a tangent to each point along the border. This is then plotted against s, which is the arc length along the boundary. Note that horizontal lines in the $\psi - s$ curve correspond to straight lines (no change in ψ) on the contour, and any vertically sloping $\psi - s$ lines correspond to a constant degree of curvature.

FUSING SHAPE INFORMATION

To form a system consensus opinion about the shape of the object, it is necessary to take the shapes arrived at while separately considering edge segment information from each of the sensors and iteratively check to see if alternate segment choices in either sensor were possible at a lower level of analysis. As was evident from the earlier discussion, the trial contours passed from the lower and intermediate levels of processing were only the best estimates of a contour given the available information from one sensor. It is possible that a different trial contour could have been formed using a slightly different combination of edge segment groupings, had additional information been provided (i.e. bias from a second sensor). Thus the proposed system will iteratively feed back such additional information about regions of an object's border after looking at both sensors' opinions of shape, possibly causing a different trial contour on the next iteration. An important observation is that consensus is sought at the higher levels of the system's analysis, namely an entire contour's shape, rather than trying to force the gray level edge segments to precisely match pixel-by-pixel. This allows the lower level analysis to proceed separately for each sensor. The orientation of the object, to some extent, is normalized out of the problem. In addition, the most prominent gray level edges in each sensor determine that sensor's evidential contribution to the analysis, as is appropriate.

The approach to this problem is as follows. First, the two sensor's $\psi - s$ shape curves will be run through a matching algorithm to look for curvature variations that best line up. The matching process shifts one sensor's shape curve until it best agrees according to a cross correlation with the second sensor's curve. Matching of these plots helps account for orientation differences between the sensors in the image plane. The goal of the matching process is to line up the discrete spatial positions on the shape map as best as is possible based on the initial information from each sensor.

Now that the shape curves have been lined up in an optimal way, it is desired to compute the agreement or disagreement between the two sensors' perceptions of an object's shape. This is done by simply computing the least squares error on a point by point basis and plotting an error curve. Regions of low agreement are now isolated by simply comparing the areas under the least squares error plot. The largest area is considered first, and then smaller and smaller regions within a predetermined bound. As this region is considered, several things occur. First, the propagated shape confidence is considered: if one sensor was considerably less confident in its analysis, that is the one considered for new trial contour formulation. The model label associated with this region of error is considered next. The local probabilistic models for direction and relative position for this label are now derived from a similar area in the second sensor's image which contains the more confident original labelings in that particular region (note that in this manner the system is biased toward the original training data until strong proof leads it elsewhere). These new model probability distributions are created for the region of concern in the first sensor's image (the one with the lowest original confidence of segments in the region of error) from the distribution of positions and directions of each edge point in the corresponding region in the second sensor's image. Region correspondence is found by referring to the points in the original data that correspond to the points lined up via the $\psi - s$ curve analysis. The new probability distribution models are now applied to the data from the first sensor in the same manner as before. These new data-related constraints are imposed on the probability space, resulting in new output probabilities reflecting the effect of the second sensor. A new trial contour is now formed based on this information and the process of comparing the $\psi - s$ curves formed from the trial contours in each sensor is repeated, as is feedback of information to the next low-confidence region in one of the sensors. In this way the entire algorithm is repeated until either no further modifications can be made or the system converges to full agreement (within an ϵ-error bound).

For the initial practical consideration of building a simplified stable working system, as soon as the intersensor correlation gets worse in any way, no further reasoning is allowed for that region and a new region is considered or the feedback process stopped and in both cases the last best result is maintained. Obviously this monotonic approach will not be able to reason out of local valleys and a more sophisticated overall optimization scheme will eventually be considered. The computational speed of the algorithm is also of concern and ways of speeding up convergence will be investigated.

<u>Example</u>

Suppose it is desired to identify a particular type of house in a scene consisting of several types of houses. The semantic framework of the front view of a house consists simply of two sides, a floor and two roof pieces, with appropriate spatial relationships. Suppose also that after being "trained" with many instances of many types of houses always viewed from approximately the same frontal direction, that the variation in the directionality of the parts of the semantic framework can be represented by the probability distributions as described earlier. Finally, for the purposes of this example, suppose that the edge operator derived segments from two different imaging sensors (e.g. infrared and visible) are as shown in figures 3a and 3b. Note in particular the slightly more sharply peaked apex of the roof in figure 3b and the problem that the linking algorithm has in choosing the correct segments to form the floor and right wall in figure 3b due to the extra line segment in the middle of the object. This extra line may be due to noise or partial obscuration of a portion of the house in the original gray level images. Also note that the initial probabilities for each of the segments derived from the model in figure 3 are shown in the single parentheses. These were derived after one stage of contextual updating.

Figure 4(a and b) shows the results of using the linking algorithm described earlier to join the segments with the highest appropriate probabilities to form trial house outlines from each sensor's images. Note the slight rounding off effect at the corners due to contour smoothing. Figure 5(a and b) shows the $\psi - s$ curves computed for these two contours after they are put into rough registration by the correlation matching algorithm described above. The correlation error curve is shown in figure 5c. Note that the points of maximum discrepancy are marked on the error curve in figure 5c and on the original linked curves in figure 4 as open circles (boundary linking start/end points are shown as filled-in circles). As can be seen by superimposing the region surrounding this maximum discrepancy point onto figures 3a and 3b, the left image (figure 3a) is where the least confidence in the original image data matching the gross house model occurred. New probability distributions in this discrepant region are formed by using the direction information from image b surrounding the same maximum discrepancy point (now mapped back into the second sensor's spatial boundary data (figure 4b)). Finally, figure 6(a and b) shows the updated boundary curves generated after a new trial segmentation using new probabilistic labelings found by comparing the raw edge direction data from image a to image b's new probability distributions. Figure 7(a and b) shows the new $\psi - s$ curves formed by the updated boundaries and figure 7c illustrates the regional improvement in the error curve. Note particularly the obvious improvement in the lower right portion of the house silhouette. At this point, either one of the consensus boundary curves could be matched to a finer or more specific set of house models (e.g colonial, ranch, etc.) described also by their $\psi - s$ curves.

SUMMARY

A complete logical strategy has been developed for the overall system of multisensor shape analysis. This approach considers low level uncertainties via a probabilistic reasoning algorithm, groups locally smooth low level information (edge segments), creates complete trial contours using an interpolation procedure and includes feedback from the high to the low levels in order to seek an intersensor consensus opinion of shape. A maximum entropy probabilistic reasoning approach to assigning and updating labelings on low level information has been developed and initial testing on simulated edge segment data performed. This approach allows the full consideration of dependent probabilistic information within event groups. Integration of the various algorithm modules as well as testing of the entire system on simulated and real data are planned as the next steps in the development process. The methodology will be initially applied to multisensor-guided, detailed classification of already grossly classified objects.

Acknowledgements

The authors gratefully acknowledge the help of Elliot Zaret in coding the $\psi - s$ and error curve analysis and the support of the Whitaker Foundation.

References

[1] D. H. Ballard and C. M. Brown. *Computer Vision*. Prentice Hall, Englewood Cliffs, 1982.

[2] R. Belknap, E. M. Riseman, and A. R. Hanson. The information fusion problem and rule-based hypotheses applied to computer aggregations of image events. In *Proceedings of the IEEE Conference on Computer Vision and Pattern Recognition*, pages 227–237, June 1986.

[3] P. C. Cheeseman. In defense of probability. In *Proceedings International Joint Conference on Artificial Intelligence*, pages 1002–1009, 1985.

[4] P. C. Cheeseman. A method of computing generalized bayesian probability values for expert systems. In *Proceedings International Joint Conference on Artificial Intelligence*, pages 198–202, 1983.

[5] J.S. Duncan. Intelligent determination of left ventricular wall motion from multiple view, nuclear medicine image sequences. In *Proceedings of the 1984 Joint International Symposium on Medical Images and Icons (ISMII)*, pages 265–269, Arlington,Va., July 1984.

[6] Kurt Konolige. *A Computer-Based Consultant for Mineral Exploration, Final Report, Appendix D.* Technical Report, SRI International, Menlo Park, California, September 1979.

[7] E. Persoon and K. S. Fu. Shape discrimination using fourier descriptors. *IEEE Transactions on Pattern Analysis and Machine Intelligence*, 8(3):388–397, May 1986.

[8] I. T. Young, J. E. Walker, and J. E. Bowie. An analysis technique for biological shape. I. *Information and Control*, 25(10):357–370, 1974.

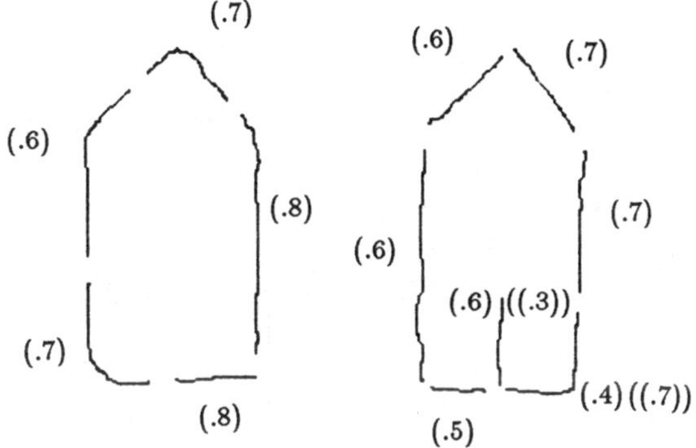

Figure 3. Simulated edge segments from test images (a) on the left and (b) on the right. The numbers in the parentheses denote maximum entropy probabilities derived from the data and the initial (single parentheses) and updated (double parentheses) probability distributions.

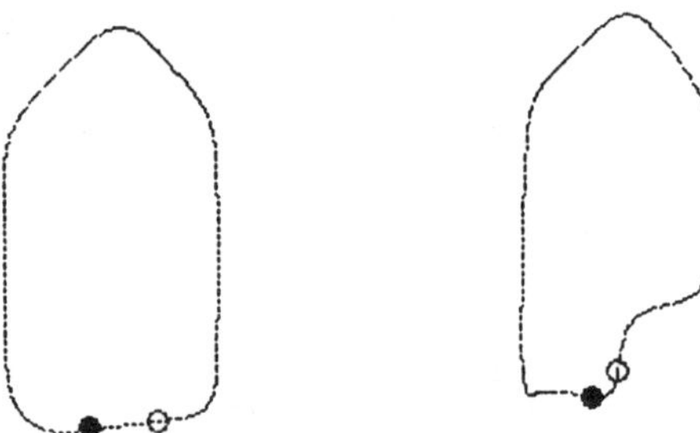

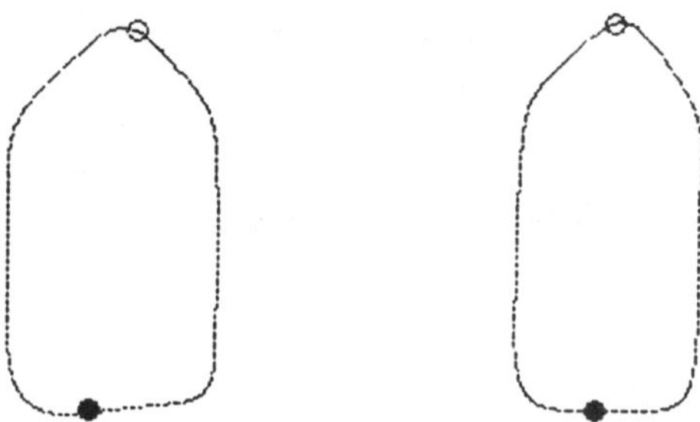

Figure 4. Complete, linked trial contours based on the initial probabilities (single parentheses in figure 3) and the linking approach described in the text. The left side (a) corresponds to figure 3a and the right side (b) corresponds to figure 3b.

Figure 6. Improved linked trial contours based on updated probabilities (double parentheses in figure 3) which were computed after one iteration of readjustment due to the error curve of figure 5c.

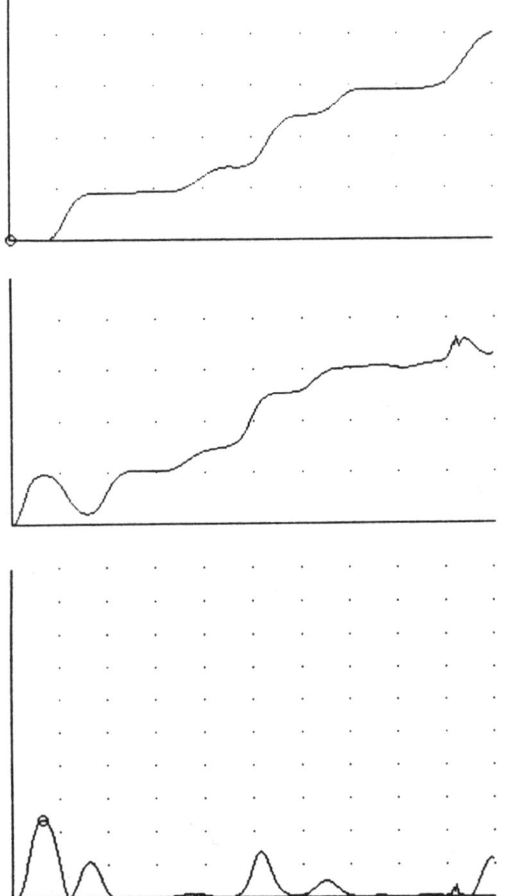

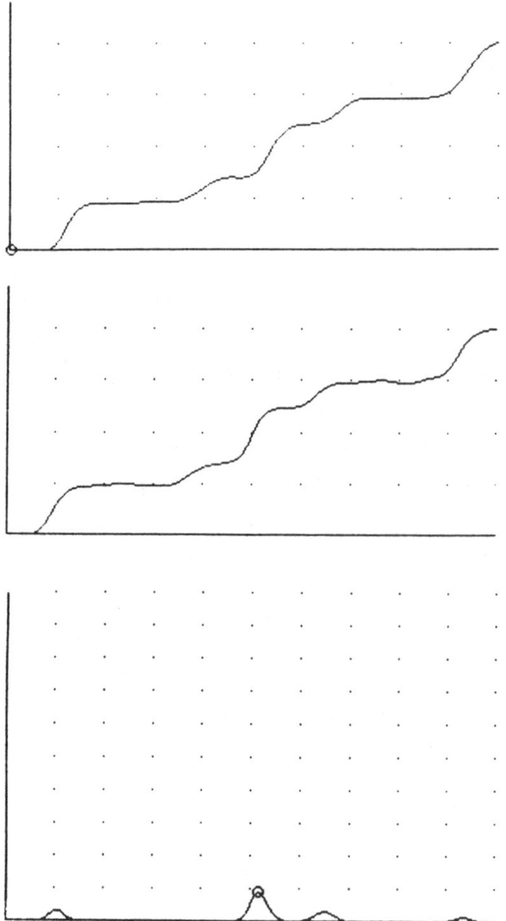

Figure 5. $\psi - s$ and error curve analysis of contours shown in figure 4. The upper two plots represent the ψ (vertical axis spacing between dots is $\pi/2$ radians) - s (equally spaced points beginning and ending at the filled-in dot of figure 4) curves for figure 4a (upper plot a) and figure 4b (middle plot b). The lower plot (c) is the least squared error curve plot between the two $\psi - s$ curves shown in a and b. Relative error is plotted vertically and the horizontal axis matches that of plots a and b. The open circle marks the point of maximum discrepancy, also shown in figure 4.

Figure 7. $\psi - s$ and error curve analysis of updated contours shown in figure 6. The upper two plots represent the ψ (vertical axis spacing between dots is $\pi/2$ radians) - s (equally spaced points beginning and ending at the filled-in dot of figure 6) curves for figure 6a (upper plot a) and figure 6b (middle plot b). The lower plot (c) is the least squared error curve plot between the two $\psi - s$ curves shown in a and b. Relative error is plotted vertically and the horizontal axis matches that of plots a and b. The open circle marks the point of maximum discrepancy, also shown in figure 6.

A FRAMEWORK FOR

MULTI-SENSOR FUSION

IN THE PRESENCE OF UNCERTAINTY

T.L. Huntsberger
S.N. Jayaramamurthy

Intelligent Systems Laboratory
Department of Computer Science
University of South Carolina
Columbia, South Carolina 29208

ABSTRACT

Analysis of input from multiple sensors offers the possibility of robust image understanding using the redundancy of information present. However, two problems need to be addressed for the design of such a system. The first is uncertainty in the output of the multiple sensors from noise and other effects. Multiple valued logic allows this uncertainty to be represented. Multisensor dynamic scene analysis within this framework can be used to resolve ambiguities which might arise from single frame processing. Second is the method and the level at which to combine the evidence from the outputs of the multiple sensors. Fusion should occur at a fairly high level in the processing sequence, and should not assume independence of sensor outputs. In this paper we present a multiple valued logic based framework for image understanding, which contains a method for representation and combination of evidence from various sensor inputs. This framework, called **FLASH** (**F** uzzy **L** ogic **A** nalysis **S** ystem in **H** ardware), will be shown to be suitable for the fusion of information from multiple sensors such as laser range finding, MMW radar, FLIR, and multispectral images.

1. INTRODUCTION

Integration of information from multiple sensors for image understanding has been the subject of recent research in the machine vision field. This process is useful for three dimensional interpretations of scenes imaged by multiple cameras [KIM85] or visible and range sensors [GIL83], and for the fusion of visible and thermal infrared sensor outputs [NAND87].

Noise in sensors and effects such as motion blur induce uncertainty into parameters derived from an image. Multiple sensors can serve to minimize these types of problems, while at the same time providing redundant information. However, there needs to be a consistent framework for the fusion and interpretation of the outputs from the multiple sensors. Multiple valued logic based sets offer such a framework with the capability of representing uncertainty and integrating information from multiple sensors.

2. FRAMEWORK FOR FUSION

A multistage system is needed since sensor fusion can occur at many different levels. This type of modularity also lends itself well to hardware implementation. FLASH is comprised of three stages. The first stage is capable of unsupervised homogeneous region identification, as well as edge detection. In this stage, individual pixels in an image obtained from a given sensor are represented by their membership values to cluster centers in a feature space. Edge location and strength are obtained using a set theoretical operator on the membership values for each region. Details of the segmentation and edge detection portions of this stage were reported previously by Huntsberger et. al. and Jacobs [HUNT85a, HUNT85b, JACO83]. This technique has been successfully tested with full color [HUNT86, JAYA85], seven-band thematic mapper [CANN86], high altitude thermal infrared [HUNT84], FLIR [KELL86], and MMW radar images [BEZD86]. For dynamic scene analysis, these operations are performed on a sequence of frames, taken four at a time. We assume here that the sequences are registered to each other ahead of time. The cluster centers for the classes of the first frame in a four frame sequence are used as reference centers for the calculation of the membership values for the following frames.

The processed output corresponding to each sensor may provide partial evidence for the presence of objects. As was noted previously by Helland, et al [HELL81], objects are broken up into constituent parts by the response characteristics of different sensors. In their study, a jeep as seen by six different sensors (Laser 0.53 μm, Laser 1.06 μm, visual, silicon TV, 3-5 μm FLIR, and 8-13 μm FLIR), was totally spread among the outputs. In order to extract a meaningful object description, it is necessary to fuse these outputs. However, fusion of sensor outputs at this early stage would be unwise without motion analysis, which determines motion characteristics of constituent portions of the images from the multiple sensors.

Stage 2 of the system is responsible for motion analysis. Motion of the objects and/or the sensors causes some changes in the frames of a sequence. By analyzing such changes over a sequence of frames, one may be able to extract motion characteristics. Changes may occur at various levels: namely, the pixel level, feature level, and region level.

Our system uses spatiotemporal changes in the shape parameters and contours of regions extracted from the processed output of each sensor. Being a region based approach, it is relatively insensitive to noise. Results from a number of experiments on full color natural image sequences were reported previously [HUNT87].

Stage 3 uses a knowledge-based systems approach to interpret the motion and shape parameters estimated by the previous stage. We have designed a multiple valued logic based PROLOG suitable for hardware implementation for this stage [HUNT85c]. A key attribute to an image understanding system is the interaction between high level knowledge in the form of object models, concepts such as occlusion and motion, and low level knowledge in the form of scene or image features.

Recently, techniques have been proposed for applying the Dempster-Shafer [SHAF76] theory for combination of evidence in the multiple valued logic domain [ISHI81, DUBO86]. The Dempster-Shafer theory allows the combination of evidence process to be treated as if there is a team of experts whose opinions must be combined to reach a conclusion. Two recent studies have shown the Dempster-Shafer approach to be more accurate for classification purposes than a Bayesian analysis of the same images [LI87, ZHAN87].

The membership values generated from the first two stages of the system can be used in the Dempster-Shafer framework as: If $m_a(X)$ is expert a's belief function for X and $m_b(Y)$ is expert b's belief function for Y, then the overall evidence for their combination or Z is given by

$$m(Z) = k \sum_{X \cap Y = Z} m_a(X)\, m_b(Y), \tag{1}$$

with

$$k^{-1} = 1 - \sum_{X \cap Y = \emptyset} m_a(X)\, m_b(Y).$$

This form for the combination of evidence assumes that the individual pieces of evidence are independent, i.e. that the observation of X has no bearing on the observation of Y. If however, the two pieces of evidence are interrelated as in

X is observed if and only if Y is observed,

as is possible with the input from multiple sensors, then the Dempster-Shafer formalism must be modified [ISHI81, DUBO86, SMET86]. The modified form given by Ishizuka [ISHI81] is

$$m(Z) = k \sum_{X \cap Y = Z} INT(X,Y)\, m_a(X)\, m_b(Y), \tag{2}$$

with

$$k^{-1} = 1 - \sum_{X,Y} [1 - INT(X,Y)]\, m_a(X)\, m_b(Y).$$

In this expression the degree of intersection of the two bodies of evidence or $INT(X,Y)$ is given by

$$INT(X,Y) = \frac{\max_{a,b}[min(m_a(X),m_b(Y))]}{\min_{a,b}[max(m_a(X)),\max(m_b(Y))]} \tag{3}$$

The degree that the capion is empty is given by $1 - INT(X,Y)$ which leads to the definition of k^{-1} in equation (2). This form of the modified Dempster-Shafer theory is similar to that of Dubois and Prade [DUBO86] and Smets [SMET86].

These alternate definitions has been shown to yield a more realistic estimate of combined non-distinct evidences [SMET86]. This property is vital for image understanding, since the Dempster-Shafer formalism will give an overestimate for the same input information. The Ishizuka modification for the combination of evidence is used in Stage 3 to combine the information from the previous stages.

3. DISCUSSION

We are in the process of developing a system for the analysis of multi-sensor dynamic scenes. Experimental evidence is accumulating to indicate that multiple valued logic sets are a good representation for the information from multiple sensors [HUNT86, JAYA85, CANN86, HUNT84, KELL86, BEZD86]. We have observed that edge and region characteristics present in this representation provide rich information about motion [HUNT87], and more work needs to be done concerning integration of the information from these operators applied to multi-sensor images using a combination of evidence approach. Preliminary results indicate that the modified forms of the Dempster-Shafer formalism defined by Ishizuka [ISHI81] or Smets [SMET86] are suitable candidates for this task. Several sequences need to be studied to ascertain sensitivity to noise of this technique.

Stage 3 is in the early experimental stages, and its development mainly depends on the choice of domain. We are investigating combination of evidence techniques suitable for the integration of motion cues available from multiple sensor edge and moving region operators. The following domains are being studied: traffic scenes, multiband remote sensing, and object detection and identification in industrial environments.

References

[BEZD86]

J.C. Bezdek and R.L. Cannon, "Algorithms for pattern recognition and image understanding systems," BAC Contract GK2337, Boeing Aircraft Corporation, Seattle, Wash.

[CANN86]

R.L. Cannon, J.V. Dave, J.C. Bezdek & M.M. Trivedi, "Segmentation of a thematic mapper image using the fuzzy c_means clustering algorithm," *IEEE Trans. Geoscience and Remote Sensing,* GE-24, 1986, pp. 400-408.

[DUBO86]

D. Dubois and H. Prade, "Set-theoretic operations on bodies of disjunctive or conjunctive evidence," *Proc. NAFIPS '86,* New Orleans, LA, 1986, pp. 107-124.

[GIL83]

B. Gil, A. Mitiche and J.K. Aggarwal, "Experiments in combining intensity and range edge maps," *CVGIP,* Vol. 21, 1980.

[HELL81]

A.R. Helland, T.J. Willett and G.E. Tisdale, "Application of image understanding to automatic tactical target acquisition," *Techniques and Applications of Image Understanding, Proc. SPIE,* Vol. 281, pp. 26-31.

[HUNT84]

T.L. Huntsberger, unpublished results.

[HUNT85a]

T.L. Huntsberger, C.L. Jacobs and R.L. Cannon, "Iterative fuzzy image segmentation," *Pattern Recognition,* 18, 1985, pp. 131-138.

[HUNT85b]

T.L. Huntsberger and M.F. Descalzi, "Color edge detection," *Pattern Recognition Letters,* 3, 1985, pp. 205-209.

[HUNT85c]

T.L. Huntsberger and W.R. Wood, "FLASH, An architecture for computer vision in uncertain environments," *Proc. IEEE Workshop. Computer Arch. Pattern Analysis Image Database Management,* Miami, Florida, 1985, pp. .

[HUNT86]

T.L. Huntsberger, C. Rangarajan and S.N. Jayaramamurthy, "Representation of uncertainty in computer vision using fuzzy sets," *IEEE Trans. Comp, Spec. Issue MVL,* C-35, 1986, pp. 135-146.

[HUNT87]

T.L. Huntsberger and S.N. Jayaramamurthy, "Determination of the optic flow field using spatiotemporal region deformations," *Pattern Recognition Letters,* in press.

[ISHI81]
M. Ishizuka, "Extensions of Dempster and Shafer's theory to fuzzy sets for constructing expert systems," Summary of Papers on General Fuzzy Problems, Rep. 7, The working group on fuzzy systems, Japan, 1981.

[JACO83]
C.L. Jacobs, "Color image segmentation: texture and a fuzzy c-means clustering implementation," M.S. Thesis, University of South Carolina, 1983.

[JAYA85]
S.N. Jayaramamurthy and T.L. Huntsberger, "Region and edge analysis using fuzzy sets," *Proc. IEEE Conf. Languages for Automation,* Mallorca, Spain, 1985, pp. 71-75.

[KIM85]
Y.C. Kim and J.K. Aggarwal, "Finding range from stereo images," *Proc. IEEE Conf. CVPR,* San Francisco, CA, 1985, pp. 289-294. "Finding range from intensity images,"

[LI87]
Z. Li, "Comparisons of reasoning mechanisms for computer vision," *Proc. AAAI Workshop: Uncertainty in AI,* University of Washington, Seattle, WA, July 10-12, 1987, pp. 287-294.

[NAND87]
N. Nandhakumar and J.K. Aggarwal, "Multisensor integration - Experiments in integrating thermal and visual sensors," *Proc. First Int. Conf. Computer Vision,* London, England, 1987, pp. 83-92.

[SHAF76]
G. Shafer, *A Mathematical Theory of Evidence,* Univ. Princeton Press, 1976.

[SMET86]
P. Smets, "Combining non-distinct evidences," *Proc. NAFIPS '86,* New Orleans, LA, 1986, pp. 544-548.

[ZHAN87]
M. Zhang and S. Chen, "Evidential reasoning in image understanding," *Proc. AAAI Workshop: Uncertainty in AI,* University of Washington, Seattle, WA, July 10-12, 1987, pp. 340-346.

MULTI-SENSOR INTEGRATED INTELLIGENT ROBOT FOR AUTOMATED ASSEMBLY

Ren C. Luo, Min-Hsiung Lin

Robotics and Intelligent Systems Laboratory
Department of Electrical and Computer Engineering
North Carolina State University
Raleigh, NC 27695-7911

ABSTRACT

The objective of this paper is to develop an intelligent robot system through the integration of multiple sensors into robot tasks.

The investigation is based on a Unimation PUMA 560 robot employing various external sensors. These sensors include overhead vision, eye-in-hand vision, proximity, tactile array, position, force/torque, cross-fire, overload and slip. The efficient machine representation of acquired sensory knowledge will enable robots to deal with the "real world". The general paradigm of a sensor data fusion system has been developed. This system will allows the robot to handle uncertainty in sensory data as well as to verify and recover sensor errors.

1. Introduction

The next generation of industrial robots will require adaptive motion control based on feedback from the work environment via visual, tactile, force/torque and other types of sensors. This will allow intelligent robots to accommodate changes in the workspace, such as changes in position and or orientation of work pieces and perform complex operations such as automated assembly and sorting.

There has been growing interest in recent years in the possible upgrading of robot intelligence using multiple visual and non-visual sensors.

Henderson et al. introduced the concept of Logic Sensor and Multisensor Kernel system [1,2]. Kak et al.[3] have presented a concept of knowledge-based robotics assembly cells, using multiple sensors. Ruokangas et al [4] have presented an Automation Sciences Testbed System.

Several other approaches for multi-sensor integration schemes have been described, for example Sensor data fusion [5], "Integration and Propagation of Geometric Sensor Observations" [6]. These approaches basically deal with specific tasks and do not lend themselves to a general multi-sensor data fusion design. While many good ideas have been developed and presented, several key issues have not yet been resolved. These issues primary consist of the effective use of available sensor information and sensor error detection and consequent compensation and recovery. Such issues must be addressed in order for the development of a multi-sensor system.

The principal technological areas of concern in this paper are those required for manufacturing activities at the "sensor and control level" and the "cell level". A multi-sensor based intelligent robot system has been presented. The approach for data fusion and its information propagation is described.

2. Basic Concept

2.1 Information Acquisition Based on Four Distinct Phases

Robot mounted sensors extend robot capabilities and can be basically grouped into four categories based upon the sensors operational ranges. These four categories best be described as "Far Away", "Near To", "Touching" and "Manipulation", respectively. First stage senses a scene from far away to acquire global information. Based upon this information, certain action may be initiated. If more information is required, one should zoom in and take a closer look at the scene of interest, i.e. to obtain local information. Again, based upon this information one could initiate certain actions. If yet more information is desired, one could proceed to the next phase, namely the "Touching" phase. Here we are just at the pre-pickup or pre-manipulation phase. The last stage would be the "Manipulation" phase.

As can be inferred by the preceding paragraphs, each phase seems to rely on a different subset of all sensors available to our multi-sensor system. Furthermore, each phase generates both common data and phase specified data. Common data would be information such as position/orientation (which is common to all phases). Phase specified data would be information which is not common to the other phases. In summary, each phase will contain a different set of data. If we were to conveniently package this information for each phase into a distinct template, we could adopt a frame type scheme for data representation. Fig. 1 illustrates the typical phase templates, where x, y, z and α, β, γ imply the object position/orientation, respectively.

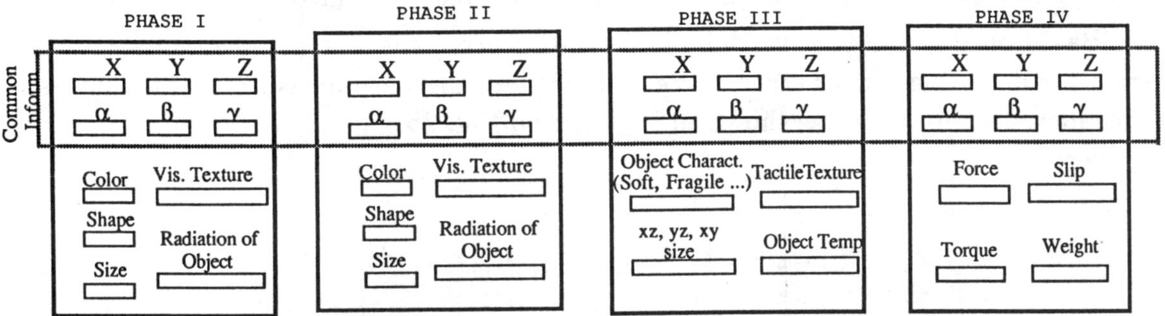

Fig. 1 Schematic diagram of typical phase templates

Having established the desirable information for each phase, the next step will be the issue of retrieving the information from all sensors used in a given phase.

3. Fusion of Sensor Data

3.1 Definition of the Distance Matrix

For fusing data describing the same object properties (e.g. object position/orientation) from different sensors, measures of confidence represent a primary means, because the data acquired by the sensors are uncertain. Errors may be generated by (1) measurement, because of the considered sensor characteristics (e.g., noise, accuracy, etc.), and (2) processing by the data interpretation algorithms.

There are a number of advantages to describing sensors by probability distributions, including an ability to integrate a variety of information types in a consistent manner, and to obtain a high degree of data compression. In addition, such statistical models have been used for a long time in other areas, and well developed methodologies exists for analyzing optimality, uncertainty and robustness.

Here we will use a probability density function (pdf) curve as the sensor's characteristic function for analyzing the confidence measures. We will define the measurement of distance matrix as a criterion for confidence measures.

The notion of a distance measure between two probability measures is widely used in statistics. Here, we will define useful distance measures as the criterion for the purpose of sensor error detection.

We can define the conditional probability function P_{ij} and P_{ji} in the form as:

$$P_{ij} = P_i\,(x_j/x_i) \quad \text{and} \quad P_{ji} = P_j\,(x_i/x_j) \tag{1}$$

As we discussed earlier, there will exist uncertainties derived from multiple sensor data, so that we need to find the relation between different sensors. If the sensor values are "close" to each other, we may fuse them together. If the values vary greatly from each other, some values may be suspected to be incorrect.

Based on this analysis, we define a new distance measures d_{ij} or d_{ji} such as a criterion for detecting sensor errors. We call this new distance measure "confidence distance measure" d_{ij} or d_{ji} as shown in Fig. 2a and Fig. 2b,

where

$$d_{ij} = 2\left| \int_{x_i}^{x_j} P_i(x/x_i)dx \right| = 2A, \quad d_{ji} = 2\left| \int_{x_j}^{x_i} P_j(x/x_j)dx \right| = 2B \tag{2}$$

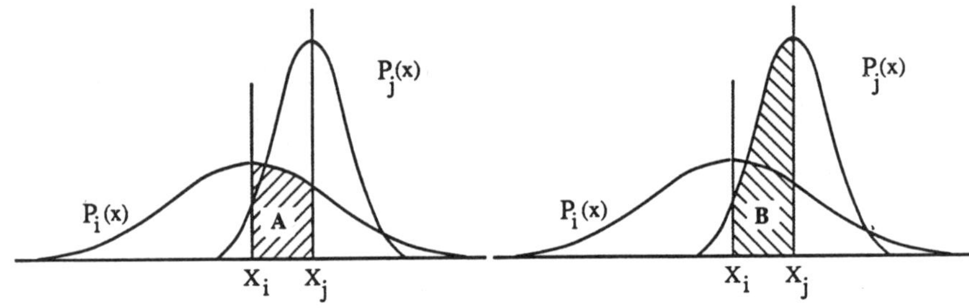

Fig. 2   Definition of "confidence distance measure" d_{ij} or d_{ji}

Here A or B is the area between sensor reading values x_i and x_j under probability distribution curve $P_i(x)$ or $P_j(x)$. In general, $d_{ij} \neq d_{ji}$ (unless the standard deviation $\sigma_i = \sigma_j$) and $0 \leq d_{ij},\, d_{ji} \leq 1$.

The advantage of this new "confidence distance measure" is that it not only provides an abstract scale value as given by the aforementioned distance measures, but it also represents the relation of the distance vs. "confidence" measures.

Basically, Gaussian distributions are the most commonly used pdf for modeling of uncertainties. Furthermore, Fukunaga et al. [7] have developed a technique which allows for testing data to determine whether or not it is a Gaussian-ness distribution. To clarify the analysis, we basically use Gaussian pdf as a sensors' distribution model. Again, $P_i(x)$ equals the probability density function of the ith sensor.

Assume we have m sensors to measure the same object property, these are x_{11}, x_{21}, $\cdots x_{m1}$, where x_{ik} means the kth data measured by the ith sensor.

If sensor i and sensor j are measuring the kth object property, then for the general case, the conditional probability function for one-dimension can be defined as

$$P_{ijk} = P_i(x_{jk} / x_{ik}) = \frac{1}{\sqrt{2\Pi}\,\sigma_{ik}(s)} e^{-\frac{1}{2}\left(\frac{x_{jk} - x_{ik}}{\sigma_{ik}(s)}\right)^2} \tag{3}$$

Hereby σ_{ik} (s) is the standard deviation of the distribution for i^{th} sensor in measuring k^{th} object property under "s" phase. In general, the standard deviation of sensor's pdf curves varied with the four distinct phases described previously.

The "confidence distance measures' can be computed by the use of the error function. The error function is defined as

$$erf(\theta) = \frac{2}{\sqrt{\Pi}} \int_0^\theta e^{-z^2}\, dz \tag{4}$$

by changing of variable and letting $x_j = x_i + \sqrt{2\theta}\,\sigma_i$ then yields $\theta = \dfrac{x_j - x_i}{\sqrt{2}\,\sigma_i}$ and

eq. (4) becomes

$$erf\left(\frac{x_j - x_i}{\sqrt{2}\,\sigma_i}\right) = 2\int_{x_i}^{x_j} P_i(x/x_i)dx \tag{5}$$

Now, from eq. (1) and eq. (5) we can compute the "confidence distance measures" as shown in eq. (6)

For the case of $x_{jk} > x_{ik}$

$$d_{ijk} = 2\int_{x_i}^{x_j} P_i(x/x_i)P_i(x_i)\, dx = 2P_i(x_i)\int_{x_i}^{x_j} P_i(x/x_i)\, dx = \frac{1}{\sqrt{2\Pi}\sigma_{ik(s)}} erf\left(\frac{x_{jk} - x_{ik}}{\sqrt{2}\sigma_{ik}(s)}\right) \tag{6}$$

Assuming we have m sensors for measuring the same object property, the general "confidence distance measures" can be described in matrix format. To simplify the matrix, we neglect the object property index k for the following analysis:

$$D_k = \begin{bmatrix} d_{11} & d_{12} & \cdots & d_{1m} \\ d_{21} & d_{22} & \cdots & d_{2m} \\ \cdot & \cdot & \cdots & \cdot \\ \cdot & \cdot & \cdots & \cdot \\ d_{m1} & d_{m2} & \cdots & d_{mm} \end{bmatrix} \tag{7}$$

3.2 Creation of the Relation Matrix

Having obtained the distance matrix ("D" matrix), we can determine the corresponding relationships of the sensors to one another. We will define a Relation

Matrix "R" by thresholding the "D" matrices by some empirically found value. The relation matrix R is defined as:

$$R_k = \begin{bmatrix} r_{11} & r_{12} & \ldots & r_{1m} \\ r_{21} & r_{22} & \cdots & r_{2m} \\ \cdot & \cdot & \cdots & \cdot \\ \cdot & \cdot & \cdots & \cdot \\ r_{m1} & r_{m2} & \cdots & r_{mm} \end{bmatrix} \tag{8}$$

where r_{ij} = threshold value of d_{ij}, and

$$r_{ij} = \begin{cases} 1, & \text{if } d_{ij} \leq threshold\ value \\ 0, & \text{if } d_{ij} > threshold\ value \end{cases}$$

3.2.1 Directed Graph Representation

The relational matrix R_k can be conveniently represented in the form of a directed graph [8] (or digraph for short). The graph is visualized by first representing all the sensors being used as nodes, and then drawing a directed arrow from node i to node j if r_{ij} equals one. The complete digraph will then represent a convenient way of visualizing the relationships among all of the used sensors, thus allowing us to look for consensus groups of sensors (i.e., with those sensor data values agreeing with each others).

We will then identify the largest connected group present in the digraph. This represents the most likely group of sensors which yield an accurate representation of the sensed data. All those sensors which are weakly supported or not supported by the largest connected group sensors would then be suspected of being in error and thus would have to be subjected to either compensation (if possible) or complete dismissal (if compensation is not possible).

3.2.2 The Strategy for Determining the Optimal Fused Sensor Data

Having identified the largest connected sub-graph, the next step will be to fuse all the sensor's data in this sub-graph and merge them together as one sensor node in the digraph. Furthermore, we have developed a strategy for determining the optimal fused data based upon this largest connected subgraph which will represent the objects property.

Assume χ contains l sets of data vectors, $\chi = \{x_1, x_2, \ldots, x_l\}$. Then since the sensor vectors are measured independently,

$$p(\chi/\theta) = \prod_{k=1}^{l} p(x_k/\theta) \tag{9}$$

Viewed as a function of θ, $p(\chi/\theta)$ is called the likelihood of θ with respect to the set of measurements[9]. The maximum likelihood estimate of θ is, by definition, that value θ that maximizes $p(\chi/\theta)$. Intuitively, it corresponds to the value of θ that in some sense best agrees with the actually measurements (i.e. the optimal fused sensor data).

For analytical purposes, it is usually easier to work with the logarithm of the likelihood than with the likelihood itself. Since the logarithm is monotonically increasing, the θ that maximizes the log-likelihood also maximizes the likelihood. If $p(\chi/\theta)$ is a well-behaved, differentiable function of θ, θ can be founded by the standard methods of differential calculus. Let θ be the p-component vector $\theta = (\theta_1, \ldots, \theta_p)^t$, let ∇_θ be the gradient operator and let $L(\theta)$ be the log-likelihood function, i.e.

$$L(\theta) = \log p(\chi/\theta) = \sum_{k=1}^{l} \log p(x_k/\theta) \tag{10}$$

Thus, a set of necessary conditions for the maximum likelihood estimate for θ can be obtained from the set of p equations $\nabla_\theta L(\theta) = 0$, where

$$\theta = \frac{\displaystyle\sum_{k=1}^{l} C_i^{-1} x_k}{\displaystyle\sum_{k=1}^{l} C_i^{-1}} \tag{11}$$

Equation (12) represent the fused sensor data value a in multi-dimensional situation. It is helpful to know the level of confidence we can have. Based on linear interpolation technique, we can derive the covariance matrix value of the fused sensor data as indicated in eq. (12).

$$C = \frac{1}{l-1} \sum_{i=1}^{l} \left[\frac{\displaystyle\sum_{j=1, j \neq i}^{l} |\theta - x_j| \, C_i}{\displaystyle\sum_{k=1}^{m} |\theta - x_k|} \right] \tag{12}$$

Apparently, the larger the covariance matrix value of the fused sensor data, the less the confidence measures will be.

After accomplishing the generation of the fused sensor template, we can update the current phase template by replacing it entirely by the fused sensor template.

4. Experimentation

As described previously, we use probability density function curve as as sensor's characteristic function for the analysis. In addition, we developed "distance matrix" and "relation matrix" based on directed graph theory to detect sensor errors and to fuse the consistency sensors together.

In order to test the aforementioned robot multi-sensor fusion system, a preliminary experimental setup has been established as shown in Fig. 3.

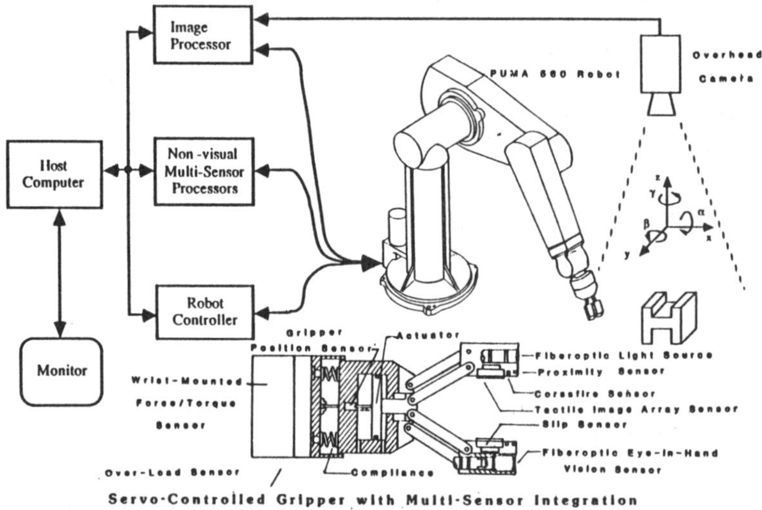

Fig. 3 The overall experimental setup

Fig. 4 shows a robot eye-in-hand vision used in the implementation. The hand is designed in parallel jaw style with hybrid position/force servo control capabilities. In addition, the hand also equipped with a LORD finger-based tactile sensor for the use of "sensing by touch" purposes. Fig. 5 illustrates the objects to be identified. Fig. 6 shows topview images of the objects after edges have been detected. Since object 1 and 3 can not be discriminated using only single topview 2-D information, we use robot hand with tactile sensor to grasp the side of the object, so that we can easily discriminate object 1 and object 3 respectively. Fig. 7 and 8 illustrates the resulting tactile data and images from object 1 and 3.

Fig. 4 Robot eye-in-hand vision system

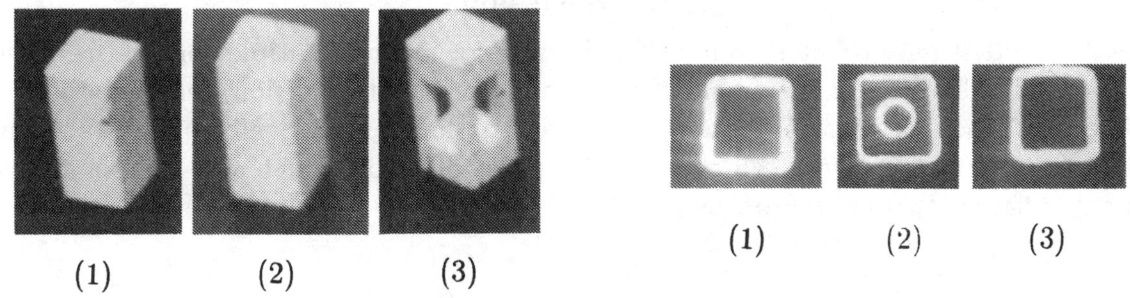

(1)   (2)   (3)

Fig. 5 The objects to be identified

(1)   (2)   (3)

Fig. 6 The edge detected topview image
of the objects

Fig. 7 Tactile image for object 1   Fig. 8 Tactile image for object 3

In general, the overall experimental setup can be divided into three categories: namely, robot, multi-sensors and computer support hardwares.

Unimation PUMA 560 together with additional external multi-sensors are used to test the success of sensor data fusion algorithms. Several sensors are used which include overhead vision, robot eye-in-hand vision, ultrasonic range sensor, tactile sensing array, wrist force/torque sensor, and finger mounted force/slip sensors, etc.

The supervisory system is a multi-user DEC VAX 11/785. Programs are also written in modular fashion in C language. The Unimation PUMA robot is a 6-axis articulated arm, with DEC 11/73 based controller; the programming language is VAL II. Vision processing is performed using a TRAPIX 5500 vision system. Programs are written in modular fashion in C language.

The VAX acts as a supervisory system, providing an interface to the user and overall task control. The VAX is responsible for some portion of each sensor subsystem set-up (i.e., calibration, communication, etc.). All sequences of adaptive commands generated for the PUMA by the VAX are communicated by use of this extensive library. Subroutines are available to perform communication, logic, and movement commands as required.

5. Conclusion

An intelligent robot system with the integration of multiple sensors has been presented. The system is capable of performing sensor data fusion, sensor data error detection , making it useful for such industrial applications as flexible manufacturing. The future research work will be on sensor coordination which will incorporate as many different types of sensors as possible.

6. References

[1] T. C. Henderson and E. Shilcrat, "Logical Sensor Systems" Journal of Robotics Systems, 1(2), 169-193, 1984.

[2] T. C. Henderson, W. S. Fai, and C. Hansen, "MKS: A Multisensor Kernel System," IEEE Transactions On System, Man, and Cybernetics, Vol. SMC-14, No. 5, September/October 1984.

[3] A. C. Kak, K. L. Boyer, C. H. Chern, R. J. Safranek, H. S. Yang, "A Knowledge-Based Robotics Assembly Cell," Proc. of IEEE International Conf. on Robotics and Automation, San Francisco, April, 1986.

[4] C. C. Ruokangas, M. S. Black, J. F. Martin and J. S. Schoenwald, "Integration of Multiple Sensors to Provide Flexible Control Strategies," Proc. of IEEE Int'l Conf. on Robotics and Automation, pp 1947-1953, San Francisco, April, 1986.

[5] S. Y. Harmon, G. L. Bianchini, B. E. Pinz, "Sensor Data Fusion Through A Distributed Blackboard," Proc. of IEEE Int'l Conf. on Robotics and Automation, pp. 1449-1454, San Francisco, April, 1986.

[6] H. F. Durrant-Whyte, "Consistent Integration and Propagation of Disparate Sensor Observations," Proc. of IEEE Int'l Conf. on Robotics and Automation,

[7] K. Fukunaga, T. E. Flick, "A Test of the Gaussian-ness of a Data Set Using Clustering," IEEE Transactions on Pattern Analysis and Machine Intelligence, Vol. PAMI-8, No.2, March, 1986.

[8] N. Deo, "Graph Theory with Applications to Engineering and Computer Science", Prentice-Hall, 1974.

[9] Duda and Hart, "Pattern Classification and Scene Analysis", John Wiley & Sons, New York, 1973.

DEALING WITH SPACE IN NATURAL LANGUAGE PROCESSING

Sergei Nirenburg
Center for Machine Translation
Carnegie Mellon University

Victor Raskin
Natural Language Processing Laborato
Purdue University

Abstract

The paper claims that spatial representation and reasoning (SRR) in robotic vision is closely related to SRR in natural language processing (NLP) because the two areas share similar issues in knowledge representation; because the way SRR is expressed by natural language cannot help influencing researchers in their developments of artificial systems of SRR; and because natural language interfaces (NLI) of a special kind are becoming increasingly essential for any type of computer system including robotic vision systems. The paper introduces a frame-based knowledge representation system for SRR, reviews NLP research on SRR, outlines SRR in natural language, and, finally, focuses on SRR in NLIs for robotic vision systems. It is demonstrated that:

- SRR in a robotic vision system is seriously affected by SRR in natural language.

- SRR in natural language is a complex, multifacted, and fuzzy phenomenon.

- Sublanguage- and meaning-based NLIs to robotic vision systems can easily accommodate all the SRR requirements of those systems.

The paper focuses on those problems of space management in natural language processing which pertain to robotics, especially to robotic vision. The relevance of NLP-related spatial research to robotics is determined by the following three considerations (in the increasing order of importance):

- Knowledge-based robotic systems and NLP systems face similar problems of knowledge representation and reasoning, including spatial representation and reasoning (SRR), and the solutions found in one of the areas may be transportable to the other.

- As the research in robotics progresses and more systems become operational on the shop floor or in a military environment, increasingly more users unfamiliar with the system design and command language will need to access them; this is a situation in which robust and non-brittle interfaces become crucial, and natural language interfaces (NLI) with a reasonably unconstrained input within a specific realistic domain are the most efficient ones for the following reasons:

  - it is natural for humans to represent, and reason about, space in natural language.

  - computer systems have to have spatial knowledge represented in frames, predicate calculus formulas or another notation that facilitates mechanical inference-making.

  - NLIs will thus provide a link between the natural language and the language of spatial representation and reasoning (SRR).

  - NLIs are becoming less costly and more feasible as the research in NLP progresses in the semantic/pragmatic direction.

- While intricate systems of geometric and/or topographic representations can, and need to, be developed artificially for robotic systems, the researchers tend to be guided by the way spatial references are made in their language.

So far, the research devoted to acquiring, representing, understanding and reasoning about spatial relations has been largely confined to the areas of vision and robotics. Much of the work in SRR concentrated on path-finding and navigation for autonomous mobile devices (cf. Meystel, 1985 for a survey). There has been a number of interesting representation (e.g., Agin, 1972; Kuipers, 1978; Davis, 1981), acquisition (e.g., Davis, 1984) and reasoning (e.g., Forbus, 1981; McDermott and Davis, 1984) efforts in the area of shape descriptions, scene descriptions, path finding, etc.

Section 1 of the paper introduces a frame-based knowledge-representation system optimal for NLP systems in general and NLIs in particular, and quite familiar to those involved in knowledge-based robotic vision. Section 2 contains a brief survey of research on SRR in NLP. Section 3 deals with the way natural languages deal with space. Finally, Section 4 discusses the optimal approach to the development of SRR modules of NLIs for robotic systems and demonstrates the adequacy of the frame-based representation for SRR information required in IMASes and other robotic vision systems.

1. Frame-Based Representation in NLP and NLIs

Frame-based knowledge representation is used in many state-of-the-art NLP systems. TRANSLATOR, a knowledge-based machine translation system (see, for instance, Nirenburg et al., 1987), uses a system of this type to represent the interlingua (IL), which is the result of a comprehensive semantic/pragmatic, syntactic, and morphological analysis of the input text in a source language, e.g., English. The information thus recorded can then be expressed in a target language in the process of generation. If the target language is another natural language, e.g., German, the system performs machine translation. But the IL information can be used for information retrieval, automatic text summarization, etc.

What follows is the IL representation of an English sentence, *Data such as the above, that are stored more or less permanently in a computer, we term a database* by TRANSLATOR's analyzer.

```
(object
 (id object1)
 (is-token-of data) *
 (subworld computerworld) *
 (quantifier (type all) (scope (and clause1 clause2)))))

(object
       (id object2)
       (is-token-of computer)
       (subworld computerworld)
       (quantifier any))

(object
       (id object3)
       (is-token-of database)
       (subworld computerworld))

(state
       (id state1)
       (is-token-of be-equivalent)
       (phase static)
       (patient1 object1)
       (patient2 (antecedent-of above))
       (time always)
       (space none)
       (subworld computerworld))
```

```
(state
     (id state2)
     (is-token-of in)
     (phase static)
     (patient1 object1)
     (patient2 object2)
     (time always)
     (space none)
     (subworld computerworld))

(state
     (id state3)
     (is-token-of  be-a-name-of)
     (phase static)
     (patient1 object3)
     (patient2 object1)
     (time always)
     (space none)
     (subworld computerworld))

(clause
     (id clause1)
     (discourse-structure (+expan clause1 clause3))
     (event state1)
     (focus state1.patient2)
     (modality conditional)
     (subworld computerworld)
     (time always)
     (space none))

(clause
     (id clause2)
     (discourse-structure (+expan clause2 clause3))
     (event state2)
     (focus time)
     (modality conditional)
     (subworld computerworld)
     (time always)
     (space (in object1 object2)))

(clause
     (id clause3)
     (discourse-structure none)
     (event state3)
     (focus object3)
     (modality real)
     (subworld computerworld)
     (time always)
     (space none))
```

```
(sentence
    (id sentence1)
    (main-clause clause3)
    (clauses clause1 clause2)
    (subworld computerworld)
    (modality real)
    (focus object3)
    (speech-act (type definition)
                (performative direct)
                (speaker author)
                (hearer reader)))
```

It is clear that there is hardly any provision for SRR in this system besides characterizing one state as IN. The space property slot remains uncharacterized throughout, and nevertheless, this system works quite well for TRANSLATOR. The reason for that is that many NLP systems (see Raskin, 1986) can get away with very little SRR. This is also the reason why NLP has not paid enough attention to SRR. It will be demonstrated in Section 4 that the representation expands easily to accommodate as much SRR information as necessary.

2. A Brief Survey of NLP Research on SRR

Winograd (1972) introduced a measure of spatial reasoning - thus, for instance, the robotic hand knew that nothing could be stacked on top of a pyramid or on top of a cube on which a pyramid had been stacked earlier and not subsequently removed. This was achieved with the help of a simple and straightforward formalism involving the categories of shape, location, and size (in our notation):

```
('space'
  ('shape' (Round Pointed Rectangular))
  ('location' (first-coordinate) (second-coordinate)(third-coordinate))
  ('size' (first-dimension) (second-dimension) (third-dimension)))
```

For size and location, Winograd used a 3D coordinate system with coordinates ranging from 0 to 1200 on all three dimensions. Thus,

```
('shape' Rectangular)
('location' (100 200 300))
('size' (400 500 600))
```

would describe a block whose front lower left-hand corner is at 100, 200, 300, and whose three dimensions are 400, 500, 600.

The robotic hand had no sensors whatsoever, and the recognition was simulated by inputting the initial parameters in symbolic form.

Winograd's effort did not, however, lead to much additional research on SRR in NLP. Moreover, neither the spatial module nor the entire system was ever scaled up. The relative lack of interest in space is even more surprising if one considers how seriously treatment of time has been approached in the NLP community over the past several years (see, for instance, Allen, 1984, Steedman and Moens, 1987).

Research by Waltz and his associates at the University of Illinois (e.g., Waltz, 1981; Boggess, 1978) was directed at the design of spatial representations for the use of natural language question-answering systems as part of their effort to relate verbal descriptions to visual representations and, more generally, to adequately analyze language descriptions of the physical world. Such representations support transitivity judgments (i.e., given as input the sequence "the goldfish is in the goldfish bowl; the goldfish bowl is on the shelf; the shelf is on the desk; the desk is in the room," the system was able to answer in the affirmative the query "Is the goldfish in the room?")

The knowledge-representation system used in TRANSLATOR already provides for more SRR than illustrated in Section 1. Its current properties set includes two SRR-related frames, 'size' and 'shape': (see Nirenburg et al. 1987, p. 97)

However, in order to be more complete (if the served domain requires) the properties should include frames for 'position' and 'distance' as well. The nature of the value-sets for these frames will be addressed in Section 4 while the issue of motion-related meaning, an important aspect of SRR, is touched upon in the following section.

3. SRR in Natural Language

Research on space representation in natural language has focused primarily on space adverbials, typically realized as prepositional phrases, such as:

```
(1)   Tom is in bed

(2)   John walked into the trap

(3)   The tree is by the house
```

Talmy (e.g., 1983) came up with the most complete representation of motion, an important aspect of SRR, to date, and it has been followed up to some extent by Herskovits (1987). Oriented primarily at linguistic description, the framework can be rendered in the frame notation roughly as follows:

```
(motion
    ('figure' object)
    ('motion' action)
    ('manner' action property)
    ('path' location property | direction property)
    ('ground' object))
```

Thus, in

```
(4)   The bottle was floating in the cove
```

the figure is 'bottle,' the motion and manner are expressed by 'float,' the path is 'in,' and the figure is 'cove.' Generally and typically, the figure and ground are expressed by nouns, the motion by verbs, the manner by adverbs (often incorporated into the verb as in the example), and the path is indicated by a preposition.

Even this one aspect of SRR as expressed in natural language clearly demonstrates its complexity. The other problems of NL-SRR are ambiguity, fuzziness, and extreme context sensitivity.

Most space prepositions double up in natural languages as temporal and abstract, such as:

```
(5)   in the house          in a minute          in a hurry

(6)   on the bed            on completion        on the way

(7)   at the market         at noon              at ease
```

In conjunction with the ambiguity of other words, there are many sentences which are ambiguous, with one SRR-related meaning and the other(s) not, such as:

```
(8)   Jim cut through the hedges
```

For NLP, this type of ambiguity is no different from any other and is treated in the same way. There can also be cases of SRR anaphora which need to be resolved. Thus, 'here' can mean 'on this chair,' 'at this table,' 'in this room,' 'in this house,' 'in this town,' etc.

More significantly, there is a considerable amount of indeterminacy, or fuzziness, in the way natural language express SRR in comparison with its precise geometry and topography. Thus, 'in the house' determines only a range of positions within the structure, and the actual object (or figure, in Talmy's terms) so located can be situated on any floor, in any room, and anywhere within each room. Moreover, 'in the house' or 'in the box' are different from 'in the city' because a city is 2D rather than 3D. Similarly, the geometric designations in natural languages are very crude and radically different from their scientific counterparts.

The context-sensitivity of SRR-related expressions in natural languages can be exemplified by the following examples:

```
(9)   The piano is in the house

(10)  Three people live in the house

(11)  Real love can be found in the house
```

The same locative expression 'in the house' has a truly SRR-related meaning in the first sentence, partially SRR-related meaning in the second, and almost entirely non-SRR-related meaning in the third. This can be demonstrated by the different inferences from the three sentences. While the piano is confined to the house, the people who live in it are not, and the love is associated with the people and not with any physical structure.

Understanding, representation and generation of SRR in natural language is an important functionality for a number of knowledge-based systems, including intelligent (natural language, graphics, and mixed language/graphics) interfaces to vision and robotic and other reasoning systems, on the one hand, and the various text understanding, skimming and generation systems, on the other.

The resolution of ambiguity, anaphora, semantic complexity stemming from context-sensitivity have to be dealt with in both kinds systems but it is the former which seem to be more affected by fuzziness.

4. SRR in NLP

Extracting meaning from text, is a *sine qua non* of any NLP system, and the only way to make this complex task feasible is by adopting the sublanguage approach. Because all computer systems deal with a very constrained domain in manufacturing, communication, or military environment, most of the ambiguity issues simply do not arise. Thus, a specific domain would deal EITHER with physical motion OR with conversation, so that 'cutting through the hedges' would be immediately reduced to only one of its meaning. It has been demonstrated elsewhere (Nirenburg and Raskin, 1987) that the word 'operator' which can have up to 7 distinct meanings in English as a whole keeps only 1.5 of them in the English sublanguage of computer science.

SRR in NLIs for computer systems, in general, and for robotic vision, in particular, should - and easily can - be flexible enough to accommodate more or less information depending on the nature of the domain and the task. A robust NLI for a typical Navigator-type program for an IMAS should be able to interpret accurately a fuzzy command such as:

```
(12) Fetch the big wrench from the shelfcase!
```
It should be able to analyze 'fetch' roughly as:

1. 'move' from your current position to any spot near the shelfcase in question

2. look for the wrench, shelf after shelf, until you find it

3. grasp the wrench

4. bring it to me

It is important here to understand the precise "division of labor" between the NLI and the robotic vision system *per se*. The former will identify the robot as the addressee of the command; it will also provide a SRR frame, whose slots will be filled by the robotic vision system. For a typical navigating task, the frame will probably be similar to the ones introduced by Kuipers in a different context (1978). In the frame notation, such a frame will look roughly as follows:

```
('motion' go-to
     ('from' location1 [the robot's current position])
     ('to'   location2 [near the operator])
     ('via'  location3 [shelfcase, where the wrench is])
     ('purpose' move (wrench location2 location3)))
```
The semantic analysis of 'the big wrench' would typically involve:

- the recognition of a wrench-type shape

- the discovery of several such objects

- the comparison of their relative sizes

- the ability to choose the biggest one

Similarly, 'the shelfcase' involves the recognition of a unique shelfcase-shaped object and the realization of its internal structure, i.e., that it consists of more than one shape. The actual IMAS domain will determine what shapes populate the subworld, and the complexity semantic analysis in the NLI will be determined by this information. Such an analysis will be always much simpler than in "the whole world."

Shape recognition is not an NLI problem. However, there is an interesting development in contemporary semantics which can make the translation from natural language into the command language of a robotic vision system easier. Shape can be described geometrically, and various methods have been proposed for that (see, for instance, Kuipers, 1978; McDermott and Davis, 1984). It can also be described as related to a prototypical shape, as in the analysis above. Semantic analysis can be also performed in terms of "prototype semantics" (see, for instance, Lakoff, 1987, and references there), a theory which attempts to determine the meaning of each word in terms of its prototype and a distance from it.

An NLI to an IMAS does not have to contain commands triggering navigation programs or include route-planning, obstacle- and collision-avoidance, etc. If 'fetch' means 'go from A to B,' such triggering occurs automatically. Similarly, the fuzziness of SRR in natural language means simply that the interface must be able to translate the fuzzy spatial expression at the input into the grid-, map- or cordinate-related notation used in the IMAS. Whether the range usually expressed by a locative in natural language is translated into a range or a random value within this range in the IMAS is a matter of convenience and design of the robotic vision system itself. This problem is simply a particular aspect of a larger issue addressed in part by Waltz and his associates (see Section 2) of generating a "scene" from its verbal description which always underdetermines reality.

Conclusion

The main points of the paper are:
- SRR in a robotic vision system is seriously affected by SRR in natural language.

- SRR in natural language is a complex, multifacted, and fuzzy phenomenon.

- Sublanguage- and meaning-based NLIs to robotic vision systems can easily accommodate all the SRR requirements of those systems.

Acknowledgments

The authors would like to thank John Brolio for the many useful discussions of the subject.

References

Agin, G.J. 1972. Representation and Description of Curved Objects. TR 173.   Stanford University AI Lab.

Allen, J. 1984. Towards a general theory of action and time. Artificial Intelligence 23.

Boggess, L. 1978. Computational representation of English spatial prepositions. TR-75. Coordinated Science Lab, University of Illinois.

Davis, E. 1981. Organizing Spatial Knowledge. TR 193. Yale University Department of Computer Science.

Davis, E. 1984. Representing and Acquiring Geographic Knowledge. TR 292. Yale University Department of Computer Science.

Forbus, K. 1981. A study of qualitative and geometric knowledge inreasoning about motion. TR 615. MIT AI Lab.

Herskovits, A. 1987. Language and Spatial Cognition. Cambridge: Cambridge University Press.

Kuipers, B. 1978. Modeling spatial knowledge. Cognitive Science 2, pp. 129-154.

Lakoff, G. 1987. WOMEN, FIRE AND OTHER DANGEROUS THINGS. Chicago - London: University of Chicago Press.

McDermott, D. and E. Davis. 1984. Planning routes through uncertain territory.   Artificial Intelligence, 22, pp. 107-156.

Meystel, A. 1985. Autonomous mobile devices: a step in the evolution. In: S. Andriole (ed.), Applications in Artificial Intelligence. Princeton, NJ: Petrocelli Books.

Nirenburg, S. and Raskin, V. 1987. The Subworld Concept Lexicon and the Lexicon Management System. Computational Linguistics, 13 (in print).

Nirenburg, S., Raskin, V., and Tucker, A. 1987. On knowledge based machine translation. In: S. Nirenburg (ed.), MACHINE TRANSLATION. Cambridge: Cambridge University Press.

Raskin, V., 1986. Natural Language Processing at Purdue University. In: V. Raskin (ed.), MATERIALS ON NATURAL LANGUAGE PROCESSING AT PURDUE UNIVERSITY AND ON COMPREHENSIVE MEANING PROCESSING APPROACH. PNLPL TR-1. W. Lafayette, IN: Purdue University, Paper 1.

Steedman M. and M. Moens. 1987. Temporal ontology in natural languages. Proceedings of 25th ACL.

Talmy, L. 1983. How language structures space. In: H. Pick and L. Acredolo (eds.), SPATIAL ORIENTATION: THEORY, RESEARCH, AND APPLICATION. Plenum Press.

Waltz, D. 1981. Toward a detailed model of processing for language describing the physical world. Proceedings of 7th IJCAI, Vancouver, B.C., -6.

Winograd, T. 1972. UNDERSTANDING NATURAL LANGUAGE. Edinburgh: Edinburgh University Press.

DEICTIC AND INTRINSIC USE
OF SPATIAL PREPOSITIONS:
A MULTIDISCIPLINARY COMPARISON

Gudula Retz-Schmidt

SFB 314

Department of Computer Science

University of Saarbrücken

D - 6600 Saarbrücken 11

Federal Republic of Germany

ABSTRACT

In this paper, principles involving the deictic and intrinsic use of spatial prepositions are examined from the viewpoint of linguistic, psychological, and Artificial Intelligence approaches. After a brief introduction to the natural-language dialog system CITYTOUR, important concepts with respect to the deictic and intrinsic use of prepositions are defined. In the following section, those prepositions that permit deictic as well as intrinsic use are listed, and the way CITYTOUR copes with them is explained. Then, the identification of the front, back, left, and right regions of a reference object is looked at in more detail. Finally, strategies concerning the deictic and intrinsic use of spatial concepts are pointed out.

The work reported in this paper was supported by the Special Collaborative Program on Artificial Intelligence and Knowledge-Based Systems (SFB 314) of the German Science Foundation (DFG), project NS2: VITRA. The system CITYTOUR was implemented by Elisabeth André, Guido Bosch, Gerd Herzog, and Thomas Rist.

1. Introduction

When describing spatial relations in natural language, we often use prepositions like "behind" or "to the left of". These kind of prepositions, which are used in order to describe the location of one object in relation to another, are called *relational prepositions* ([8] p. 45]), *directional prepositions (Richtungspräpositionen)* [36], or *projective prepositions* ([16], p. 156). Some of these prepositions can be used in different ways, depending on the particular point of view (cf. [9] p. 1). Thus, if we say "The post office is behind the church.", it can either mean that we want to locate the post office in relation to the church from the point of view of the speaker, or with respect to the orientation of the church itself. The former is usually called *deictic use*, the latter *intrinsic use* [35].

In this paper, several approaches to the problem of the deictic and intrinsic use of spatial prepositions are examined. These approaches belong to different disciplines, such as linguistics, psychology, and Artificial Intelligence (AI). After a brief, general description of the natural-language dialog system CITYTOUR, several issues concerning the deictic and intrinsic use of spatial prepositions are discussed, and CITYTOUR is compared to other approaches in more detail.

2. The System CITYTOUR

The system CITYTOUR ([2] and [3]) is part of the project VITRA (VIsual TRAnslator), which is concerned with the natural-language description of visual, in particular spatial, information. Experimental studies are being carried out in the way of designing an interface between image-understanding and natural-language systems. CITYTOUR [1] operates in the domain of city and traffic scenes. It answers natural-language questions (in German) about the spatial relations between objects in a scene. An example of a scene is shown in the right window in fig. 1. It is a part of the city center of Saarbrücken. Another scene used is the traffic scene "Durlacher Tor". Here, the input data for CITYTOUR are actually provided by a vision system [2], namely, the system currently being developed at the IITB of the FhG in Karlsruhe ([30] and [37]). CITYTOUR deals with spatial relations, in particular, between non-moving objects (called *static objects*) or between a moving (called *dynamic object*) and a static object. In the system CITYTOUR, static objects are represented by means of the following characteristics: their *center of gravity*, their *closed polygon*, their *delineative rectangle*, and their *prominent front* - an intrinsic property of the objects which determines their intrinsic orientation (cf. section 5). Dynamic objects are represented as a sequence of space-time-coordinate pairs, called *trajectory*. So far, like in city maps, only two dimensions in the horizontal plane are considered. The vertical dimension is ignored.

In addition to the issue of the deictic and intrinsic use of spatial prepositions, which is dealt with in more detail in the following sections of this paper, degrees of applicability of spatial prepositions and the semantics of path prepositions were investigated within the framework of CITYTOUR. Since it seems inappropriate to assume a fixed borderline which separates the area in which a spatial relation (e.g. "x is behind the church") holds from the area in which it doesn't hold, in CITYTOUR, degrees of applicability of spatial prepositions are calculated. These depend on the size of and on the distance from the reference object, in relation to which another object is being located. The degrees of applicability are expressed by FUZZY values. In natural-language answers, they are described by means of linguistic hedges (like "directly" or "approximately") (cf. [16] p. 181ff., who speaks of *graded concepts* (p. 184)).

As examples of path prepositions, the prepositions "along" and "past" were examined. In order for the relation "along" between a trajectory and a static object to hold, the trajectory has to follow the contour of the object much more closely than in the case of the relation "past" (cf. [10] p. 123ff.). Therefore, in order to be appropriate, the representation for the static object needs to be more detailed in the case of "along" than in the case of "past". In CITYTOUR, the closed polygon is used for the calculation of "along", and the delineative rectangle (which is a rougher representation) for "past".

A more detailed description of those aspects of CITYTOUR that won't be dealt with in this paper can be found in [2] and [3].

3. Definitions

According to [36] and [13] (p. 6f.), directional or projective prepositions have three arguments. The first argument is the object that is being located. Henceforth, I will call it *subject*. The second argument is the

---

[1]   the system is implemented in FUZZY and ZetaLISP on a Symbolics 3600

[2]   so far, only in the case of moving objects; the data about static objects are still entered manually with the aid of a graphics editor

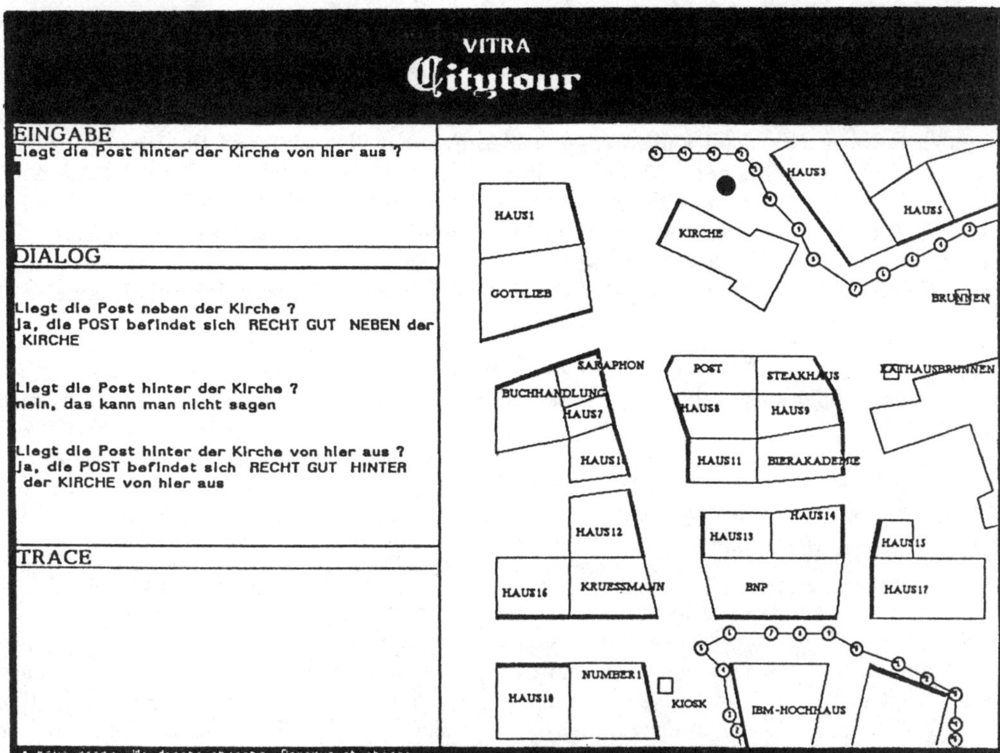

Fig. 1: CITYTOUR's windows on the screen

object in relation to which the subject is being located. I will refer to it by *reference object*. The third argument is the *point of view* from which the subject and the reference object are viewed [3] . Different terminologies can be found within the relevant literature. The first argument is called *figure* [20], *trajector* [33], or *located object* [13], the second *ground* [20], *reference object* [16], *anchor* [7], or *landmark* [33], and the third *point of observation* [16], *perspective* [7] or *point of view* [7]. Vandeloise calls the third argument *point of reference* or *(virtual) viewpoint*, depending on whether it is consciously or unconsciously taken on by the speaker [33]. Other terms often used for the third argument are *origo* ([21], [22], [29], [32]), which goes back to [6], and *reference point* ([5], [7], [22], [32]). Additional terms are listed in [29] (p. 12f.). Ehrich, in analogy to Reichenbach's three-part system for the interpretation of tenses ([27] p. 288ff.), distinguishes between the *speaker's place*, the *denotation space*, and the *reference space* [11]. Her *denotation space* comprises our *subject* and *reference object*; and our *point of view* corresponds to her *reference space*, which can coincide with her *speaker's place* (cf. below).

For the most part, we will restrict ourselves in this paper to those kinds of localizations in which the subject is outside the reference object. Now, the intrinsic and deictic use of spatial prepositions can be defined in the following way: We speak of *intrinsic use* if the point of view coincides with the reference object. In this case, the point of view is usually omitted in the natural-language description. The subject is being located with respect to the intrinsic orientation of the reference object (this aspect will be dealt with in section 5). An example is "The post office is behind the church.". If the point of view coincides with the speaker's location, we speak of *deictic use*. In this case, the subject is being located with respect to the line of sight from the speaker's location to the reference object. An example is "From here, the bank is behind the department store.". The hearer's location might also serve as the point of view, but is used less frequently than the speaker's location (cf. [7], section 6).

Levelt and Bürkle et al. use the terms *intrinsic* and *deictic system* ([23], [7]). Saile speaks of *objective* and *subjective interpretation* [28]. Rauh uses the terms *non-egocentric* and *egocentric use* [26].

In the example "The supermarket is behind the post office, as seen from the town hall.", we have neither intrinsic nor deictic use. If the point of view is given (often it will be explicitly mentioned in the description) and doesn't coincide with the location of the reference object, we will speak of *extrinsic use*. The subject is

---

[3]   either in actual fact or mentally, through an act of imagination

being located with respect to the line of sight from the point of view to the reference object. Since, in the case of deictic use, the point of view coincides with the speaker's (or hearer's) location, deictic use is a special case of extrinsic use (cf. [36]).

A third way of classifying localizations by means of relational prepositions is that of Herrmann et al. [15]. They distinguish between *two-point* and *three-point localizations*. Examples of the former are: "The ball is to the right of me.", "The ball is behind you." (which - in our terminology - would be regarded as examples of intrinsic as well as deictic use since the reference object as well as the point of view are the speaker's or hearer's location), and "The ball is in front of the car." (which we would regard as intrinsic). Examples of three-point localizations are "The ball is to the right of the lamp, as seen from my point of view." and "The ball is in front of the block, seen from your point of view." (which we would call deictic). Examples of extrinsic use, which would also be three-point localizations, are not given in their paper.

4. Which Prepositions can be Used Deictically and Intrinsically?

As stated in section 1, only some relational prepositions allow deictic and intrinsic use. In particular, most authors ([10], [15], [16], [25], [28], [32], [35], [36]) agree that "in front of", "behind", "to the left of", and "to the right of" belong to this group. In [32] they are classified as belonging to the *secondary deixis system*, in contrast to "here" and "there", which belong to the *primary deixis system*. In addition to "in front of", "behind", "left of", and "right of", Saile includes "beside". Miller, Johnson-Laird as well as Wunderlich, Herweg include "over" and "under".

According to some authors ([1], [8], [16], [18], [24], [25], [35]), the vertical dimension has the status of a priviledged direction since it is fixed by the gravitation of the earth, whereas in both horizontal dimensions, man can move freely. Thus, the vertical dimension can be conceived of as being the *primary dimension*. Moreover, the human body is asymmetric in the front/back dimension, enabling man to distinguish more easily between front and back than between left and right. This permits the less salient distinction between the front/back dimension as the *secondary dimension* and the left/right dimension as the *tertiary dimension* ([18], [24] p. 690f., [28] p. 75f.). For prepositions describing verticality, deictic use is not possible (cf. [33] p. 47f.). Instead, we can distinguish two uses based on different concepts of verticality. One is based on the intrinsic top and bottom of the reference object (Clark calls it *intrinsic verticality*) and thus can be regarded as intrinsic use. The other is based on the gravitation of the earth (Clark calls it *geological* or *gravitational verticality*). This is another kind of extrinsic use, different from that defined in section 3. We will go into it more closely in section 5. Thus, ambiguities can occur if objects that usually stand upright are lying horizontally, as in the example "There is a fly three inches above the lady's knee." (cf. [8] p. 44, [35] p. 347). However, Adorni et al. argue that gravitational verticality is more absolute than intrinsic verticality, and thus has priority ([1] p. 42). In CITYTOUR, this problem doesn't occur because only the two horizontal dimensions are considered.

CITYTOUR can operate with the following spatial concepts:

(1) the relational prepositions "vor" ("in front of"), "hinter" ("behind"), "links von" ("left of"), "rechts von" ("right of"), and "neben" ("beside") in their *locative (static) use*, like in "Die Post ist hinter der Kirche." ("The post office is behind the church.")

(2) the relational prepositions "bei" ("near"), "an" ("at"), "in" ("in"), "auf" ("on"), and "zwischen" ("between") in their locative use, like in "Der Springbrunnen ist auf dem Marktplatz." ("The fountain is on the market-place.")

(3) the prepositions "vor", "hinter", "links neben", "rechts neben", and "neben" in their *directional (dynamic) use*, like in "Sie ging links neben das Theater." ("She went to the left of the theater.")

(4) the path preposition "vorbei an" ("past"), like in "Er ging an der Schule vorbei." ("He went past the school.")

(5) combinations of "vor", "hinter", "links an", "rechts an", and "neben" with "vorbei", like in "Sie ging vor der Kirche vorbei." ("She passed in front of the church.")

(6) the path prepositions "entlang an" and "entlang" ("along"), like in "Er ging an der Fabrik entlang." ("He went along the factory.") and "Sie ging die Hauptstrasse entlang." ("She went along Main Street.")

(7) the verbs "abbiegen" ("turn off") and "einbiegen" ("turn into")

(8) the verbs "anhalten" ("stop") and "anfahren" ("start off"), possibly with specifications of the locations of the corresponding events by means of relational prepositions (cf. [37]).

Intrinsic as well as deictic use is possible in the cases (1), (3), (5), and (8). This also holds true for extrinsic use in general (cf. section 3). Thus, questions like "Where is the supermarket, as seen from the town hall?"

can be answered "The supermarket is behind the post office, as seen from the town hall." However, this type of question is rare in human conversation.

In contrast to CITYTOUR, the system ALVEN, which recognizes motion concepts and which also utilizes spatial concepts such as "rightwards", explicitly dispenses with the participation of the observer in the description process and thus cannot distinguish between intrinsic and deictic use ([31] p. 565). In Badler's system too, only intrinsic sides of objects are stored and can be used for localizations ([4] p. 49).

In the following, we will restrict ourselves to the relational prepositions "in front of", "behind", "to the left of", and "to the right of" in their locative (static) use. I shall now describe how their applicability is determined in CITYTOUR: The area around a reference object is partitioned into four half-planes - a front, a back (cf. figs. 2a and 2b), a left and a right half-plane. The half-planes are aligned to the sides of a delineative rectangle around the reference object. In the case of intrinsic use, the delineative rectangle that is oriented by the prominent front of the reference object is used, as can be seen in fig. 2a. For deictic use, the delineative rectangle that is oriented by the observer's position is taken (cf. fig. 2b). It is then determined in which half-plane(s) the subject is located so that the appropriate spatial preposition can be selected for the description.

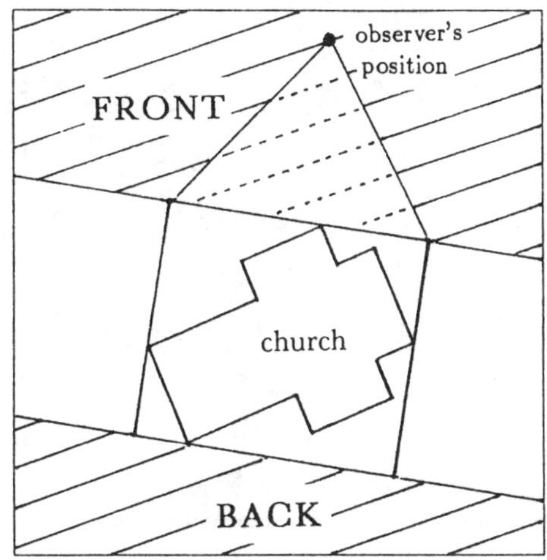

Fig. 2a: The front and back half-planes in intrinsic use

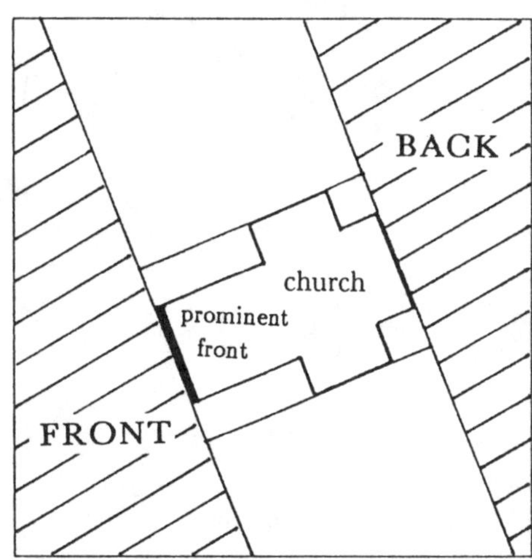

Fig. 2b: The front and back half planes in deictic use

The observer in CITYTOUR is assumed to be inside the scene; that is, sitting in a bus (which is marked on the screen as a large dot; cf. fig. 1) and asking someone who is sitting near him (and thus can be regarded as having the same point of view) and who knows more about the city (e.g. the guide of a sightseeing tour) about the locations of buildings, streets etc.. The bus can be moved within the scene so that the observer's position changes. The questions are answered by CITYTOUR either with respect to the intrinsic orientation of the buildings etc., or with respect to the observer's position (cf. sections 3 and 5). So, for the actual user of the system, we have the case of *analogical deixis* ([21], [22], [26], [29]) because, when he asks "Ist die Bank links von der Post von hier aus?" ("Is the bank to the left of the post office from here?"), with the deictic expression "here", the point of view is not his actual position in front of the screen, but the observer's position within the scene. The same is true for the user's interpretation of the system's answers. This kind of analogical deixis can be viewed as a case of *"extrinsic use in disguise"* because, in effect, what the user asks is "Ist die Bank links von der Post vom Bus aus gesehen?" ("Is the bank to the left of the post office as seen from the bus?").

5. How are the Front, Back, Left, and Right Regions Determined?

In order to determine which relational preposition is appropriate to describe the location of a subject in relation to a reference object, the front, back, left, and right regions around the reference object have to be identified.

In extrinsic and, in particular, in deictic use, they are identified by means of the *line of sight* from the point of view to the reference object. The side facing the point of view is the front. The opposite side of the reference object is its back. The regions adjacent to the front and back are the front and back regions resp. (cf. [5] p. 83). This is the way the front and back regions are assigned to an object in the Indo-European and many other languages; the reference object is treated "as if it were the other person in a canonical encounter, a person facing directly towards the speaker." ([8] p. 45). In Hausa, the opposite way (called *tandem principle*) is chosen: the reference object can be thought of as looking in the same direction as the speaker, i.e. as having the same line of sight. Thus, the back is facing the point of view, and the front is on the far side of the reference object (cf. fig. 3a) (cf. [18], [35], [36]). The assignment of left and right regions to the reference object doesn't follow the proper rules of canonical encounter (cf. [8] p. 46f.) (cf. fig. 3b). The application is not reversed but maintained. This is expressed more appropriately by the term *Spiegelbildprinzip (mirror principle)*, used in [36] (cf. fig. 3c). Herskovits uses a different terminology. Her term *encounter situation* (where the base axes of the coordinate system are in *mirror order*) denotes the same relationship between speaker and reference object as the term *mirror principle* (fig. 3c) ([16] p. 157ff.).

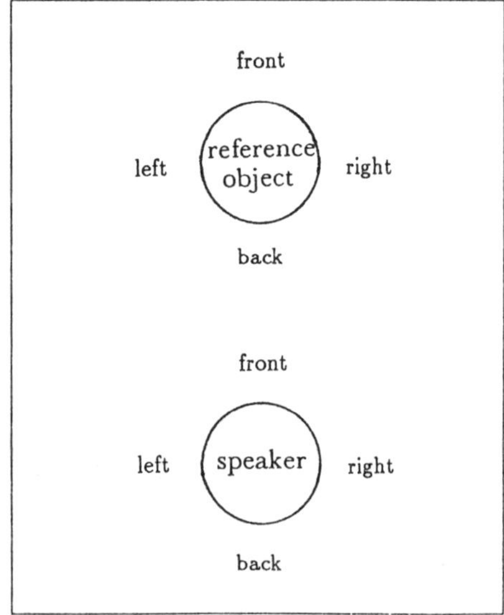

Fig. 3a: The tandem principle

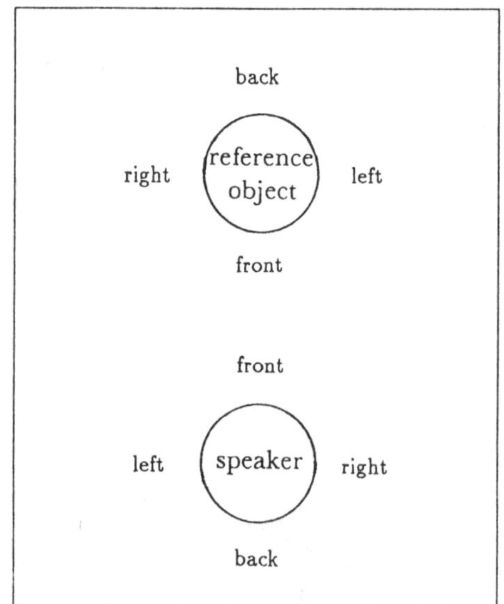

Fig. 3b: The (proper) canonical encounter

In intrinsic use, the top, bottom, front, back, left, and right regions are determined by means of the corresponding sides of the reference object. Instead of *intrinsic*, often the term *inherent* is used (e.g. in [36]). Clark, for instance, speaks of *inherent front* (which we would call *intrinsic front*) to differentiate it from the *egocentric front (deictic front)* ([8] p. 46). Lyons uses the term in a different way: he distinguishes between *inherent orientation* and *canonical orientation*. When a certain orientation is an indispensable characteristic of an object (e.g. a top in the case of mountains, buildings, or trees, a front in the case of human beings or animals), he speaks of inherent orientation. When an object is usually but not necessarily oriented in a certain way, he speaks of canonical orientation ([24] p. 697f.). Since, for us, this difference is irrelevant, we will subsume both terms under *intrinsic orientation*. Cresswell and Dirven speak of *conventional front* ([9] p. 26, [10] p. 113). Saile uses the terms *objective front* (in the case of intrinsic use) and *subjective front* (in the case of deictic use) ([28] p. 71).

Because of the symmetry in the left-right dimension, intrinsic left and right sides of objects are rare (cf. [33] p. 194). Because of this and because of the dominance of gravitation in the vertical dimension (cf. section 4), the determination of intrinsic fronts and backs seems to be the most interesting case. Once the intrinsic front is identified, the left and right regions can be deduced (cf. below).

According to Miller and Johnson-Laird, the intrinsic front is the side lying in the characteristic direction of motion (e.g. for arrows, bullets, torpedos), the side containing the perceptual apparatus (e.g. for people, animals, dolls, cameras), or the side characteristically oriented to the observer (e.g. for cars, chairs, clothing, desks, radios, mirrors). Examples of objects that have no intrinsic front are tables, vases, trees, blocks, cubes, balls, and stars ([25] p. 403, [28] p. 69, 72, [36]). These criteria are adopted or only slightly changed by many other authors ([5] p. 83, [7] p. 9, [18], [24] p. 698f.). According to Lyons, *confrontation* (i.e. the canonical encounter) and the canonical *direction of locomotion* serve to identify the canonical front. For Bennett, the inherent front is the side that normally leads when the object moves (e.g. for busses), or the side which is most

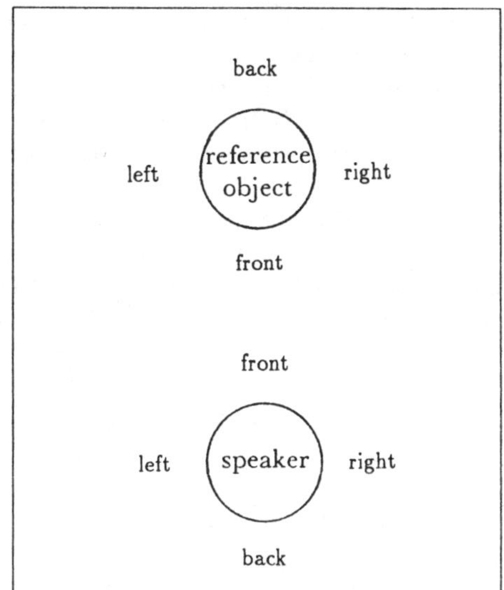

Fig. 3c: The mirror principle

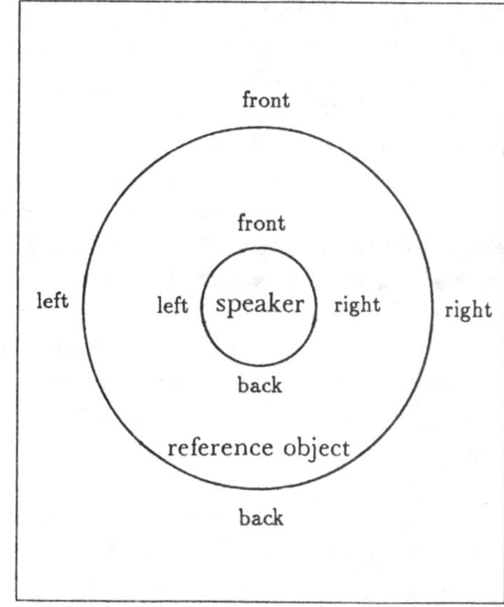

Fig. 3d: The coincidence situation

frequently seen (e.g. for stations). According to Bürkle et al., the intrinsic front is either defined by means of anthropomorphic criteria (the side with perceptual apparatus, e.g. for cameras, or the side that leads in motion, e.g. for locomotive engines), or by means of familiarity conventions (the way things are worn, e.g. for clothes, or handled, e.g. for cupboards or typewriters, or the direction in which one moves with them, e.g. for cars). Herskovits, in addition to *the way objects are used* (e.g. main access to buildings, rooms, or open spaces), and to *anthropomorhic metaphora* (i.e. resemblance to human beings, e.g. with respect to normal direction of motion, facial features, or other striking features), states *symmetry* as a criterion to determine the intrinsic fronts of objects ([16] p. 165ff.).

Conflicts can occur if two or more criteria contradict each other. Fillmore argues that in the case of animals, the criterion based on the perceptual apparatus outweighs the criterion based on the direction of motion since we speak of crabs as moving sideways, not as having their heads on the sides of their bodies [12].

Once the intrinsic front of a reference object is identified, the question still remains open as to whether the intrinsic front is seen from the outside of the reference object, as in the case of desks, radios, or mirrors, or from the inside of the reference object, as in the case of cars, chairs, or clothing (cf. [25] p. 403). If the intrinsic front is the same, regardless of whether the reference object is seen from the inside or from the outside, the difference in the line of sight doesn't have any effect on the assignment of the front and back regions, since the front region is always adjacent to the intrinsic front, and the back region to the intrinsic back of the reference object. But it does affect the determination of the left and right regions, since, if the reference object was seen from the outside, the left and right regions would be assigned according to the mirror principle (cf. fig. 3c), whereas if it was seen from the inside, they would be assigned according to the coincidence situation (cf. fig. 3d) (cf. [25] p. 401, [28] p. 76]). The latter also holds true in the case of animate beings (with a perceptual apparatus that defines their fronts) as reference objects, to which left and right sides will be assigned in analogy to human beings (cf. [25] p. 401). The term *coincidence situation* is used by Herskovits to denote the situation in which observer and reference object coincide (here, the base coordinate axes are in *basic order*). It is in contrast to the term *encounter situation*, which denotes the situation in which observer and reference object are opposite each other (cf. above). This distinction is - according to Herskovits - independent of the distinction between intrinsic and deictic use ([16] p. 159, 163).

Conflicts in the identification of the left and right regions can occur in those cases in which people can take on a characteristic orientation with respect to the object inside as well as outside it, as in the case of chairs or cars. Another source for conflicts - even in the identification of intrinsic fronts - is that the intrinsic front of an object is different, depending on whether it is seen from the outside or inside (like in the case of churches or theaters) (cf. [16] p. 161, 165f.). In CITYTOUR, the intrinsic front (of the buildings) is always assumed to be seen from the outside. Hence, the left and right regions are assigned according to the mirror principle. If a reference object doesn't have an intrinsic front (e.g. a tree), a front can still be *contextually induced* or *projected* on it (cf. [18], [25] p. 398f., [28] p. 69, [33] p. 196, [36]). In this case, Miller and Johnson-Laird speak of it as being an *accidental front*. An accidental front can be induced on an object in different ways. According to to Hill, Miller, Johnson-Laird, and Vandeloise, an object can acquire an accidental front through other objects in its vicinity (e.g. the front of a tree standing in a yard in front of a house will be the side facing the street) (cf. [25] p. 398f.). Wunderlich and Herweg use the criterion of accessibility (also cf. [16] p. 167): the front of a reference object is the side that is sooner accessible inside a container, the side that is sooner accessible at a material boundary, the side that is sooner accessible by a particular moving subject, or the side that is sooner accessible because of the reference object's own actual motion. The first two conditions of Wunderlich and Herweg can be subsumed under Miller's and Johnson-Laird's criterion of contextual induction through other objects in the vicinity. While a criterion for the determination of intrinsic fronts was the way objects usually move or are worn, a criterion for the contextual induction of fronts can be the way objects actually move or are worn in the particular situation (cf. [36], [16] p. 161, 165). Finally, the vertical axis, determined by the gravitation of the earth, can also serve to impose sides (in this case tops and bottoms) on objects. In section 4, this was called *geological* or *gravitational verticality*.

If an accidental front is contextually induced onto an object which is then used as a reference object to locate a subject, we have another kind of *extrinsic use*, different from that defined in section 3. Herskovits doesn't distinguish between intrinsic use and this latter kind of extrinsic use. She subsumes intrinsic sides and contextually induced sides (where a certain side is intrinsic to an object other than the reference object) under *priviledged directions* (cf. [16] p. 169).

CITYTOUR, as well as other systems that distinguish between deictic and intrinsic use, at the moment, evades most of the problems mentioned in this section. Contextual induction of fronts is not yet considered, and intrinsic fronts are not determined by the system, but defined beforehand.

Kautz accepts the *orientation* of objects as primitive ([20] p. 2-18). In [1] (p. 39), the *privileged direction* of an object is indicated by the x-axis of a particular cartesian triple associated to the object. This is in accordance with Saile's view that, in human memory, intrinsic fronts - regardless of how they have been determined - are stored in the internal lexicon ([28] p. 71).

In CITYTOUR, the intrinsic fronts are the *prominent fronts* of the buildings (e.g. the west facade of a church or the main entrance of a public building). The prominent fronts have to be defined by the user when the scene is built up. They then become part of the representation of the static objects (cf. section 2).

6. When are Prepositions used Deictically and When Intrinsically?

Sentences like "The post office is behind the church." are ambiguous because they can either be used deictically, with the point of view being omitted, or intrinsically (cf. [5] p. 83, [8] p. 46, [24] p. 698f., [28] p. 67f.). Apart from ambiguities between intrinsic and deictic use, ambiguities among deictic use (between speaker or hearer as the point of view), among intrinsic use (between the different criteria in determining the intrinsic front and the left and right regions), and between intrinsic and extrinsic use (since even an object with an intrinsic front can acquire an accidental front; cf. [36]) can occur.

Ambiguities between deictic and intrinsic use can be avoided by means of explicitly stating the point of view (using expressions like "from here") or by reformulating the sentence in a way that it can only be interpreted intrinsically. Examples in German and French are: "Das Taxi steht, von mir/dir/ihm/... aus gesehen, hinter dem Lieferwagen." (deict.) vs. "Das Taxi steht an der Rückseite des Lieferwagens." (intr.) ([28] p. 69), "C'est ma soeur a gauche de Jean." (deict.) vs. "C'est ma soeur a la gauche de Jean." (intr.) [18], and "Ronald est devant l'arbre." (deict. or intr.) vs. "Ronald est en face de l'arbre." (intr.) ([33] p. 193f.).

Miller and Johnson-Laird claim that ambiguities between deictic and intrinsic use are resolved in the following way: Intrinsic interpretations usually dominate deictic ones. Thus, deictic use has to be marked explicitly by means of expressions like "from my point of view" or "as I am looking at it". For interpretations, this means that "people first determine whether the landmark has intrinsic parts. If it does, they try to interpret the spatial relation intrinsically unless they are explicitly informed to the contrary. If the landmark does not have intrinsic parts relevant to the spatial indication, they must rely on context to provide a deictic interpretation. If both strategies fail, they may ask for more explicit information." ([25] p. 398f., cf. [28] p. 69f.).

In the generation of descriptions, CITYTOUR follows this strategy. Intrinsic use is treated as the unmarked case, i.e. if possible, prepositions are used intrinsically. If intrinsic use is not possible because the reference object doesn't have a prominent front, the deictic system can be used without explicit mention. If intrinsic use is possible, the deictic system can be used, but has to be marked explicitly by means of "von hier aus" ("from here").

The claim that intrinsic use dominates deictic use is not generally accepted. According to Levelt, individual preferences determine whether the intrinsic or deictic system is used [23]. Ullmer-Ehrich showed in an experiment that the use of spatial concepts depends on the kind of text produced. In room descriptions, which are often structured as a *gaze tour*, the deictic system is predominant. Ambiguity between deixis and intrinsics is avoided "by using temporal in place of spatial expressions, which - due to the underlying tour format of the descriptions - provide the desired singularity of descriptions." ([32] p. 247f.). In contrast to Levelt, Bürkle et al. found through experimenting that the selection of deictic vs. intrinsic use is not a matter of individual preferences, but that it depends on more general conditions of the communication situation ([7] p. 34). The deictic system is predominant; it is the default or canonical case ([7] p. 33, 38, 39) and can be modified within certain limits by the communication situation. If the perceptual field is not shared by speaker and listener, the predominance of deictic use is less striking than otherwise ([7] p. 30f., 33). Deictic use is often marked explicitly by explicit mention of the point of view (speaker) ([7] p. 32). The selection of the point of view also depends on the kind of listener. If the listener is specifically in need of information (like a child) or authorized for receiving exact information (like a professor), the amount of listener-oriented localizations (i.e. listener as point of view) increases ([7] p. 36, 39). Vandeloise calls this *transfer by intermediate person* and views it as a manifestation of the *principle of cooperation* ([33] p. 192f.).

These results suggest that speaker-oriented deictic use is easiest for the speaker, whereas listener-oriented deictic use is easier for the listener. Intrinsic use may take on an intermediate position (cf. [25] p. 402), although it also seems plausible that it is, for the speaker, as difficult as the listener-oriented deictic system, and, for the listener, as difficult as the speaker-oriented deictic system. But the simplicity with which locative expressions involving deictic or intrinsic use can be interpreted, probably also depends on the situation (how speaker and listener are located in relation to each other), and on the context (how preceding locative expressions were used). Herrmann et al. showed in experiments that the cognitive effort for listener-oriented deictic use depends on the relative positions of listener and subject with respect to the speaker's location [14].

Herskovits gives a list of criteria that can determine the speaker's choice of the *frame of reference* (i.e. the front, back, left, and right region of the reference object) as well as a few heuristics for the selection among them ([16] p. 172f.). Her specification is not restricted to the distinction between intrinsic and deictic use (which is not explicitly dealt with), but is concerned with the determination of the frame of reference in general.

7. Conclusions

Some aspects of spatial prepositions that are rarely dealt with in the relevant literature, like extrinsic use and the dynamic uses of "in front of", "behind", "to the left of", and "to the right of" as well as combinations of these with other prepositions, like "past", can be handled by CITYTOUR (cf. section 4).

On the other hand, so far, CITYTOUR can only cope with some of the aspects discussed in this paper. Extended versions of the system could possibly include the use of the actual direction of motion of a dynamic object for determining its actual front in order to extend the set of possible reference objects to dynamic objects. This would be a kind of extrinsic use in the sense that a front is contextually induced on an object (cf. section 5, [16] p. 160, [36]). Another plausible extension could allow for the intrinsic fronts not to be pre-defined, but to be detected by the system, using the position of the buildings with respect to streets and squares as well as a more exact representation of the objects including the location of entrances, outdoor stairs etc.. For this purpose, however, more experimental data about the way how people determine intrinsic fronts would be needed.

References

[1] Adorni, G.; Boccalatte, A.; DiManzo, M. (1981): Object Representation and Spatial Knowledge: An Insight into the Problem of Men-Robots Communication. In: Proc. of the 7th Conference of the Canadian Man-Computer Communications Society, Waterloo, Ontario, p. 37-45.

[2] André, E.; Bosch, G.; Herzog, G.; Rist, T. (1986): Characterizing Trajectories of Moving Objects Using Natural-Language Path Descriptions. In: Proc. of the 7th ECAI, Brighton, July 1986.

[3] André, E.; Bosch, G.; Herzog, G.; Rist, T. (1987): Coping with the Intrinsic and Deictic Uses of Spatial Prepositions. In: Jorrand, Ph., Sgurev, V. (Eds.) (1987): Artificial Intelligence II. Methodology, Systems, Applications. Amsterdam: North Holland.

[4] Badler, N.I. (1975): Temporal Scene Analysis: Conceptual Description of Object Movements. Report TR-80, Department of Computer Science, University of Toronto.

[5] Bennett, D.C. (1975): Spatial and Temporal Uses of English Prepositions. London: Longman.

[6] Bühler, K. (1934): Sprachtheorie. Jena: Fischer.

[7] Bürkle, B.; Nirmaier, H.; Herrmann, T. (1986): "Von dir aus..." Zur hörerbezogenen lokalen Referenz. Bericht Nr. 10, Arbeiten der Forschergruppe "Sprechen und Sprache im sozialen Kontext", Heidelberg/Mannheim.

[8] Clark, H.H. (1973): Space, Time, Semantics, and the Child. In: Moore, T.E. (Ed.) (1973): Cognitive Development and the Acquisition of Language. New York, London: Academic Press.

[9] Cresswell, M.J. (1978): Prepositions and Points of View. In: Linguistics and Philosophy 2 (1978) 1, p. 1-41.

[10] Dirven, R. (1981): Spatial Relations in English. In: Radden, G.; Dirven, R. (Eds.) (1981): Kasusgrammatik und Fremdsprachendidaktik. Trier: Wissenschaftlicher Verlag.

[11] Ehrich, V. (1982): *Da* and the System of Spatial Deixis in German. In: Weissenborn, Klein (1982).

[12] Fillmore, C.J. (1971): Toward a Theory of Deixis. Paper read at Pacific Conference on Contrastive Linguistics and Language Universals, University of Hawaii, January 1971, Mimeographed.

[13] Hays, E. (1987): A Computational Treatment of Locative Relations in Natural Language. MS-CIS-87-31, LINC LAB 58, Department of Computer and Information Science, School of Engineering and Applied Science, University of Pennsylvania, Philadelphia, PA 19104-6389.

[14] Herrmann, T.; Bürkle, B.; Nirmaier, H. (1987): Zur hörerbezogenen Raumreferenz: Hörerposition und Lokalisationsaufwand. Bericht Nr. 12, Arbeiten der Forschergruppe "Sprechen und Sprachverstehen im sozialen Kontext", Heidelberg/Mannheim.

[15] Herrmann, T.; Bürkle, B.; Nirmaier, H.; Mangold, R. (1986): VOHILIRE: Untersuchungen zur hörerbezogenen Objektlokalisation. Bericht Nr. 7, Arbeiten der Forschergruppe "Sprechen und Sprachverstehen im sozialen Kontext", Heidelberg/Mannheim.

[16] Herskovits, A. (1986): Language and Spatial Cognition. Cambridge: Cambridge University Press.

[17] Hill, C. (1982): Up/Down, Front/Back, Left/Right. In: Weissenborn, Klein (1982).

[18] Jarvella, R.J.; Klein, W. (Eds.) (1982): Speech, Place and Action. Chichester: Wiley.

[19] Kautz, H.A. (1985): Formalizing Spatial Concepts and Spatial Language. In: Hobbs, J.R. et al. (1985): Commonsense Summer. Report No. CSLI-85-35, CSLI, Stanford University, Stanford, CA 94305.

[20] Klein, W. (1978): Wo ist hier: Präliminarien zu einer Untersuchung der lokalen Deixis. In: Linguistische Berichte 58 (1978).

[21] Klein, W. (1982): Local Deixis in Route Directions. In: Jarvella, Klein (1982), p. 161-182.

[22] Levelt, W.J.M. (1982): Cognitive Styles in the Use of Spatial Direction Terms. In: Jarvella, Klein (1982).

[23] Lyons, J. (1977): Semantics. Volume II. Cambridge: Cambridge University Press.

[24] Miller, G.A.; Johnson-Laird, P.N. (1976): Language and Perception. Cambridge: Cambridge University Press.

[25] Rauh, G. (1984): Aspekte der Deixis II: Deiktische Dimensionen und die Verwendung deiktischer Ausdrücke. A 123, Duisburg: L.A.U.D.T.

[26] Reichenbach, H. (1947): Elements of Symbolic Logic. New York: MacMillan.

[27] Saile, G. (1984): Sprache und Handlung. Braunschweig: Vieweg.

[28] Sennholz, K. (1985): Grundzüge der Deixis. Bochum: Brockmeyer.

[29] Sung, C.-K.; Zimmermann, G. (1986): Detektion und Verfolgung mehrerer Objekte in Bildfolgen. In: Hartmann, G. (Ed.) (1986): Mustererkennung 1986. Berlin: Springer.

[30] Tsotsos, J.K.; Mylopoulos, J.; Covvey, H.D.; Zucker, S.W. (1980): A Framework for Visual Motion Understanding. In: IEEE Transactions on Pattern Analysis and Machine Intelligence, Vol. PAMI-2, No. 6, November 1980.

[31] Ullmer-Ehrich, V. (1982): The Structure of Living Space Descriptions. In: Jarvella, Klein (1982).

[32] Vandeloise, C. (1984): Description of Space in French. Ph.D. Thesis, Department of Linguistics, University of California, San Diego.

[33] Weissenborn, J.; Klein, W. (Eds.) (1982): Here and There. Amsterdam: John Benjamins.

[34] Wunderlich, D. (1985): Raumkonzepte. Zur Semantik der lokalen Präpositionen. In: Ballmer, T.T.; Posner, R. (Eds.) (1985): Nach-Chomskysche Linguistik. Berlin: deGruyter.

[35] Wunderlich, D.; Herweg, M. (forthcoming): Lokale und Direktionale. To appear in: Schwarze, C.; Wunderlich, D. (Eds.): Handbuch der Semantik. Königstein: Athenäum

[36] Zimmermann, G.; Sung, C.K.; Bosch, G.; Schirra, J. (1987): From Image Sequences to Natural Language: Descriptions of Moving Objects. Report No. 17, SFB 314, Dept. of Comp. Sc., University of Saarbrücken.

MONITORING AN ASSEMBLY TASK BY PERCEPTION REQUESTS

Tapio Heikkilä   Paavo Kärkkäinen   Sakari Pieskä

Technical Research Centre of Finland
Electronics Laboratory
P.O.Box 181, SF-90101 Oulu, Finland

ABSTRACT

Reliability and flexibility are general requirements demanded from modern robotic assembly systems. As demands for accuracy are increasing
within new application areas, needs for sensory feedback to adapt to
arising uncertain and erroneous situations are clear. Problems in providing an assembly robot with a real-time control system and sensory
enhancements are addressed and solutions relying on knowledge-based
techniques are presented with experimental examples from a pilot
assembly system.

INTRODUCTION

The concepts of control structures, programming languages and sensor distribution for assembly tasks are important factors in robotics. Execution of complex assembly operations requires decisional capabilities available on-line in order to cope with the various events, eg part verification, measurement of physical properties, failure detection etc. To perform reliable assembly and at the same time maintain flexibility advanced sensory technologies must be used /1, 2/. The need for utilization of perceptional knowledge in monitoring and controlling robotic equipment is clear. There may arise various erroneous situations during robot operations due to the modelling and tolerance errors from different sources. Common aspects related to knowledge engineering in robotics may be found from /3 - 5/.

The advantages of using knowledge engineering are apparent. Firstly, the chosen approach makes possible to easily customize the system for different applications, because the system structure is modular: control knowledge is clearly separated from the domain knowledge. Secondly, it enables use of incomplete and uncertain knowledge, and thirdly, the system may be built in such a way that it can improve its performance gradually as information is gathered during operations. Often all these imply use of different type of knowledge representation methods /6 - 9/.

In this paper we address the problems in providing an assembly robot with a real-time control system with sensory enhancements. The main task of the system is planning and monitoring the assembly execution by coordinating the robot behaviour and associated peripheral devices in insertion of electronics components.

CONTROL PRINCIPLE

In the case of robots working in a well structured environment and performing predefined tasks repeatedly, most decisional problems may be addressed off-line. However, there are several phases during on-line task execution, which require confidence measures for correct decisions. In some cases in order to make correct interpretations about the state of the system the inclusion of multiple sensing systems is required.

We have established an experimental assembly system to study the problems in the robotic insertion of electronic components into printed circuit boards /10/. The major functional components of the assembly system are described in Figure 1.

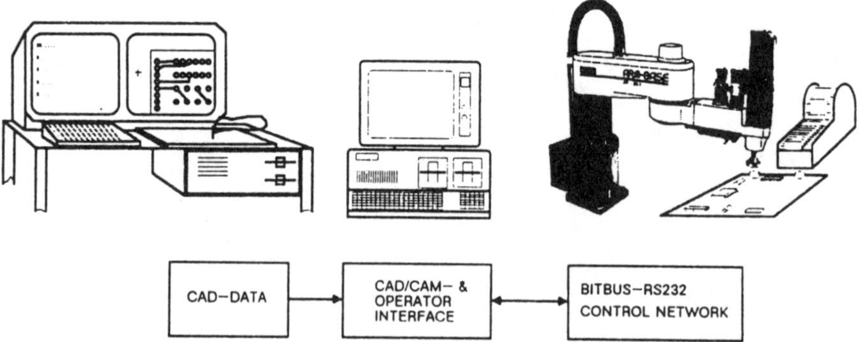

FIGURE 1. The principal components of the assembly system.

The system comprises an ordinary scara-type robot, a personal computer (PC) and a distributed control network. Other system components include a servo-controlled multi-sensor gripper with exchangable fingers, component feeding devices and a measurement station for inspection of component leads. The use of small fiber-optic intensity modulated sensors distributed in suitable places in the system has been emphasized in applying sensory techologies /11/.

The general control principle of the assembly system is based on hierarchy (Figure 1, /12/): The cell PC creates an assembly plan (as assembly parameters) from CAD- and cell device definitions and passes the parameters to the device controller network, which is finally responsible of controling the physical equipment.

In the off-line plan generation the reference values, i.e. the assembly parameters for the assembly sub-operations, are evaluated. When needed, also proper sensor-based actions to adapt to the arising errors are mapped as functional perception requests into the assembly plan. During on-line execution of a certain action, acquiring a value of the expected quantity from the sensor defined at the appropriate time indicates either success of the operation or implies a correcting procedure to be called.

<u>SENSOR SYSTEM</u>

The sensory system applied consists of components communicating by asynchronous message passing. The assembly system uses distributed microcomputer modules for sensory integration and sensory processing. The units compose a control network in which each node has specific functions related to sensory data acquisition, processing and verification. There are four types of sensors used in the system currently. The use of them is illustrated in Table 1.

TABLE 1. Sensors in the electronics assembly unit.

MEASURED VARIABLE	TYPE	PRINCIPLE
gripping forces	force	strain gauge
gripping diameters	proximity	fiber-optic (intens.modul.)
component lead position	proximity	fiber-optic (intens.modul.)
component position	proximity	fiber-optic (intens.modul.)

In the gripper there have been integrated force sensors and proximity sensors for controlling the movements of the gripper fingers. Because both these are available independently for each of the fingers and the controlling is performed with separate DC-motors (one for each finger), there are a variety of ways to apply force- and proximity-feedbacks to adapt the gripping system to the changes and errors due to the product variations and erroneous situations.

There are also two different observation sensors, one integrated into the gripper and the other in a separate measuring station. Both these are based on fiber-optics and they utilize the robot arm movements in

the sensing process. The former one is used to define correct positions
of components or other elements in the environment by moving the robot
arm and scanning their bodies with a vertical light beam. The accurate
position of the observed element can be defined by locating the edge
values from the scan profiles. The latter one is used to define the positions of the component leads in respect to the robot gripper. The robot
passes the component by a measuring head, and then a 1-dimensional pin
image scan profile is captured. From the image data the position of reference pins may be extracted. The principal structure of the pin image
station may be found from Figure 4.

There are many possibilities to utilize the services of the sensory sub-
systems. Some examples of such perception requests are given in Table 2.

TABLE 2.   Sensor - perception request -connections.

SENSOR	PERCEPTION REQUEST BASED OPERATION
finger position/force	proximity-based grip force-based grip combined force-proximity grip
component proximity scan	component presence verification component position definition
pin image	component position definition pin-figure verification

The sensory sub-systems are integrated to the assembly system with a
distributed microcontroller network. The basic principle is illustrated
in Figure 2. The synchronization of the assembly work cycle relies on
the robot controller, which utilizes the services of the sensor modules
by passing the perception function codes via the network. The software
in the device controllers is fixed.

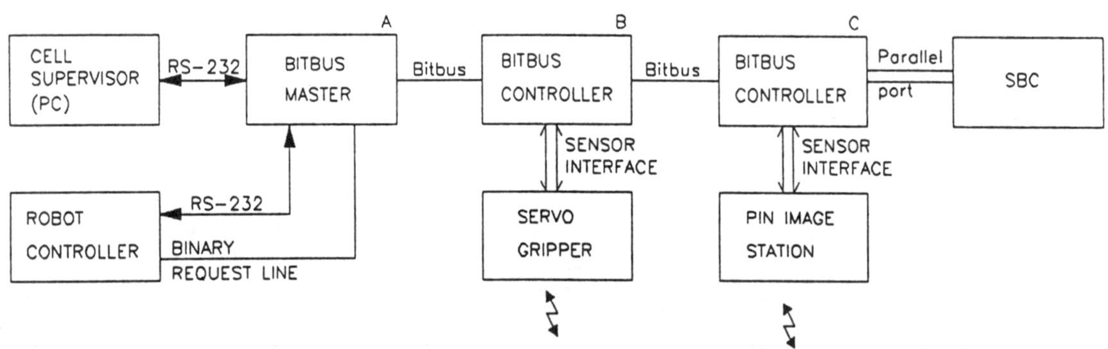

FIGURE 2.   Integration of the sensor modules.

WORLD MODELLING

The control of the robotic assembly system relies on a world modelling
system. In the model the essential elements of the system are described

related to each other. The model enables the utilization of the geometric knowledge about the assembly equipment together with the geometric knowledge acquired from the CAD design.

The selection of the model elements is based on classification of the
components, initially made in the CAD-design phase. For each class there
are model elements describing all the component and assembly equipment
properties specific for that individual class. Some physical devices may
be modelled in different ways for different component classes and thus
the modelling yields descriptions of ways to use the assembly system
rather than pure physical properties of it. This naturally gives a great
freedom to use the system in desired ways.

Also the components are included in the model. All properties of the
class to which the component belongs to are inherited by the individual
component.

Each model element includes:

- a frame:
  description of the geometric relation to a reference element (eg a
  component in the board or a component in the pin image station).
- element specific parameters:
  types, identification codes, reference values for sensory subsystems.

The model data is extracted from the CAD-database with a specific post-
processor routine and with an expert system (see later) from the assembly equipment data base. The role of the model in the system is illustrated in Figure 3.

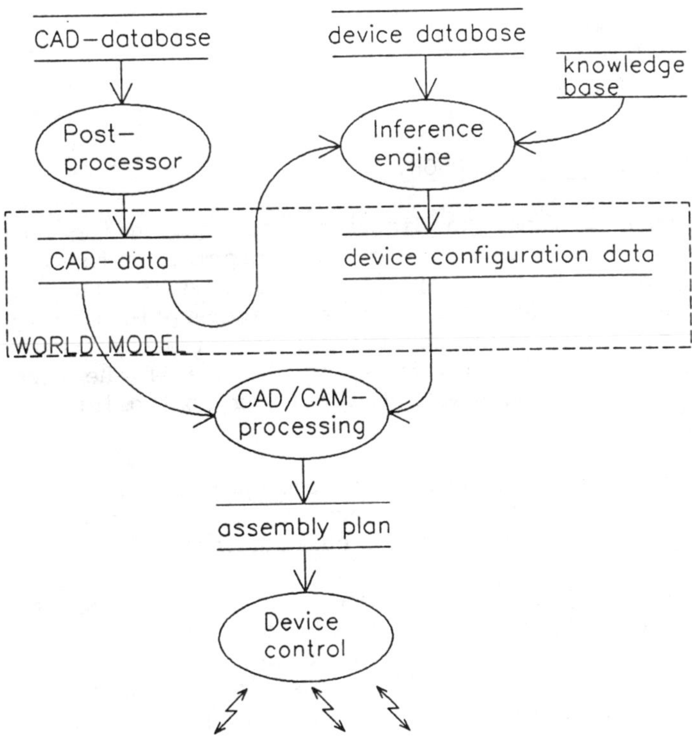

FIGURE 3. Assembly control model.

Based on the model data the control parameters, eg the robot positions, pin image reference data, gripping diameters etc., are defined. For the calculation of robot positions, each spatial state related to the assembly has to be considered and a corresponding geometric link to be solved. As an example, a spatial state related to component inspection is illustrated in Figure 4.

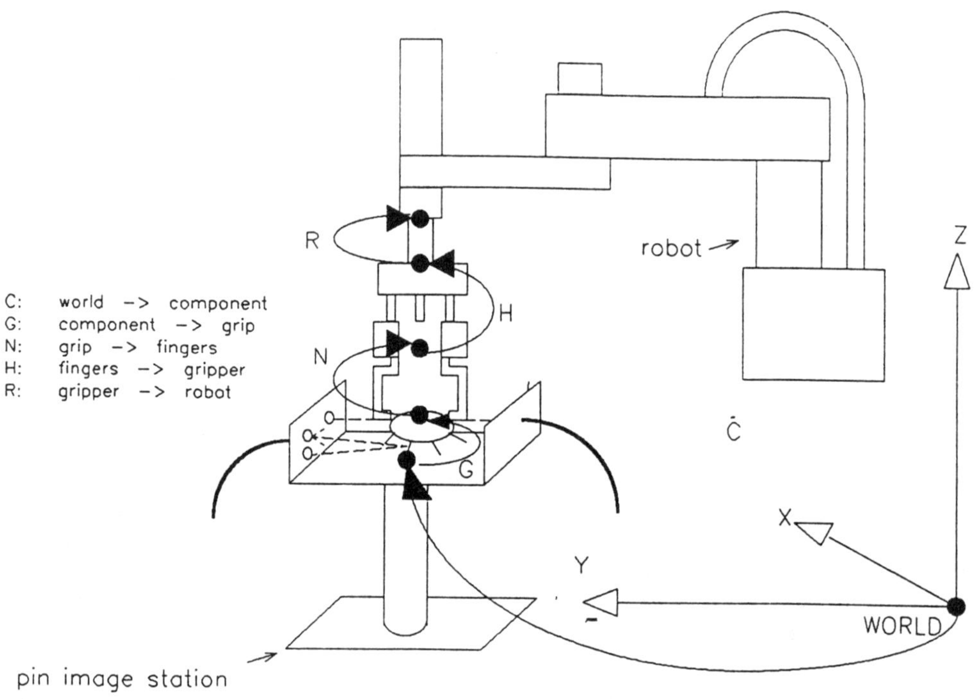

FIGURE 4.   Component inspection.

MODELLING THE SENSORY UNITS

The sensory units are used to find the discrepancies between the modelled and measured values of the elements and pass information to other sub-units for correcting operations. Examples of this kind of functions are the operations of the pin-image station and the fiber-optic scanning sensor of the robot gripper. Both these observe certain element/elements modelled and yield correcting position values for the use of the robot arm position control. The sequence, where the calling controller uses the services of the sensory unit is:

1) The sensory unit gets a service request from the calling controller.
2) The sensory unit acquires the data to be measured and analyzes it.
3) The sensory unit passes the results to the calling controller.

The results from stage 2) are for the force sensors simple like approving/disapproving the observed operation. For the position sensors the situation is more complicated and in the following the concentration has been laid on these. The sensory units used in position correction are modelled in a same principle. Their task is to indicate positional differences between the model values and the situation during the assembly execution, particularly in a pre-defined frame (a sub-link, i.e. a frame or a set of sub-frames related to the spatial state). The results have to be given in a frame that the calling procedure is able to utilize, so the analyzed results have to be transformed to this goal frame. The process of the sensory unit may be described with the following procedure:

1) Capture the image profile sample queue, $\overline{S}_i$.
2) Extract the features $\overline{F}_{i,s}$ from the sample queue; typically the vertices.
3) Define the differences $\overline{F}_{i,d}$ between the modelled features $\overline{F}_{i,m}$ and the features extracted from the samples $\overline{F}_{i,s}$.
4) Transform the feature increments to position increments $\overline{R}_{i,s}$ in the observed frame; $\overline{R}_{i,s} = f(\overline{F}_{i,d})$.
5) Transform the position increments from the observed frame $\overline{R}_{i,s}$ to the goal frame $\overline{R}_{i,g}$ with the trans formation matrix $\overline{RR}_{s,g}$:

$$\overline{R}_{i,g} = \overline{RR}_{s,g} * \overline{R}_{i,s}.$$

In the electronics assembly the modelling may be simplified to a four degree-of-freedom system and then the transformation from initial frame (i) to a goal frame (g) may be described with a matrix

$$\overline{RR}_{i,g} = \begin{bmatrix} \cos\omega & -\sin\omega & 0 & x \\ \sin\omega & \cos\omega & 0 & y \\ 0 & 0 & 1 & z \\ 0 & 0 & 0 & 1 \end{bmatrix}$$

where ω = orientation between the z-axis of the coordinate systems and

$(x\ y\ z)^T$ = translation vector of for the origin between the coordinate systems.

Using the modelling principle described above helps us to define several ways to use the sensory units. Again we have a description of a way of operation rather than a pure description of a physical model. The transformation examples described above are applied in robot position control and so the matrices are related to cartesian coordinate systems. However, the same principle may be used also in other type of cases, where low level processes are discussing with each others, and suitable transformations to interpret the parameters (features) are needed.

PERCEPTION REQUEST LISTS

As described above, the use of sensors and sensory sub-systems relies on the functional requests passed via the device control network. For each type of assembly tasks they are described as request lists loaded in the robot control unit which performs the synchronization of the work cycle. The request lists (one perception list/one component class) may be given directly to the model by an ordinary operator, but this requires from the operator a great deal of expertise and knowledge about the components and the system equipment. In addition, this might become a time consuming task, because it would tie the operator to the assembly system every time, when control information for a new assembly is defined. To overcome these problems a knowledge-based approach with expert system technique is applied. In fact, an embedded expert system is used to define not only the perception request lists but all the device specific information to the model.

The logic and knowledge that the operator would use in defining the sensor-based operations lies in the form of rules in a knowledge base. Rule-based description is suitable in this case, because the type of the problem is combinatorial. Typical objects in representing the knowledge are components, feeders and the perception requests, and typical attributes are the classes, types, names and other object specific properties. The rule-base is analyzed before the CAD/CAM-processing, because the outputs of the expert system act as initial model values for the use of the CAD/CAM-algorithms.

A simple example illustrating the definition of the perception list is represented below.

Let's assume that the component inspection station has such constraints, that it can inspect only regular type components. Dual_In_Line (DIL) components are in this case regular, because the spacing between the component leads are similar. Also if a radial component has only two pins, it may be considered regular. With these facts, the rules for generating a perception request for component lead inspection would be as:

```
IF the component_group is DIL
THEN the pin_row is regular

IF the component_group is radial
AND the number_of_pins = 2
THEN the pin_row is regular

IF the pin_row is regular
THEN request is check the component_leads
```

CONCLUSIONS

Flexible and reliable operation of robotic systems implies proper use of advanced sensor and software technologies. In this paper we have described a method with which to approach the solutions for problems arising in precision assemblies. The implementation has been carried out in a test system, from which examples were given.

Key ideas are to utilize the knowledge about the parts and sub-elements of the the assemblies and also about the assembly equipment in planning and monitoring the assembly tasks. Strategies defining how to use the sensory sub-systems are defined by a heuristic description in a knowledge base with rules. The domain knowledge is described separately in a world model.

Applying knowledge-based principles yields freedom to use the systems in desired ways and the features of the arising problems may be better considered. Although our application example is in the area of precision assembly, the basic principles applied may be used also more widely.

References

1. Sanderson, A. C., Perry, G., Sensor-based robotic assembly systems:
    research and applications in electronic manufacturing. Proceedings
    of the IEEE, Vol. 71, 7/1983, pp. 856 - 871.

2. Latombe, J.-C., Information processing for robots. Computers in
    Mechanical Engineering, pp. 17 - 23 (September 1984).

3. Rembold, U., Levi, P., Sensors and controls for autonomous robots.
    International Conference on Intelligent Autonomous Systems.
    Amsterdam, December 1986.

4. Malcom, C. A., Ambler, A. P., Some architectural implications of the
    use of sensors. International Conference on Intelligent Autonomous
    Systems, Amsterdam, December 1986.

5. Harmon, S., Biancini, G., Pinz, B., Sensor data fusion through a
    distributed blackboard. IEEE Conference on Robotics and Automation,
    San Francisco 1986.

6. Hayes-Roth, F., The knowledge-based expert system: a tutorial. IEEE
    Computer, September 1984, pp. 11 - 28.

7. Rosenman, M. A., Gero, J. S., Design codes as expert systems.
    Computer-aided design, Vol. 17, No 9, 1985, pp. 399 - 409.

8. Wang, C.-H., Spihari, S. N., Object recognition in structured and
    random environments: locating address blocks on mail pieces. Pro-
    ceedings of the 5th National Conference on Artificial Intelligence,
    Philadelphia, August 1986, pp. 1133 - 1137.

9. Gevarter, W. B., Expert systems: limited but powerful. IEEE
    Spectrum, August 1983, pp. 39 - 45.

10. Kärkkäinen, P., Heikkilä, T., Niemelä, U., Supplementing a standard
    robot arm with multi-sensor capabilities. IFAC Symposium on Low Cost
    Automation, Valencia, November 1986.

11. Kopola, H., Nissilä S., Myllylä, R., Kärkkäinen, P., Intensity modu-
    lated fiber optic sensors for robot feedback control in precision
    assembly. 4th International Symposium on Optical and Optoelectronic
    Applied Science and Engineering. SPIE Proceedings, Vol. 798, Hague,
    March 1987.

12. Heikkilä, T., Kärkkäinen, P., Niemelä, U., A hierarchical robot con-
    trol system for flexible assembly in electronics. 8th International
    Conference on Assembly Automation, Copenhagen, March 1987.

A QUALITATIVE APPROACH TO ROBOT EXPLORATION AND MAP-LEARNING

Benjamin J. Kuipers and Y.T. Byun

Department of Computer Sciences

The University of Texas at Austin

Austin, Texas 78712

ABSTRACT

This paper describes a qualitative method for a mobile robot to learn a map of an unknown environment. Other researchers have aimed for metrical consistency in the map, whereas we aim to make *a topological model* of the environment at the beginning to which metric information can be added later. This strategy is inspired by the qualitative methods that humans use to build cognitive maps of new environments. The topological model consists of nodes and arcs corresponding to distinctive places and local travel paths linking nearby distinctive places. *A distinctive place* is defined as the local maximum of some measure of distinctiveness appropriate to its immediate neighborhood, and is found by *a hill-climbing search*. Local travel paths are defined in terms of *local control strategies* required for travel, rather than in terms of metrical distances and directions. This topological model, defined in terms of sensorimotor procedures, allows us to control cumulative error. Our qualitative approach can be robust against various possible errors in the real world. We also adopt human-like reasoning about large-scale space to help a mobile robot explore the environment efficiently and construct a consistent topological map. We describe a working simulation in which a robot with range sensors explores a variety of 2D environments.

Support for this research is provided by NASA, under grant number NAG9-200.

1. INTRODUCTION

Existing strategies for robot exploration and map learning of an unknown 2-D environment have concentrated on trying to build accurate metrical maps. We review their spatial representation methods and discuss their difficulties in section 1.1. Then we introduce briefly our qualitative approach using a topological model in section 1.2.

In section 2, we talk about the topological model, its components including distinctive places and local control strategies, and how to define them in detail. In section 3, exploration strategies observed in human reasoning on large-scale spaces are discussed, which help find the interesting places globally and build a map which is free from topological errors. In section 4, we show our simulation result of a simple environment. The current simulation assumes that sensory information is free from errors. However, our approach is designed to be robust in the presence of various types of errors, as discussed in section 5. We summarize our preliminary results and discuss future work in section 5.

1.1 Review of related works

Building a model for the world has been studied [Brooks, 1985; Giralt, 1983; Laumond, 1983; Chatila and Laumond, 1985; Iyengar et.al. 1985; Koch et.al. 1985; Turchan and Wong, 1985; Crowley, 1985; Moravec and Elfes, 1985; Rosenberg and Rowat, 1981; Miller, 1985; Lozano-Perez, 1981]. Basic spatial representation methods used in their works belong to one or a mixture of Skeleton, Generalized-cones, Convex polygon, Voronoi diagram, and Configuration space. They either describe the environment directly with x and y coordinates of sets of line segments and points, or use a projection on a rasterized map.

In most traditional approaches, the assumption is that every object in the world consists of points and lines connecting pairs of points. Most use a 2-D cartesian coordinate system, so each point has explicit X and Y coordinates. Eventually every object in the world is described by a sequence of coordinates, or every free space is described in the same manner. The main issue is to find such points and give them (x , y) coordinates and then represent the world mainly by those points and connecting lines. The position of a mobile robot itself is also represented by x and y coordinates. Some difficulties of these methods are the following.

- It is very hard to describe a real world by using only points and lines connecting points. The world models in most cases have only polyhedral objects, but do not accept curved objects from which it is hard to find meaningful points.

- Because of noise and inaccuracy in sensory input, and slip and miscalibration in motor output, it is very hard to find accurate x and y coordinates of points and the position of robot itself. Therefore, it is difficult to maintain metric consistency.

- Since our understanding about the world or representation is quite different from these methods, communication between robots and men may be difficult to achieve naturally. (eg. "Take the third left")

- Since the map uses an absolute coordinate system, devices whose output cannot be used to determine coordinates of points in the environment are difficult to use meaningfully. (eg. A system recognizing visual landmarks without measuring the distance)

Brooks [1985, 1986] makes similar criticisms of traditional approaches, and proposes to solve some of them by using a relational map of the world. The relational map is not yet fully specified, but includes such features as metrical range bounds of distances between pairs of places. Our topological approach has a significantly different character.

1.2 Concept of a Topological model

The basic description of the environment in our qualitative approach is a topological model built from an unknown environment. The model consists of a set of nodes and arcs, where nodes represent distinctively recognizable places in the environment, and arcs represent travel paths connecting them.

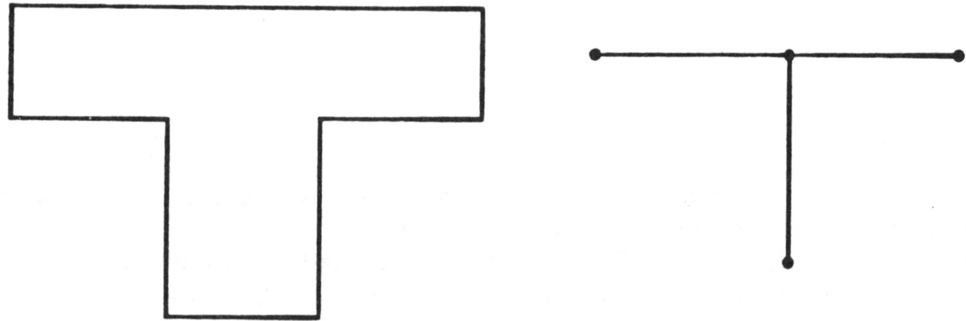

Figure 1. A T-shaped space, and a simple topological model

Figure 1 shows a simple 2-D environment and one possible corresponding topological model. The nodes and arcs are defined procedurally in terms of the sensorimotor capabilities of the robot in our approach.

A place in the environment corresponding to a node in the topological model is *locally distinctive* within its immediate neighborhood by one geometric criterion or another. We introduce locally meaningful "distinctiveness" measures defined on a subset of the sensory features, by which some distinctive features can be maximized at a distinctive place. We define the *signature* of a distinctive place to be the subset of features, the distinctiveness measures, and the feature values, which are maximized at the place. A hill-climbing search is used to identify and recognize a distinctive place when the robot is in its neighborhood. When returning to a known place, the hill-climbing search is guided by a known signature. When exploring, both the signature and the local maximum must be found.

Travel paths corresponding to arcs are defined by local control strategies which describe how the robot can follow the link connecting two distinctive places. This local control strategy depends on the local environment and there may be several possible strategies. For example, in one environment, following the midline of a corridor may be reasonable; in another environment, maintaining a certain distance from a single boundary on one side may be reasonable.

2. DEFINING A TOPOLOGICAL MODEL

Studies of the human cognitive map [Lynch, 1960; Kuipers, 1978, 1979, 1982, 1983b; Piaget and Inhelder, 1967; Siegel and White, 1975] suggest that the basic element of a useful and powerful description of the environment is a topological description. In the human case, a topological model is built first and a metric map is built on top of the topological model. However, the topological model is central to the cognitive map, in that it provides the greatest combination of useful route-finding capability along with tolerance for inaccurate information by maintaining topological consistencies rather than metric consistencies. These studies and some preliminary investigations of the problem of robot exploration [Kuipers, 1983a, 1985] led us to search for an approach to spatial exploration and map-learning that will be robust under circumstances of moderate accuracy of input and output operations.

2.1 Qualitatively defining distinctive places and travel paths

In order to find distinctive places, we must determine which sensory characteristics provide the distinguishing features by which a place becomes distinctive locally. This allows us to formulate a locally meaningful "distinctiveness" measure. We hypothesize that any reasonably rich sensory system will have distinctiveness measures that can be defined in terms of low level sensory input. Topologically distinctive places can be defined as local maxima of one or more of these distinctiveness measures. Then we perform a hill-climbing search around the neighborhood looking for the point with maximum distinctiveness. For instance, for a robot with several sonar-range finders, the extent and quality of symmetrical regions in the array of measured distances can be used as a distinctiveness measure. The hill-climbing search tries to find the place which maximizes the symmetry across lines or the center of the robot. Note that it is not necessary for a place to be globally distinctive; it is only necessary for it to be distinguished from the other points in its immediate neighborhood.

In order to find the distinctive places, we consider a stream of sensory information which changes only as the result of motion of the robot, but we do not attempt to determine the shapes of objects in an absolute coordinate system. All distinctiveness measures are considered initially and one or more of them are used to define the maximum distinctiveness for a place. When a distinctive place is identified, it is defined in terms of the distinctive features that it maximizes, and is added to the topological model with a qualitative description of the sensory vector. In the process of route-following, once the robot has travelled along an arc so that it believes that it should be in the neighborhood of a particular place, it uses the stored definition of the place (its signature) in order to know what features it should attempt to maximize to find the place.

Travel paths are defined in terms of local control strategies. Once a distinctive place has been identified, the robot moves to another place by choosing an appropriate control strategy. While following a path with a chosen strategy, the robot continues to analyze its sensory input for evidence of new distinctive features. Once the next place has been identified and defined, the arc connecting the two distinctive places is defined in the topological model in terms of the local control strategy required to follow it.

The paths followed during exploration are defined by some distinctiveness criterion that is sufficient to specify a one-dimensional set of points. Therefore, following our control strategies, the robot will follow the midline of a corridor, or walk along the edge of a large space, but will not venture into the interior of a large space, where the points have no distinctive characteristics.

When the robot is following a known path from one node to another, it starts by using the hill-climbing algorithm to locate itself at the distinctive place corresponding to the first node. It then follows the travel control strategy associated with the arc. The strategy is intended to bring the robot directly to the destination place, but due to sensory or motor errors, it may end up somewhere in its neighborhood. Then the hill-climbing algorithm brings it to the distinctive place corresponding to the destination node.

2.2 Experimental sonar robot and simulation environment

As a specific instance of a robot, to test our approach, we currently define NX, with 16 sonar distance sensors covering 360 degrees with equal angle difference between adjacent sensors, two tractor-type chains, and an absolute compass.

Table 1. Robot components

COMPONENT	USAGE
16 sonar range-finders	Measure distances for each direction
Two tractor-type chains	Movement effector
An absolute compass	Global orientation

Our simulation has been done on the Symbolics 3600 and a program has been written in Common lisp. Figure 2 shows the simulator with the example environment and topological map to be discussed in section 4. The program allows users to use different numbers of sonar range-finders, (4 * i) where 2 < i < 9. The range of measured distance of each sonar sensor is from 18 to 220 pixels. A number 30 is used as a minimum safe distance.

At the right top corner of the simulation window in Figure 2, measured distances for the 16 sonar range-finders are displayed. At the left top corner, the result of analysis of each distinctiveness measure considered in the current simulation is displayed and it scrolls horizontally.

In the middle top, an energy pair supplied to two tractor-type chains is shown. If both Left and Right have the same positive numbers, NX moves straight forward. If both of them are positive and one is larger than the other, the result is motion forward and turning slowly to the right or to the left. If one is positive and the other is negative, and their absolute values are identical, the robot turns in place to the right or to the left by some amount. While NX moves, it decides the energy pair continuously and the energy pair is displayed.

While NX is moving from one place to another, it keeps a record of number of rotations of each chain. This information, called the Travel List, will be used to give rough information about the shape of the path and the relative position of two places. For instance, TL ((30 30)) means that NX has moved straight, whereas TL ((20 12) (20 30)) means that NX has moved forward and turned to the right slowly, and then moved forward and turned to the left slowly. Notice that we will not use this information to derive X and Y coordinates of the robot.

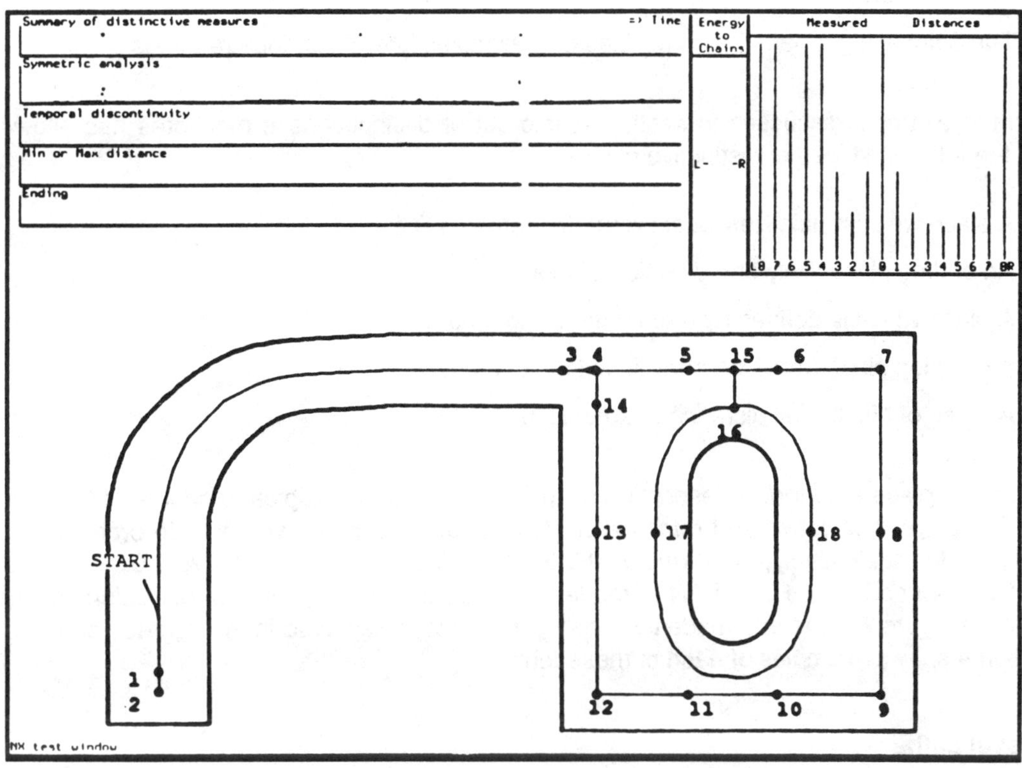

Figure 2. A curve and room environment

As mentioned earlier, we hypothesize that these robot components are able to provide sufficient richness to distinguish many interesting places and to describe the structure of the given environment. However our approach and the result do NOT depend on a good choice of sensors. These are chosen only for the simplicity and concreteness of our initial studies. We hypothesize that any sensorimotor system which provides sufficiently rich sensory input, and takes sufficiently small steps through the environment, can use our approach. However it may be true that with a very rich sensory input such as vision, the search for an appropriate signature in a given neighborhood is more difficult, as is the problem of avoiding too many distinctive places.

2.3 Distinctive places

The individual distinctiveness measures are an open-ended, ad hoc set of measures specific to the given type of sensor. For our current robot, the measures we can define include the following.

- Extent and quality of symmetry across a line.

- Extent and quality of symmetry across the center of the robot.

- Temporal discontinuity in one or more sensors, given a small step.

- Number of directions of reasonable motion into open spaces around the robot.

- Temporal change in number of directions of motion provided by the distinct open spaces, with small step.

- The point along a path that minimizes or maximizes lateral distance readings.

In the example discussed in section 4, this set of distinctiveness measures has allowed us to detect the following types of distinctive places:

- A place which maximizes local symmetry across a line.

- An ending place (only one direction of motion).

- A place which is defined by a temporal discontinuity.

- A decision place (three or more directions of motion).

- A place of Min lateral distance to an object.

Once a place is found, a description of the place in the topological model is of the form (place index, signature, qualitative and quantitative description of sensory vector). In order to describe a sensory vector qualitatively, the terms, FULL-FAN, R-HALF-FAN, L-HALF-FAN, OPEN-SPACE, and OTHERS are used. The FULL-FAN is made by a wall without any serious occlusion. A FULL-FAN example in Figure 2 is the one made by sensors from 1 to 7 displayed in the right-top corner. Table 2 in section 4 shows examples of each of these terms.

2.4 Travel paths

When leaving the current distinctive place, NX analyzes its sensory input to select the local control strategy most appropriate to the immediate environment. The currently studied strategies are:

- Follow-Midline

- Walk-along-Object-Right

- Walk-along-Object-Left

- Blind-Step

While following a path, NX continues to analyze its sensory input for evidence of new distinctive features. Once the next distinctive place has been identified and defined, the arc connecting the two places in the topological model is defined in terms of the control strategy required to follow it.

A set of sequentially-tested production rules selects a proper local control strategy depending on the current sensory information. Each rule consists of assumptions and a decision for the local control strategy. An example is listed below.

```
(defrule l-c-strategy-rule10 ()
   (if    (>= (number-of f-fan) 2)
          (two-walls-are-near-to-each-other)
          (two-walls-are-almost-opposite-directions))
   (then (proper-l-c-st is follow-midline)))
```

If the assumptions underlying the current control strategy become false while NX is moving, it chooses the next acceptable strategy and continues its exploration.

3. EXPLORATION

3.1 The Current Position

While NX explores the given environment, it attempts to maintain the current position (CP). The CP is described by the current place index, the current orientation in degrees, and a travel path through which NX has come to the current place from the previous place, for example, (place-2 0.0 path-1). Whenever NX believes it is in the neighborhood of a distinctive place, it attempts to reach the place using hill-climbing search. If the place was previously known, NX already knows its signature, and the hill-climbing algorithm knows what properties to maximize. If the place is new, NX must also determine the appropriate distinguishing characteristics for this place.

As part of the description of the current place, NX determines the set of distinct directions for leaving that place. These will include the reverse of the direction of approach, the direction that NX will depart on, and possibly additional directions that will be placed on the Exploration Agenda.

3.2 Determining the Current Place

When NX reaches a place during its exploration, the identification of the place is the most important task in order to build a consistent topological map. Moreover, since the high level descriptions of places are qualitative, we may apply constraints from the exploration history to restrict the set of previously seen places that might match the current place.

While NX explores, it uses the *Exploration Agenda* to keep the information about *'where'* and *'in which direction'* it should explore further to complete its exploration of the given environment. If (Place1 Direction1) is in the Exploration Agenda, it means that NX has visited Place1 already and went in some other direction. Therefore NX should visit Place1 later and go to Direction1 direction or it may return to Place1 from ((Direction1 + 180) MOD 360) direction, in order to delete (Place1 Direction1) from the Exploration Agenda.

NX attempts to minimize the number of elements in the Exploration Agenda. If the Exploration Agenda is empty when NX gets to a place, it means that there are currently no places with unexplored directions, so the place must be new, unless NX has intentionally returned to a previously known place through a known path. If the Exploration Agenda is not empty when NX gets to a place, the current place could be one of the places saved in the Exploration Agenda. This is only possible when the current place description is the same as that of a place saved in the Exploration Agenda, and the difference between the current orientation and the orientation of the stored place is 180 degrees. In our future work, discussed in section 5, we expect to expand the use of relative positional information to decide what the current place is.

Current and stored place descriptions are compared using their qualitative descriptions, allowing a certain amount of looseness of match to provide robustness in the face of small variations in sensory input.

The *Rehearsal procedure*, based on an observation of Kuipers [1977, 1985], is useful to distinguish between places whose sensory images are identical, but which can be distinguished by their spatial context. If the current place description is very similar to one recorded previously, NX considers the previously known distinctive place as a candidate match, and attempts to determine whether or not the current place is actually the same as that place. NX constructs a route between the known place and some nearby distinctive place. It then tries to follow that route and return to the current place. If the route performed as predicted, then the current place matches the previously known one, and NX has identified the current place. If not, then the current place must be a new place with the same sensory description as the old one.

3.3 Global exploration strategy

The experimental version of NX has no goal other than determining the complete topological structure of its environment. NX has two strategies for efficiently exploring its environment:

G1. Try to explore an unexplored area rather than an explored area.

G2. Try to minimize the number of elements in the Exploration Agenda.

Rule G1 is natural since it is unnecessary for NX to visit previously visited places without a special reason like the Rehearsal procedure. Rule G2 helps minimize the matching problem for new places. For example, after a "loose end" has been added to the Exploration Agenda, NX uses heuristics to try to come back to the place through an unexplored path. Therefore NX tries to explore one area at a time completely in terms of a topological model instead of having a lot of unexplored places and directions in the Exploration Agenda, to reduce the problem of identifying the current place. If there is a conflict between G1 and G2, G2 dominates.

4. SIMULATION RESULT

We can illustrate our approach to exploration with an environment consisting of a curved corridor leading to a room containing an oval object (Figure 2). The initial location for NX is shown as START. Table 2 shows a fragment of the internal description that is created.

NX initially selects an appropriate local control strategy, and follows the midline of the corridor until it finds the first distinctive place, place-1, which is characterized by the maximum degree of symmetry in the sonar image. As shown in Table 2, the distinctive feature, SYMMETRY, which makes this place distinctive is saved in the topological model, with the description of sensory information. The list (51) in RAW-DATA of the first *FULL-FAN* (Table 2) designates the distance reading from sensor 0 which defines the front of NX. The sensory description is made in the clockwise direction, starting with the segment including sensor 0. There are two directions for NX to move from place-1. Since there is nothing in the Exploration Agenda, it prefers the direction which requires no Turning action. Therefore it continues its exploration downward, and puts into the Exploration Agenda the one unexplored direction from place-1.

By maintaining the same control strategy and moving downward, it finds another distinctive place, place-2, an ending place, defined by reaching the minimum legal distance from the wall while following the given local control strategy. It saves place-2 and a travel path linking place-1 and place-2. Table 2 also shows the description of path-1 by the first node of path-1 and the orientation when NX leaves the node, the second node of path-1 and the orientation when NX reaches that node, the local control strategy, the travel list, and the rough distance between two nodes.

Since there is only one direction to the open space at place-2 and NX has come to place-2 from that direction, it turns around at place-2 and moves along a curved corridor with a Follow-Midline control strategy until it gets back to place-1. It recognizes place-1 from the stored description, removes the remaining direction from place-1 from the Exploration Agenda, and continues moving upward.

While using the Follow-Midline local control strategy, it gets to place-3 which is defined by a temporal discontinuity. DISCONTINUITY-TYPE-3 in Table 2 means that there is a sudden increase of measured distance on the right side when NX follows the midline of the corridor from place-1 to place-3. Notice in Table 2 that the Travel List of path-2 encodes its shape and length.

When the previous control strategy was Follow-Midline or Walk-along-Object left or right, there is no more than one FULL-FAN, and the signature of the current place is a temporal discontinuity, then NX uses the Blind-Step strategy until it finds place-4, detected by symmetric information. It chooses the open direction which doesn't require it to make a turn action. The current place and an unchosen direction are recorded in the Exploration Agenda. The next local control strategy is Walk-along-Object-Left.

Place-5 is defined by a temporal discontinuity. DISCONTINUITY-TYPE-1 in Table 2 means that there is a sudden decrease on the right side. NX then finds place-6 which is also defined by a temporal discontinuity. Detecting place-5 and place-6 by DISCONTINUITY-TYPE-1 and DISCONTINUITY-TYPE-3 in a row makes it consider that there may be an object on the right side and this information is added to the Exploration Agenda. Notice that place-15 is not detected while NX is moving from place-5 the first time, because it doesn't know what's coming next.

Table 2. A map description of an example

```
-------------------------------------------------------------------------------------
| Node |      Criteria      | Orientation |                                         |
|-------------------------------------------------                                   |
|                                                Sensory      Information            |
|                                                                                    |
-------------------------------------------------------------------------------------
| 1     SYMMETRY                  180                                                 |
| ((*FULL-FAN* L-WING-WIDTH= 2 R-WING-WIDTH= 2 SHORTEST-DIST= 51 RAW-DATA= (72 55 (51) 55 72)) |
|  (*FULL-FAN* L-WING-WIDTH= 2 R-WING-WIDTH= 3 SHORTEST-DIST= 51 RAW-DATA= (72 55 51 55 72 132)) |
|  (*OPEN-SPACE* WIDTH= 1)                                                            |
|  (*FULL-FAN* L-WING-WIDTH= 3 R-WING-WIDTH= 2 SHORTEST-DIST= 51 RAW-DATA= (132 72 55 51 55 72))) |
|                                                                                    |
| 2     ENDING                    180                                                |
| ((*FULL-FAN* L-WING-WIDTH= 3 R-WING-WIDTH= 3 SHORTEST-DIST= 30 RAW-DATA= (55 42 32 (30) 32 42 55)) |
|  (*FULL-FAN* L-WING-WIDTH= 1 R-WING-WIDTH= 3 SHORTEST-DIST= 51 RAW-DATA= (55 51 55 72 132)) |
|  (*OPEN-SPACE* WIDTH= 1)                                                            |
|  (*FULL-FAN* L-WING-WIDTH= 3 R-WING-WIDTH= 1 SHORTEST-DIST= 51 RAW-DATA= (132 72 55 51 55))) |
|                                                                                    |
| 3     DISCONTINUITY-TYPE-3       90                                                 |
| ((*OPEN-SPACE* WIDTH= 1) (*R-HALF-FAN* WIDTH= 2 RAW-DATA= (182 184)) (*OPEN-SPACE* WIDTH= 2) |
|  (*R-HALF-FAN* WIDTH= 3 RAW-DATA= (38 49 91)) (*OPEN-SPACE* WIDTH= 1)               |
|  (*FULL-FAN* L-WING-WIDTH= 3 R-WING-WIDTH= 3 SHORTEST-DIST= 35 RAW-DATA= (91 49 38 35 38 49 91))) |
|                                                                                    |
| 4     SYMMETRY                   90                                                 |
| ((*OPEN-SPACE* WIDTH= 2) (*OTHERS* RAW-DATA= 138) (*OPEN-SPACE* WIDTH= 2)           |
|  (*FULL-FAN* L-WING-WIDTH= 1 R-WING-WIDTH= 1 SHORTEST-DIST= 51 RAW-DATA= (93 51 91)) |
|  (*OPEN-SPACE* WIDTH= 1)                                                            |
|  (*FULL-FAN* L-WING-WIDTH= 3 R-WING-WIDTH= 3 SHORTEST-DIST= 35 RAW-DATA= (91 49 38 35 38 49 91))) |
|                                                                                    |
| 5     DISCONTINUITY-TYPE-1       90                                                 |
| ((*OPEN-SPACE* WIDTH= 3) (*R-HALF-FAN* WIDTH= 2 RAW-DATA= (78 109)) (*OPEN-SPACE* WIDTH= 1) |
|  (*OTHERS* RAW-DATA= 185) (*OTHERS* RAW-DATA= 142) (*OPEN-SPACE* WIDTH= 1)          |
|  (*FULL-FAN* L-WING-WIDTH= 3 R-WING-WIDTH= 3 SHORTEST-DIST= 35 RAW-DATA= (91 49 38 35 38 49 91))) |
|                                                                                    |
| 6     DISCONTINUITY-TYPE-3       90                                                 |
| ((*FULL-FAN* L-WING-WIDTH= 3 R-WING-WIDTH= 4 SHORTEST-DIST= 35 RAW-DATA= (91 49 38 35 38 49 91 (142)))|
|  (*R-HALF-FAN* WIDTH= 3 RAW-DATA= (142 154 201))                                    |
|  (*OPEN-SPACE* WIDTH= 2)                                                            |
|  (*OTHERS* RAW-DATA= 78)                                                            |
|  (*OPEN-SPACE* WIDTH= 3))                                                           |
|                                                                                    |
|             .                        .                        .                    |
|             .                        .                        .                    |
|                                                                                    |
| 15    MIN-DISTANCE               90                                                 |
| ((*FULL-FAN* L-WING-WIDTH= 3 R-WING-WIDTH= 4 SHORTEST-DIST= 35 RAW-DATA= (91 49 38 35 38 49 91 (188)))|
|  (*OTHERS* RAW-DATA= 203) (*OPEN-SPACE* WIDTH= 1)                                   |
|  (*FULL-FAN* L-WING-WIDTH= 1 R-WING-WIDTH= 1 SHORTEST-DIST= 69 RAW-DATA= (95 69 90)) |
|  (*OPEN-SPACE* WIDTH= 1)                                                            |
|  (*OTHERS* RAW-DATA= 193)                                                           |
|  (*OPEN-SPACE* WIDTH= 1))                                                           |
|                                                                                    |
|             .                        .                        .                    |
|             .                        .                        .                    |
|                                                                                    |
| 18    SYMMETRY                    0                                                 |
| ((*FULL-FAN* L-WING-WIDTH= 1 R-WING-WIDTH= 1 SHORTEST-DIST= 197 RAW-DATA= (213 (197) 213)) |
|  (*FULL-FAN* L-WING-WIDTH= 3 R-WING-WIDTH= 3 SHORTEST-DIST= 109                     |
|                                               RAW-DATA= (213 154 118 109 118 154 214))|
|  (*FULL-FAN* L-WING-WIDTH= 1 R-WING-WIDTH= 1 SHORTEST-DIST= 198 RAW-DATA= (214 198 214)) |
|  (*FULL-FAN* L-WING-WIDTH= 3 R-WING-WIDTH= 3 SHORTEST-DIST= 35 RAW-DATA= (214 49 38 35 38 49 214))) |
|                                                                                    |
```

```
--------------------------------------------------------------------------------
| ARC |First node  |Second  node|    Local control      | Chain Program        | Total  |
|     |place degree|place degree|      Strategy         |                      | length |
--------------------------------------------------------------------------------
|  1  | (1 180)    | (2 180)    | FOLLOW-MIDLINE         ((13 13))                  13   |
|  2  | (1 0)      | (3 90)     | FOLLOW-MIDLINE         ((72 72) (57 51) (60 48)        |
|     |            |            |                         (19 17) (175 175))      373   |
|  3  | (3 90)     | (4 90)     | BLIND-STEP             ((21 21))                  21   |
|  4  | (4 90)     | (5 90)     | WALK-ALONG-OBJECT-ON-LEFT-SIDE ((59 59))          59   |
|     |            |            |                                                        |
|     |     .      |     .      |                                    .                   |
|     |     .      |     .      |                                    .                   |
|     |            |            |                                                        |
| 14  | (14 0)     | (4 0)      | BLIND-STEP             ((18 18))                  18   |
| 15  | (5 90)     | (15 90)    | WALK-ALONG-OBJECT-ON-LEFT-SIDE ((28 28))          28   |
| 16  | (15 180)   | (16 180)   | BLIND-STEP             ((23 23))                  23   |
| 17  | (16 270)   | (17 180)   | WALK-ALONG-OBJECT-ON-LEFT-SIDE ((41 41) (34 38) (44 44))  121 |
| 18  | (17 180)   | (18 0)     | WALK-ALONG-OBJECT-ON-LEFT-SIDE ((38 38) (44 52) (40 42) (42 50) |
|     |            |            |                                    (40 40)) 213        |
| 19  | (18 0)     | (16 180)   | WALK-ALONG-OBJECT-ON-LEFT-SIDE ((44 44) (30 42) (38 42))  121 |
--------------------------------------------------------------------------------
```

It continues following the same control strategy and finds place-7, which is detected by symmetric information. At place-7, NX rotates itself to the direction in which it can continue to use the Walk-Along-Object-Left control strategy. Once Walk-Along-Object left or right has been chosen, NX prefers to use the same contol strategy until it returns to a previously seen place. It continues from place-8 through place-14 in a similar way.

After moving past place-14, NX tries to find a node matching the available sensory information. By considering the Exploration Agenda, sensory data, Travel List, and orientation, it guesses that the place after place-14 may be place-4 which it visited before. Comparison of all information returns an affirmative answer and NX follows a rehearsal procedure to confirm its hypothesis. If the current place is place-4, it should be able to find place-5 with the same control strategy used before to find place-5, and place-3 with the same control strategy used before from place-3 to place-4. It executes that procedure and confirms that the current place is place-4.

In the Exploration Agenda, NX has the information that there may be an object to explore. It goes to place-5 and finds a place which has the minimum distance to the object, while moving to place-6. Place-15 is defined by the minimum lateral distance on the right side, and NX turns to the right to face the object.

NX knows that turning to the right at place-15 results in facing to the object with the minimum distance to the object. NX uses the Blind-Step control strategy, since it will take NX to the object. Place-16 is an ending place, defined when the current control strategy brings the robot to the minimum legal distance to the object. Then it uses the Walk-along-Object-Left control strategy to explore the object. It finds two other maximally symmetric places (place-17 and place-18) and comes back to place-16. Finally, it confirms its exploration of the object by trying to return to place-15, place-5, and place-4. Since it is at a known place and the Exploration Agenda is empty, NX halts.

Figure 3 presents the results of exploration of additional environments.

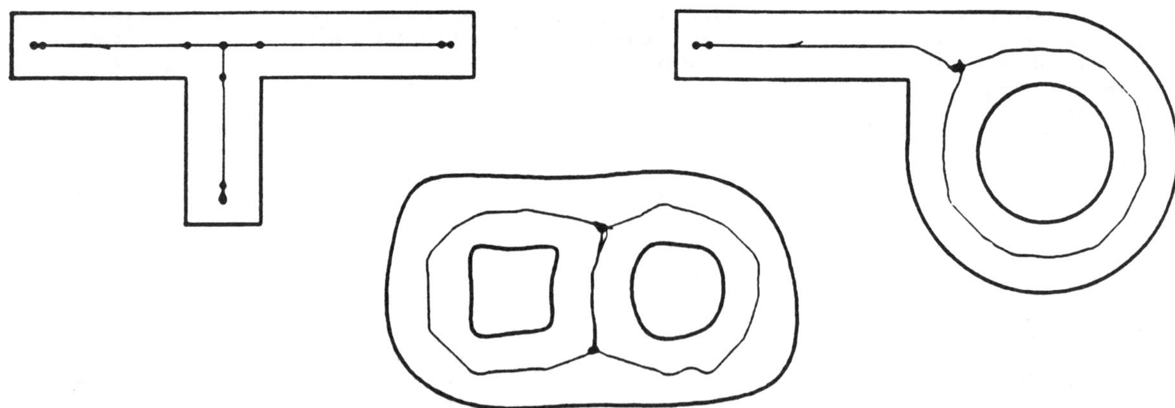

Figure 3. Environments and Topological Models

5. DISCUSSION and FUTURE WORK

We have described our method for qualitative exploration, resulting in a topological map of an unknown environment. Our pilot studies have convinced us that the qualitative method avoids many of the difficulties of traditional approaches. Once the topological map is complete, we should be able to build a metrical map of the distances and directions between places, and of the shapes of walls, without suffering from cumulative metrical error. Below, we briefly summarize some of the key elements of our approach, and some of the directions of our future research.

- Errors occur in sensory devices as well as in the movement actuator. Although there are slippage and miscalibration in the motor, local control strategies are in effect continuously and allow the robot to follow a path. When traveling from one place to another along a known arc, the local control strategy will correct for small initial and subsequent errors to bring the robot into the neighborhood of the place at the other end of arc. At that point, the hill-climbing algorithm can be counted on to minimize moderate amounts of error. Since we do not use metric information from the motors to find the current position, small motor errors should not degrade the performance of our approach. However, since the motor information helps to describe a path or an object approximately, they are recorded. Systematic error is only partially corrected in our approach. NX finds places which are distinctive according to its own perception of the world, but not necessarily geometrically. Random error may bring NX near to a previously defined distinctive place, but not to exactly the same location. In neither case, is there harm to the topologically described map. Therefore our approach to building a map is robust in terms of topological consistency.

- Our method does not restrict the shape of objects in the environment, whereas others have allowed only particular shapes of objects. Our final goal is to build a robot which can explore a real world, not an artificial one.

- Our model has basically successive layers. Sensorimotor description is assimilated into the topological model, and metrical relations will be built on top of topological spatial relations. In other aspect, it will be represented in multiple layers in abstraction. Several distinctive places will be combined together to make one higher-level place representing all of them (e.g. places 3,4, and 14 in figure 2).

- In order to add more shape analysis, we plan to use the sensory history from which qualitative description as well as metrical information can be extracted. For instance, when NX moves from place-1 to place-3 with the Follow-Middle control strategy, then at place-3, it should be able to say that there is an almost straight wall continuously on the left side and there is a corner on the right side. More metric information, like the distance between the two walls, can also be added.

- Information about relative positions of objects in terms of global orientation seems to play an important role in human reasoning [Hutchins, 1983; McReynolds, 1951; Piaget and Inhelder, 1967]. Although the current simulation uses a compass for global orientation, this assumption will be relaxed and a local orientation will be used. Then each local orientation frame will be incrementally linked to the others. Relative positional information between places, like place-3 being on the left side of place-4 in a particular orientation frame, will be added onto the topological model.

- We hypothesize that any sensory system which has the ability to recognize and identify distinctive places can be used in our method. It means that our approach is largely independent of particular sensory devices and movement actuators.

References

R.A.Brooks (1985) Visual Map Making for a Mobile Robot, IEEE, International Conference on Robotics and Automation, pp 824-829

R.Brooks (1986) A Robust Layered Control system for a Mobile Robot. IEEE Journal of Robotics and Automation VOL RA-2 No.1, pp 14-23

R.Chatila and J.Laumond (1985) Position Referencing and Consistent World Modeling for Mobile Robots, IEEE, International Conference on Robotics and Automation, pp 138-170

J.L.Crowley (1985) Navigation for an Intelligent Mobile Robot, IEEE Journal of Robotics and Automation, Vol RA-1, No.1, pp 31-41

G.Giralt (1983) Mobile Robots, Robotics and Artificial Intelligence, Edited by M.Brady L.A.Gerhardt and H.F.Dividson, NATO ASI series, pp 375-393

E.Hutchins (1983) Understanding Micronesian Navigation. Mental Models edited by D. Gentner and A.L. Stevens, pp 191-225. Lawrence Erlbaum Associates, Publishers.

S.S.Iyengar, C.C. Jorgensen, S.V.N.Rao, and C.R.Weisbin (1985) Learned Navigation Paths for a Robot in unexplored Terrain, IEEE the 2nd Conference on AI Application, pp 148-155

E.Koch, C.Yeh, G.Hillel, A.Meystel and C.Isik (1985) Simulation of Path Planning for a system with Vision and Map Updating, IEEE International Conference on Robotics and Automation, pp 147-170

B.Kuipers (1977) Representing Knowledge of Large-Scale Space, Cambridge, MA:
    MIT AI Lab TR-418

B.Kuipers (1978) Modeling spatial knowledge. Cognitive Science,2:pp 129-153

B.Kuipers (1979) Commonsense knowledge of space: Learning from experience. in proceedings of
    IJCAI. Stanford, California, pp 499-501

B.kuipers (1982) The 'Map in the Head' Metaphor. Environment and Behavior 14; pp 202-220.

B.Kuipers (1983) The cognitive map; Could it have been any other way? In H.L. Pick. Jr. and
    L.P. Acredolo (Eds.), Spatial orientation: Theory, Research, and Application.
    New York: Plenum Press. (a)

B.Kuipers (1983) Modeling human knowledge of routes: Partial knowledge and individual
    variation. in procedings of AAAI, Washington,D.C. (b)

B.Kuipers (1985) The Map-Learning Critter. UT AI Lab TR-18

J.Laumond (1983) Model Structuring and Concept Recognition: Two Aspects of Learning for a Mobile
    Robot, in proceedings of IJCAI, pp 839-841

T.Lozano-Perez (1981) Automatic Planning of Manipulator Transfer Movements, IEEE Trans. on
    Systems Man and Cybernetics, pp 781-798

K.Lynch (1960) The Image of the City. Cambridge: MIT Press

J.McReynolds (1951) Geographic Orientation of the Blind. Ph.D. dissertation in U.T.

D.Miller (1985) A Spatial Representation System for Mobile Robots, IEEE International Conference
    on Robotics and Automation, pp 122-128

H.Moravec and A.Elfes (1985) High Resolution Maps from Wide Angle Sonar, IEEE Robotics and
    Automation. pp 116-121

J.Piaget and B.Inhelder (1967) The Child's Conception of Space. New York: Norton

R.S.Rosenberg and P.F.Rowat (1981) Spatial Problems for a simulated Robot. IJCAI '81, pp 758-765

A.W.Siegel and S.H. White (1975) The Development of Spatial Representations of Large-Scale
    Environments. In H.W.Reese (Ed.), Advances in Child Development and Behavior;
    Academic Press

M.P.Turchan and A.K.C. Wong (1985) Low Level Learning for a Mobile Robot: Environment Model
    Acquisition, IEEE the 2nd conference on A.I. Application, pp 157-171

PERCEPTUAL ORGANIZATION USING INTERESTINGNESS

Daryl T. Lawton and Christopher C. McConnell

Advanced Decision Systems
201 San Antonio Circle/ Suite 286
Mountain View, California 90035

ABSTRACT

We treat image segmentation as the application of rules which organize symbolic image structures into qualitatively significant groupings based upon general perceptual criteria. We present a general architecture for grouping processes and a format for describing the rules, image structures, and relationships to which they apply. A basic idea is focusing the application of grouping rules upon the *interestingness* of image structures and relationships. Following Lenat, who faced a similar problem in rating the significance of mathematical theorems, image structures and relationships are ranked according to several attributes such as size, contrast, extent and type of similarity, and the number of groupings a structure is associated with. Interesting objects are then selected based upon their sorted position in different subsets of these lists. Using interestingness to focus control yields a simple loop in which relations between objects are computed, attributes of these relations are sorted to determine interestingness, the selected relations are used to direct the application of grouping rules which produce new objects and relationships which are then added to the rankings and evaluated. Processing is implemented as a pyramid of uniform nodes in which the interesting structures from one level are passed to higher levels to allow for rapid communication and relating non-locally adjacent structures into groups.

INTRODUCTION

Grouping processes in visual perception were initially studied by the gestalt psychologists ([Kanizsa - 79], [Kohler - 47], and [Kubovy - 81]) who attempted to understand how the visual system could organize locally, disconnected events into coherent, meaningful, and global perceptions. Their approach involved establishing different measures for "form goodness" which the vision system was sensitive to and would use to organize perception. Measures reflected such things as perceptual symmetry, connectedness, and smoothness. These in turn corresponded to very general attributes of world objects such as the continuity and smoothness of structure independent of particular object properties. Little resulted from this work in terms of mechanisms for determining these measures.

Developing computational processes for perceptual organization is fundamental to computer vision. Researchers have discovered over the past decades that active, intelligent processing must occur at all levels of image understanding. Undirected segmentation and feature extraction processes have proven to be too brittle, resulting in insufficient structures for interpretation or discovery about the world. Early computer vision work reflecting gestalt principles is found in the line trackers and region growers which would optimize measures such as average curvature or compactness using established AI search techniques to form more complete contours and regions. Recent research in perceptual grouping has involved two major trends in computer vision. The first of these is a modern framework which stresses the fundamental role of symbolic and relational representations in vision ([Marr - 82], [Binford - 81]). Perceptual organization in this framework is expressed as rule-based operations applied to a rich set of extracted symbolical relations and objects. This is in juxtaposition to earlier approaches where image processing was treated more or less as some set of filtering operations which would result in image to image transformations but not explicit structural relations. This made the manipulations necessary for shape recognition, for example, quite difficult. Interestingly, psychologists working in perceptual organization are developing rule-based models independently of work in computer vision [Rock - 84].

The second trend stresses the extraction of robust, qualitative information from images as opposed to exact quantitative information about environmental depth. This is partially in response to the difficulties with SHAPE-FROM-X techniques in working with complex, unconstrained, natural imagery ([Verri and Poggio - 87]). Because of this, it is no longer clear that the recovery of exact depth is a necessary first step in recovering surfaces for invariant similarity to object models. Researchers ([Witkin et.al. - 83], [Lowe - 85], [Binford - 81]) are attempting to establish more reliable, qualitative structures which can be extracted from images. The processes proposed for doing this are non-semantic grouping operations sensitive to such things as coincidence, symmetry, and pattern repetition. This approach involves an object modeling methodology in which objects and events are represented in a form compatible with predictions of qualitative image structures.

We use grouping processes to organize the vast amount of symbolic information describing extracted image structures into a definable set of structures which correspond directly to the components of object and event models. These can be used to direct the access operations over a data base of object models. The grouping processes can also be run from predictions which are imprecise and qualitative. Finally, they serve as a focus of control mechanism to determine significant image structures to direct instantiation over a set of object and event models.

<u>SYSTEM ARCHITECTURE</u>

We begin by describing the attributes and representations for groups and the processing which forms them. The general attributes of perceptual groups are shown in figure 1. The different types of groups are organized into the attribute inheritance hierarchy shown in figure 2. These different types of groups can combine when groups are formed; thus a transformation group can have the attributes of both an expansion and a displacement group. There is also no necessary distinction between whether the components of a group are separated in space or time: there can be a sequential group of different types of transformations to reflect the changes in a structure over time.

Instances of groups exist in two different ways: as objects with attributes specified by a given group type and as spatially distributed structures in a **label plane** (Figure 3). A label plane is an abstract image in register with a sensor surface where each pixel consists of a list of pointers to all objects which occur at and occupy the pixel. Objects at different times and the shape descriptions associated with objects are identically distributed in the label plane. Virtual perceptual structures, such as that shown from the famous Poggendorff illusion (Figure 4), are extracted by grouping operations which connect aligned linear structures to form an instance of a sequential linear contour group. Associated with this group instance is a shape description (which is itself a group--this recursiveness is important) which is deposited in the label plane and treated as an object for further grouping operations, such as the extraction of the perceived, but invisible, relational junctions. The label plane acts as a spatially indexed data base for groups. The neighboring perceptual objects in a label plane could have been extracted at different times or correspond to objects extracted with procedures using different parameters. This enables grouping operations to be applied across spatial resolutions, time, or parameterization of spatial description. Complicated queries can also be performed with respect to a label plane, such as searching through a parameterized neighborhood to find an adjacent object with specified properties.

The grouping architecture consists of virtual processors called **grouping nodes**. The grouping nodes are organized in a coupled hierarchy (Figure 5) with respect to the label plane for extracted perceptual objects. Each grouping node is a local processor which directs the application of grouping rules to extract perceptual structures. The arrangement of grouping nodes also serves as a basis of communication and applying grouping rules to non-adjacent perceptual structures which are contained in areas of the label plane effected by non-adjacent grouping nodes. Significant groups at one level are made available to higher level grouping nodes for the application of rules in a more general context with other groups extracted over a large area of the label plane. Groups at one level of the hierarchy can be used to bias and direct the application of grouping rules at lower levels in the grouping node hierarchy, as in rapidly establishing a repeating structure or aligning distant structures. The processing flow at each grouping node is organized in the simple loop shown in figure 6. Initially, an image is obtained and conventional edge, region, motion, shape description processes are used to extract initial groups. For example, edges are obtained using the Canny operator [Canny - 83a], they are thinned, traversed, and critical points extracted along them using multi-resolution curvature descriptions. From these, instances of connected sequential and junction-type groups are extracted. If curves are extracted at different spatial resolutions or different parameterized shape descriptions are used, then each of these is represented as a separate instance of a group. In this way, the potential relations between the contours at different spatial resolutions can be determined by grouping processes.

The relations between groups in the label plane are determined and stored in different types of **similarity objects**. There are three different types of similarity objects: 1) those for describing the similarity of feature attributes; 2) those for describing the similarity of attributes which

Bookkeeping Attributes: Several different types of information such as inherited group types, subgroups, supergroups and creation time.

Group Membership Attributes: Specifies what is required to be a member of the group.

Total Group Attributes: Attributes which describe the characteristics of the group as a whole.

Shape Description: Structural characteristics of the group and its components.

Assimilation Measures: A set of numbers between 0 and 1 describing the fit of potential group members to the defined requirements of each inheritance group type.

Neighborhood Constraints: Methods for establishing areas in which to form groups with other groups.

Figure 1: General Attributes of Perceptual Groups

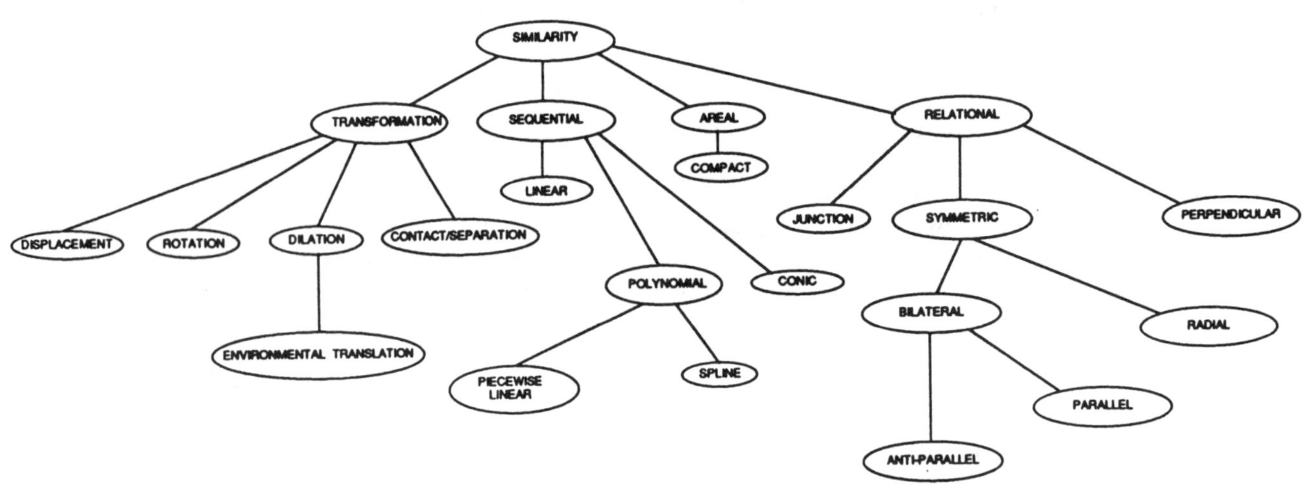

Figure 2: Group Type Inheritance Hierarchy

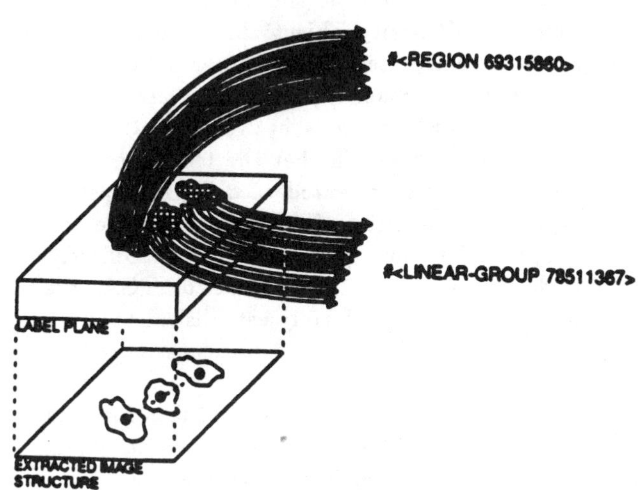

Figure 3: Label Plane

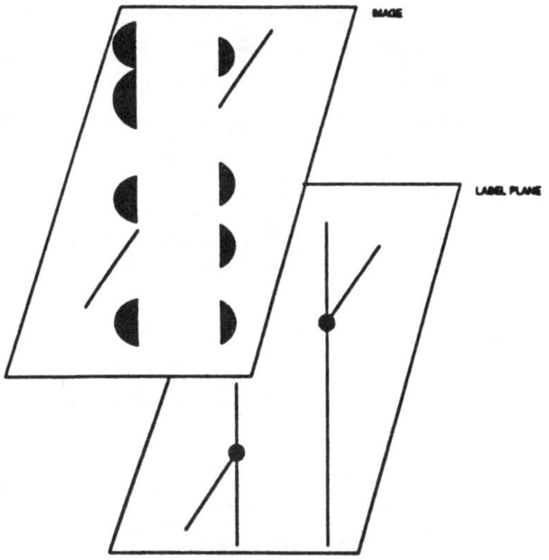

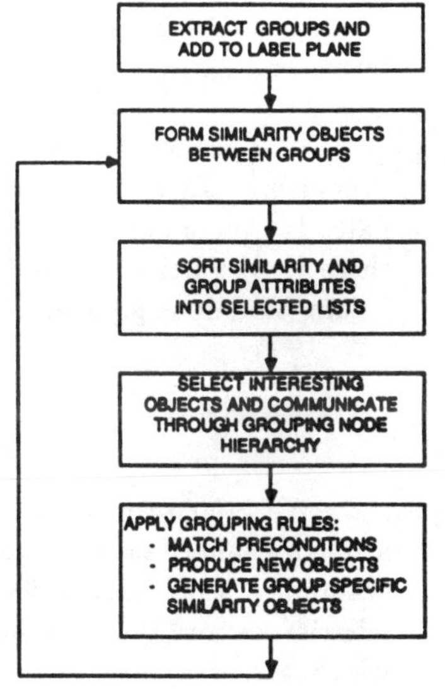

Figure 4: Poggendorff Illusion

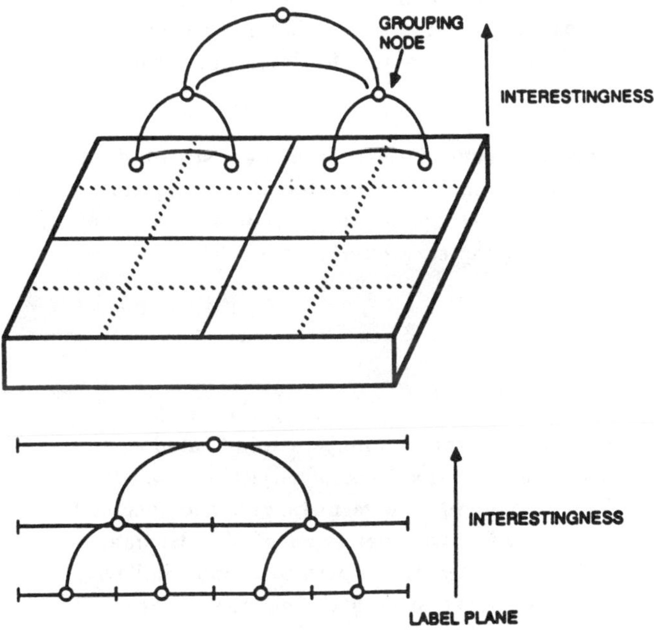

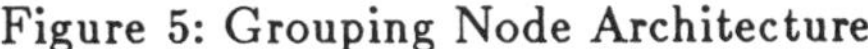

Figure 5: Grouping Node Architecture

Figure 6: Processing Flow

are spatially distributed over a structure; and 3) those for describing the similarity of composite structures which consist of multiple groups. The kind of similarity object that is established between groups is determined by the type of group and the attributes being compared. Different similarity objects can be extracted between the same pair of groups because of different ways attributes of groups can be related or compared. A basic distinction is between whether one group assimilates another group to the properties which define it or whether the two groups are combined to produce a new group. This difference is explicitly represented as different types of group attributes: the Total Group Attributes (TGAs) for the properties of a group as a whole and the Group Membership Attributes (GMAs) for the properties of components of a group. Different similarity objects can be produced between groups depending on whether GMAs or TGAs are being compared. At this stage of processing, similarity objects are uniformly established between adjacent groups in the label plane.

Different attributes of the similarity objects and groups are sorted into several lists for such things as size, feature similarity, normalized measures which reflect the extent to which an object has been assimilated to a group, summary statistics for all the similarity objects generated for a particular group and time since an object was involved in a grouping operation. These different rankings are then combined by a modifiable selection criteria to select the interesting [Winston - 84] similarity objects and groups to focus the application of grouping rules to them.

The selected interesting objects at one level of the grouping-node architecture are then made available to higher level grouping nodes for consideration in a larger context. Grouping rules are then applied to the selected interesting similarity objects and groups to produce new group instances. The applied grouping rules have preconditions which must match the attributes in the selected similarity objects or groups. The grouping rules can result in new groups, in extending a group by assimilating something to it, merging groups, generalizing or specializing the defining attributes of a group, or generating a more complicated similarity object to determine structural transformations.

Processing continues, as it started, with additional groups derived from new sensor data. Processing can continue indefinitely as less and less interesting similarity objects become candidates for the application of grouping rules. Processing can be stopped using criteria such as when there is a sufficiently uniform covering of an image with extracted groups or when all structures belong to unique groups.

<u>GROUPS</u>

We refer to perceptual objects as groups. The different type of groups are indicated in the attribute inheritance diagram in figure 2. Groups are objects in the sense of object-oriented programming: they have defined attributes, associated methods, can receive messages, and specified inheritance and type combinations. In addition to groups, we have other types of objects: images which are arrays of values derived from sensors or feature extraction operations and similarity objects which are used to describe relations between groups. We stretch the concept of group a bit to include other common image processing objects such as histograms. The term group follows the use of gestalt psychologists and others. It is also easily confused with the notion of group as an algebraic structure, especially when we refer to things such as transformation groups, but the meaning should be clear from context

Groups consist of the following attributes:

Bookkeeping Attributes. Bookkeeping attributes keep track of several different types of information such as the list of inherited group types applicable to a group, the immediate component groups, super groups, and feature images groups are in register with. Groups are recursive so they can be consist of different types of groups resulting in potential groups of arbitrary complexity.

Group Membership Attributes. (GMAs) The group membership attributes specify what is required to be a member of a group. It is used to determine the extent to which something is assimilated to an existing group. The group membership specification can be a set of attributes and their required values or it can itself be a group which serves as a structural template specifying the characteristic structure making up a group. The group membership specification can be an instance of a transformation group to deal with successive changes in structure.

Total Group Attributes. (TGAs) The total group attributes refer to the properties of a group as a whole. This distinction between a group as a collection of related entities or as a complete object in its own right has implications for how relations between groups are determined and the type of rules which form groups. When two groups are combined based upon their total group attributes, this generally results in a new type of group. When groups are combined based upon their group membership attributes, one of the groups will usually assimilate the other. The same sets of groups can be combined to form different types of groups because of this.

Shape Description. The shape description specifies the structural characteristics of a group. For similarity groups this is several simple shape features such as centroid, minimum bounding rectangle and orientation axes. An important property of a shape description is that it is itself an instance of a group which can be deposited as an object in the label plane and can be involved in grouping operations. This allows for uniform grouping operations to be applied to groups consisting of disconnected elements. One benefit of treating shape descriptions as groups is the distinction between shape as something to which grouping rules can be applied and shape as an attribute of objects disappears. For example, the centroids associated with regions are themselves degenerate regions, the axis associated with parallel edges are themselves curves. The shape descriptions associated with objects can usually be expressed in terms of basic object types such as curves, regions, and junctions to allow grouping operations to be applied to the shape description associated with objects. For transformational groups, shape properties refer to the characteristics or the history of a transformation. The grouping rules associated with forming a given type of group specify the type of shape description that get's deposited in the label plane. There is an explicit linkage between groups which are shape descriptions and the groups they describe.

Assimilation Measures/Methods. These are methods for evaluating how well all the components of a group fit to the defining characteristics of the group or how well another object fits these characteristics. The assimilation measures can be functions of attributes found in the TGAs, the GMAs, and the shape descriptions. For a linear sequential group, these refer to the fit of the elements to a parameterized description of the line. Assimilation measures are constrained to evaluate to between 0 to 1. Multiple assimilation measures are generally associated with a group corresponding to the group types which are combined.

Neighborhood Determination Constraints The neighborhood determination constraints determine the areas in the label plane over which similarity objects with other groups are extracted. These fall into a small number of general classes, such as a uniform expanding neighborhood or a directed, cone shape neighborhood.

SIMILARITY GROUP

A similarity group is the most general type of group in the hierarchy. It is specialized with respect to the attribute inheritance hierarchy as the nature of the similarity is refined. All of these attributes are inherited by their children in the inheritance hierarchy. The basic attributes are:

Bookkeeping:

- **Types** -- all of the group types that apply to this group.

- **Components** -- The groups that make up this group.

- **All-components** -- All of the groups and subgroups that make up this group.

- **Parent-Similarity-Object** -- The similarity object that this group was created from.

- **Children-Similarity-Objects** -- All of the similarity objects that have been created from this group.

- **Children-Groups** -- All of the groups that were created from this group.

- **Feature-images** -- The images that the components of this group came from.

Total Group Attributes:

- Attribute and values that are found in all of the component groups. Examples include color, orientation, contrast, etc.

- Attribute and values that describe the group as a whole, such as size, the bounding rectangle, and the axis of symmetry

Shape: These attributes include the groups that are used to describe the shape of the group as a whole. Shape measures that are not expressed as groups such as compactness are found in the Total Group Attributes. Examples include centroids, spine networks, junctions, etc.

Group Membership Attributes: These attributes describe the characteristics that the components of the group have in common. There are two general classes:

- **Similar attributes** -- these are the attributes and the defining values for attributes that are similar between all of the group's components. Examples include red between certain values, or matching a group that describes a components shape.

- **Difference attributes** -- these attributes describe the differences found in common between the components. With two components, this is just the mapping between all of the non-similar attributes. With more than two components, these attributes become similar attributes if they are similar across three components. Examples include a edges with a constant change in orientation, or a constant change in intensity.

Assimilation: Each assimilation measure is a number between 0 and 1 that describes how well this group assimilates its components. Different rules express this assimilation measure in different ways. Examples include the average similarity of all of the similar components, or the ratio of the number of similar attributes in the Group Membership Attributes to the maximum number of similar attributes in the component groups.

Neighborhood: Uniform area around the group.

SIMILARITY OBJECTS

Much of the processing involved in building groups involves determining how groups are related with respect to group membership criteria or whether an instance of a new type of group should be instantiated based upon the relation between the groups. We use different types of similarity objects to describe the relations between groups. Computationally there is a wide variety of approaches and problems in realizing object similarity. We first distinguish between some basic types of attributes which can be associated with objects in general. One type is for **feature attributes** which are described by scalar values or a simple structured object, such as matrix describing moments. Another type is for **indexed attributes** for values associated with an object which are indexed by positions with respect to the object, such as the gradient vectors or curvature estimates along a curve. Another general type is **composite attributes** which are relational structures for describing characteristics such as shape. An example is breaking a curve into sub-curves and junctions reflecting curvature extrema at different levels of smoothing. In our work we have found it useful to distinguish between three different types of similarity objects corresponding to these types of attributes. There are some computational expense related characteristics for determining the type of similarity object to create between objects. Feature attribute similarity is generally inexpensive to compute but, unless the groups are locatable as points, does not specify a transformation relating different objects. Indexed attribute similarity does this, but at the expense of searching over the set of potential transformations relating the groups. This is also an issue with similarity for composite objects, since each primitive component can be matched in these different ways and explicit type of transformation needs to be determined for each component and also for the object as a whole. Because of this, initial similarity objects are usually based upon feature attributes, with the generation of the other types based upon the application of specific grouping rules.

Attribute Similarity Functions

To realize similarity determination we have a database of functions called attribute similarity functions that map a pair of type attribute values onto the range between 0 and 1 for such things as orientation, the area, and the variance of feature attributes. The methods associated with these functions can be specific to the objects they are applied to.

Attribute Similarity Structure

This type of similarity describes the relation between objects based upon the differences in their attributes such as size, length, average-contrast, and orientation. Attribute based similarity doesn't necessarily determine the geometric transformation which relates two objects which are highly correlated. One exception to this is an oriented point-object, like a junction which has a precise location associated with it. When a similarity is determined for it, the transformation is based upon the change in position and orientation. Extended objects, such as curves or composite objects can be similar based upon several attributes without knowing what the transformation relating them is. Associating such a geometric transformation with such extended or composite objects is done in three different ways: 1) a specific method is used over the determined attributes based upon the centroid and orientation attributes of the objects; 2) The determined attribute similarity is used to apply a transformation to the object with the type of similarity using one of the different types of similarity described below; 3) The object is decomposed into point objects such as its junctions and these are matched using relaxation-style similarity.

Indexed Similarity Structure

Some of the attributes associated with objects are indexed by positions with respect to the object, such as positions in a region, along a curve, or in an image. Index attributes can be compared for different objects by applying a transformation to the indices of one of the objects, performing a pointwise-comparison of attributes, and then summing these point-wise comparisons in some way. A common example of this is associating with each point along a curve object a vector containing the gradient values with respect to the image from which it was extracted. The indices can then be translated with respect to another gradient image and the extent of similarity determined by finding the average value of the normalized inner-product between gradient values along the curve and those found in the corresponding position in the gradient image. Note that objects of different types can be compared with respect to each other and that objects needn't be of the same dimensions. This type of similarity is described by the Indexed-Similarity-Structure.

Composite Similarity Structure

Complex perceptual objects consist of relations between objects, such as a network of curves and junctions associated with a region spine shape description or the set of curves which make up an instance of a perceptual group. These structures can be matched using attribute and indexed similarity structures, but these are insufficient to describe the independent similarities of the components. This type of similarity is described by a composite-similarity-structure which describes for each primitive component of an object what's it initial potential similarities are, what the best similarity is with respect to some local transformational consistency determined by a relaxation procedure [Barnard - 80], and a similarity-description-function which determines the extent of subcomponent similarity. Associated with the entire structure is a composite similarity value which associates, recursively, with each subcomponent up to the level of the entire structure, the total extent of similarity.

Composite similarity is usually invoked by the occurrence of a strong similarity between a component object of one group or to determine the similarity objects of several adjacent objects under the constraint of similar motion. By restricting the neighborhoods to which the subcomponents can determine their potential similarity relative to the entire object they are being matched to it is possible to get the effect of applying the global transformation to the object and allow some jitter to each component as it finds it's best similarity. The relaxation-similarity-state is initialized to the values found in the corresponding similarity object.

<u>GROUPING RULES</u>

Grouping Rules are applied to a similarity object or a group and produce either an updated version of a group or an instance of a new type of group. One set of rules create groups from similarity objects. There are different types of grouping rules reflecting whether the rule is specializing or generalizing a group with respect to the group inheritance hierarchy or the GMAs which describe a group. Other classes of rules deal with the generation of more detailed similarity objects for indexed and composite structural relations and distributing information about groups over the grouping node hierarchy. In the abstracted grouping rules which follow, boldface items correspond to TGAs, italics to GMAs, with capitalized items corresponding to constants. Some example rules, in particular classes are:

Group Membership Attribute Creation

CONDITION: There are attributes in the similarity object that compares the Total Group Attributes of one group to the Total Group Attributes of the other group that have a similarity above threshold.

ACTION: Create a group. Add NEW-GROUP to the group's **types**. Set **components** to be the two groups being compared. Set the Group Membership Attributes of the group to include the similar attributes and their composite values from the Total Group Attribute to Total Group Attribute match object, and the differences of all of the remaining attributes.

Group Membership Attribute Generalization

CONDITION: There are attributes in the match object that compares the Group Membership Attributes of one group to the Group Membership Attributes of the other group that have a similarity above threshold.

ACTION: Create a group. Add MERGED-GROUP to the group's **types**. Set **components** to be the combination of the **components** of the two groups. Set the Group Membership Attributes of the group to include the similar attributes and their composite values from the Group Membership Attribute to Group Membership Attribute match object.

Total Group Attribute Specialization

CONDITION: One of the group's **types** is MERGED-GROUP, the groups in the components both have a type of SEQUENTIAL-GROUP, and the **first** or **last** component of the first group is the closest group in the first group to the **first** or **last** component of the second group.

ACTION: Add SEQUENTIAL-GROUP to the group's **types**. Set **order** so that the components are still in an ordered list.

Match Generation Rules

CONDITION: *Shape* has an acute junction.

ACTION: Look for acute junctions in a larger neighborhood around the object. If a similar junction is found, then form an indexed match object that describes how well the whole shape can be found in that position.

INTERESTINGNESS

The application of grouping rules is directed using an interestingness criteria applied to groups and similarity objects. This is an agenda-based method to restrict the complexity of matching grouping rules to similarity objects and also to limit the number of groups that are created to those satisfying general perceptual criteria. This is a fundamental problem in rule-based inference systems working with large data bases of assertions. Our approach is related to that of Lenat [Lenat - 82], who faced a similar problem in rating the significance of mathematical theorems to direct experimentation. Rule application is directed by forming several sorted lists ranking many different attributes of groups and similarity objects. The interesting objects are then selected based upon their sorted position in different subsets of these lists. Using interestingness to focus control yields a simple loop in which relations between objects are computed, attributes of these relations are sorted to determine interestingness, the selected relations are used to direct the application of grouping rules which produce new objects and relationships which are then added to the rankings and evaluated. Interestingness is also used to organize the flow of information in the grouping pyramid. Lower nodes pass their interesting groups up to higher node for combining them in more global contexts to increase processing speed.

There have been attempts to develop measures which express the extent of structural significance from simple shape properties [Attneave - 57], information theory [Lowe - 85], group theory [Levitt - 84], and [Grenander - 81]. A general difficulty with such attempts is trying to compress structural information into a single measure. In addition, natural images are not binary dot patterns. The richness of information in natural images as a basis of attribute and structural correlation should make it simpler to extract information. In addition, the direction of the grouping process should be modifiable based upon model based predictions and the current stage of processing.

The implemented mechanisms for forming attribute lists and sorting them are very general. It is possible to form new ones during processing. Attribute lists we commonly use are:

- group assimilation measures

- best assimilation measure for a group with its neighbors

- change in the best assimilation measure

- number of similar attributes

- attribute similarity values

- time since a grouping rule was applied to a structure or some composite object containing the structure

Interesting objects are selected by union and intersection operations over subsets from the minimal and maximal subsets of these lists.

Processing Example

Figures 7 through 9 show a simple segmentation example using a two level rule-based grouper applied to an image of a fern leaf. Figure 7 shows the initially extracted groups derived from the Canny edge operator and the extraction of topological junctions and distinctive curvature junctions at both levels of the grouper which are used for reference for displaying selected groups at different stages of processing. Super-imposed on this are the extracted groups after a few stages of processing. The succeeding figures display selected groups at the end of processing cycles which are part of sequential groups with GMA's consisting of anti-parallel groups. There are, in addition to these displayed groups, a large number of groups at each location in the label plane at the positions indicated by the initially extracted contours and junctions. The number of such groups indicates the complexity of the segmentation. The figures show the development of an extended sequential group with a GMA describing a constrained anti-parallel structure continued along the length of the fern leaf.

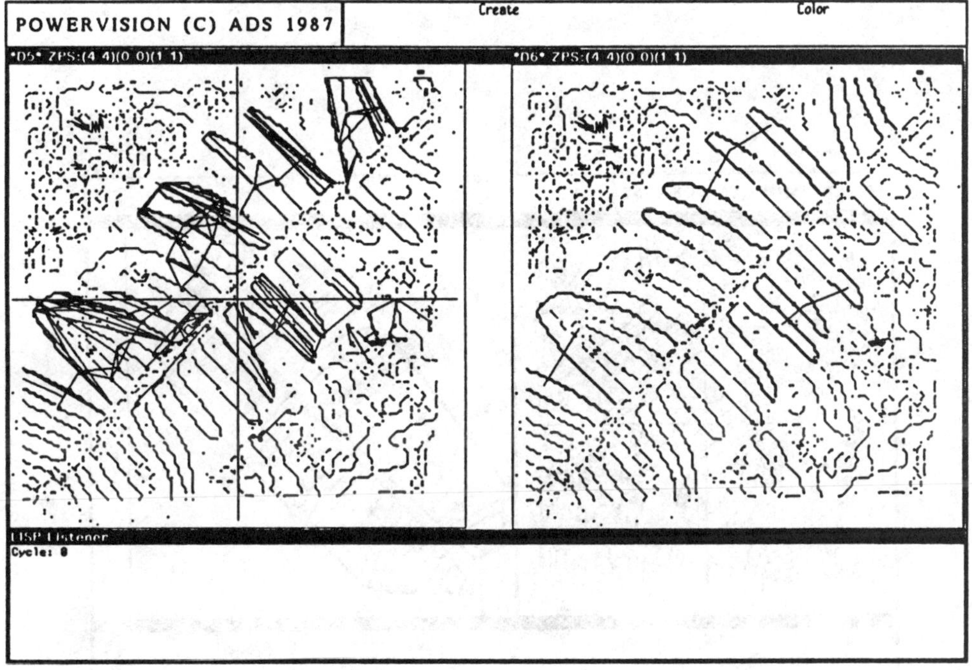

Figure 7: Fern Leaf 1

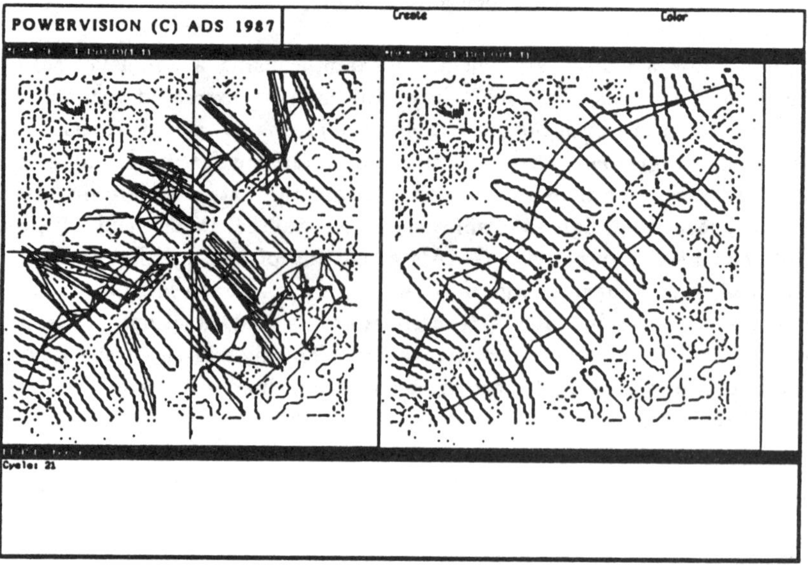

Figure 8: Fern Leaf 2

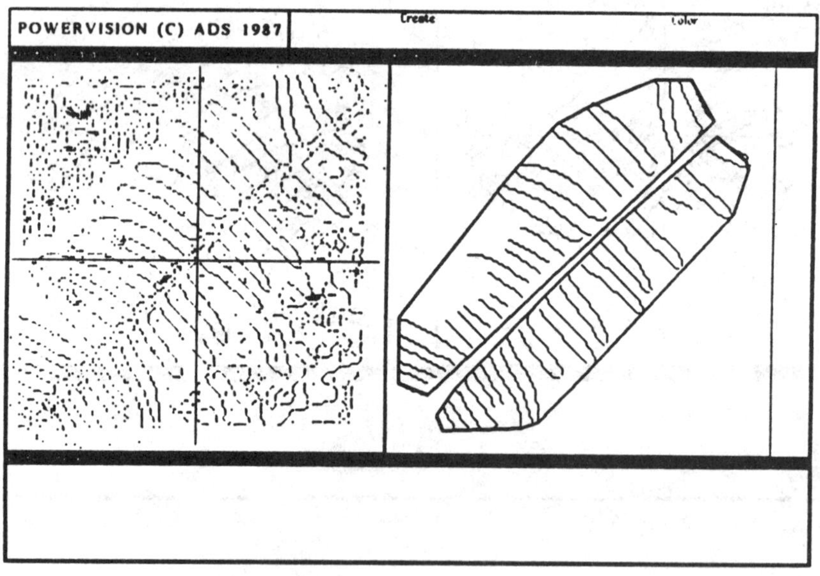

Figure 9: Fern Leaf 3

ACKNOWLEDGEMENTS

This document was prepared by Advanced Decision Systems (ADS) of Mountain View, California, under U.S. Government contract number DACA76-85-C-0005 for the U.S. Army Engineer Topographic Laboratories (ETL), Fort Belvoir, Virginia, and the Defense Advanced Research Projects Agency (DARPA), Arlington, Virginia. The authors wish to thank Tod Levitt and Ellen Toyofuku.

References

F. Attneave, "Physical determinants of the judged complexity of shape", *J. Exp. Psychol.*, vol 53, pp. 221-227.

S. Barnard and W. Thompson, "Disparity Analysis of Images", IEEE PAMI, Vol. PAMI-2, No 4, July 1980.

J.F. Canny, "Finding Edges and Lines in Images", Technical Report, Artificial Intelligence Laboratory, June, 1983.

U. Grenander, "Regular Structures" from *Lectures in Patter Theory vol.3*, Springer-Verlag, NY, 1981.

G. Kanizsa, "Organization in Vision", New York: Preaeger, 1979.

W. Kohler, "Gestalt Psychology", New York: Liverright, 1947.

M. Kubovy, and J. Pomerantz, "Perceptual Organization", Hillsdale, N.J.: Erlbaum, 1981.

D. B. Lenat, "AM: Discovery in Mathematics as Heuristic Search", in *Knowledge-Based Systems in Artificial Intelligence*, edited by R. Davis and D. B. Lenat, McGraw-Hill Book Co., NY, 1982. Based on a PhD thesis, Stanford University, Stanford, CA, 1977.

T.S. Levitt, "Domain Independent Object Description and Decomposition", from *Proceedings of the National Conference on Artificial Intelligence*, AAAI, Austin TX, August 6-10, 1984.

D. Lowe, "Perceptual Organization and Visual Recognition", Kluwer Academic Pub., Boston, MA, 1985.

D. Marr, "Vision", W.H. Freeman, New York, New York and San Francisco, California, 1982.

I. Rock, "Perception", Scientific American Library, NY, 1984.

A. Verri and T. Poggio, "Qualitative Information in the Optical Flow", in Proceedings Image Understanding Workshop, Los Angeles, CA, Feb, 1987, pp. 825-834.

P. H. Winston "Artificial Intelligence", Addison-Wesley Publishing Co., Inc., 1984.

A.P. Witkin and J.M. Tenenbaum, "On the Role of Structure in Vision", in Human and Machine Vision, J. Beck, B. Hope, and A. Rosenfeld (Eds.), Academic Press, 1983.

TERRAIN ANALYSIS FOR TACTICAL SITUATION ASSESSMENT

Drew McDermott and Andrew Gelsey
Yale University Computer Science Department
New Haven, Connecticut

Abstract

Tactical situation assessment is the problem of analyzing incoming military-intelligence data about enemy activities, in order to produce estimates of their intentions and capabilities. An important prerequisite to this assessment is the analysis of the terrain to find militarily significant features, such as cover and concealment, avenues of approach, and obstacles. We are studying two classes of algorithms: for region segmentation and line-of-sight calculations. The former use a variant of the symmetric-axis transform to find the widths of regions, which are then segmented into the longest possible areas of constant width. The latter find pairs of pixels that can "see" each other, first at a coarse level, then at progressively finer levels of resolution. Many of the pieces of these algorithms can profit from parallelism, and we are exploring implementation on a Connection Machine.

1   Defining the Problem

The problem of *tactical situation assessment* is to analyze incoming intelligence data about enemy activities, and produce estimates of their intentions and capabilities. Defined this way, it is fairly open-ended, and the current project[1] allows several approaches.

A "complete" solution to this problem would require solving all of several major AI research areas, including planning and plan recognition, since a complete assessment of what the enemy was up to would require "getting into his head" and understanding his plans. While that is an interesting and worthwhile direction for research, we have opted to make use of the computer's skills in other directions. Hence we are focusing on the tactical-situation assessment process organized into two phases:

1. Find militarily significant features of the terrain. "Significant features" change only occasionally, so the output of this phase can be used repeatedly for detailed analysis of a particular area.

2. Match up intelligence reports with those features in order to infer which ones the enemy is making use of and how. If we are under heavy attack on the right, and observations report that the enemy has howitzers in that sector, which would be useful if he could take a certain hill in that sector that we currently hold, then it is plausible that the hill is his goal.

The program will be concerned with battlefields several kilometers on a side, about the size a division is concerned with. The program has access, we suppose, to an excellent map of the region, giving elevation and feature data at a resolution of about 100 meters square. The enemy ("Red," as opposed to friendly "Blue") is assumed to be working with a division or two, and hence the program will have to think about the movement and location of units down to about battalion size.

Note that the problem is a level above the raw sensor-fusion problem. We assume that elementary intelligence data have already been sorted out, with some duplication and noise eliminated. However, the overall report will still be spotty and unreliable. The presence of noise is going to make it difficult to apply detailed plan recognition to each such event. That is why we have opted for a "mass matching" process.

Most of our work so far has been on Phase 1, finding significant features. We will justify our approach to Phase 1 by describing how Phase 2 will make use of the output of Phase 1, a *terrain analysis graph* that describes militarily significant features of the area, such as "attack site" and "avenues of approach." Figure 1(a) shows a fragment of a typical contour map, and Figure 1(b) shows part of the terrain-analysis graph for it.

2   Hypothesis Formation

In a real tactical situation, there will be reams of data coming in about enemy behavior, typically about a certain type and size of force observed doing some activity at a location and time. The time stamps on the data give us some estimate of how out-of-date they are. Such time stamping

---

[1] Funded by the US Army's Center for Signals Warfare, under grant DAAB10-86-K-0604

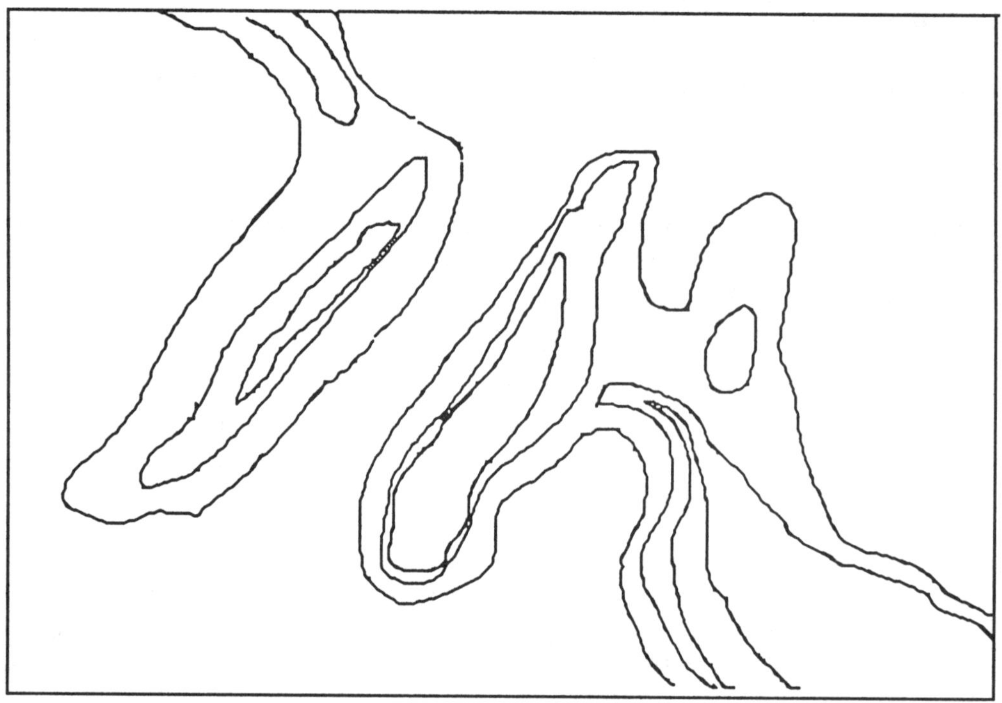

(a) Contour Map

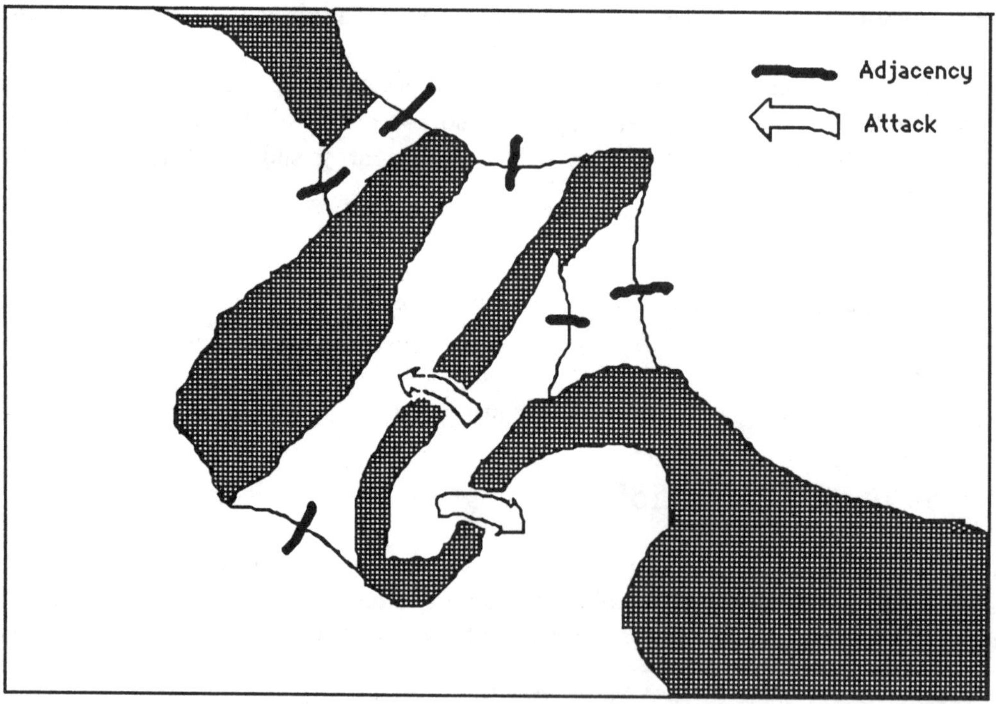

Figure 1: Example map and its analysis

may also give us some idea of the speed and direction of movement of enemy units, provided we can identify a unit at one time with a unit at another.

Given a terrain-analysis graph and a set of observational data, we must combine the two in order to come up with an overall hypothesis about what the enemy is actually threatening to do. There are two components to this overall hypothesis: A proposed arrangement of enemy forces, both observed and unobserved; and a proposed set of targets for those forces. The second component is largely dependent on candidate targets, which are computable in advance from the terrain-analysis graph. Enemy forces may then be matched to targets and conduits to them in order to guess at their arrangement and destination.

Here are some of the ways a piece of terrain can be classified as a target worth attacking and occupying:

1. The program is told that it is an objective of one side or the other. Major objectives are few in number and change quite infrequently, so it seems reasonable to just tell the program what they are. (We have in mind a major railhead or other objective that Red or Blue is supposed to take or keep.)

2. It affords an effective attack site toward current or anticipated force-concentration areas. That is, if a force were located on this site, it could attack enemy forces. Deciding this depends on line-of-sight calculations, but also on the piece of terrain being accessible with the appropriate weapon systems.

3. It affords an effective attack site toward an avenue of approach for one side or the other.

4. It blocks communication and transportation for enemy forces. An example would be a bridge, road, or railroad.

These categories are close to what military people call *key terrain*, a piece of ground worth occupying for its use in further military operations. Except for the first, all of the items in the list can be easily computed from the terrain-analysis graph, which represents explicitly what areas can be used to attack a given area, and what conduits are narrow bottlenecks between areas.

The hypothesized arrangement of enemy forces depends on the observed arrangement, plus consideration of what could be hidden in various areas. For example, suppose that one of our outposts is under attack. It is at the end of a wide valley that would be suitable as an avenue of approach, not just toward the outpost, but toward some large and tempting target that the outpost is shielding. We would not be surprised to see a larger-scale attack on the large target, although of course the whole thing might be a feint. It depends on what has been observed in the wide valley.

We are trying to avoid coming up with a detailed plan that the enemy might be following. Hence we are led to thinking of enemy activity as an "inanimate" phenomenon. Hydraulic and gaseous analogies come to mind. Observed enemy units are like test particles that indicate the densities and velocities of larger forces. If a large number of test particles are observed in an important area, then chances are the enemy is indeed using that area for the purposes implied by the terrain analysis graph. In general we must accommodate incompleteness in the data by transforming observed activity levels into ranges. The low estimate may actually be lower than the observed activity level, if there is a good chance of duplication of reports. The high estimate may be much higher than the observed level, if there are few reports, many enemy units unaccounted for, poor visibility in the area, and so forth.

Suppose we perform such calculations on all observations over time. We will be left with range estimates of how many forces are in each spot at each time. The next step is to link the time segments up. Here we invoke "conservation of mass." We can't have a large force proposed in a place at a time segment without a hypothesis about where they came from. Hence we expect to see flows of force masses from one terrain region to another over time. If we have excellent data on the size of a force at one time segment, and the estimated size is within the "exaggeration factor" of the observed force in a nearby place in the next time segment, we give more credence to a high-side estimate of the size of the later force. We know that big force went *somewhere*.

At some point in here we must make use of the force types. Two forces over time cannot be identified if they seem to have radically different properties. But we don't want to be too sticky about this, lest we get bogged down in the combinatorics of deciding exactly which observation is interpreted as what. We want to group observations together into force masses early in the game, and think in terms of masses. The process is guided by terrain; two objects that are fairly big and fairly close together with respect to the terrain-analysis graph should be lumped together. Once the observational data have been fitted to a time schedule, we must predict which way the forces will flow in the future. If a force has entered a region from one direction, we will simply assume, if the area is not an ultimate target, that they are headed toward the most important further regions reachable from there. The further destinations will be weighted by their importance and size relative to the force. We assume that most of the force will head toward the most important region that can hold it.

3   Terrain Analysis

The previous section is only a sketch of an approach to analyzing intelligence data. To be able to fill in the gaps, we must first convince ourselves that the required terrain-analysis graph can be constructed in reasonable time. This graph must show militarily interesting features of the area, and the relations between them. We take our principal inspiration from standard ideas of military theory. The US Army *Combat Intelligence* manual emphasizes finding *terrain features* and focusing on how the enemy might exploit them, and how we might defend or counterattack. In particular, it distinguishes four "military aspects" of terrain: observation and fire, concealment and cover, obstacles, and avenues of approach. Naturally, these concepts have not required formal definitions in the past, when they were to be manipulated by human intelligence officers. We must supply such definitions.

The observation–fire pair is complementary to the concealment–cover pair. What is crucial to all these concepts is the idea of "line of sight." If a person at point A is to observe an object at point B, there must be a line of sight between them; and if the object at B is to remain concealed, there must not be. It is not always necessary that a defender be visible from the position of an attacking weapon, but he must be visible from whoever is controlling the fire of that weapon. Obstacles and avenues of approach ("conduits") are another complementary pair. A "space" is a patch of terrain that is not an obstacle in an area that is mostly obstacle; it becomes an avenue of approach if it is shaped so as to lead somewhere interesting. Such corridors are interesting as possible loci of force movements. Spaces in general are interesting because the value of a candidate for key-terrain status depends on whether there are any ways of getting to it.

Most of our research to date has therefore focused on segmenting the map into coherent regions, and finding possible attack relations between them.

3.1   Segmentation

One defining characteristic of a region should be that it has approximately uniform cover, concealment, soil conditions, and so forth. However, we are currently focusing on two factors: steepness and shape. Regions can be classified as passable or impassable, and the key question about passable regions is what directions they allow movement in. Further partitioning regions based on local conditions will be easy to do later. With these simplifications in mind, we can think of the map initially as partitioned into two "regions": *spaces* in which fighting can occur and *obstacles* where it cannot.

The next step is to break the level area down into smaller regions, either *corridors* or *rooms*. A corridor is a long, thin region, suitable as an avenue of approach. A room is a blob with no particular direction. A room can also be used an avenue of approach, but detecting forces there gives no clue as to what direction they're going. Finding these regions is just like the corresponding problem in vision, but easier, we hope. For one thing, we are assuming noise-free maps. For another, our maps are physically significant elevations, not gray levels, and so the regions we find are likely to make sense. (There is no occlusion problem, for instance.) In many cases, it does not matter too much if the program finds too many corridors; it may slow down later processing a bit, but won't change its results. But there are cases where finding a large number of rooms is a signal that analysis has gone off track. In Figure 2, on the right side there is a tolerably traversable area broken up by some hills. Rather than analyze it as several little rooms and corridors, we would like to classify it as one big room made less trafficable by hills.

The algorithm works as follows:

1. It finds the Manhattan distance from each pixel to the nearest obstacle pixel, and notes local maxima of this distance. We expect that along the ridges in the middles of regions this distance increases slower than elsewhere, so that local maxima of this function show the approximate location of the ridges and the approximate width of the region at those points.

2. Local maxima are propagated to their neighbors as far as they go while still decreasing. When propagation from a higher maximum hits a region occupied by a lower one, the lower one wins if it is far from the higher's center of propagation. Hence all the pixels in a corridor leading to an approximately circular room will tend to become marked with the corridor's highest ridge value; while the room will be marked with the ridge value in its center.

3. Groups of adjacent pixels with the same width are lumped into regions.

4. Region boundaries are approximated as polygons. Adjacency relations between regions that share a boundary are noted.

5. Each region is examined and split into subcorridors if possible. A corridor is detected as a subregion with one or two sides much longer than its width.

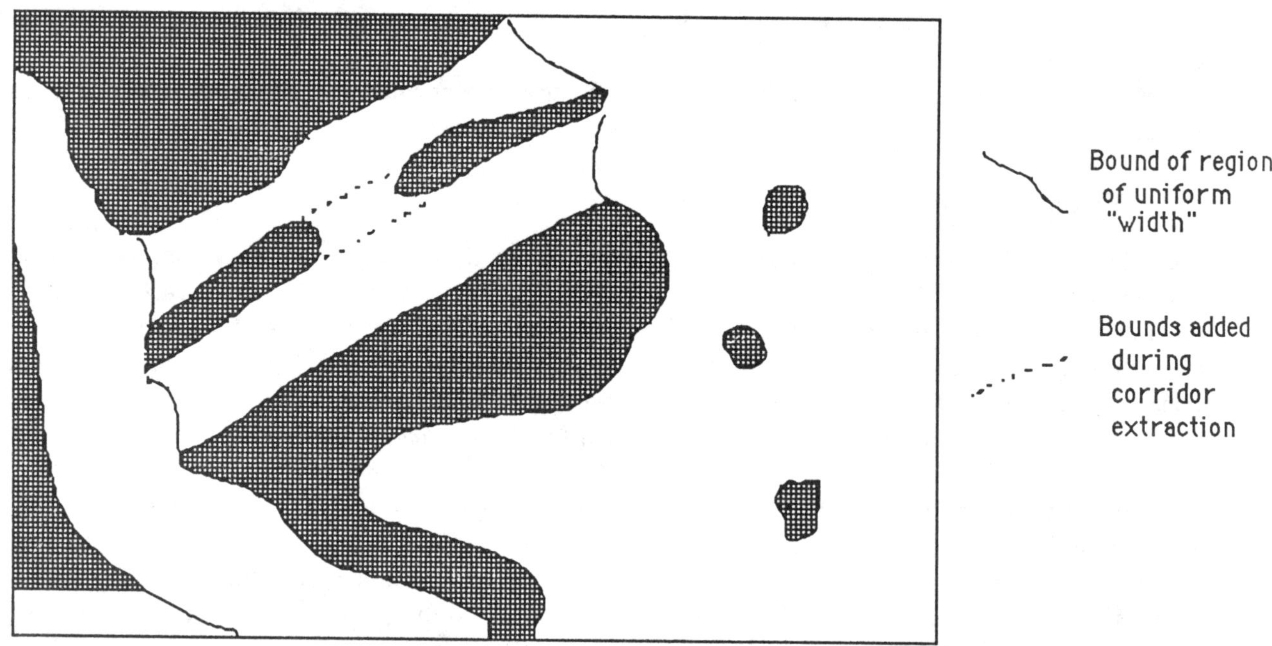

Figure 2: Finding the Right Rooms

The first step implements a thinning algorithm such as those described in (Pavlidis 1977, Ballard and Brown 1982). This phase, and most of the rest of the steps through Step 4 can be done by parallel operations on all parts of the map at once. We are exploiting that fact by implementing them on a Connection Machine. See below.

3.2   Lines of Sight

Simultaneously with segmentation, another algorithm must find all pairs of pixels that are visible from each other. In the terrain-analysis graph, one region A will then be considered as a potential attack site on another B if some pixels of A can see some of B.

There are two ways to approach the line-of-sight problem, at the region level or the pixel level. At first glance, it looks as if we are mainly interested in line-of-sight relations between areas, and hence it might be wise to postpone line-of-sight calculations until after segmentation is done, and then search out from each region to find places to attack it from. We have not been able to think of a plausible algorithm for doing this, and so have opted for finding all pairs of pixels that can see each other, and clumping together pixels in region A that can be used to observe pixels in region B.

It may sound as if just storing the intermediate results of this computation would be prohibitive. A map typically consists of about 10^4 pixels, so we might have to examine and output 10^8 pairs. Fortunately, we can use hierarchical techniques for representing and computing the pairs. The line of sight from most pixels terminates fairly quickly; when a pixel has a long view, it can typically cover a wide area as well. These facts suggest analyzing the map at a coarse resolution first, using "fat" pixels that cover many actual pixels. There are three possible outcomes to a comparison between two pixels $P1$ and $P2$ at the coarse level:

1. You can see $P2$ from any point in $P1$. (*Complete visibility*)

2. You cannot see $P2$ from any point in $P1$. (*Complete invisibility*)

3. You can probably see some point in $P2$ from some point in $P1$.

If the outcome is 1 or 2, then we can stop, storing the result at the coarse level. Future retrievals from any pixel covered by $P1$ or $P2$ must be careful to check the higher-level pixels to catch such relationships.

If the outcome is 3, then the algorithm must recurse, checking all pairs of sub-pixels, one drawn from $P1$ and one from $P2$. The recursion ceases with pairs that can see each other completely or not at all; or with pairs of elementary pixels, for which outcomes 1 and 3 are counted the same. This algorithm will work well if it reliably verifies that any point in $P2$ can be seen from any point in $P1$. In this case, broad, gently sloping areas will be analyzed at a coarse level, and recursion can cease early.

We obtain the coarse levels in the obvious way: Map pixels are clumped into two-by-two groups, making coarser pixels four times as big. These are then clumped in the same way, and so on, until a single fat pixel is obtained covering the whole map. We will use the word *pixblock* to cover these things, and count individual pixels as zero-level pixblocks. With each pixblock we store its maximum and minimum altitudes, that is, the max and min of the altitudes of any sub-pixel; and its maximum slope, that is, the maximum gradient within it.

It remains to describe the algorithms for testing pixblock intervisibility. There are three cases: testing whether $P2$ is completely visible from $P1$, testing whether whether $P2$ is completely invisible from $P1$, and testing whether a pixblock is completely visible to itself (i.e., is flat enough that all its sub-pixblocks are completely visible to each other). Of these, we will focus on the first case. The third is basically a matter of whether the maximum slope inside the pixblock is small enough that given a "periscope" of height h we could see over any hill. The second case, complete invisibility, depends on whether some other pixblock gets in the way; our analysis of the first case will give the flavor of what is needed here.

The complete visibility test comes down to whether the least advantageous view from one pixel can be blocked. In figure 3, looking at the map from the side, we have labeled the higher pixblock H, the lower L, the potential blocker B. (B may $= H$, but the case $B = L$ will be considered separately below.) We have put H on the right, but of course the direction from L to H is arbitrary. In this context, we treat pixblocks as circles, and neglect the fact that L, B, and H are not in general quite collinear. We give each pixblock r and y coordinates, r representing distance from the side of L opposite H. We use subscripts u and d to represent the "up" and "down" sides of a pixblock. That is, r_{Hu} is the distance of the far side of H from the opposite side of L. Although we will use the symbol r_{Ld}, it is always the case that $r_{Ld} = 0$. In general a pixblock represents several pixels, so the y coordinate of a pixblock ranges from y_0, the height of the lowest pixel in the block, to y_1, the height of the highest. L and H are so labeled that $y_{L0} < y_{H0}$. (The terms "up" and "down" are convenient given that H is higher than L, but an object on the u side may well be lower than an object on the d side of a pixblock.)

B cannot block the view from H to L if its highest point cannot get in the way. We don't know exactly where its highest point is, so we assume the worst case, that the lowest point of H is its u side, the lowest point of L is its u side, and the highest point of B is its d side, so that the d corner of B sticks as far as possible into the line from the u corner of H to the u

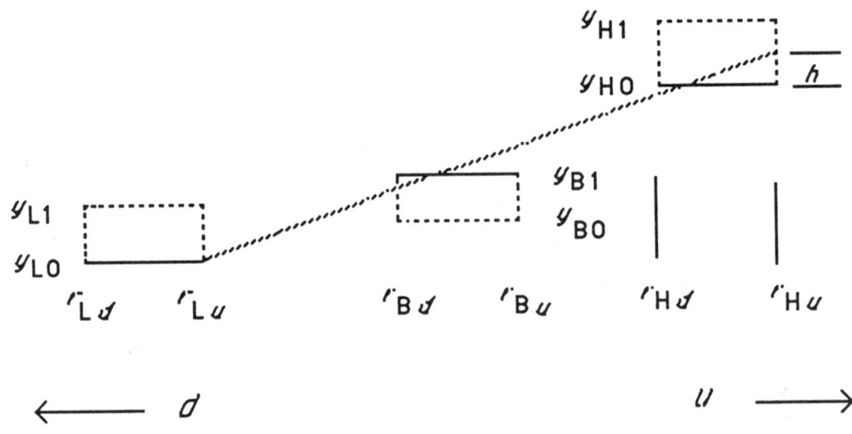

Figure 3: A Pixblock with a View

corner of L. In other words, B may block the view only if

$$\frac{h + y_{H0} - y_{L0}}{r_{Hu} - r_{Lu}} < \frac{y_{B1} - y_{L0}}{r_{Bd} - r_{Lu}} \tag{1}$$

If this condition is falsified for every possible blocker B, then L is completely visible from H. (The special case $B = L$ must still be dealt with.)

Unfortunately, this analysis is too pessimistic. It works well for large flat areas, in which the maximum and minimum heights within a pixblock are about the same. But for a gently sloping area, the large pixblocks will be treated as if they were sawtooth cliffs in the wrong direction. That is, in the worst case, the highest part of each pixblock could be on the d side, and each would block the view from its u neighbors. To remedy this problem, we observe that the value of y on the boundary of a pixblock cannot be greater than the y_1 of the neighbor on that boundary, nor less than y_0 of that neighbor. If the slope within the pixblock is arbitrarily high then this fact will not matter, since y can reach any value within ϵ of the boundary. But if the maximum slope is low, as in a gently sloping area, then we can get better estimates for y_{H0} and y_{B1}.

To formalize these observations, let P be a pixblock, and let Q and R be the two pixblocks on its d and u sides, respectively. Define

$$y_{Pd} = \min(y_{P1}, y_{Q1})$$

and

$$y_{Pu} = \max(y_{P0}, y_{R0})$$

that is, the true maximum downside and minimum upside y values for P. If

$$\text{max slope in } P \approx \frac{y_{Pu} - y_{Pd}}{r_{Pu} - r_{Pd}} \geq 0$$

then P is *smoothly sloping up*. If a pixblock is smoothly sloping up in this sense, then it can't do much more than rise from d to u. If H is smoothly sloping up, then substitute y_{Hu} for y_{H0} in formula 1. If B is smoothly sloping up, then substitute y_{Bd} for y_{B1}.

It remains to deal with the case where $B = L$. Now the d side of B cannot obstruct the u side of L. Instead, the danger is that the slope of L may be so high that some hump in it could obscure the other side. We can define the concept of "smoothly sloping down" exactly analogously to smoothly sloping up. If L is smoothly sloping down, then it is guaranteed not to be self-obstructed from H. Otherwise, the worst case is trying to see the d corner of L from the u corner of H. If

$$\frac{h + y_{H0} - y_{L1}}{r_{Hu} - r_{Ld}} < \text{ max slope in } L$$

then L may be self-obstructed from H. (As before, if H is smoothly sloping up then use y_{Hu} instead of y_{H0}; and if L is smoothly sloping up, then use y_{Ld} instead of y_{L1}.)

4   Conclusions

This is very much work in progress. Our tentative conclusions so far are that tactical situation assessment requires detailed terrain analysis, followed by matching intelligence data with significant terrain features. The terrain analysis requires grouping pixels into regions and finding relations among them. While there are good algorithms for doing these things, they will require parallel hardware for efficient execution.

We are currently coding the algorithms in *Lisp for the Connection Machine. (Hillis 1985, Thinking Machines Inc. 1986) The code for region segmentation is mostly written and is being debugged. The code for line-of-sight calculations is more speculative. We have not yet explored ways of parallelizing it, although at the pixel level where it would do the most good there are probably many opportunities for doing so.

Acknowledgements

Thanks to CSW, TASC and HERO for military education. Jeff Maier of TASC discussed with us in depth what was required in a terrain-analysis graph.

References

Dana Ballard and Christopher Brown 1982 *Computer Vision*. Prentice-Hall

Daniel Hillis 1985 *The Connection Machine*. MIT Press

T. Pavlidis 1977 *Structural Pattern Recognition*. Springer-Verlag

Thinking Machines Incorporated 1986 *The Essential *Lisp Manual*. Unpublished memo.

Free Space Modeling and Geometric Motion Planning Under Location Uncertainty

Alex C-C Meng
Artificial Intelligence Lab.
Texas Instruments, Inc.
P. B. Box 655474, MS 238
Dallas, Texas 75265
meng@ti-csl.ti

Abstract

This paper addresses the Motion Planning under Location Uncertainty problem for Autonomous Air Robots maneuvering in a large 3-D space. Presumably, the air robot navigates by some passive navigation scheme based on imaging sensors. Depending on the ground sampling and estimation, its exact location is therefore fuzzy and can only be estimated to within a certain range. We will describe a real-time motion planning system that navigates the autonomous air robots in a 3-D real world while coping with the instantaneous change of uncertainty of its current location. We will also show that the complete maneuvering is collision-free. The system use layered 2-D elevation slices to approximate the real 3-D space and a circle in the given 2-D slice to model the uncertainty or the fuzzy range. Facing real world complexity, including obstacles with random shapes, we use a spatial graph based on the *Voronoi Diagram* to model the skeleton or the passing channels of the free space. By imposing the *proximity* property on the Voronoi Edges we can model the safe world for any given fuzzy range at a given time. The basic idea is that the system will maintain a snapshot of the world that is safe to travel at any time t with the given uncertainty range r and plan a path on that safe world in real time. Since the robot always travels along the paths that are collision-free at any time by definition we can show the complete maneuvering is collision-free. A motion simulation system has been implemented on a TI Explorer Lisp Machine.

Problem Statement

This paper studies the motion planning problem for Autonomous Air Robots maneuvering in 3-D space. Presumably, the robot is navigated by some passive navigation scheme [HOLLISTER81] using imaging sensors or even by dead-reckoning. The exact location of the robot can only be estimated inexactly. The size of the error depends on the ground sampling and estimation each time. The uncertainty of its current location will be modeled as a circle with the fuzzy range as its radius at the given altitude. For any given start and goal positions, the motion planning under location uncertainty problem is the path generation problem coping with the instantaneous change of the uncertainty of the robot's current location and insuring that the complete maneuvering is collision-free. The robot has a passive navigation device the motion planning system can query. For any given time time t the navigation device will return the center of its location estimation c and a fussy range r, i.e. the robot can be in any position inside the circle with its origin at c and radius r.

Existing Methods for Path Planning

The general schemes to solve the Find-Path problem in Robotics and Computational Geometry can be characterized by the way the approaches represent the free space. We can categorize two basic approaches: one represents the obstacles explicitly as geometrical shapes, like polygons, and the free space is defined implicitly by being outside of those obstacles. The shortest path in a 2-D space can be found by searching the Visibility Graph [WESLEY79]. But to extend this approach to the 3-D shortest path problem incurs a very high computational cost [SHARIR84]. The other basic approach represents the free space explicitly and finds the path directly inside the free space. Brooks [BROOKS83] represents the free space as generalized cones where the central axes of these cones form a connected graph of passing channels. The path finding process searches for the path on the connectivity graph. By definition, the path found is therefore a safe path (i.e., collision-free), but not the shortest path. This paper will model the free space bounded by randomly shaped obstacles on Digital Geometry using the *Voronoi Diagram*.

Free Space Modeling

Most of the research on mobile robots in Robotics focuses on a controlled environment such as the blocks world rooms, corridors and hallways or simple polygonal obstacles. In the case where the air robot is maneuvering in a large 3-D space, if we take a horizontal contour slice for a given altitude, the world model consists of randomly shaped natural obstacles (e.g., mountains) and artificial obstacles (in our example represented as circles). See Figure 1.

Considering a 2-D contour slice, an obstacle O is defined by its closed boundary geometrically; let *Bound(O)*, *Int(O)* denote the boundary and interior of O respectively and $O = Bound(O) \cup Int(O)$. A point p is in free space iff p doesn't belong to O for every O in the given world model. The distance between a point p in free space and an obstacle O is defined by *distance(p,O) = MIN { d(p,q) | q $\in$ Bound(O) and d(p,q) is the Euclidean distance between two points p and q}*. To represent the free space bounded by the obstacles, the geometrical concept, known as a *Voronoi Diagram*, is used to characterize the skeleton or passing channels of the free space between adjacent obstacles. Consider the region defined by the obstacle O as follows: *T = { p | p is in free space and distance(p, O) < distance(p, Ô) for any other obstacle Ô }*. We will call it the *Voronoi Region* defined by O. The *Voronoi Diagram* for a given world model is the set of points that do not belong to any Voronoi Regions, i.e. the set of points in free space that maintain equal distance between two adjacent obstacles (two obstacles are adjacent iff the Voronoi Regions they define are adjacent). In other words, the Voronoi Diagram partitions the 2-D plane into disjoint regions. Figure 1 shows the Voronoi Diagram for a 2-D world model with altitude at 2000 feet. (Note that here we treat the four external boundaries as a single obstacle.)

We can interpret the Voronoi Diagram into edges and nodes symbolically as follows: let the Voronoi Edge between two adjacent obstacles, O_1 and O_2, be the set of points: *{ p | distance(p, O_1) = distance(p, O_2)}*. The edge has two end points and we can order the points in sequence from one end to the other. Define a Voronoi Node as an intersection of Voronoi edges, except for some rare cases, every Voronoi Node is the common intersection of exactly three edges of the Voronoi Diagram [PREPARATA85] (see Figure 1). In fact, we use this property of the Voronoi node to interpret those edges of the Voronoi Diagram into the Voronoi Graph [MENG87a]. The Voronoi Graph is defined by the set of Voronoi Edges and Voronoi Nodes. After interpretation, the Voronoi Graph is the spatial graph that represents the skeleton of free space for the given world model. Abstractly, it is just a mathematical graph defined by nodes and adjacency between nodes (i.e., edges), but geometrically, the nodes denote exact locations in the 2-D contour map and the edges can only be traversed from end to end in a unique way, defined by the sequence of edge points. The Voronoi Graph represents the skeleton of the free space. When traversing the Voronoi edges, the path is collision-free.

[SHARIR84] has shown that the computational complexity of planning a collision-free path in 3-D space directly is doubly exponential. Even a polynomial time approximation algorithm is still not practical [PAPADIMITRIOU85]. Our approach to the 3-D space is to use the layered 2-D contour slices starting from the given *base altitude* and slice the world incrementally every x feet. When x approachs to 0, the layered 2-D slices approach the real 3-D space asymptotically. A chosen optimum altitude will be given to the system as the *reference altitude* and the robot will try to stay as close as possible to the reference altitude. The *start* and *target* position will be given on the contour slice of the reference altitude, the final position of the robot will project on the target position on the reference altitude but may be on different altitude depending on the uncertainty measure at that time.

Global Path Finding Process

The research on the path planning problem in robotics focuses on environment-dependent local sensory-driven navigation, i.e. performing a perception-action cycle. When dealing with a large space, path planning just based on local sensory information may not lead to a globally good path. Moreover, it can lead the robot into traps, for instance, into a U-shape obstacle. We will describe a path planning process that searches the spatial connectivity graph defined by the obstacles known as the *Retraction* method [YAP83].

For any given set of obstacles and two positions in free space S and T, the Find-Path problem is to find a path of continuous movement from S to T that is collision-free. If both S and T are on the Voronoi Graph, then the edges that S and T are on are called retraction edges and are denoted as S-edge and T-edge, respectively. We will adjoin S and T as two new nodes and split S-edge and T-edge into two subedges intersecting at S and T, respectively. Considering the new graph as a mathematical graph, the path finding algorithm can be one of these shortest path search algorithms found in the shortest path research on a finite graph. Here we use Dijkstra's shortest path algorithm. The proof of collision-freeness of the path found follows directly from the definition of the Voronoi Graph that lies in free space. The path plan so derived is a sequence of edges to be traversed.

If S or T are inside some Voronoi Region, let S be inside the region defined by obstacle O. Let $p \in Bound(O)$ and $d(p, S) = distance(S, O)$, i.e., p is the closest point on O to S. Draw the half line from p to S and it will intersect a Voronoi Edge, call it S-edge, the retraction edge, and the intersection point $\hat{S}$, the retraction point. The line segment between S and $\hat{S}$ is collision free. Similarly, retract T to $\hat{T}$. The complete path starts at S, moves in a straight line to $\hat{S}$, then follows the shortest path from $\hat{S}$ to $\hat{T}$ as described above and finally moves from $\hat{T}$ to T in straight line. One example of the path is shown in Figure 2.

The path generated by the Retraction method is not the shortest path in the given world model but is a globally good path, an improvement can be found in [MENG87b]. Moreover, the path will improve when the number of obstacles increases.

Path Finding Under Location Uncertainty

When the robot is uncertain about its location and can only estimate it to within a fuzzy range r, we can view the robot as a disc with the radius r. Assuming the uncertainty r is fixed, the path planning problem is the Find-Path problem for the disc from two given positions S to T. Define the property called proximity for a given point p as follows: *p-proximity(p) = MIN { distance(p, O) | for any obstacle O in the 2-D world model}*, i.e., the distance from p to the nearest obstacle. Define the proximity for a Voronoi Edge E by *E-proximity(E) = MIN { p-proximity(p) | p $\in$ E }*, i.e., the proximity property of an edge is the safe distance the moving object can maintain when traversing along the edge. For any proximity measure r, let the proximity graph r-V-graph be the graph with a collection of edges as follows: { *E | E-proximity(E) $\geq$ r* } and the nodes are those intersections of edges or ends of edges. In other words, the r-V-graph represents the skeleton of the free space that is all the traversal edges or valleys between obstacles that the moving point object can maintain at least r distance away from the obstacles, i.e., a horizontal clearance of r. Figure 3 shows the 1500-V-graph, the spatial graph with a horizontal clearance of 1500 feet.

For the disc with fixed radius r, we can use the center to represent the disc, reducing the Find-Path problem for a disc from S to T to the Find-Path problem for the point object from S to T on r-V-graph, which is solved by the same Retraction method described above. Figure 4 shows the path for the same start and goal positions as Figure 3 while the moving object is a disc with a radius of 1500 feet.

When the robot is traveling with the uncertainty changing from time to time, the problem is how to guarantee that the robot with any given estimated uncertainty will always travel along safe valleys only. We have th following:

Algorithm 1 *Let the uncertainty measure at time t-1 is r_1. For the time t and the new uncertainty measure r_2, if $r_2 > r_1$ then starting from the current contour slice, increases its altitude until a new safe $r_2 - V - graph$ can be found such that there's a path on $r_2 - V - graph$ from the current location to the target location. If $r_2 < r_1$ then starting from the current contour slice, find the lowerest altitude up to the reference altitude such that there exists the $r_2 - V - graph$ and there's a path from the current location to the target location. If $r_2 = r_1$ then continue on the current path.*

Observation 1 *The complete maneuvering is collision-free can be shown inductively. For any given time instant t and the uncertainty measure r at time t, the robot will be traveling on the graph r-V-graph by the above method which is collision free.*

For any given instant t with uncertainty r, the proximity graph r-V-graph represents all the safe valleys for that instant that the robot can travel. The path planning problem at time t becomes the shortest path search problem on the r-V-graph. The generation of the subgraph r-V-graph can be done in linear time respect to the number of edges.

Path Plan Execution

A path plan will consist of a sequence of path segments to be traversed in order. The path segment will be described as a triplet : (FROM FOLLOW TO). The FROM part is the starting position; the TO part is the ending position; and the FOLLOW part is a Voronoi edge, a portion of a Voronoi edge, or a line segment. For each path segment, these edge points in sequence will give the general directional directives for the robot's local navigation system. The robot will perform the local sensory-driven navigation by tracking these edge points optimized with respect to its motion constraints (turn radius, etc.), speed etc. Along with tracking, the passive navigation system will report the new uncertainty measure back to the path planner to generate a new safe path.

To demonstrate the instantaneous change of uncertainty, the simulation system receives a simulation sequence in terms of time and uncertainty. A simulation is a list of pairs in which the first entry indicates the total time unit the robot moves with the uncertainty given in feet as the second entry of the pair. A sample run of the motion simulation based on the simulation sequence ((5 300) (7 1000) (10 1500) (5 1000) (10 1800) (15 1500) (10 2000) (15 1800) (10 1500) (20 1000)) is shown in Figure 5, where the varying circles represents the changing uncertainty. This example shows the movement in a two-dimensional case. When the uncertainty range is so large that the proximity graph becomes disconnected, ·i.e. there is no safe path from S to T for the given uncertainty in that 2-D world model, this brings about a three-dimensional situation.

In the three-dimensional real world, the number of obstacles tends to decrease as the altitude increases, so the robot with a large fuzzy range will have a better chance to fly through. For the given altitude e, if there is no path from S to T at this altitude, then the robot will try to move to a 2-D slice world with a higher altitude and will eventually reach a completely free space if no safe path can be found in these 2-D slices. Similarly, whenever the uncertainty decreases, the robot will try to reduce its altitude when a safe path is available at a lower altitude until it reaches the base altitude, which is chosen as the optimal altitude for the robot. [Figures 6,7,8,9,10] show the complete maneuvering based on the following simulation: ((5 300) (7 800) (10 1200) (15 1500) (10 1800) (15 2000) (5 2300) (10 1500) (10 1200) (5 1000)). The robot starts from the altitude 2000 feet and increases to 2200, 2400 feet and eventually reaching to the completely free space. It then reduces its altitude when the uncertainty decreases and finally arrives at 2000 feet.

Conclusion

This paper presents a solution for the motion planning under location uncertainty problem of Autonomous Air Robots maneuvering in a large 3-D space. The free space model is based on the Voronoi Diagram. By interpreting of the diagram into a spatially-oriented graph representing the skeleton of the free space, we can solve the Find-Path problem by a path search on the graph. By imposing the proximity property on the edges of the graph and maintain the snapshot of the world that is safe at time t with instantaneous uncertainty r. Therefore the robot always travels along an edge path proven to be collision-free.

References

[BROOKS83] R. Brooks, "Solving the Find-Path Problem by Good Representation of Free Space," IEEE Trans. on System, Man, and Cybernetics. Vol. SMC-13 No. 3, 1983. Also in AAAI 82.

[HOLLISTER81] F. H. Hollister, "Bearings-only Passive Ranging Using Kalman-Bucy and Moore-Penrose Methods," Proceeding of the SPIE, Aug. 1981.

[MENG87a] A. C-C. Meng, "Computing and Interpreting the Weighted Voronoi Diagram of Randomly Shaped Obstacles On Digital Geometry," Technical Report, Texas Instruments, Inc. 1987

[MENG87b] A. C-C. Meng, "Free Space Modeling and Geometric Motion Planning Under Unexpected Obstacles," Technical Report, Texas Instruments, Inc. 1987

[PAPADIMITRIOU85] C. H. Papadimitriou, "An Algorithm For Shortest-Path Motion In Three Dimensions," Information Processing Letters 20, 1985.

[SHARIR84] M. Sharir and A Schorr, "On Shortest Paths in Polyhedra Spaces," Proceeding of 16th ACM Symp. on the Theory of Computer, 1984

[PREPARATA85] F. P. Preparata, M. I. Shamos, Computational Geometry, Springer-Verlag 1985.

[WESLEY79] T. Lozano-Perez and M. A. Wesley, "A Algorithm for Planning Collision-Free Paths Among Polyhedral Obstacles," CACM, Vol. 22, Oct. 1979.

[YAP83] C. DUNLAING M. SHARIR and C. K. YAP, "Retraction: A New Approach To Motion Planning," ACM 15th Symp. on The theory of Computer, 1983.

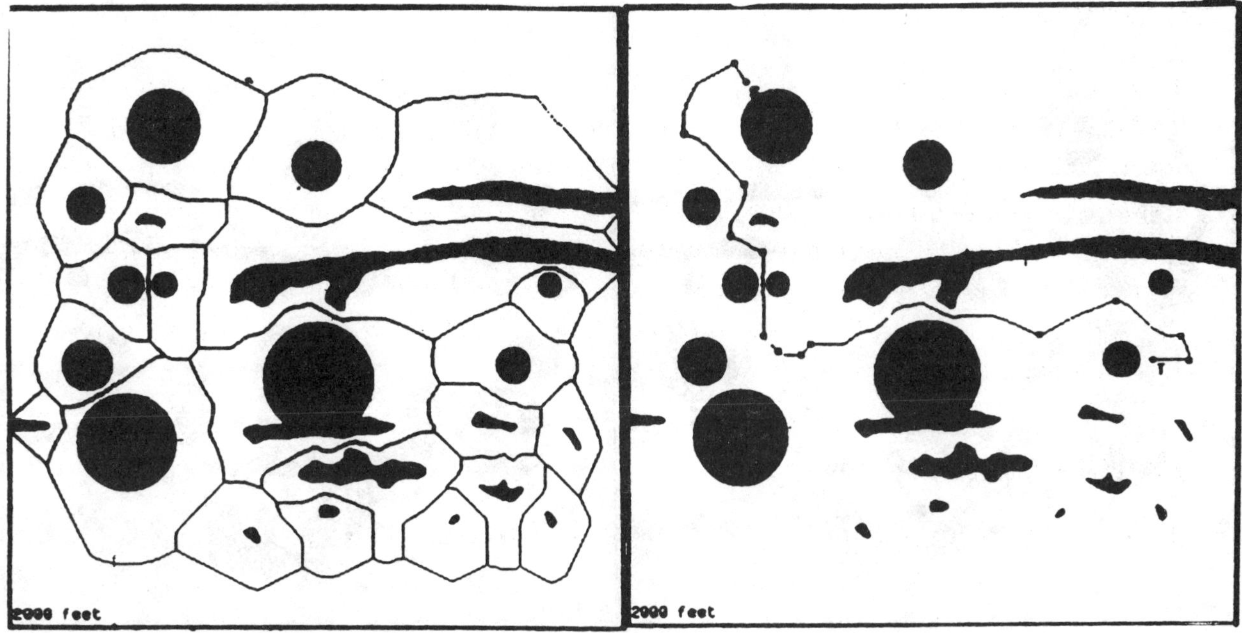

Fig. 1   Fig. 2

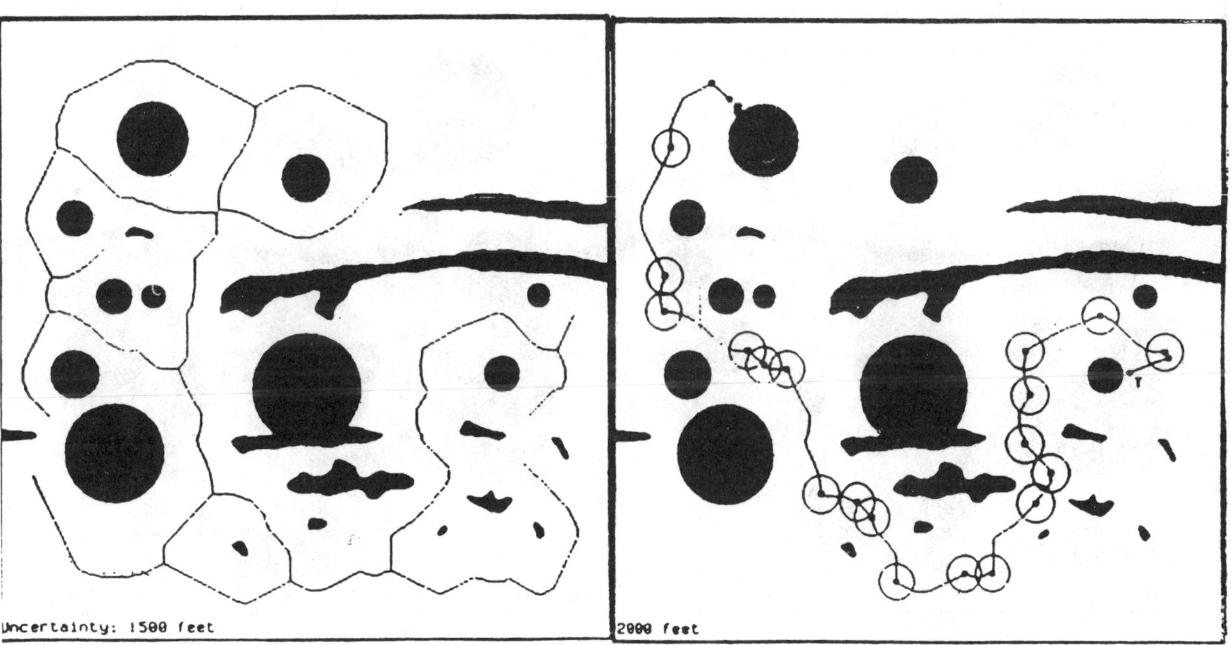

Fig. 3   Fig. 4

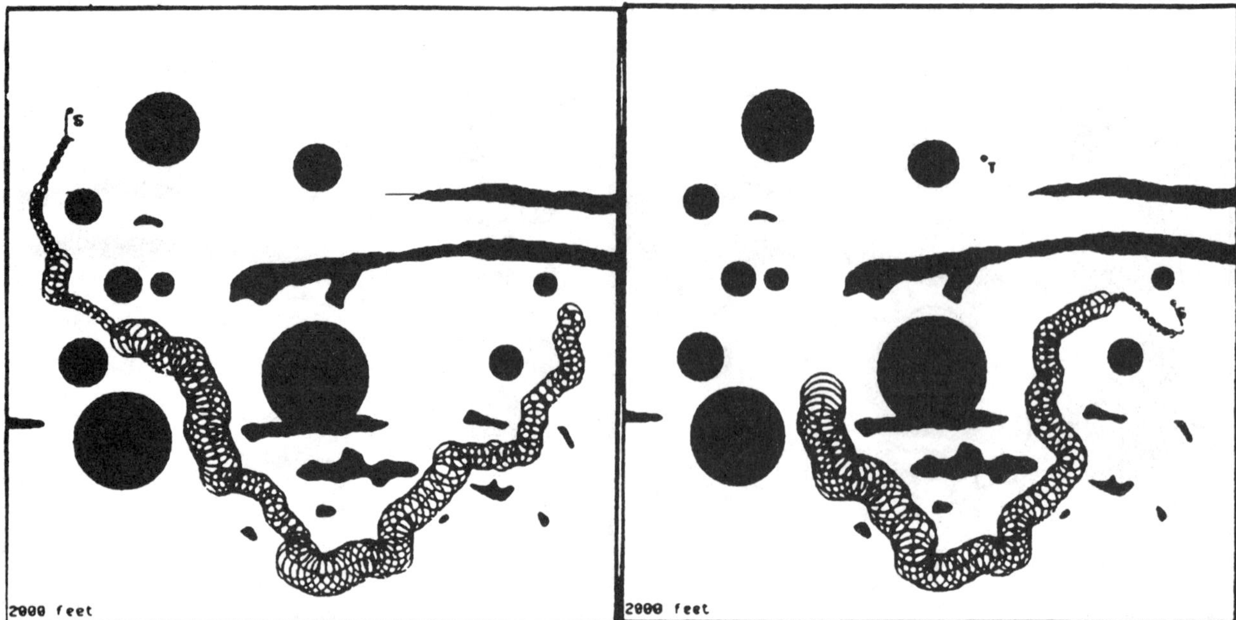

Fig. 5   Fig. 6

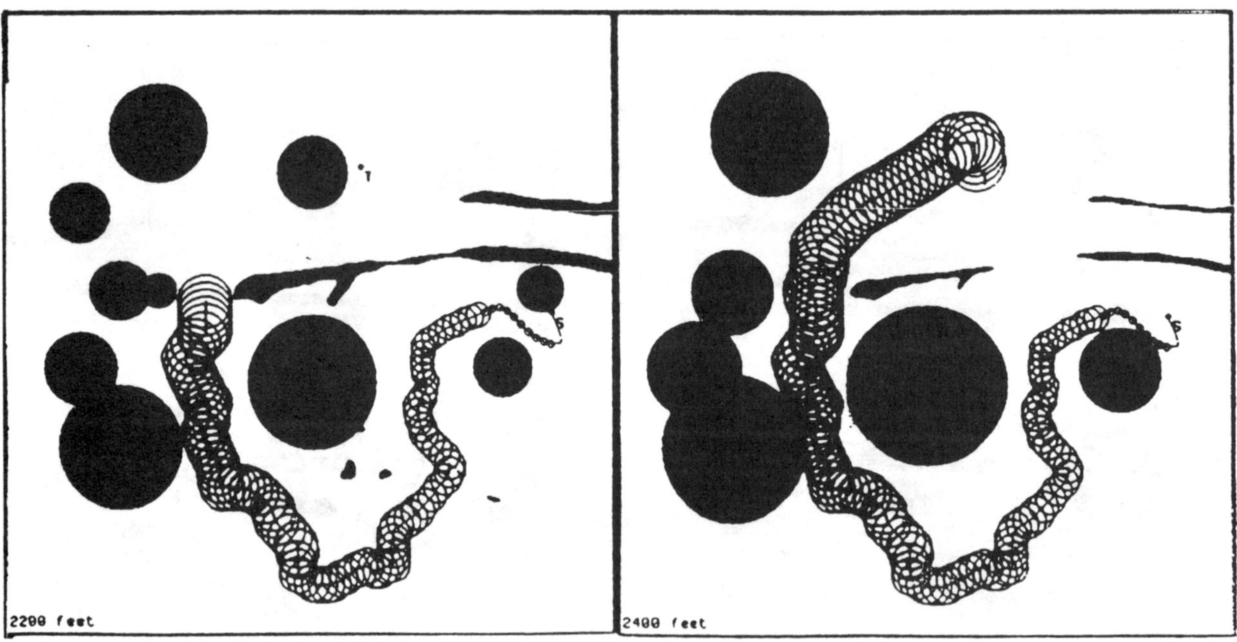

Fig. 7   Fig. 8

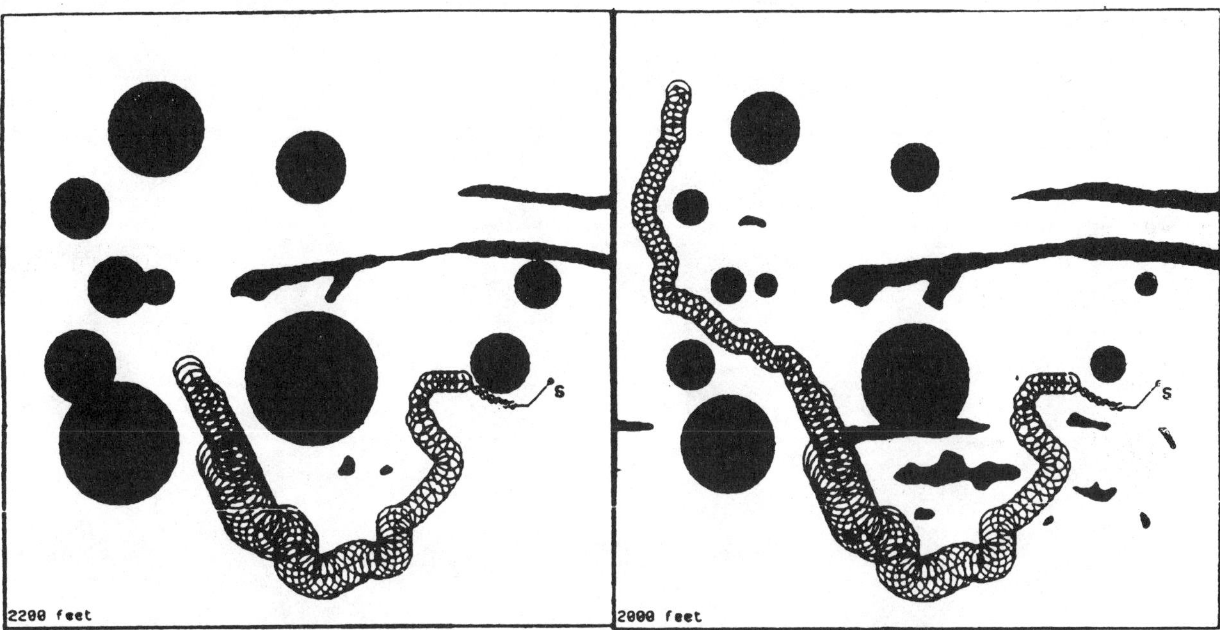

Fig. 9

Fig. 10

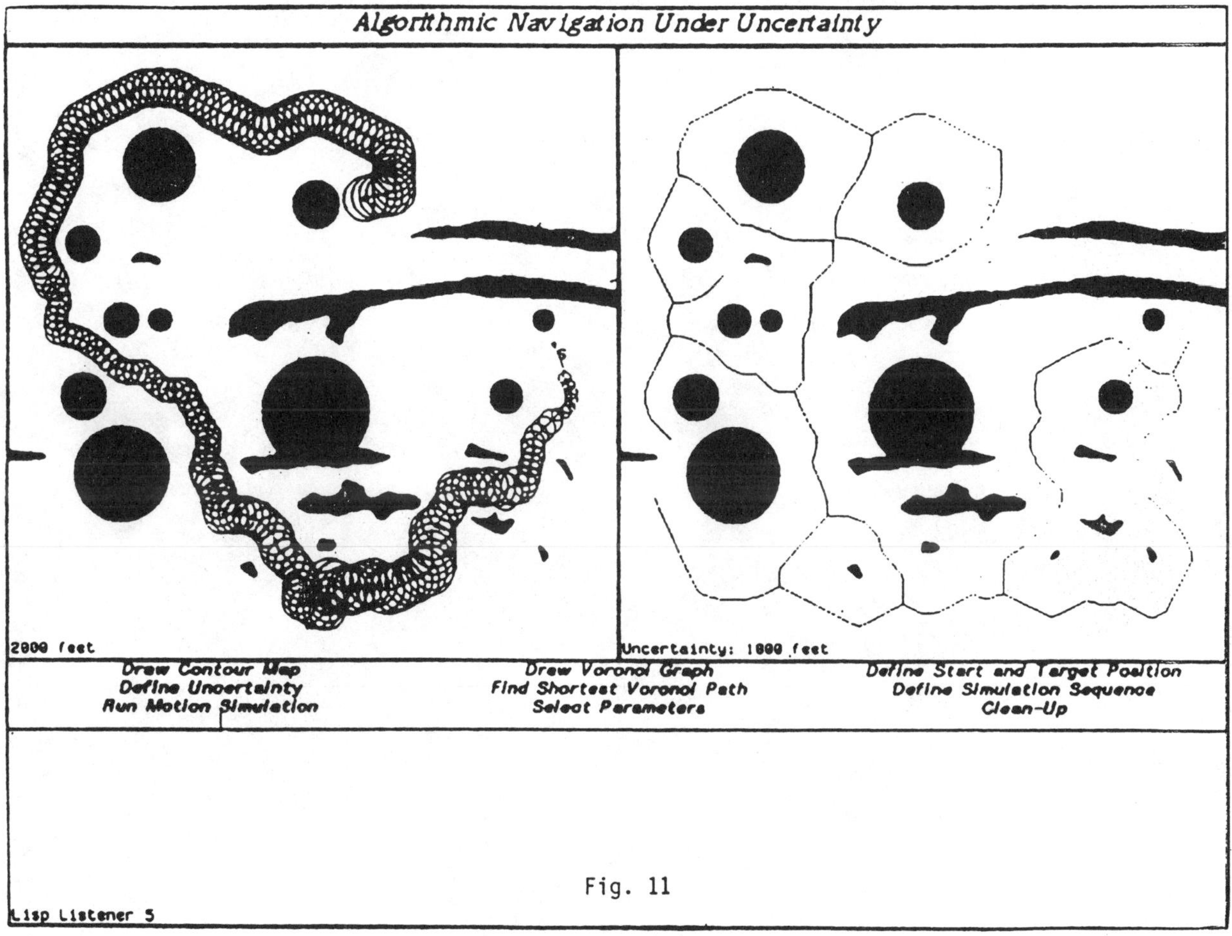

Fig. 11

AUTHOR INDEX